Writing
THE MODERN
HISTORY OF IRAQ
Historiographical and Political Challenges

Writing
THE MODERN
HISTORY of IRAQ
Historiographical and Political Challenges

Editors

Jordi Tejel
Graduate Institute of International and Development Studies, Geneva

Peter Sluglett
National University of Singapore

Riccardo Bocco
Graduate Institute of International and Development Studies, Geneva

Hamit Bozarslan
École des Hautes Études en Sciences Sociales, Paris

World Scientific

NEW JERSEY · LONDON · SINGAPORE · BEIJING · SHANGHAI · HONG KONG · TAIPEI · CHENNAI

Published by

World Scientific Publishing Co. Pte. Ltd.
5 Toh Tuck Link, Singapore 596224
USA office: 27 Warren Street, Suite 401-402, Hackensack, NJ 07601
UK office: 57 Shelton Street, Covent Garden, London WC2H 9HE

British Library Cataloguing-in-Publication Data
A catalogue record for this book is available from the British Library.

Cover art courtesy: Ismail Fattah, Standing Faces (Wujuh Waqifa), 1998. Photo: S. Naef, 2000
(Exhibition of Iraqi Painters, Paris, Maire du 9ème arrondissement, 22 June–1 July, 2000).

First published 2012 (Hard cover)
Reprinted 2015 (in paperback edition)
ISBN 978-981-4730-38-9

WRITING THE MODERN HISTORY OF IRAQ
Historiographical and Political Challenges

ISBN 978-981-4390-55-2

In-house Editor: Sandhya Venkatesh

Typeset by Stallion Press
Emial: enquiries@stallionpress.com

CONTENTS

ACKNOWLEDGMENTS

During the fall of 2007, Jordi Tejel and Anna Neubauer, on behalf of the Swiss Society for Middle East Studies and Islamic Civilization (SSMEIC) based in Bern, and Riccardo Bocco, on behalf of the Centre on Conflict, Development and Peace-building (CCDP) of the Graduate Institute of International and Development Studies in Geneva, met to discuss the possibility of convening an international conference on contemporary Iraqi studies in the social sciences.

In the aftermath of the American invasion of 2003, the establishment of an international commission to 're-write' contemporary Iraqi history to accompany the long-term process of national reconciliation ended in failure and the project was abandoned after a year of meetings and conferences. The idea of the conference to be held in Geneva stemmed, therefore, from the will to bring a critical spirit to bear on some of the more debated and often controversial items facing social scientists dealing with the recent history of Iraq. Peter Sluglett and Hamit Bozarslan joined the steering committee to finalize and advertise the content of the symposium. An international conference was organized on 6–8 November 2008 at the Graduate Institute in Geneva.

Bringing together thirty junior and senior researchers of different nationalities and from different disciplines (history, sociology, political science and anthropology), it was intended that the symposium should take stock of the historiography produced on and in the country over the past half century, that it should discuss the prevailing narratives and paradigms of interpretation of Iraqi politics, society, history and culture, contribute to assessing areas where research is lacking, and suggest new grids of analysis.

The meeting was made possible thanks to the financial support of the Swiss National Science Foundation, the Gerda Henkel Stiftung, the Union Pétrolière Suisse, the Swiss Academy of Humanities and Social Sciences, the SSMEIC and the CCDP. We are also particularly thankful to Dr. Oliver Jütersonke, head of research at CCDP, and the Centre's administrative

assistant, Ms Sandra Reimann, for having facilitated the practical organization of the event at the Graduate Institute. Finally, Ms Mimi Kirk has
patiently prepared the index of this volume.

Although the publication of this volume has taken more time than fore-
cast, the different topics approached have not lost their timeliness. Most of
the conference papers have been included in the volume and a few others
were commissioned in the aftermath of the symposium. We sincerely thank
all the contributors to the volume for their work, their willingness to adapt
and revise their texts, and above all for their patience.

The Editors
August 2012

Note on Transliteration and References

1. Transliteration has been kept as consistent and simple as possible. No
   diacritical marks have been used.
2. The electronic references cited in each paper can be found at the end
   of the paper: full titles of books and articles can be found in the
   Bibliography.

INTRODUCTION

Riccardo Bocco and Jordi Tejel

The official aim of the American invasion of Iraq in March 2003 was to put an end to Saddam Husayn's regime and establish a viable democracy that would, it was hoped, serve as a model for other Middle Eastern countries. New institutions and elites were to replace the old ones. The period of Ba'th party domination (1968–2003) was to come to an end through the "de-Ba'thification" of Iraq along the lines of the de-Nazification of Germany after the Second World War. Thus the Coalition Provisional Authority (CPA), led by L. Paul Bremer, issued a decree on May 16, 2003 promoting the de-Ba'thification[1] of Iraqi society in order to lay the foundations for a "new" Iraq. This process, which was abandoned in 2004, had been applied mostly to military and educational institutions.

As for the latter, the ideologues of the CPA particularly targeted history and historians, ignoring both the intellectual openness of some Iraqi historians and the existence of a dissident historical tradition.[2] The de-Ba'thification policy had two objectives as far as the re-writing of Iraqi history was concerned. On the one hand, CPA officials favored the production of new textbooks, complete with a USAID-approved "re-interpretation of Iraqi, Arab, and Islamic history" (Al-Takriti, 2005, p. 25). On the other hand, educational reforms were aimed at the replacement of an academic system perceived as dominated and shaped by the primacy of "ideology" with a new system, inspired by some American experiences, founded on the values and ethos of the Liberal Arts (Méténier, 2006, p. 261). In this sense, the CPA encouraged a couple of pilot efforts: The "American Liberal

---

[1]The idea of de-Ba'thification was originally promoted by some Iraqi exiles in the United States. For an account of the evolution of de-Ba'thification policies between 2003 and 2004, see Saghieh (2007: 203–223).
[2]See Méténier (2006: 261–284).

Arts University of Iraq" and the "College of Democracy," both located in Northern Iraq.

In the post-Saddam era, the writing of past and recent history was thus assigned a major role in establishing the basis for a national and state identity that would be recognized as legitimate by the majority of Iraqi citizens. In contemporary Iraq, however, where there is a significant vacuum of state power in some parts of the country, the reification of boundaries between Sunnis and Shi'is and the continuous movement towards autonomy in the Kurdish regions, appears to correspond very little to the model of a "bourgeois democracy" (Sluglett, 2004, pp. 126–127) that would require the integration and adherence of its citizens. Furthermore, and as Charles Tripp puts it, since the very beginning of the Iraqi state in the 1920s, there have been very different, contrasting, and competing ideas about the future and nature of Iraq (Tripp, 2007, pp. 1–2).

Although many Iraqis tried to assess the idea of politics as civility (Zubaida, 2003, pp. 47–61), most political, tribal, and religious actors, even those who challenged the established order, tended to exploit existing networks of family, kin, tribe, ethnicity, or religion to assert control and eventually bring others into line with their vision for the country. This process has always been disruptive: The state has frequently been captured by distinct, usually unrepresentative groups, and it has generally been incapable of socializing the population into accepting the ruler's vision of society and history other than by resorting to forms of coercion. Furthermore, despite the material resources available to them and their authoritarian methods, "Iraq's rulers have had little success in forcing the histories of Iraq's various communities to conform with their own timetables and objectives" (Tripp, 2007, p. 4). In Tripp's view, authoritarianism combined with the habit of exploiting the fault lines among different sectors in the population has actually deepened social fragmentation. In doing so, Iraqi rulers have subverted the very idea of a "national community," the final political goal invoked by all of them. In that sense, at least to some extent, the Iraqi case conforms to Migdal's analysis of state/society relations, in that patrimonialism and authoritarianism in Iraq have taken their toll: "state policy implementation and the outcomes in society have ended up quite different from the state's original blueprints" (Migdal, 2001, p. 12). In other words, like many other states in the region, the Iraqi state actually implemented a self-destructive policy in that its "practices" have often contradicted the "image" of itself that it has constructed of a dominant, integrated, and autonomous entity.

Indeed, in spite of Ba'thist policies (e.g., purges, intellectual isolation), especially since 1979, the regime, characterized by authoritarian rule[3] and the monopolization of resources by an *'asabiyya*, or even a "dynasty" (Bozarslan, 2003, pp. 31–46), was unable to ensure that the multiple histories of the Iraqis were subsumed into a single narrative of state power. The "long decade" of the embargo during the 1990s and the collapse of the regime in 2003 have only multiplied the number of Iraqi narratives.

The "state of violence" (Gros, 2005) into which Iraqi society has sunk since 2003 has reactivated some of the old narratives used by Iraqis to understand and to justify their political engagement over time. These narratives have an impact on their visions of life and of the world and eventually nourish both new self-perceptions and perceptions of the "Other" which in turn reinforce collective imaginaries (Ypersele, 2006, p. 38). In such a context, the uses and abuses of memory (Todorov, 1995) and history by diverse political parties, communities or groups, whether ethnic or sectarian, are a common feature. In that sense, narratives of victimhood provide particular opportunities for constructing, or reinforcing, a sense of endangered group belonging or identity.

With Iraq facing the danger of implosion, which groups — or even segments of the population with their own sub-Iraqi and trans-border references — will be able to impose their visions of history? Is Iraq facing an unavoidable "fragmentation of collective memory"? What is the experience of Iraqi Kurdistan, autonomous *de facto* since 1991? Is Iraq moving towards communalist historical accounts based on wounded memories or on discourses of victimization? Some chapters included in this volume seem to confirm this trend, especially amongst Kurds and Shi'is, each group claiming an "incomparable" and "unique" form of suffering.

Interestingly, the discourse of victimization of some Iraqi groups must also be analyzed through the lens of a broader phenomenon. Since the 1990s, different conflicts of memory have emerged more generally amongst "minorities" (e.g., Jews, homosexuals, Afro-Americans, etc.), which have suffered

---

[3]It is clear that Saddam Husayn's power was a complex network of patronage and association as well as of mutual dependence. Nevertheless, in the final analysis it was Saddam Husayn who decided which individuals should benefit from privileges, and "which should be reminded of his power in some exemplary way and how far competition amongst them should be encouraged as a means of fragmenting them and harnessing their ambitions to his cause" (Tripp, 2007: 260).

in the past either massive massacres[4] or strong discrimination. This trend confirms the integration of Iraq, and the Middle East in general, into what Wolfram Eberhard has called *Weltzeit* (universal time), that is, "the time that characterizes an epoch-making context" (Reinhard, 2000, p. 3). Related to this, the claims of some Iraqi actors and the trial of Saddam Husayn place Iraq in the same "regime of historicity" (Hartog, 2003) as European countries marked by some common features: The wish for reparations for past crimes and "mistakes"; the growing intervention of justice within "historical events"; the reading of history through the lens of victimhood; and finally, the growing intervention of international institutions in the master narratives of national and regional histories (Rousso, 2009, p. 215).

What is the historian's role in the face of a sort of "competition" between victims leading to an inevitable "abuse of memory?" Can, or should, (s)he adjudicate between competing versions of the truth (Rousso, 2009, p. 3)? In order to avoid this kind of trap, historians have underlined the necessity of a critical "re-historicization" of memory and its political as well as identity stakes (Ypersele, 2006, p. 198).[5] Yet in the face of the "crisis" of History as a science partly due to the "democratization" of the public debate on "historical events" (Gallerano, 1995; Hartog, 2000, pp. 1–14) and to new social demands ("applied history"), the question of the relationship between societies and their past, present and future seems far from closed (Delacroix *et al.*, 2009).

On another level, is it conceivable to write a "distant" history of some Iraqi events? The memory of the present is extremely volatile and fragile. It is also deceptive, because it is saturated with emotion and passion as well as being exposed to an excess of information, to acts of disinformation or misinformation and, in the end, to a lack of meaning (Bozarslan and Harling, 2007, pp. 9–15). The challenges faced by researchers concern the analysis of the past, both in its own terms and also from the point of view of the present. In this respect, the trial and execution of Saddam Husayn raised many questions. The trial was conceived as a moment of memory, but also as an "instrument of history," hence the necessity of recording it. But what role has been played by historians? How will it be possible from now on to discuss and write the history of the darkest pages of the Ba'thist regime, now that justice has already spoken its last word? Broadly speaking, can

---

[4]On some of these violent chapters through history, see the volume edited by Mark Levene and Penny Roberts (1999).
[5]See also Bédarida (1997), Chaumont (1997), Rousso (1998), and Todorov (1995).

(Iraqi) historians write a history "on line" (Hartog and Revel, 2001, p. 21)? Can they refuse to do so?

Taking into account all the elements mentioned above, it seems clear that working out a new historical narrative centered on the state is problematic at the very least. Therefore, what materials are needed to reunite plural memories? What should be the aim? After the radical redefinition, through state coercion, of categories such as "bottom," "top," "power", or "society" between 1979–1991, and the devastating effects of the embargo on Iraqi society and of three wars (1980–1988, 1991, 2003) over a period of only 23 years, is it still possible to lay the foundations for a history less centered on power (*hukumat*) and more concerned with transversal dynamics? Is it possible to move in a different direction by focusing on a "History from below"? Can the Iraqi context offer opportunities for a renewed resort to subaltern studies among historians?

The material challenges are also considerable. For historians, written documents and archival materials are essential, although a very wide range of sources is commonly used today. Henri-Irénée Marrou used a very telling image to underline the importance of written materials for historians: "history is made from documents in the same way as the internal combustion engine runs on fuel" (Marrou, 1954, p. 65). In 2003, however, with the fall of the Iraqi regime, many institutions, libraries and archives — including the Baghdad Museum, the National Archives, the Awqaf Library, the Iraqi Academy of Sciences, and *Bayt al-Hikma*[6] — were looted and/or destroyed. Some documents have been recovered, but others have disappeared for ever. While electronic archives may be available, there are difficulties with scientific control and verification. Consequently, the question arises of the multiplication of sources (written and oral, local, etc.), and of methodological approaches. In this respect, fieldwork might be able to provide a new empirical construction of objects of study and thus of categories of analysis closer to the reality of the internal dynamics of Iraqi society.

Finally, the human dimension cannot be ignored. By 2005, an estimated 10–15% of Iraq's 16,500 instructors spread across some 20 universities had left the country (Al-Takriti, 2005, p. 24). Others resigned then and subsequently because of death threats from Islamist groups and other gangs: some three hundred have been killed. In this state of violence, what does it

---

[6]For a detailed account, see Watenpaugh *et al.* (2003).

mean to be a historian in Iraq today, and what meaning do Iraqi historians give to their scholarly discourse?

$$***$$

The history of contemporary Iraq is of course first the history of all Iraqis. Nevertheless, it is not only Iraqi actors who have left their imprint on the history of Iraq. Certainly, the British mandatory authorities transformed Iraqi society. As well as implementing a number of infrastructural projects, British policy in Iraq created a class of Iraqi clients, including former Sharifian officers, large landowners and tribal leaders. These "collaborators," so to speak, became the elites of the Iraqi state until the overthrow of the monarchy in 1958, and although they were under the influence of British advisers, politicians like Nuri al-Sa'id also left their imprint on the history of Iraq.

Likewise, the interventions of the United States, first in 1991, and more decisively in 2003, have dramatically changed the course of Iraqi history. Following the example of British policies during the mandate, US policy since 2003 has also encouraged the emergence of a new class of Iraqi clients, which in turn will leave its mark, either positively or negatively, on the history of Iraq. In this respect, what place should "the Other," Great Britain (1914–32/1958) and the United States (since 1991/2003), occupy in Iraqi contemporary history?

Furthermore, taking into consideration that the de-Ba'thification of Iraqi history, encouraged by the United States, was one of the main ideological projects of these new Iraqi elites in 2003, how far has the process of de-Ba'thification of academic institutions, and of history, actually gone? Is it already possible to assess the emergence of a "new history" (Iraqi, Arab, and Islamic) promoted by Washington?

The history of Iraq is made up above all of successive and radical breaks (*coups d'état*, changes of regime, military invasions), whose chronological markers are easy to identify. Nevertheless, a narrative exclusively based on these disruptive moments may lead us to observe Iraqi society through the lens of political violence, making Iraqis the champions of violence in the Middle East.[7] Ultimately, it represents a succession of tragic events, which might incline us to assume a sort of fatality in the country's evolution

---

[7]For a critical insight on this grid of analysis, see Loulouwa Al-Rachid and Edouard Méténier (2008: 114–133).

towards the present.[8] Although researchers cannot ignore these disruptions, is it not also necessary to establish a link between the moments when the breaks occur and the longer term, in order to shed light on the period under study?

After the Ba'th party seized power, historical and political science research concentrated almost entirely on the analysis of the political system, the regime and the ruling clique (Aburish, 2000; al-Khalil, 1990; Baram, 1989, pp. 447–493). Nevertheless, as Hamit Bozarslan suggests (Bozarslan, 2007, pp. 13–29), research between the early 1990s and the American invasion of 2003 also focused on tribal and communal phenomena as new grids of analysis (Jabar, 2003, pp. 69–109; Luizard, 2002; Sakai, 2003, pp. 136–161). Yet if we accept that these categories should not be considered essential — in other words, that they are fluid and sometimes the product of constant construction by political powers as well as by researchers — ought they not to be examined critically? For the period until the late 1970s, Hanna Batatu underlined the diversity of Iraqis, not only in ethnic or sectarian terms, but also in social and economic ones (Batatu, 1978, pp. 13–36). More recently, Yitzhak Nakash has shown that the Iraqi Shi'is are by and large recent converts to Shi'ism, a "result of a development which took place mainly during the 19th century as the bulk of Iraq's Arab nomadic tribes settled down and took up agriculture" (Nakash, 1996, p. 4).

Yet the fluidity of sectarian and ethnic boundaries does not imply that they are empty of meaning. As mentioned earlier, within certain contexts (e.g., war, harsh dictatorship), they have often become salient and have determined the collective belonging of individuals or groups, and, eventually, their political engagement. Therefore, instead of rejecting the validity of works focused on power, clan, tribalism and sectarianism as grids of analysis, it seems more appropriate to multiply the sites of observation and the levels of analysis (between the local, the regional and the global, and between internal and external) so that our perspectives on Iraqi or even Middle Eastern history can be renewed. In this sense, the essays assembled in this volume seek to open new avenues for research that can contribute to a fuller — albeit incomplete — understanding of the history of Iraq.

---

[8]Other authors explain the present situation by invoking the 'artificial character' of the Iraqi state. Thus the Iraqi nightmare is the result of the union of three distinct and homogeneous groups (Kurds, Sunnis, and Shi'is). See for instance Peter Galbraith (2006). This version of Iraqi history has been contested convincingly by Reidar Visser.

DEALING WITH THE PAST: METHODOLOGICAL ISSUES

Peter Sluglett

In 1991, and again in 2004, I first co-authored, and then authored, two essays on the European language historiography of Iraq that focused principally on its modern history (Marion Farouk-Sluglett and Peter Sluglett, 1991; Sluglett, 2004). It has also been my good fortune to have written reviews of many of the leading works of modern Iraqi history over the past several years,[1] and I can say with confidence that the field has grown greatly in breadth, depth and stature, and has acquired many accomplished and distinguished practitioners since I entered it in 1976.

So what is the task of the historian? In general, I believe that (s)he should engage as far as possible with *primary sources*, and is professionally obliged to be as honest and truthful as possible. In addition, (s)he should be very aware first, that no sources are ideologically neutral, and second, that (s)he comes to a particular topic with many assumptions, preconceived ideas and so on of which (s)he may not be fully aware. I very much like this passage from Hobsbawm's introduction to *Nations and Nationalism* (1990), where he says:

> Nationalism requires too much belief in what is patently not so. As Renan said, "Getting its history wrong is part of being a nation." Historians are professionally obliged not to get it wrong, or at least

---

[1]The most recent include Tareq Ismael (2008) in *International Journal of Middle East Studies*, 43, 2011, pp. 559–561; Eric Davis (2005), in H-Levant, December 2009; Kenneth L. Brown (2004), in *International Journal of Middle East Studies*, 39, 2007, pp. 647–650; Reidar Visser, (2005), in *The International History Review*, xxix, 1, March 2007, pp. 183–185; Hanna Batatu (2004), in *Democratiya* (on line: www.democratiya.com), March–May 2006; Toby Dodge, (2003), in *International Affairs*, January 2005, pp. 237–239; Pierre-Jean Luizard (2002) in *Times Literary Supplement*, 7 March 2003, pp. 4–5. Other books long overdue for review glare balefully at me from my bookshelf as I write.

> to make an effort not to do so. To be Irish and proudly attached
> to Ireland — even to be proudly Catholic-Irish or Ulster Protestant-
> Irish — is not in itself incompatible with the serious study of Irish
> history. To be a Fenian or an Orangeman, I would judge, is not so com-
> patible . . . unless the historian leaves his or her convictions behind when
> entering the library or the study (Hobsbawm, 1990, p. 12).[2]

My own sympathies have always been with the left, and particularly the Iraqi left, and I find the intolerance and historical questionableness of most nationalist writing or apologetics quite hard to stomach. I also think that originality is important, and lack of originality, or the retracing of steps along well worn paths without due acknowledgement, and poorly documented, unapologetic, or unacknowledged ideological bias, is one the main reasons for the impatient and irascible reviews I have written from time to time.

In the past, one of my main concerns was to highlight the kind of bias in Western history-writing on Iraq best illustrated by Majid Khadduri's two later volumes, *Republican Iraq* . . . (1969) and *Socialist Iraq* . . . (1978), especially the latter,[3] whose main aim was to portray all the Iraqi regimes after 1963 in as sympathetic a light as possible. Apart from the fact that neither contains a bibliography or footnotes, my main academic criticism of the two books was their heavy reliance on official publications and inter-views. Since the interviews were invariably with members of the regime of the day rather than the opposition, the results were inevitably extremely biased. Furthermore, Khadduri described institutions such as the various provisional constitutions and the Revolutionary Command Council (RCC) in such a manner as to suggest that they had some relationship to the way in which the country was actually run. In fact, all the constitutions were sus-pended after 1958, and while the RCC was nominally the country's supreme executive body and its members 'elected' by the Ba'th Party, all important decision-making and politics took place among a small circle of individuals already dominated by Saddam Hussein in the late 1970s, which also oversaw all appointments to the council's ranks.

---

[2]Renan's original words are: "L'oubli, et je dirai même l'erreur historique, sont un facteur essentiel de la formation d'une nation, et c'est ainsi que le progrès des études historiques est souvent pour la nationalité un danger." *Qu'est-ce qu'une nation? Conférence faite en Sorbonne le 11 mars 1882*, Paris, C. Lévy, 1882, pp. 7–8.

[3]See my review in *International Journal of Middle East Studies*, 13, 1982, 370–372. These strictures do not apply to *Independent Iraq 1932–1958: a Study in Iraq Politics* (1960), which is still a useful reference for the events of that period.

Again, although Khadduri might have claimed that his own craft, political science, precluded him from making forays into economic and social analysis, the virtual absence of this dimension renders much of the political conflict he describes incomprehensible. Even in his capacity as a political scientist, he does not attempt to explain what Ba'thism actually was in practice or what 'socialism' meant to those who ruled Iraq, still less what it meant to those who bore the brunt of it. Two quotations from *Socialist Iraq* convey the general atmosphere:

> The leadership has been able to maintain on the whole a high degree of stability and continuity by applying various measures of conformity, including disciplinary action.

> More important perhaps are [Saddam Hussin's] potentials in prudence, flexibility and resourcefulness . . . These qualities, combined with integrity and high moral courage, are his Party's best promise for the country's future leadership.

Although such naivety seems quite laughable today, and I very much doubt whether either *Republican Iraq* or *Socialist Iraq* are still widely read, this was the sort of thing that people, including, most damagingly, US policy-makers, wanted to hear, especially in the late 1970s and the early 1980s, when Saddam Hussein's regime seemed to be all that stood between "us" and the mullahs in Teheran. At that stage, this sort of writing (and compare Christine Moss Helms, *Iraq, Eastern Flank of the Arab World,* 1984) was almost all there was; several years would pass before accessible "alternative" reading would appear, including Samir al-Khalil's *Republic of Fear* (1989) and our own *Iraq since 1958: from Revolution to Dictatorship* (1987).[4] Batatu's masterpiece had appeared rather earlier, but apart from the fact that it is not aimed at the casual reader, the last hundred-odd pages of the book dealing with the period between 1963 and 1977, are its weakest part.[5] At that time, one also had to contend with the curious notion, which died hard in the minds of many European leftist intellectuals, that Saddam Hussein actually was the doughty crusader against imperialism that he claimed to be.

****

---

[4]Christine Moss Helms (1984); Samir al-Khalil (sc. Kanan Makiya) (1989); Marion Farouk-Sluglett and Peter Sluglett (1987, 2001).
[5]Hanna Batatu (1978). See my "Hanna Batatu and the Historiography of Modern Iraq", in Chris Toensing and Mimi Kirk (2011, pp. 7–27).

In their introduction to this volume, Riccardo Bocco and Jordi Tejel ask
historians to refocus their attention on a fairly catholic range of themes,
including subaltern studies, the *longue durée*, continuities and ruptures, and
the "history of all Iraqis". Of these, I wonder whether subaltern studies, the
holy grail of much early modern and modern historiography over the last
few decades, is really feasible in Iraq (and here I am not speaking of research
based principally on oral history). In the Indian sub-continent, where such
writing originated, the voice of the subaltern is filtered through a mountain of administrative, ethnographic, judicial and census data, collected by
officialdom over many generations.[6] Much of that kind of archival material
for Iraq perished in the aftermath of 2003, but in addition, access to the
country, and perhaps more crucially, access to source materials within the
country, was generally denied to foreign scholars after the Revolution of July
1958.[7] Thus two of the three major anthropological studies of Iraq, Robert
Fernea's work on the al-Shabana, and Shakir Salim's *Marsh Dwellers of the
Euphrates Delta*, were based on fieldwork carried out in the 1950s, while the
third, Edmund Leach's short study of the economy and society of southern
Kurdistan, is the fruit of research going back to the late 1930s.[8] The only
more recent study based on fieldwork that I know of, a doctoral thesis on
Madinat al-Thawra (subsequently Madinat Saddam, now Madinat al-Sadr),
submitted (presumably) by an Iraqi to the EHESS in Paris in 1979, does not
seem to have been published, either in whole or in part, in any European
language (al-Ansari, 1979).

In the 1960s, 1970s, and 1980s, when the Iraqi government still had
money to send students abroad, a number of Iraqis produced doctoral theses on humanities and social science topics at British universities.[9] A large
number of them remain confined (by their authors' wish) to the shelves
of the library of the British university from which their authors graduated, and they have generally not been published in book or article form in
any European language. In addition, increasingly severe censorship, and a
great measure of self-censorship, combined with the economic deprivations

---

[6]See, for instance, C. A. Bayly (1983) or F. G. Bailey (1996).

[7]Archaeology seems to have been the exception here: for example, the Chicago Oriental
Institute excavated at Nippur in 1987, while the British School of Archaeology in Iraq
excavated at 'Ana earlier in the 1980s, and at Samarra' in 1986.

[8]See Shakir M. Salim (1962), Robert A. Fernea (1970), and E. R. Leach (1940).

[9]Many of these are listed in my compilation, *Theses on Islam, the Middle East and
North-West Africa 1880–1978 accepted by Universities in the United Kingdom and Ireland*,
London, Mansell (1983).

of the 1990s and early 2000s, meant that Iraqi academics living in Iraq were generally unable to publish academic studies of their country. Lack of access to economic and other data meant that much of the best scholarship on Iraq written in Arabic during that period by Iraqis living in exile (such as Hadi al-'Alawi (d. 1998), Falih 'Abd al-Jabbar and 'Isam al-Khafaji), concentrated on analytical rather than empirical issues, such as the nature of the *rentier* state, the interpretation and significance of modern Islamic thought, and forms of cultural discourse, all concerns widely shared by their contemporaries in other Arab countries.[10] Of course one of the major consequences of the persistence of the brutal and despotic regimes under which the population of Iraq had suffered for so long was that many of its most talented citizens were forced into exile, and that Iraqi scholars could only express themselves freely outside their country. Sadly, this situation seems to have changed little since 2003: many of the academics who returned to Iraq with high hopes after the US invasion have found it impossible to go on living there.

For most of us engaged in the kind of intellectual production exemplified by the contributions to this book and to others like it, the notion of a "history of all Iraqis" probably comes closest to what we would think it our business to be engaged in. While we might focus on the recent history of, say, the Kurds or the Shi'is, we would probably not seek to privilege the suffering of one group over the other. By the same token, few of us would regard Saddam Hussein's idiosyncratic "Project for the Rewriting of History",[11] as a proper exercise of the historian's craft. Unless we are forced to participate in the production of hagiography of various kinds, as must

---

[10]Hadi al-'Alawi (d. 1998) wrote *Fi'l-din wa'l-turath* [On Religion and Heritage] (1973); *Fi'l-siyasa al-islamiya* [On Islamic Politics] (1974); *al-Mu'jam al- 'Arabi al-jadid* [The New Arabic Lexicon] (1983); *al-Mar'i wa'l-la-mar'i fi'l-adab wa'l-siyasa* [The Visible and the Invisible in Poetry and Politics] (1998).

Falih 'Abd al-Jabbar has published *Ma'alim al-'aqlaniyya wa'l-khurafa fi'l-fikr al-siyasi al-'Arabi* [Signs of rationality and irrationality in Arab political thought] (1992); *al-Dimuqratiyh al-mustahila, al-dimuqratiya al-mumkina: namudhaj al-'Iraq* [Impossible democracy, possible democracy; the example of Iraq] (2002). He has also published in English: see his two important edited collections (2002), and (with Hoshem Dawod, 2003). 'Isam al-Khafaji has published *Dawra al-Tatawwur al-Ra'smali fi'l-Iraq, 1968–1978*, [The Role of Capitalist Development in Iraq 1968–1978] (1983), summarized and reviewed by Marion Farouk-Sluglett in *MERIP Reports* 125–6, July–September 1984, pp. 51–52. al-Khafaji also has a major book in English: *Tormented births: passages to modernity in Europe and the Middle East* (2004).

[11]Described so vividly by Eric Davis (2005, see note 2 above).

have been the case with so many of our Iraqi colleagues, we think it beneath us to write "official" or "partisan" history. Mercifully, most of us will never have to, or have had to.

There are four very different essays in this section, written by young historians who have already made major contributions to the historiography of Iraq. Orit Bashkin's "Advice from the Past: 'Ali al-Wardi on Literature and Society" looks at attitudes towards the role of intellectuals in Iraqi society, with special reference to the *oeuvre* of one of the most prominent of these, the sociologist 'Ali al-Wardi (1913–1995). Bashkin examines the notion of the intellectual as professional, expert and technocrat, as purveyor, conveyor, and critic of cultural production, as pioneer and upholder of the "modern" activities of the state, and finally as a revolutionary, urging or seeking the overthrow of the colonial regime.

In the early days of the Iraqi state, the view of the intellectual-as-agent-of-modernity, essentially carried over from the post-1908 Ottoman Empire, seems to have been paramount. This gradually transitioned into the notion of the politically neutral intellectual-as-expert, with appropriate professional or technical training, who would be able to solve the state's practical problems (infant mortality, illiteracy, eco-systems and so on). Here the intellectual is primarily *in the service of*, rather than critical of, the state. This seems to have been the view of authors like Fadil al-Jamali and Sami Shawkat, while Sati' al-Husri ascribed greater agency to intellectuals, whom he thought of both as vital "instigators of change" and "builders of the modern state". Of course much of this discussion is rather vaguer than the reader might like, since "our own" definition of "intellectual" is probably much more restricted than that of the Iraqi writers being considered here, for whom the label seems to have applied to anyone with a university degree or professional qualification.[12]

Iraqi leftists in the 1930s, 1940s, and 1950s saw the role of the intellectual as being in the service of the people, a revolutionary vanguard, while believing that literature should either be in response to, or expressing, the needs of society. As elsewhere in the leftist third world at the time, the writer/intellectual in the colonial state should be concerned primarily with facilitating or explicating the process of national liberation, or with tradition

---

[12]Thus the contributors to this volume would probably regard describe themselves as "intellectuals", but they would probably not think of "their" doctor or lawyer in the same way unless the doctor/lawyer happened also to be a novelist, philosopher, historian or poet in his/her spare time.

and national history rather than with the rarified world of "high culture". Of course, in the Iraqi (or Algerian, or Palestinian) context the (leftist) intellectual was spied upon and "hunted down" by the state; his commitment to the national struggle was his chief virtue, and his outspokenly critical attitude to the *status quo* his badge of courage. Prominent poets and writers of the medieval period were invoked as advocates of social justice, while almost all post-second world war writers were deeply critical of the Hashemite state, in this way fulfilling their "historic role".

The rest of the article is devoted to al-Wardi's *oeuvre*, and his influence on his contemporaries during his lifetime and on young Iraqis today. al-Wardi's *Usturat al-adab al-rafi'* (1957) is about the position of the writer in society. The writer, al-Wardi says, is dependent either on political patronage or on those who buy his work; in order to become (at least relatively) prosperous he has to praise the actions of the regime, or at least mute his criticism. He is irritated by the common man, who either does not buy his work, or prefers trashier or less serious books or magazines. al-Wardi thinks that writing is only meaningful when addressed to people under specific historical circumstances, when it aims to change their attitudes. It is the duty of the writer to oppose and expose oppression, and to make sure that his words reach as wide an audience as possible in order to change hearts and minds. In a novel interpretation, al-Wardi takes the Qur'an as a prime example of a text with enormous social implications, both in its day and ever since; in addition, he tried to put forward a new vision of Iraqi society, part of his commitment to the notion that literature should have meaning. "The true intellectual [in al-Wardi's work]," Bashkin says, "is a secular, democratic critic, conscious of issues relating to social justice and attentive to matters concerning language, history, sociology and culture." Here, as in the work of other leftist writers of the period, the intellectual is a revolutionary social critic. Of course, this was written before 1958; after that, and especially after 1963, many intellectuals were co-opted or bought by successive regimes. On the other hand, many, as we know, could not be bought, although they were obliged to write their critiques from exile and many died there of old age or illness before they could return. By writing or blogging, their contemporary counterparts bravely continue the agenda of committed activism "charted out by al-Wardi half a century ago."

Johan Franzén's paper, "Writing the History of Iraq: the Fallacy of 'Objective' History" raises a number of interesting issues. As noted elsewhere in this volume, especially by Fanny Lafourcade and Peter Harling, the process of de-Ba'thification after 2003 was both inadequately thought out and insensitively or subjectively applied. Clearly, it was important to disband the *mukhabarat*, and to put torturers and murderers on trial.[13] However, the use of the process in a blanket and undifferentiated manner, under institutional arrangements controlled almost entirely by politicians returning from exile, meant that the dragnet was applied on a far broader basis that it need have been. Instead of promoting "truth and reconciliation", de-Ba'thification became politicized, a means of settling scores or neutralizing potential political rivals. In addition, some of those with useful connections to the current regime managed to escape punishment or removal from office.

Drawing on telling examples from Northern Ireland and post-Dayton Bosnia, Franzén underscores the dangers of separate sectarian educational systems and the rewriting of post-conflict history by those who administer such systems. In Iraq, the failure to engage seriously in national reconciliation has created an atmosphere of "empowerment through suffering", especially among the Shi'is who dominate the government, and to some extent, at least in the minds of some Sunnis, creating a witch hunt. As the examples in Peter Harling's paper show, some Shi'is evidently supported the regime of Saddam Hussein during the *intifadha* in 1991, while some Sunnis rose up against it; since people do not wear the same ideological clothes all the time, sectarian labels are not always accurate predictors of behavior.

Franzén's concern is with a specific aspect of the post-conflict process, the rewriting of history, and, in particular, with attempts on the part of those in charge to "white out" anti-Americanism and anti-imperialism in classroom textbooks. He contends that anti-imperialism had long been at the heart of Iraqi education, and it was part of a concerted effort to promote a sense of belonging and national identity. Under the mandate, British officials left education largely in Iraqi hands, and educational provision expanded considerably after the end of the mandate in 1932. Franzén discusses the contributions of Sati' al-Husri, Fadhil al-Jamali and Sami Shawkat rather more generously than I think they deserve — partly because, while fostering a sense of love of country is one thing, the political ramifications of notions

---

[13]There is a large literature on this topic in comparable situations elsewhere in the world; see, for example, the references in Greg Grandin (2005, pp. 46–67). Although the parallel may seem remote, El Salvador's "negotiated transition" from a twelve year civil war (1980–1992) between guerrilla fighters and an "establishment" supplied and armed by the US, to relative peace and prosperity ever since, is instructive in the Iraqi context; see Elizabeth Jean Wood (2003, pp. 78–107).

of the "Arab homeland", the "Arab people", and *qawmiyya* have generally been pretty negative as well as almost entirely a-historical. As I often ask my students, "When was the Arab nation?"

The next section of the paper covers Saddam Hussein's "Project for the Rewriting of History" (mentioned above), which involved the arabization of pre-Arab Iraqi history, and the jettisoning of the notion of an Iraqi national history. It is good to note that the project never really met its goals, but on the other hand, anti-imperialism had become internalized in the minds of most of the population as early as the 1920s and 1930s. While I am not sure that I follow Franzén's evaluation of the curious process of the fictionalizing of some parts of Iraqi history by the Ba'th, I am in complete agreement with the idea, which must be common in the reconstruction of the history of all colonized states, that the national struggle, the independence struggle, and the struggle against imperialism are all "fundamental and vital part[s] of Iraqi historical memory...". While admitting the very great difficulties confronting the writing of a pluralist "history of all Iraqis", containing "multiple historical narratives" one can only applaud Franzén's conclusion that this is the only viable, and professional, way forward for historians of Iraq, both Iraqi and non-Iraqi.

Reidar Visser's "The Sectarian Master Narrative in Iraqi Historiography: New Challenges since 2003", is an eloquent and well-argued plea directed towards journalists and other "analysts" of current events, who are far too ready to resort to neat or stereotypical explanations of events. In particular, Visser criticizes the widespread tendency to reduce almost every instance of conflict in Iraq to primordial sectarian-based animosity. It would be foolish to deny the existence of sects, or of sectarian hostility, but it is sloppy, as well as misleading, to imagine that everything that happens or has happened in Iraq can be traced back to that single source. One obvious point, especially in southern Iraq, is that many of the conflicts are *intra*-Shi'i; different Shi'i groups, parties, militias or interests are fighting over the same turf, with nary a Sunni in sight.

A good way to nip this sort of one-size-fits-all thinking in the bud would be for journalists to avoid starting sentences with "Sunnis fear...", or "Shi'is think...".[14] In addition, Visser briefly raises the larger question, which has

---

[14]While Joe Biden might once have thought in terms of "Sunnistan" and "Shi'istan", most Iraqi Arabs do not want "a separate territorial space". Mercifully, the "Biden plan" (www.planforiraq.com), aired by the Senator in October 2006, fell out sight after his promotion. A separate Kurdistan, on the other hand, though undoubtedly a high-risk

certainly had resonance over the past eight years, of whether, like the British in India, the occupier actually *needs* the notion of the constant potential for sectarian violence to legitimize (his) continuing occupation — on the grounds that withdrawal would lead to civil war. Charitably, Visser prefers a more innocent explanation (faced with a thoroughly bewildering situation, the journalist searches for the explanation (s)he finds easiest to grasp), but it might also be wise to "hold that thought". If feelings or emotions are held to be primordial or atavistic, this may lead to the conclusion that solutions or attempts at reconciliation are unattainable, because the parties involved are not rational beings (that is, they "really hate each other"). The incidents and episodes that Visser recounts show only too tellingly how simple repetition makes statements "acquire the quality of truisms". Greater analytical effort, and greater attention to detail on the part of both those who produce and those who consume the news, are clearly necessary.

The last paper, Peter Harling's "Beyond Political Ruptures: Towards a Historiography of Social Continuity in Iraq", is probably the most challenging of the four. Harling's concern is the period between1968 and about 2008: I have made an effort to provide a "straight" narrative history of the years between 1990 and 2003 (Sluglett, 2010, pp. 13–33), but it is clear that Harling has had access to sources which enable him to bring far greater insights to the table. In essence, what happened after 2003 was not created out of nothing: hence the seizure of initiative by Muqtada al-Sadr and his followers was "predictable" in the sense that almost all other forms of political organization had been banned, exiled or exterminated, and the divisive ethno-sectarian model which the US seized upon as "natural" was largely dictated by influential political exiles in London and Washington. Of course, as Harling says, very few outsiders had been able to observe what was happening in, say, the Iraqi provinces, between the mid-1980s and the fall of the regime. To that extent, US notions of what might reasonably have been expected to be in place on "the day after surrender" — were based almost entirely on ignorance or wishful thinking.

Harling makes the sensible point that sectarianism was revived, rather than created, by the occupation. In my view this had been in the offing at least since the late 1970s and then more obviously during the Iran–Iraq war, where Shi'is could be represented as a kind of permanent fifth column, and men were offered substantial sums to divorce their "Iranian" wives.

---

strategy for those who support it, seems less completely farfetched. See Peter W. Galbraith (2006).

Sectarianism continued with the *intifadha* in 1991, and with the overall neglect of the south during the sanctions in the 1990s and 2000s. I had not previously encountered the suggestion that Harling makes to the effort that since the regime no longer had the means to be omnipresent, it actually became less totalitarian during the 1990s — and "mere survival [became] the main organizing principle of both polity and society." If the state apparatus was in some sense in retreat, and total repression was no longer an option, some freedom of association or organization may have been possible.

Harling discusses some other examples of US myth-making: the "traditional tribal structures", which had largely disappeared by the 1960s, were revamped by the regime in the 1980s and 1990s, making the shaykhs part of the state's clientele. These tribal leaders were "powerful" to the extent that they were able to attract the regime's munificence; loyalty to the regime dissolved the moment it fell, and the leaders were correspondingly helpless without regime support. Judging by their early embrace of "the tribal leaders", the US administration must have thought that the social meaning of tribal affiliation, and the dependence which this implied, had been somehow frozen in time. In fact, by the early 2000s, the rural population of Iraq was only 33% of the total (about the same, incidentally, as Italy [32%] and Japan [34%]).[15] Even the most amateur anthropologist must have wondered what effect massive rural to urban migration, and the wholesale abandonment of agricultural labor which this implied, might have had on "the tribes".

Harling's insights are so numerous and so perceptive that I can only single out a few of them. For instance, the idea of the entire "Sunni community" as permanent recipients of the regime's benevolence is neatly deconstructed. In addition, the regime's tolerance or encouragement of Wahhabi/Salafi influence in the 1990s evidently caused massive social dislocation and the marginalization of much of the Sunni population, especially in the rural areas and in small towns, and of course Salafism became the main motor of the Sunni insurgency, first with al-Qa'ida, and then against it in the course of a conservative backlash. The intra-Shi'i struggle, on which Visser has written here and elsewhere, is also described, particularly the socio-economic rift between the followers of the *marja'iyya* on the one hand and the Sadrists on the other.[16] The latter were mostly poorer ("detribalized") rural migrants,

---

[15]Data from the World Bank: http://data.worldbank.org/indicator/SP.RUR.TOTL.ZS.

[16]Many of whom had originally been roused by the "anti-American and anti-Iranian rhetoric" of Muqtada al-Sadr's father, Ayatullah Muhammad Sadiq al-Sadr, assassinated by the Ba'th in 1999.

whose economic opportunities, always fairly limited, had become even more circumscribed with the sanctions, which they associated with the US, and for whom "suits" like Ahmad Chalabi and his circle must have seemed like visitors from another planet. In the last section of his paper Harling analyses the "civil war" which took place in and around Baghdad in 2006 and 2007, the result of "multiple and intersecting dimensions of past identity formation and social organizational trends"; "one can only wonder", as he says, "how a brutalized society can deal with so many discontinuities."

All four papers, each replete with deep insights and an unblinking sense of the magnitude of the task that lies ahead, are infused with a common humanity and a desire to encourage reconciliation and the construction of a decent future for Iraq. This can only be based on a major effort to come to terms with the past, a process that will take years, perhaps decades. On the other hand, the more is known — or least so one hopes — the more reconstruction can be effective. The experience of post-civil war Lebanon (where particular forms of sectarian division have long been seen as a set of primary social givens), may give some hope. Thus the Israeli attack on Qana (near Tyre) in April 1996, in which only one of the hundred dead was Christian, and which took place in a region where Muslims and Christians had fought each other bitterly during the civil war which had ended only five years earlier, is commemorated as a *national* tragedy, and in an important sense Rafiq Hariri, assassinated in February 2005, while self-evidently a Sunni Muslim, "managed to transcend ethno-religious boundaries to be remembered as a martyr for both Christian and Muslim communities."[17] Whether or not this can be described as "progress", power in Lebanon is no longer monopolized by an alliance of Maronites and Sunnis (as it was until about 1980), but by Sunnis and Maronites and/or Shi'is and Maronites. It is much too early to predict whether historical memory can be transformed in Iraq (as may or may not be taking place in Lebanon); I can only hope fervently that it will, and that it will also make whatever positive contribution that 'telling the truth' can bring to the table.

---

[17]Lucia Volk (2010, pp. 154–188, here 187). For a generally less optimistic view, see Sune Haugbolle (2010).

ADVICE FROM THE PAST: 'ALI AL-WARDI ON LITERATURE AND SOCIETY

Orit Bashkin

In this essay, I look at some representations of the functions of intellectuals in modern Iraqi society as articulated in the print media of the Hashemite period. In doing so, I wish to underline the richness of this intellectual field and to illustrate that the public sphere was typified by competing definitions of the term "intellectual".[1] I then address the writings of an extremely important sociologist and theoretician, 'Ali al-Wardi (1913–1995), on this question. I underscore Wardi's secular and democratic critique, yet argue that despite his original and pioneering arguments, his views reflect discourses current in Iraq in the 1940s and the 1950s. Finally, I reflect on the ways in which Wardi's insights might inform our thinking about contemporary Iraq. His ideas, I propose, are both universal *and* specific to the Hashemite context, and therefore could help us understand modern Iraqi history on the one hand, and modern intellectual history on the other.

Iraqi intellectual history has tended to focus on intellectuals who were affiliated with the state and active during the interwar period, thus

---

[1] I warmly thank Peter Sluglett. The term used by most writers to signify the word intellectual is *adib*, a writer or an author. The word originated from the medieval concept of *adab*, meaning "prose literature" or "culture", but was transformed in the modern Arab context into a concept specifying a writer that publishes views on important philosophical and ethical issues in the public sphere. The word *muthaqqaf* was often used in the essays I reviewed to designate an educated man or a thinker. Another term is *fannan*, meaning artist or a creative person (although in the early 1920s it also retained the Ottoman meaning of a man with a proficiency in a particular scientific domain). *Mutakhassis* signified a technocrat, or an expert in a discipline.

neglecting other important voices in the public sphere.[2] However, as shown by Silvia Naef (2001, pp. 255–268) and Sami Zubaida (2002, pp. 205–215), the biographies of leading poets, novelists and writers can also serve as interesting case studies for historians of modern Iraq (see also Walther, 1996, pp. 219–241; Masliyah, 1996, pp. 161–167). For example, the fascinating biography of the celebrated poet Muhammad Mahdi al-Jawahiri (b. 1900) (his political poetry; his involvement in the anti-Hashemite opposition and in the institutions of the state during the first years of Qasim's regime) could teach us much about the changes taking place in the Iraqi public sphere. Similar observations could be made with respect to the biographies of neoclassical poets like Maʿruf al-Rusafi (b.1875) or modernist ones, like ʿAbd al-Wahhab al-Bayati (b.1926). Furthermore, historians of modern Iraqi culture should look at many of Iraq's intellectuals as interesting theoreticians, whose work could guide our research on Iraqi society, in both the past and the present.

Not surprisingly, Iraqi intellectuals have been asking themselves similar questions to the ones posed by their European and American peers. Edward Said identified two main streams of thought concerning the roles that intellectuals play in society. The first sees the intellectual as a man belonging to a small, gifted group of morally and ethically committed thinkers, blessed with the sensitivity to reflect about the nature of the universe (Said, 1996, pp. 3–45; and also Shils, 1958–1959, pp. 5–22). Michel Foucault has shown that this perception of the "universal intellectual" became politically significant from the 18th century onwards, when thinkers, often jurists, resisted abuses and injustice in the name of the rule of law (Foucault, 1984, 51–75; Said, 1996, pp. 9–10). The second position that Said identified sees intellectuals as functionaries in their societies. Antonio Gramsci underscored the links between the intellectual and modern capitalist society, which produced a line of professionals, such as technocrats and political economists. These "organic intellectuals" systematized new political and cultural structures and were closely linked to their class (Gramsci, 2000, pp. 300–322; Said, 1996, pp. 8–11; in Iraq, see Davis, 2005, pp. 1–29). Foucault located the rise of the professional-intellectual in the post World War II era, which gave birth to the "specific intellectual," i.e., an expert, who worked within a discipline with claims to or qualifications in specialized forms of knowledge. The specific intellectual had a direct and localized relation to scientific knowledge and to academic and political institutions (Foucault, 1984,

---

[2]For a critique of Iraqi intellectual history, see the introduction in Bashkin (2008).

pp. 51–75). Demand for the creation of such professional technocrats was not unique to Europe, and became an important part of interwar discussions in the Middle East. For example, urban elites in both Syria and Egypt championed the training of a new generation of professionals (engineers, social-scientists etc) that could assist the emerging nation state, replace the colonial elites equipped with similar bodies of knowledge, and benefit the nation's education systems (El Shakry, 2001; Zeifa, 2004, pp. 497–536).

Said's definition of "the public intellectual" (Said, 1996, pp. 11–12) is greatly influenced by the argument of Jean Paul Sartre (Sartre, 1988) that writers needed to respond to the demands of their society. No matter how critical they were of the public, writers related to the public's dominant conceptions of society and literature. For Said, the public intellectual is an individual who articulates an opinion "to, as well as for", the public, and challenges well-accepted conventions and dogmas. The intellectual does so in a particular context, yet acts on the basis of universal principles, such as belief in the universality of human rights. A public intellectual, furthermore, operates outside the realm of the state, and resists specialization, since becoming an institutionalized expert means exposure to political pressures (Said, 1996, pp. 11–12, 41).

In Iraq, the tensions regarding the duties of intellectuals as recognized by Said (private/public; universal/specific, ethical/professional) assumed immense importance. These debates signified the relationship between the intellectual on the one hand, and the state, i.e., political parties, disciplinary institutions, the royal court and British colonialism, on the other. While some thinkers championed complete segregation between the intellectual and the political system, others saw the political sphere as the only legitimate realm in which they could realize their objectives, and they utilized the state's institutions to propagate and implement their ideas. Those who supported the latter option often felt that intellectuals ought to be trained within specifically defined disciplines. In the last decade of the Hashemite state, however, the intellectual became a committed revolutionary, seeking to overthrow the regime.

Representations of the Iraqi Intellectual

In the 1920s, intellectuals believed that they were agents of progress, urbanism and modernity. Inspired by discussions about constitutionalism and democracy in Iran and in the Ottoman Empire (especially around 1900–1912), intellectuals felt that men of thought instigated historical change. In many ways the budding Iraqi public sphere of the 1920s was a continuation of a local-Iraqi Ottoman public sphere that had emerged in Iraq after 1908, and persisted into the first decade of the Iraqi state (Davis, 2005, pp. 29–55; Watenpaugh, 2006, pp. 31–121). It was within this sphere that the role of the intellectual was debated.

An article in the daily *al-Dijla* suggested that intellectuals constituted a group that voiced public opinion, and critiqued the decline in their society. Whereas in the past, the power of reason (*'aql*) had been inferior to that of the body, currently human reason had advanced to an unimaginable extent. Knowledge was therefore the ruler of the present time (*sultan al-'asr*).[3] Many journalists, moreover, agreed that intellectuals had a moral duty to critique the faults of political regimes and to strive to create a better society.[4] Novelist and short-story writer Mahmud Ahmad al-Sayyid (b.1904) offered a different perspective. He perceived the intellectual as being inherently powerless, while the rich and the dishonest acquire the respect of the people.[5] al-Sayyid explained that even in the middle ages writers were dependent on affluent rulers and were subsequently forced "to ornament their words, fearing the rage of the Sultan."[6] Sadly, very few changes occurred in the modern age. The state, in his view, was always immoral, albeit powerful, while intellectuals, men of high standards, who refused to yield to its powers, were extremely weak. Nevertheless, despite this weakness, he believed that intellectuals must pronounce their opinions, and make them known to the public, for eventually they would generate change.

Other intellectuals, however, took issue with such positions. In an article published in the prestigious Egyptian cultural journal *al-Hilal*, the Iraqi writer 'Atta Amin (b. 1897) denied both the ethical functions of intellectuals and their ability to change society. In his view, politicians and generals were the important elements in society, while intellectuals usually replicated prevalent views without advocating any particular change. As evidence, he considered the stance of intellectuals towards murder. Theoretically, there was no crime more serious than the killing of another human being. Nonetheless, thinkers cheered Brutus for killing Caesar and poets like Friedrich von Schiller extolled the Swiss hero Wilhelm Tell, although Tell

---

[3] *al-Dijla* (No. 41, 2), August 10, 1921.
[4] *al-Rafidain* (No. 45, 12), March 1, 1921,
[5] al-Sayyid, "*Qissat al-da'if*," 156; see also al-Sayyid, "*al-Siham al-muqabila*," *A'mal*, 207, al-Sayyid, "*al-Dhi'b al-bishri*," *A'mal*, 238–241.
[6] al-Sayyid, "*Qissat al-da'if*," *A'mal*, 152–153.

had murdered an Austrian governor. The reasoning behind such justifica-
tions was that these murders were politically necessary. Therefore, despite
the consensus among people concerning the condemnation of the murder of
someone like Abraham Lincoln, eventually intellectuals — just like politicians — judge actions by their final results. Furthermore, regardless of forms
of political organization, the world has remained lawless and unethical.
According to this rather Machiavellian account, intellectuals were utterly
immersed in the political, unethical realm, and their writings echoed, rather
than altered, popular consensus.[7]

The gradual growth of the Iraqi state and the development of its institutions during the interwar period produced the view of the intellectual as an
expert and a nationalist, who supported the various projects of the state.
Demand for the employment of professional technocrats began as early as
the 1920s. The daily *al-'Iraq* reported that the Iraqi nation needed professionals more than food, and specified that the nation required "men who
specialize in arts, sciences, and administration."[8] Every branch of knowledge
needed specific laws and rules. Ma'ruf al-Rusafi, Anastas Karmili (b. 1866)
and Jamil Sidqi al-Zahawi (b. 1863) demanded a more professionalized literary criticism, based on impartiality, objectivity, and aesthetic and artistic
merit, as well the contribution of the particular work to the nation,[9] while
the literary journal *al-Yaqin* advocated the professional and scientific study
of history.[10]

In the 1930s, bureaucrats like Sami Shawkat (b. 1893) and Fadil al-Jamali
(b. 1902), reduced the intellectuals into mere technocrats, who could create
national subjects through the production of modern knowledge. Individuals
like Jamali had in mind a professional elite that would take responsibility
for solving Iraq's demographic problems, educating its peasants and women,
and constructing a history that evoked national zeal and loyalty to the
Hashemite dynasty. Shawkat, it seems, never perceived intellectuals as critics
of the state, and constantly called upon artists, writers and poets to assist in
the national project. Moreover, he made no distinction between journalists,
writers, and social scientists, since all needed to "gather information on our

---

[7] *al-Hilal* (Vol. 30, Part. 5), February, 1922.
[8] *al-'Iraq* (No. 513, 127), January, 1922: see also: *al-'Iraq* (No. 608, 1), May 18, 1922;
al-Dijla (No. 56, 3), September 1, 1921; *al-Rafidan* (No. 18, 1), October 21, 1921; *Istiqlal*
(No. 105, 1), June 9, 1922.
[9] *al-Amal* (No. 59), December 10, 1923. Reprinted in Ahmad Matlub (1968: 32).
[10] *Yaqin* (No. 17), February 17, 1923.

social illness" and provide treatment for the nation's problems (Shawkat, 1939).[11] Jamali deemed leaders and experts as essential elements in national politics, blessed with the ability to reform Iraqi society. He envisaged a body of technocrats, working together in the ministries of education and health, and attempting to reform the socioeconomic conditions of Iraq's tribal populations (al-Jamali, 1934).

Of all Iraqis, the nationalist educator and writer Sati' al-Husri (b. 1862) expressed most admiration for intellectual activity. To Husri, intellectuals were the motivating power behind revolutions and he esteemed the writers, philosophers and thinkers who stimulated social change. Thus he argued that the perception that the termination of slavery was a mere by-product of economic development, in particular of the industrialization of the American North, did injustice to one of the greatest American intellectual projects, namely the anti-slavery campaign. Husri asserted that one could not dismiss the various discussions, speeches, electoral campaigns and activities of writers over almost four decades prior to the American Civil War as trivial (al-Husri, 1962, pp. 387–395). Husri similarly portrayed the Enlightenment as a movement of historical change that occurred thanks to the efforts of philosophers, such as Voltaire, Diderot and Rousseau, who looked differently at questions of social order, progress and freedom.[12] His own writing focused on intellectuals who lived in periods of transition: Tolstoy at the time when imperial Russia was debating its position between East and West, or Fichte at the birth of German nationalism. This enabled Husri to present them both as generators of change and as individuals reflecting on the changes occurring in their societies.[13]

Nonetheless, Husri also wished to employ technocrats in the service of the nation. He referred to "techno-psychology", that is, the science of orientation, and professional and vocational guidance, which elucidated the motivations behind the selection of a particular profession, and served to envisage the functions these professionals would fulfill in the state. Moreover, while in the West physical, practical and theoretical inclinations generally guided an individual when choosing a profession, in the East individuals saw

---

[11] *Istiqlal* (No. 3521), December 15, 1939.

[12] Husri's views of the Enlightenment were published in his essays about Rousseau (1928/1962, pp. 240–242, 255–257).

[13] Husri published a special issue of *Majallat al-tarbiyya wa'l-ta'lim* in 1928 dedicated to Tolstoy, in which he wrote three essays on Tolstoy, reprinted in *Ahadith* (1962, pp. 283–309); On Fichte's impact see Cleveland (1971, pp. 85–86).

their higher education as a way of obtaining a position of power within the state. The control of the state over the market made it the only institution capable of granting fixed salaries to its employees, regardless of unstable political and economic conditions. Easterners thus looked at officials with fear and jealousy, and government positions became a sort of a magnet to educated young men. It was accordingly the role of intellectuals *inside* the state, like teachers or psychologists, to encourage educated youth to work in institutions *outside* the state (al-Husri, 1962, pp. 95–107, 120–133). Husri's call for technocrats to work outside the sphere of the state did not mean that he did not regard the state as an important key to intellectual activity, especially through its involvement in the cultivation of modern education. He was certain, however, that the growth of an educated, economically independent, middle class would improve Iraq's socio-cultural conditions and foster its national revival.

Husri's writings contained two contradictory poles: Respect, on the part of Husri, the writer and the intellectual, for the power of intellectuals to change society, and on the other hand the desire of Husri the bureaucrat to capitalize on the activities of modern intellectuals for the sake of the state. Like many of their contemporaries, Husri, Shawkat, and Jamali felt that the national revival needed able men, and that the state ought to produce, and subsequently employ, professionals and administrators who would pave the path to a modern nation.

The interwar Left, however, propagated other visions. Addressing their young readership through letters, epistles, books and newspapers, Iraq's social democratic group *al-Ahali* (established in 1932) propagated the image of writers and thinkers as men committed to the Iraqi working classes and free of the state's manipulation. The intellectuals' role *vis-à-vis* the state was consequently defined as exposing its failures. Motivated by a belief that intellectuals should be an integral part of the society they sought to change, writers affiliated with *al-Ahali* did outline various domains in which the state should employ the services of intellectuals, like mass education and the construction of cooperative villages. These writers accentuated the fact that intellectuals could play a role in the state, although in their opinion this was not the corrupt Iraqi state of the present, but rather the just social-democratic community of the future. Their construction of a combative, active intellectual managed to destabilize the image of the weak, tormented intellectual of the 1920s as articulated by al-Sayyid, on the one hand, and that of the expert-administrator and bureaucrat, on the other. The group's intellectuals had indeed functioned as critics of the state. They criticized

British influence in Iraq's politics and economy, protested its dysfunctional land regime, its legal codes and its electoral and educational systems, and, more broadly, exposed the gaps between the Iraqi national discourse, which hailed the nation's progress, and Iraq's bitter socioeconomic realities.[14]

These positions regarding the roles of intellectuals should be grounded within the specific context of the interwar period. The Hashemites, in particular King Faysal I, as well as the Sharifians and Iraq's landed and military elites, realized that the newly established state needed trained professionals. The Hashemite Court, moreover, employed the services of poets and writers as part of its patronage system.[15] Nonetheless, the binaries ethical/unethical, strong/weak, nationalist/critic, articulated by Iraqi writers, registered the doubts of intellectuals regarding their position in the nation. The debates on intellectualism expose the historical setting in which Iraqi intellectuals sensed the power of the new state and the potentialities it offered them. Some chose to challenge the state, while others advocated accepting its authority.

During the 1940s, the Iraqi Communist Party (henceforth ICP), and particularly its leader, Fahd (Yusuf Salman Yusuf, hanged in 1949), viewed the intellectual as a significant agent in the future revolution. The ICP was established in the mid-1930s, and became active in Iraq's socio-cultural and socio-political life in the 1940s and 1950s. Fahd was familiar with Leninism (through Stalinist lenses) and wished to apply a Leninist model of a revolutionary avant-garde leading both the proletariat and the peasantry (Salman Yusuf/Fahd, 1976).[16] The Iraqi communists viewed the intellectual as an organizer. Organization was decisive in the context of peasant and tribal revolts, groups whose dissatisfaction with their social conditions was not yet channeled into making fundamental changes in Iraq's social realities. The role of intellectuals was therefore to give meaning to these events and to shape them into a coherent movement. The communist intellectual, however, was a man of the *avant-garde*. He was interested in the most novel ideas and literary genres, which were entirely different from the creations of reactionary writers, and committed to advancing experimental forms of art and literature (Fahd, 1976, pp. 153, 183, 329–330; Khayri, 1976, pp. 46–52).

---

[14]On the group and the Left of the 1930s, see Bashkin (2008), Jamil (1983), al-Wakil (1980).

[15]On the relationship of the educated elites and the state, see Bashkin (2008), Yousif (1991, pp. 172–196).

[16]On the ICP, see Ismael (2008).

There was nothing particularly original about Fahd's thinking. In fact, such ideas featured in many publications by communists in the third world and in Eastern Europe. Their importance, however, emanated from the fact that many of the intellectuals at the time identified with and were inspired by communist and socialist publications, and reproduced them in their own essays. The vocabulary advanced by Fahd, in other words, was to be found in the ICP's press, in its leaflets, and pamphlets, and it was discussed in cell meetings, as well as in literary salons and cultural journals.

The perception of the intellectual as a man propagating progressive literature and art was also found in the articles of Husayn Muhammad al-Shabibi (hanged alongside Fahd in 1949), in particular "The Scientific Tendency in Literature (*adab*)" (1939), and "Who are the Writers (*udaba'*)?" (1941). True writers, he elucidated, wished to liberate the people in nonviolent ways. As literature reflected relations of production, both writers and critics should take into account the context in which they write, and look at society, its modes of production and prevalent types of regimes. Shabibi condemned writers, who, convinced of their uniqueness and irreplaceability, associated their writings with high taste and excluded the people from the dual processes of writing and reading. Endeavoring to please a small and exclusive cluster, they divorced literature from popular culture and from the people. On the other hand, communist writers did not think in terms of abstract art or art for art's sake. Rather, they were conscious of their readership. The communist party, nevertheless, should always allow freedom of expression, in which true avant-garde intellectuals write and critique (al-Shahir, 1978, pp. 96–101).

Shabibi's views differed from Fahd's postulations, particularly in his view of the nonviolent diffusion of revolutionary knowledge through literature. Fahd, conversely, romanticized the Russian intellectuals, "who carried weapons in their right hand, and a pen in their left; those who imprisoned themselves in factories to create fine weapons." He also believed that Iraq was in need of rapid industrialization, which in turn required the service of specialists (*fannaniyun*) and technocrats, who would invest every effort to establish industries in the country. The experts could even be foreigners, or Iraqis educated abroad, who had learned the newest methods of industrialization.[17] Both Fahd and Shabibi's views, nonetheless, mirror Lenin's *What*

---

[17]Fahd, "Heavy Industry — The Root of Our Economic Struggle," *al-Majalla* (No. 4), March 1, 1941. Reprinted in *Kitabat* (1976, pp. 415–417).

Needs to Be Done? especially Lenin's call for a popular, yet not vulgar, literature, read by both the people and the elite (Lenin, 1963, p. 152). Both writers, however, also appropriated some of the positions towards popular literature articulated by Iraqi and Egyptian critics. Many other Arab critics, not necessarily communists, articulated the necessary correlation between literature and popular taste, and between artistic works and the milieu in which they were produced. Likewise, the view of literature as transmitting the traditions and the history of a particular space was underlined in the writings of many nationalist intellectuals.[18]

The Iraqi political context, in which ICP members were constantly persecuted by the government, gave birth to an image of the intellectual as a man constantly hunted by the state and willing to become a martyr for the causes he held dear. Fahd argued that the communists "do not like prisons and do not enjoy having their houses searched by the police and being terrorized by them." The communists in Iraq saw "faces of spies following them like shadows", yet endured these violent measures, thinking they were "a shining example to their class and to humanity in its entirety" (Fahd, 1976, p. 68).

The positions of *al-Ahali* and the communists viewing the intellectual as an individual located outside the state, exposing its weaknesses, and in the case of the communists, laboring for the coming revolution, became dominant during the 1940s and 1950s. After the Second World War, and particularly in the 1950s, intellectuals, including radical Pan-Arab nationalists, grew more critical of the Hashemite state. One of the major catalysts that affected the thinking of Iraqi and Arab intellectuals at the time was the writings of Jean-Paul Sartre and his notions of the intellectual's commitment (*iltizam*) to his or her society. Writers were not to write for the aesthetic pleasure of writing, but rather to expose, to critique, and to cure (Sartre, 1988; Bashkin, 2008, pp. 87–123). As Jabra Ibrahim Jabra noted, Sartre's name became an emblem to all writers who believed in the links between writing, politics, and justice, despite the fact that such writers might have not read all (or even any) of Sartre's works (Jabra, 1980, pp. 7–22; 2005, 82–83). For Iraqi nationalists, the commitment of the *littérateur* to the national struggle produced literature committed to Arab causes, such as Palestine and Algeria. Sartre's initial support for the Soviet Union and his

---

[18]On how Egyptian intellectuals viewed the relations writer-context, see Semah (1974) and Musa (1956).

trips to the Soviet Union and Cuba in 1954 made him very important to Iraqi communists.[19] This conversation kindled further interesting questions: What is the relationship between commitment and Marxism? Did the notion of commitment exist in the Arabic literature of the past? How should it affect contemporary poetry, prose and the plastic arts? How should the Arab public be addressed, changed, and revolutionized? By what means?

Already in the 1940s, social realists (in literature and art) declared that literature corresponded to the needs of society. Novelist 'Abd al-Majid Lutfi, for example, argued that literature was the product of both spiritualism and freedom, and that it was a medium that played a vital role in exposing national and social problems (Lutfi, 1944, pp. 4–6). The left-leaning intelligentsia as well as the radical Pan-Arabists used the notion of commitment to highlight their support of the aspirations of the people, on the one hand, and their critique of the state, on the other. The Iraqi literary market was influenced by contemporary French literary theory, since some literary critics had acquired their training in France (Rossi, 1958, pp. 61–65; Mahdi, 2001). Similarly, poets like Badr Shakir al-Sayyab (1926–1964) and Buland al-Haydari (1926–1996), all emphasized the link between the writer, his goals, the society surrounding him, and his commitment to changing it.[20] Sayyab further projected the question of *iltizam* onto the Arab past. For him, the poet Abu'l-Tayyib al-Mutanabbi (915–965) struggled for rebellion, the poet Abu'l-'Ala' al-Ma'ari (973–1057) advocated social justice, while the prose writer al-Jahiz (781–868) was the first Arab to be interested in the conditions of the people. al-Sayyab was pleased with the new directions taken by modern writers like Najib Mahfuz, and repeatedly emphasized that literature should come from the soul of the writer and ought not to be calling for despair and defeat, but ought rather to radicalize Arab readers.[21]

In the post-war era, most of Iraq's prominent writers were affiliated with the anti-Hashemite opposition (social-democratic, communist or nationalist) and were consequently persecuted by the state. Thus, while the generation of the 1920s and 1930s accepted the cooperation with the state (working as technocrats and experts in its services), by the 1950s, radical nationalists

---

[19] On the commitment to the Palestinian cause in Bayati's works, see Kadhim (2001, pp. 86–106).

[20] *al-Adab* (No. 4, 4, 84–86), April 1956. See also the reflections on Iraqi paintings by Shakir Hasan, and his views on the relationship between art and human existence: *al-Adab* (No. 4, pp. 74–5), April 1954, 2nd year.

[21] *al-Adab* (No. 4, 10), October 1956.

and Marxists alike had come to argue that they needed to be located out-side the realm of the state. This connoted a universal, existentialist position, on the one hand, yet also a very particular Iraqi position, which regarded the Hashemite state as hopelessly irredeemable, on the other. Such posi-tions conveyed the growing dissatisfaction of the new generation of Iraqi *effendiyya* with the policies of the state. The concept of revolution, essential to large groups of intellectuals, such as the communists and the Ba'thists,[22] became of immense importance. Iraqi writers felt that their works should in one way or other facilitate the coming of this revolution, motivated by the belief that culture and politics could not, and should not, be separated.

Wardi's Complaint

'Ali al-Wardi was an Iraqi Shi'i writer and thinker, who received his PhD in sociology from the University of Texas in 1950. He taught sociology in Baghdad University, where his classes became extremely popular. Unlike many of his Pan-Arab contemporaries, Wardi's work is typified by a genuine interest in Iraq (rather than the wider Arab Middle East): Its social geog-raphy, political economy and its various modes of state power. Wardi pub-lished numerous studies of Iraqi history and sociology, mostly dealing with the relationship between Iraq's tribal and settled communities. His research has assisted many Western historians, especially scholars of the Shi'is in Iraq, because of his analysis of tribal history. In addition, his research paid much heed to Iraq in the Ottoman period, which he depicted not simply as an era of oppression, but also as a period that profoundly influenced the character of the modern Iraqi state. On the other hand, he tried to analyze events in Iraq by using methodological tools borrowed from modern sociol-ogy, history and anthropology as well as from a comparative perspective. In recent times, numerous websites operated by young Iraqis have been dedi-cated to 'Ali al-Wardi (Luizard, 1995, pp. 120–126) and his works (including one on Facebook!).

Wardi's *The Myth of Elite Literature* (*Usturat al-adab al-rafi'*), published in 1957, deals brilliantly with the new currents in the intellectual field of the 1950s, yet offers new theoretical insights regarding the position of the writer in society. A writer, argued Wardi, sells his merchandise in the market like

---

[22]On the concept of the revolution and linearity as reflected in the thinking of the Ba'th, see Bashkin (2006, pp. 59–86).

any other merchant. The lofty image of the intellectual as a man producing his work solely for the sake of knowledge is itself a representation cultivated by writers who served in the courts of sultans (*udaba' al-salatin*). Relying on the upper classes, and echoing their contempt for the lower classes, these writers have depicted themselves as somehow separate or apart from the rest of the population. There was no reason, however, to bemoan the golden status of the writers in those days, since such adulation implicitly means hailing the authoritarianism of the writers' patrons.

Regrettably, contemporary Iraqi writers are still enslaved to norms that presume that the author is located above the people and in the service of powerful political patrons. For instance, newspaper editors who praise a particular politician are later astonished to discover that the public rejects their products, and thus complain bitterly about the decline in the status of the Arab writer. Such editors do not understand that the public rejects this system of patronage. In a similar vein, Iraqi intellectuals who sharply criticize the ways in which the poor are treated, immediately turn silent once they assume a position of importance in the state. These intellectuals approach the common man with much contempt and arrogance. Not only do they want him to labor all day so that he will buy what they write (which bears no relevance to his life), but they are also irritated with him when he prefers buying products of lower artistic value, like magazines which show nude girls, or remind him of the bygone days of the magnificent poets of the past. Mockingly, Wardi added that had the poets Abu Nuwas (750–810), Jarir (c.650–728) or Farazdaq (c.641–728/730) been with us today, they would have probably published in, or at least read, similar magazines.[23] Most important, however, was the relationship between the writer and the political system. The dependence of modern writers on political patrons caused the public to distrust their words and to believe in rumors, because the public connected intellectuals with the state. By not fulfilling their true calling as intellectuals, such writers have made the words "nation" and "people" meaningless. In addition, contemporary misunderstandings of the significance of pluralism in society have produced ridiculous claims about the significance of the national consensus and unity of opinion that entirely missed the importance of intellectual creativity and diversity.

---

[23] Abu Nuwas is known for his wine- and love poetry (for males and females); Jarir and Farazdaq are famed for mastering the *hija'* genre and the impertinent and colorful imagery they employed when mocking their rivals.

For Wardi, writing turns meaningful when it is addressed to a people situated in a particular socio-historical context, and aimed at changing particular mentalities. Wardi warned his fellow writers to be very aware that the poor needed bread much more than they needed poets, writers, and men of religion. The poor, however, also needed the producers of a new democratic theory, or a contemporary Voltaire, Rousseau, or Diderot. Sartre, Wardi added, called upon writers to take on the responsibility for solving the problem of oppression. Writers must therefore name things and unmask certain phenomena. Thus blacks in America will continue to be oppressed as long their oppression remains unexposed. Oppression in itself, wrote Wardi, did not generate a social movement calling for change. It was the power of the pen, however, to direct, to highlight, and to make oppression known. Writers, then, should not only be interested in the production of the text, but also in its distribution and in its ability to affect and change their audiences. A true intellectual was thus a person with a social message, a revolutionary and a man of vision: a Moses to a contemporary Pharaoh or a Muhammad to a contemporary Abu Jahl and Abu Sufyan.[24]

An example of the power of a text to transform social realities was the Qur'an. Challenging Muslim tradition that looked at the Qur'an as a linguistic miracle that could not be imitated by any human being (*mu'jiza, i'jaz al-Qur'an*), Wardi proposed to look at the Qur'an as a social text. Muslims, he argued, were too busy exploring the literary aspects of the text without paying heed to its social message that challenged the values of the *jahiliyya*. Whereas both the Qur'an and *jahili* poetry reflected the same historical context, *jahili* poetry perpetuated local tribal values, while the Qur'an offered a new ethical vision. The transformation from a social text to a linguistic miracle should be attributed to sultans who did not want readers to ponder on the ethical and social meanings of the Qur'an. Moreover, rulers like the third Caliph 'Uthman ibn 'Affan (644–656) repressed the multiplicity of Qur'anic interpretations, by imposing one particular reading of the text.[25] The text's social meanings had thus escaped its readership (Wardi, 1957).

---

[24]On Abu Jahl, see W. Watt (2008). On Abu Sufyan see also W. Watt (2008). Available on-line, http://www.encislam.brill.nl/subscriber/entry?entry=islam_SIM-0254.

[25]Wardi refers here to the canonization of the text of the Qur'an under the rule of the third rightly-guided Caliph, Uthman ibn 'Affan, during which variant readings (*qira'at*) of the sacred text were suppressed and destroyed. This last reference could be read as a sectarian remark, reflecting Wardi's Shi'i origins. In my opinion, however, it attests more to Wardi's general attempt to provide his readers with a secular and sociological analysis of the Qur'an. On the *qira'at*, see Paret *Kira'a* (2008). Available on-line: http://www.encislam.brill.nl/subscriber/entry?entry=islam_SIM-4383.

Wardi's book created some noise at the time of its publication. Eminent literary scholars argued that as a sociologist he was writing about matters beyond the scope of his discipline. For his part Wardi insisted that he could provide insights on the connections between politics, patronage, culture and literature, precisely because he was not an expert on meters, prosody or rhyme. He asserted that his critics failed to understand that sociology was a discipline aimed at studying various social phenomena expressed in literature, history, economy, science, religion and art. Moreover, he averred that the modern intellectual was aware of the fact that his opinions, and his very understanding of the concept of "truth," were affected by psychological and social factors. Therefore, such intellectuals have been very careful in the claims they have made (Wardi, 1957, pp. 48–51).

Much like Sartre, Wardi presumed that a writer had a commitment to freedom and to a universal battle against oppression. For this reason, he emphasized the need to shy away from an imagined golden past, and to acknowledge the authoritarian culture of the previous sultans, in the hope of making a better, more democratic future. Wardi himself, moreover, interwove his opinions about a variety of political and social affairs into his book: he criticized the tribal order and land regime in Iraq, which turned sheikhs into compliant functionaries serving the state rather than their tribesmen. He attacked religious leaders who turned sectarianism into a useful vehicle for achieving positions of power in society, and disparaged the presumption of certain moralists to pass judgment on individuals for "sexual deviation," without realizing that sexual conduct is a private affair, and without grasping that sexual behavior is also a product of social and psychological factors. The fact that Wardi intertwined his political agenda into a text about literature served his point well; it indicated to readers that the book was not simply an academic discussion of literary matters, but provided a new vision of Iraqi society for its intellectuals.

Wardi's book was original and innovative. It merged sociological theories, historical observations, medieval poetry, and Qur'anic interpretation alongside indirect references to Marx and Sartre. On the other hand, many of his ideas could be contextualized within the Iraqi intellectual domain. The intellectual elites of the 1950s, i.e., Iraq's modernist poets, writers, and painters, as well as its Marxist and Ba'thist writers, were mostly secular. The secularism of Wardi's text, which sees the Qur'an as articulating a new set of values befitting a specific historical and cultural context, is a product of this environment. At the time that this text was published, debates about the Islamic past took up much space in the Iraqi intellectual domain and Wardi took part in these discussions. The intellectual was thus a man giving a secular meaning to the sacred within time and space. Wardi's text also reflects his commitment to Sartre's ideas. As noted, at the time of the book's publication, the word *iltizam* was current in the writings of radical nationalists like Sayyab as well as in the publications of the radical Left. Although Wardi did not use the word *iltizam* often, Sartre's assertion that literature should have meaning, and that it should be read within a socio-political and socio-cultural context, echoes throughout the book. Furthermore, Wardi outlined his own political agenda, which included a critique of Iraq's land regime and the ways in which the sectarian problem was manipulated by various politicians. Ideas of left-leaning intellectuals, especially Marxists, shaped Wardi's argumentation; his book speaks of intellectual production and the distribution of intellectual capital, and considers literature as an ideological tool produced in a specific market and distributed to the reading publics. Transregional influences, such as Wardi's references to the works of the Egyptian writers Salama Musa (especially his support of Musa's call to simplify the writing of Arabic, 1956) and Taha Husayn (especially his critique of *Fi'l-shi'ir al-jahili* for failing to see that both *jahili* poetry and the Qur'an were responses to the context of *jahili* Arabia[26]) are important in understanding Wardi's reasoning (Wardi, 1957, pp. 62–63, 159, 301). The text mocks intellectuals on a number of occasions: their everlasting search for recognition and fame, their disrespect for their audiences, their preposterous self-importance, and their reliance on the state. At the same time, however, he also called on intellectuals to be committed to their public, to their society, and to their nation, and to work on their behalf. This call was shared by many of Wardi's radical peers.

Particular and universal, emblematic of, and in opposition to, the Iraqi intellectual field, *The Myth of Elite Literature* was, and still is, an important prism through which we can think about Iraqi intellectuals. The true intellectual in the work is a secular, democratic critic, conscious of issues relating to social justice and attentive to matters concerning language, history, sociology and culture.

---

[26]In his book on *jahili* poetry, Taha Husayn argued that *jahili* poetry might have been created at a later period than that of pre-Islamic Arabia. The book, because of its secular and rationalist approach to the Qur'an, was a topic of much controversy. Significantly, Wardi did not critique Husayn's methodology, namely, his rationalist approach to the sacred scripture, but rather Husayn's inability to look at both the Qur'an and the *jahili* poetry as representing two conflicting ideologies, yet addressing the *same* milieu at the *same* period (Husayn, 1926). Husayn published a revised version of his arguments in Husayn (1927).

Words of Advice

The questions posed by Wardi and several other intellectuals of his time reveal a changing relationship to the Iraqi state; they disclose a transformation in the representation of the intellectual from a man committed to the national project (as seen in the works of Jamali and Shawkat) to a revolutionary critic. Although we find representations of both approaches throughout the Hashemite period, the representation of the intellectual as a revolutionary becomes more pronounced in the 1940s and 1950s. Unsurprisingly, in these decades many members of the intellectual elite sharply criticised the Hashemite state. These representations thus correlate with significant socio-political changes within Iraqi society.

Nonetheless, such questions are also important for the present. Wardi's mockery of his peers, his *La Trahison des clercs*, to borrow Julien Benda's famous title, could also be employed as a way of thinking about the collaboration of Iraqi intellectuals with the antidemocratic regimes that emerged after 1958, and their betrayal of pluralistic and humanistic principles. While 'Abd al-Karim Qasim's revolution enjoyed the enthusiastic support of Iraqi leftist intellectuals in its early stages, more perilous forms of affiliation between the state and its intellectuals came into being after 1963, and more dramatically after 1968. Even communist intellectuals, motivated by the Ba'th-communist rapprochement in the very late 1960s and 1970s and supportive of such major social transformations as the nationalization of oil, were willing to work with the regime for a while.

To their great credit, however, most leading Iraqi intellectuals did not simply become obedient collaborators who supported, or were supported by, a "republic of fear". They also adopted the strategies proposed by Wardi, even under the Ba'thi regime, and often paid a heavy price for their stance. Furthermore, works like Wardi's, and more broadly, the views (and often the political actions) of his peers, show that not all intellectuals accepted the patronage of the state during the 1950s. Rather, they criticized the state, and functioned as Saidian "public intellectuals." This line of thinking was most apparent in the 1950s, but prevailed in the 1960s, 1970s, 1980s, and 1990s. For example, many of Iraq's canonical poets and novelists chose to write about Iraq from exile ('Abd al-Wahhab al-Bayati, Gha'ib Ta'ma Farman, Buland al-Haydari, Muhammad Mahdi al-Jawahiri, and Sa'di Yusuf, to name just a few), because they were persecuted by the regime and wanted no share in Ba'thi oppression. They wrote in Arabic for Iraqi and Arab audiences, detailing and analyzing dictatorship and its causes. I imagine that most of them thought that they would be able to come home some day. When we think today about the possible reconstruction of a shared Iraqi cultural ethos, whose texts might inspire young Iraqis, works such as Wardi's, and others written during the Iraqi cultural renaissance of the 1950s, immediately come to mind. Moreover, many of these works are already part of the Iraqi cultural and literary canon. Similarly, thinking about the present, we ought to appreciate the bloggers, human rights activists, writers and journalists who work in Iraq, despite horrific conditions, and continue writing, knowing full well that an unsympathetic portrayal of a militiaman or a politician could come at a very heavy price. More than anything, such intellectuals remain loyal to the agenda charted out by Wardi half a century ago.

WRITING THE HISTORY OF IRAQ: THE FALLACY OF "OBJECTIVE" HISTORY

Johan Franzén

The modern history of Iraq did not commence with the Ba'th regime — nor does it end with its demise. Yet, one of the few American policies to be more or less fully implemented following the 2003 invasion was to "de-Ba'thify" the Iraqi army and civil service. Thousands of government employees lost their jobs after the old regime crumbled. One of the cornerstones of this "de-Ba'thification" was to change the nature of Iraqi history teaching, deemed "propagandistic" by the Americans. Thus, one of the very first projects to be launched by the new Coalition Provisional Authority (CPA) during the summer of 2003 was the revision of Iraqi history textbooks. Under the leadership of Fu'ad Husayn, an Iraqi professor living in Holland, a team of 67 Iraqi teachers set out in May 2003 to revise the Iraqi school curriculum. In the process, no less than 563 texts were severely edited and revised.

Under pressure to prepare the new schoolbooks for the coming school year, the Ministry of Education simply erased all sections that were considered 'controversial', meaning all references to the US, Shi'is, Sunnis, Kurds, Kuwaitis, Jews or Iranians. Thus, half the texts used to teach modern history disappeared at one go (Asquith 25 November 2003). On March 31, 2004, 'Ala' al-Din 'Alwan, a former official at the World Health Organization, was put in charge of the Ministry of Education. During the summer of 2004, the US put together a team of educationalists and sent them to Iraq to oversee the curriculum revision. In a project funded by the United States Agency for International Development (USAID), Iraqi officials and teachers began tearing out pictures and effacing references to Saddam Husayn and the Ba'th Party in millions of school textbooks (Wang, 2005).

What purpose does, or did, this "de-Ba'thification" serve? Is rewriting the history of Ba'thist Iraq really going to solve any of the fundamental problems facing post-Saddam Iraq? It is clear from the procedural brusqueness of the project that its underlying premise was that history teaching is equivalent to propaganda, and perhaps also that exchanging one mode of education for another would *ipso facto* transform the recipients of the "new history" into malleable pro-Western youngsters ready to accept "democracy" and American liberalism. In other words, it is a case of removing malign propaganda and replacing it with benign. However, as will be argued in this chapter, any attempt at targeting anti-Americanism, seen as an inherent part of Ba'thist history teaching, will ultimately strike at the very core of the Iraqi self-image. One of the fundamental pillars of "Iraqist" ideology is the notion that the Iraqi state and territory has been gradually appropriated by the "Iraqi people" through a continuous and hard-fought battle against Western "imperialism".

Recent examples of the ambiguous role of post-conflict history education to promote reconciliation can be seen around the world. A major component of the educational debate in conflict-torn societies is over the nature of any new history curriculum (Pingel, 2008, p. 182): Should it convey a multi-perspective approach or one based on ethnicity or nationality? In many conflict-ridden countries, including Iraq, history education has attained an unenviable position; although chronically underfunded and conspicuously lacking resources in terms of qualified teachers, appropriate academic materials and professional educationalists, it has often been expected to promote peace by fostering a new ethos of peaceful co-habitation (Pingel, 2008, p. 184). In such cases, the new authorities demand that history should serve the objectives of the post-conflict regime, with the result that educational aims become contradictory, because not only is the history curriculum expected to explain what happened but it is also charged with presenting a new narrative at odds with the old one, a narrative whose goal it is to unite the fragmented country. "Thus," commented Pingel (2008, p. 184), "before history instruction has really started and can draw on viable research or documentation, governments often anticipate the challenge of an open, serious, and in-depth historical debate and either prescribe a new core narrative or put aside history instruction altogether."

Post-conflict regimes have dealt with history in different ways. In Rwanda, a new narrative was introduced presenting the idea that the country was harmonious before the arrival of colonialism. The fall of *apartheid* in South Africa initially created much historical debate and willingness to create a new South African history, but once it became clear that such an endeavor would require much time and re-open many wounds it lost its appeal. In Bosnia, the 1995 Dayton Accords officially divided education into separate systems for the three "constituent peoples" — Serbs, Croats and Bosnians (Pingel, 2008, pp. 185–186). There, "education, as it is organized and conceived, has continued to deepen intra-national divisions and aims to create or consolidate ethnically-pure territories." (Torsti, 2007, p. 79). In Torsti's opinion (2007, p. 90), history education in post-conflict Bosnia has remained as dogmatic as in the Tito era. In Northern Ireland, too, the segregation of education has been pivotal in sustaining the conflict (Torsti, 2007, p. 92). Thus, the provision of history education in post-conflict states has been used both to provide "national" reconciliation and as a means of separating these states into mutually antagonistic entities. The common denominator is that education, and above all history teaching, has been seen as a vehicle to achieve *political* objectives. However, to be able to provide an inclusive, multi-perspective history education, the task of bringing about reconciliation must be addressed separately from, and preferably prior to, the introduction of a new history curriculum. If not, the curriculum of the day will only reflect the political color of the current constellation in power.

In Iraq, no substantial political reconciliation has yet taken place. Although provisional plans for "transitional justice" were considered after the overthrow of the regime in 2003, these have all failed to materialize due to a variety of logistical, security and administrative constraints (al-Marashi and Keskin, 2008, pp. 246–247). Another reason for the absence of reconciliation has been that the new Maliki government has invoked the collective suffering of Shi'is under the Ba'thists as a way of consolidating its own rule (al-Marashi and Keskin, 2008, p. 246). Such political usage of historical memory, while understandable given the immense suffering of various groups during the Ba'thist era, is hardly conducive to reconciliation. "Empowerment through historic grievance," as Jeremy Black has commented (2008, p. 227), "is a source not only of division but also of a reluctance to search for the compromises necessary if life is to continue both within and between communities." Reconciliation was also problematic for the Maliki government for more practical reasons; as long as the process could stay focused on the Ba'thist era, any crimes and grievances unearthed would strengthen the new regime, but if it were to continue into the era of post-2003 sectarian violence and the government-sponsored death squads during al-Maliki's own incumbency, its moral force would be undermined, or become untenable (al-Marashi and Keskin, 2008,

p. 247). In June 2006, the Iraqi government did announce another attempt to implement a "Reconciliation and National Dialog Plan," but although the endeavor gained the support of the three major parliamentary blocs, it was rejected by the Sunni political parties (al-Marashi and Keskin, 2008, pp. 253–254), almost certainly because it was viewed as a witch hunt.

Political reconciliation between Baʻthists, Kurdish nationalists, Shiʻi and Sunni political parties, as well as those who still cherish a vision of a united polity, such as the Iraqi Communist Party (ICP), is a major concern, and until agreement has been reached on Iraq's future, any hope of achieving a "new Iraqi history" is futile. What is needed in current circumstances is to allow various groups and communities to develop and sustain *their* historical narratives, providing these do not aim to dismember the Iraqi state. Although it is important to acknowledge the political socialization that comes with education, especially history teaching, and recognizing that to allow multiple histories to flourish may create stronger divisions in the short run, the effect of introducing "official" history teaching at odds with parts or all of oral, family and community history could be much more detrimental in the long run. If current differences between political groups working from a "Sunni", "Shiʻi", or "Kurdish" platform are given too much leeway, Iraq might end up like Northern Ireland where the perennial conflict between groups based on "catholic" and "protestant" identities has become cemented to the degree that these identities have come to seem irreversible.

In the process of creating and sustaining mutually antagonistic identities in Northern Ireland, the segregation of education has been pivotal (Torsti, 2007, p. 92). Bosnia, too, should serve as a stark warning. There education was federalized, allowing the three groups acting from different identity platforms — Serbs, Croats, and Bosnians — to gain control over education in areas where their ethnicity was the majority, thus creating, in the words of Pingel (2008, p. 186), a "playground for cultural separatism." Instead of implementing a "Bosnian" curriculum conducive to reconciliation between the warring groups, schools were allowed to teach their "own" history and emphasize the cultural differences of their ethnic group, thus slowly putting down boundary markers between incipient "nations". (Pingel, 2008, p. 186). It is therefore important to recognize that while allowing for a multitude of narratives and perspectives and giving space to the whole range of suppressed histories that have existed clandestinely, history teaching in post-Saddam Iraq must not be separatist lest Iraq turned into another Northern Ireland or Bosnia.

The inherent weakness of the American "de-Ba'thification" policy vis-à-vis Iraqi society and especially as regards the provision of history education is clear when taking a longer view. Not only have the Americans failed to punish most of the former senior Ba'thists with blood on their hands (with the exception of those in the notorious deck of cards) while at the same time managing to alienate large sections of the population by collectively punishing low-level Ba'thists and bureaucrats by dismissing them *en masse* (al-Marashi and Keskin, 2008, p. 247), but their actions on education are yet another example of the conspicuous lack of historical thinking among American policymakers. The idea that history teaching was only taken over and used for propagandistic ends *by the Ba'thists* is a canard. History education serving nationalist objectives is not a novel concept — it predated the Ba'thi regime by many decades, and is a familiar phenomenon in the wider Arab world. Rather than viewing it as a cunning scheme to dupe the young generation by an "evil" regime, as is the implicit American view of Ba'thi history education, this paper argues that it is necessary to nuance the picture somewhat and recognize some of the positive effects of nationalist education for an artificially created state. For all its historical simplification, ideological reductionism and historical vilification, Iraqi nationalist history education, over the years, has been instrumental in fostering a sense of "Iraqiness" among its recipients. As such, it is an integral part of the multifaceted and enigmatic "Iraqi identity".

To understand more fully the role which nationalist history education has played for Iraq it is necessary to consider how it developed. When the modern Iraqi state was created as a combination of the former Ottoman *wilayas* of Basra, Baghdad, and Mosul and entrusted as a League of Nations mandate to Great Britain after World War I, British officers on the ground became the new rulers of the land along with local landowning and politico-bureaucratic elites. Yet, despite exercising much influence in most areas of policy through subtle usage of advisers in Iraqi ministries, one of the areas that seemed of least interest to British officials on the ground was education. Consequently, Iraqi civil servants were given considerable latitude within the Ministry of Education (Sluglett, 2007, p. 197). Although British officials were against the expansion of education, arguing that it would ultimately create a class of educated unemployed youths susceptible to radical political ideas (Franzén, 2008, p. 102), Iraqi nationalists in the Ministry of Education nevertheless managed to expand the educational system and increase its budget allocations throughout the mandate (Sluglett, 2007, p. 205). Following Iraqi independence in 1932, this process was further intensified. Thus, from a mere 600 secondary school places at the beginning of the monarchy in 1921, the Iraqi school system provided no less than 28,000 in 1948 (Batatu, 2004, p. 477). The provision of modern education to ever-wider segments of the population over time created a new social force — a radicalized intelligentsia.[1] As the new education was largely unconnected to traditional loyalties of tribe and religion, it meant that its recipients became more susceptible to new political ideas and *Weltanschauungen*. Thus, ideas of pan-Arabism (*qawmiyyah*), Iraqism (*wataniyyah*) and Communism (*shuyu'iyyah*) soon spread.

Crucial for this development were early Arab educationalists working in the new Iraqi state, such as Sati' al-Husri, Fadil al-Jamali, and Sami Shawkat, all of whom served as Directors-General of the Ministry of Education in the 1920s and 1930s. While all three played important roles in the political development of Iraq under the monarchy, with al-Jamali serving as Prime Minister during a short spell in the 1950s and Shawkat promoting paramilitary extra-parliamentary opposition movements in the late 1930s and early 1940s, al-Husri stands out in terms of importance for the development of Iraqi education. Abu Khaldun Sati' al-Husri (1881–1968) was of Syrian origin but born in Yemen where his father had been sent as a judge; before the fall of the Ottoman Empire, he had studied political science in Istanbul. As Faysal and his *sharifian* entourage moved from Syria to Iraq following their ousting by the French in 1920, al-Husri accompanied them and began teaching at the Higher Teachers Training College in Baghdad. He was appointed Director-General of Education by King Faysal, and from this position, he was instrumental in shaping the curriculum, selecting (and often writing) the textbooks and disseminating pan-Arabism to the young generations who were growing up in the early years of the Iraqi state (Abdi, 2008, pp. 10–11).

To al-Husri, history instruction was of special importance. In his view, history was one of the vital factors creating a "spiritual kinship" (*al-qarabah al-ma'nawiyyah*) between people (al-Husri, 1974, p. 42). Accordingly, history was seen as the embodiment of the nation's consciousness and memory. The "spiritual kinship" brought about by history was considered stronger than material kinship (al-Husri, 1974, p. 44). "The dominated nation that forgets its history," he argued (1974, p. 44), "has lost its awareness and

---

[1]For a discussion of this social stratum, which some have called the "new effendiyyah", see Eppel (1998).

consciousness. This awareness and consciousness will not return to it until it starts to remember that history and returns to it." For that reason, occupied and dominated nations, the fate that had befallen the "Arab nation" since falling under the yoke first of the Ottomans and then of British and French imperialism, had to combat the history of the dominating nation and exert every effort to efface that history (al-Husri, 1974, p. 44). Following this blueprint, al-Husri's ideas of using history to form a "spiritual kinship" among the individual subjects of the new Iraqi state were put into practice. Aiming at eradicating the impact of "foreign" domination and bringing about a new sense of pride in *'urubah* ("Arabness"), al-Husri's curriculum marked the beginning of nationalist history teaching in Iraq.

Early on, al-Husri employed Darwish al-Miqdadi, a Palestinian graduate of the American University of Beirut. Like al-Husri, he was a philosopher and theoretician of Arab nationalism. While working in Iraq, al-Miqdadi elaborated the notion of the nuclear "Arab Homeland" (*al-Watan al-'Arabi*), thought to comprise Syria, Iraq and the Arabian Peninsula. This concept was then fully developed in his 1931 seminal work *Ta'rikh al-Ummah al-'Arabiyyah*, which became a standard history textbook for Iraqi schools (Abdi, 2008, p. 11). When Iraq gained independence in 1932, the scope of nationalist research and teaching widened. al-Husri was appointed Director of the Department of Antiquities and quickly started working on a new Antiquities Law that was eventually adopted in 1934. Among the growing number of educated nationalists, there was a sense that archaeology, a favorite pastime of some British administrators during the mandate, had robbed Iraq of its national heritage.[2] Thus, with the new law and a focus on Iraqi interests over foreign, al-Husri laid the foundations for an indigenous Iraqi archaeology (Abdi, 2008, p. 15). From then on, this nationalistically driven archaeology became the backbone for history teaching, a phenomenon that gradually helped shape an incipient "Iraqi" identity.

These efforts to inject a nationalistic content into education initially had a willing backer in Iraq's first king, Faysal I. Although at all times aware of his own tenuous position and always careful not to upset relations with the British, he was a staunch backer of al-Husri. Faysal's son, Ghazi, who ascended the throne in 1933 upon his father's death, was even more of a

---

[2]See the article by Magnus Bernhardsson.

nationalist. Yet, his short rule, which ended with his death in a mysterious car accident in 1939, was at all times marred by his awkward relations with the British. During his time in power, nationalist military officers and members of the new intelligentsia, as well as disgruntled elements of the old politico-bureaucratic elite, made inroads into the centre of power. Through a series of military coups (1936–1941) they managed to take over the government and steer Iraq in a direction at odds with British intentions. However, the British eventually thwarted this development; they defeated the Iraqi army in a short war in 1941 and imposed a second military occupation. Britain made sure things returned to normal and reinstated Faysal I's cousin 'Abd al-Ilah, who had been acting as regent for the underage Faysal II since 1939. During his term in power, which lasted until the 1958 Revolution,[3] no attempts were made at officially appropriating and restructuring Iraqi history. In fact, the few publications on Iraqi history during this period were mostly in English and aimed at a Western audience (Davis, 2005, p. 311).

The Revolution that occurred in July 1958 swept away British influence and the power of the old landed classes whilst bringing to the center of the state nationalist military officers and members of the new intelligentsia, the recipients of al-Husri's nationalist history curriculum over the preceding decades. The revolution also marked the intensification of nationalist education and the first coherent attempt to appropriate the country's past and channel it into a restructuring of historical memory. 'Abd al-Karim Qasim, the leader of the Free Officers responsible for the military action that overthrew the monarchy, was instrumental in this state project. In the words of Davis (2005, p. 110), "Qasim's injection of the state into the realm of reassessing culture and the past represented the first systematic effort in modern Iraq to officially restructure historical memory." However, while al-Husri's efforts had been grounded in a pan-Arabist (*qawmi*) project with the ultimate aim of signing up Iraq to a larger Arab unity scheme and fulfilling the "eternal mission" of reuniting the "Arab nation", Qasim's ideological predilection was more Iraqist (*watani*). Immediately challenged by his erstwhile brother-in-arms, 'Abd al-Salam 'Arif, who joined the Iraqi Nasirists and pan-Arabists in calling for Iraq's merger with the United Arab Republic (UAR), which had been formed between Egypt and Syria in February 1958, Qasim came to the conclusion that Iraq's interests were best served by the

---

[3]Officially, King Faysal II was crowned in 1953 but 'Abd al-Ilah continued to run affairs along with the British.

preservation of the territorial state.[4] Thus, in order to offset the tide of pan-Arabism which had been on the rise in Iraq and the rest of the Arab world after Nasser's triumphant defiance of Britain and France during the 1956 Suez crisis, Qasim began using pre-Islamic and pre-Arab symbols, such as the Akkadian sun, which became the symbol of the revolution and part of the flag of the new republic (Davis, 2005, p. 111).

In the struggles that ensued between pan-Arabists and Iraqists, more and more efforts were put into officially reshaping the public's self-perception through a concerted campaign of rewriting and refocusing Iraqi history. For this purpose, Qasim set up the Ministry of Guidance, which to all intents and purposes was a Ministry of Propaganda.[5] He also enlisted the support of the ICP, which had decided to support Qasim against the pan-Arabists for ideological reasons. The ensuing alliance between Qasim and the Communists, which was not without its frictions and which ultimately ended in tragedy for both parties when Qasim was overthrown in an Arab nationalist coup in 1963, shaped the development of nationalist education during Qasim's time in power. ICP members and sympathisers and other intellectuals of Iraqist leanings, who almost to a man hailed from the new generations that had received modern education since the inception of the Iraqi state, began filling key positions in Qasim's new Ministry of Guidance and other important ministries. There, they began building an impressive infrastructure with a radio and TV network and a new Directorate of Folklore (Davis, 2005, pp. 110–111). The dominance of Communists meant that much effort was exerted on recording and writing the history of the "lower classes" by stressing folklore. Historical narratives of marginalized groups were thus brought into the realm of "Iraqiness" through the recording of customs, oral history, traditions and so on in this Communist "history from below"-project. This documentation was then published by the Ministry of Guidance through its Committee for the Celebration of the 14 July Revolution (Davis, 2005, pp. 122–123).

The years following Qasim's overthrow in 1963 until the seizure of power of the Ba'th Party in 1968 were an interlude. While Communists and other supporters of Qasim were purged from the Ministry of Guidance, sometimes

---

[4]For a more in-depth treatment of these events, see Farouk-Sluglett and Sluglett, 2001: 55–60.

[5]That this was the case can be deducted from its name in Arabic, "*Wizarat al-Irshad*," with *irshad* having the religious connotation of guidance on the "right" way or of keeping someone on the straight and narrow.

with loss of life, the ministry itself had come to stay. Thus, although Iraq under the 'Arif brothers[6] once again tried to steer its orientation back towards pan-Arabism and a focus on Islamic history, the phenomenon of mass political socialization through manipulation of historical memory that had been institutionalized with Qasim remained in effect.

The Ba'th Party's arrival in power through a bloodless coup in 1968 marked a new stage in officially sponsored state history. Realizing its own tenuous social support base and the continuing affinity for Iraqist *wataniyyah*, especially in its communist variety, among large parts of the population, the Ba'thists moved quickly to address the problem. Using a "stick and carrot" policy vis-à-vis the two main rival political parties — the Kurdistan Democratic Party (KDP) and the ICP — to neutralize them politically, it began a massive redirection of official history in order to off-set them both culturally and ideologically. The Ba'th Party thus started its Project for the Rewriting of History (*Mashru' I'adat al-Ta'rikh*), which although not officially launched until 1979, had in fact begun shortly after the party came to power in 1968 (Davis, 2005, p. 148). The aims of this project were political and of a fundamentally long-term nature; it sought to build a new public sphere and reshape Iraqi political identity, largely to negate the legacy of Iraqist history instruction and propaganda (Davis, 2005, p. 148). Another key motivation behind the project was to under-mine the widespread appeal of the ICP by appropriating its monopoly on mass history and folk culture (Davis, 2005, p. 150). Thus, over the course of the 1970s, the Ba'thists sought to create a new *wataniyyah* to offset the Communist-progressive *wataniyyah* that had been the dominant ideology amongst the majority of the Iraqi intelligentsia since the 1950s, and which had enjoyed much support among the population as a whole by virtue of its inclusivism and reluctance to stress sectarian affiliations. Accordingly, Ba'thist intellectuals, historians and archaeologists began propagating the idea of an "Iraqi people" which had existed since the beginning of time and for which Arab-Islamic civilization (always the main historical focus of the pan-Arabists) was just one of many great civilizations to have existed in

---

[6]'Abd al-Salam 'Arif (1921–66) was President of Iraq between 1963 and 1966; he had played a major role in the overthrow of the monarchy in 1958, but joined forces with the Ba'thists to overthrow 'Abd al-Karim Qasim in February 1963. In November 1963 he expelled the Ba'thists from the government and seized full power. After his accidental death in April 1966, his brother, 'Abd al-Rahman 'Arif (1916–2007) became President until his removal by the Ba'thists on 17 July 1968.

"Iraq" (Baram, 1991, p. 100). To underpin this major academic effort, state funding for archaeology was increased immensely under the Ba'thists (Abdi, 2008, p. 18).

The Ba'thi master plan was to Arabize Iraq's ancient civilizations through "academic research" in order to appropriate them for political purposes in a bid to bring about a new Iraqi identity — a new Iraqi man carrying the pride of history on his shoulders. Thus, unlike the appropriation of ancient civilizations under Qasim, who had showed no concern about their ethnic content, the Ba'thists, whose underlying ideological platform was ethnic (*qawmi*) Arab nationalism, needed to Arabize these civilizations to make them "useful" for modern political purposes. However, few within Iraqi academia would initially sign up to the new Arabization policy. Opinions ranged from those who saw Iraq merely as the cradle of the great ancient civilizations to those who considered modern Iraqis as the offspring of these civilizations (Baram, 1991, p. 97). Indeed, during the 1960s and early 1970s only a few attempts had been made to make Arabs out of the Akkadians, Babylonians and other Semitic peoples (Baram, 1991, p. 99).

Nevertheless, the transition from regarding the modern inhabitants of "Mesopotamia" (*bilad al-rafidayn*) as having only a spiritual connection with the ancient civilizations into regarding "Mesopotamians" as a distinct ethnicity was not as difficult as might be imagined. In fact, archaeologists, who, as we have seen, were a key component of nationalist history instruction in Iraq, had been teaching the idea of the common origin of the "Semites" in the Arabian peninsula since the early days of the monarchy. In line with this kind of thinking, "Mesopotamians" were seen as Arabians. Since this notion had been an accepted axiom since the 1930s, the historians, archaeologists and politicians of the 1970s had all been raised on this nationalist history (Baram, 1991, pp. 101–102). Accordingly, the leading Iraqi archaeologist Taha Baqir[7] argued in 1977 that there was no "doubt that, historically, the correct name for these people... called Semites is... the people of the Arab peninsula or simply Arabs."[8] Having thus both construed "Mesopotamians" as a distinct "people" and established their "Arabness", Iraqi academics and

---

[7]Taha Baqir (1912–1984) was a Shi'i who served as curator of the Iraqi National Museum 1941–1953 and who was appointed Director of Antiquities in 1958. Following the 1963 coup, he was relieved of his posts and later lived in exile in Libya. He was brought back by the Ba'thi regime in 1970 and made a member of the Iraqi Academy of Sciences (Abdi, 2008, p. 16).

[8]Taha Baqir, *Afaq 'Arabiyyah*, March 1977, quoted in Baram, 1991, p. 102.

Ba'thi intellectuals started to describe Iraq's Persian, Hellenistic, Sasanian, and Ottoman eras as somehow not part of the legitimate history of the Iraqi *watan* (Baram, 1991, pp. 109–110).

Yet, despite this bending of the narrative to serve political purposes, it is important to recognize that this phase in Iraq's modern history was just that: a result of political struggles. The Ba'th Party did not seize power in a political and historical vacuum but in the midst of fierce struggles with the supporters of Iraqism, such as the ICP and the Kurdish nationalists (KDP). It is against the backdrop of the successful manipulation of historical memory carried out under Qasim, especially by the communists in the Ministry of Guidance, and the increasingly separatist inclinations of the Kurds (as shown in the Kurdish wars of the 1960s), that the Ba'th's preoccupation with history teaching must be understood. Ba'thist intellectuals and academics began stressing "Iraqiness" and tried to create a new Iraqi *wataniyyah* in order to undermine the legacy of Qasim's and the ICP's *wataniyyah*, despite the fact that since its creation in the 1950s the Ba'th Party had given every appearance of being a staunchly *qawmi* party striving towards Arab unification. The fact that the Ba'thi regime initially was reluctant to stress the "Arabness" of this new *wataniyyah* and that it did so systematically only by the late 1970s is indicative of its political concerns once having seized power. As the regime was initially trying to entice both the KDP and the ICP into political cooperation, it was keen to be seen to be fostering an inclusivist *wataniyyah* that was not explicitly "Arab". That way, the Ba'thists intended that Kurds should also feel part of the new Iraqi identity. After 1975, when relations with the Kurds had deteriorated into open war, and the ICP had been subdued politically by the formation of the so-called "Progressive National-Patriotic Front" (*al-Jabhah al-Wataniyyah wa'l-Qawmiyyah al-Taqaddumiyyah*) in 1973, the inclusivist *wataniyyah* was dropped in favor of one based on a common Sunni-Shi'i "Arab" historical memory (Baram, 1994, p. 304).

Nevertheless, although the Ba'thi restructuring of historical memory to serve its political purposes may appear to have been a sinister plan to "poison" the minds of the younger generations, and American post-invasion policy in Iraq posits that "de-Ba'thification" is the antidote that will cleanse and purify the new generations, it is important to recognize that this phenomenon was far from being as systematic and policy-driven as has been made out. Senior Ba'thi officials and political activists were in the main focused on daily politics and international relations, and had little time for, or indeed the appropriate level of education to grasp, academic research into the ancient past. Like most members of the Ba'thist leadership, Saddam Husayn had only the most "rudimentary education and superficial knowledge of the past" (Abdi, 2008, p. 28). It is therefore unreasonable to argue that he, or indeed the leadership, was directly responsible for the appropriation of Mesopotamian imagery for nationalist purposes. In fact, most of the initiatives to do so originated within lower levels of the state and academia, and even in the wider society (Abdi, 2008, pp. 28–29). Yet, the essence of Iraqi *wataniyyah*, even in its Ba'thist variety, continued to be anti-imperialism and notions of *watani* struggle against outside domination. Thus, "de-Ba'thification" means not only removing the legacy of Saddam Husayn, or the Ba'th Party, but by attacking these latter aspects of Iraqi nationalism it strikes at the heart of Iraqi identity — an identity that had been building for a long time before Saddam Husayn's rise to power and for which the Ba'thist restructuring of historical memory was but the last link in a long chain.

This is the key to any understanding of the teaching of Iraqi history in the past and, indeed, for planning for its future. It is important to understand that to "de-nationalize" history teaching entirely more or less equals going back to square one, as most history instruction in Iraqi history has been nationalist and anti-Western. This type of socialization through history teaching is not unique to Iraq and is not completely negative. In fact, the sense of pride and positive ideas of national identity it has (at times) instilled in a heterogeneous population that, through no fault of its own, was bundled together in a colonial state has made the Iraqi polity relatively stable over the past nine decades, despite several attempts by supra-national and irredentist movements to destabilize it. Thus, demonizing these aspects of Iraqi history teaching through schemes of "de-Ba'thification" is dangerous and might lead to the erosion of the tenuous Iraqi identity that still exists. Although the Ba'thi regime might have been an authoritarian and fierce regime, loathed and detested by many, the principal ideological notions on which its legitimacy originally rested, that is, the principles of anti-imperialism, support for Palestine and solidarity with the Arab and Muslim world as well as notions of historical greatness fuelling a sense of *watani* and/or *qawmi* pride, are tenets that are part and parcel of Iraqi identity. This identity has been hard-fought throughout the last nine decades and due to the tenuous territorial, linguistic, cultural and sectarian nature on which it rests, it is extremely volatile. Thus, when one of the cornerstones of "de-Ba'thification" appears to be to ensure that future Iraqi regimes are pro-American and are prepared to sell out the country's resources to the lowest (!) bidder, it is not far-fetched to argue that such a venture seriously undermines Iraqi nationalism. For instance, Fu'ad Husayn, who headed the post-invasion textbook revision team, admitted that he had been instructed to consider anything anti-American found in textbooks as propaganda and these passages were subsequently removed (Asquith, 25 November 2003). However, such blatant manipulation of history, ironically resembling Ba'thist practices, will never further American aims. This is not only because most Iraqis find it hard to accept the benign nature of American intentions behind the invasion in the short run, but, crucially, because anti-imperialism (of which anti-Americanism forms a part) is a fundamental and vital part of Iraqi historical memory and thus, in the long run, attacking or discrediting that notion will ultimately create more resentment of Western policies in Iraq.

So, what is the solution for Iraqi history-writing? This chapter has tried to nuance and historicize an aspect of the debate surrounding the American policy of "de-Ba'thifying" both Iraq and its history. While there are no obvious ready-made solutions for post-conflict societies such as Iraq, it is evident that the long-term objective must be to foster political reconciliation. The fact that no serious attempts at reconciliation have been implemented in Iraq in the years that have passed since the toppling of the *ancien régime* is not only due to the chaos that has plagued Iraq for the past years, but is also indicative of the fact that the country is still under occupation. Political reconciliation dictated by a regime supported by an occupying power is extremely hard to achieve, and would probably not stand the test of time. The same argument could be used for the problem of Iraqi history writing. As with the rest of Iraq's current problems, what is needed is reconciliation in order to attain an acceptable historical narrative of the Iraqi past. Yet this cannot be achieved as long as the country is under occupation. Thus, the prospect of writing the new history of Iraq must be regarded as a long-term objective, not a quick fix.

Instead, what is needed in the current climate is the liberation of history from the shackles imposed on it over the last decades. Thus, rather than introducing a new, officially approved, historical account from above, which would be very difficult to implement in any case because of the unwillingness of teachers and educationalists to teach accounts that are at odds with their own narratives or those of their families, communities, or political affiliations, a multifaceted and multi-approach history must be allowed to come into being. If Iraq is really to become the pluralist, multicultural, and, crucially, democratic society that American policymakers dream of, it will only develop in that direction if Iraqis are taught that historical accounts and narratives are multifaceted and that acknowledging your enemy's grievance and story does not mean surrendering your own account, but might in the long run facilitate political reconciliation and a non-sectarian and peaceful future for Iraq. Only when communities and groups that have seen themselves as victims of political persecution for decades, for whom grievances have become an important part of their identity and self-perception, become able to develop and sustain their historical narrative for a significant time, will it be possible for them to take steps towards political and historical reconciliation. Equally, those civil servants, administrators, academics and others that worked directly or indirectly for the Ba'thist regime, and even those who were ideologically committed to it, and perhaps even those ideologically committed to the cause, must be allowed to come to terms with the past and develop their own historical accounts. "De-Ba'thification" has acted as a form of collective punishment for large parts of Iraqi society, especially ideologically, and its main achievement has been to create more "victims" for whom this particular grievance has become part of their self-identity.

Thus, only with the passage of time and with the development and sustaining of multiple historical narratives will Iraqis be able to come to terms with their past. However, it is important to stress that unless these narratives are focused on Iraq as a historical and political entity they may undermine the territorial integrity of the Iraqi state and serve those minority groups who wish to see the Iraqi state dismembered. For this, the example of history instruction in Bosnia and Northern Ireland serve as stark and negative examples. There, history has been taught on sectarian grounds, to schoolchildren who are completely separated from one another, and this has significantly strengthened the divides in the respective countries over the years. In order to avoid a similar scenario, which seems plausible in the current circumstances of Iraq, it is imperative that history instruction is universal and unitary while multifaceted and allowing multiple approaches.

THE SECTARIAN MASTER NARRATIVE IN IRAQI HISTORIOGRAPHY: NEW CHALLENGES SINCE 2003

Reidar Visser

Reading reports by Western newswire services, one could get the impression that the celebration of 'Id al-Fitr at the end of Ramadan in Iraq in September/October 2008 had seriously accentuated sectarian tensions in the country. One AP article was headlined "Iraq's Sunnis celebrate Eid festival" and asserted that "Sunnis and Shiites both celebrate Eid, but often begin the festival on different days. In the past, that difference has sometimes underlined tensions between the two sects."[1] Two days later, another headline, this one from AFP: "Iraq attacks kill 26 as Shias mark Eid."[2] The theme of sectarian tension was reiterated in the text of the report, which maintained that "the latest wave of attacks came as Iraq's Shia majority celebrated Eid, a day after Sunni Muslims began to mark the end of the dawn-to-dusk fasting month of Ramadan." Similar tendencies could also be seen in a story in *The New York Times*:

> Suicide bombers killed about two dozen people on Thursday in attacks on two Shiite mosques in East Baghdad during a holiday to mark the end of the holy month of Ramadan. The attacks were the second wave this week during a lengthy public holiday for observances of Id al-Fitr, which is celebrated at different times by different Sunni and Shiite congregations.[3]

---

[1] "Iraq's Sunnis Celebrate Eid Festival amid Security," AP, 30 September 2008.
[2] "Iraq Attacks Kill 26 as Shias Mark Eid," AFP, 2 October 2008.
[3] Stephen Farrell, "Suicide bombers kill at least 20 in Baghdad," *The New York Times*, 3 October 2008.

In reality, Iraqis celebrated Eid on three different days in 2008. Most Sunnis celebrated on 30 September, some Shiʻis on 1 October, and other Shiʻis on 2 October. Muslim scholars often disagree on which day to start the celebrations and the preceding fast, which is based on the sighting of the moon. Thus, this year, there was a three-way disagreement, which separated not only Sunnis from Shiʻis, but also Shiʻis following Ali al-Sistani (who celebrated on 2 October) from those following other grand ayatollahs.[4] Another intra-Shiʻi dimension to this are the frequent disagreements between Iranian and Iraqi scholars, with Iraq's Sistani very often taking a different line from the leading clerics of Iran, as was the case in 2008, and as had happened earlier, for instance in 2002.[5] Despite these cross-cutting cleavages, however, Western media have fairly consistently tended to show a preference for highlighting the sectarian aspect of the controversy.[6]

This chapter seeks to describe the problem of a "sectarian master narrative" in sources on Iraqi history from the period after 2003, and to suggest methodological approaches that might ameliorate the problem. It should be stated at the outset that this is not a search for narratives representing some kind of higher truth as opposed to the "fabrications" of mainstream Western journalism. Nor is it an attempt at pretending that sectarianism does not exist in Iraq — it does, and in many different forms. But it is becoming a real problem for historians that so much source material relating to Iraq — such as newswire reports and stories in leading Western newspapers — is increasingly afflicted with a bias towards episodes and developments that focus exclusively on tension between the two main sectarian groups. Conversely, news from Iraq relating to intra-sectarian disagreement or inter-sectarian cooperation quite consistently receives less attention from the international press. Given the continuing security problems in Iraq, a rather limited selection of journalists remains responsible for much of the outside world's knowledge about key political developments in the country, and dealing with their biases often requires careful consideration of sources and interpretations.

---

[4]For one example, see the *bayan* by Muhammad Saʻid al-Hakim dated September 30, 2008 in which he cites the sighting of the new moon in Australia and South Africa as a sufficient basis to start the Eid on 1 October.

[5]"al-Iraniyyun yasumuna al-khamis," <http://www.islamonline.net>, 6 November 2002 (accessed 5 April 2009).

[6]For another example, see "In Iraq, Split Shiite-Sunni Start to Ramadan Serves to Reinforce Sectarian Division," AP, 24 September 2006.

How the Sectarian Master Narrative Works

The identification of sectarian or communal master narratives in Western analyses of foreign countries is far from new. In the 1980s, the Indian historian G. Pandey singled out the British designation of "communal conflicts" in Banaras — Hindus versus Muslims — as a relevant case. In Pandey's view, the British portrayed local politics as "the reflexive actions of an irrational people" which "but for the imposition of government would lead to a civil war" (Pandey, 1989, pp. 151–152, 166). Pandey's analysis is based on the assumption that the colonial power deliberately plays up local sectarian conflicts in order to justify its own presence:

> By the later 19th century, it is no longer the power of the English sword, nor simply the superiority of English science and commerce, but also the argument that the 'natives' are hopelessly divided, given to primitive passions and incapable of managing their own affairs, that legitimises British power (Pandey, 1989, pp. 151–152).

Many poststructuralist writers similarly voice skepticism against meta-narratives precisely because they are seen as being the product of the powerful forces in the world. But it is also perfectly possible to think of master narratives as something originating in a more innocent desire in ignorant individuals to navigate and interpret a complex world of which they have only limited knowledge. In the case of Iraq, this explanation should be particularly relevant, with the enormous number of persons in the United States and the international community who suddenly became engaged in 2003 in producing knowledge about a country they did not know much about prior to the invasion (Visser, 2008a, pp. 83–99).

A good example of how the bias towards sectarian readings is created could be seen in the reporting in the international media of an incident that took place in Diyala governorate on August 19, 2008. On that day, special security forces from Baghdad raided the office of the provincial council, killing the secretary of the governor. On the surface, it seemed like an archetypical intra-sectarian affair: All the key players involved — the governor, the special forces, and the commander of those forces — were Shi'is.

Nevertheless, in the Western media, even this episode prompted a quest for sectarian motives. For example, a *New York Times* report datelined 20 August asserted that "Iraqi security forces burst into the Diyala provincial headquarters to arrest a Sunni member of the provincial council but ended up firing at a federal lawmaker [...] the secretary of the provincial council was killed." The report continued, "the target of the raid was Husayn al-Zubaydi, head of the security committee on the Diyala provincial council, who is in custody. Mr. Zubaydi, like most citizens of Diyala, is Sunni, but the local government is dominated by Shi'is because many Sunnis boycotted the last election." In other words, the apparent intra-sectarian aspect of the affair was a mere misunderstanding!

Had the *NYT* reporters bothered to follow Diyala politics before it became headline news, they would have known that only weeks earlier the same "Shi'i-dominated" local council had engaged in yet another act of intra-Shi'i conflict — and one which cannot possibly be dismissed as a "mistake" in the heat of a battle or a misunderstanding between various arms of the security forces: they had sacked the local police commander, Ghanim al-Qurayshi, a Shi'i and a powerful figure who had earlier been appointed by the interior ministry (and whose appointment would have been unimaginable had he not enjoyed strong support from at least some forces within the Maliki government).[7] But this important piece of information was never given serious weight by the leading Western journalists in Baghdad. Quite the opposite: later in the day, Robert H. Reid of AP covered the same story, and with an even stronger emphasis on supposedly sectarian dimensions. According to Reid:

> Iraq's largest Sunni party accused government security forces of sectar-
> ian bias Tuesday after soldiers arrested a Sunni university president and
> a Sunni provincial council member northeast of Baghdad [. . .] The raids
> in Diyala province follow an Iraqi crackdown there against US-backed
> Sunni Arab volunteers who turned against al-Qaeda and joined the fight
> against the terror movement [. . .] The moves are likely to heighten Sunni
> suspicions about the Shiite-led national government at a time when the
> US sees progress in tamping down the sectarian hatreds that brought
> Iraq to the brink of civil war two years ago.

The description of the key personalities in the story was particularly tendentious. After having used sectarian adjectives in front of almost every noun in the story, Reid suddenly omitted a reference to the Shi'i identity of the governor, which would have muddied the sectarian narrative in his story: "The troops stormed the office of the provincial governor, Ra'd Rashid al-Tamimi, triggering a gunfight that killed his secretary and wounded four of his guards, police said." He then resumed in his more habitual style:

---

[7] "Qa'id shurta diyala al-muqal: a'da' majlis al-muhafaza aqaluni li-sahbi hamayatihim" [The sacked police commander of Diyala: the members of the provincial council dismissed me because I withdrew their special protection force], *Aswat al-Iraq*, 12 August 2008.

"The Sunni head of the provincial council's security committee, Hussein al-Zubaidi, was arrested, police said." Later, Reid did consider the information about the sacking of the police commander by the provincial council, but failed to explain that this action had been taken by a Shiite-led majority, thereby again perpetuating the sectarian master narrative: "Sunni trust in the government is tenuous, especially in Diyala. Last week the provincial council voted unanimously to fire the Diyala police chief, Maj. Gen. Ghanim Qureyshi, for alleged abuse of power against Sunnis." The headline, too, left no doubts about what sort of perspective the writer wanted to get across: "Iraqi Sunnis Outraged over Diyala Raids, Arrests."[8]

The example from Diyala is typical. The cumulative effect of stories of this kind on Western knowledge of Iraqi history after 2003 is impossible to overestimate. At the macro level, one consequence is that the birth of a cross-sectarian current in Iraqi parliamentary politics in October 2006 went unnoticed for a long time, and while the Arab media finally discovered it in the summer of 2008 (and gave it the name the 22 July front), US media and policy-makers alike remained ignorant about it until the open quarrelling between different Shi'i factions during the months leading up to the January 2009 local election made it impossible to maintain the fiction of a monolithic Shi'i community (Visser, 2008b). An additional worrying sign is that increasingly some segments of the Arab media are deliberately copying Western story formats in a way that makes it more and more likely that they too soon will show a special appetite for sectarian motives that can create sensational headlines.

Three Kinds of Imposition of Sectarian Themes

For analytical purposes it may be useful to distinguish between different ways in which historical sources become biased towards sectarianism in ways that say more about the authors of the sources than the historical incident that the sources purport to depict. At least three such different kinds of bias stand out; articles in the mainstream media often represent a mix of these ideal types.

The first category is best described as sectarian ornaments or "noise". In it, the theme of sectarianism is clearly thrown in just for good measure, without having any plausible link to the story that is reported. Sometimes this

---

[8] "Iraqi Sunnis Outraged over Diyala Raids, Arrests," AP, 19 August 2008.

can be very obvious and easy to detect. A rather glaring example occurred in the October 21, 2008 edition of the *New York Times*. According to a report from an Iraq correspondent:

> Meanwhile, intra-tribal violence erupted in the village of Sakhreya in Central Iraq just a few hours after American troops withdrew from the immediate area, resulting in up to 15 deaths, witnesses and Iraqi police officers said. It was unclear whether the fighting had occurred Tuesday or earlier. Sakhreya lies in a disputed area between Babil Province, which is mostly Shiite, and Anbar Province, which is overwhelmingly Sunni. One of the branches of a Sunni tribe in the village supported the insurgency while another branch backed the Americans, a local farmer said.

The casual reader of the *New York Times* would be forgiven for concluding that this was yet another example of how the "main sects" of Iraq were engaged in civil strife best characterized as "chronic". But of course, a closer look shows that the sectarian themes were entirely irrelevant in this case, which concerned an intra-Sunni dispute in an area that just happened to be situated on the border between a Shi'i-majority governorate and a Sunni-majority governorate, without the relationship between the two administrative entities having any plausible relation to the story.

In other cases, the sectarian dimension is introduced more discreetly, often, it seems, by "independent" Westerners who consider themselves far above the "mainstream media". A good example is the film "Iraq in Fragments" by James Longley. The director is passionate about his desire to convey a sense of the "real Iraq": in his production notes, he refers to how "I did not just want to bring the viewers into Mohammed's [an Iraqi resident of Baghdad] neighborhood — I wanted to put them inside his head. I wanted them to see what he saw, hear what he heard, including the sound of his own thoughts." Based on these aspirations, he proceeded to make a film in three parts, one from a Sunni-dominated area of Baghdad, one from Nasiriyya in the Shi'i-dominated South, and finally one from the Kurdistan region.

Of course, in a country of nearly 30 million, when the model is tripartite, it is very easy to find three individuals that can vouch for a particular kind of narrative. But these immense methodological problems notwithstanding, the movie's reception among Western audiences has been nothing short of jubilant. In *Entertainment Weekly*, Lisa Schwarzbaum gave the move an "A" and declared, "Longley looks and listens, with nonjudgmental sensitivity, as Sunni, Shiite, and Kurdish Iraqis explain their colliding, intractable, invaded worlds, and their rising frustrations. He lets people be people, not position-holders. The calm poetry of the cinematography offsets the mess of the politics to stunning effect." Another reviewer in the same publication described "Iraq in Fragments" as a "patient, lyrically photographed, closely observed meditation that pays calm attention to aspects of Sunni, Shiite, and Kurdish daily life." *In These Times* focused on the same subject: "Not a moment from these Sunni, Shiite and Kurdish daily lives is familiar from US news programs, and it's all eye-opening."[9]

Somewhat more challenging are those cases where sectarian motives are seamlessly imposed on players in Iraqi politics. For example, during the parliamentary debate in September and October 2006 about the law for implementing federalism, Reuters reported "Majority Shiites want to create an autonomous region in their oil-rich southern heartland. Minority Sunnis fear this would siphon oil wealth from Baghdad and could tear the country apart."[10] What the report fails to disclose, however, is that only a small segment of the Shi'i community were in favor of the establishment of this kind of federal region. In reality, significant numbers of Shi'i parliamentarians boycotted the final vote on the federalism bill in October, while a great numbers of others voted for it but without expressing any affection for the particular vision of a Shi'i region in the "oil-rich southern heartland". Nevertheless, the journalist in this case managed to create a polarizing and sectarian effect.

A similar case occurred in November 2008, when AP reported from Baghdad that "Miles of concrete blast walls and dozens of fortified checkpoints dissect the city. Some neighborhoods remain almost entirely walled off, and sectarian hatreds that boiled over into a bloodbath in 2006 and early 2007 simmer below the surface."[11] But the specific indications of sectarian hatred were nowhere to be found; the only voices that come to the forefront in this report are those of the journalist himself as well as the occupation authorities, whose ideas about sectarian hatreds that demand concrete walls in order to be tackled are taken at face value. And while these cases are mostly easy to detect given the conspicuous absence of quoted statements, they are now becoming so frequent that their cumulative impact on the newspaper source material for the post-2003 period in Iraq cannot be ignored.

---

[9] From excerpts of "critical responses" at http://<www.iraqinfragments.com/critics/index.html> (accessed 5 April 2009).

[10] "Iraqi Parliament Debates Autonomy," Reuters, 27 September 2006.

[11] "Security Offers Comfort to Baghdad," AP, 2 November 2008.

Perhaps the toughest challenge relates precisely to this cumulative effect: statements about Iraqi politics are repeated so many times that they acquire the quality of truisms. One particularly recurrent example concerns the way in which the Iraqi debate about oil and oil resources is misrepresented in Western (and indeed some Arab) media.

In May 2008 CNBC reported, "While the [Iraqi] legislature squabbles over how to divvy up the petrol pie insurgents continue to puncture already fragile pipelines."[12] Similarly, in October that year, AP stated in one of its reports, "Among other things, the [oil] law would set the rules for foreign investment in Iraq's oil industry and determine how oil revenues will be shared among Shiites, Sunnis and Kurds."[13] What both reports fail to acknowledge is that Iraqi oil politics is not at all about "divvying" the oil wealth between the different communities. Although this kind of portrayal and the choice of words may come across as fancy in American journalese, it is simply an inaccurate rendering of the debate that is taking place in Iraq with respect to oil. In the first place, the biggest problem in passing oil legislation in Iraq has not been related to distribution at all, but to the signing of contracts — an area where the two biggest Kurdish parties with their calls for an extreme degree of decentralization face off against almost everyone else, regardless of whether they are Sunnis or Shi'is. Secondly, to the extent that distribution is an issue at all, almost all Iraqis insist on a distribution that would be on a strict demographic per capita basis, with no other differentiation between governorates or sects. Besides the influence of Iraqi nationalist rhetoric on this issue, part of the reason may also be that another frequently heard cliché about Iraqi politics — that of the "oil-rich Shiite South" — is also highly misleading. This kind of language would suggests that all the land between Basra and Baghdad is full of oil (hence the idea of "Shi'i oil"), but the geological facts are that 60% to 70% of all of Iraq's oil is situated in a single governorate in the far South (Basra), and with another 10% or so in the two neighboring governorates of Maysan and Dhi Qar (Revenue Watch Institute/Mehaidi, 2005). In other words, there is not much more oil in Najaf than in Anbar, and when this point is realized (along with the unpopularity of the idea of a single Shi'i federal region, another pet theme of Western reporters in Iraq), most of the rationale for the entire project of "divvying up" the energy resources on some kind of

---

[12] CNBC, "Fast Money," 28 May 2008.
[13] "Iraq's Cabinet Sends Hydrocarbon Law to Parliament," AP, 27 October 2008.

communitarian basis has evaporated, and the futility of concepts such as 'Shiʻi oil' should be evident.

In the most extreme cases, nifty journalists even invent laws and institutions that do not exist in Iraqi reality. This became evident for instance in the case of the resignation of the speaker of the Iraqi parliament, Mahmud al-Mashhadani, in December 2008. The reasons for Mashhadani's resignation were complex, and came despite the fact that he retained the support of a significant cross-sectarian alliance (the so-called 22 July parties, which include Sunnis and Shiʻis as well as Islamists and secularists). Nevertheless, the Western media soon focused on his ouster as something that had been prompted by 'Shiʻi and Kurdish' demands. Some journalists went much further: according to an AFP report from early February 2009 (when the question of a replacement for Mashhadani remained pending), "under Iraq's complex political rules, Sunni Arabs have the right to nominate the speaker."[14] It would be interesting to know exactly what "complex rules" AFP is referring to here. For while there is certainly a lot of informal sectarianism in Iraqi politics (as well as some instances of formal or near-formal sectarianism, such as the institution of the transitional tripartite presidency during the 2005–2010 parliamentary cycle, as well as the much-repeated constitutional requirement that key assemblies be representative of all the "elements" or *mukawwinat* of Iraqi society), there is certainly no requirement for the speaker to belong to any particular sect. Similarly, the requirement in the bylaws of the Iraqi parliament that the speaker selection should reflect the "balance" of the assembly may be freely interpreted in whatever way one wishes — it could refer to sect, but it might equally refer to ideological division. As a reflection of this, Mashhadani, the ousted speaker, actually suggested that a Shiʻi Sadrist candidate would be best suited to succeed him — an arrangement that would have been constitutionally impossible according to AFP's exegesis of the Iraqi constitutional framework.

How the Sectarian Master Narrative can be Counterbalanced

In 1925, Stephen Longrigg, the British civil servant and Iraq historian, characterized a work on the Persian Gulf by an official of the Indian government as "a remarkable storehouse of misprints and errors [...] of use only when it quotes dispatches verbatim" (Longrigg, 1925, p. 340). In other words, it

---

[14] "Iraq's Parliament Fails to Elect New House Speaker," AFP, 9 February 2009.

is possible to make use of poor sources, as long as one exercises caution. What follows is a brief list of methodological suggestions for dealing with reporting with a sectarian bias on the post-2003 situation in Iraq.

1. Use local sources as far as possible. A wealth of daily newspapers from Iraq is available on the internet, as well as news services from most governorate councils and governorates. The daily record of the Iraqi parliament is another useful source. In general, Jean Francois Lyotard's ideas about "petit récits" are of obvious relevance in the Iraqi context.

2. Avoid as far as possible sources where format counts more than content. This means most major English-language media institutions, but also often front-page stories in the biggest Arab and Iraqi newspapers like *al-Hayat*, *al-Sharq al-Awsat* and *al-Zaman*. The choice of words in many of these stories is governed more by the ever-changing trends of Western journalese than by realities on the ground. Even "independent" (though often NGO-supported and educated) Iraqi news agencies such as *Aswat al-Iraq* are beginning to copy the formulas of Western journalism.

3. Exercise particular caution with statements purporting to represent motives but without any clear quotation, such as "Shi'is think...," "Sunnis are afraid...," "Kurds want..."

4. Identify a multitude of variables instead of focusing on the sectarian ones only. Hanna Batatu mapped the monarchical period of Iraq according to sectarian criteria, but he also described variables such as occupation, social class, family backgrounds and migration stories, thereby managing to put sectarianism into perspective.

5. Focus on intra-sectarian dynamics to get the full picture. Relevant examples include internal Shi'i controversies about federalism: Should there be no federal entities South of Kurdistan, a single big Shi'i region, or multiple regions, for example with Basra as a one-governorate federal region? Or consider the standard image in the Western media of the Iraqi security forces as loyal to the Islamic Supreme Council of Iraq (ISCI). Recently, repeated episodes in the south have exposed severe internal friction between al-Da'wa and ISCI about control of the police commanders in the various governorates.[15] More generally, the splits inside

---

[15] See for example "Dhi qar: kutlat al-majlis al-a'la tutalibu bi-ib'ad al-ajhiza al-amniyya 'an al-muhasasa al-hizbiyya," [Dhi Qar: the Supreme Council bloc demands that the security services be purged of the system of party quotas], <http://www.nasiriyah.net>, 27 February 2008 (accessed 5 April 2009).

the Shi'i Islamist camp before, leading up to and after the provincial elections of January 2009 provide instructive insights into the dynamics inside what are often construed as monolithic communities. In those elections, some Iraqi Shi'i parties — most notably ISCI — clearly tried to appeal to sectarian interests, for example through suggesting that voters should choose candidates who followed a "Husayni" approach. Conversely, Nuri al-Maliki's coalition emphasized professionalism as well as a strong state. Similarly, attitudes towards Iranian influence make an interesting point of entry for investigating intra- Shi'i differences.

6. Accept instances of inter-sectarian cooperation as one would have accepted them in a Western context. All too often, episodes of inter-sectarian cooperation in Iraq are dismissed "because in reality these players hate each other" (Galbraith, 2008). But in political science elsewhere in the world, what is often significant is how players behave and not what they think. In US politics, instances of Democrats cooperating with Republicans are often hailed as attempts to "reach across the aisle" in a spirit of "bi-partisanship."

7. When describing sectarian tension, be precise and do not impose or import motives from Western settings. One of the big problems with Western accounts of the constitutional debate in Iraq are the frequent attempts to draw parallels to the Balkans and the assumption that sectarian tension necessarily translates into a desire for separate territorial space (Visser, 2007, pp. 801–822). The recourse to artificial concepts never used by Iraqis themselves such as "Sunnistan" and "Shi'istan" for the imagined federal regions for the two sects is a good example.

8. Question the representativeness of individuals who speak in the name of sectarianism. For example, who is an Assyrian in Iraq? What about those Christians who prefer to describe themselves as Chaldeans and see themselves as Iraqis rather than as an ethnic minority in search of a homeland (Joseph, 1983)? Historically, the most ardent "Assyrianists" among the Iraqi Christians are also the smallest and by far the most recent addition to the Christian community — the Nestorians, previous inhabitants of the Hakkari mountains who were settled in Iraq after the First World War. Similar questions of representativeness can be raised about websites such as Nahrainnet, which claims to speak for the Sadrists, but which for a long period did not produce first-hand materials from Muqtada al-Sadr himself.

9. A relatively small number of Western journalists with big microphones account for a disproportionate amount of the information about

post-2003 Iraq available to the general public in Western countries (Qassim Abdul Zahra of the AFP — probably a pen name — is a good example). Many of their stories say more about their own personalities than they say about Iraq. Keep track of these writers to better understand the reports they are writing.

10. Consider investigating expressions of sectarianism through other channels than those primarily referred to by Western journalists. When it comes to issues like oil and federalism, the distance between Western writers and the situation on the ground is simply too big for their articles to make any meaningful contribution. While sectarianism certainly exists in Iraq, it is often expressed quite subtly. In particular, while the façade and rhetoric is often kept immaculately Iraqi nationalist, a look at recruitment patterns to parties and organizations often reveal tendencies that can clearly be described as sectarian.

11. Give due attention to forces that unify, and do not dismiss them out of hand as Ba'thist propaganda. It is significant when Iraqis come together across sectarian lines to celebrate national heroes, be they contestants in the Arab world's idol competition or the national soccer team (which performed brilliantly in the Asia Cup in 2007).

12. Explore the limits of sectarianism by asking critical questions. For example, do the Shi'is have an idea about a "Shi'i homeland"? The marginal project of a Shi'i federal region has already changed its name twice (from *Iqlim al-Wasat wa'l-Janub* to *Iqlim Janub Baghdad*), and does not appear to be in a position to be a serious rival to "Iraq" as a territorial framework of identity.

None of these practical suggestions can eliminate bias. That is not the intention either. Mankind needs biases to think and communicate: Without models, we would be mute and in chaos. But in writings on Iraq since 2003, the sectarian master narrative has become influential to a point where it is all-pervasive and thereby could have a decisive influence on how new histories of Iraq are written. In this context, every little attempt at disturbing the dominant storyline will be a small step in the right direction. Once more, contributors to the *Subaltern Studies* series can come to the rescue with parallels from India:

> If the small voice of history gets a hearing at all in some revised account of the Telangana struggle, it will do so only by interrupting the telling in the dominant version, breaking up its storyline and making a mess of its plot [...] What precise

form such a disorder may assume is hard to predict. Perhaps it will force the narrative to stutter in its articulation instead of delivering in an even flow of words; perhaps the linearity of its progress will dissolve in loops and tangles; perhaps chronology itself, the sacred cow of historiography, will be sacrificed at the altar of a capricious, quasi-Puranic time which is not ashamed of its cyclicity (Guha, 1996, pp.1–12).

Electronic references

Revenue Watch Institute/Mehaidi, K (2005). Geographical distribution of Iraqi oil fields and its relation with the new constitution. Online. Available HTTP: <http://www.iraqrevenuewatch.org/> (accessed 5 April 2009).

Visser, R (2008). Five years on: The Pentagon still struggling to make sense of Iraq. Online. Available HTTP: <http://historiae.org/pentagon.asp> (accessed 1 October 2008).

BEYOND POLITICAL RUPTURES: TOWARDS A HISTORIOGRAPHY OF SOCIAL CONTINUITY IN IRAQ

Peter Harling

Attempting to understand present-day Iraqi tribal, religious, class, political, generational, geographical, and social fault lines makes little sense without taking the long view. In the wake of the 2003 invasion and the subsequent ill-conceived US occupation policies, the collapse of the Iraqi state created a socio-political discontinuity — almost an aberration — leaving a vacuum that quickly filled up with identity politics, ethno-sectarian entrepreneurs, social outsiders and communal structures. None of these, however, appeared *ex nihilo*, but rather constituted indices of continuity, albeit distorted. This article will attempt to illuminate the underlying dynamics of contemporary socio-political trends in Iraq by connecting them to several of the profound transformations the country had already witnessed under the former regime.

To date, few scholarly works have successfully incorporated Iraq's pre- and post-2003 eras into a meaningful historiographical continuum. Although Saddam Husayn has departed this realm, the legacy of his regime has not yet faded, and indeed continues to affect Iraq. The period between the 1968 *coup d'état* and the 2003 US invasion was formative, yet remains under-studied. Scholars and policymakers alike have tended to simplify the complexities and ambiguities of this 35-year period, arguing that the former regime erased both society and politics, leaving post-invasion Iraq a blank slate. A vast body of emerging work either overlooks the previous era completely, treating it as a Dark Age of social immobility and debilitation, or relies on generalities and assumptions that are just as sweeping as they are questionable.[1]

Regrettably, the academic body of knowledge on the Saddam era is patchy; even its corner stone studies are decontextualized and unsupported by related pieces of work (Chaudhry, 1991; Fernea and Louis, 1991; Graham-Brown, 1999; Rigaud, 2003; Steavenson, 2009, etc.). Clearly, Iraq's inaccessibility to scholars and researchers from 1968 to 2003 contributed to the dearth of sociological studies. The literature that does exist centers on issues of power, the regime's repressive social engineering, and its antagonistic foreign policies. In this respect, studies of Iraq are not much different from studies of the Middle East in general (Khalidi, 1991), most of which have focused on the politics of regime-society relations and elites rather than larger segments of society and informal social structures and processes. This scholarly bias was magnified in the case of Iraq because Saddam's regime was viewed through the lens of a deterministic and totalitarian school of thought mostly imported from the field of Soviet studies (al-Khalil, 1989). Furthermore, any academic scrutiny of social trends unrelated to the regime ran the risk of being dismissed as trivial, naïve, or worse — malevolent, by focusing on anything other than the severity of repression.

Such theoretical and ideological limitations, as well the practical obstacles to conducting field research, have made it tempting and expedient to ignore the Saddam era altogether. In very practical terms, the general assumption that Iraqi society was defeated and chaotic greatly influenced the United States' post-invasion attempts at social engineering.

A serious sociological analysis capable of bridging the 2003 rupture must examine historiographical continuities, whereas analyses focused narrowly on the issue of power tend to emphasize political discontinuity and social dysfunction. In Iraqi historiography, attention to political disruptions at the national level too often obscures processes of identity formation and social organization at the infra- or supra-national levels.

---

[1]This is especially true of the growing number of personal accounts from US and British officials deployed in Iraq (Etherington, 2005; Bremer, 2006). But more academic literature is by no means immune. In an otherwise thoroughly researched book, Adeed Dawisha devotes only 30 pages to an era that lasted over 30 years, and concludes on this cliché: "Saddam's Iraq was a country that was held hostage to the will and whim of one omnipresent tyrant" (Dawisha, 2009).

The 2003 Rupture/Transition

Much can be learned from the abrupt 2003 transition itself, particularly the depth of what can be termed a "national deconstruction process" (Harling, 2007a), which was only prolonged by a highly disruptive US occupation. The fall of the regime gave way to a desolate landscape: state institutions were thoroughly looted, often by employees ransacking their own sources of income,[2] revealing a powerful survival ethos focused on instant gain in the face of uncertainty. Previously powerful tribal leaders appeared bewildered and helpless;[3] exiled Islamist parties returned, and upon discovering that they had no significant social base, turned to US sponsorship, militia activity and sectarianism. Former regime officials were at pains to reorganize themselves into an effective opposition.[4] While the traditional Shi'i *marja'iya* was challenged by an expansive Mahdist movement,[5] the Sunni religious establishment, which had by and large been associated with the regime, was overtaken by a rising, if disorganized, Salafi undercurrent.

The 2003 rupture created an extraordinary "bestiary" of political and religious tendencies,[6] whose proliferation and weaknesses paved the way for the US administration's social engineering pipedreams (Harling, 2007a). The former regime's monopoly of the public sphere, which had rendered Iraqi society largely invisible to itself, gave way to a multitude of political players espousing fragmented, conflicting, and hyperbolic identities. All were striving to distinguish themselves from each other by stressing their "genuine" Iraqi credentials (as opposed to the allegedly "false pretences" of their rivals), in order to carve out a share of the emerging public space.

This unstable political environment of fading institutions and surplus symbols was vulnerable to the occupier's own intentions and designs. Not only was the United States in a position to fill in the void left by the former

---

[2] Author's observations, Baghdad, April–May 2003.
[3] Author's meetings with tribal leaders from the Dulaym, Shammar Sayih, Albu Muhammad, Bani Ka'b, and others, Baghdad, Tikrit and Basra, April–May and October–November 2003.
[4] Author's meetings with former security officials, Baghdad, October–November 2003.
[5] Interestingly, one of Ayatollah 'Ali al-Sistani's first decisions was to enact a *fatwa* banning the practice of self-flagellation, ahead of the April 2003 'Ashura processions, which drew massively from what was to become the Sadrist current; his ruling was ignored. Author's observations, April 2003.
[6] The expression is borrowed from a presentation given by Loulouwa al-Rachid at a seminar on "Iraq's Future" at the Institute of Political Science, Paris, attended by the author in March 2005.

regime, but large swathes of Iraq's political elite, disoriented and fractured as they were, also expected it to do so. Ordinary citizens themselves, who often were suspicious of the elite's background and intentions, at first pinned their hopes on the possibility of a benevolent occupation (Baran, 2004).

The establishment of a political system based on simplistic ethnosectarian calculations was the outcome both of US misconceptions and the returning exiles' need to endorse whatever power-sharing agreement could best foster their ambitions. Communal narratives flourished throughout the diaspora during the 1990s, as exiled politicians failed to articulate any credible ideological vision. Long before the regime was toppled, ethnosectarianism had become the organizing principle structuring relations between the various opposition groups.

The challenges posed by the exiles' lack of social base in post-2003 Iraq became obvious as the country's socioeconomic fabric, political institutions, and national identity quickly unraveled. This state of affairs initially precluded any structured opposition from the inside and generated indeterminate and easily exploitable rifts.[7] In this context, sectarianism emerged as a resource offering nominal representativeness to figures devoid of social backing, thus enabling them to displace the dominant fault line which, in the few months immediately after the regime's collapse, came to oppose "exiles" to "insiders".[8]

Arguably, the dismantling of what remained of the state, through the decreed dissolution of the security apparatus and the infamous "de-Ba'thification" project, reflected the new elite's desire to forestall any potential resistance to their flimsy hold on power. In fact, the opposite happened. De-Ba'thification was made to accommodate partisan ambitions and sectarian narratives rather than the requirements of state-formation and transitional justice. Demotions were frequently based not on past crimes, but rather on the need to make room for political appointees in reaction to the Sunnis' alleged domination of the former regime. Although sectarian narratives had already appeared in the wake of the 1991 repression (al-Rachid and Méténier, 2007), the regime had simultaneously manipulated and contained them. The former exiles' resort to these narratives breached what was left of the dam of a unified Iraqi nationalist ideology.

---

[7]Gordon, M. "The Last Battle," *New York Times*, 3 August 2008.
[8]Remarkably, this fundamental divide, although it continues to inform Iraq's political structure, has essentially been ignored in journalistic commentary and academic writings.

Narratives of victimhood hardened along ethno-sectarian lines as the US occupation discriminated against Sunnis allegedly beholden to Saddam Husayn (Harling, 2006), nurtured uncompromising Shi'i claims of "ownership" over the Iraqi state, and acquiesced in unrealistic Kurdish ambitions (both territorial and ideological). The 2005 polls and a rushed constitutional process anchored these dynamics within the political system, guaranteeing enduring violence pending sustainable agreements on power sharing, resource allocation, and territorial dispute resolution.

As Iraq began to founder, rather than taking stock of the side effects of their policies and correcting their course, US officials developed their own narrative of externally driven violence, focusing on al-Qa'ida and regional spoilers. US policies clearly contributed to a number of other troubling trends, of which we can list but a few.

The Sadrist current developed a dialectical relationship with the occupier (Harling and Nasser, 2007). The United States responded to the politicization of Iraq's Shi'i under class, animated by social grievances, political exclusion, patriotic feelings, and Mahdist inclinations, by furthering its marginalization while simultaneously ensuring its utmost visibility (to others and to its nascent self) in the mainstream media. An intra-Shi'i struggle for power deepened when Washington took sides with a coalition of conservatives against these revolutionary masses.[9] Furthermore, the occupation's view of Tehran's interference solely through the lens of subversive action overlooked an Iranian strategy of influence over and investment in both militant groups and "legitimate" players. While the US focused single-mindedly on so-called "special groups," Iran exploited multiple channels of leverage, from humanitarian aid to theological scholarships and religious tourism (Harling and Nasser, 2006).

The occupation factor, however, should neither be overstated nor ignored. It may be tempting, for instance, to reconstruct sectarianism as an exogenous and manipulative device introduced by the United States (Ismael and Fuller, 2009), or, on the contrary, as the consequence of centuries of hatred and decades of totalitarian rule that the occupier simply "inherited" and now had to contain (Bremer, 2006). In fact, the invasion revealed, enabled, and exacerbated pre-existing phenomena more often than it generated them in and of itself. Ironically, many of the challenges that US

---

[9]Malley, R and P Harling. "Containing a Shiite symbol of hope," *Christian Science Monitor*, 25 October 2006.

authorities confronted after 2003 derived in part from past US policies, e.g., blind support for Saddam Husayn in the 1980s and a blanket chastisement of his people after the invasion of Kuwait in 1990.

As every historian knows, contemporary socio-political trends almost always have deep roots in earlier periods. Some of the more dramatic recent developments in Iraq have stemmed from undercurrents largely unnoticed during the former regime, which only accelerated as the post-invasion power structure evolved. To be sure, Saddam Husayn's initial, oil-fuelled drive toward national modernization, mobilization, and aggrandizement suppressed alternative social trends such as tribalism, Islamism (both Sunni and Shi'i), non-Ba'thist forms of Arab nationalism, and of course communism. The mechanics of Ba'thist repression have been the focal point of academic and journalistic literature alike since the early 1990s, obscuring a host of nuanced and systematic shifts in the regime's rapport with society.

Indeed, Saddam Husayn's personal power was built at the expense of the country's institutions, including the regime's own social foundations, such as the president's tribe and family, the security apparatus, and the Ba'th party, not to mention the state (Baran, 2004). This process went against Ba'thist ideology, using the oil rent and an assertive foreign policy as sources of legitimacy. Around 1990, Iraq moved away from its earlier, quasi-totalitarian model toward a less ambitious and more normative system, turning mere survival into the main organizing principle of both polity and society (Hiltermann, 1999; Harling, 2007b).

Devoid of an organizing and integrative project, and increasingly the object of its own violence, the regime was consumed by a need for demonstrations of loyalty. Thus, as the threat of the US/UK invasion materialized in 2002, Iraqi military preparations had little connection with any military rationale; rather, they were driven by the need to display zealous steadfastness.[10] Saddam's overwhelming distrust of his own armed apparatus, and the latter's valuation of cronyism over professionalism, seriously undermined the Iraqi military's performance during the 2003 invasion (Baran, 2003; Woods,

---

[10]Illustrations abound, although none can surpass a video discovered after the war in which senior officials (notably the head of Military Industrialization) present Saddam with such innovative weapons as slingshots and crossbows, which they flaunt as an asset to face off the most powerful army in the world. The video was clearly designed for archival rather than propaganda purposes and was not shown to the public at the time. Shane, S. In Video, Hussein Uses Slingshots and Bows to Rally Iraqis for War. *New York Times*, 24 November 2006.

2006). Tellingly, the regime's inner core put up the least resistance, proving that pageantry had pervaded the system, substituting itself for any other form of cohesion (notably the notion of *'asabiya*). Saddam's perpetuation, regardless of predictable cost, of the last remnant of his greatness — the myth of Iraq's possession of weapons of mass destruction (Duelfer, 2004) — dramatically revealed the extremes to which the regime was willing to go to assert an image of power to the detriment of the state's institutional capabilities to uphold it.[11] This transformation provided an expanding space for social dynamics that the regime, instead of repressing, sought more often to contain, arbitrate, and manipulate. Many of these trends, which have yet to be fully identified and understood, were themselves rooted in socioeconomic developments that long-predated the Saddam era.

Tribal "Loyalties"

The "tribe," as a social subunit as well as a theoretical construct, has witnessed so many profound transformations and diverse uses in both academic and lay literature since the nineteenth century that the word has become semantically slippery. As the United States struggled to find a "unified field theory" through which to understand and control Iraq, "the tribe" assumed disproportionate importance and erroneous meanings among policymakers and media analysts.

The tribe's "traditional" role was primarily one of protection from the hazards of nature (illness and death), as well as threats posed by other tribes (raids, vendettas, displacement provoked by competition over trade routes or fertile land), and later by forms of state authority (levies and conscription). Cohesion derived from common descent, biological or fictive, which provided collective solidarity and socio-political capital in a highly formalized "pedigree" system structured by professed lineage (for instance, claims to descent from the Prophet or from a number of prestigious pre-Islamic tribes). Reconstructed narratives (stories of bravery, munificence or acumen) also established the tribes' credentials, and geographical or economic differentiation (Bedouins, semi-nomadic sheep and camel breeders, sedentary cultivators, and Marsh Arabs) determined a caste-like social hierarchy.

---

[11] An interesting example in this respect is the deployment around Najaf of troops in 1999 dressed in protective suits as a way of cowing the population into submission following the assassination of Muhammad Sadiq al-Sadr (Rohde, 2010).

A tribal leader's authority was established not simply by lineage, but more importantly, by his ability to serve the community's interests by upholding the tribe's reputation through rituals of honor, generosity, and (in some cases) combat, while mitigating disputes and violence through negotiation skills and marital strategies.

In the late Ottoman period and under the Iraqi monarchy, many prominent tribal chieftains (*shuyukh*) forged a *de facto* alliance with the government. They gained tax exemptions, ownership of land, and discretionary rule over their subjects in exchange for assuming functions of social control that transformed their clansmen into an indebted work force, preyed upon by their leaders' private armies who exerted new forms of violence aimed at dominating rather than protecting the tribe (Batatu, 2004). The emergence of a state further alienated the *shuyukh* from their social base by incorporating them into a centralized apparatus of power and urbanized elite.[12]

Early Republican policies put an end to this state of affairs by redistributing the land and challenging the tribal frames of reference that still enjoyed a quasi-monopoly over Iraq's rural society. During the 1980s and 1990s, however, Saddam Husayn's regime gave renewed prominence to the tribes by co-opting some of them within the security structure and ostensibly promoting tribal culture (Yaphe, 2000; Jabar and Dawod, 2003). Wrongly understood as a "resurgence" or "revival", this was in fact a novel phenomenon (Baram, 1997). The *shuyukh*'s basis of authority was neither protective nor predatory now. In this new configuration, the regime provided the *shuyukh* with resources (employment, social recognition, tolerance of criminal activities — notably smuggling — and occasionally weapons) from which they derived their newfound power in the context of a two-tier patronage system. Only by becoming the regime's clientele could the *shuyukh* secure access to assets indispensable to inducing their tribesmen's support (Baran, 2004).

The *shuyukh*'s clout was thus conditioned on absolute loyalty to the regime's core interests, rather than the traditional sources of their authority (i.e., the lineage and the capacity to protect the tribe), or more recent power bases (land tenure and internal coercion). There were in essence no "powerful" tribes; the more affluent were simply the ones most dependent

---

[12]In an interview with *Niqash*, Falih 'Abd al-Jabbar made this very illuminating remark: "The creation of the Iraqi state in 1921 contributed to the legitimization of the historic disintegration of the tribes: Agricultural stability, the emergence of private property, migration to cities, the emergence of private owners independent of their tribes, etc. We see that in parliament, the tribe became part of the parliament, not the opposite" (Jihad, 2008).

on the regime's benevolence. At the same time, while tribal pageantry came dramatically to the fore in the regime's media, actual practices systematically demeaned the tribal value system, degrading the legitimacy of the *shuyukh* and forcing tribes to betray their kin rather than to defend them (International Crisis Group, 2008b).

The dynamics of this complex relationship illuminate much of Iraq's tribal landscape since the 2003 war. Tribal "loyalty" to Saddam Husayn dissolved as soon as the prospect of his demise became tangible; tribal delegations from cities like Falluja or Bayji attempted to negotiate their surrender in the immediate aftermath of the US takeover of Baghdad.[13]

Although some US officials viewed the tribes, intuitively and early on, both as potential allies and as real threats (thanks to erroneous conceptions of revenge as a key component of tribal ethos),[14] they failed to engage with them effectively and thus missed an important opportunity to foster political cohesion. They were confused by the proliferation of self-proclaimed *shuyukh* volunteering their services, each one of them boasting "hundreds of thousands" of supporters,[15] and were consequently reluctant to invest seriously in any of them. When they did decide to extend them resources, however, they failed to understand that tribal "loyalty" could only be durably bought if betrayal came at great cost, hence the unsuccessful attempts at co-opting tribes to protect pipelines, in a context where "guards" were inclined to stage attacks themselves to maximize their profits. Finally, the United States opted for the notion of tribal "representation" within the nascent political system, as if the few figures they handpicked meant anything to the many they had not.

Revealingly, whereas the extent of shaykhly authority and autonomy historically had been an antithetical function of the expansion or retreat of central power (Baran, 2004), the complete collapse of the state left the *shuyukh* helpless. Accusations of opportunism and self-interest were rife among their tribesmen. Tribal leaders in and around Basra were subdued by

---

[13] Author's observations and interviews, April–May 2003.

[14] Internal Coalition Provisional Authority correspondence made available to the author. The issue of "revenge killings" was misunderstood. The tribal ethos in fact seeks to circumvent vendettas, and usually succeeds in doing so. Revenge killings take place precisely when the mitigation/litigation procedures (*fasl*) are impaired. Tellingly, the United States registered considerable success in upholding the policy of paying "blood money."

[15] In the early stages of the occupation, a number of federations, associations, and unions of tribes emerged, generally centred around one egotistical figure or another, and failed to gain any traction.

Islamist parties and militias in an expression of vendetta dynamics, which the latter won.[16] In the alleged tribal stronghold of Anbar, lack of popular support in an increasingly dangerous environment forced many previously "powerful" *shuyukh* into exile — notably to Jordan and Syria. Others threw in their lot with Islamist insurgent groups.[17] An illuminating example is that of the case of Sattar Abu Risha, a pioneer of the struggle with al-Qa'ida in Iraq. He succeeded in maintaining influence thanks to autonomous resources, namely the spoils of banditry along the Baghdad–Amman highway — competition over whose control was, incidentally, the tribe's initial bone of contention with al-Qa'ida (Biddle, 2008; International Crisis Group, 2008b).

The *sahwat* phenomenon[18] enabled a wider tribal elite to return to power through a more formal relationship with a new sponsor, the United States, which was now willing to provide them with necessary resources. The tribes' loyalty was further assured by their own fear of retribution from al-Qa'ida if coalition backing were to be withdrawn. Although Prime Minister Nuri al-Maliki has proved reluctant to embrace the Sunni tribes' participation in the *sahwat*, he has made good use of his control over state resources to secure his own tribal base through the *isnad* councils — whose members receive stipends in exchange for their support of Maliki's security-related (and electoral) undertakings — in the South and along the Kurdish–Arab boundary, particularly in the run-up to the January 2009 provincial elections (International Crisis Group, 2009). On that occasion tribes entered the race independently in scattered places, such as Ramadi, Tikrit, and Samawa, regions of the country where tribal structures remain predominant. Elsewhere, tribes put themselves up for auction, eliciting patronage from a range of parties and lists in exchange for their pledges of "loyalty".

Another interesting trend is the replication, in a disjointed and *ad hoc* fashion, of a model of rurally based control of the cities, a distinctive feature of several authoritarian regimes in the region. In 2008, a frequent complaint voiced by inhabitants of towns such as Falluja, Mosul, and Ba'quba was that local security forces (namely the police in Mosul and the *sahwat* in the

---

[16]In Basra, for instance, even the Garamsha tribe, self-sufficient and cohesive due to its involvement in organized crime, was ultimately cowed (International Crisis Group, 2007).

[17]The Zawba' and 1920 Revolution Brigades provide an example of tribally structured insurgent activity.

[18]The word *sahwat*, which initially designated a tribal movement, has come to encapsulate whoever joined US-sponsored proxies fighting the insurgency.

other cases) were staffed by individuals hailing from peripheral areas, who were perceived as unwelcome interlopers by the urban elite.

The relevant fault line, however, is not between tribalism and more "civil" forms of social organization, in as much as tribes are dependent upon and transformed by the civilian apparatus of the state more than they are capable of challenging it. What requires greater attention is an urban/rural divide that played out in numerous arenas, and even within the boundaries of the capital. Despite a history going back centuries, modern Baghdad was shaped by two socio-political processes interacting intensively in a relatively short time frame. On the one hand, the capital city grew quickly thanks to rapid urbanization fuelled by accelerated rural to urban migration. This resulted not only in an expanding state bureaucracy, but also in the construction of middle-class neighborhoods to house the influx of people from the countryside, which dominate the city's structure to this day (Luizard, 1994). On the other, the well-established elites that existed in nineteenth century Baghdad (Ottoman-era notables, Jews, traders, and craftsmen) were soon to be decimated.

Thus the seat of power in Republican Iraq was never the home of deeply rooted urban elites, in contrast with, say, Damascus. In the 1970s and 1980s, Iraq's urban/rural divide opposed not so much the capital against the country's rural areas, but rather, a recently urbanized elite against more venerable ones (within Baghdad itself but also as in towns such as Najaf, Karbala, Hilla, Falluja, Tikrit, and Mosul).

Sunni Arab Trends

The existence of the tribes as specific social actors enjoying particular ties with the state is evidence enough to dismiss any vision of an amorphous Sunni Arab "community" defined, as much of the literature available on contemporary Iraq suggests, by the collective loss of power in the post-2003 period. As argued elsewhere (Harling, 2006), this pervasive misconception among US officials led to a self-fulfilling prophecy; prejudiced policies fostered a shared Sunni Arab identity informed by a narrative of victimhood.

If one postulates that the Sunni Arabs were by and large the beneficiaries and backers of the former regime, it becomes difficult to comprehend their limited inclination to defend it, their surprisingly arduous struggle to reorganize in any meaningful opposition after its demise, and the rise of Salafism as the driving force behind a nascent insurgency over Ba'thism, tribal and professional networks, as well as against the non-Salafi versions of Islam promoted under Saddam. Part of the explanation can be found in the regime's previously mentioned inclination to undermine its own ideological and institutional pillars, and to undercut the tribes as autonomous and coherent social sub-units (Baran, 2004).

Other segments of Sunni Arab society were also undermined during the former regime. Saddam Husayn promoted a new rural elite at the expense of the old urban classes in such towns as Baghdad, Mosul, and even in his hometown of Tikrit. What middle classes emerged through the state-building process were later debilitated by the collapse of the oil-rent patronage system during the grueling decade of the US-imposed embargo (Darle, 2003). The Sunni Arab business class, a mix of long-urbanized families and *nouveaux riches* hailing from the countryside (Khafaji, 2004), had become too intertwined with the regime and too reliant on crony-capitalism to prosper in the post-Saddam environment. For its part, Iraq's Sunni religious establishment was weakened both by the regime's thorough repression of the Muslim Brotherhood in the late 1960s and early 1970s, and the systematic manipulation of all other home-grown trends of religious thought thereafter.

Nonetheless, while Saddam Husayn flaunted the much-publicized "National Faith Movement," a crude form of propaganda that did great harm to many prominent preachers (Baran, 2004), he partly tolerated a *Wahhabi* undercurrent that percolated into Iraq throughout the 1990s.

Salafi attire, notably the characteristically short *dishdasha*, became increasingly stylish around some mosques, even in Baghdad.[19] Incidents of religiously motivated violence against Christians were reported, particularly in the city of Mosul, while attacks on liquor stores and cinemas occurred, for instance, in Falluja (Hashim, 2006).[20] As of 2000, the introduction and possibilities of the internet were not lost on a number of religious figures who had already become active members of a globalized *umma* by the time the regime was toppled.[21] Moreover, despite the authoritarian nature of the regime, it was not completely insulated from the "Afghan Arab" phenomenon, as later evidenced by the itineraries of some insurgent leaders in Falluja (Hashim, 2006).

---

[19] Author's observations, 1998–2003.

[20] Attacks on Christian-owned liquor stores also occurred in Basra, indicating a wide-ranging shift toward more conservative mores throughout Iraq's Muslim society (Harling, 2000).

[21] Author's interviews with religious figures in Falluja revealed a remarkable network of contacts forged through the internet, predating the regime's demise, May 2003.

The security apparatus sought to track down and suppress known Jihadist figures (Rohde, 2010), and Salafi figures within the elite itself were harassed if not arrested (Steavenson, 2009). But few paid attention to the social ramifications of this phenomenon. In some parts of the country, quietist forms of Salafism filled the gap left by a retreating regime whose ideological tenets were increasingly difficult for Iraqis to identify with. A town like Dhulu'iya, north of Samarra', became a Salafi stronghold after its inhabitants were purged from the security apparatus following the discovery of a plot involving some of their kin.[22]

As the regime collapsed, this social disorganization left the Sunni Arabs, in what had become a sectarian-oriented political setting, devoid of any credible political representatives, in contrast to the Kurds and the Shi'is. Their comprehensive marginalization on the basis of the Kurdish and Shi'i victimization narratives and resulting US support, combined with the fact that the occupation took more antagonistic forms in predominantly Sunni Arab areas, quickly led to a situation in which a Sunni Arab identity could only assert itself in radical opposition to the political process. This also meant that Sunnis could only organize "underground," making it all the more difficult for any clear representation to emerge.

One should not, however, envisage an entirely atomized Sunni Arab society. The insurgency initially grew out of a myriad of professional, familial, tribal, religious and neighborhood networks, and small-scale systems combining several of these categories.[23] Although discredited and struggling to rationalize the Party's crimes and failures,[24] Ba'thists came to form a web of outcasts loosely held together by their common predicament. Former colleagues, sacked from the military and security apparatus, offered

---

[22]The locality of Qaraghull, near Yusifiya, South of Baghdad, is another example. Home to the Qaraghull tribe, affiliated with the Dulaym, its residents were purged from the security apparatus as a result of tensions with the regime in the 1990s. They turned to a simple, pious life of Salafi inspiration, and the area rapidly turned into an al-Qa'ida stronghold after Saddam Hussein's demise. Author's observations, prior to and after the 2003 war.

[23]Author's observations, October–November, Baghdad, 2003.

[24]The Ba'th was associated with the humiliating 2003 defeat, only the latest of a long series of debacles. As mass graves dating back to the repression of the 1991 revolts were discovered and exhumed throughout the South, the Party strove to justify them through communiqués explaining that the graves contained the many civilian casualties caused by the coalition's onslaught at the time, buried hurriedly because of the prevailing conditions. Naturally, this argument failed to convince anyone other than hard-core Ba'thists themselves. Author's observations, October–November, Baghdad, 2003.

a source of invaluable know-how (more so than leadership, given the culture of blind obedience nurtured under Saddam's regime). The existence of strong local bases of identity (in Falluja, Mahawil, Albu 'Itha, Abu Ghrayb and Mosul, among others) also played a role. Mosques provided legitimacy and connected people of different backgrounds.[25] Finally, a significant pool of recruits was to be found among the country's despairing youth, whose hopes of social fulfillment had been ruined by a debilitated educational system, a maimed and humiliated national army, an economy under embargo, and, as a more general consequence, diminished marital prospects.

In this complex and fragmented landscape, Salafism became the easiest common denominator of political organization, given its remarkable plasticity in mobilizing the armed struggle. Both foreign and domestic enemies (the United States, Iran, Shi'i parties, former exiles) could readily be labeled infidels, whereas other frames of reference could never have encompassed these trends into a single enemy category. The considerable financial assets accessible to Jihadists, the spectacular nature of their deeds, and their mastery of communication tools within the globalized media sphere, contributed to the inordinate role of Salafism as the insurgency gained speed. All alternative narratives — Ba'thism, nationalism and anti-imperialism — receded from the public eye as insurgent propaganda emphasized an ever-more Salafi image. But these narratives also buttressed individual perspectives among fighters animated by many different motives — some of them as undramatic as revenge or unemployment.

As examined in more detail elsewhere (International Crisis Group, 2008b), Salafism also served as a springboard for outsiders who, in their drive to insert themselves into the insurgency and the wider Sunni Arab society, resorted to an increasingly rigid and coercive form of Salafism at the expense of its doctrinal foundations. They challenged the social order by turning their violence against traditional elites (tribal *shuyukh*, the non-Salafi religious establishment, modernized urban middle classes, what remained of the business class, etc.), and thus alienated the very segments of society that resistance movements are usually careful to placate.

In a dislocated society, extreme forms of violence became a primary source of social mobility, financial gain and political capital (notably for menial workers in both rural and urban settings, as well as youth). Interestingly, the pauperized masses, as a reservoir for mobilization, have been as

---

[25] Author's observations, October–November, Baghdad, 2003.

crucial to Sunni as Shiʻi militant organizations. Empowered Salafi militants dismissed deep-seated frames of reference, brushing aside Iraq's national identity (by supporting the establishment of a sectarian Islamic state), tribal customs, popular religious practices, a measure of cross-sectarian conviviality, and numerous other codes of behavior such as deference to elders, the well to do, and the learned. Tellingly, some attempted to marry themselves forcibly into the local tribal society, against the *shuyukh*'s will (Kilcullen, 2007).

This upheaval prompted a conservative backlash, which came to be known under such labels as "Concerned Citizens," "Awakening Councils," and "Sons of Iraq." This hodgepodge of actors crystallized in reaction to the social disruption described above, a dynamic that US forces, in the context of the "surge," quickly capitalized upon. The notion that the United States would prove a far more powerful, wealthier, and less brutal ally against Iran than al-Qaʻida could ever be, certainly played a role in the success of the surge, if only as a convenient rationalization. Naturally, along with the conservative component of Sunni Arab society, a number of opportunistic outsiders also joined in, dropping the Salafi mantle as easily as they had adopted it (International Crisis Group, 2008b).

It has yet to be seen whether further elections will progressively allow not only for a fair representation of the Sunni Arab constituency on a national level, but also instate a sustainable balance between diverse Sunni elites struggling to reassert themselves. Tribes co-opted by the United States — often those that enjoyed similar relations with the former regime — are challenged by those left out, who flaunt their "authenticity". Finally, homegrown religious elites have yet to recover from nationalization under the former regime and marginalization as a result of an imported Salafi trend.

This picture is still far from complete without factoring in strong local identities. Mosul's ethno-sectarian makeup, its military traditions, and commercial ties to northeast Syria and Turkey make it infinitely different from a town like Ramadi. Mosul's resilience as a centre of armed opposition owes much to its geographical location (straddling the Arab–Kurdish fault line), its distance from Baghdad, and scarce resources (justifying the lack of interest demonstrated until recently both by the Iraqi government and US occupation forces), tribal and family connections in neighboring Syria, and mountainous topography.

Other examples of potentially significant local dynamics abound. The longstanding rivalry between Samarra' and Tikrit, the latter having been promoted by Saddam over the former as the seat of power within

Salah al-Din governorate, has re-emerged since 2003. The indiscriminate targeting of individuals hailing from Samarra' in retaliation for the bombing of the city's Shi'i shrines in February 2006 forced many to relocate to their town of origin, provoking a consolidation of local identity whose effects are yet to be understood. In Diyala and in the Sunni enclaves south of Baghdad, even less is known about the manner in which sectarian consolidation may impact socio-political mobilization. Falluja's tightly knit society, both victimized and galvanized by resistance to the occupation, presents another identity crucible deserving greater scrutiny.

As the scramble for power and resources shifts from an armed conflict opposing sectarian coalitions and centered on the capital and its institutions, to more diverse and localized struggles, often pitting kin against kin, these social fault lines will likely come to the fore.

An Intra-Shi'i Struggle

Since 2003, a class struggle within Iraq's Shi'i Arab society, suppressed under Saddam Husayn but nevertheless dating back for decades, has opposed the so-called Sadrist phenomenon to a conservative coalition comprising the *marja'iya*, its tribal following, formerly exiled Islamist parties, and urbanized elites.

The Sadrist current's powerbase is geographically centered in the areas that received the bulk of the rural exodus under the monarchy (Batatu, 2004). Particularly affected were the current governorates of Maysan and Dhi Qar, especially the population living in the marshes. The exodus spawned shantytowns on the periphery of Baghdad, Basra, and other towns throughout the South, where rural migrants settled in makeshift neighbourhoods called *sarayif*, in reference to huts built out of reeds.

As described elsewhere (Harling and Nasser, 2007), the Marsh Arabs traditionally formed an insular society, geographically isolated and largely self-sufficient, differentiated in culture and cult, cut off from the influence of both the religious sanctuaries of Najaf and Karbala and the modernist powerhouses of Baghdad and Basra. They were also positioned disadvantageously in the traditional tribal hierarchy, in which Bedouin raiders occupied the dominant position and marsh dwellers (who were buffalo breeders and rice cultivators) the lowest. As outsiders simultaneously feared and exploited by urban elites, they retained this insular quality in the slums where they settled in the urban areas (Farouk-Sluglett and Sluglett, 2001).

The development projects that turned these slums into genuine neighborhoods in the late 1950s and early 1960s, reflecting efforts at social control rather than urban integration, did little to alter this state of affairs. Residents often retained strong ties to their cultures and villages of origin, and were thus slow to integrate into their new environment. Popular forms of religiosity, tribal custom, and a tradition of civil disobedience in the face of state authority translated from the marshes to the outskirts of major cities. From the beginning, the *sarayif* were a breeding ground for proletarian movements (both secular and Islamist), and a refuge for criminals and deserters. al-Thawra, also called Saddam City, most recently Sadr City, and perhaps the best example of the *sarayif* phenomenon, developed its own, very specific, and partly underground culture under the former regime (Rigaud, 2003):

After the war in 1991 and the state's breakdown as a result of the embargo along with the regime's withdrawal from the social sphere, these neighborhoods only became increasingly insular.[26] Their youth in particular were denied any prospects of social mobility through education or even incorporation in the army, where wages barely sufficed for a recruit to survive as an individual, let alone establish a family. Limited financial and social capital hampered opportunities for emigration, leaving menial jobs and criminal activity[27] as the only viable economic choices.[28] With the US military build-up in late 2002-early 2003, many inhabitants of central Baghdad, regardless of confessional identity, were fearful that the aftermath

---

[26] Even the public transport system did not extend to the more remote parts of Fadihat al-Thawra, whose potholed and sewer-inundated roads were served by an improvised system of British-era jeeps used as collective taxis. Water was scarce (in contrast to electricity, which was required for security reasons). Education standards were particularly low. (Author's observations prior to the war.) A second rural exodus took place in the 1990s due to the regime's policy of draining what was left of the marshes. This new wave of migrants merged with the previous one; in Baghdad, they congregated, notably, in the neighborhood of Fudhayliya.

[27] The open-air marketplace called Suq Umm Raydi, dubbed the "thieves' market," thrived as the major commercial zone and source of employment within Fadihat al-Thawra. The neighbourhood also provided cheap labour to the more reputable trading platforms of al-Jamila, Shurja, and al-Baya', as well as unskilled workers in numerous other fields of activity, from printing to gardening. (Author's observations prior to the war.)

[28] This in part explains why the regime succeeded in luring many of them into the ranks of the *Fida'iyu Saddam*, which could offer a sense of accomplishment otherwise largely unavailable to them. Harling, P. "Iraq's Lost Generation," *al-Quds al-'Arabi*, 11 December 2007.

of the regime's fall would unleash the "mob" (*al-ghawgha'*), emerging from the suburbs to prey upon upper- and middle-class neighborhoods.[29]

Casting blame on the suburbs for the looting of Baghdad only hid a more troubling reality: a pauperized middle-class had ransacked the state's bureaucratic infrastructure, of which — tragically — it had been a product. Sophisticated operations mounted by organized criminal networks, a systematic Kurdish *razzia* on consumer goods and construction materials whisked off to the North or smuggled into Turkey and Iran, the frenzied efforts of former regime officials to grab as much as possible before all was lost, and the keen interest shown by outside powers and profiteers, all contributed to a complex situation irreducible to the actions of the *ghawgha'*.[30] The looting of Baghdad revealed a predatory culture spawned by the decade-long embargo (al-Rachid and Méténier, 2007), which was by no means only an outgrowth of the suburban under-class.

The emergence of the Sadrist current in 2003 revealed the existence of new crosscutting fault lines within Iraqi Shi'i society. Sadrist militants and cadres were most often very young, in their 20s and early 30s, meaning they belonged to the generation deeply fashioned by the embargo.[31] The grueling effects of US-sponsored sanctions, which permeated every aspect of their daily lives and epitomized the perceived viciousness of Washington's policy, planted the seeds of a bitterly anti-American worldview. If there were any defining political moments to their lives, these were the decay, in the late 1980s, of the army into which many of them had been recruited,[32] the repression of the 1991 revolts, in which youthful urbanites were let down both by the United States and the Iranian-based Islamist Badr militia (Cockburn, 2008), the advent and assassination of the populist Ayatollah Muhammad al-Sadr, dubious US air strikes such as Operation Desert Fox in 1999, and the charade of haggling and tensions over weapons of mass destruction. Neither the quietist *marja'iya* in Najaf nor the Islamist parties now returning from exile had ever meant anything to these Sadrists in the making. Rather, they brandished their sufferings in the face of such parties as SCIRI (since

---

[29] Author's interviews, Baghdad, December 2002–February 2003.

[30] Author's interviews and observations, May 2003.

[31] Harling, P. "Iraq's Lost Generation," *al-Quds al-'Arabi*, 11 December 2007.

[32] The army, previously a vector of social integration, became the very opposite after the war on Iran. Young soldiers, whose description evoked Sadrists-to-be, were seen walking into Kuwait after Iraq's invasion, wearing tattered uniforms and sandals instead of boots. They partook in the looting out of sheer misery. Author's interview with a Palestinian witness of these events, April 2009.

renamed ISCI) and al-Da'wa, whose claim to monopolize Shi'i representation and control the state was generating a strong and wide-ranging reaction
of popular rejection.[33] As a result and as seen above, the Shi'i parties first
leaned heavily on US support, later resorting to sectarianism as a source of
legitimacy. A Sunni/Shi'i fracture soon replaced the insider/exile divide.

Similarly, Sadrists vocally challenged the *marja'iya*'s own claims to religious leadership on the basis of its silence under Saddam and estrangement
from ordinary people. Instead, they invoked the example of Muhammad al-
Sadr, a figure first promoted by the former regime to outshine 'Ali Sistani,
and then assassinated once he had succeeded in doing so (Baran, 2004;
Visser, 2008). By eradicating the Islamist parties in the early 1980s, hem-
ming in the *marja'iya*, and retreating from society, the regime virtually guaranteed the huge appeal of the particular form of religious-based mobilization
engineered by Muhammad al-Sadr in the 1990s. His plebeian, nationalistic,
anti-American, and anti-Iranian rhetoric electrified Iraq's Shi'i under-class.
Tellingly, his assassination prompted riots, especially in the former *sarayif.*

When the Islamist parties and the *marja'iya* resurfaced in 2003, they
progressively coalesced Iraq's Shi'i middle class, the commercial elite living
off the pilgrimage industry, and tribes that historically enjoyed close ties
with the sanctuaries of Najaf, Karbala, and Kadhimiya.[34] One of the most
seminal and vicious conflicts since 2003 has been an intra-Shi'i class struggle
opposing social outsiders, represented by the Sadr current and other formations of similar extraction, to this coalition of conservatives (International
Crisis Group, 2006). Although both coalitions seem to have evaporated as
a result of the Sadrists' disarray and the rivalry among former exiles, the
assertiveness of the Shi'i under-class is unlikely to diminish.[35]

In Iraq, another deeply ingrained Shi'i fault line opposes the Middle
Euphrates to the far South. Shi'i representation has long been the preserve
of elites originating from central Iraq and resented by the periphery (Visser,
2007). Besides the marsh areas, the city of Basra has developed its own
strong local identity as a cosmopolitan seaport and the country's economic

---

[33]Author's observations in the months following the invasion.

[34]Interestingly, when the Sadrists besieged Sistani's quarters in April 2003, demanding
he leave the city, the Ayatollah called upon the Middle Euphrates tribes for protection.
These are deeply enmeshed with the commercial and religious elite within Najaf, and thus
have an interest in preserving the status quo.

[35]An interesting analogy may be drawn, tentatively, with Iran, where a proletariat of
Mahdist inclinations appears very much at odds with the traditional religious elites and
the Bazaar.

powerhouse, commandeered and exploited by Baghdad (Visser, 2005). Here we see a degree of continuity between the former regime's practices and those that now prevail in the post-2003 order, nurturing an unremitting if subdued conflict (International Crisis Group, 2007; International Crisis Group, 2009).

Yet, regardless of the divisions described above and despite the suppression of its religious and political representatives under Saddam, post-2003 Iraqi Shi'i society has displayed a relatively high degree of social organization, at least in comparison with the Sunni, and — even more so — with the progressive components of Iraqi society. Its demographic weight aside, this advantage contributed heavily to its recent ascendency. The fight for control of the capital illustrates the changing socio-political positioning of Iraq's Shi'is.

What the Civil War Revealed

The term "civil war" will be used here, somewhat inadequately,[36] to describe one of many forms of violence within a multilayered and ever-shifting state of conflict (Bozarslan and Harling, 2007). Implicit in this analysis is the contest over territory between two sectarian coalitions mobilizing — often coercively — the symbolic, financial, and paramilitary resources of their respective power bases. This particular episode of the Iraqi conflict took place in and around Baghdad throughout 2006 and 2007.

For the armed groups involved, the fight consisted in holding ground, building or enforcing popular acquiescence, connecting strongholds, securing control of key positions, and undermining their opponents' own footing. In doing so, they resorted to gruesome practices against civilians, whose commission was rooted in complex strategies informed by the combatants' intuitive, and at times sophisticated, understanding of the socioeconomic factors at play. Indeed, civil war dynamics revealed the complexity and diversity of Baghdad's make-up, which to a large extent determined the course of the fighting.

Arguably the most remarkable and decisive feature of the civil war was the role played by the *sarayif*. The four Baghdad neighborhoods in which the Sadrist current established itself (al-Thawra, al-Fudhayliya, al-Shu'la

---

[36]This episode and its consequences will be examined more extensively in a forthcoming publication.

and al-Washshash) are all former *sarayif*, whose youth filled the ranks of the Sadrist militia, the Mahdi Army.[37] Densely populated, socially cohesive, and economically underprivileged, the *sarayif* constituted impenetrable strongholds and unlimited reservoirs of recruits that the Mahdi Army utilized to expand into the mixed and middle-class quarters.

Within the territories they controlled, these competing forces engaged in systematic sectarian cleansing, while deftly ministering to the needs of those displaced from other quarters. In taking over predominantly Sunni districts, Mahdi Army fighters sought to "soften up" these areas by disrupting their economic fabric, using methodical attacks on shop owners to erode social cohesion, and by forcing residents to flee in search of basic goods, thereby cutting opponents off from their own social base. Finally, they strove to isolate Sunni bastions from each other, and more importantly, from the Sunni hinterland.

Sadrists easily and fully rationalized these tactics, which were carried out in collusion with state institutions controlled by the more "legitimate" Shi'i parties; police forces either turned a blind eye or facilitated the Mahdi Army's freedom of movement, while some ministries contributed to social dislocation by selectively denying the provision of basic services (Dodge, 2008). Although Baghdad has been routinely described as the seat of Sunni power, the Sunni landscape was in fact far more diverse and fragmented. Only a few strongholds were cohesive enough to resist.

The quarters of al-Ghazaliya and al-'Amiriya in Western Baghdad were originally mixed, built on land distributed by the former regime to government employees, including officers in the security apparatus and the armed forces (many of whom rapidly sold off their properties).[38] A number of inhabitants were migrants from neighboring al-Anbar, a connection strongly revitalized in 2004 by a massive influx of displaced persons from that violence-ridden governorate. As middle class Iraqis — more inclined and able to seek refuge abroad — left the area, the latter came to look like an eastern edge of al-Anbar wedged deep into the capital.

al-Saydiya and parts of Dawra offer a rare case of disenfranchised Sunni neighborhoods in a city whose Sunni component was largely middle class and mostly state-employed. A strong connection developed with the nearby

---

[37] The Sadrists' role has been documented extensively elsewhere (International Crisis Group, 2006; International Crisis Group, 2008a) and will only be summarized here.

[38] Author's interviews, Baghdad, 2000–2003.

rural surroundings, particularly Albu 'Itha (a village co-opted into the intelligence apparatus in the 1980s) and 'Arab Jbur (agricultural land held by former regime figures). al-Fadhil, a Sunni quarter in the oldest part of town, characterized by a strong local identity and tightly-knit society, also became a Sunni stronghold, as did another historical neighborhood, al-'Adhamiya, a commercial hub centered on the religious sanctuary of Abu Hanifa.

These exceptions aside, large swathes of Baghdad fell into the hands of Shi'i forces, primarily the Mahdi Army. The Iranian-born Badr brigade, for its part, maintained its hold on older, central, middle class neighborhoods characterized by a well-established Shi'i constituency, such as al-Karrada and Shaltshiya. al-Kadhimiya, the Shi'i counterpart of al-'Adhamiya, on the other hand, was the site of a *modus vivendi* between various armed Shi'i factions.

The civil war was anything but an a-historical event. Multiple and intersecting dimensions of past identity formation and social organization trends informed both its course and its practices. More fundamentally, the civil war profoundly transformed the capital's social landscape, along with the make-up of the state institutions it shelters. Indeed, the neighborhoods most severely affected were mixed, middle class quarters, many of which were built on land distributed by the former regime in the 1970s and 1980s to civil servants of all kinds — doctors, Ministry of Foreign Affairs employees, teachers, military officers, bank employees, intelligence personnel, etc. — as well as Christian neighborhoods.

These mixed residential areas, often lacking cohesive local identity, difficult to defend, inhabited by a typically non-combative and already depleted bourgeoisie, were easy prey for armed groups from all sides. The hemorrhaging of these quarters' populations was aggravated by their inhabitants' ability to find refuge abroad. Moreover, armed groups (both Sunni and Shi'i) composed of social outsiders systematically targeted representatives of Iraq's modern and cosmopolitan middle class (notably doctors, professors, engineers and the like). These quarters were, however, the seat of what was left of a mixed, progressive and technically skilled population that was both the product and the basis of a modern state. As human capital was displaced and driven into exile, the state apparatus was purged and positions divvied up on the basis of political, sectarian and family affiliation.

Territorial conquest, by the Mahdi Army for instance, may since have been reversed, but it will take generations for Iraq to repair the damage done to its residual middle class, a crucial underpinning of any functioning state.

The ease with which this middle class espoused a sectarian narrative casts doubt on its recent turnaround and rediscovery of nationalism, which is likely a reaction to the huge price it paid for its previous identification than the product of a clear, stable, self-generating identity.[39] Chillingly, the middle class seems just as passionately disposed to embrace forms of Arab nationalism promoted by the government in its bid against Kurdish ambitions, a struggle underpinned by ethnic narratives that may cost the country even more than their sectarian equivalents.

This inability to articulate a vision of its own translates into what could be called a missing "political centre," leaving "a vacuum in which fringe groups and opportunists could flourish without opposition" (Etherington, 2005). The intellectual elite in particular has failed to produce a trans-sectarian and class narrative for anything other than its own consumption (Chatelard, 2009). Pushed into internal enclaves or the exiled diaspora, this elite is incapable of providing a counterweight or alternative to the fringe groups and opportunists mentioned above, largely because the latter have appropriated the means of mass communication.

Over the past several decades, a process of "national deconstruction" has transpired through the dispersion of the country's modern and cosmopolitan middle class (Zubaida, 2008), the utter destruction of the educational system, the army's reformulation around the requirements of repression and patronage rather than national integration, and the erection of communal barriers (both conceptual and physical), which the most recent shift at the level of political rhetoric will do little to attenuate.

---

[39] An additional question to be raised here is whether the middle class can be anything more than what it has been in the past, namely a clientele at the disposal of an unaccountable state. Indeed Iraq's "middle class" should not be understood as the concept is used elsewhere. It was essentially the product of a rentier state, defined above all by its yearning for a certain life style based on free education, state employment, urban amenities, and all the trappings of modernity — from the Western style villa to the private car to holidays abroad. In exchange for this comfort, the middle class appeared willing to weather extraordinary abuse by the regime. Tellingly, the latter's policy throughout the war with Iran was to make it, precisely, as imperceptible as possible to the population of the capital. Middle class Baghdadis interviewed by the author in the late 1990s essentially repressed any memory of the massive deportations from their midst of colleagues and neighbours of alleged Iranian origins in 1980. In a society where information, whenever deemed relevant, flowed relatively well through informal channels, they displayed a remarkably weak understanding of the nature of the Anfal campaign. Rather, they clung to the myth of a "golden age" of comfort and consumption which they contrasted with their suffering under the embargo.

In that sense, the official and media depiction of a situation that is supposedly "returning to normal" has been stunningly shallow. Just as the rural
exodus toward the capital more than half a century ago shaped recent events,
one can only wonder what the magnitude of Baghdad's recent transformations holds for the future. It is striking, for that matter, that a historiography
of Iraq's contemporary population movements has yet to be written, considering their massive scale, numerous variations, and crucial relevance to
our understanding of the country's contemporary socio-political dynamics.

Conclusions

In sum, the former regime neither homogenized Iraqi society nor completely
atomized it — with the possible exception of its more "progressive" segment,
born out of the modernizing policies pursued in the 1970s and early 1980s
(Darle, 2003). Rather, it eclipsed Iraqi society by monopolizing public space.
In 2003, when the myth of national unity finally caved in along with the
institutions designed to uphold it, the former regime's discredited imagery
gave way to prolific, disjointed, and divisive narratives. Collective memory
itself, increasingly forged in enclaves insulated from each other (in the diaspora and, within Iraq, in various social sub-units), fragmented dramatically
(Chatelard, 2009).

Needless to say, political actors exploited such antagonisms as their
primary source of legitimacy, and outside sponsors were quick to pick
and choose whichever faction suited best their interests (Harling, 2007a).
Internal players developed their own means of mass communication (CDs,
websites, printing houses, television channels, etc.), supporting an increasingly decentralized production of meaning. These narratives relate competing historiographies structured around traumatic events (al-Rachid and
Méténier, 2007), and are above all focused on victimhood, making them
almost entirely unacceptable to one another. Unfortunately, these narratives resonate all too easily with much of the existing body of academic
work on Iraq.

A more constructive narrative might emerge from a historiography that
delves into trends of social movement and identity formation, scrutinizing both moments of disruptive transition (that often take place within
a national storyline of wars, coups, repression, etc.) and elements of continuity entailing a deeper examination of infra- and supra-national dynamics, as exemplified by the emergence in Iraq of a Salafi school of thought.
Delving into localized and regional trends would help end a tradition of

"Iraqi exceptionalism", which compares the former regime's unique repressiveness in order to obscure social trends it simply was blind to.

Further consideration should also be given to disruptions themselves as an element of continuity. Several years of US occupation have only added to a long series of ruptures, and one can only wonder how a brutalized society can deal with so many discontinuities. In post-2003 Iraq, coping strategies derived from previous periods offered a response to forms of violence at times remarkably similar to those of the past (from the perpetrators' immunity to the arbitrariness of their motives, to their actual *modus operandi*).

Understanding the state of violence and fragmentation to which Iraq descended is in itself an exercise in juggling multiple frames of reference. By highlighting this fluidity, and thus challenging fixed and essentialist narratives, writing the history of Iraq may help Iraqi society to project an image of itself it will ultimately be able to live with.

Electronic references

Biddle, S (2008). Stabilizing Iraq from the Bottom Up. Statement before the Committee on Foreign Relations of the US Senate, 2 April 2008. Online. Available HTTP: <http://www.google.fr/url?q=http://www.cfr.org/content/publications/attachments/Biddle%2520408%2520Testimony.pdf&ei=26ndSfLUN92QjAfv5PikDg&sa=X&oi=spellmele-on_result&resnum=1&ct=result&cd=1&usg=AFQjCNH7EnIhcWdoH0FvroS3Kp5-sJ9J4g/> (accessed 9 April 2009).

Duelfer, C (2004). *Comprehensive Report of the Special Advisor to the DCI on Iraq's WMD*. Online. Available HTTP: <http://www.cia.gov/library/reports/general-reports-1/iraq_ wmd_2004/index.html/> (accessed 9 April 2009).

International Crisis Group (2006). *Iraq's Muqtada Al-Sadr: Spoiler or Stabiliser?*, 11 July 2006. Online. Available HTTP: <http://www.crisisgroup.org/home/index.cfm?action=login&ref_id=4210/> (accessed 9 April 2009).

———— (2007). *Where Is Iraq Heading? Lessons from Basra*, 25 June 2007. Online. Available HTTP: <http://www.crisisgroup.org/home/index.cfm?action=login&ref_id=4914/> (accessed 9 April 2009).

———— (2008a). *Iraq's Civil War, the Sadrists and the Surge*, 7 February 2008. Online. Available HTTP: <http://www.crisisgroup.org/home/index.cfm?action=login&ref_id=5286/> (accessed 9 April 2009).

———— (2008b). *Iraq after the Surge 1: The New Sunni Landscape*, 30 April 2008. Online. Available HTTP: <http://www.crisisgroup.org/home/index.cfm?action=login&ref_id=5415/> (accessed 9 April 2009).

———— (2009). *Iraq's Provincial Elections: The Stakes*, 27 January 2009. Online. Available HTTP: <http://www.crisisgroup.org/home/index.cfm?action=login&ref_id= 5883/> (accessed 9 April 2009).

Jihad, AT (2008). Faleh Abdul Jabbar: No Innate Tribalism, *Niqash*. Online. Available HTTP: <http://www.niqash.org/content.php?contentTypeID=75&id=2310&lang=0> (accessed 9 April 2009).

Kilcullen, D (2007). Anatomy of a Tribal Revolt. *Small Wars Journal*. Online. Available HTTP: <http://smallwarsjournal.com/blog/2007/08/anatomy-of-a-tribal-revolt/> (accessed 9 April 2009).

Visser (2007). Basra, the Reluctant Seat of Shiastan. *Middle East Report*, 242. Online. Available HTTP: <http://www.merip.org/mer/mer242/visser.html/ (accessed 9 April 2009).

―――― (2008). *The Sadrists of Basra and the Far South of Iraq. The Most Unpredictable Political Force in the Gulf's Oil-Belt Region?* Norwegian Institute of International Affairs. Online. Available HTTP:<http://english.nupi.no/content/download/4400/61587/version/2/file/WP-734-Visser.pdf/> (accessed 9 April 2009).

Woods, K *et al.* (2006). *Iraqi Perspectives Project. A View of Operation Iraqi Freedom from Saddam's Senior Leadership*, Joint Center for Operational Analysis and Lessons Learned. Online. Available HTTP: <http://www.jfcom.mil/newslink/storyarchive/2006/ipp.pdf> (accessed 9 April 2009).

THE MONARCHIST ERA REVISITED

Jordi Tejel

Historians often argue that writing history calls for a certain temporal distance between themselves and the object of their study. According to this vision, historians would be the holders of the final truth of a given event, and this "truth" would be obviously out of reach of the event's contemporaries. The privilege of the historian would be based on the temporal distance vis-à-vis the event analyzed and the access to archival materials that "reveal" what the main actors of the past concealed from their contemporaries. In that sense, societies would only be capable of appropriating their past after a certain lapse of time. Yet, in spite of the existence of the "time factor" and the availability of a significant amount of documents, writing the history of the monarchist era (1921–1958) in Iraq is far from being an easy task for at least two interrelated reasons.

First, British sources have tended to dominate scholarly research on the colonial period, although the mandate archives certainly do give researchers a great deal of information on the principal actors. Furthermore, the British (and French) materials, particularly local police intelligence reports, also tell us a good deal about unofficial activities. Nevertheless British sources often reflect colonial fears and colonial perceptions of Iraqi society, thus limiting the value of some of the observations made by British officials.

Thus, in order to shed a light on Iraqi social and intellectual history both diversification and multiple sources (memoirs, press, and pamphlets) are needed, including oral histories. This is the main, and generally successful, claim of Hala Fattah's piece in this section. Yet, as the author shows, "remembrance" of the past is evidently selective, and as such is very much a product of the present. Therefore oral history must be carefully analyzed, keeping in mind that it should be seen as composed of constructed memories, which call for an "intervention" on the part of the historian. Thus although oral histories may add authenticity to printed sources and even correct them, historians must insert "constructed memories" into the structure in order to ensure a full understanding of the period under scrutiny.

The other major obstacle to a "normalized" writing of the royalist period is the interference of the colonial "other". What place should the British occupy in contemporary Iraqi history? How can we describe the relationship between Iraqi actors and British representatives during the mandate and after until the revolution of 1958? Did British officials favor the construction of the Iraqi state or, on the contrary, did they act as an obstacle to its completion?

Taking into account the obstacles mentioned herein, the new momentum of mandatory studies (Méouchy, 2002; Mizrahi, 2003; Méouchy and Sluglett, 2004; Tatchjian, 2004), as well as the renewal of approaches — oral history, the study of mobilizations "from below" (Lockman, 1996; Provence, 2005) and of symbolic and discursive fields (Gelvin, 1998) — to contemporary Middle Eastern histories, a re-evaluation of the monarchist era in Iraq seems all the more necessary. Without drawing up an exhaustive list, one can suggest two themes with which the chapters in this section are directly or indirectly concerned and through which the monarchy deserves to be revisited: the continuities and discontinuities between the age of Empires and of nation-states, on the one hand, and British influence in Iraq until 1958 on the other.

Should we view the royalist era as a period of rupture from the Ottoman past, or as a phase of transition towards political modernity in 1958 with the acquisition of real independence? Should we consider the monarchist era as a failed experiment in "bourgeois democracy", setting the stage for Ba'thist authoritarianism under Saddam Husayn or as a historical period on its own with a much a more pluralistic political and intellectual sphere than is generally thought? An analysis of the mandatory archives, journals, memoirs, and interviews suggests that the Hashemite period must be considered both a phase of continuity from the Ottoman era and as a time of change.

The traditional narrative associated the installation of the Hashemite dynasty in Iraq with the beginning of a modern state on the shaky foundations of a corrupt Ottoman administration. This perception of the legacy of the Ottoman Empire profoundly shaped British interactions with Iraqi society, and more importantly, the British reforms of the Iraqi state (Dodge, 2003). Recent work has challenged the idea of the introduction of "modernity" in Iraq by the British (Dodge, 2003; Visser, 2007). Throughout of the 19th century, various Ottoman sultans had launched various projects of reform seeking to modernize not only the structures of the Empire, but also Ottoman society. The Gülhane decree, promulgated on November 3, 1839, represented a major effort to fend off the collapse of the Ottoman Empire. It constituted the point of departure of a vast program of reforms known as the *Tanzimat* ("reorganization"), which shook the country institutionally, economically, and socially. Eventually the Ottoman Constitution of 1876 inaugurated a new era marked by new goals: administrative centralization, modernization of the state apparatus, the westernization of society, and the gradual secularization of law and the educational system.

Although the intellectual "public sphere" (Habermas, 1989) expanded dramatically during the monarchy, its existence preceded the arrival of the British in Iraq. In that respect, the British did not themselves introduce "modernity" in Iraq. As Hala Fattah suggested during the colloquium in Geneva, the British "dialect" of modernism was merely one of many cultural "dialects" of modernism. Some of the European debates such as secularism or the territorial basis of the state that flourished in the West also formed part of Ottoman debates. Thus, although Middle Eastern history has its own singularity, one should underline the "synchronism of political, social and cultural events which have gone beyond the narrower concerns of countries and acquired general historical significance" (Schulze, 2000, p. 6). By the same token, and as Hala Fattah asserts, the notion of Iraq as both a historical and political category was already present, at least amongst urban populations, in the late Ottoman era and the first years of the Iraqi state. Another question is what it meant to be an Iraqi at those times. Fattah's paper gives some answers to this broad question.

Continuity was at times encouraged by the British colonial power enabling the survival, or even the strengthening, of some "traditional" features of Iraqi society such as the patronage system linked to land ownership or the role played by tribal chiefs as mediators between state and society (Batatu, 1978; Tripp, 2007). By the same token, the legacy of the ethnoreligious organization of the Ottoman Empire was by no means entirely eradicated, and continued to shape notions of polity and community long after the fall of the Ottoman state.

At the same time, Hashemite Iraq also witnessed new developments, one of the most important of which was the "progressive re-adjustment of boundaries between the state and local communities as a result of the emergence of new political and social forces" (Fuccaro, 2004, p. 581). The transformation of the *millets* (Christians and Jews) into "minorities" within the framework of the nation-state system (Méouchy, 2004, p. 39) is a good example of this re-adjustment. Thus the Iraqi constitution of 1925 (Organic Law) opened the door to legal recognition of a special status for those groups. However, the recognition of (religious) "minorities" paralleled the emergence of other "minorities," whether "ethnic" ('The Kurds') or "sectarian" ("the Shi'is").

The interwar years were times of great upheaval and confusion for the inhabitants of the provinces of the former Ottoman Empire. By 1920 the region outside Anatolia had been transformed into five new states (Iraq, Lebanon, Palestine, Syria, and Transjordan) by the Permanent Mandates Commission of the League of Nations under the temporary tutelage of Britain and France. Given the wider cultural-political atmosphere of the time, the various national and nationalist movements which had begun to develop in the very last years of the Empire (especially after 1909) continued to gain momentum, with the additional impetus in the mandated states of the presence of a new colonial "other".

The "Kurds" like the "Shi'is" (Nakash, 1993), as well as the "Sunnis", had never constituted a monolithic entity, and had always been divided socially, economically and politically. Furthermore, as Hala Fattah puts it, communitarian, sectarian, and ethnic identities became progressively subordinated to an expansive Iraqi nationalism, which at times seemed to threaten British projects in Iraq and the Middle East. However, the umbrella of Iraqi identity never covered all groups and, moreover, it "began to fray at the edges, and the politicized distinctiveness of communities, sects and ethnicities re-emerged as an important factor in the national body politic" (Fattah, 2010, p. xxx).

The British vision of Iraqi society as a country divided between three monolithic blocs (Sunni Arabs, Shi'i Arabs, and Kurds) certainly encouraged the reification of sub-Iraqi identities. For instance, Britain's exploitation and manipulation of the Kurds between 1918 and 1925 is well known. Yet it would be a quite a stretch of the imagination to suggest that the British "created" "minority" movements such as the Kurdish nationalist movement in order to delay the completion of the Iraqi state. Thus during the interwar era, Kurdish nationalism in Iraq, like Arab nationalism, echoed trans-border dynamics (Bozarslan, 1997) affecting a wider space, in Iran, Syria and Turkey. It must also be remembered that relations between the British and the Kurds were not always easy (Sluglett, 2007, pp. 127–129), and more important, that the colonial power played a crucial role in jeopardizing the consolidation of an urban Kurdish nationalist movement in Sulaimaniyya, the cultural and intellectual centre of Iraqi Kurdistan (Tejel, 2008). Interestingly, the minority question had two apparently contradictory outcomes; on the one hand, it contributed to frustrate the process of nation-building in states like Iraq and Syria; on the other hand, it nurtured the articulation of 'state nationalism' in those countries (Fuccaro, 2004, p. 583). Although Iraqi and Syrian nationalists, as opposed to pan-Arabist nationalists (see Davis, 2005, pp. 29–108), focused primarily on getting rid of British and French control over their states during the 1920s and 1930s, they started to see the "minorities" as an obstacle to the full completion of their state-building project.

Another new development of the Hashemite period was the consolidation of Baghdad as the center of gravity for aspirations to power. Although other cities like Najaf, Basra and Mosul still played a significant role in the territory of Iraq, the state centered on Baghdad progressively reinforced its power of attraction not only amongst the Sharifians but also amongst tribal shaykhs, Kurdish chieftains and the notables of the major cities of Iraq, the latter seeking to protect their interests when major decisions were taken in the Iraqi parliament (Tripp, 2007, pp. 50–51). On another level, continuing a process that had begun before World War I, Baghdad became a cultural center where intellectual clubs opened and newspapers appeared. Baghdad attracted not only Iraqis but also Arab intellectuals and activists from Syria, Palestine, and Egypt, strengthening the idea of a broader Arab identity amongst some segments of the Iraqi intelligentsia.

Pan-Arabism was not completely new on the Iraqi landscape at the time of the British mandate. Nevertheless, pan-Arab narratives evolved within a changing political context after the creation of the Iraqi state. During the 1920s and 1930s, pan-Arab narratives still emphasized the spirit of Arabism, as a product of language and history. Yet, pan-Arab narratives started to blame Ottoman, British, and French domination to explain why the Arab lands, which shared a common and ancient culture, seemed unable to achieve political unity. In that sense, pan-Arabism, along with communism, had the potential to stir up anti-British propaganda. At least to some extent, this explains why British officials came to view pan-Arabism as a pretext to facilitate pro-German activities in Iraq and in the Middle East in the late 1930s and during World War II. Nevertheless, the pan-Arab discourse was a complex phenomenon in which a multiplicity of influences (Arab *nahda*, Islamism, Italian, German and British narratives, etc.) came together (Bashkin, 2009, pp. 139–40).

Thus, different actors with different purposes could mobilize pan-Arabism. It could become a major field for anti-British activities as well as for real demonstrations of Arab solidarity; the Hashemite elite could even exploit it in order to gain some national legitimacy in the face of local criticism, while a younger generation of pan-Arab nationalists could get inspiration from it to challenge not only British domination but also the state and its Western institutions, which put Arab unity in jeopardy. As Peter Wien suggests, the "Rashid 'Ali movement" of 1941 seems to be the culmination of various different interacting trends in Iraq during the interwar period.

In *Iraqi Arab Nationalism* (2006), Wien described the events of 1941 as the culmination of a process of generational change. In his contribution to this volume, Wien underlines the plasticity of ideologies as well as of the official version of past events at various different times in recent Iraqi history. Thus whereas the Qasim (1958–1963) and 'Arif (1963–1968) regimes do not seem to have regarded the "Rashid 'Ali movement" as a seminal event in Iraqi history, the Ba'thist leaders showed increased interest in the episode after 1968, using it as a means of legitimizing their "revolutionary" deeds and credentials. Wien's case study illustrates through an observation of the symbolic field that while the monarchist era was regarded by a wide range of opposition movements as a corrupt period in Iraqi history — due to the failure of Iraqi political actors to challenge the colonial power — some chapters could be revised with new interpretations and goals, if needed.

As mentioned before, the second theme through which the monarchist era should be re-considered is the place of the colonial "other", the British, in contemporary Iraqi history. Indeed, one can establish two different, although not necessarily opposing, narratives about the place of British representatives in Iraq during the monarchy. The first insists on the key role played by the British in the construction of the Iraqi state (Longrigg, 1953) and the British influence on the Hashemite elite during the mandate (1921–1932), and on until the establishment of the republic in 1958. The British were at the same time the driving force behind the construction of the Iraqi state — artificial (Galbraith, 2006) or imposed (Luizard, 2002; Luizard, 2009) on the Shi'is and Kurds — and the main cause of the "national incompleteness" of Iraq. The Hashemite elites, large land-owners, tribal chiefs, bureaucrats and certain intellectuals would constitute the army of Iraqi "collaborators" needed to maintain British control over Iraqi affairs. Thus the outward appearance of Iraqi citizenship actually masked a system of colonial domination.

Without denying the colonial character of the British presence in Iraq, a second reading suggests a more balanced reading of the British role in Iraq and relations between British and Iraqis. In a very stimulating volume on the French mandate in Syria and Lebanon, Nadine Méouchy and other contributors draw a complex picture reflecting the "ambiguous" relationship between the French officials and local populations (Méouchy, 2002). Seemingly, while studying the intellectual public sphere in Iraq under the monarchy, Orit Bashkin challenges the categories of "colonized" and "colonizer," since both were changed and transformed during a period of colonial interaction which blurred any clear-cut "boundary" between the "self" and the "other". The outcome of this relationship would be the emergence of a "hybrid" Iraqi political and intellectual culture (Bashkin, 2009, pp. 3–5).

Sara Pursley's piece offers a very meaningful example of this "hybrid" culture. In the early 1920s, the new Iraqi elites, like elites elsewhere, viewed the educational system as a tool to build a homogeneous national identity. The educational program implemented by the intellectual and educator Sati' al-Husri represents the best example of this view. For al-Husri, director general of the Ministry of Education and later director of Antiquities, national education and military service were the most appropriate means of creating effective national loyalty (Tibi, 1981, pp. 116–132). In fact, Husri hoped that students would become soldiers, disciplined "guards" of the nation. Although he was interested in European history and Western educational models — such as those of Maria Montessori (1870–1952) or Johann Heinrich Pestalozzi (1746–1827) — which he had studied in France, Switzerland, and Belgium, al-Husri defended the necessity for Iraqis to find an "Arab alternative" in the face of the colonial (British) educational system, which sought to "transform the colonized subjects into functional workers" (Bashkin, 2009, pp. 252–253).

However, al-Husri's influence on the Iraqi educational system after the 1930s was challenged by a younger generation of intellectuals. In this section Pursley discusses the effects of the implementation of new ideas, namely the curriculum "differentiation" of students according to different "categories" (urban, rural, tribal, female, and Kurdish), into the Iraqi education system by a group of American-trained Iraqi educators such as Matta 'Aqrawi, influenced by the pragmatist school of educational theory.

Pragmatists pretended to propose educational practices more connected with "real life" than al-Husri's visions of the importance of history as a means to shape Iraqi national identity. Teachers were to be sent to the villages to demonstrate to the peasants the most efficient ways of improving their economic conditions. Pursley's study focuses on the differentiation of curricula by sex, which sought to prepare the future "mothers of the nation." Interestingly, the author points out that despite the conservative approach of pragmatists regarding gender, the effects of this policy went far beyond the educators' expectations, in that, as elsewhere (Childress, 2008, pp. 553–569), the education of girls fuelled attitudes which challenged the traditional division of gender roles in society. Women college students subverted the programs of the Ministry of Education and played an important role in the massive demonstrations of 1952 that heralded the end of the monarchist era.

Albeit from different approaches, the contributions to this section show that a careful reading of the monarchist era can give us a nuanced picture of the political and cultural debates that animated Iraqi society during the first half of the 20th century, which the violence and authoritarian practices of subsequent regimes have attempted to conceal.

WHAT DID IT MEAN TO BE AN IRAQI DURING THE MONARCHY? A PRELIMINARY INVESTIGATION BASED ON ORAL INTERVIEWS WITH IRAQIS IN JORDAN AND THE UNITED KINGDOM

Hala Fattah

As we all know one of the central preoccupations of a certain type of right wing, neo-Orientalist discourse is the de-legitimization of the notion of "Iraq", both as a historical as well as political category.[1] My colleague Reidar Visser has been at the forefront of those who have demolished what has now become the rather less convincing notion of an artificial Iraq, possessing neither historical roots nor contemporary legitimacy (Visser, 2009, pp. 143–54). But if we move away from the unrepresentative and shallow debate on Iraq at foreign policy forums and think tanks in the West, and talk to Iraqis themselves about what Iraq meant or means to them, then the whole notion of Iraq as a contrived and unnatural development falls apart. In fact, when the issue was brought up at an informal seminar attended by many Iraqis in late 2009 in Amman, Jordan, it barely registered among the Iraqis in the room. Nobody had the slightest doubt that Iraq had pre-modern

---

[1] I am grateful to Professor Keiko Sakai and Professor Hidemitsu Kuroki, of the Tokyo University of Foreign Studies and The Japan Center for Middle Eastern Studies in Beirut respectively, for giving me the opportunity to present this paper at the International Workshop on the Future of Iraq that took place in Beirut, Lebanon on the 16th to 17th of January 2010. I am also indebted to TAARII of Chicago, Illinois; the Mary Ann and Lawrence Tucker Foundation of Connecticut, and the Toyota Foundation of Japan for their invaluable help in the oral history project[s] I undertook from 2004 to 2009.

roots and was a solid, if constantly changing national, social, political, and cultural reality.

The question then becomes how to document this changing national reality in the face of assaults on its existence. For this article, I want to weave together a few choice statements by Iraqis themselves on the evolving meaning — or meanings — of Iraq and the historical development of the nation-state over the past 90 years. I began my project by concentrating on the history of the Hashemite period, which covered the first 37 years of what has been termed Iraq's modern history. I talked to about 60 Iraqis in both Jordan and in the UK, most of them octogenarians who had lived active professional lives and were discerning spectators of Iraqi history. Although I came away with the realization that there was no way that one could limit Iraqis to a neatly structured description of the Hashemite era, because Iraqis wanted to talk about everything, especially the last painful years under Ba'thist rule, I decided to confine myself only to the Hashemite period (1921–1958) for this article because of time constraints.

To begin with, there were pitfalls in asking Iraqis about the generation of their fathers, and how their parents became Iraqis. Under the influence of post-colonial theory, which presupposes that "becoming national" is an evolutionary progression (Eley and Suny, 1996, pp. 3–37), I made what was perhaps a questionable assumption from the very beginning. I felt that I should concentrate on the *process* of becoming Iraqi because I thought that assuming a national identity would involve several stages of development, not the least of which was the construction of a national culture that would provide a referent for future generations. As it turned out, becoming Iraqi was very easy, or so my respondents asserted. At least in the early stages of national development, it seemed as if passing from an Ottoman to an Iraqi identity was relatively painless. Of course, it must be said at once that many of the 80-year old Iraqis that I talked to were the second generation to have been brought up under the auspices of an Iraqi state; the first generation (who had grown up under the Ottomans) had long since died off and whatever ambivalence they might have had towards the new Iraqi state had died with them. Still, talking to people who had been young men and women in the 1930s and 1940s seemed to be a valid exercise, especially since many of them had imbibed their parents' reactions to the creation of the Hashemite state and were ready to relay them to the interviewer at second hand. At the same time, perhaps one of the most important factors for the relative ease underlying the transition to becoming Iraqi is that some evidence points to the existence of an amorphous, generalized Iraqi identity in the late 19th and early 20th centuries in the towns that were to become the bedrock of modern, post-1921 Iraq (Visser, 2009, pp. 143–154). That it had not as yet become articulated as Iraqi nationalism was not in itself a problem; the important thing was that the seeds of an Iraqi nation were already manifest in the major urban centers of geographical Iraq.

One of the most delightful accounts of the development of his family's Iraqi identity was provided to me by an elderly Iraqi who had been the chief engineer at the port of Basra from the 1960s onwards. Originally from Syria, with relatives who had lived in Istanbul throughout the period of Ottoman rule, he explained the almost *accidental* way that his father — and therefore his whole immediate family — had become Iraqi. Retracing his family's history from Ottoman times onwards, he recalled:

> After World War I, Muhammad Bahjat [the subject's uncle] became the Director of the Sultaniya school in Istanbul, after having been educated at the Jesuit University in Beirut [...]. Sati' al-Husri [Iraq's most important Arab nationalist thinker in the 1920s and 1930s] was himself from Aleppo. And his house was close to ours in Aleppo. When my uncle Bahjat traveled from Beirut to Istanbul [to take up his post], he met Sati' al-Husri at the train station. So one of them asked the other: Where are you going? [My uncle Bahjat] said: I am going to Istanbul. Sati' al-Husri said: I am going to Faysal, come with me. But [my uncle Bahjat] declined, saying I am going to live on the shores of the Bosphorus. And Sati' al-Husri went to Faysal [...]. Then my father, Muhammad al-Katib, finished secondary school in Aleppo and enrolled in the medical school in Istanbul. Among his classmates were [Iraqi students] such as Sami Shawkat, Hashim al-Witri, Jalal 'Azzawi, Fa'iq Shakir and Isma'il al-Saffar. Sa'ib Shawkat was two years below my father at the medical school in Istanbul. My father graduated from the military medical school in 1917. He graduated second in his class. And because he was one of the followers of the 'new' era and an adherent of Arab nationalism, the Ottoman government sent [him] to the military front because Turkish intelligence had him listed as a supporter of Arab nationalism. [He was sent to] *Jenna qala'* (the citadel of Jenna), near Gallipoli, on the Sea of Marmara, and the Bosphorus, and near Istanbul [...]. My father was sent to that area to cure the sick and help the injured [...]. After the war, my father left Istanbul and went to Aleppo. There, he joined the Ramadhani hospital as well as the army of Faysal [ibn al-Husayn, then King of Syria,] as a medical lieutenant [*naqib tabib*]. And he stayed there until Faysal left Syria. So he came to Iraq, accompanying Faysal, in 1922 [...] and he settled in Basra, and did very, very well at work. Then he got married in 1923, and I was born in 1926.[2]

---

[2]Conversation with H.A.K. Amman, 2006.

This account is remarkable because of its attentiveness to the *fluidity* of becoming Iraqi. First, the subject's uncle is casually asked (at a train station, no less) by Sati' al-Husri, who was to become the chief theoretician of Iraqi Arab nationalism, to change his plans on the spur of the moment and come to Iraq to serve Faysal I, the first king of the country. Presumably, had the subject followed al-Husri's call to follow him to Iraq, he too would have accepted Iraqi nationality, just as al-Husri did. However, even though the subject's uncle continued to Istanbul, and became a Turkish citizen after Turkey became an independent state, the subject's father, who had gone to school in Istanbul with Iraqi students as a matter of course, went on to become Iraqi. After all, he had joined Faisal's fledgling administration in Syria, and after Faysal was expelled from Syria by the French and became king of Iraq, the subject's father left for Iraq as well and took Iraqi citizenship. So we have two brothers: one became a Turk, the other an Iraqi. And it probably was as easy for the one as for the other to "become a national" of each of their respective adopted countries.

Of course, the volatility of the inter-war years lent itself to such new beginnings. New states were being born, and empires were dying. Identities were in constant flux, and affiliations were being created and recreated. At the same time, it must be remembered that not everyone who became an Iraqi came from outside the country; those people whose families had been in the country for a long time, also rapidly assimilated into the new nation-state, even as they fought to conceptualize Iraq according to their traditions and cultural affinities. For instance, Kadhim Abu'l-Timman, one of the uncles of Ja'far Abu'l-Timman, one of the leading Iraqi nationalists in the interwar years, signed a petition in 1919, along with many other Iraqis, for Iraq to become an Islamic state (al-Timimi, 1996, p. 66). Obviously many models for the Iraqi state were offered by many Iraqis but in the end, it was British power that configured the state system in Iraq.

But what happened after the Iraqi state became entrenched in the 1920s and 1930s? What did it mean to be an Iraqi during that period? Another respondent provided yet another fascinating answer. The son of a provincial governor who traveled all over Iraq deputizing for the central administration in Baghdad had this to say:

> I consider [the idea of what it means to be an Iraqi] an important question. And it is a very important question for Iraqis as a whole. The question is taking on even more significance today. We did not feel that we were from Kurdish or Arab tribes. We always felt Iraqi. We always felt we should live and work in this country. Even though our parents spoke Turkish, we did not lean towards learning Turkish or Kurdish,

but remained committed to the Arabic language and Arab culture. And I have never in my life called myself a Kurd. I never told anyone that I belonged to the Diza'i tribe or anything like that. Our sense of affiliation and identity was always Iraqi [...]. Also [our sense of identity] was shaped in our house. We were brought up to believe that we were Iraqis, and that this was our country and we were to live in it, to the point where, wherever my father was, Kirkuk, Diwaniya, Hillah, or Ramadi, we never said we were Kurds or Arabs or anything of the sort. For instance, in our family, the wife of our uncle Amin was a Turcoman from the Naftaji family. Never, not even for a day, did we consider her a Turcoman [...]. My relative Samiha [...] sent her daughter and son to Kirkuk for the holidays so that they would learn languages [Turkish and Kurdish] just because they were additional languages that [her children] could converse in. My maternal uncle speaks Kurdish as well as other languages but he never once said: We are Kurds, even though he was an important army officer and known as being a Kurd.

And he went on:

And I can tell you in all honesty that even at school, we never asked if anyone was a Shi'i or a Sunni or a Kurd, or even a Christian. Lots of my schoolmates at school thought I was a Christian. Why? I do not know. Perhaps because I had a ruddy complexion and was very fair. But the point was even though we never asked about these differences, we knew from a person's accent that he was from a family in Karbala or other places. My cousin got married to a man from the Astarabadi family [Shi'is from Baghdad] and no-one objected. On the contrary, her husband is a capable and wonderful man and forms part of our group of friends. He quickly became part of the family. In our family, there were never any of those sentiments; *we were Iraqi*.[3]

To my mind, the punch line, "we were Iraqi," says it all. In the subject's mind, being Iraqi meant belonging to different social, ethnic, sectarian, and religious backgrounds, acknowledging it and moving on. Being Iraqi meant learning ideals of loyalty and self-sacrifice to the nation *at home*, and only secondarily at school. And finally, being Iraqi meant knowing all the languages and cultures of the region but using Arabic both out of choice as well as necessity, because it had become the *lingua franca* of the Iraqi state, if not completely that of society. Thus, an Iraqi identity solved a lot of problems: Whether undertaken as a conscious choice or not, becoming Iraqi in the early 20th century meant taking the middle road between a jumble of different ethnicities and sects. It also meant assuming the trappings of a secular, all-inclusive, political identity that relegated sub-national categories to

---

[3]Conversation with H.M. Amman, 2006.

the *cultural* sphere, as manifestations of the whole. That is to say, communitarian, sectarian, confessional, and ethnic identities became subordinate to an expansive Iraqi nationalism that grouped all sub-national identities under its wing almost as cultural artifacts, to be enjoyed in private.

However, as the Hashemite era wore on, the umbrella of Iraqi identity began to fray at the edges, and the politicized distinctiveness of communities, sects and ethnicities re-emerged as an important factor in the national body politic. Sometime in the 1940s and 1950s, sub-national categories became politicized. An agricultural engineer had this to say of the 1950s.

> I remember going to an interview at the College of Agriculture in 1954. At that time, I had high grades so I was assured of a scholarship. The Dean of the College of Agriculture was an Englishman and as he was asking me about my personal details, he asked me what my religion was and when I told him [I was Muslim], he asked me if I were Sunni or Shi'i. I felt as if I had been attacked with a knife in my back. In the South, there are no Sunnis and we were not used to the presence of Sunnis amongst us. In Hilla, for example, there are only two places which contain Sunnis and we coexisted with them as brothers. I never heard the word, Sunni even though the wife of my grandfather, Salman Barrak, was a Sunni. Sectarianism was not present. It is only present when two people of different sects sit together and talk together and you hear bad things about the other person and so you begin to dislike him. We never passed through something like that, even though the government was in the hands of Sunnis and we were oppressed. That is why I had a problem. For example, if I wanted to enter into government service, I would have to pretend to be Sunni. But in the South, there was no such thing; in fact, teachers' jobs were available to all, no matter their background [...]. My wife [who is Sunni] used to always ask me this question: "Why are you Shi'is always complaining?" I would always reply that we are not complaining, we just want our rights. I would tell her: "We are fighters!" One day, the principal of the primary school where my wife worked, [and the principal] was a Shi'i although her husband was a Sunni, was nominated as an assistant administrator for her school. But when the nomination reached the Ministry of Education, they asked to see the nominee and they insulted him, and they asked the principal why she could not find a Sunni to fill the position. The position was only that of an assistant administrator of a primary school. So the principal came to see Laila, my wife, because she knew I was Shi'i and she told her: "Have you ever heard of anything so ridiculous?" So then my wife said to me, "Oh, you are right, you Shi'is really are oppressed!" I replied, "And it's only now that you realize this?"[4]

---

[4]Conversation with A.B. Amman, 2007.

Although sectarian and ethnic identities re-emerged in the last years of the Hashemite period, it is also true that there was an ebb and flow in the politicization of sub-national identity. Sectarian and ethnic identities were not always in conflict with the overarching political ideology of Iraqi nationalism, at least not in the Hashemite period. In fact, one of the ways to redress discrimination against minorities must have occurred through the activation of back channels. Thus, personal networks were frequently mobilized to correct social injustices or right political wrongs. As one Kurdish gentleman from the Jaf tribe recalled:

> When Mas'ud Muhammad, a well-known Kurdish opposition leader in parliament died [during the monarchy], there was an interesting story behind it. He had apparently gone up to Nuri al-Sa'id and told him: our [Kurdish] region requires a lot of services. Nuri al-Sa'id asked him what these were, and Mas'ud Muhammad said: First, we need a good road from Kirkuk to Koi Sanjaq; second, the cost of tobacco should go up [because the Kurdish cultivator was not making any money] and third, you have exiled a number of Barzani chiefs to the South so perhaps you can bring them home. Before replying, Nuri al-Sa'id told him to get in the car, and they went to see the Minister of Commerce and Nuri al-Sa'id ordered him to issue a directive to raise the price of tobacco being sold on the Iraqi market. Then he took him to the Minister of Communications [so that he would issue a directive to build a road between Kirkuk and Koi Sanjaq]. And all this, without police protection or a fleet of security guards on motorcycles accompanying Nuri's car. By God, at the end of the day, he had gotten the budgetary committee to meet and the costs of paving a road from Kirkuk to Koi Sanjaq had been estimated. And as for the Barzanis, he issued an order for them to return to their ancestral lands. And at the end of it all, they cut him up into pieces and his grandchildren were not allowed to receive Iraqi passports.[5]

An Iraqi of Shi'i background concurred:

> I graduated [from AUB] with a good grade point average [...] I returned to Najaf to the family house and one day, I picked up *al-Zaman* newspaper and read that the Ministry of Education had decided to appoint [me] as a school teacher in a secondary school [...] so I started teaching at that school. Who was with me? [The scion of an important family in Mosul]. Also with me were Ali Sa'ib and Khalil al-Daghistani. I used to teach Commerce and Business Studies. Then one day, I read an announcement in the papers that the Ministry of Foreign Affairs wanted applicants, starting from the most junior level. So I went and applied but I did so quietly, so that none of my family or friends knew, including [my friend from Mosul]. But then I met him at the interview!

---

[5]Conversation with S.J. Amman, 2006.

He asked me why I had not told him that I was applying. The minister was Arshad al-'Umari, God have mercy on him, whose daughter [Su'ad] I praised a great deal [...]. Anyway, [the friend from Mosul] and I presented our applications. We were about 30 applicants in all and they wanted six or seven people. I passed the exam. Oh, I forgot, before we entered the exam room, Arshad al-'Umari said he wanted to see us. He was a real character (said in English). We entered one by one. [My friend from Mosul] entered before me. When I entered [al-'Umari] asked me: What is your full name? [I told him]. He then asked: where are you from? I told him I come from Najaf. He then asked me: What does your family do? I told him they were grain merchants. He asked me if I was employed. I said yes, I teach in secondary school. He said: Well, you see then, you are employed. We only take on people who have no occupations [...]. By the life of my only daughter, Raya, I said to him: Well, [my friend from Mosul] was here before me and he teaches at the same school I do. Did you tell him the same thing? He shouted at me: The interview is over. Get out!

And this particular respondent went on:

Now, the Ministry of Foreign Affairs and Parliament were in Bab al-Mu'adham. I went to see Shaykh Muhammad Ridha al-Shabibi, who was the Speaker of the House. His brother was the famous Muhammad Baqir al-Shabibi, the poet of the 1920 revolution. I entered into his office where two members of parliament were sitting already. One of them was Sayyid Husayn al-Naqib al-Rufa'i and the other was his son, the surgeon Dr. 'Ali al-Naqib. I knocked on his door and he asked me to come in. I presented myself, I said I am [so-and-so]. He said: I know your uncles, Hajji Isa and Hajji Musa. We are all from Najaf. What can I do for you, my son? I told him I wanted to take the Foreign Service examination, and told him the whole story. He lifted the phone and dialed Arshad al-'Umari's number and told him: I know this young man and I know his family. So Arshad al-'Umari told him to send me to the Foreign Ministry for the exam. I passed the exam and I was appointed to the Ministry.[6]

What I would like to suggest here is that, in contrast with what my respondents in the oral history project[s] had asserted earlier on, "becoming Iraqi" was indeed a process, and a very complex one at that. Fluid and nebulous at first, Iraqi identity eventually became more specific, even as it took on the contours of the colonial-era nation-state that sought to shape it. Sometimes this was a highly contentious undertaking; for, as Orit Bashkin's work reveals, Hashemite ideology frequently clashed with distinctive notions of what it meant to be an Iraqi, whether espoused by liberal or left-leaning

---

[6]Conversation with K.K. Amman, 2005.

opposition politicians, newspaper editors and columnists, or novelists and short story writers (Bashkin, 2009). Moreover, the ideal of the great tent of Iraqi nationalism, as relayed to me by one of my interlocutors, was not itself a universal belief espoused by all Iraqis, because of the historic fissures built into the Iraqi fabric from the nation-state's first inception. For Sami Zubaida, for instance, there were at least four different social groups — the *effendiyya* or urban officials; the ex-Ottoman officers that came to Iraq with Faysal ibn al-Husayn; the clergy, both Shi'is and Sunnis, and the tribal leadership of the mid-Euphrates as well as Tigris districts — that constituted the "fragments" that imagined the new nation-state of Iraq, and they all had different visions of what this would entail (Zubaida, 2002, pp. 208–211). My interlocutor, himself the son of an Iraqi bureaucrat — the "[m]ost "national" of all strata in an incipient nation-state" (Zubaida, 2002, p. 211) — saw the world differently than other embryonic "nationals" in Iraq.

Finally, the constant bargaining between state actors enjoined to uphold the philosophy of the ruling elite and other groups in society pressing to take advantage of state-supported privileges (whether these were educational or administrative positions or entry into the diplomatic corps) rendered "the process of becoming Iraqi" a constant negotiation between unequal partners. By virtue of the undemocratic and unsystematic nature of the post-colonial Iraqi state, patronage networks stepped in to fill an immense breech in Iraqi society and, as time went on, gradually opened up more cracks in the social and political foundations of the new state.

Of course, all oral history tends to reflect the views of the moment so that it cannot be viewed as a completely accurate recollection of the past. Thus, idealized notions of a just and egalitarian state serving its people, or the reverse, ideas of a state that was riddled with discrimination against certain sects and ethnicities, are as much a product of the present as they are of an earlier period. Nonetheless, while oral histories can never be seen as entirely valid recollections of yesteryear and must be viewed alongside a wide variety of archival and documentary evidence, they provide unique glimpses of the past that provide many more questions than answers, and in the process open up new vistas of research for scholars and laymen alike.

FROM FORTY-ONE TO
QADISIYYAT SADDAM:
REMARKS ON AN IRAQI
REALM OF MEMORY

Peter Wien

This article traces several interpretations of the 1941 military coup and so called "Rashid 'Ali movement" between World War II and the early 1980s, situating this high watermark of Arab nationalist trends of the interwar period in the evolution of nationalist mythology in the post revolutionary period. According to the dominant interpretation, the first post-revolutionary regime in Iraq under 'Abd al-Karim Qasim tried to install a distinctly Iraqi narrative, emphasizing the country's pre-Islamic Mesopotamian past. After the interlude of the rule of the 'Arif brothers (1963 to 1968), the Ba'thist regime — first with Hasan al-Bakr as president, but under the ever growing influence of Saddam Husayn and finally under his presidency from 1979 on — moved forcefully to an implementation of an Arab ethnocentric state ideology that rejected the earlier Iraqism of Qasim's regime as *shu'ubiyya*, interpreting it as undermining the pan-Arab identity of the state, instigated by Iranian agents. The term *shu'ubiyya* refers back to the medieval Islamic period, when — in the eyes of 20th century Arab nationalists — "Persian imposters" started to interfere in Arab government and culture, pretending to be Arab through their use of the Arabic language. In addition, Saddam Husayn integrated the Mesopotamian narrative into his game of ideological inclusion and exclusion, in that he claimed the Mesopotamian past as equally Arab and non-Arab, thus opening access for non-Arab communities such as the Kurds to be part of the national community (Baram, 1994, p. 302; Bashkin, 2009, p. 170; Davis, 2005, p. 131).

Evidently, it is more difficult to manipulate the memory of recent events than the memory of mythical times. The memory of the 1941 revolt is a case in point, as it became part of the foundation myth of the Iraqi army. The state had no power to decide if this particular event fitted into its national narrative, which for many was an immediate, or un-mediated, personal memory. Instead, the rulers had to adapt their national narrative to this memory. The fact that the memory was suppressed, as was apparently the case during the later years of the monarchy, turned it into a dissident memory and motivation for the army's Free Officers to act during the revolution.

The findings of this article cannot yet be fully conclusive, due to the limited available sources. I have examined a sample of remembrances as reflected in the Iraqi press following a sequence of ten year anniversaries of the 1941 events in 1951, 1961, 1971, and 1981. The sample was limited to the material available at the Library of the Congress, so that in cases where I could not find any, or only limited references, this may have been due to gaps in the Library's holdings. Even though the present study consequently remains a sketch, I believe that, in the wake of these remembrances, the 1941 revolt has become one of Iraq's "Realms of Memory" ("Lieux de Mémoire"). I will henceforth refer to this realm as "Forty-One," as opposed to "the 1941 revolt," which would mark the historical record of the events. Following Pierre Nora, realms of memory form the nation's points of reference in both positive as well as negative senses, either for identification or dissociation (Nora, 1996). While in open, pluralistic, and democratic societies, such realms are marked though a process of negotiation and debate that takes place in the public sphere, the manipulation of history and of the realms of memory has been a constant feature of the Iraqi state in its efforts to impose an official narrative of state identity on its peoples. My analysis of the various newspaper articles starts from the assumption that the images presented by the newspapers reflected the official narrative of the regime, since the various dictators would not have tolerated an open discourse about the definition of right and wrong with respect to the nation's past.

Forty-One in Perspective

The Rashid 'Ali movement of 1941 is generally considered as the climax of an extreme pan-Arab nationalist trend that came to dominate Iraqi politics during the period of military coups between 1936 and 1941. During the months of April and May 1941, four Iraqi officers, Salah al-Din al-Sabbagh, Kamil Shabib, Fahmi Sa'id, and Mahmud Salman, the so-called "Golden

Square," helped install a "Government of National Defense" in Iraq, headed by Rashid 'Ali al-Kailani, supported by the Grand Mufti of Jerusalem Amin al-Husayni, then in exile in Baghdad, and backed by a number of civilians of a younger generation. Only two months later, the second British occupation of Iraq put an end to this so called "Rashid 'Ali movement" ("Harakat Rashid 'Ali"). In spite of this short term, the movement is considered as a seminal event in Iraqi history and in the wider history of Arab nationalism.

I have described the events of 1941 elsewhere as the culmination of a process of generational change, both in terms of the personnel in the "Government of National Defense," and the readiness of young Arab nationalists in Baghdad to resort to violence, erupting in the events of the "Farhud" pogrom against the poorer strata of Baghdad's Jewish population. For the first time in Arab history, the movement produced an alliance between radical Arab nationalist intellectuals and Arab officer-politicians. Rashid 'Ali al-Kailani was in fact more of a figurehead than a leader. There was a circle of Arab nationalist fanatics around Yunus al-Sab'awi, the civilian spokesman of Arab nationalist extremism among the youth between the late 1930s and 1941, who were at odds with both Rashid 'Ali and the Mufti. The Four Officers stood some way off from these rivalries, but were certainly in charge as far as the military decisions were concerned that led to the disastrous defeat of May 1941 (Wien, 2006). It is arguable that the defeat of the Iraqi army by the long time imperialist overlord Great Britain, the subsequent re-installation of a pro-British regime and the humiliating trial and public execution of the Four Officers after the war drove many Iraqi military men into opposition to the monarchy, which would eventually find its expression in the Free Officer conspiracy (Davis, 2005, p. 69). Arab nationalists perceived those who had participated in "Forty-One" as the forerunners of a new generation of Arab nationalists that had been willing to challenge pro-imperialist trends in Iraq, but who failed because imperialist proxies such as Nuri al-Sa'id and the regent 'Abd al-Ilah had betrayed them. The failure of 1941 and the government's short-lived alliance with Nazi Germany discredited Arab nationalism in the immediately post-war period, however, and gave considerable credibility to the Iraqi Communist Party that had in fact acted as an Iraqi nationalist party (Davis, 2005, p. 275). The myth of the nationalist uprising of 1941 and its "martyrs" survived nevertheless, and became increasingly prominent under the post-1968 Ba'th regime in particular, as I will show.

Engineering Public Memory Under Qasim

The sources that I used for this study do not mention any public commemoration of the "Forty-One" events in Iraq prior to the Revolution of 1958: Hence the 10th anniversary in 1951 seems to have passed unnoticed. This is not surprising if we consider that the Old Regime, once reinstalled after the war of May 1941, made every effort to present the followers of the Rashid 'Ali movement as proxies of Nazism. To publish about "Forty-One" in Iraq was difficult. The memoirs of Salah al-Din al-Sabbagh and 'Uthman Kamal Haddad, the private secretary of the Mufti Amin al-Husayni during these events, appeared in Syria and Lebanon (Haddad, 1956). The eminent Iraqi historian 'Abd al-Razzaq al-Hasani, himself an Arab nationalist who spent several years in jail after 1941, also published his views about recent events in Iraqi history in Lebanon. This did not spare him from the rage of the Regent 'Abd al-Ilah, who summoned him to the palace to debate his views of the "Forty-One" movement (Bashkin, 2009, p. 129).

The record for the post-1958 period is different. The years of 'Abd al-Karim Qasim's rule saw numerous confrontations between the President and the Pan-Arab and Nasserist faction under 'Abd al-Salam 'Arif's leadership, especially during the Shawwaf rebellion in Mosul in 1959 (Davis, 2005, p. 109; Tripp, 2007, pp. 147, 158). The record of the remembrance of the "Forty-One" events, however, supports a more nuanced view of the prevailing state narrative under Qasim. According to this view, Qasim was forced to negotiate his position as a "Sole Leader" of Iraq between the diverse ideological currents in the country. "Forty-One", therefore, had to be included in Qasim's vision of the state, but it was reinterpreted as representing the army's struggle against imperialism, thus to some extent taking the narrative out of the hands of the pan-Arab nationalists. In addition, Qasim himself (b. 1914) was awarded an indirect role in the events.

By the 20th anniversary of "Forty-One" in 1961, Qasim had distanced himself from the communists who had been instrumental in his rise to power in 1958 and 1959. He had abolished political parties and clamped down on the relatively free press of the years between 1958 and 1960. He had become a military dictator whose legitimacy rested on an elaborate personality cult, but which also led him to neglect the interests of his fellow officers. The major goal of the remembrance of "Forty-One" was therefore apparently to present the 1958 revolution under the leadership of President Qasim as its fulfillment. The most notable feature of the newspaper coverage of this anniversary is the fact that the remembrance was not about the "Forty-One" movement as such, but rather about the execution of the members of the coup leadership in May 1942. The main headline on the front page of *al-Akhbar* read "Glory and Eternal Life to the Martyrs of 1941." The actual coverage of the anniversary took place on page five, with a number of articles of varying lengths praising the *shuhada'* of 1941. A small text box in the upper right corner quoted Qasim and thus set the tone for the entire page: "The Army emanates from the people, it is merged with the people, it rests on the people, and both work for the benefit of the country." A longer article by Sajjad al-Ghazi presented an interview with Muhammad Salman, Minister of Oil under Qasim and a brother of Mahmud Salman, one of the martyrs who had died on the gallows in 1942. Muhammad Salman himself was also a former officer, who had been among the exiles who took refuge in Nazi Germany after 1941. Qasim had called him back to Iraq after the revolution. The interview itself is not very substantial. Muhammad Salman's major revelation in the exchange is that British intrigue had tried to provoke a falling out between the officers during the revolt, but to no avail. More interesting are the numerous references to Qasim. The article asserts that the revolution of 1958 had sparked the memory of the martyrs anew, who had died on the gallows on May 5, 1942. They had been an elite of "Free Officers," which is an anachronism with respect to the "Forty-One" movement, as the Four Officers were by no means clandestine conspirators. Instead, it was a reference to 1958. The interview's attempts to create continuity went even further: The elite that preceded the Four Officers in the uprising (*intifada*) of 1936 and those who had been martyred in all other revolutions and uprisings of the Iraqi army and people, "what else were they but forerunners of the gigantic labor that the savior (*munqidh*) of the country and hero of the 14 July Revolution, Qasim, had completed" (Batatu, 1978, pp. 5–6).

Of course, this version promoted by the press under Qasim differs greatly from the "actual" events of 1941, which sheds light on the demands and challenges to Qasim's rule that the new nationalist narrative about "Forty-One" was trying to absorb. The last quote, for instance, is a drastic re-interpretation of the pan-Arab nature of the "Forty-One" movement. The assumption that a line of continuity existed between the 1936 military coup and the "Forty-One" movement disregards the fact that Bakr Sidqi, the Kurdish general who was the driving force of the coup (Qasim himself was of partly Fa'ili Kurdish origin), was slain in a counter coup in 1937 by pan-Arab officers who in turn pushed the Four Officers into the limelight of Iraqi politics. In addition, Baghdad became a hot bed of pan-Arab activism with the arrival of the Mufti in 1939. His role in the events of 1941 is notorious. It is remarkable that the words nation (*umma*) and fatherland (*watan*) are used several times in the 1961 article, but only once towards the end of the article does the nation receive the adjective "Arab." In two instances, the executed rebels are described as "heroes of Arabism" (*"abtal al-'uruba"*), but when the interviewee speaks of the army and the people, they are distinctively Iraqi.

Another remarkable discrepancy between 1941 and Qasim's "Forty-One" is the choice of persons to be remembered. It seems that its Realm of Memory was mostly occupied by the execution of the martyrs, and that this realm was most strongly established in the officer corps. In 1961, the only civilian name still associated with the movement was Yunus al-Sab'awi. His execution alongside the Four Officers, which made him the only civilian among the "Forty-One" leaders that was actually put to death, is the most obvious reason for his inclusion. Still, this conceals the fact that "Forty-One" was in large part a civilian middle class movement. The fact that the 1961 version of "Forty-One" completely ignored Rashid 'Ali al-Kailani is, however, not surprising, because the former Prime Minister, who had returned to Iraq from exile after the revolution, had organized an abortive attempted coup that was uncovered late in 1958.

Further articles on the commemorative page of *al-Akhbar* mentioned that Qasim had revived the 5th Division during the Revolution. In 1941, when Fahmi Sa'id was its commander, Qasim had served in it. Finally, a poem by the Arab nationalist poet Ma'ruf al-Rusafi, probably written soon after the execution, lauded the four officers as stars in the sky, "setting like suns [...] A time of good fortune will come from [the setting]/the gloom of disaster will be cleaned from it [...]."

The Ba'th and the Mosul Spring Festival

In 1971, Rashid 'Ali returned to the realm of "Forty-One". Even if it is hard to make conclusive statements on the basis of a relatively small sample of newspaper articles, it seems that the "Takriti Ba'th" (Davis, 2005, p. 318) that came to power in the so-called corrective revolution of 1968 did not initially value "Forty-One" as much as Qasim did. Indeed, *al-Jumhuriyya*, the major government newspaper, honored the 30th anniversary of "Forty-One" with a short article only, almost in passing. This is in itself remarkable, because "Forty-One" should have been closer to the pan-Arab emotions of the Ba'thists than to Qasim. In contrast to what happened 10 years later, as we shall see below, the remembrance in 1971 still depicted "Forty-One" as a straightforward struggle against the imperialists and their helpers in Iraq. The fact that this was a movement of the army and the people for the liberation of the country was more central than the fact of the martyrdom of the — mostly military — leaders of the movement. The new Ba'thist interpretation continued Qasim's theme that "Forty-One" had been an effort of "Free Officers," but it added the contribution of "civilians who were faithful to the greatest of fatherlands and its unity." Rashid 'Ali was even mentioned first among the leaders of the revolt. The article called it "an exemplary Arab nationalist Revolution in spite of its outcome," thus openly acknowledging its failure, although, as we shall see, this became less of a feature in subsequent commemorations.

The military re-interpretation of "Forty-One" prevailed in army circles, however, as the 1971 Mosul Spring Festival shows. The festival, first held in 1969, was a means for the new regime to build public legitimacy (Baram, 1991, p. 53). In contrast with the Mesopotamian references that Qasim had used to underline his Iraqist nationalism, the Ba'thists tried to reconcile the Mesopotamian past with Arab nationalist ideology (Davis, 2005, p. 150). During the staging of the festival in April 1971, which took the form of a series of floats representing different periods and events, "Forty-One" found its way into a historical chain linking the Stone Age, Sumer, Hammurabi, and Nebuchadnezzar's victory over the Jews (who stood in for the Zionists), to the Islamic conquests and the fall of Baghdad in 1258. There was a remarkable leap from the Mongol invasion in 1258 to the next float, which represented the British occupation of Iraq in World War I. On the one hand this underlined the usual Arab nationalist disdain for the Ottoman period, but it indirectly credited the British for "awakening" Arab Iraq, which was certainly unintended.

The floats were pulled through the streets of Mosul on two consecutive days, 10 April, marking the formal opening of the festival, and again on 11 April. The festival itself lasted until 18 April. All themes were represented on decorated floats. *al-Jumhuriyya* reported that more than a thousand Boy Scouts (*kashshaf*) populated the floats, acting as cavemen, kings, and warriors.

The organizers had arranged the 20th century floats — undoubtedly the centerpiece of the procession — as a chain of revolutions that started in 1920 and culminated in the corrective revolution of 1968. The revolutionary cortège thus included the 1958 revolution as well, depicting the people breaking free from their chains and a soldier ramming his bayonet through a crown. It was followed by a float representing the Mosul crisis of March 1959. A column supported a bowl with planted flowers and girls in white clothes holding and tending to flowers, standing for the purity of Arab Nationalism. They were surrounded by the people who pushed back raging troops trying to rape the girls. A picture of 'Abd al-Wahhab al-Shawwaf, the declared "leader of the Mosul revolution," was carried in front of the float. The fact that the events in Mosul had their own float represents a particularly Ba'thist appropriation of Iraq's revolutionary history. When the Mosul garrison rose up against 'Abd al-Karim Qasim's regime under the leadership of a group of Arab nationalist Free Officers in March 1959, the communists helped to suppress the revolt, which they considered a counter-revolution. According to the Ba'thist version in 1971, the uprising of 1959 was an unsuccessful attempt by the people of Iraq to preserve the purity of the revolution. The military played a strong role in this, and 'Abd al-Wahhab al-Shawwaf embodied it. This alleged merit, however, was not fully justified. According to Hanna Batatu, few of the officers had any affiliation with the Ba'th party. Others were close to 'Abd al-Salam 'Arif, or had their own personal ambitions. al-Shawwaf joined the conspiracy only late, but managed to attach his name to it as "the leader of the revolution" in a manifesto broadcast on the morning of March 8, 1959. He was the scion of a landed and religious family, a self-declared wealthy man, who had once leaned towards the communists. All this combined did not make him a very likely ally or precursor of the Ba'th, and it was probably to his advantage that he was killed during the rebellion and thus became a *shahid* (Batatu, 1978, pp. 871, 881). In any case, the Shawwaf rebellion served the Ba'thist narrative as an attempt to salvage the Iraqi revolution through a genuine Arab nationalist uprising, which was "hijacked" and abused by Qasim and the ICP.

The float of what was now called the "Revolution of May 1941" was placed three positions in front of the 1958 float. There was one for the foundation of the Ba'th party in 1947, and another depicting the partition of Palestine in 1948 in between. Apart from an article about "Forty-One" that appeared in *al-Jumhuriyya* a few days later, the version presented by the float was as much an aberration of the historical record as the version of the Qasim period. There was no mention of Rashid 'Ali al-Kailani, and the movement was reduced to the events of May 1941, ignoring the fact that the "Government of National Defense" had come into office a month earlier. This, and the very peculiar, if not rather extravagant design of the float indicates that the design of the procession as a whole had not been predetermined by the party leadership in Baghdad; most probably, the task of decorating the thematic floats was given to committees from local institutions. In the case of the "Forty-One" float, it was probably the local Air Force base. The float carried an "abstract depiction" of the May Revolution, with a figurative monument for the martyrs of the revolution. Unfortunately, the newspaper report does not mention who was included in this set up. Wings were attached to both sides of the monument representing the Air Force. The article explained that this monument should convey the contribution of the Air Force to the liberation of the country. This was a very creative interpretation of the 1941 events indeed, because the war of May 1941 is best known for the short lived and unsuccessful involvement of German and Italian airplanes, but not for any heroic deeds of the Royal Iraqi Air Force. A portrait of President al-Bakr was attached to the front of the vehicle, surrounded by the emblazoned wings of the Air Force. On the top of the vehicle was a depiction of the sun of the Ba'th, surrounded by the flags of the Republic, the flag of the Air Force, and the flag of the party. In sum, this was a strange appropriation of the 1941 revolt by the Air Force and the Ba'th party, since both had little or nothing to do with it.

Qadisiyyat Saddam

Once he came to power, Saddam Husayn made new efforts to manipulate the Iraqi national narrative with an increased interest in fabricating historical depth in order to define the nature and identity of the state and its citizens reaching back to the Mesopotamian period (Davis, 2005, p. 148). "Forty-One" made a grand return, too, after Iraq declared war on Iran. In 1981, Rashid 'Ali disappeared again in a militarized narrative that was remarkably similar to Qasim's version, although with the marked difference that "Forty-One" now had become as much a part of Iraq's struggle against Iran and Zionism as against imperialism and the reactionary *ancien régime*. The integration of the Ba'thist corrective revolution and of the war against Iran into a grand revolutionary history of Iraq with a strong emphasis on the role of the military in that history may have been particularly necessary because the new regime had steered away from military dictatorship and a "Free Officer" regime to a totalitarian party dictatorship since 1968. Both the outbreak of the war against Iran and its unexpectedly long duration made it painfully clear to Saddam Husayn, who had no military credentials, that he was again dependent on the Iraqi officer corps. In times of war, when skills and experience were more important for an officer than ideological reliability, the loyalty of the officer corps to the Ba'thist regime was far from assured. Arguably therefore, it was opportune for Saddam Husayn to emphasize revolutionary continuity, to show respect for the military component, and as a part of that, to integrate and re-interpret "Forty-One".

He therefore developed a particular interest in the integration of "Forty-One" and its so-called martyrs into a national effort to re-assess Iraqi history at a time when the state had to justify the deaths of thousands of young men on the battlefields of the Iran–Iraq war (Davis, 2005, p. 184; Wild, 1982, p. 169). Madiha al-Salman, the widow of Mahmud Salman, mentions in her memoirs that shortly before he took over the presidency in 1979, Saddam Husayn had invited the families of the *shuhada'* to a celebration of those whom he called the "first martyrs" (al-Takriti, 1990, p. 256). Husayn honored the martyrs of "Forty-One" as forerunners of the 1968 Revolution, which in turn was the "legal heir of the sacrifice, heroism, and witness of all the good and honorable sons of this people." The 1968 revolution was thus a continuation and fulfillment of the 1941 revolution and elevated its martyred heroes to an appropriate place in the pantheon of Iraqi historical memory.

Two years later, on the occasion of its 40th anniversary, the absorption of "Forty-One" into Saddam Husayn's propaganda machinery was complete when — in the context of the Iran–Iraq war — it became a part of the "Qadisiyya" myth. al-Qadisiyya was a decisive battle during the early Arab-Islamic conquest of the Sasanian Empire, sometime between 635 and 637 (Streck *et al.*, *Encyclopedia of Islam* 2009). al-Qadisiyya played a role early in Iraqi Arab nationalism, promoting the steadfastness and masculinity of the early Islamic warriors among Iraqi youth (Wien, 2006, p. 100). The topic offered itself for further exploitation after Saddam Husayn's miscalculation that the attack on Iran would lead to a swift victory over a regional rival severely weakened by the Islamic revolution. Confronted with early setbacks for the Iraqi army, Husayn's propaganda re-interpreted the war as an epic struggle between Arabs and Persians, or in other words: Saddam's Qadisiyya. This, however, only added a new shade to the militarized "Forty-One" narrative familiar since Qasim's time. The emphasis remained on the martyrdom of the Four Officers and Sab'awi, although *al-Jumhuriyya's* new revolutionary continuity was careful to leave out Qasim. The headlines read: "The continuing heroic struggle: From the May Revolution to Saddam's Qadisiyya," and "Saddam's Qadisiyya recalls the glories of May and immortalizes the revolution of liberation and honor."

al-Jumhuriyya dedicated more than a full page to the commemoration of "Forty-One", thus pushing its meaning as a symbol of revolution even further than that had been the case 10 years earlier. For the Arab nation — now clearly and up-front *al-umma al-'Arabiyya* — the grand revolution of "Forty-One" was outstanding among the revolutions of the Arab people against imperialism and its agents. An elite of "fearless and free leaders of the army," had the support of "the forces of patriotism (*wataniyya*) and nationalism (*qawmiyya*)" — that is, including both the Iraqi and wider Arab fatherland — in their fight against "imperialism, Zionism, and reaction," all key terms in the article to describe "Forty-One's" foes. In *al-Jumhuriyya's* new interpretation, it was an anti-Zionist revolt. The circumstances of World War II had offered a chance to uproot Zionism in Palestine and to push back its perilous influence and potential expansion in the rest of the Arab lands. "Forty-One" had been a lesson that the Arabs had taught the imperialists, and according to the article, it had been a vast popular effort. The failure of the revolt plays only a minor role in this propaganda effort, because in this narrative, the trajectory of "Forty-One's" revolutionary momentum points towards the Ba'th party, and further on towards what the newspaper described as its heroic efforts to safeguard the Eastern border of the Arab nation against the leaders of Iran and the agents of a new imperialism. Another article presents the Persian leaders as — supposedly anti-Arab — racists. Already in 1942, they had betrayed the leaders (and later martyrs) of the revolution when they had handed them over to the "reactionary forces" in Iraq for execution, in spite of their status as political refugees in Iran. The following quote is a summary of the claim to continuity between "Forty-One" and the rule of the Ba'th:

> The martyrs of the May revolution dedicated their souls as a sacrifice for the sake of Iraq's honor and that of the Arab fatherland. At the same time the Brave of the Second Qadisiyya wage their historical battle on the eastern border of the Arab fatherland defending the same principles and goals that these martyrs died for [...] Indeed, Saddam's Qadisiyya is an extension of this liberating revolution [...]

Khayr Allah Tulfah and the Four Officers

It seems that a somewhat enigmatic personality in the powerful circles of the Ba'thist regime played a particular role in the veneration of the "martyrs" of 1941: Khayr Allah Tulfah, the uncle, foster father, and father-in-law of Saddam Husayn, and the father of Saddam's cousin 'Adnan, who later played an important role as a military leader during the war against Iran and reached a level of public appreciation unbearable to the regime. It did away with 'Adnan in 1989 in a helicopter crash that was declared an "accident" (Abdullah, 2006, p. 60; Tripp, 2007, p. 240). His father Khayr Allah Tulfah was made governor of Baghdad after the 1968 coup (Batatu, 1978, pp. 1084, 1092; Tripp, 2007), and features prominently in the "psycho-biographies" of Saddam Husayn that became a popular genre prior to the 2003 invasion. According to these studies, Saddam was deeply impressed by Khayr Allah's stories about the heroism and betrayal of the Four Officers during the 1941 movement, when he had been a co-conspirator as a young officer in Baghdad. Apparently, Tulfah was dismissed from the army and spent several years in prison after Rashid 'Ali's downfall (Davis, 2005, p. 249; Post and Baram, 2003, p. 165). The credibility of this story may be questionable, particularly the likelihood of a young Takriti officer having access to the circles of the Iraqi general staff in 1941. Nevertheless it seems to provide the missing link between the 1941 coup and Saddam's regime of terror, which Western observers used as questionable evidence to present Saddam as the inheritor of Iraq's assumed "Nazi legacy." I have mentioned earlier that the historical record does not support this view of the 1941 movement at large. Nevertheless, Tulfah played a central role in the sanctification of the members of the 1941 movement.

In the early 1970s, Tulfah was the president of an Iraqi veterans' association (*Jam'iyat al-Muharibin*). *al-Jumhuriyya* reported on May 7, 1971, that he had handed an "Arab sword" as a gift to president Hasan al-Bakr. A photograph on page one shows two other men next to Tulfah in the president's office in the Republican Palace. All the men appear to be in their fifties or sixties, and hence maybe they were not just veterans, but also combatants during the nationalist struggle of 1941 and the following years. The image evokes the impression that symbolically, Tulfah, whose career as a *muharib* had ended with the 1941 movement, passed on the sword of the Arab struggle, and thus the legacy of the *shuhada'*, to the Ba'thist president.

A year earlier, Tulfah had participated in an event that arguably gave the Four Officers the strongest public visibility since their public executions: Their re-burial in Baghdad. Madiha al-Salman recounts briefly in her memoirs that the government of the "revolution" of 1968 had made the momentous decision to transfer the bodies to the martyrs' cemetery at Umm al-Tubul. The children of the martyrs participated along with their families, together with 'Abd al-Jabbar Shanshal, chief of the general staff, and, notably, Khayr Allah Tulfah (al-Takriti, 1990, p. 254). Already in 1961, *al-Akhbar* had reported that, after the execution, the bodies of the martyrs had been buried secretly, and the government (the "executioners of imperialist machinations") had banned the relatives from bidding them farewell in appropriate obsequies. A guard detachment had been stationed next to the graves for a long time because "imperialism and its helpers trembled for fear of them both alive and dead!" Madiha al-Salman complained that 'Abd al-Karim Qasim had rejected her family's request to build a mosque [!] as a mausoleum for the remains of the *shuhada'* (al-Takriti, 1990, p. 254).

One of the publications that appeared in the 1980s as part of the effort to re-assess Iraqi history from the point of view of its usefulness for the current regime was a new edition of Salah al-Din al-Sabbagh's memoirs (al-Sabbagh, 1983). Once more, we encounter Khayr Allah Tulfah, this time as the author of the foreword to the new edition. His praise for Sabbagh as a model of manliness, courage and true commitment to the Arab cause is exactly what we would expect in an Arab nationalist's sanctification of a *shahid*. Tulfah stressed that one would not find a page in the glorious history of the Iraqi army that was not enlightened by this shining episode in Iraq's recent history. He called upon old and young to follow this example. The most interesting part is a story that allegedly, Ghazi al-Karim, a former member of parliament and close friend of the Regent 'Abd al-Ilah had referred to Tulfah, which turns Tulfah's praise of Sabbagh into an outright apotheosis.

Sabbagh was sentenced to death in Iraq after the Syrian authorities handed him over to the Iraqi authorities for trial after the end of World War II, giving in to pressure from the British and the regent. Tulfah's informant reports that at 11 o'clock on the night before the execution, he had been at 'Abd al-Ilah's house when the regent ordered that Sabbagh should be brought before him. The leader of the Four Officers had a long beard, because he had no permission to shave in prison. He wore prisoner's clothes and slippers on his feet. In fact, Tulfah's image of Sabbagh resembles that of a saint and hermit, if not that of Christ before Pilate. 'Abd al-Ilah turned to him and said: "Is this what you wanted, Salah?" He answered: "This is what you wanted, 'Abd al-Ilah. I wanted to preserve the honor of the country and its Arabness, but you insisted on its humiliation and insult." 'Abd al-Ilah replied: "You have been condemned to death, and it is your right to appeal the sentence." But Salah al-Din replied: "Wa'llah! Oh 'Abd al-Ilah, death is more dearer to me than standing before the person that greeted me." Tulfah explains this confusing reply as Sabbagh's reaction to the humiliation of his court martial, whose presiding judge had been Sabbagh's subordinate before his exile. 'Abd al-Ilah replied: "So you do not regret what you set in motion?" Sabbagh said: "On the contrary, I am proud. I am confident that history will record my deeds in shining letters, and it will write in shame about people other than me." Here, 'Abd al-Ilah replied angrily: "Then the gallows await you in three hours." Salah al-Din smiled and said: "'Abd al-Ilah, the land that you are running down is better than it seems."

Conclusion

The veneration of the martyrs of 1941 thus reached a high point in the sanctification of their leader Salah al-Din al-Sabbagh. During the one and a half decades before the downfall of the monarchy, their memory had become an integral part of the *esprit de corps* of the officers who would overthrow the ancient régime. In spite of the fact that "Forty-One", which in the meantime had become a "lieu de mémoire" of Iraqi Arab nationalism, does not seem to fit into the ideological set-up of the Qasim years, even he and his propagandists felt compelled to include it in the national revolutionary story. During the Ba'thist years, "Forty-One" seems to have remained a military realm of memory, which Saddam Husayn was eager to see integrated into his myth of a second Qadisiyya. "Forty-One" then became all but a forerunner to the eternal revolutionary struggle of the Ba'th party.

One can only speculate about the diffusion of this commissioned mythology among the Iraqi population at large. It remains to be seen how contemporary Iraqi historians and publicists perceived and continue to perceive of the history of 1941. The years since the fall of Saddam Husayn's regime have brought forth an increasing number of books re-assessing Iraq's history in the 20th century. The Qasim years from 1958 to 1963 have been of particular interest to writers who are trying to present the first republican president as an example of a benevolent dictator and non-sectarian leader. It is more than likely that an event as deeply rooted in Iraqi "public memory" as the 1941 movement will have produced a similar output of publications. For a conclusive version of this research, they would also have to be taken into account.

BUILDING THE NATION THROUGH THE PRODUCTION OF DIFFERENCE: THE GENDERING OF EDUCATION IN IRAQ, 1928–1958

Sara Pursley

In 1952, an American educator named Ava Milam was sent to Baghdad by the Food and Agriculture Organization (FAO) of the United Nations to evaluate the state of female education in Iraq. The report she authored, which followed several months of field research, criticized the Iraqi public school curriculum for girls, especially at the secondary level, for being too similar to the curriculum for boys. It recommended that female secondary school students, in both the "literary" and "scientific" tracks, be required to study female-specific subjects for at least 20% of the time they spent in school, up from 6% to 7% of the current curriculum. Loosely categorized under the term "home economics," such subjects included "food, clothing, shelter, family relationships, and child development" (Milam, 1952, p. 1). The proposal is noteworthy in part because a controversy had emerged in Iraq during the mid-1940s over the addition of *any* home economics requirement to the girls' secondary school curriculum, especially in the scientific track.[1] One argument against it was that many girls in this track were preparing for public school examinations to enter college science programs, in competition with boys who did not have similar requirements. Given the importance of

---

[1] Part of this debate was carried out in the journal of the Ministry of Education, which added some home economics requirements to the girls' secondary school curriculum from 1940–1943. For an article in the journal opposing differentiation in the science curriculum, see 'Abir (1942).

these exams, it is difficult to imagine how the FAO proposal would not have adversely impacted an Iraqi girl's chances of pursuing a higher education, especially but not exclusively in science.

Milam was something of an American home economics missionary during the first decade of the Cold War. Prior to arriving in Iraq, she had helped to establish programs in China, Korea, the Philippines, and Syria. Interestingly, when she wrote her memoirs, she devoted a whole chapter to her experiences in Iraq but did not discuss the substance of the FAO report she authored. The impression conveyed to the reader is that her mission was part of the global postwar march of American-style liberation and scientific know-how; she was helping to make modern education available to women in a traditional country that resisted such education on principle. For example, she claimed that the female educators she assisted in Iraq faced opposition from male officials, who "violently opposed" teaching subjects such as political science to women (Milam, 1969, pp. 333–334). This account may refer to a controversy over the content of a political science textbook, which preceded and had nothing to do with Milam's work in Iraq. But its inclusion in her narrative is striking, and indeed misleading, given that she had proposed a significant reduction in the periods of study in academic subjects, including political science, for all girls in Iraq's secondary schools.

Milam's 1952 FAO report and her 1969 memoirs point to a number of problems in writing a history of gender in Iraq under the monarchy (1921–1958). The first is the powerful Orientalist narrative that posits the West as the origin of all liberatory tendencies, especially those related to women. In this familiar framework, the East is *always* out of time with the West. Thus, in Milam's memoirs, Iraq in the early 1950s is somehow not contemporaneous with the United States in the early 1950s, where the "cult of domesticity" was celebrating its golden age. Instead, 1950s Iraq is implicitly confronted with American standards of the late 1960s, after the feminist movement had launched an attack on mandatory gendered education. In both 1952 and 1969, Milam represented herself as an agent of progress in a traditional country; what had changed during those years were the American definitions of progress and tradition. Thus, looking back in 1969, Milam could simply suggest, without elaborating, that her work in 1952 had the effect of expanding academic education to Iraqi women, which was the exact opposite of its actual effect. What had *not* changed in the intervening years was the underlying conviction that progress is always of Western origin. As we know, the persistent appeal of this narrative still shapes many discussions of Iraq in the Western media, notably when American-style women's liberation was regularly invoked in defense of the US-led invasion in 2003.

The second difficulty is that the discourses of feminine domesticity prominent in many Arab countries during the modern period have often been associated with anti-colonial nationalist ideologies. However, the most influential advocates of mandatory female education in domesticity from the 1930s to 1958 in Iraq were Western-aligned Iraqi bureaucrats and Western, mainly American, advisors. Pointing out that "Iraqi national elites were profoundly immersed in Western culture" during this time, Orit Bashkin has proposed that Homi Bhabha's notion of "colonial hybridity" is more useful than colonizer/colonized models for analyzing national discourse in monarchical Iraq (Bashkin, 2009, p. 3). I would add that this immersion was not restricted to the "public" masculine sphere as the location of scientific modernity, and did not mark off the "private" feminine space for the preservation of tradition and cultural authenticity, the model posited by Partha Chatterjee's famous argument about inner and outer domains in the Indian anti-colonial nationalist movement. Calls to protect the Iraqi/Arab domestic sphere and Iraqi/Arab femininity from modern/Western decadence did emerge, but not primarily in response to the colonial policy or any other practice of a Western state, either during or after the British mandate. Instead, they were primarily a response to the indigenous nationalist and communist youth movements in Iraq during the 1940s and 1950s, and were commonly invoked to justify practices that in fact accelerated and deepened the influence of Western bureaucratic specialists and knowledge on the attempted reconstruction of the Iraqi domestic sphere. One example is Ava Milam's mission to Iraq, organised in response to a request from the monarchy to the FAO for assistance in redesigning female secondary education, which, it was feared, was producing leftist revolutionaries rather than domestic mothers and housewives.

A third difficulty is the tendency in many studies of Iraq to emphasize — and assume an opposition between — unity and difference, citizenship and sectarianism, nationhood and fragmentation. In the history of education, these analyses are often primarily concerned with whether schools were working to produce loyalty to an Arab nation or an Iraqi nation, with bureaucratic struggles between the two kinds of nationalisms, and with the degree to which the unification process succeeded or failed (Davis, 2005, p. 58; Simon, 2004, p. 69; Sousa, 1982, p. 100). Clearly, education policy under the monarchy often did aim to suppress certain *kinds* of difference, especially those related to some forms of social class and religious sect; for example, it attempted both to limit enrollment and to impose a uniform curriculum in private religious schools. But it also often worked to produce, reconfigure, or normalize other kinds of difference, such as those marked by divisions of Arab/Kurd, urban/rural, tribal/settled, and male/female. Moreover, these differences should not necessarily be seen as opposed to the aims of state-building and national unity, whether Arab or Iraqi, nor as simply an elite strategy of divide and conquer. For instance, the pedagogical process of constructing differently gendered citizens was understood by many policymakers precisely as a means of ensuring the nation's future survival and prosperity.

This essay traces certain historical forces that shaped the emergence of a "cult of domesticity" in Iraq from 1928–1958 and its effect on the experience of female students. It challenges Orientalist narratives that continue to assume, against all evidence to the contrary, that Western influence in 20th-century Iraq tended to weaken gender constructs that assign women a predominantly domestic and reproductive role in the household. More broadly, it proposes that the writing of Iraqi history must pay attention to Iraq's national particularity while also situating that particularity within a wider global framework. Iraq was hardly unique in being influenced by modern discourses of feminine domesticity and practices of gendered education in the 20th century. But these practices developed in Iraq in historically specific ways due to a unique convergence of local, national, and global forces. Among other factors, they were shaped by the pro-Western alignment of the monarchy, especially after the start of the Cold War; the ideological conflict between Arab nationalism and American-style pragmatism among education officials; ongoing struggles over land reform, industrialization, and peasant migration; and the emergence of a revolutionary generation of educated urban youth in the postwar period.

The basic historical narrative of this essay runs as follows. A shift occurred in Iraqi education policy during the years preceding and immediately following World War II. During the 1920s, the school system was dominated by Sharifian Arab nationalists, especially the well-known intellectual Sati' al-Husri. But in subsequent decades, their power in the Ministry of Education was increasingly challenged by a new group of US-trained Iraqi educators influenced by the pragmatist school of pedagogical theory associated with the philosopher John Dewey. Among the most prominent in this latter group were Muhammad Fadil al-Jamali and Matta 'Aqrawi, both of whom received their doctoral degrees in the 1930s from the Teachers College of Columbia University, where Dewey had taught until his retirement in

1929. This new generation of educators was perfectly poised to lead the Iraqi school system into a global postwar age marked by the expansion of American power and influence and by the dawning of the "age of development" with the founding of the World Bank in 1944 and of the United Nations and its development organizations, including UNESCO, in 1945.

The new Iraqi educators were supported by the reports of American education commissions and international development teams that came to Iraq beginning in the 1930s, but with increasing regularity in the early 1950s. Both groups consistently argued that the Iraqi public school curriculum was not sufficiently differentiated by sex. They recommended that girls from the primary through the secondary levels, and in many cases at the college levels, be required to take courses in home economics, a field developed in the United States during the late 19th century that by this time was receiving substantial US government support (Elias, 2008). This discourse joined the conceptual language of pragmatism with an emerging ideology of national development. Among other relevant aspects of this ideology was its emphasis on technical, rather than structural, solutions to underdevelopment, and its conception of the importance of a scientifically managed and feminine-oriented domestic family space for improving national health and productivity, molding future citizens and workers, and fostering the growth of a national consumer market.

Between 1932 and 1958, Iraqi officials implemented these recommendations through revisions to curricula, textbooks, teacher training programs, and the construction of new schools. In what might seem to be a paradox, the differentiation of the curriculum by sex was paralleled by the expansion of coeducation in Iraq at the primary and postsecondary levels during this same period. An Iraqi girl entering the public education system in 1926 was certain to study in a school populated only by other girls, but she was almost equally certain to study the same material and follow the same course of schooling as a boy at her grade level. A girl entering the system in 1956 might or might not attend a coeducational primary school, but either way she would follow a girls-only curriculum for approximately 20% of the time she spent in that school. It seemed that the more girls mixed with boys, and women with men, in the public sphere, the greater became the impetus to produce differences in their learned modes of being and thinking.

This narrative does not address all historical forces relevant to the gendering of Iraqi education. For example, it leaves out the militarist forms of nationalist pedagogy that gained prominence in the late 1930s and early 1940s and which focused partly on the formation of strong and disciplined male bodies (Makiya, 1989; Simon, 2004; Wien, 2006). While its gender aspects are under-examined, the militarist movement in education has received more recent attention than the effects on Iraqi schools of Western specialists, global and domestic economic forces, and postwar political upheaval in Iraq. I have chosen to focus here on the latter issues.

Masculine Time, Feminine Space, and Arab Unity: Sati' al-Husri and the Schooling of Iraqi Girls in the 1920s

Sati' al-Husri was director general of Iraqi education from 1921–1927 and held other posts in the Ministry until 1936. His philosophy of Arab nationalism is relevant to understanding Iraqi education in the 1920s for several reasons. First, as the most famous Arabist intellectual in Iraq during this time, he was in many ways the ideological spokesman for the Sharifian brand of Arab nationalism dominant among the entire cohort of bureaucrats serving under King Faysal. Second, the highly centralized structure of the education system, and the consolidation of most power under the director-general rather than the minister of education, meant that al-Husri exerted a powerful influence on every aspect of Iraqi public education during its formative years (Simon, 2004, pp. 69–72; Sluglett, 2007, p. 197).

al-Husri believed that language and history were the only legitimate foundations of modern nationhood. Like Faysal, he was committed to the stabilization and eventual independence of the Iraqi state, intellectually as a "province" of the Arab nation and pragmatically as the political domain over which he had a bureaucratic mandate. But he always maintained that Iraq had no lasting legitimacy as a nation because it only had — as he saw it — a geographically determined identity. At the same time, the desired Arab nation was lacking one of the two essential components of nationhood: A shared historical memory among those who spoke Arabic. One of his most unwavering convictions was that the "return of national consciousness to a conquered nation can only be accomplished through the recovery of its historical memories" (Husri, 1967, p. 481). The answer was public schooling. A rigorously uniform modern education would instill in Arab youth the sense of a unified history that would enable them to someday unite politically as a modern and sovereign nation-state.

Education was a critical tool of nationalism for al-Husri, not only because it molded the sensibilities and aspirations of the rising generation, but because it did so by removing youth from the harmful influence of their families, especially their illiterate and superstitious mothers. For this reason, he viewed compulsory military service as the second crucial institution for the formation of national identity. Like schools, the military removed youth from their families and particular identities and enabled them to feel the existence of a larger force, the nation. In fact, the military was an even more effective nationalist force than the school, for the simple reason that it removed boys from their families for longer periods of time. A school could take a child from his family "every day for a few hours only," and then must return him, "allowing him to live and sleep in his home, spending the remaining hours of the day with his family." But the military "demands his separation from his original family and private life [...] for a long period of time" (Husri, 1967, p. 309). These two institutions were so indispensable to the construction of every "modern social order" that, according to al-Husri, every (male) individual in the nation should be forced to join both of them, "in a particular stage of his life, passing through the school in his childhood and through the barracks in his young adulthood" (Husri, 1967, p. 308).

These views had several implications for the schooling of Iraqi girls in the 1920s. First, as a progressive modernizer and an opponent of illiteracy, al-Husri supported the education of women, at least in theory, and the number of girls in Iraqi schools expanded steadily under his watch. Between the 1920–1921 and 1931–1932 school years, the number of girls attending primary school rose from 3,049 to 8,532 and those in secondary school from 0 to 176 ('Aqrawi, 1942, p. 157; Kadry, 1958, p. 6). Second, during al-Husri's service as director general of education from 1921–1927, the public school curriculum for girls was identical to that for boys ('Aqrawi, 1942, p. 196). This was consonant with his view that uniformity in the curriculum would create unity in the nation, and that the academic subjects of history and language were the most essential for the formation of national consciousness. In 1928, al-Husri did support the addition of a home economics requirement in primary school, and he later agreed with the pragmatists that some differentiation of the curriculum on the basis of sex was necessary. However, he continued to argue against them that such differences should apply only to the "details" and should not affect the "essentials" of education. Most importantly, female and male students should progress through the national school system following identical temporal rhythms of intellectual development and bureaucratic order. Thus, al-Husri sharply criticized a proposed reform in 1931 that had girls and boys studying different subjects at different grade levels, arguing that to the extent they were studying the same subjects it was a national imperative that they study them at the same time (Husri, 1967, p. 132).

Third, in spite of these two trends, al-Husri's conceptions of Arab nationalism and Arab youth were consistently masculinist in tone and vision. He often seemed pessimistic or apathetic about actually overcoming women's illiteracy, and impatient with pragmatist proposals to reform the family through the school.[2] He never seemed able to explain, or was never very interested in explaining, how his vision would bring the stagnant feminine space of the family into the progressive masculine time of the nation. It was certainly not through that most masculine of public institutions, the military, which, as we have seen, he deemed even more critical than the school to the formation of Arab identity. The essentially masculine bent of al-Husri's nationalism may help to explain why the increase in female students under his leadership was not matched by an equivalent increase in new schools for girls. Some of his pragmatist critics would later use this point to suggest that the expansion of girls' education in the 1920s was fueled from below by popular demand rather than from above by genuine government support ('Aqrawi, 1942, pp. 156–158).

Learning by Doing: Pragmatist Philosophy and the Differentiated Curriculum

Global, national, and local factors contributed to making 1932 a pivotal year in the eventual convergence of developmentalism and pragmatism in the school system, and for the influence of this convergence on the classroom experience of Iraqi girls. Globally, the great depression was transforming the landscape of public schooling, accelerating the acceptance of new educational philosophies that emphasized the relationship between national education systems and the growth and resilience of national economies. The American pragmatist school of education, and kindred philosophies of education for "real life" emerging in Europe, attracted worldwide interest, influencing educational policy from Turkey and China to Brazil and the Philippines, in part through the development of programs such as the International Institute at the Teachers' College of Columbia University (Popkewitz, 2005; Steiner-Khamsi, 2004).

Columbia Teachers College was the institutional heart of the global pragmatist movement in education. In the late 1920s and early 1930s, it

---

[2]For example, see 'Aqrawi's analysis of Husri's curriculum for the teaching of "moral and civic information" (1942: 192).

forged agreements with Iraq, and many other governments, to co-sponsor some of the country's top college graduates to pursue advanced degrees in education. Among the Iraqi students completing their doctoral work at Columbia in 1932 was Fadil al-Jamali, who became director general of Iraqi education in the 1930s, and would serve as prime minister in the 1950s. al-Jamali and his friend Matta 'Aqrawi, who also received his PhD from Columbia, would lead the movement to join pragmatism and developmentalism in the Iraqi school system, in direct and often very public conflict with Sati' al-Husri.

On a national level, Iraq gained its formal independence in 1932 and entered the League of Nations, although Britain maintained significant influence over the Iraqi government and official control over its foreign policy. But following the Anglo-Iraqi treaty of "independence," certain elements of the monarchical regime — pushed by the economic crisis, a growing opposition movement, and personal interest — attempted to lead the country toward full political and economic sovereignty by marshalling its natural and human resources in a state-led modernization plan. One aspect of this was a shift in dominant statist perceptions of rural Iraq, from seeing the countryside primarily as "the basis of a distinctive moral order" to viewing it also "an area of human and material resources to be pressed into service for the benefit of those who controlled the state" (Tripp, 2000, p. 78). In the end, these elements were never able to guide a successful economic development project, a failure that contributed to the monarchy's fall in the revolution of 1958. One reason was that a critical requirement of industrialization, land reform, was consistently blocked by the large tribal landowning class that had been deliberately strengthened by both British and monarchical policy. So long as state planners were unable or unwilling to directly challenge the economic interests of this class, which remained an important base of political support for the monarchy, they were largely restricted to technical approaches to development (Haj, 1997).

Within the Ministry of Education itself, tensions that had been simmering for several years, including a struggle over female education, became a matter of public controversy in 1932. The first home economics requirement for girls had been added to the primary school curriculum in 1928, and the first "vocational" secondary school for home economics was established in 1932. But conflicts over the seriousness with which officials were implementing these projects erupted in the Iraqi press after the 1932 publication of the report of the Monroe Commission, which criticized the Ministry of Education for, among other things, its lack of genuine attention to home

economics in the education of Iraqi girls. The commission was led by Paul
Monroe, al-Jamali's dissertation advisor at Columbia Teachers' College.

Before examining how the new educational approach helped to reshape
female education after 1932, this rest of this section will explore some of
its basic philosophical differences with the "old" approach, that is, with the
concepts and practices of education developed by al-Husri and his cohort of
Sharifian Arab nationalists during the 1920s. First of all, there were some
similarities. Both philosophies were based on faith in progress and modernization; embraced science and technology; affirmed the connection of public
education to both economic development and nationalism (usually Arabism,
though some of the pragmatists leaned toward Iraqist nationalism); assumed
that the nation's backwardness could only be overcome by uprooting local
customs, traditions, and superstitions; and believed that these obstacles
to progress were particularly strong within families and among women.
These shared assumptions formed the background of consensus within which
debates between the "old" and "new" educators played out after 1932. For
our purposes, there were three critical differences in the new philosophy: (1)
the primacy of economic development over nationalism as the first aim of
public schooling; (2) activity-based learning over so-called "passive" learning; and (3) a differentiated rather than uniform curriculum.

For al-Husri, the dominant aim of public schooling was Arab unity; economic advancement could not be fully pursued until that goal was met.
National unity was important to the new educators, but they tended to
conceive of economic development as the primary aim of public schooling.
al-Jamali — who never relinquished his own commitment to the Arabist
dream — argued explicitly for this reconceptualization in his Columbia
Teachers' College dissertation. He wrote that of the three main problems facing the school system — economic reconstruction, nationalism, and morality — the first was the most challenging and demanded the most concerted
attention from education officials (Jamali, 1943, p. 7). By the end of World
War II, if not earlier, al-Jamali's argument was considered axiomatic; officials consistently articulated the primary mission of the school system to be
the nation's scientific and industrial development (Rawi, 1948, p. 3). This
being the case, its classroom methods and its curriculum had to advance
that aim. The philosophy of pragmatism, as interpreted by educators in
Iraq, provided the conceptual vocabulary for translating national development plans into pedagogical practice.

Of special interest to the new educators was pragmatism's emphasis on "activity-based" learning. In this view, education was not about

transmitting knowledge from one generation to another, which they often denigrated as "stuffing children's heads with facts." Instead, it was about developing the whole child — mentally, physically, and morally. The aim of schooling was to instill the particular habits, capabilities and sensibilities that the modern world demanded if a nation was to develop rather than disappear: From habits of hygiene that would reduce child mortality, to problem-solving abilities that would enable the future citizen to manage the complexity of modern life, to a sense of agency that would empower the future worker to shape his or her physical environment. 'Aqrawi wrote that "the fundamental aim of primary education" was "nothing less than the reconstruction of the whole life and behavior of the child along lines that will lead to his physical, psychological, and social moral growth. Information in order to be functional and useful must be translated into action" ('Aqrawi, 1942, p. 198).

The pragmatists criticized Iraqi education on the grounds that the curriculum was too "scholarly," "bookish," and disconnected from "real life"; students were "passive" while the teacher was "active"; teaching was "subject-centered" rather than "child-centered"; and learning was about "memorization" rather than environmental "problem-solving." al-Jamali wrote that since the present curriculum was "literary and nonpractical," it lacked "direct bearing on the social and economic life of the people to-day [...] There is a maximum of inert memory work and a minimum of activity and thinking." Thus, schools were turning out "nonproducers" (Jamali, 1934, p. 10). The pragmatists regularly mixed criticisms of overly "academic" or "literary" approaches to education with criticisms of "inert memory work," as if the two things were identical. But there was a coherent logic running through such arguments. They consistently advocated pedagogies that motivated students to "activity," by which they usually meant physical activity, and those that related to "real life," by which they usually meant either the development of healthy bodily habits (e.g., of hygiene) or training for future manual work (agricultural, industrial, or domestic).

The widespread association of pragmatist philosophy and vocabulary with American-style democracy has influenced the study of pragmatism outside the US.[3] But the drive for "activity-based" and "real-life" pedagogies in Iraq did not necessarily represent the forces of democratization and

---

[3]For an example of this tendency in Iraqi historiography, see Simon (2004: 87). For a more critical discussion of the global traveling of pragmatist theories, see Popkewitz (2005).

individualism against authority and despotism. An example of how such discourse could be employed to foster a different *kind* of discipline among students is suggested in the following observation of an Iraqi classroom by a mission of the American Council on Education, which toured the country in the late 1940s under the direction of Matta ʿAqrawi:

> In one village school first-grade children were being given a practical lesson in the use of soap; those whose use of it was ineffective were sent back to the water tap to clean their hands and faces. The Commission found this a refreshing departure from the predominantly academic and detached-from-life atmosphere of the schools (Matthews and ʿAqrawi, 1949, p. 155).

The problem with the typical Iraqi classroom was not so much that children were being controlled by their teachers, but that they were being controlled in a nonproductive way, one that did not compel them to *action*.

The pragmatist emphasis on activity-based over academic learning was also related to its prioritization of primary over secondary and higher education in Iraq. In fact, al-Husri's most effective and devastating critique of the Monroe report was one that linked it, rather convincingly, to British colonialist policy in this regard. While it was widely believed that the British feared secondary education because they thought it would produce nationalists, the pragmatists insisted that their argument for privileging primary education was based on the importance of activity-based learning and the fact that modern psychology had revealed the significance of the child's earliest years for his or her future development (Jamali, 1938, p. 166). Unfortunately for their argument, the Monroe report had explicitly warned against the expansion of secondary education in Iraq, since "we have a very definite impression that a surplus of academically prepared youth will become a menace to the political stability of any country. In several countries of the Orient such a situation is now quite obvious" (Monroe, 1932, p. 38).

al-Husri pounced on this argument in a series of open letters to Paul Monroe published in the Iraqi press: "Do you believe that 'political stability', regardless of its type, is in the best interests of the country under any circumstances? Could you clarify for us which 'countries of the Orient' have fallen into political or social troubles due to their abundance of educated citizens?" He went on to argue that countries under the control of colonial or other harmful powers required not stability but revolution (*inqilab*). Only a government that ruled by promoting the "genuine aspirations of the nation" could meaningfully claim that stability was in that nation's interests, and such a government had nothing to fear from educating its citizens beyond the age of childhood. "I will concede to you that an abundance of educated citizens may lead to instability in the first type of political situation, but I believe you will concede to me that this is not the kind of stability that is in the genuine interests of the nation." Finally, al-Husri chided Monroe that, "as you know," in 1932 the number of intermediate school students in Iraq was only slightly above 2,000, the number at the preparatory level of secondary school did not exceed 300, and the total number of secondary school graduates since the Iraqi state was established had not yet reached 700. By contrast, "if secondary education had expanded in this country at the rate it has expanded in yours, the number of our secondary school students would now be 125,000" (Husri, 1967, pp. 237–239).[4]

The third difference in the new philosophy was its criticism of the uniformity of the public school curriculum, which al-Husri considered a hard-won nationalist achievement. In a bold and direct swipe at al-Husri himself, 'Aqrawi wrote in his dissertation that "the course of study, the methods of teaching, inspection, examination, and textbooks are all directed towards one end: Uniformity, or as one of the protagonists of the system prefers to call it: 'the unity of education.'" Against this nationalist uniformity, the pragmatists argued that education should be differentiated according to the "varieties of life and environment" found in Iraq. But they advocated a particular kind of differentiation. They shared al-Husri's concern that British policy had fostered sectarianism in Iraq by funding Christian schools in an attempt to produce civil servants loyal to Britain. "Difference" and "variety" of the positive type were not those that fostered national fragmentation but those that would help further the state's larger economic plan. Thus, the curriculum for a child living in a reed hut and engaged in the raising of buffaloes should differ from the curriculum for a child living in an urban industrial community ('Aqrawi, 1942, pp. 135, 209, 215).

The question of uniformity versus difference in the curriculum became one of the main sources of conflict between the pragmatists and their opponents. al-Husri insisted that differentiation would divide the nation and block future unity. Other critics argued that it was also regressive because it would track youth into their future careers from the time they entered

---

[4]al-Husri's critique points suggestively to the possibility that American educators such as Monroe may have interpreted central pragmatist concepts such as the "activity-based curriculum" differently depending on whether they were writing about American or Iraqi schools.

primary school. In response, some pragmatists protested that their understanding of a differentiated curriculum was not synonymous with occupational specialization or social stratification. The point, they argued, was not to teach students *particular* crafts, or to tie them to particular future vocations, but rather to create modern, industrious citizens, confident in their ability to shape their environment through their own activity. Since the environment of rural students was different from that of urban students, it followed that they should use different curricula ('Aqrawi, 1942, p. 215).

But there were many ambiguities in pragmatist proposals for differentiated education. The reports of international specialists, from the 1932 Monroe Commission to the World Bank and UN missions of the early 1950s, consistently emphasized the importance of agricultural education to Iraq's future development. They were clear that rural schools must aim at keeping peasant youth in the rural areas, both to increase agricultural production and to minimize political instability in urban areas. The Monroe report argued that the rural curriculum should "increase among rural youth respect for manual labor and the desire to have a part in the basic economic activities of agriculture which has always been the chief means of support of the people of this ancient land" (Monroe, 1932, p. 120). The emphasis on agricultural production as the key to national development was joined to the pragmatist philosophy of "learning by doing," or the activity-based curriculum, to argue for near-universal vocational education. "The village or farm boy particularly learns by seeing and doing. His best education cannot come from books [...] Schoolroom work of an academic character should have a definite place, but a subordinate one" (Monroe, 1932, p. 29). Similarly, a 1952 World Bank mission argued that Iraqi schoolchildren "passively absorb information and learn comparatively little by actually doing things." It recommended that Iraq's existing "book schools" be transformed into "work schools," which would "inculcate an appreciation of the value and dignity of hard, manual work" (International Bank for Reconstruction and Development [IBRD], 1952, pp. 64, 402, 391).

A major stumbling block to implementing an activity-based and urban/rural differentiated curriculum in Iraq, according to many of its own advocates, was that manual laborers in Iraq did not want to send their children to school in order to become manual laborers, and peasants did not want to send their children to school in order to become peasants. This problem was often blamed on "traditional" Arab understandings of education, which had "been handed down through the ages to the present generation" and "makes both teachers and parents put undue stress on subject matter in the schools. We can see its effects in the fact that many a parent looks with suspicion at such things as physical education, manual training and the like" ('Aqrawi, 1942, p. 177). The World Bank agreed that the "[e]radication of this aversion to manual work should form an important objective of educational policy at all stages." For good measure, the bank supported its recommendation with a Qur'anic verse on God's appreciation of manual labor (IBRD, 1952, p. 418).

The argument for differentiating the curriculum by sex emerged out of the same logic, linking the aims of development to the conceptual vocabulary of pragmatism. But there were differences in how the "varieties of life and environment" in Iraq were envisioned when it came to gender. 'Aqrawi proposed five different public school curricula: For urban, rural, tribal, female, and mountain-dwelling Kurdish students ('Aqrawi, 1942, p. 216). Among several noteworthy aspects of this proposal is that one kind of difference — that of being female — not only overlaps with but trumps every other kind of difference, so that urban, rural, tribal, and mountain-dwelling Kurdish girls would all follow the same curriculum. It turned out that differentiation itself was sex-specific, relevant only to male students. 'Aqrawi suggested that this is because female students were likely to be future homemakers and thus their environment and the materials they worked on were the same, regardless of where they lived, an explanation that arguably contradicts his claim that curriculum differentiation was not about tracking youth for future vocations ('Aqrawi, 1942, p. 237).

The notion that female education should be uniform while male education was differentiated was a recurring theme in the new discourse. Thus, in the early 1940s al-Jamali, 'Aqrawi, and other pragmatists launched a campaign to modify the academic preparatory school curriculum, which was divided into literary and scientific tracks in both boys' and girls' schools. For the boys' curriculum, they proposed increasing the level of differentiation from two to four tracks, corresponding to science, mathematics, literature, and social science. At the same time, they proposed eliminating differentiation altogether in the girls' schools, so that all female secondary students would follow the same curriculum, oriented toward domestic skills. The proposals were temporarily instituted and then revoked after generating much controversy. But they remain a striking example of the gendered nature of pragmatist education for "real life." While in al-Husri's worldview, the household represented particularity, fragmentation, and immersion in local difference, in the pragmatist vision it promised to be a unifying element, the one universal environment found in every corner of the nation. But this national uniformity was produced through the difference of gender.

What the School Builds the Home Destroys:
The Gendering of Education, 1932–1952

Not all pragmatist proposals were implemented, even when their strongest theoretical advocates reached positions of power in the ministry. In the 1960s and beyond, educators would still be complaining that Iraqi classrooms fostered passive learning, with the teacher in front lecturing to students sitting quietly in their chairs. The question of agricultural and other vocational training remained a topic of much dispute — as well as public resistance — and the cause of many confusing shifts in policy. But some pragmatist proposals had dramatic and lasting effects on the Iraqi school experience. One of these was the differentiation of the curriculum by sex, instituted through the gradual expansion of mandatory home economics for female students.

In many ways, home economics was treated like the other types of vocational education in Iraq — agricultural, commercial, and industrial — which were specifically designed for boys in secondary school. Yet it was unlike those in important ways, not least in that, by the mid-1940s, it was taught to all girls at every age and level of schooling. Contrary to the claims of many pragmatists, the differentiation of the curriculum by sex aimed in part at enabling and disabling particular vocational skills and therefore futures. But that was not all it did. It also aimed at enabling and disabling certain capabilities, motivations, habits, social behaviors, and mental approaches to problems. This process of enabling and disabling was a process of constructing gendered citizens.

In 1932, the Monroe report praised both the Ministry of Education and the Iraqi public for the quantitative expansion of girls' education up to that time, commenting that "no feature of the educational situation offered more surprise to the members of the Commission than the very genuine interest that everywhere appeared in the education of girls and women" (Monroe, 1932, p. 56). But it criticized the education of girls on qualitative grounds, arguing that it should be "differentiated from that of the boys" (Monroe, 1932, p. 162). The report is clear that it was a girl's future status as a mother that made her gendered education essential:

> To expect a modern school to translate scientific knowledge into the habits and customs of a people without the education of women is a vain hope. Nor can social life be modernized when the school instructs in one set of ideas and the home in another (Monroe, 1932, pp. 133–134).

The sense that ignorant women were undoing the work of the school was not limited to Western specialists. The Iraqi educator 'Abd al-Razzaq al-Hilali compared children to raw materials and schools to factories, writing that you don't put raw materials into a factory without first "spending a lot of time rinsing and scrubbing off the harmful substances" attached to them. Yet in Iraq, children were allowed to enter school covered with all the "harmful substances" — i.e., the ignorant customs and superstitions — picked up in their families, so that "what the school builds the home destroys" (Hilali, 1946, p. 18). While al-Husri and other nationalists were in complete agreement that feminine ignorance in the household was a barrier to progress, the pragmatist belief that environmental influences in the child's earliest years were irreversible significantly amplified this threat in their understanding. As one educator put it, the child in the early stage of life is like "a malleable instrument in the hands of his mother: Easy to influence, quick to submit." Unlike al-Husri, the pragmatists believed that if a woman was ignorant, her child could not be saved by national institutions such as the school and the military. Instead, "the child will be a victim of her ignorance" (Sa'id, 1949, p. 85).

In primary school, differentiation of the curriculum was accomplished primarily though the subject of "drawing and manual arts," a focal point of pragmatist reform efforts as it seemed the most amenable to an activity-based approach. In 1928, it was allotted 11 periods in the six years of primary school, and these decreased as the pupil progressed from first to sixth grade ('Aqrawi, 1942, p. 181). It was seen primarily as a way of teaching motor skills to very young children. In the 1930s and 1940s, it became increasingly differentiated by sex as its time in the schedule steadily lengthened. For girls, the subject was changed to cover "needlework and embroidery, knitting, and making such things as doilies, aprons, and baby clothes. They also learnt how to wash and clean clothes, polish windows and furniture, and prepare the tea table" (Matthews and 'Aqrawi, 1949, p. 152). By the 1945–1946 school year, it comprised 22 periods of primary school, third only behind Arabic and math, and its allotted time increased rather than decreased as the pupil advanced from first to sixth grade. Rather than teaching young children motor skills, it now seemed designed in large part to produce gender difference as the child developed. The additional time in the curriculum was created by reducing the periods of Arabic, English, geography, history, and religion. Besides math, the only subjects not affected were the other three activity-based, real-life subjects favored by the pragmatists: Object lessons and hygiene, civics and morals, and physical education and singing. The last of these was also newly differentiated by sex, so that an Iraqi girl now followed a female-only curriculum for about 20% of the time she spent in primary school (Matthews and 'Aqrawi, 1949, p. 149).

Home economics at the secondary school level developed in two different ways. The first was the foundation of a "vocational" home economics secondary school in 1932, with an enrollment of 53 girls. Its main function was to train teachers for girls' primary schools, a role that became more important as these schools expanded their home economics curriculum. But in 1946, its mission was modified to encompass the "dual purpose" of producing teachers and "intelligent homemakers," and in 1952 it was modified again so that its primary aim was to train homemakers (Matthews and 'Aqrawi, 1949, p. 177; Ministry of Education, 1952, p. 60). The school — at least in official discourse and actual curriculum — thus moved further and further away from the concept of vocational training for feminine occupations outside the home and toward the notion of homemaking as the primary vocation for which the school existed. Yet it is clear that only a tiny fraction of future Iraqi homemakers were expected to attend this school, and in that sense officials could hardly have been very optimistic about its impact on society as a direct form of vocational training. In addition, whatever the school's mission might claim, its graduates remained in high demand as primary school teachers and recruits for the higher teachers' training college. The modifications in the school's mission thus represented primarily a discursive/political shift that also had effects on the content of girls' education.

The second change to female secondary education was the modification of the curriculum in the academic (nonvocational) schools. Revisions in 1940–1943 added two mandatory periods of home economics for the three years of intermediate school and the two years of preparatory school. As in primary school, the curriculum became more differentiated as the student advanced through the grade levels. In addition to the two core courses required for all five years of secondary school, girls at the preparatory level were required to take additional courses. Those in the scientific track took two periods covering medical aspects of child-care and hygiene, and those in the literary track took four periods in child psychology and development (Matthews and 'Aqrawi, 1949, pp. 166–168).

At the higher education level, Queen 'Aliya College for women in Baghdad overhauled its curriculum in 1946–1947, changing its areas of specialization from literature, chemistry, social work, geography, history, and physics to home arts, education, English, fine arts, and secretarial work (Kadry, 1958, p. 12).

Unfit for Marriage and Motherhood: The Crisis of Girls' Education and the Age of Development, 1952–1958

In the 1957–1958 school year, on the eve of the July 1958 revolution that toppled the Hashemite monarchy, there was still a significant sex disparity in Iraqi education. The ratio of female to male primary school students was 1:3, with about 22% of Iraqi girls and 65% of boys aged 6–12 attending school. But the quantitative expansion of girls' education between 1932 and 1958 was not insignificant. The number of girls enrolled in primary school increased from 8,532 to 108,552 and those in secondary school from 176 to 13,627 ('Aqrawi, 1942, p. 157; Qaysi, 1983, pp. 46, 51).

In 1952–1953, the ministry launched its most comprehensive home economics campaign to date. The campaign was driven by political and economic factors, both global and domestic. Politically, it was motivated by the growing sense among Iraqi officials that the female education system was not only failing in its primary mission of training modern mothers capable of raising strong and healthy citizens, but that it was having the opposite effect: Producing a generation of educated Iraqi women who were *resistant* to marriage, domesticity and motherhood, and who seemed to believe that they could better serve the nation's interests by overthrowing the existing political order than by learning how to efficiently manage a household. The increasing political unrest in Iraqi society, and particularly the rising popularity of the Iraqi Communist Party (ICP) among students, was a clear subtext in many of the discussions around the "crisis" of girls' education. Moreover, there is much anecdotal evidence to suggest that the widespread anxiety among officials that female students were especially attracted to Marxist thought in general, and the ICP in particular, was not unfounded. These fears could hardly have been assuaged by the foundation of a women's front of the ICP in 1952, and still less by the 1948 *Wathba* and 1952 *Intifada* uprisings, which shook the monarchical regime to its foundation and in which leftist students of both sexes played a major role.

In 1953, one year after the *Intifada*, the foundation of the communist women's league, and the completion of Ava Milam's FAO report, the ministry devoted a full issue of its journal *al-Mu'allim al-Jadid* (The New Teacher) to the crisis and future of girls' education in Iraq. The articles in this issue are primarily an attempt to justify the ministry's decision to overhaul and expand the home economics curriculum, a process that had already begun. As Safa' Khulusi explained the perceived problem: "For a quarter of a century we have forgotten the difference between a woman and a man [...] and have given the woman a man's education." The result is that "a class of women has appeared in Iraq who despise cooking, housework and child raising [...] We have made women unfit for marriage and motherhood" (Khulusi, 1953, pp. 61–63).

As a historical narrative, the argument had some flaws. In fact, it was in September 1928, or exactly one quarter of a century before this article appeared, that a sex-differentiated curriculum was *introduced* in Iraq, with the addition of a home economics requirement in primary school. And, as have seen, by 1953 no female student in Iraq's primary or secondary school system was receiving a "man's education." Only when she reached the college level could an Iraqi woman receive the same education as her male counterpart, and even then only outside Queen 'Aliya women's college and the higher teacher's training college, where most women at this level were enrolled. But the issue was obviously not about historical research. It was about the politicization of Iraqi youth in the postwar period, and the sense that this tendency was both more prevalent and more dangerous among female students. Another article asserted that "materialist philosophies" (i.e., communism) had convinced women that the mere "affirmation of a woman's femininity" was "a sign of reaction and backwardness [...] with the aim of destroying her rights and enslaving her" (Bazzaz, 1953, pp. 45–46).

In *al-Mu'allim al-Jadid* between 1952 and 1954, proposals to address the crisis of girls' education were diverse, from courses on sex education to more religious study. But in the end, the solutions pursued by the ministry were oddly familiar: More differentiation in the curriculum on the basis of sex, and more attention to "real-life" rather than "academic" learning for female students. Thus, even the curriculum in the vocational home economics school was found to be too scholarly, and a new one was drafted, "with the aim of minimizing the hours of theory and emphasizing the hours of practice, so that the graduate of this school is first and foremost a housewife" (Ministry of Education, 1952, p. 60).

Ironically, it became common in this period to blame the West for the purported emphasis on academic rather than real-life learning in Iraq's schools, which had filled girls' heads with frivolous and/or rebellious ideas. The Arab nationalist professor 'Abd al-Rahman al-Bazzaz wrote that in a developed country, where citizens had the luxury to pursue knowledge for its own sake, it might make sense for the state to provide an intellectual education for all youth. In a developing country like Iraq, however, it was inappropriate and dangerous: "Science for science's sake, education for education's sake, art for art's sake, does not work for us today" (Bazzaz, 1953, p. 41). But this discourse in fact echoed the decades-long criticism of Iraqi education by Western specialists, and was invoked for the same purpose: To argue that a girl's education should be determined by her sex and focus on domestic skills.

The political motivations driving the new campaign dovetailed with economic factors, national and global. Shortages during World War II had sparked the growth of some domestic industries in Iraq, mostly in consumer goods such as textiles, soap, shoes, and cigarettes. This process was largely reversed after the war by "the flooding of the home market with foreign industrial goods," especially textiles (Haj, 1997, p. 56). But in both cases, expansion was limited by Iraq's small consumer market. This constraint was ultimately a structural one, linked to the agrarian crisis, which ensured the subsistence-level poverty of most Iraqis. But government officials were motivated to find technical solutions to the country's economic woes, and their optimism soared after the renegotiated oil treaty of January 1952 vastly increased state revenues, "opening possibilities for economic development throughout the social order" (Haj, 1997, p. 70).

At the same time, the Point Four agreement signed with the US in 1951, the World Bank mission in 1952, and programs established by UN agencies between 1951 and 1954, provided unprecedented levels of foreign expertise for state-led development projects. The larger context was the global expansion of American political power and consumer exports, the pro-Western alignment of the Iraqi monarchy as Cold War divisions deepened, and the dawning of the age of development with its dominant institutional conviction (at least in the "free world") that the problems of underdeveloped nations could be overcome through the opening of national markets and the proper application of technical know-how.

As with previous home economics programs, those promoted by postwar development specialists aimed to improve health and productivity and shape the nation's future citizens and workers. But there was a greater emphasis on education that would improve household budgeting among the poor, create new desires for the comforts and pleasures of bourgeois domesticity, and teach women purchasing skills. One aspect of the shift was a conceptual reorientation of women's household labor from the sphere of production to that of consumption. Thus, while the curriculum established in 1943 covered "sewing, embroidery, knitting, cooking and home cleaning" the FAO now recommended that "more attention be given in schools to clothing selection, dress design and textiles, and that less emphasis be placed on embroidery" (Milam, 1952, p. 3). A more detailed 1954 FAO report explained that the education of intelligent female consumers in the purchase of manufactured textiles would be based on the "results of research conducted in [Western] universities, government departments and industries on fibers and fabrics, textile finishes and textile strength etc along with courses on art principles and design" (Brodie, 1954, p. 2).

In the end, the 1952 FAO proposal to triple home economics requirements in girls' secondary schools was never fully implemented, in part because it required a dramatic increase in the number of female teachers qualified to teach home economics, and this target was not reached prior to the 1958 revolution. But FAO representatives were actively involved in the initial stages of the project. These centered on the preparation of teachers, through yet another overhaul of the curriculum at Queen 'Aliya college and the construction of new "vocational" secondary schools for home economics in numerous Iraq provinces, to supplement the one in Baghdad. The number of students attending these schools increased more than tenfold between 1952 and 1958, from 236 to 2,528 (Batatu, 1978, p. 477). In 1954–1955, for the first time, it exceeded the combined number of female students attending the women's teacher training institutes for primary school and the higher teacher's training college for secondary school (Hasan, 1957, pp. 3–4).

UNESCO also sent specialists to help train peasant women in home economics at the Dujaila Land Settlement Project. Somewhat counter-intuitively, experts attached to the UN's education wing, UNESCO, were thus leading the home economics program for adult peasant women, while those attached to its agricultural organization, FAO, were leading the Baghdad-based program to expand home economics in the school system. The field of home economics was seen as critical to all aspects of national development, and thus the jurisdiction of various UN agencies over its expansion in developing countries was often unclear. Officially, the UN had designated FAO as the organization responsible for knowledge production and program implementation in home economics, which became a source of conflict between it and UNESCO over the Iraq-based programs in the 1950s.

The fact that home economics was officially housed at FAO and not UNESCO reflects the constitutive connection of home economics to agricultural development in the US, where the field first emerged at the rural land-grant universities and aimed specifically at the education of farm women. It also reflects the importance of food and nutrition at the micro-economic level to development ideology in the postwar period, and the related fact that food consumption as well as production fell within the purview of the FAO. The focus on nutrient consumption as an issue of individual knowledge and choice is related, in turn, to a number of important development concepts in this period, not least of which was the notion that national development was blocked not only or even primarily by global economic forces or national political structures but by local human ignorance and underdevelopment, especially of women. These beliefs helped to reshape the classroom experience of many Iraqi girls between 1952 and 1958, while the country's political and agrarian crises continued to deepen.

RETHINKING THE BA'THIST PERIOD

Hamit Bozarslan

For any observer of the Middle East, the Iraqi Ba'th regime, which left behind at least 500,000 victims of state coercion and hundreds of thousands of dead on the battlefields of the First and Second Gulf Wars (1980–1988, 1990–1991), constitutes an enigma. This enigma becomes particularly profound when one takes a broader historical perspective into account and compares the trajectory of Iraq with the two other Arab countries which experienced similarly radical regime change in the 1950s and 1960s: Egypt and Syria.

Like the previous or subsequent military coups in Syria and Egypt, the Iraqi military coup in 1958 was also an outcome of massive urban contestation and mobilizations which took place in the period both before and after the creation of Israel. In the three countries, the "military option" and authoritarianism were widely welcomed by the urban population as the only way of creating a national "power" able to resist "Zionism" and "imperialism". Likewise, in the three countries, wide sections of the intelligentsia legitimized the military coups. One observes, however, that by 1958, a specific "Iraqi pattern", different from those of Syria and Egypt, had already come to light and had some effect in determining the country's evolution over the coming decades. Obviously, in Syria and in Egypt the "revolutionary regimes" also instituted single-party rule; in Syria, but also, to a lesser degree, in Egypt, opposition groups were brutally repressed. The suppression of the Muslim Brothers' revolt in Hama (1982) showed that when threatened, this "other Ba'thist regime" could act as brutally as its Iraqi counterpart. Still, within a couple of decades, both regimes had transformed themselves into bureaucratic and authoritarian structures whose main aim

143

was to ensure their own survival, and for the most part did not institution-alize wide scale coercion as the cornerstone of their rule. In contrast to these "hard" or "soft" authoritarian trajectories, Iraqis first endured a dramatic increase in political violence between 1958 and 1968, which occasionally took the shape of *pogroms*. Thereafter Iraq underwent a very harsh dicta-torship between 1968 and 1979, and with Saddam Husayn's accession to the presidency, experienced what many scholars (Makiya, 1989; Saghieh, 2007), including myself, have described as a totalitarian regime between 1979 and 1991–1992.

Why did such experiences occur in Iraq and not in the two other Arab countries, not to mention other Arab states? There is no simple answer to this question; one can only suggest that a combination of distinctive factors may have contributed to this Middle Eastern "singularity". The first factor is historical: Since the formal independence of the country in 1932, the various regimes in Iraq achieved an almost total autonomy of action at the domestic level and acquired, more than in Egypt or Syria, the *habitus* of using massive coercion to overcome social, political, ethnic, and sectarian conflict. The suppression of the Assyrians in 1933, and of the Kurds and Shi'is at various historical moments thereafter, transformed internal war-making into an efficient power-building instrument. Second, the country's military and civil elites have been exposed, much more than their Syrian and Egyptian counterparts, to the impact of the interwar ideologies and to the social-Darwinist versions of Arab nationalism (Wien, 2006). While being an important stronghold of British domination in the Middle East, the Iraqi monarchy itself contributed to the wide-scale spread of ideological radicalism. The processes of radicalization that took place in Iraq were also different from those in Egypt and Syria. It is true that the 1948 *Wathba* was much less violent than the Egyptian revolution of 1952, but symbolically, in its claims and its anti-monarchist and anti-imperialist slogans, it was the bearer of an unprecedented degree of radicalization in the Arab world. In a certain sense, it was the continuation of this process well after the 1958 coup that created a paradoxical situation and led to a radical bifurcation, both in ideological and axiological terms.

A third element concerns the country's social and demographic fabric: If Iraq was not more or less "artificial" than neighboring Syria, it was eth-nically, religiously, and politically much more plural than Syria, not to mention Egypt. Thus, only the protection of its internal plurality at the cost of the "national unity" that the military regimes and the Ba'th dic-tatorship tried to impose upon the society could have prevented the use of unlimited violence and state coercion to resolve internal conflict. Even before the 1968 coup, the campaigns against the Jews, the Kurdish revolt of 1961, and Qasim's decision to suppress it by military means, and finally, the wide scale massacres of communists and Nasserists during the first Ba'th military coup of 1963, left very few chances for peaceful coexistence between the various ethnic and sectarian communities and the main political actors. They also led to the redefinition of ethnic, religious and political "otherness" as potential expressions of enmity, betrayal and "vital threats" to the nation. Finally, in contrast to Syria and Egypt, Iraqi oil revenues have allowed the state to win a large degree of autonomy *vis-à-vis* society; reinforced by the "security rent", i.e., direct financial aid or credits obtained from the Western countries or from the Arab world, in the 1980s, which allowed the state to develop its internal coercive organs (Middle East Watch, 1994).

***

After the country became independent in 1932, and after Bakr Sidqi's military coup in 1936, the army played an important role under both the monarchy and the republic between 1958 and 1968. It protected the state and used massive coercion on its behalf, and was thus at the same time one of the key threats to the state. The 1958 military coup showed that radical, nationalist and/or left-wing currents were widespread within the military, not only among the young officers born after the foundation of the state. In spite of this historical legacy, however, the Iraqi military's evolution has followed a radically different path from that of its Syrian and Egyptian counterparts. There is no doubt that the political arena in these two countries has been to a large extent marked and controlled by strong leaders; still, the military as an institution continued to play an important role and ultimately remained the main pillar of both these authoritarian regimes. But the personalization of the Syrian and Egyptian regimes did not take place at the expense of the military *mu'assassa*. On the contrary: Hafiz al-Asad and his son Bashar, Nasser and his successors Sadat and Mubarak, were all keen to improve the economic conditions of the military caste either through policies of privileged resource allocation or through the use of legal and illegal resources such as trans-border commerce and economic enterprises. To some extent, they were able to remain in power thanks to their capacity to arbitrate internal conflicts between military commanders. They also created new intelligence organs, but the military in these countries challenged these new organs' growing influence by transforming themselves into a sort of *mukhabarat*.

In contrast, in Iraq, the fate of Qasim, and subsequently of the regime of the 'Arif brothers, showed that military cohesion was far too weak and that neither military resources nor internal *esprit de corps* could serve as the basis of a durable power system. It is true that Hasan al-Bakr, the mentor of Saddam Husayn and officially president between 1968 and 1979, was from the military; but everyone knew that his space of maneuver was rather narrowed by Saddam Husayn, who was not a soldier but a Ba'thist *pistolero*, and by a range of different parallel and personalized security organizations that were already under his command. With Saddam officially in power in 1979, the military lost any kind of autonomy, and, like the Ba'th Party itself, became totally subordinated to the new *ra'is*.

The Iraqi Ba'th regime was both a product of the Iraqi crisis of ungovernability that the militaries were unable to resolve, and an answer to it. However, it is astonishing to observe that the Ba'th regime's long-lasting political stability was not linked to its efficacy as the country's *de facto* single party. On the contrary, by the end of the 1960s, the Party had already become an empty organ.

More than to any party network, Saddam Husayn owed his success to four distinct but complementary power-building resources. The first resource was that of traditional *'asabiyya*; as Khayrullah Tulfah, the uncle of Saddam Husayn put it bluntly, "kinship is thicker than ideology" (Aburish, 2000, p. 23). The successful use of the mechanisms of *'asabiyya* transformed the Takriti Sunni tribes (rather than the Sunni community as a whole, as is often wrongly alleged), and among them, *primus inter pares*, the Albu Nasir, Saddam Husayn's own tribe, into the basis of the durability of power. Therefore, the 'Sunni domination paradigm' in Iraq should be questioned, historicized and much more nuanced. A careful reading of the Ba'th period shows that the social basis of power was more regional than sectarian, but it was certainly highly cohesive. The second resource was radically distinct from the first, and allowed the ruler to dispose of wide autonomy *vis-à-vis* his social basis, including his own tribe and his family: A "household *'asabiyya*" (Hourani, 1990, p. 308) which included "slaves, mercenaries, and bureaucrats" allowed the creation of a reservoir of loyal men highly instrumental in controlling the society. The third resource was a pan-Iraqi and pan-Arab nationalist *da'wa*, which, in contrast to the regime's jealous attachment to Iraq as a sovereign state and despite the strength of Iraqi nationalism, was exacerbated at the official level in order to give suprapolitical legitimization to the ruler. Very distinct from cultural forms of Arab nationalism, including the brand advocated by Sati' al-Husri, this

nationalism appeared to be social-Darwinist in ideology as well as in practice. Finally, the last resource was Saddam's ability to create a modern
bureaucratic apparatus, including but not exclusively, in the area of state
coercion.

The mobilization of these resources also showed the regime's skill to combine very classical and very modern registers of power. Obviously, far more
than Qasim, the 'Arif brothers or his mentor Hasan al-Bakr, Saddam Husayn
had the profile of a *malik*; neither his very repressive politics, nor his often
clement, even "generous" attitudes, were perverse by-products of his system.
On the contrary, they were heuristic behaviors attesting that his personal
sovereignty could not be restricted by any external or internal mechanisms
of check and balances. His novel, *Zabiba and the King*, written in the aftermath of the 1991 War, gives us a fairly accurate vision of what he meant
by state and politics: A domain governed solely by a cruel but wise and
just tyrant. But at the same time, he was also the *malik* of a quite different profile than the classical power-holders in Islamic societies — a *malik*
with a social-Darwinist vision of the world and Bismarckian projects for
his country and for the Arab world. Obviously, in his understanding, the
state was a *dawla*, whose leadership was decided by destiny, rather than a
Weberian construct. But this *dawla* was also of an entirely new kind: The
classical ideal of the Islamic state understood as a guarantor of *nizam* and
the administration of *'adala* was replaced, in his "political philosophy", by
permanent turmoil, fear and uncertainty for everyone, including those in
power. The durability of Saddam Husayn's state depended not only on its
capacity to organize repressive politics against large sections of the society,
but also on the *malik*'s own skill to exert a high degree of internal coercion
within the state apparatus.

Here, again, there is a sharp contrast between the Iraqi and Syrian systems. In Syria, as long as he did not join the opposition, any dignitary could
choose to resign. Not only was "exit" possible, but internal conflicts within
the state have always existed and except in a very few cases (such as the
marginalization of Rif'at al-Asad, brother of the Syrian president, in the
1980s), were peacefully arbitrated by the *ra'is*. Obviously, some important
former leaders, as Salah al-Din Bitar, were assassinated under the Asad
regime, and others have been imprisoned or exiled, but I am not aware of
a single public purge within the inner circles of power. In Iraq, in contrast,
Saddam Husayn's accession to the presidency in 1979 was accompanied by
massive coercion within the state, with about a third of the Ba'th leadership
executed after a dramatic speech on the part of the *rais* accusing them of

betrayal. While other internal purges were not as bloody, they showed that while anyone could be dismissed by the ruler, no one could opt out of his own free will. The notion of "exit" that Albert O. Hirschman considers as one the main alternatives to "loyalty" and "voice" was simply unthinkable in the Iraq of Saddam Husayn.

***

For more than a decade, researchers have agreed on the massive coercion utilized by the state against Iraqi society under the Ba'th regime, particularly under Saddam Husayn's presidency, but the degree of coercion *within the state* during the same period has not been sufficiently studied. This is an extremely crucial issue in political sociology and political science, not least because it often (but not always) constitutes a distinctive feature of totalitarian regimes. The question of internal coercion is very different from that of the existence or nonexistence of internal conflicts and competing forces within a totalitarian state. As many scholars have remarked, there were many serious internal conflicts within the Nazi regime that the Führer was not always able or willing to arbitrate. One of the features of Nazism, however, was its ability to use coercion within the state apparatus, and even within the Nazi Party. The extermination of the SA as early as 1933 is the most important manifestation of this internal "purification". This episode had its own logic and was part of a specific political agenda, but it also has to be understood as a clear signal of the readiness of the regime to use massive coercion against any political group or any section of the society. The same observation can be made concerning the Soviet Union. What made the Stalinist regime totalitarian was not the "totalization" of power through an internal chain of command, but the capacity of the regime to use internal coercion within the state and to maintain its cohesion by spreading fear among all the ruling elite. The Moscow trials in 1936 left no doubt that anyone within the leadership could become a target of state coercion, which had a tremendous impact on society as a whole. Similarly, the elimination of some high-ranking communist leaders during the Cultural Revolution in China by 1966 was, I believe, the founding act of the Maoist totalitarian regime, which was indeed very different from the previous Communist single party regime. In each of these cases, the passage to a totalitarian order was also a necessary condition for regime consolidation and continuity. This internal coercion had a further implication: It was impossible to leave the ruling circle, or the security apparatus or the organization of the single party organizations. Thus, at least for a given period, the state ceased to be a field of power relations as is the case under many other authoritarian regimes.

Once again, the organic unity of the state does not prohibit internal conflicts within the high-ranking elite; as Chérine Chams shows, an elite shift was almost institutionalized throughout the Saddam decades. The internal turnover was ultimately decided by Saddam Husayn himself, but it was also linked to the search for the most rational choices in the economic and bureaucratic fields. Opting for a particular economic policy to the detriment of another is undoubtedly evidence of the existence of internal debates and even conflicts. But the actors in these internal competitions were entirely subordinate to the personal allegiance of the ruler, who destroyed the very possibility of the existence of factions or autonomous bodies within the state. Moreover, as the two Gulf Wars attest, the ruler had unrestricted autonomy of action, and while he could adopt a rational reform policy in the economic or bureaucratic fields, he could also fix a millenarian military horizon, which might well lead to the undermining of his "positivist" reformist measures.[1] The simultaneous institutional and cognitive impossibility of creating autonomous entities and spaces within the state explains largely why in Iraq, as in other totalitarian regimes, the military also became totally subordinated to the ruler's will. Obviously, in Saddam Husayn's Iraq, the army continued to play a role as the defender of the state and its war-making arm, and, when required, it was also used as a coercive force within the country. But in this second role it was largely marginalized by the internal security organizations, which were in charge of spying on the army as well as on each other.

***

Of course, massive intra-state coercion, or the use of coercion against different social, political, ethnic, and sectarian categories, does not mean that the leader had effective control of the totality of the state apparatus; internal or not, coercion is rather an outcome of a process that the chief sets in motion. Undoubtedly, it is legitimized by the reference to the chief and the sacralised cause that he incarnates, but as Achim Rohde's comparative reading shows, the ruler does not necessarily master the disruptive coercive process in its entirety. This process, however, gives birth to other systemic effects as well as to blind and exclusive allegiance to the chief. The process may be more or less haphazard, but it has a strong political meaning, convincing the society,

---

[1] On the paradoxical link between positivism and millenarianism, see Leca (1984).

and more importantly, every collective entity and every individual, of the utter impossibility of any kind of organized or individual resistance and of the absolute necessity of a unquestioning and "natural" obedience. That is probably one of the most important reasons why social and political violence or protest is impossible under totalitarian regimes: Collective violence ceases in fact to be an axiological repertoire because it becomes meaningless. While coercion makes terrible sense under these regimes, violence is scarcely unintelligible. No wonder then, except in the Kurdish regions — where the control of the state was relatively weak and the geographical conditions for a long-lasting guerrilla war existed — there was almost no manifestation of violent contest in Saddam Husayn's Iraq between 1979 and 1991, either in the urban or in the rural areas, or in the Sunni areas, or, except for a few short-lived episodes, in the South.[2]

The transformation of the society into an ensemble of individuals disconnected from any autonomous social structures is indeed an absolute condition for the creation of mechanical obedience, even when the price of obedience is very high. Parallel to this obedience, however, the territories of resistance are also largely redefined under totalitarian systems: while not compromising or in some cases, not compromising quite so much, becomes a form of dissidence, individual lives, and occasionally, limited social, scientific or artistic circles, are transformed into the main spaces of passive resistance.

***

The totalitarian shift in a regime's trajectory means a total occupation of the space of visibility by the presence, symbols, monuments and agents of the state. This occupation is not the kind of occupation that becomes a part of the urban landscape and that everyone integrates without either challenging it or living under its permanent threat. There is a qualitative distinction between the control of authoritarian regimes and totalitarian regimes over space; in the first case, power is "routinized" and the effective presence of the state manifests itself through punctual excursions like police raids.

---

[2]The 1991 *Intifada* which followed the massive defeat of Iraq in the Second Gulf War showed that there was a difference between mechanical obedience to the ruler and his legitimization. After having been abandoned by the Americans, the society broadly speaking became victims of fear; the Republican Guard and the security apparatus remained loyal to the Ruler, and even within the army very few decided to opt for dissidence; the efficiency of the repression in some symbolic places as Najaf was enough to suppress the uprising, which opened the way to massive executions within the Shi'i community.

In the second, totalitarian control, this presence is articulated by the sense of permanent fear and it is efficient enough to create the impression that the state is effectively or potentially present in every aspect of daily life.

The shift to totalitarianism also means a radical change in political language, where concepts of "betrayal", "traitors", or "enemies" occupy a central place. Those concepts were obviously present in Iraqi (and Middle Eastern) political language especially after the 1948 defeat. In fact, in the worldview of many contesters in the 1950s and 1960s, the Arab leaders had not only been unable to defend the Arab lands, but betrayed the nation only in order to protect their own positions, and did so deliberately. In Egypt and in Syria, the concepts of betrayal and internal enmity were widely used to apply either to the *anciens régimes* or to opposition groups. In Iraq however, these concepts were used in rather a singular manner — they were at once vague and codified. They were vague, in the sense that the category of "traitors" and "enemies" was not defined *a priori*. On the contrary, a Kurdish leader like Jalal Talabani could become a would-be-"friend" at least for a short period in 1983, but other previously unsuspected categories and groups, like high-ranking Ba'thists, could also be defined as traitors and enemies. At the same time, these concepts were extremely codified, not least because the "traitors" and "enemies" were regarded, by their very existence, as vital threats to the society and were indeed "biologically" dealt with: It was often not only the "enemy" and the "traitor" but also his/her family and offspring were transformed into a single block of enmity. As in totalitarian regimes, the moment of execution of the "enemy" was celebrated as "a monument erected in the name of trust in the Revolution" — according to Tariq 'Aziz — the bodies of "traitors" were transformed into symbols of a war going well beyond an individual's own person.

***

In contrast to the 1979–1991/1992 period, the second period of Saddam Husayn's rule was not marked by massive or systemic use of state coercion. Paradoxically, the regime not only survived the calamitous Second Gulf War, but retained an astonishing durability. There are many explanations for this: As David Baran has shown, Saddam Husayn was no longer obliged to bear the burden of socialism, Ba'thism or even Arab nationalism or to suffer any kind of ideological constraint (Baran, 2004). He had a free hand to offer a large space of maneuver to non-state actors, including some religious groups, to rehabilitate tribalism as an important element in Iraqi society and invent a new political engineering based on policies of resource alloca-tion to selected tribes. Coercion did not disappear even after the extremely brutal repression of the *Intifada* and the massive spate of executions which followed, but it became random and targeted, namely, the authors of real or would-be military coups, young men who tried to escape from military service and women accused of prostitution. The random nature of the new forms of coercion had still a strong political meaning: Their high visibility (amputations, public displays of heads ...) (van der Stoel, 1992) showed that the regime could target anyone, at any time. That was also the mean-ing of the last plebiscite, which took place shortly before the 2003 invasion, in which Saddam Husayn obtained 100% of the vote. This did not of course mean that he wanted the Iraqis and the outside world to believe that 100% of Iraqis had actually voted for him. Rather, the meaning of the plebiscite was that when required, the leader was able to use 100% coercion.

A final issue that should be mentioned here is the legacy of this period. At present the situation in Iraq cannot afford the luxury of the kind of reflective evaluation that would try to understand the dynamics of state coercion between 1968 and 2003, and its disruptive and irreversible effects on the society. The 'de-Ba'thification' process that Fanny Lafourcade analyses in her article, and the intense violence which followed this disastrous step (which had been decided upon without remotely taking Iraq's historical circumstances into account) does not provide the detachment needed for such a critical reading of the past. Iraq has first to staunch the bleeding of its tragedies since 2003. There is no doubt, however, that future generations of Iraqis will need to try to understand why their country, of all Arab states, exhibited such extremes of brutality.

DIGGING THE PAST:
THE HISTORIOGRAPHY OF
ARCHAEOLOGY IN MODERN IRAQ

Magnus T. Bernhardsson

As the art historian John Malcolm Russell has pointed out, virtually all the territory of Iraq is an archaeological site (Russell, 2001, p. 45). The area now called Iraq was, of course, the "cradle of civilization" and the site of many great ancient civilizations such as the Assyrian and Babylonian Empires. It is in Iraq that the earliest evidence of formal institutions and material culture has been discovered. The region between the Tigris and the Euphrates Rivers, known as Mesopotamia to the Greeks, was home to the historic cities of Babylon, Nippur, and Uruk, where humans first developed alphabets and techniques of irrigation.

For the last 200 years, archaeologists have discovered both priceless and mundane objects from a myriad different eras from these important civilizations. These artifacts now fill museums, libraries, and private collections around the world. The story of how these archaeological objects were discovered and deciphered is a fascinating one, filled with intrigue, luck, scientific brilliance as well as some occasionally questionable ethics. It involves colorful and resourceful characters, such as Hormuzd Rassam, Leonard Woolley, Sati' al-Husri, Austen Henry Layard, and Gertrude Bell. At the same time, it is an unusual and somewhat contradictory story in the history of science because some of the most spectacular finds and discoveries took place in the 19th century when archaeology as a discipline was still in its infancy and its methods were rudimentary and amateurish by today's professional standards, in contrast to what has happened in other scientific disciplines where important discoveries have tended to be cumulative. Yet archaeology is not all about discovering spectacular objects, even though that may be what drives the public perception. Contemporary archaeology is also about preservation and interpretation. In its early days in the nineteenth century, archaeologists focused on individual objects. Today, however, they are more concerned with context, and tend to focus on historic sites as a whole — to think about relations between the objects rather than the objects themselves. The painstaking and patient work of the last 100 years has yielded invaluable information about the cultures of ancient civilization and provided people with inspiring stories from the past. Because of advances in archaeological knowledge, our knowledge about the great ancient civilizations is now considerable although much work still remains to be done.

A number of historical artifacts have been excavated in Iraq over the last two centuries. Yet as the archaeologist Zaynab Bahrani has suggested, this number pales in comparison with the amount of archaeological objects that still remain unearthed (Bahrani, 2004, p. 47). Around 10,000 historic sites have been identified in Iraq and only about 1,500 have been researched, a history that still has to be dug and discovered. These antiquities are a great cultural resource for the nation of Iraq, comparable in value to its other major resource — oil.

Like oil, archaeology has brought benefits to the Iraqi people. Yet at the same time, Iraqis have not had the opportunity to capitalize fully on this great cultural resource. Instead, they have seen so many of their historic treasures leave the country that little has been left behind for the nation at large. During the first decades of the twentieth century, foreign interests dominated archaeology and crafted legislation that proved more favorable to Western than to Iraqi institutions. But as with their relations with foreign oil interests, only at a much earlier juncture, Iraqis gradually gained more control of archaeological affairs within their own boundaries. By World War II, the Iraqi Law of Antiquities had made it impossible for foreign archaeologists to take unique objects outside the country except on loan (Bernhardsson, 2005). The laws made it clear that archaeological artifacts belong to the Iraqi people and therefore should remain in Iraq. After World War II, Iraqis were fully in control of archaeological matters. Iraq's first foreign-trained professional archaeologists, Fu'ad Safar and Taha Baqir, returned from their studies at the University of Chicago and started their own excavations at 'Aqar Quf, a ruined ziggurat near Baghdad.

In 1952, Safar and Baqir spearheaded the establishment of the Faculty of Archaeology at the University of Baghdad, which would become the main department educating Iraqi archaeologists. They published a world-class archaeological journal called *Sumer* and worked on developing the National Museum into an impressive institution that housed some of the world's most priceless artifacts. In 1966, the Museum moved to its current location on the west side of the Tigris. The art deco structure had 28 halls and housed over 200,000 objects. Increasingly, however, archaeology became subservient to the political goals of the government and science, especially under the regime of Saddam Husayn (Baram, 1991). Perhaps no politician realized the immense political potential of archaeology better than Husayn (Bernhardsson, 2005). As with so many other aspects of Iraqi society and culture, archaeology became utterly subsumed into Husayn's cult of personality and essentially an extension of his rule.

During the era of sanctions (1990–2003), Iraqi archaeologists and archaeology became isolated from the outside world, and because of the crippling restrictions on dealings with Iraq there was little serious archaeological activity or internal investment. As has been well documented, the National Museum was attacked and plundered during the chaos and anarchy of the US led invasion of Iraq in 2003, and over 10,000 objects disappeared. Other regional museums were similarly destroyed. These were calamitous and tragic events that were catastrophic for the Iraqi people and the world at large. Priceless historical objects went missing. Though some of the looted artifacts have resurfaced, thousands of antiquities are still missing. For the last eight years, since the occupation of Iraq, there has been a surge in looting of archaeological sites that has caused irreparable harm. It will take years before the full extent of the damage will be known.

Archaeology in Iraq, therefore, has been closely tied to Iraq's political trajectory and therefore intrinsically related to the overall political process. In many ways, the story of archaeology and its trajectory is a mirror of the overall political development of the country. Just like its political history, archaeology in Iraq has gone through five periods: (1) "international" (1808–1921); (2) "national" (1921–1941); (3) "independent" and "sanctioned" (1941–2003); and (4) "fragmented" (2003–present). The distinct historical context of each of these eras is clearly represented in the historiography. Each epoch has its own questions, philosophy, and focus, and some periods have attracted more attention than others. The main actors are different and the assumptions and stakeholders have changed. Furthermore, each era has its own set of scholars or commentators from different disciplines and backgrounds.

In many ways, the historiography of archaeology in Iraq resembles the historiography of oil. Iraq is depicted a "source nation", with seemingly endless reservoirs, that supplies the worldwide antiquities and art market. The mental picture is similar, showing the removal of the material at a remote and barren site, the means of transport to the outside world, and its eventual deposit at convenient access points. Foreign interests question whether the Iraqis have the technical capacity to manage this unique resource properly, and therefore seek to take its management out of Iraqi hands. Yet a critical difference between archaeology and oil is that antiquities are theoretically returnable. Once they have left the country, there is a chance that they will at some point return back "home" — back to Iraq. Furthermore, at some point the oil wells in Iraq will run dry. Yet historical artifacts are a never-ending and perpetual source. Each generation leaves behind its own remains for future generations to uncover, study and collect. With its ties to Iraq's distant past, archaeology will undoubtedly play an important cultural and political role in the future. As Iraq's fortunes have yet to be forged and as the nation seeks to rebuild and heal its many war wounds, it is likely that the nation will seek inspiration from its storied history. Antiquities can be unifying symbols, reminding Iraqis of Iraq's glorious past and its future potential. They can also be manipulated to justify questionable political action. As the history of archaeology in Iraq suggests, the fate and fortunes of the nation are closely tied to the fate of its historical artifacts. It is therefore useful to consider how each distinct phase of archaeology in Iraq has been studied and presented.

The International Period 1808–1921

During the "international period", Western archaeologists, especially British, French, German and American, dominated the scene. Iraqis played limited roles — primarily as manual laborers at various sites — while foreigners sought to claim Mesopotamian antiquies as theirs. They excavated mostly at pre-Islamic sites, especially those that had clear Biblical connections, including Nippur, Babylon, Kuyunjik, and Nineveh. The early pioneers such as Austen Henry Layard, Henry Creswicke Rawlinson, and Robert Koldewey viewed the historical objects that they uncovered as universal and belonging to them since these artifacts represented an earlier period of mankind's cultural development. They were going back to their "cradle" — tracing the infancy of their own history. Such assumptions made it natural to produce a sense of ownership over the objects. As richly described in contemporary accounts, they went through great difficulties in transporting the artifacts back to Europe to adorn the new national museums in Berlin, Paris, or London. These objects were well received and were great adornments for the imperial powers. In a sense, they were trophies indicating the imperial reach and success of the respective powers (Bernhardsson, 2005).

The scholarship on archaeology in this period is substantial, and sufficiently varied to appeal to a wide range of audiences. The literature covering this stage is probably the most "archaeological" and traditional, focusing on who found what, where, and how. Often this is practitioners' history, portraying the archaeologist as a hero who finds priceless and beautiful objects in a hostile environment against all odds. Typical examples of this genre are works both by academic archaeologists (Roux, 1980; Larsen, 1996; Russell, 1997) and by those who write for a more general audience (Kubie, 1964; Ceram, 1967; Fagan, 1979). These writings do not consider the local cultures or inhabitants and do not pay attention to Iraqis except perhaps as obstructions or annoyances to the archaeologist class. In particular, works for the general public offer a very uncritical portrayal of archaeological activity, and do not raise any ethical questions about whether or not the archaeologists should have removed the objects and who actually owns them. Of course, archaeology is rare among the academic disciplines in that it has a large popular following and it is therefore not surprising to find books on Iraqi archaeology with a more popular bent. There are other works about this period that do not follow this traditional approach and are more concerned to place archaeology in its intellectual and political context (Kuklick, 1996; Foster *et al.*, 2005) and offer a much more critical approach. Works written in the last 15 years are much more aware of the ethical dimensions of the archaeological enterprise and question the motives and methods of the pioneering archaeologists whose careers and discoveries had been lionized a generation earlier.

The National Period 1921–1941

This period has not garnered as much scholarly attention as its predecessor, although it is rich in potential and implications. The interwar years were a transitional period marked by intense negotiations between the British and the Iraqis and the beginnings of Iraq's national preoccupation with archaeology. This epoch was initially dominated by the British but eventually became a struggle between Iraq and Britain over antiquities. During these years, important foundations were set for Iraqi archaeology such as the development of the Antiquities Law and the establishment of the National Museum. Most of the sites excavated during this period were pre-Islamic, although largely through the efforts of Sati' al-Husri, the first Iraqi director of antiquities, Islamic sites also started getting some attention. Initially many of the excavated artifacts were exported out of the country, but by the late 1930s, very few objects were leaving Iraq legally. Consequently, the national collections of Iraq started to grow exponentially.

Like the "international period", the scholarship of the interwar period can be divided between, on the one hand, scholars who are more focused on archaeology as a science and discipline (Lloyd, 1947; Mallowan, 1959; Matthews, 2003) and on the other, those who are interested in archaeology's relationship with other political trends such as nationalism, orientalism, and imperialism (Davis, 1994; Bahrani, 1998; Bernhardsson, 2005, 2007; Goode, 2007).

In the last 20 years, archaeologists have been much more conscious of the ethical dimensions of their craft and more critical of the history of the discipline (Trigger, 2006). Furthermore, scholars outside archaeology have started to study the political dimensions and implications of archaeology (Kohl and Fawcett, 1995; Kohl *et al.*, 2007). Because the Middle East has such a rich archaeological legacy, the story of how archaeology intersected with foreign interests, nation building, modernity, and the arts, is rich with potential. In recent years, several substantial works on these developments have been studied, particularly in relation to Egypt (Reid, 2002; Colla, 2007). In Iraq, the focus has largely been on Iraqi–British relations and how the Iraqis were consistently trying to assert more control over archaeological matters (Bernhardsson, 2005). Because Iraqi national identity was still being forged in the decades leading up to World War II, attention has also been paid to how archaeology helped to establish the cultural basis for a shared Iraqi nationalism.

The Independence and Sanctions Periods 1941–2003

By this time Iraq had full control of its archaeology, though its room to maneuver was severely restricted during the years of the economic sanctions imposed by the United Nations. Archaeology became a popular and prominent discipline in Iraqi society and archaeologists played key roles in the public sphere. What is particularly exciting during this period is how archaeology came to be represented in a number of different spheres. For example, inspired by Mesopotamian history, Iraqi artists such as Jawad Salim and Fa'iq Hasan incorporated ancient themes into their art to develop a unique Iraqi aesthetic in the late 1940s and 1950s (Shabout, 2007). Salim, a very prominent painter and sculptor, had worked at the National Museum for several years and was thus intimately familiar with the material culture of ancient Iraq. The 1950s were also a vibrant time in literature and Iraqi poets and writers such as Badr Shakir al-Sayyab also introduced ancient history and motifs into their literature. The historiography of this period is not very extensive. There were several works by Iraqi archaeologists, including articles in the journal *Sumer* but also in other more general archaeological works or extensive museum guides and directories (Safar, 1974; Baqir, 1986; Basmachi, 1972).

The most important general work exploring the political and cultural ramifications of archaeology for this time period is Amatzia Baram's *Culture, History and Ideology in the Formation of Ba'thist Iraq.* Using an array of different sources, both literary and visual, Baram's work demonstrated how the Ba'thist government under Saddam Husayn incorporated Mesopotamian themes into its political discourse and enterprise in order to instill a distinct and unified national identity. Exploring such venues as the regional festivals, folklore, or the proliferation of public images of Nebuchadnezzar, Baram argues that archaeological motifs and images were critical in the articulation and maintenance of Ba'thist ideology under Saddam Husayn. As this book demonstrates, Iraqi identity is not an either/or manifestation of Iraqi particularlism or pan-Arabism. Rather, archaeology enabled Iraq to develop a unique identity that integrated the Islamic and pre-Islamic periods into Iraqi nationalism. The scholarship on archaeology under the sanctions regime is basically nonexistent and as in the case for many other subjects in Iraqi history, this important time period is essentially a big black hole.

The Period of Fragmentation, 2003–present

Unlike other periods which sought the centralization of governmental control over archaeology and sought to preserve and protect antiquities, the most recent years have been characterized by the fragmentation, destruction, and atomization of Iraqi artifacts. Whereas in earlier eras archaeology was an important means of demonstrating and justifying the oneness of the nation, in the first years of the 21st century, archaeology has splintered. Archaeology in Iraq has thus entered a new and unknown historical phase. The implications of the most recent developments are far from clear or predictable and troubling times lie ahead. Yet what is evident is that just as the National Museum was ransacked and burst asunder, there has been a simultaneous explosion in archaeological writing.

The reaction of the scholarly community to the looting of the National Museum in April 2003 was immediate and forceful. Initially, journalists such as Robert Fisk, Anne Garrels, and John Burns, covered this calamity extensively. The descriptions that first came out of Baghdad were almost apocalyptic in nature suggesting that a catastrophic destruction had just taken place. What made the news so damning and outrageous is that archaeologists and other scholars had warned the US military authorities that, based on experience from other turbulent times in recent Iraqi history, such as during the *Intifada* in 1991, Iraqi museums would be vulnerable to plunder and opportunistic raids (Gibson, 2003). When US troops entered Baghdad and the grip that Saddam Husayn's government held on Iraqi society loosened, anarchy and chaos ensued. During this mayhem, gangs attacked the National Museum under the nonchalant eyes of US soldiers. The public around the world responded vigorously to these reports. The US government faced immediate and vehement criticism of its handling of this issue — which would prove to be symbolic of the widespread mismanagement that was to come. Even though the destruction was not as catastrophic as initially feared, Iraqi archaeology suffered irreparable damage. During a few hours in April 2003, several thousand years of Iraqi history vanished in one of the most dramatic episodes of memoricide in recent history. Indeed, many early commentaries compared it to the ransacking of Baghdad in 1258 by Gengis Khan.

A number of archaeologists immediately wrote impassioned and powerful newspaper articles about the destruction (Deblauwe, 2003) and eventually articles started to appear in journals and magazines. An early account and cataloging of this destruction was an online report by four historians (Edouard Méténier, Jens Hanssen, Keith Watenpaugh, and Hala Fattah) who traveled to Iraq in the summer of 2003 to observe the damage (Watenpaugh *et al.*, 2003). These scholars looked at the damage done to a number of cultural institutions including the National Museum.

In subsequent years, a number of important works have appeared that have cataloged and discussed this damage (Polk and Schuster, 2005; Gharib, 2008; Emberling and Hanson, 2008; Rothfield, 2009). Some attention has been paid to the ramifications of this destruction for Iraq's legal or cultural heritage (Stone and Bajjaly, 2008; Rothfield, 2008). In addition, especially between 2003 and 2007, a number of websites tracked missing objects from the National Museum and closely followed developments in archaeological matters.

Not all the writings on the looting have been entirely critical. Writing in the tradition that resembles earlier practitioners' histories of archaeology, an American military official, Matthew Bogdanos, a colonel in the United States Marine Corps, published his memoirs in 2005 that recounted his role in tracking down some of the plundered artifacts from the Museum (Bogdanos, 2005). While the actions of Bogdanos and his staff clearly facilitated the return of some important objects, his book is essentially a justification and a defense for the US occupation of Iraq. Bogdanos claims that the Assyriologists and other scholars who lamented the ransacking of the Museum and criticized the US military for not assuming responsibility to protect the major cultural sites have missed the point. Calling the critics "armchair archaeologists", Bogdanos has stated that the US military did everything in its power to try to prevent the looting and puts the blame squarely on the looters and also implicates some of the Museum staff in the looting by name. Bogdanos' work does correct some inaccuracies and myths that have circulated relating to the looting. But unlike most academic works on archaeology in recent years, his work shows no awareness of the ethical and political dimension, and he ignores the fact that the US occupation raises serious moral issues. Further, he does not sufficiently address the ethical and legal responsibilities of the US to protect and preserve Iraq's cultural institutions. Though he himself was not seeking to remove any archaeological objects from the country (Bogdanos clearly believes that they are Iraqi property) like some of the archaeologists of the 19th and early 20th century, it is possible to see links between his presence and attitude to the foreign archaeologists operating in Iraq over a hundred years ago.

Hence in some respects, archaeology in Iraq has come full circle. What started as an unsystematic, disorganized plundering of Iraqi sites which then developed into a more careful, transparent, organized, and centralized activity in the course of the 20th century, has now become chaotic and anarchic once more. Iraqi archaeological sites are constantly being ransacked and objects are leaving the country in droves, showing up on the black market in Asia, South America, Europe, and North America.

Hence the political challenges facing the writing of the history of archaeology in Iraq are immense. Given the centrality of archaeological remains to Iraqi culture, their importance for the rebuilding of the country — culturally, economically, and psychologically — it is important that scholars on Iraq should pay more attention to archaeology. The subject is rich with both important and interesting implications. Though it is easy to become pessimistic about the current state of affairs and the future potential of the country, the history of archaeology suggests that Iraq has faced immense challenges before. Iraqis can seek inspiration from this long and storied history and take pride in their material culture. It is probable that once the current situation is stabilized that Iraq will once again return to its independent stage between the early 1940s and the 1970s, when Iraqis had full control in defining, articulating, and executing archaeology.

TOTALITARIANISM REVISITED: FRAMING THE HISTORY OF BA'THIST IRAQ

Achim Rohde

This chapter outlines a novel approach to studying the history of Ba'thist Iraq, based on comparative historiography and a critique of the totalitarianism paradigm that has long been predominant among scholars of Iraq.[1] It was epitomized in the single most influential book written on Iraq under the rule of Saddam Husayn: Kanan Makiya, then publishing under the pseudonym Samir al-Khalil, in his seminal study *Republic of Fear* argues that Ba'thist Iraq should not be considered an ordinary authoritarian system like many others in the contemporary Middle East, but rather be taken as a full fledged totalitarian system, very much like such 20th century dictatorships as Stalinist Russia, Fascist Italy or Nazi Germany (al-Khalil, 1989).[2]

Reflecting the gist of Makiya's argument, comparisons between Saddam Husayn and Adolf Hitler became a standard trope in global media discourse during the 1990s. In the run up to and during the Gulf War of 1991, numerous references linking Saddam and Hitler appeared in the US media.[3]

---

[1]This chapter is an adapted version of the introduction to my book *State-Society Relations in Bathist Iraq. Facing Dictatorship* (Rohde, 2010), which is built along the approach outlined here.

[2]In a similar vein, see Reeva Simon, *Iraq Between the two World Wars* (2004: 169), where she reiterates the case for Iraqi "exceptionalism" in the Middle East, based on its history of anti-British militancy inspired and partly supported by Germany, and presents Saddam Husayn as the "necessary climax" and ultimate proof of this argument.

[3]Philip K. Lawrence (1997: 171) claims to have found 1,170 references linking Husayn and Hitler in the US print media during 1991. The Gannet Foundation (1991: 42) counted 1,035 Husayn–Hitler linkages in the US media between August 1990 and January 1991.

The application of a Hitler image to the Iraqi dictator was still visible in 2003, when he was depicted in much of the US and other Western media as a danger to humankind. Among intellectuals, too, there were heated debates on the Saddam–Hitler linkage, as was illustrated by the reception among Arab intellectuals of Hans Magnus Enzensberger's 1991 essay (originally published in *Der Spiegel*) depicting Saddam Husayn as a reincarnation of Hitler.[4] While Adonis, who was arguing against the invasion of Iraq, dismissed Enzensberger's comparison as "exaggerated to the point of mystification,"[5] Kanan Makiya accepted it in principle and criticized Adonis for failing to grasp the truly monstrous nature of the Iraqi regime (Makiya, 1993, pp. 250–251). Under the influence of the 1991 Gulf War and the failed Intifada against the regime that erupted in its aftermath, Makiya publicly distanced himself from the kneejerk anti-imperialist reaction popular among Arab intellectuals and their rejection of the US-led war against Iraq. His second major work, *Cruelty and Silence*, is an emphatic account of the Iraqi *Intifada* that turns into a sharp critique of Arab intellectuals, whom Makiya accuses of moral corruption and a lack of intellectual honesty, contrasting their apparent silence in the face of home-made tyrants like Saddam Husayn with their attempt to locate all evil in the world squarely in the camps of Western imperialism.

Makiya's sweeping indictment of Arab intellectuals was widely and critically received in Middle East studies circles.[6] His line of thought helped to give legitimacy to the US-led invasion of Iraq and the toppling of Saddam Husayn in spring 2003.[7] Numerous other members of the former (exiled) Iraqi opposition have also characterized Ba'thist Iraq as an example of late 20th century totalitarianism and have linked Ba'thism and Nazism in terms of both their respective ideologies and their political practices (Humadi, 1995, pp. 50–52; al-Khafaji, 2000, p. 287; al-Kayssi, 2000, pp. 31–39; al-Saleh, 2001, pp. 5–49; Jabar, 2001, pp. 14–31; Ismael, 2001, pp. 80, 209; 'Aboud, 2002, pp. 58–74; Fakhir, 2004, pp. 23–32). Yet, most

---

[4] "Hitlers Wiedergänger," *Der Spiegel*, February 4, 1991. Reprinted in the *Los Angeles Times*, February 14, 1991.

[5] "The Prayer and the Sword: Or Savage Democracy," *al-Quds al-'Arabi*, March 11, 1991.

[6] Among the many critical reviews of Makiya's book, see Ahmad (1993: 178–179); Said (1991: 15–20); Abu Khalil (1993: 695–706); Trabulsi (1994: 61–63); Rabbani (1994: 58–60). For Makiya's polemic response to some of the equally polemic accusations levelled against him, see his introduction in *Cruelty and Silence* (1993).

[7] The debates of GW II between Arab intellectuals repeated themselves regarding the war of 2003 (Ofteringer, 2003: 50–53).

such comparisons boil down to generalizations pointing to the state terror and the leader syndrome as common features of both systems. If so many scholars agree on describing Ba'thist rule in Iraq in the context of 20th century totalitarianism and fascism, the lack of comparative historiography in this regard is striking. Even Makiya's work, by far the most serious, was inspired mainly by Hanna Arendt's groundbreaking work on totalitarianism and pays little or no attention to more recent debates on the totalitarianism paradigm, or to the well researched recent histories of Nazi Germany to which he so insistently alludes in his characterization of Iraq under the rule of Saddam Husayn.[8] The same appears to be true for those who equally strongly dismiss such comparisons, but do not bother to root their rejection in any argument other than the fact that their political opponents are using it.[9] It becomes regrettably evident here that linking Ba'thism and Nazism as well as rejecting such comparisons are both part of a moral, rather than an analytical discourse that easily lends itself to value-guided political arguments. In fact, the Ba'th themselves have denounced political opponents by linking them to Nazism (Bengio, 1998, pp. 61, 170). Little is served by adding to these controversies. I rather take them as a point of departure for developing a conceptual frame for the historiography of Ba'thist Iraq. I will now mention a number of specific trends in scholarly debates on the history of Nazi Germany that might help construct a more critical perspective of the history of Ba'thist Iraq.[10]

Comparative Perspectives

To emphasize the historical uniqueness of Nazi Germany and the unprecedented dimensions of its crimes, first and foremost the attempted complete

---

[8]See the interview with Makiya in which he defended the invasion of Iraq in 2003 as a just war against fascism, in *Der Spiegel*, April 14, 2003. In a later interview he described Iraq under Saddam Husayn as "one big concentration camp." See *Die Welt*, December 6, 2005.

[9]In this vein, As'ad Abu Khalil has an article in which he reviews some examples from among the many popular and academic works on Islam and the Middle East published recently in the US, which in his view demonstrate the resurgence of the classical Orientalist paradigm in the US after 9/11. While I would not argue with Abu Khalil regarding the general validity of his critique, given the continuing commercial success of Orientalist luminaries like Bernard Lewis, Abu Khalil himself is not above occasionally placing apologetics before sound arguments (Abu Khalil, 2004: 130–137).

[10]An inspiring work in this regard is Schaebler (1999: 17–44).

physical destruction of European Jewry, is to state one of the most obvious differences between the two systems. Nothing that Saddam Husayn's regime ever devised came close to reaching the dimensions of the Holocaust, not merely because it lacked the resources, but simply because it never thought of it. However, in order to demonstrate uniqueness, comparison is a necessary tool. The historiography of Ba'thist Iraq cannot ignore what appears to be a genocide committed against Kurds, carried out during and eclipsed by the Iran–Iraq war in 1987–1988 (HRW, 1995; Salih, 1995, pp. 24–39; Bruinessen, 1994, pp. 141–170).[11] Comparing the Holocaust and the Iraqi Anfal campaign does not relativize the former's uniqueness. To compare does not mean to equate, let alone to weigh up different crimes against each other. An eminent historian of the Holocaust like Yehuda Bauer emphasized its singularity by comparing it explicitly with other historical cases of genocide. His intention was to lay out a comparative framework for genocide research based on understanding the unprecedented character of the Holocaust. The UN genocide convention of 1948, which was formulated under the impact of the Nazi death camps, defines as genocide "acts committed with the intent to destroy, in whole or in part, a national, ethnical, or religious group as such." For the sake of accuracy, Bauer suggests reserving the term genocide for the partial murder of any such group, and the term Holocaust for total destruction (Bauer, 2001, pp. 10–11).[12] The uniqueness of the Holocaust as a radicalized form of genocide is not only evident in terms of its dimensions, but also in its nonpragmatic, ideological motivation. Proponents of comparative genocide research have at times criticized the notion of the singularity of the Holocaust as a historical and tending to portray the Nazi death camps as beyond rational understanding (Schaller *et al.*, 2004, p. 18). For his part Yehuda Bauer describes the Holocaust as a combination of ideological motives put in place by a powerful modern state machine in an unprecedented, (i.e., neither inexplicable nor unrepeatable) manner, thus turning it into a seismograph for exploring humanity's destructive capabilities in

---

[11] For a Kurdish account of the Anfal, see 'Abd ar-Rahman (1995). The title designates the Anfal as "burnt offering," in allusion to the term Holocaust. Among the first writings to indicate the scale of the Anfal, based largely on eyewitness accounts and official documents seized by Kurdish Pershmerga in 1991, is Kanan Makiya, *Cruelty and Silence* (1993), in particular Chapters 4 and 5.

[12] For recent studies on the Holocaust in comparative historiography, see Gellately and Kiernan (2003); Weitz (2003); Jones (2006).

general — and eventually, for learning how to prevent such deeds.[13] The simultaneity of a seemingly irrational ideological fanaticism and the instrumental rationality of a modern state machine which came into being in Nazi Germany remains a conceptual challenge for historians until today. Despite important differences between competing schools of Holocaust historiography, scholars have come a long way towards bridging the gaps between their respective interpretations of how and why the Holocaust happened. The important impact of structural factors (the composition of the German bureaucracy, economic, social, and political crises, the war etc.) that pushed the Nazi system towards the physical destruction of European Jewry, is commonly acknowledged. But no one seriously disputes the central role of ideology in motivating and justifying the Holocaust, namely, the impact of what was termed "redemptive anti-Semitism" (Friedländer, 1997, p. 101).[14]

In contrast to more standard conclusions stressing the mainly ideological mechanisms underlying the Holocaust, Bauer also identifies pragmatic motives (territorial expansionism, political control etc.) at the root of the Holocaust itself as well as with most other historical cases of genocide, such as the murder of native Americans at the hands of European settlers in the formative period of the USA, or 20th century cases like the massacres of the Khmer Rouge in Cambodia or the slaughter of Hutus in Rwanda (Bauer, 2001, p. 45). As I understand it, the distinction Bauer makes seems somehow static, as pragmatic and ideological motives were intertwined in most cases of genocide. Reviewing the Iraqi Anfal campaign against the country's Kurdish minority between 1987–1988 in the context of comparative genocide research helps to understand the character and the composite structure of the Ba'thist state and society at that stage, as compared to other 20th century dictatorships.

Which ideological and/or pragmatic motives fuelled such atrocities? To what extent were ordinary Iraqis involved in the perpetration of the Anfal massacres? How were the regime's crimes perceived in Iraqi society as a

---

[13]Bauer has himself polemically attacked what he called the mystification and trivialization of the Holocaust visible for example in the work of Elie Wiesel (Kieser and Schaller, 2002: 42 ff). For more on this debate, see Postone and Santner (2003).

[14]That is, a pseudo-messianic ideology of national salvation, which saw in the Jews a corrupting parasitic force bound to rule the world, whose elimination would give rise to a racially pure and supreme Aryan race, which would then be the legitimate rulers of the world. See also Burleigh and Wippermann (1991).

whole? Makiya's sweeping condemnation of Iraqi intellectuals and artists leaves no doubt as to his conviction that under the Ba'th regime not only had civil society been destroyed by a totalitarian state that imposed itself on pre-existing societal structures, but that the regime also succeeded in penetrating the hearts and minds of the people with terror and fear. This brought about the destruction of almost all traces of independent rational thinking in Iraqi society, and the regime obtained the acquiescence or active consent of even the most educated and critical minds (al-Khalil, 1991, pp. 117, 128–129).[15] To the extent that the Ba'th managed to capture the state and to penetrate all parts of society, Iraqis were mobilized and absorbed into the expanding totalitarian state machine.

This way of thinking considers that the ascent of Saddam Husayn to the Iraqi presidency and his successful installation of a highly personalized dictatorship sealed the depoliticization of Iraq by marginalizing even the Ba'th Party as the last formal collective political structure with any significance that remained operative in the country. Eventual cracks and fissures in the mask of national unity and in the tyrant's total control over state and society are dismissed as mere ephemeral phenomena lacking any wider significance. No alternative political realm could possibly evolve inside the totalitarian system due to the silencing of political dissent and public debate under the Ba'th regime. Hence resistance could only come from outside the system, from clandestine opposition groups engaging in armed struggle against the regime. This argument rests within the parameters of liberal political theory, according to which state and civil society are clearly separate entities, where the realm of politics is constituted in the arena of public debate, and bargaining takes place between various social actors on the one hand and the state on the other (al-Khalil, 1989, pp. 125, 127–128).

As in the Iraqi case, a number of early works on the history of Nazi Germany had emphasized the autonomy of Adolf Hitler within the system and his central role in shaping the course of events. But since the 1970s, historians have challenged the Hitlerism argument by focusing their research on the performance of the Nazi system in various interdependent sectors. They have held that exclusive focus on the tyrant and his quasi-hypnotic powers tends to render inexplicable both the mechanisms at work within the system and their impact on society. Focusing solely on Hitler and his ideological

---

[15]Terri de Young has noted Makiya's slide into apocalyptic discourse and the dehumanising and totalising effects on the way he presents events inside Iraq (Young, 1998, pp. 10–12). See also, 2005, p. 295, note 32.

goals risks obscuring numerous important factors like the state, the economic and war context, and the active consent of a majority of Germans, but also the resistance of a minority among them regarding the regime's policies, etc. Proponents of this line of interpretation portrayed Nazi Germany as a quasi-anarchic polycratic system characterized by a diffusion of power between the state, the party and other institutions as well as informal networks of corruption and patronage. In their search for the mechanisms that made the Nazi system work as well as it did, structuralist works have sometimes come close to drawing the picture of a weak dictatorship torn apart by crises and internal contradictions. However useful it may have proved in developing a more detailed and complex view of German history under the Nazis, this line of thought ultimately fails to explain the existence of a state machine intent on unleashing World War II and on organizing and perpetrating crimes of hitherto unimaginable dimensions.[16] Unlike Marxist-inspired structuralist thought, the "intentionalist" view, with its proclivity for the theory of totalitarianism, sees the rise of Nazism mainly in terms of a revolution against constitutional democracy based on an authoritarian ideology and an expanding modern state machine. In an influential early work, Carl Joachim Friedrich and Zbigniev Brzezinski set up a list of criteria defining "totalitarian dictatorships" that include (1) an ideology aimed against enemy classes or racialized groups, (2) a terror system targeted against enemy classes or racialized groups, (3) a state-led command economy, (4) a monolithic one-party system with an almighty leader at its helm, (5) state controlled media, and (6) a monopoly of the means of coercion (Friedrich and Brzezinski, 1965).[17] More recently, historians have demonstrated the limited analytical value of such a static and idealized concept of totalitarianism by testing its validity on various empirical examples, including Nazi Germany itself (Bauer, 2001, p. 37). Moreover, the disruptive effects that authoritarian pressures have on the efficiency of a state machine are often underestimated when looking at this kind of polity.

The thorough penetration of state structures by the Nazi party and its tendency to act as a parallel power structure that controlled and often bypassed formal state structures generated a degree of friction within the system that compromises the perceived absolute control that regimes like Hitler's were able to exert on the system as a whole. This has been

---

[16] For a helpful survey of the main lines of research and interpretative paradigms regarding the history of Nazi Germany, see Hildbrand (2003).

[17] See also Söllner *et al.* (1997); Maier and Schäfer (1996–2003).

demonstrated, for example, by various scholars of Nazi Germany who in their discussions of the role of the German bureaucracy in perpetrating the Holocaust pointed to an increasing trend towards internal friction and inefficiency along the way, a far cry from the perceived monolithic structure of totalitarian systems (Bauer, 2001, p. 55). Yet, if internal friction and the diffusion of power among various actors in Nazi Germany compromised its perceived totalitarian character, the central role of the dictator himself as an integrative figure who managed to control this "authoritarian anarchy" often remains unaccounted for (Kershaw, 2004, pp. 242–243). Many contemporary scholars, including researchers with a Marxist background, have accepted the use of a refined and empirically oriented concept of totalitarianism that takes into account the specificity of each single case.[18] Ultimately, neither the "structuralist" paradigm, which leans towards economic, administrative, ethnic or communal factors, nor the "intentionalist" paradigm with its emphasis on ideology and a seemingly all-pervasive state leviathan, offer a sufficiently complex analysis of the kind of polities under scrutiny here. The relative autonomy and central role of the dictator within such systems, the character and the limitations of his power, remain conceptual challenges for both approaches.

One way of evaluating the power of a dictator is to analyze specific sectors of the governmental system according to the degree of the dictator's involvement in them, the level of coercion applied to sustain the system's functioning and the degree to which such policies were "successful." Among the few authors who have followed such a route with respect to Iraq under Saddam Husayn is David Baran, a French social scientist who conducted field research in Iraq both before and after the fall of Saddam Husayn's regime. His work portrays various sectors of the governing system, challenging its perceived homogeneity and purely repressive character (Baran, 2004). Baran argues that an exclusive focus on the dictator and his repressive apparatus amounts to a mystification of totalitarian systems that helps to condemn such regimes on moral grounds, but is only partly capable of analyzing the range of techniques of governance which they apply, and the degree of their success or failure (Baran, 2004, p. 294). He selects various sectors of the former Iraqi system, e.g., the military industrial complex,

---

[18] A proponent of a refined concept of totalitarianism is Wolfgang Kraushaar (1993: 6–29). Critical of the analytical value of such theories is Wolfgang Wippermann (1997). For a defence of the totalitarianism paradigm in the light of recent challenges, see Pyta (2006: 141–156).

the security apparatus, the Ba'th party etc. and then points out areas of friction and disorder and the range of governmental techniques applied by the regime in the various sectors that were far more flexible than the rather static mechanisms of central governance based on pure repression, particularly during the last decade of Saddam Husayn's rule. He argues that the presence of a degree of fluidity is the key to understanding the regime's longevity (Baran, 2004, pp. 18–19). A similar picture emerges from the account of Pierre Darle, a French social scientist who uses mainly linguistic and psychoanalytic methodology. Darle spent 18 months doing field research in Iraq between 1998 and 2001, interviewing Baghdadi middle class professionals like teachers, architects, engineers, and artists, enquiring into their attitudes towards the regime and the character of their relationship with the government. He focuses on the rising communalism observed in Iraq during the 1990s and portrays the regime's governing techniques and state-society relations in late Ba'thist Iraq as marked by a growing ambiguity that eventually allowed for the (re-)emergence of autonomous social spaces, while the regime "s'est contenté depuis 1991 d'une légitimité *a minima*, reposant sur sa qualité d'unique rempart contre l'anarchie" (Darle, 2003, p. 12).

To what extent, then, did the Ba'th manage to penetrate and control Iraqi society? What was the role of the dictator within the system? How did the crises that the regime had to manage in the course of the 1980s and 1990s affect its highly centralized command structure in terms of its performance in various sectors? Many scholars of Iraq consider that repression, the destruction of the institutions of civil society and the regime's skillfully employed 'divide and rule' tactics intensified the vertical and horizontal fault lines in Iraqi society, leading to a renaissance of ethnic, communal, and religious group loyalties, most notably in the 1990s.[19] The generally fragmented character of Iraqi society has often been emphasized in the context of the history of Iraq as a modern nation state. Such works refer to the rifts that divide the three main ethnic/religious groups (Sunni Kurds, Sunni Arabs, Shi'i Arabs) and the rural–urban divides as the main structural problems that have impeded the emergence of a viable Iraqi polity. Many scholars have highlighted the longstanding dominance of the Sunni Arab minority in Iraqi politics, initiated by the Ottomans and then transformed by the British. When it comes to understanding the history of Ba'thist Iraq,

---

[19] For a poignant discussion, see Zubaida (1991: 197–210).

scholarly debates between "structuralists" who point to the tensions built into the modern Iraqi nation-state from its inception, and "intentionalists" who rather emphasize the dictator's actions as being at the root of this fragmentation, are reminiscent of debates among historians of Nazi Germany (Blackwell, 2005, pp. 445–446).

True, Saddam Husayn's system of rule was built not only on thorough control of the state's repressive apparatus, but increasingly also on informal networks of patronage, held together by kinship and material interests. This process became most visible in the years after the war of 1991, when the dictator openly aligned himself with various tribal groups at the expense of formal party and state structures (Baram, 1997, pp. 1–31). Yet, a focus on structural factors as vertical fault lines runs the risk of overestimating the power of communal identities like ethnic, religious or tribal affiliation in Iraqi society over the years. At times this perspective tends to paper over the historical mutability and heterogeneity of the three groups mentioned and to ignore the active manipulation of such identities by the Iraqi Ba'th regime, whose long term impact on society in general remains unclear (Bengio, 1999, pp. 149–167; Simon, 1997, pp. 87–104; Lukitz, 1995). Although it has been convincingly argued that "the significance on a day-to-day level of an individual's regional background, family, clan, and tribal affiliation continues to be more pronounced [in Iraq] than in the long-established, settled urban and rural societies in some of the neighboring states," (Farouk-Sluglett and Sluglett, 1991, p. 1411)[20] there is a degree of skepticism concerning the normative power of communal loyalties in Ba'thist Iraq (al-Khafaji, 2003, p. 79; Dodge, 2003, p. 159). It is certainly the case that such identities are not fixed formulae but are being "constantly redefined and reconstituted, politically and socially" (Davis, 2005, p. 24). In order to develop a framework for understanding how the Ba'th regime managed to administer this diverse population, Pierre Darle regards the fragmentation of its discourse as a divide and rule technique designed to separate the various constituencies comprising Iraqi society and thus to *demobilise* them (Darle, 2003, pp. 155–6). Still, can one assume a total eclipse of dissent and public debate in Saddam Husayn's Iraq? Is the increasingly amorphous structure of the regime's system of governance after 1991 more than just a different way of securing the control of the population (Blackwell, 2005, p. 451)?

---

[20]See also Zubaida (2002: 205–215).

Recovering or Inventing Public Opinion and Dissent in Baʻthist Iraq

Using terror to discipline the population and to destroy autonomous social structures was integral to the Baʻthist system of rule, and a very effective one, too, insofar as regime survival was concerned. But in order to assess the regime's capability to shape society according to its wishes, one must look beyond the question of sheer regime survival. Even in a society so heavily controlled by the state, where public opinion surveys did not exist and where individual opinion did not necessarily reflect the public mood but rather the degree of coercion exercised by the regime, it would be an over-simplification to write the Iraqi public entirely out of the script. This is not to say that the thorough penetration of the Iraqi population by the party and the state left room for anything remotely resembling a liberal Western civil society. However, this study assumes that the party and state organs did not simply impose their structures on a passive society, but were themselves also transformed by their massive expansion and by the incorporation of ever-wider groups within Iraqi society into their ranks. The evolution of the Iraqi state was part and parcel of the socio-economic transformations Iraq underwent during the twentieth century. Recent studies on German society under Nazi rule have shown similar effects following the expansion of the party in the course of the 1930s and 1940s, pointing to the growing fragmentation of the Nazi movement into its constituent parts after its seizure of power as well as to the less than smooth incorporation of civil society into its ranks, particularly on the local and district levels, eventually raising the question of "who was leading whom?" (Noakes, 2004, p. 208).[21] All governments struggle to attain hegemony; in authoritarian states this is generally achieved through a combination of repression, censorship and propaganda. Repression and censorship, however, have rarely succeeded in silencing oppositional voices completely, and propaganda, for its part, does not invent entirely new discourses. Its success depends partly on its ability to confirm and manipulate existing opinions and attitudes rather than to alter them radically. Thus, even at the height of its power the Baʻth regime tried to achieve cultural hegemony not by imposing its original pan-Arabism, but rather by absorbing and transforming popular discourses on Iraqi national history through a state-sponsored historiography that increasingly sidelined party doctrine

---

[21]For a regional focus on the interactions between the state and party organisations and the population, see Broszat (1977–1983).

(Baram, 1991; Davis, 2005). Official discourse thus reflects a certain implicit interaction between the ruler and his subjects, rather than the mere imposition of certain values from above. It is this kind of interaction that needs to be rendered visible.

How is it that scholarly literature on resistance activities in Ba'thist Iraq focuses almost exclusively on elite politics, on (rumors of) coup attempts from within the Iraqi army or clandestine oppositional groups? On the one hand, it reflects the scarcity of reliable data on developments in Iraqi society and the need to rely heavily on official Iraqi sources or on opposition sources. There was an upsurge of publications by members of Iraqi opposition movements after the war of 1991, when their exiled members started to take on a higher public profile than in the previous decade, while access to reliable data concerning developments inside Iraq remained as scarce as ever, due to regime censorship and the lack of opportunities to conduct field research (Farouk-Sluglett and Sluglett, 1991, p. 1409). The omission of any discussions of internal dissent and the focus on elite politics in the study of Iraq under the Ba'th may, however, also reflect the *a priori* assumptions of the scholars themselves regarding the thorough destruction of civil society and the absence of any form of political bargaining under a violent totalitarian regime.

Ba'thist Iraq is not among the countries where any of the transitions towards greater political freedom observed elsewhere during the 1990s have taken place. Iraq was never a serious field for research on the concept of civil society, which has attracted so much attention in Western academia, including Middle East studies since the end of the Cold War. Numerous works have heralded the transition from authoritarian political systems to liberal democracy, highlighting the role of autonomous organizations and civil society in former Communist and Third World countries (Poznanski, 1992; Chandhoke, 1995; Norton, 1995). Others have emphasized the programs of economic liberalization introduced by most formerly state-capitalist Arab states since the 1980s, and have pointed out that economic liberalization does not automatically lead to the emergence of an autonomous civil society or to democratization. For a variety of reasons, authoritarian regimes have shown remarkable resilience in most countries in the region (Posusney and Agrist, 2005). Still, even skeptical voices can point to emerging civil society *activities* in Middle Eastern countries in the fields of social welfare, health and education, art and culture, which may be considered a response to the state's partial withdrawal from the public sphere in the course of economic liberalization (Niblock, 1993, pp. 55–87; Richards, 1993, pp. 217–227;

Niblock, 1998, pp. 221–233; Pawelka, 2000, pp. 389–413; Lawson, 2005, pp. 19–43). Scholars investigating processes of transition in Middle Eastern societies have argued that it is not sufficient simply to analyze the formal structures of oppressive authoritarian systems. Mounia Bennani-Chraïbi and Olivier Fillieule opt instead for a more dynamic framework that renders visible the different patterns of interaction between the ruler and the ruled, the ways in which official discourse is received, negotiated, and contested among various audiences (Bennani-Chraïbi and Fillieule, 2003, pp. 28–29; Wedeen, 1999; Pratt, 2007; Cronin, 2008). Eric Davis, who portrays the ambiguity of state-sponsored historiography and the spread of oppositional literature published outside Iraq during the 1990s, takes these findings as evidence of the existence of "counter-hegemonic discourses" among educated Iraqis inside the country, particularly during the regime's latter years (Davis, 2005). Davis, Darle and others have noted the perseverance and/or emergence of autonomous social spaces in arts, literature, and poetry during the 1990s (Darle, 2003, pp. 74–82; Rigaud, 2003, pp. 197–218; al-Musawi, 2006). Darle ultimately seems to rule out the possibility of a subversive dimension to these more or less informal structures and practices, and instead emphasizes their stabilizing function within the system. Still, he assumes that the regime's ambiguous policies during the 1990s were the result of an implicit bargain that it struck with various social actors (Darle, 2003, p. 160).

State-Society Relations in Liberal and Authoritarian Systems

The historiography of Ba'thist Iraq should thus move beyond the dichotomous conceptualization of liberal vs. totalitarian polities, of state versus civil society etc. that are prevalent in most of the studies discussed above. An alternative understanding of state-society relations that transcends the dichotomy of these concepts is based on the ideas of Antonio Gramsci and Michel Foucault. For Gramsci, the state is not simply an instrument of coercion in the hands of the ruling class that either remains detached from the rest of society or entirely incorporates society into its formal structures. It also includes a range of social practices in the fields of cultural and ideological production designed to foster the active consent of its subject citizens to its rule (Gramsci, 1971, pp. 244, 263). The Gramscian *raison d'état* reaches deep into the spheres of mentalities, opinions and ideas. The techniques of the modern state machine are often applied outside formal state structures and do not necessarily include explicit regime coercion. If successfully applied, the ruling elite of a state may thus gain hegemonic status, i.e., the active consent or at least acquiescence of its subjects/citizens in its rule. The activities of the government should not be regarded as restricted to what can be termed the political arena in a narrow sense of the word. Neither is its power demonstrated solely by sheer regime survival. Its hegemony in various spheres is dependent on the daily cooperation of the people and is therefore never to be taken for granted.[22] In order to investigate state-society relations in the Middle East, all the various formal and informal aspects of state power need to be addressed (Davis, 1991, pp. 1–35).[23]

The possibly productive rather than merely repressive character of state power in Gramscian thought corresponds with Foucault's network-like concept of the workings of power in modern societies. Foucault has highlighted the productive role of power for the creation of individual and collective identities and for the functioning of modern societies. He developed a technical or administrative concept of the microphysics of power that he contrasted with a juridical understanding of power as originating in a subject-center, i.e., a ruler or a state (Foucault, 1976). He analyzed the emergence and meaning of modern forms of government as rooted in notions of sovereignty (monarchical rule, later constitutions, laws, parliaments), the expansion of disciplinary regimes (schools, hospitals, prisons, factories, armies etc.) and the development of state bureaucracies and administrative apparatuses aimed at maintaining and improving the well-being of the population through what he called bio-political interventions in the areas of health, habitation, urban environment, working conditions and education. His concept of "governmentality", describing ways of thinking about government and the techniques of governing society by regulating the psychological, biological, social, and economic processes that constitute it, is increasingly being applied in the social and political sciences (Foucault, 1991, pp. 87–104). According to Foucault, nonliberal state systems of the 20th century do not constitute a separate

---

[22]Davis has noted the potential of Gramscian thought for an analysis of Iraqi history that is informed by the perspectives of subaltern classes (Davis, 1994: 276). In the same vein, see Ayubi (1995). For a broader view, see Jabar (1997). With regard to nationalist narratives, the Iraqi Ba'th regime's struggle to achieve hegemonic status has been illustrated particularly with regard to state-sponsored activities in the fields of historiography and art (Baram, 1991; Davis, 2005).

[23]From a more state-centered, yet not altogether distant perspective, see Anderson (1999: 39–56, particularly 52). See also Mitchell (1991: 77–96).

order, but are instead specific historical expressions of modern "govern-mentality", which places the population, rather than the territory (as in pre-modern times), at the center of politics and tries to shape it in its image. Nazi Germany stands out in this context as the most radical his-torical example of a "gardener state" that systematically connected various nodes of bio-political racism that had evolved in 19th century Europe to the exercise of state sovereignty, thereby establishing a "positive relationship between the right to kill and the assurance of life" (Stoler, 1995, p. 84).

Foucault's theories thus challenge the perception of Nazi policies as being characterized by an ultimately self-destructive and irrational ideological drive, as argued by Yehuda Bauer in his comparative framework for geno-cide research. If anything, Foucault points to the self-destructive dimension inherent in the rational functioning of the Nazi state (Dean, 1991, p. 141). For the most part, mirroring Foucault's own concern with 18th and 19th cen-tury Europe, the "governmentality" concept is applied to the emergence and transformations of the modern liberal welfare state. But although Foucault did not follow through his agenda of portraying the emergence of mod-ern "governmentality" until the great totalitarian systems of 20th century Europe, he never recognized a normative distinction between liberal and authoritarian modes of government, be they Stalinist or Fascist.[24]

In Foucault's view all modern political systems work on the same mode of "governmentality" based on notions of bio-politics and sovereignty. At various occasions in the 20th century, authoritarian systems have evolved out of liberal polities. The most recent examples of such trends can be observed in a number of Western democracies since the events of 9/11 and the ensuing "war against terrorism" (Bigo and Tsoukala, 2008). Liberalism itself includes a despotic dimension that is directed (with varying degrees of intensity) against those groups within liberal polities deemed not to qualify fully for the rights of enlightened subject citizens (Balibar, 2004). Foucault's analysis raises the disturbing question of whether and to what extent the rationality of mass murder might be located within the logic of modern "governmentality" itself. Although, according to Mitchell Dean, "[t]he study of 'governmentality' is yet to open up the extensive discussion of authoritarian and nonliberal 'governmentality'", Foucault's work suggests that "authoritarian 'governmentality' is [...] an element in liberal forms of

---

[24]For a philosophical work that takes Foucault's "governmentality" concept as a point of departure and posits Auschwitz as the ultimate symbol of modern "governmentality", see Agamben (1998, 2005).

rule as well as a genre of political rationalities unto itself" (Dean, 1991, pp. 145, 147).

Foucault's main interest was to highlight the decentralization and the transformations that the art of government underwent after the emergence of modern juridical and administrative apparatuses in European states. He tended to downplay the significance of states as a focus of political struggle. Wondering whether modern states indeed possessed the unity and functionality ascribed to them, he preferred to see them rather as a "composite reality," as a "mythicized abstraction" (Foucault, 1991, p. 103). He has been criticized for ignoring the ability of states to grant authority to certain power fractions within society. A state can grant stability to certain (im-)balances of power by "freezing" specific historical moments of the continuous power struggle within society (Neocleous, 1996). This point is particularly valid regarding dictatorships such as Ba'thist Iraq. However, tyranny does not automatically imply the overwhelming strength of such states *vis-à-vis* their subject-citizens. Arguably, the violent and oppressive character of many regimes in this region is a sign of their inherent weakness, their failure to obtain the active consent of their citizen subjects to their rule, or in Gramscian terms, hegemony. In order to account for the Ba'th regime's relative strength or weakness, it seems useful to distinguish between its regulative/normative power over the population on the one hand and its ability to secure the accumulation of capital needed to sustain itself on the other. Gerhard Hauck has observed that in numerous African countries states gradually transfer parts of their sovereign power to private interlocutors, who at times act as para-sovereigns, thus contributing to a considerable degree of chaos and fluidity within the system. Instead of taking these indicators merely as signs of the erosion and weakness of such states, Hauck examines the functionality of such "public-private-partnerships" in sustaining the ruling elite's ability to control vital resources. He concludes that the weakening of the normative/regulative power of many such states has actually served the interests of the ruling elites, whose continued control of material and financial resources may well rest on their alliance with other actors within their territory, thereby securing their power even against rising opposition (Hauck, 2004, p. 417; Daloz, 1999). This characterization seems to mirror the changes the Iraqi governing system underwent under Saddam Husayn, particularly during the 1990s.

Michel de Certeau has argued that Foucault's focus on the mechanisms of power does not take sufficient notice of the actual process of transmission and implementation of state policies, which is far less smooth then often thought (Bennani-Chraïbi and Fillieule, 2003, p. 30; de Certeau, 1990, pp. 105, 146–147).[25] It would thus be simplistic to assume that the "fierce" state personified by Saddam Husayn stood as the sole subject agent over the rest of society (Ayubi, 1995). In this sense, focusing on the microphysics of power allows us to reach a deeper understanding of state-society relations in Ba'thist Iraq than would be possible by confining our scrutiny to the repressive state apparatus (Rohde, 2010).

Conclusion

Scholarly accounts of Iraq's recent history spend time and energy describing the regime's narrowing power base and the contraction of the state after 1991, all the while highlighting its continued oppressiveness. Rarely have scholars focused on the regime's more subtle governing techniques and on the functionality of its survival strategies under the circumstances imposed on the country during this period. Nor did they evaluate the impact of these policies on the governing apparatus and on the relationship between the regime and the Iraqi population. Such works therefore do not account for the complexity and vitality of the Iraqi system, or for Saddam Husayn's ability to integrate an increasingly fluid and ambiguous system of rule. These developments entailed an erosion of the Iraqi state to a degree that anticipated the failed state that it turned out to be in 2003. Numerous indicators pointing in this direction all through the 1990s were not sufficiently taken into account by most researchers and politicians in favor of invading Iraq. They miscalculated the effects of removing the dictator, who had hitherto managed to prevent the country's slide into open chaos as much as he had been the cause of this tendency in the first place (Le Vine, 2006).

Pending more detailed archaeology, it is suggested here that instead of clinging to a rather static and idealized notion of totalitarianism, the history of Ba'thist Iraq might be more aptly framed with recourse to the concept of fascism, understood by Robert O. Paxton as a dynamic and non-linear process comprising several phases. Such processes can be observed at various times in different regional settings in Europe and beyond (Paxton, 2006; Wippermann, 1997).

---

[25] In this vein, see the elaborate discussion of the mechanisms of authoritarian rule in Syria by Lisa Wedeen (1999: 67–86). A similar argument has been put forward by miriam cooke (2007).

HOW TO "TURN THE PAGE"[1]? THE NATIONAL IRAQI LEADERSHIP AFTER 2003 AND THE DE-BA'THIFICATION ISSUE

Fanny Lafourcade

Societies emerging from periods of war or political repression deal with the past in different ways. They can ignore it and pass amnesty laws that pardon past offenders. Or they can confront it by recognizing past crimes, pursuing criminals, establishing truth commissions, putting programs in place to remove past offenders from the public sector, and providing reparations and apologies to victims. All these activities comprise the main components of "transitional justice", which can be defined as a "set of practices, mechanisms and concerns that arise following a period of conflict, civil strife or repression, and that are aimed directly at confronting and dealing with past violations of human rights and humanitarian law" (Stover *et al.*, 2008).

Very often, societies emerging from armed conflict or authoritarianism go through complex and delicate processes regarding their past. Confronting this past can take place many years after the facts, once the transition to democracy is secured. In Spain, for example, on November 20, 2002 — 27 years after the death of Franco — members of parliament passed a resolution condemning his coup and giving moral recognition to the victims of his repression (Labelle *et al.*, 2005, p. 274). In Chile, in spite of the work of

---

[1]This is the title of a famous speech given by Ambassador Paul Bremer, then head of the Coalition Provisional Authority, on April 23, 2004. As the military campaign in Falluja had caused many civilian deaths and profoundly shocked many Iraqis, particularly Sunnis, Paul Bremer's speech encouraged Iraqis to support and participate in the "Reconstruction" project of the CPA, and announced the easing of the de-Ba'thification policy. . . . . Paul Bremer, *Turning the page* (2004).

the Truth and Reconciliation National Commission (Rettig Commission), convened in 1990, whose aim was to tackle some of the abuses of the military junta led by Augusto Pinochet, in particular the disappearances of leftist activists, the former dictator and the main leaders of the junta continued to be protected for years by an amnesty law and many occupied official positions, notably in the Senate. It was only after the arrest of Pinochet in London in 1998 and the attempt to extradite him to Spain that gave human rights defenders a new impetus to reopen the file and address pending issues such as the broader use of violence and torture against thousands of Chileans (Grandin, 2005, p. 65).

The situation may be different when political regimes have collapsed as the result of military defeat and external intervention, as in Germany or Japan in 1945. In Germany, de-nazification started as early as January 1946 by the Allied forces occupying the country. By the beginning of 1947, 90,000 Nazis were being held in detention camps and 1,900,000 people were denied any other than manual work.[2] In addition, the idea of the collective guilt of the German people underpinned such measures as the forced tours of concentration camps organized for German civilians by the Allies. By 1948, however, with the Cold War clearly in progress, the United States focused increasingly on the threat posed by the Eastern Bloc and handed over the de-nazification process to German institutions. The main criteria for prosecution became personal guilt rather than group membership in the Nazi party or its affiliated organizations, which concerned approximately six million people. Five categories of individuals were distinguished: "guilty", "compromised", "little compromised", "followers", and "exonerated" (Vincent, 2008).

Increasingly, most of the "de-nazified" were classified as "followers" largely because the experience of these former Nazi officials as managers and civil servants was urgently needed to run the newly established German institutions. What was supposed to be a mass purge became, therefore, a mass rehabilitation. Between 1949 and 1954 a series of amnesty laws were passed and the numbers of suspected war criminals to be prosecuted was limited to those convicted of penal offences. While "these measures created a sense of unity centered on the new state and its leader, Adenauer" (Saghieh,

---

[2]Herbert Hoover's press release of The President's Economic Mission to Germany and Austria, Report No. 1: German Agriculture and Food Requirements, February 28, 1947, http://www.trumanlibrary.org/whistlestop/study_collections/marshall/large/documents/ index.php?pagenumber=4&documentid=24&documentdate=1947-02-28&studycollection id=mp&nav=OK.

2007, p. 213), the experience profoundly influenced German society. Until now, Germans have had a complex relationship with their Nazi past, filled with a sense of collective culpability — it reemerged for example in 1968 as a part of the broader student protest movement (Labelle *et al.*, 2005, p. 276).

The examples of Chile and Germany show that the issue of national reconciliation is much broader than straightforward transitional justice measures and involves complex personal, psychological, and collective memory processes that can span over one or several generations. Moreover, while these measures are necessary steps to enable subsequent processes to take place, the way they are implemented is profoundly linked to the political environment in which they emerge. Whether they are considered as a way of democratizing institutions as in Chile, or as obstacles to the reconstruction of a democratic state as in post-1948 Germany, transitional justice measures are often time-bound, incomplete and designed according to expedient political considerations. In Chile, for example, the report of the Rettig Commission, while addressing important human rights issues, was also a justification of the coup led by Pinochet, and the violence of the regime was presented as a necessary step in the process of the restoration of state sovereignty — allegedly threatened under Allende's previous regime (Grandin, 2005, p. 56).

In Iraq, de-Ba'thification was designed on the lines of the original German model. Just as British civil servants in Iraq in the 1920s had been strongly influenced by the Indian colonial experience (Dodge, 2003, p. 63), the United States' occupation of Germany and Japan was very much an initial source of inspiration for the American administration in Iraq (Feldman, 2004, p. 1).[3] This was particularly the case for Ambassador Paul Bremer, head of the Coalition Provisional Authority (CPA) between May 2003 and June 2004, as he admits himself (Bremer and Mac Connell, 2003, p. 17).[4] Not surprisingly, the de-Ba'thification of Iraqi institutions and society was his very first decision, taken immediately after his arrival in Iraq in May 2003 (CPA, 2003c).

This paper looks at the evolution of the de-Ba'thification policies and processes after 2003. Much has been written on the CPA's errors and particularly on the adverse effects of the de-Ba'thification policy on attempts

---

[3] "I glanced around at my new colleagues. Those who were awake were reading intently. When I saw what they were reading, though, a chill crept over me, too. Not one seemed to need a refresher on Iraq or the Gulf region. Without exception, they were reading new books on the American occupation and reconstruction of Germany and Japan."

[4] "America and its allies have not taken on a job this big since the occupations of Germany and Japan in 1945 [...] Let's keep in mind the relevant lessons of Germany and Japan."

at state building in Iraq after 2003 (Sluglett, 2006). Yet little has been said about the fact that an important segment of the new Iraqi leadership supported the CPA's approach to de-Ba'thification. As early as September 2003, with the creation of the Supreme National Commission for de-Ba'thification (CPA, 2003e), the issue was transferred almost entirely to Iraqi hands. But while this sensitive matter was supposed to be at the core of a sound investigative and transitional justice process intended to foster genuine national reconciliation, it actually became the catalyst for a worsening fracture over power-sharing in post-Ba'thist Iraq.

The real or perceived excesses of the process contributed to persuade Sunni Arabs that it was and still is a tool of sectarian politics and exclusion, paving the way for a Sunni post-2003 "culture of rejection" and generally undermining any real possibility of national reconciliation. In spite of the emergence of an alternative view, denouncing the excesses and adverse effects of the process, and in spite of increasing American pressure for reform, the post-Ba'thist Iraqi leadership still largely favors the system put in place in 2003, as shown by the Justice and Accountability Law adopted by the Iraqi parliament in January 2008. Therefore, instrumental in raising political tensions among Iraqi communities, the de-Ba'thification issue is still a central factor in the fragmentation of the Iraqi polity.

This paper is based on some of the findings of my doctoral research on the Iraqi national leadership after 2003. In addition to interviews with Iraqi politicians, US officials, as well as Iraqi citizens and civil society activists, sources include official communiqués and websites of the different political forces, press statements and publications of many Iraqi politicians between 2003 and 2007. They also include the testimonies, publications and press statements of US officials involved in the Iraqi political process, as well as CPA orders and regulations.[5]

The Central Role of Ahmad Chalabi

With the collapse of Saddam Husayn's regime, the Ba'thist political and administrative leadership was removed from Iraqi society and institutions, through the de-Ba'thification of the Coalition Provisional Authority (CPA),

---

[5]Due to constraints on access to the field, my sources are far from exhaustive and information gathering has often been limited by security concerns. My fieldwork was relocated to Amman from 2004–2005, and part of the Iraqi political spectrum, for this reason, may be underrepresented in the research sample.

and the search for the 55 "Most Wanted" Ba'thist personalities, includ-
ing Saddam Husayn himself, and his sons (CPA, 2003c). To replace
it, a national post-Ba'thist leadership emerged, as a result both of the
American administration's policies and the internal dynamics of Iraqi soci-
ety. The Iraqi Governing Council (*Majlis al-hukum*) (July 2003) and the
September 2003 and June 2004 governments were entirely appointed by the
Coalition Provisional Authority while the Transitional National Assembly
(TNA) (January 2005), the Council of Representatives (*Majlis al-nuwwab*)
(December 2005) and the governments of April 2005 and June 2006 were
outcomes of the January 2005 and December 2005 general elections.

At least in 2003, the issue of de-Ba'thification was one of the key elements
of cohesion of this composite and pluralistic group.[6] Moreover, at this initial
stage, there seemed to be a general consensus in Iraq over the principle of
de-Ba'thification. As 'Ali,[7] a sculptor, put it, "something had to be done to
exclude those Ba'thists from the new Iraq."[8] That is why he was "so upset
with Jay Garner" for "The Americans c[a]me, they destroy[ed] everything,
and they remove[d] just Saddam and t[ook] back the others." But Jay Garner
did not have a precise idea about the de-Ba'thification process: 'real agents'
of the Party should "first be arrested, then be judged."[9]

Building on this broad but somewhat ill-defined consensus, Ahmad
Chalabi emerged as the key player in the process of de-Ba'thification. Ahmad
Chalabi is an Iraqi politician and businessman who had founded the Iraqi
National Council (INC) with United States support in 1992. The INC was
then supposed to act as a platform for the Iraqi opposition in exile. Ahmad
Chalabi managed to gain supporters from within the United States administration and Congress, lobbied continuously for a United States military
intervention to oust the Ba'thist regime, and played a key role in building
the case for the 2003 US invasion of Iraq.

First of all, Ahmad Chalabi played a crucial role in the initial design
of the process implemented by the CPA and Paul Bremer (Stover *et al.*,
2008, p. 19), the famous "Order 1: Debaathification of Iraqi society" (CPA,

---

[6]This new national leadership did not speak and still does not speak with one voice.
Political views, ideological backgrounds and intellectual references have differed. One of
the points of disagreement among the new leaders has been over the place of religion in
politics, as shown during the debates around the writing of the Constitution.

[7]In order to protect my interviewees, I have changed their names. This does not apply to
public figures such as politicians.

[8]Interview with the author. Damascus, December 2003.

[9]*Ibid.*

2003c). Second, he ensured that his followers in the INC participated in all stages of the process, recovering part of the former regime's archives that had disappeared in the April 2003 lootings, assisting United States personnel in the screening of Iraqi civil servants, providing them with translators and conducting the inquiries, etc. Within the CPA, the general understanding of Iraqi society and history was rather weak. Less than a dozen people had any real command of Arabic,[10] and among them, only two were in Bremer's immediate circle — Ryan Crocker, who later became US ambassador, and the late Hume Horan — but they were both marginalized within the CPA (Sluglett, 2006, p. 363). At the operational level, the CPA lacked the basic knowledge to implement de-Ba'thification, which is why they relied so heavily on Ahmad Chalabi's men.

Moreover, Ahmad Chalabi lobbied tirelessly in favor of a quick handover to the Iraqis. This occurred within six weeks, with the Iraqi Governing Council seizing the initiative and creating the Higher National de-Ba'thification Commission (HNDBC) (CPA, 2003a, 2003b). Unsurprisingly, this also resulted in the early control of this new institution by Ahmad Chalabi and his aides (Stover *et al.*, 2008, p. 21).

A Specific Narrative on the Ba'th Era

Political leaders always put in place strategies of appropriation, modification, and even manipulation of national historical memory (Davis, 2005). This is why it is possible to analyze the narrative produced by the players in the de-Ba'thification process as an attempt to appropriate Iraqi historical memory. This narrative focuses on the Ba'th era and holds several elements. The Commission was supposed to be a memory institution, but also had an operational role since it had to prevent the return of the "dark period" (*fatra muzlima*), of the "era of domination of the Saddamist Ba'th" (*hiqba al-tasallut al-ba'thi al-saddami*), with its "appalling crimes" (*al-mahazir al-bashi'a*), namely the "mass graves" (*al-maqabir al-jama'iya*), perpetrated by "Saddam and his clique" (*Saddam wa azlamihi*) (Mahdi, 2004). The mass graves, the use of torture, as well as the Halabja massacre, are key elements in this narrative.

---

[10]Interview with a former employee of the Coalition Provisional Authority. Washington DC, August 2005.

Beyond this will to denounce past crimes and violations of human rights was a notion of how the Ba'th Party had interacted with Iraqi society. The term "de-Ba'thification", rather neutral and almost scientific, has less weight than the Arabic (*ijtithath al-ba'th*): Ba'thist elements had to be "extirpated" or "uprooted" from Iraqi society. The Arabic expression is of agricultural origin and signifies "completely uprooting a harmful and parasitic plant" (Saghieh, 2007, p. 204). The complexity of the relations between the Ba'th Party and Iraqi society, the subtlety of domination mechanisms in Ba'thist Iraq, do not have a place in this narrative.

Instead, such a narrative relied heavily on a schema highlighting the regime's repressive dimension above all. Kanan Makiya's *Republic of Fear* (published under the name of Samir al-Khalil), describing the Ba'thist repressive machine of the 1980s, had become the major reference for many exiles as well as for the United States administration (al-Khalil, 1989). This work was very much influenced by Hannah Arendt's work on totalitarianism (Arendt, 2002), and while not demonstrating it, considered Iraq's Ba'thist regime as being totalitarian in nature.[11] It emphasizes the role of fear in Ba'thist Iraq and the isolation of the individual in an atomized society where traditional hierarchies have been destroyed by the regime.

What is de-Ba'thification?

The implementation of de-Ba'thification matched this specific narrative. De-Ba'thification describes a twofold process. One was the complete dissolution of the Iraqi army as well as certain organizations (mostly security-related) that were either notorious for their role in enforcing Ba'th Party rule, or whose resources might offer the party a means to return to power. These organizations included the Iraqi army, the intelligence services, the Olympic committee and others (CPA, 2003d). The other process was the dismissal of thousands of civil service employees from their positions (CPA, 2003c). Actually, the dismissal procedures involved two categories of persons: All individuals in highest-level management positions (level of director general and above), regardless of their party membership; and all individuals who were members of the top four ranks of Iraqi Ba'th Party membership, regardless of the level of their civil service position (CPA, 2003c). Therefore, individuals were not dismissed on the basis of individual deeds or

---

[11]The nature of the Ba'thist regime has not yet been the object of a systematic analysis.

other criteria of integrity, but on the basis of their party rank, and of their real or supposed administrative responsibilities. The assumption underpinning these procedures was that the members of the Ba'th Party elite could not have reached a certain rank in the party without either having committed acts that seriously violated human rights standards or without being deeply corrupt. Some of those dismissed became eligible for civil service pensions — but they risked losing them if they appealed their dismissals. From the beginning there was a parallel but unclear process of exemption and reinstatement, influenced partly by the technical and political needs of the CPA and later the Iraqi government.

As we can see, the Commission focused primarily on the issue of the purging of the Iraqi administration. The other aspects of transitional justice processes were taken in charge either by the United States or by NGOs. One of the aims of Iraq Memory Foundation of Kanan Makiya (The Iraq Memory Foundation [al-Mu'assassa al-dhakira al-'Iraqiyya]), for example, which is supported by the United States, is to gather evidence and testimonies on Ba'thist crimes. But apparently it is more focused on the collection of Ba'thist archives and its role as a memory institution has not really been activated yet. USAID's mass graves program was very much publicized in the first weeks after the 2003 war: The Agency funded local NGOs or directly supervised the exhumation of graves, the compilation of lists of missing Iraqis, suspected mass grave sites, confirmed victims, and documents relating to disappearances (USAID, 2004). A later decree, issued on December 10, 2003, created the Iraqi Special Tribunal for Crimes against Humanity (CPA, 2003f) to prosecute Iraqi nationals or residents of Iraq accused of genocide, crimes against humanity and war crimes. Bremer also mandated a series of other administrative and institutional directives, including the establishment of a property claims commission, a central criminal court, and a task force on victim compensation.

But none of these measures really helped to trigger any collective work on the Iraqi past. The Iraqi Special Tribunal, for example, has so far treated two cases — Dujayl and Anfal. While the two cases were easily documented, and the culpability of those prosecuted — among them Saddam Husayn — was easily established, political interference and procedural weaknesses undermined the legitimacy of the trials. The trials — and particularly Saddam Husayn's — were supposed to act as tools with which Iraqi society might tackle its immediate past. But the defects described above undid the pedagogical aims they were supposed to achieve. Above all, Saddam Husayn's execution on 30 December, 2006 was perceived as an act of sectarian revenge and fueled profound resentment among the Sunni community (Stover *et al.*, 2008, p. 16).

The Excesses of de-Ba'thification

The de-Ba'thification process itself was rapidly criticized, particularly its excesses and the revengeful spirit of its promoters (Saghieh, 2007). One of the main criticisms has been that de-Ba'thification went much further than was indicated in the text of Order 1. Until now, the extent of de-Ba'thification remains a sensitive issue and official figures are not available. But several estimates have been published at different points in time. It comes as no surprise that estimates emanating from Iraqi (and US) authorities are much lower than those emanating from other sources. According to Mith'al al-Alusi, Director General of the Commission, 60,000 persons have been removed from the Iraqi administration (Mahdi, 2004). In May 2005, the newspaper *al-Dustur* reported that 90,000 persons would have been excluded (Institute for War and Peace Reporting, 2005b). But, according to other sources, de-Ba'thification has far exceeded these figures and more than 200,000 people would have been excluded from administrative positions (Commission Des Recours Des Réfugiés, 2005). To these figures we should add the 400,000 members of the Iraqi Army and the 100,000 former members of other repressive, security and intelligence agencies.

The truth is probably somewhere in the middle. According to interviews conducted with ex-Ba'thists, it seems highly probable that the de-Ba'thification went much further than Order 1. Fear of revenge or of public humiliation often encouraged ex-Ba'thists who were in theory not under the provisions of the de-Ba'thification process not to come back to work.

"I had to leave Iraq, because of the security and the economic situation. I can say I am a political figure in the country — I am against this clique monopolizing power nowadays. I've been advised to leave the country. First, I refused. But there is a practical dimension: I have a book to finish, and there, there is no electricity, no telephone, you can't travel. That is why I thought it was better to come to Amman."[12]

This Ba'thist professor will later acknowledge that he "received threats." In addition to this "self-de-Ba'thification," in April–May 2003, there was a

---

[12]Interview with a Ba'thist university professor. Amman, November 2005.

degree of spontaneous de-Ba'thification which may have further encouraged some Ba'thists to choose to go into hiding or to flee the country. In ministries, trade unions, and other associations, general assemblies were convened and pronounced the dismissal of ex-Ba'thists.[13]

Moreover, the Commission has been denounced as being secretive, all-powerful, and manipulative. The loss of the Ba'th Party's archives in March–April 2003 gave disproportionate powers to Commission members. Political and personal considerations entered into play and were mixed with the highly political and sensitive task they were entrusted to perform. Procedures for appeal were not clear. Exemptions and reinstatements were technically possible, but depended on ill-defined and often changing criteria. Moreover, the Commission had the ability to go beyond the dispositions of Order 1: According to legal dispositions, even simple members (*'udu* and *'udu 'amil*) of the Party can be excluded if they are considered a threat to security (CPA, 2003c).

As a result, the Commission wielded enormous power over the lives of thousands of people with little or no accountability (Stover *et al.*, 2008, p. 22). Nepotistic practices were common: In many places, previous civil servants were replaced with members, friends and allies of the new masters of Iraq — that is, members of the political parties of the former opposition to Saddam Husayn, the INC, SCIRI/ISCI, Da'wa, Iraqi National Alliance, etc. On the other side, there was an obvious impunity gap — hundreds of thousands of lower-level Ba'thists (many of whom may have been guilty of abuses) retained their civil service positions and others who have been dismissed but were well-known abusers have not suffered any other penalty. That is why the Commission has increasingly appeared as a political tool in the hands of the post-2003 political leadership.

In addition to enforcing civil service dismissals, the Commission has intervened in judicial appointments at the Iraqi High Tribunal, including shortly before the release of verdicts in the Dujayl case where several members of the Iraqi special tribunal were dismissed because of the commission's accusations: for example, Sayyid Hamish, the deputy presiding judge, was dismissed after his past membership in the party was revealed in January 2006. The Commission interfered in the political process. According to *al-Zaman*, the Iraqi Electoral Commission denied a request from the

---

[13] Interviews of the author with several Iraqis, mainly students and artists who witnessed this spontaneous de-Ba'thification in their institutions. Amman, Baghdad and Damascus, 2003–2004.

de-Ba'thification Commission in November 2005 to exclude 51 individuals from running on party lists in the December 15 elections because they were insufficiently involved in Ba'th activities to be excluded from civil office (Cole, 2005).

Increasingly, the de-Ba'thification process came to be perceived as a "de-sunnization" of Iraqi institutions and society, a collective punishment by the new Shi'i masters and their allies, the Kurds. On the other side, opponents of the process were characterized as frustrated Ba'thists refusing to lose their grip on power and Iraqi resources. Their demands were therefore not received as legitimate.

The stigmatization of the Sunni community in post-Ba'thist Iraq is obvious. The belief that the Ba'th Party was primarily a tool of domination of the Sunni Arab community has become part of the narrative of the new leadership. It is shared also by many Americans, as expressed for example by Paul Bremer in his memoirs:

> For almost three decades, the Baath Party had subjugated Iraq. Like the Nazis and Soviet Communists, the Iraqi Baathist Party — dominated by Saddam *and other Sunni Arabs* [Stressed by the author] — had controlled not only political life, but Iraq's entire society through a combination of police state terror and toadyism, while mismanaging a corrupt command economy [...] (Bremer and MacConnell, 2003, pp. 38–39).

While victims of de-Ba'thification protested,[14] their voices were not relayed at the political level by their so-called "representatives", understandably, since the members of the *Majlis al-hukum* had been nominated by the United States. Soon, they had the feeling that they did not have access to the Green Zone, the seat of the CPA and nascent Iraqi institutions, or to decision makers.[15]

The Emergence of an Alternate Voice

While it had been broadly consensual in 2003 among the new Iraqi leadership, the dominant narrative was increasingly challenged by an alternative one, relaying critiques of the de-Ba'thification process and developing another discourse on Iraq's Ba'thist past. This narrative appeared as a discourse of the Iraqi leadership in the spring of 2004. In March 2004, Mas'ud

---

[14]Several demonstrations involving sacked Iraqi officers were held in May and June 2003.
[15]Interview with a Sunni politician. Amman, April 2005.

Barzani, head of the Kurdistan Democratic Party (KDP), demanded that de-Ba'thification should be abandoned (Saghieh, 2007, p. 215). After the nomination of Iyad 'Allawi as Prime Minister in June 2004, de-Ba'thification was further criticized, with increasing pressure being put on the US administration. In April 2004, Bremer stepped back on the de-Ba'thification policy and announced his intention to dissolve the Supreme National Commission for de-Ba'thification two months later.[16] Since then, criticisms have been increasingly vocal. The general conference of Iraqi tribes for example, called in August 2006 for an end to de-Ba'thification[17] (Haymas, 2006). The denunciation of the process as a sectarian or "racist" purge has been voiced in the political arena by the Tawaffuq Party (Accord Front). For example, 'Abd al-Mutlaq al-Jubburi, a former deputy prime minister and senior Accord Front lawmaker, told parliament in December 2007: "The de-Ba'thification law was set up not to uproot a party but to uproot a section of the Iraqi people."[18]

According to this alternative narrative, it is possible to distinguish between "good" and "bad" Ba'thists. Individuals should be judged according to their criminal responsibility and not according to their membership to the categories established by the policy of de-Ba'thification. This distinction is possible first of all because membership in the Ba'th party was so widespread. Under Saddam Husayn's rule, many people, particularly civil servants, were almost obliged to be members of the party, to protect their family or keep their job. Therefore, the de-Ba'thification process has often been unfair. Moreover, as valued managers, former Ba'thists, are needed in the new Iraqi state. De-Ba'thification has prevented a number of skilled managers and professionals from participating in the reconstruction of Iraqi institutions, thus delaying or even preventing such a reconstruction. This opinion was expressed by Iyad 'Allawi, while a member of the Iraqi Governing Council: "Overnight we saw most of the civil bureaucracy disbanded and many honest civil servants unjustly sent home penniless [...]."[19]

---

[16]But this decision is contested by several members of the interim government and the Commission has not been dissolved.

[17]See the article by N. M. al-Haymas, "Asha'ir al-'Iraq tushakkilu lijanan li-bahth ijtithat al-ba'th wa'l-hiwar ma'al-muqawama wa hal al-milishiyat," *al-Sharq al-Awsat*, August 28, 2006.

[18]Reuters, December 3, 2007.

[19]See his article "In Search of Justice, Not Vengeance," *The Washington Post*, December 28, 2003.

Two elements have often been highlighted: Education and security. The dismissal of several thousand teachers and professors has been denounced as absurd since Party membership was a prerequisite for employment by the Ministry of Education. But, above all, security considerations have proved decisive. The decision to dissolve the Iraqi army was widely blamed as a major trigger of the insurgency and a severe hindrance to improving security:

> At a single stroke we also sent home 400,000 Iraqi soldiers, most of them patriots, and in the process created a vacuum in which insurgents, terrorists and criminals have flourished ('Allawi, 2003).

This has been mainly the approach adopted by the US: In April 2004, Ambassador Bremer declared that a large number of officers who had served in Saddam's army would be recalled to rebuild the new Iraqi army (Bremer, 2004). Shortly after Bremer's statement on the reintegration of former Iraqi army officers into the new army, the Iraqi minister of Defense, 'Ali 'Abd al-Amir al-'Allawi, met with more than 50 former senior army officers of the rank of brigadier-general or higher, to discuss the structure of the new army (*al-Sharq al-Awsat*, 2004).

The best example of this new approach was the creation of the Falluja Brigade in May 2004. After a month of intensive fighting in Falluja, a former intelligence officer was given the responsibility of ensuring the security of the city, and above all ensuring that foreign fighters were handed over to the US military. He was given the responsibility of a brigade composed mainly of ex-Ba'thists.

For some, this difference between "good" and "bad" Ba'thists is equal to the difference between Ba'thists and "Saddamists", or Saddam Husayn's partisans. Many people were members of the Ba'th Party, because they had no choice. But the true criminals were Saddam's followers. As Justice Minister Malik Duhan al-Hasan said, "dealing with all Ba'thists the same way is wrong."[20]

It is interesting to note that this distinction is being used by the ex-Ba'thists themselves. When recognizing their past membership,[21] many

---

[20]See "My Hands Are Not Stained With Blood," *The Washington Post*, February 3, 2005.

[21]Membership in the Ba'th Party is now something to be hidden after 2003 in Iraq, something shameful. Among the ex-Ba'thists that I met, the majority did not acknowledge their past membership — they only mentioned for example that they have been forced to leave Iraq after 2003, or "advised to leave", because of threats. Few ex-members of the Ba'th have therefore recognized their past membership. When they did so, they immediately asked for this information not to be mentioned in the research.

ex-Ba'thists that I met during my research systematically distanced themselves from Saddam Husayn's policy and recognized that "errors were made" under Ba'th rule.[22] In their view, Saddam Husayn, perverted the Ba'th:

> Saddam Husayn did not have an ideology, only a disproportionate love for power [...]. Saddam Husayn is a criminal. But the Party as a party does not belong to him.[23]

Moreover, parts of this alternate narrative are completely at one with the results of research I conducted during the spring of 2001 on the Iraqi university system. I found, for example, that in Ba'thist Iraq, individuals were first and foremost concerned for their own survival in a very difficult economic and political environment. In this context, membership in the party was very often purely instrumental. That is why for the Party, the university system represented a unique opportunity to try to encourage new members to join, because they were automatically attributed supplementary credits during exams. For students with other resources (financial, social, political), it was not an option. It could become one for others. Once "in the system", the incentive was very strong to keep using the membership and then the rise within the party as a tool of social promotion (Lafourcade, 2001). In 2001, the ideological dimension of the regime had become almost entirely rhetorical, and resembled very much what Lisa Wedeen has described for Syria in 1999 (Wedeen, 1999). In any case, the totalitarian nature of the Ba'thist regime was very doubtful.

A Minority Discourse

Under Iyad 'Allawi's government, changes were clear. In September 2004, he sought to limit the powers of the de-Ba'thification Commission, demanding that his ministers cease to have dealings with the former Commission and making it more complicated for its members to enter the "Green Zone" and have access to the CPA and Iraqi government officials (Saghieh, 2007, p. 220). At the same time, Ahmad Chalabi's honeymoon with the US administration came to an end and his offices and belongings were searched on several occasions and even sacked by American forces during 2004. We lack accurate figures and precise reports on the number of Ba'thist reintegrations, but it seems that it took place particularly in the military. The creation

---

[22]Interview with a Ba'thist, ex-member of Parliament. Amman, April 2008.
[23]Interview with a competitor on the 158 list. Amman, December 2005.

of the "Falluja brigade" is an example of this new policy. Nevertheless, it remained a case-by-case policy and the Law remained unchanged.

The reason is simple: The reintegrations caused enormous anger within the Shi'i leadership, which has always remained the strongest advocate of de-Ba'thification. While the Shi'i leadership is quite pluralist and has many different viewpoints on major issues such as the American occupation, the relations between state and religion, etc. — it has generally been united since 2003 on the issue of de-Ba'thification. The announcement of the creation of the Falluja Brigade, for example, provoked a unanimous outcry among its ranks. On May 2, 2004, the former Ba'thist Major-General Jasim Muhammad Salih al-Muhammadi, from the disbanded Republican Guard, the commander of the Brigade, entered Falluja with his 200 ex-Ba'thists, wearing his Republican Guard uniform and carrying the Iraqi flag. The Da'wa party immediately issued a statement that the return of the Ba'thists was casting doubt on the credibility of democracy (Raphaeli, 2004). In his Friday sermon in the Kufa Mosque, Muqtada al-Sadr said that the Americans were trying to restore the Ba'thists, and that this decision showed "American hatred of the Iraqi people and [was] a reward to the Ba'thists for the gift they presented to the occupier, which is Iraq" (Raphaeli, 2004). The distinction between Ba'thists and Saddamists was rejected by this trend. For example, the newspaper *al-Mu'tamar*, organ of Ahmad Chalabi's INC was particularly vehement against the 'profiteers' who joined the party to keep their jobs, retain their food ration coupons, or avoid losing their electricity (Raphaeli, 2004).

The United States backed off immediately. It named retired Major-General Muhammad Latif as the commanding officer of the Falluja Brigade; General Latif studied at a British military academy and spent years in Saddam's prisons, and was thus a much more acceptable figure. But, in spite of this decision, demonstrations were organized in Baghdad by the Supreme Council of the Islamic Revolution in Iraq (Raphaeli, 2004). Later on, when Iyad 'Allawi was designated Prime Minister, his past as a member of the Ba'th Party in the 1970s, the Ba'thist past of several ministers, and the restrictions put on the de-Ba'thification commission have been extensively criticized. For example Nuri al-Maliki declared in October 2004 that "['Allawi is] outside the law and [that] the de-Ba'thification commission has the right to remove all traces of the Ba'thists" (Saghieh, 2007, pp. 220–221).

After the elections of January 2005, which constituted a relative setback for 'Allawi, and a large victory for the Shi'i list — and Ahmad Chalabi was part of it — the tendency was clearly reversed and the Commission resumed its activities. De-Ba'thification remained very popular within the Shi'i community:

> Chalabi deserves to be elected because he called for de-Baathification, [a move] against the Baath Partywhich destroyed us and our country [...]. Now we're showing our gratitude by voting for him (Institute for War and Peace Reporting, 2005a).

There was thus no reversal of the de-Ba'thification policy. Re-integration remained very circumscribed, limited to the security field and generally received no publicity at all.

The de-Ba'thification Issue and the Iraqi Civil War

2005 was a crucial year in the triggering of the Iraqi civil war, although the year had started with the first free elections in Iraq's history. But the impact of those elections was much different from what had been expected. They clearly contributed to increase latent sectarian tensions among the Iraqi communities, particularly between Sunnis and Shi'is. Due to military operations against the Sunni city of Falluja — which was supposed to have been harboring al-Qa'ida and other Sunni jihadist groups since April 2004, most Sunni political formations and personalities chose to call for a boycott of the vote. As a result, the electoral turnout was very low in Sunni provinces. In al-Anbar, for example, it reached only 2%. In the Transitional National Assembly elected in January 2005, only 7 out of 275 members were Sunni, while Sunni Arabs represent approximately 20% of the Iraqi population.[24] Later attempts to include Sunni personalities in the committee in charge of the writing of a new constitution for Iraq, during the summer of 2005, failed — and the Sunnis increasingly protested that their claims were not taken into account by the new masters. One of their first claims was for a reform of the de-Ba'thification process. This is explicitly mentioned, for example, on the program of the 158 List ('Adnan al-Dulaymi) for the elections of December 2005.

All this reinforced the perception within the Sunni community, of a "de-sunnization" of the country, and many Sunnis believed that official institutions were being used to implement this policy. Even their participation in the elections of December 2005 did not change the situation:

---

[24]The last census considered reliable was conducted in 1956.

They perceived the rule of the majority as a *de facto* tyranny of the majority — their minority status in post-Ba'thist Iraq, as well as the strong Shi'i-Kurdish alliance on major political issues, prevented them from having a decisive input in the political arena. This undoubtedly played a crucial role in increasing tensions between the communities in Iraq. Sectarian violence was clearly on the rise during the year 2005. By summer, all the elements of a civil war were already in place; a vicious circle of violence and revenge was going on. When the "transitional" period came to an end with the adoption of a new constitution by a referendum in October 2005 and other general elections in December 2005, violence became overwhelming, especially after the Samarra bombing in February 2006. For many, the political process had come to a dead end.

The Battle turns Parliamentarian

This is one of the main reasons why the United States increasingly pressurized both Sunni and Shi'i factions to agree on de-Ba'thification reform. It was one of the main benchmarks imposed by the American administration on Nuri al-Maliki's government in June 2006. United States pressure and the devastating effect of communitarian violence progressively convinced an initially reluctant Shi'i leadership to engage in some reforms. But the Shi'i leadership itself has proved divided on the question. Promulgated in June 2007, the "Accountability and Justice" Law has been facing strong opposition, particularly from the Sadrists. As a result, several drafts circulated, emanating from different political forces, in an attempt to find a compromise between parliamentarians. Through fragments of parliamentary debates available in the Iraqi media, it appeared clearly that what was at stake was a partial reintegration of lower rank-Ba'thists. Falah Shanshal, the head of the parliament's de-Ba'thification Committee and a Sadrist leader, said this would give an opportunity to many of Saddam Husayn's supporters to return to their posts, "resulting in many tragedies" (Voices of Iraq, 2008). For other members of the Shi'i coalition, such as the Da'wa party, the idea was possible, but with guarantees. As Haidar al-'Abbadi, a leading figure of the Da'wa Party, pointed out:

> Former Ba'th Party members should vow not to return to their old practices before they return to their positions. [...] Damages should be paid to those who have been harmed by the former regime's policies and former Ba'thists should receive their retirement rights (Voices of Iraq, 2008).

Sunni Arabs views also differed on the law. While 'Adnan Dulaymi's Iraqi Accord Front (IAF) welcomed it, the secular National Dialog Front (NDF) led by Salih Mutlaq rejected it (Voices of Iraq, 2008). Opponents of the law objected to clauses in the legislation that banned anyone who had served in Husayn's special security organs from working in the new forces. Another contentious section involved members from the fourth-highest level of the Ba'th Party. The law would block them from serving in the country's judiciary council or the Foreign, Interior and Defense ministries. High-ranking officials who had been reintegrated could be fired again, paving the way for a new purge.

Finally, the law was passed with 150 votes out of 272 members of the parliament. But debates around the adoption of the Law (Majlis al-Nuwwab, 2008) provoked such a polarization of the *majlis al-nuwwab* (Council of Representatives) that the presidency council hesitated to ratify it. In an attempt to avoid a deadlock, Vice President Tariq al-Hashimi declared that the presidency council would submit amendments to parliament in the coming weeks but would not prevent the law from being implemented.

The 2008 Law, a Victory for Opponents of de-Ba'thification Reform

The new law does not mark the major change that some reformers had hoped. On the contrary, it may be seen as a major victory for the de-Ba'thification Commission and opponents of de-Ba'thification reform:

> The new law gives the de-Ba'thification Commission a new name, but preserves much of the old system. The new Supreme Commission for Accountability and Justice will have the same staff and much of the same structure as its predecessor (International Center for Transitional Justice, 2008).

The Commission's powers were strengthened, its reach extended (to a number of organizations not previously affected, including the Iraqi judiciary), and some of the target groups affected were changed. All former employees of Ba'th-era security intelligence agencies now had to be dismissed from government employment and pensioned off, regardless of whether or not they were party members (except for individuals who worked in the Ba'th-era Defense ministry, military or police forces). This clearly enables a new purge to take place. On the other side, many ex-Ba'thists were officially reinstated, pensions rights were clarified, and an independent appeal mechanism was created, the Cassation Chamber. Individuals who were at the level of *firqa* (group) member are now permitted to return to government service — counting in descending order from the highest level of leadership, a *firqa* member was the sixth rank of party member (International Center for Transitional Justice, 2008).[25] The results of these two different tendencies (a new purge vs reinstatements) are impossible to measure since some reinstatements had already taken place since late 2006 (International Center for Transitional Justice, 2008).

But the law introduced one major change, namely the principle of individual responsibility. The Justice and Accountability Law acknowledges the idea of instrumental membership of the Ba'th Party and recognizes the need to reintegrate these Ba'thists. If an individual belongs to a category of membership that would benefit from the new law but is convicted by a court of having committed crimes or embezzled public funds, then he or she will forfeit their pension and/or return rights. Part of the narrative on "good" and "bad" Ba'thists has therefore been integrated, as clearly indicated in the law:

> This law was enacted to [...] take into consideration the existence of bogus memberships in the Party of some segments of the populations who do not believe in the dictatorial ideas of the Ba'th and its oppressive practices (Majlis al-Nuwwab, 2008).

But, while this principle is recognized, the general approach does not change: It is yet to consider group membership rather than individual wrongdoing. Those targeted are party members above the rank *'adu firqa*, and members of security agencies. As a result, it is doubtful that the new law will change much. The narrative of the ex-Ba'thists ("we are Ba'thists but we are innocent") is still not recognized as legitimate. They are even more stigmatized. The validity of Ba'thist ideas should be, in their view, recognized: "The de-Ba'thification Law is even worse than the old one [...] it

---

[25]There are two major exceptions, however: *firqa* members who held the highest civil service positions may not return; and *firqa* members who held or hold positions in certain sensitive ministries, the Supreme Judicial Council, and key leadership offices may not continue in or return to these positions.

is against Ba'thist ideas themselves, civil society, Arabism."[26] According to them, the law is still inspired by revenge and fanaticism:

> If Ba'thists have to be put aside from the political game, it should be the people who decide so. This is democracy. This is the contrary of what the fanatical Shi'is are doing.[27]

In September 2008, 'Ali al-Lami, a protégé of Chalabi and a member of the commission was accused by an anonymous American official of giving the names of Ba'thists to death squads (al-Hayat, 2008). For ex-Ba'thists, instead of punishment and revenge, what should be sought for and promoted is a spirit of reconciliation. Here, the model is the Truth and Reconciliation Committee of South Africa as "with this law, the civil conflict will never end." Thus, "we should have followed the South African example. We should start again from scratch — do not forget that in Nuremberg there were only 94 persons: this is very few."[28]

Revenge vs Reconciliation

To this day, the Iraqi polity is divided on how to handle its immediate past. Instrumental in this fragmentation and the triggering of the Iraqi civil war; de-Ba'thification has become one of the flash points of the conflict. Even if the security situation improved in 2008 after more than a year and a half of intense violence between communities, it still remains fragile. In order to consolidate the security achievements of the past years, a national reconciliation strategy for Iraq seems more pressing today than ever before. This should include non-partisan work on Iraq's Ba'thist past, that could best be effected by setting up a truth and reconciliation commission.

Electronic references

al-Hayat (2008). Mudir hay'at ijtithath al-ba'th zawwada al-majm'uat al-khassa ma'lumat sahhalat qutl 'iraqiyin [The director of the de-Ba'thification Committee provided 'special groups' information facilitating the killing of Iraqis]. 9 September. Online. Available HTTP: <http://www.daralhayat.com/arab_news/levant_news/09-2008/Item-20080908-42ffd428-c0a8-10ed-01ec-19d7bf8293eb/story.html> (accessed 9 April 2009).

---

[26]Interview with a Ba'thist ex-member of Parliament. Amman, April 2008.

[27]Interview with a competitor on the 158 list. Amman, December 2005.

[28]Interview with a non-Ba'thist ex-member of Parliament (1980–1984). Amman, April 2008.

al-Sharq al-Awsat (2004). Wazir al-difa' al-'iraqi yaltaq dibatan sabiqin [The Iraqi defense minister meets former officers]. 30 April. Online. Available HTTP: <http://www.asharqalawsat.com/details.asp?section=4&article=231514&issueno=9285> (accessed 9 April 2009).

Bremer, P (2004). *Turning the page.* Online. Available HTTP: <http://www.cpa-iraq.org/transcripts/20040423_page_turn.html> (accessed 14 December 2006).

Coalition Provisional Authority (2003a). *Memorandum 1: Implementation of De-Baathification Order 1.* Online. Available HTTP: <http://www.cpa-iraq.org/regulations/20030603_CPAMEMO_1_Implementation_of_DeBa_athification.pdf.> (accessed 14 December 2007).

—— (2003b). *Memorandum 7: Delegation of Authority Under De-Baathification Order No 1.* Online. Available HTTP: <http://www.cpa-iraq.org/regulations/20031104_CPAMEM0_7_Delegation_of_Authority.pdf> (accessed 14 December 2007).

—— (2003c). *Order 1: De-baathification of Iraqi Society.* Online.Available HTTP: <http://www.cpairaq.org/regulations/20030516_CPAORD_1_DeBa_athification_of_Iraqi_Society_.pdf> (accessed 31 October 2006).

—— (2003d) *Order 2: Dissolution of Entities.* Online. Available HTTP: <http://www.iraqcoalition.org/regulations/20030823_CPAORD_2_Dissolution_of_Entities_with_Annex_A.pdf> (accessed 14 December 2006).

—— (2003e). *Order 5: Establishment of the Iraqi De-Baathification Council.* Online. Available HTTP: <http://www.cpa-iraq.org/regulations/CPAORD5.pdf> (accessed 14 December 2007).

—— (2003f). *Order 48: Delegation of Authority regarding an Iraqi Special Tribunal.* Online. Available HTTP: <http://www.iraqcoalition.org/regulations/20031210_CPAORD_48_IST_and_Appendix_A.pdf> (accessed 14 December 2006).

Cole, J (2005). Saturday, November 26, 2005, *Informed Comment. Thoughts on the Middle East, History and Religion.* Online. Available HTTP: <http://www.juancole.com/2005_11_01_juancole_archive.html> (accessed 9 April 2009).

Commission Des Recours Des Refugiés (2005). *Irak: les baasistes dans l'après Saddam Hussein.* Online. Available HTTP: <http://www.commission-refugies.fr/IMG/pdf/Irak-les_Baasistes_de_l_apres_Saddam_Hussein.pdf> (accessed 14 December 2006).

Majlis al-Nuwwab (2008). *Qanun al-hay'a al-wataniya li'l-musa'ala wa'l-'adala.* Online. Available HTTP: <http://www.ictj.org./static/MENA/Iraq/20080112.DBLaw.arabic.pdf> (accessed 12 February 2008).

The Iraq Memory Foundation [al-Mu'assasa al-Dhakira al-'Iraqiyya]. Online. Available HTTP: <http://www.iraqmemory.org/en/index.asp> (accessed 12 February 2008).

United States Agency for International Development (Usaid) (2004). *Iraq's Legacy of Terror. Mass Graves.* Online. Available HTTP: <http://www.usaid.gov/iraq/pdf/iraq_mass_graves.pdf> (accessed 12 February 2008).

Voices of Iraq (2008). "Parliamentarians share thoughts on debaathification law, 10 January." Online. Available HTTP: <http://www.iraqupdates.com/p_articles.php/article/25994> (accessed 9 April 2009).

DEALING WITH VICTIMHOOD: WHOSE MEMORIES OF MASS VIOLENCE? BETWEEN ORAL AND OFFICIAL HISTORY

FRAGMENTED MEMORY, COMPETING NARRATIVES: THE PERSPECTIVE OF WOMEN SURVIVORS OF THE ANFAL OPERATIONS IN IRAQI KURDISTAN

Karin Mlodoch

Introduction

Over the years since the fall of the Ba'th regime in 2003, there has been an increasing fragmentation of Iraqi society along ethnic-national and religious lines. This cannot simply be explained by the power vacuum in the aftermath of the US-led intervention: It is also the reflection of decades of dictatorship and violence, which have exposed large swathes of the population to massive violence and loss and has destroyed individual and social structures throughout Iraq. The relatives of the Shi'i victims of the mass executions in the South, the survivors of the poison gas attacks and the Anfal operations in Kurdistan, the victims of mass deportation in the Iraqi marshes, the relatives of executed political prisoners and members of persecuted religious minorities: All are still waiting for the opening of the mass graves found after the fall of the regime, and for evidence, justice and compensation. At the same time, ongoing violence by different actors — terrorist groups, occupation forces, militias, and criminal gangs — continues to claim numerous new victims, some of them undoubtedly the former perpetrators. The current national political debate is characterized by competing and conflicting memories and narratives of the past and present with victimhood of past and current violence being a significant argument to legitimate power claims on the national level. At the same time the debate on how to deal with the legacy of the Ba'th regime, initially pushed forward by the Coalition Provisional Authority in the aftermath of the intervention, has been pushed off the political agenda by the urgency of the need for an inclusive national compromise to end the violence. Apart from the highly contested tribunals against Saddam Husayn and his immediate circle at the Supreme Iraqi Criminal Tribunal and the precipitate execution of Saddam Husayn, and an equally precipitate (although subsequently revised) law for the de-Baʻthification of the political and military apparatus, no institutional steps for dealing with the past are currently in sight.

In contrast with the great significance surrounding the memory of violence and victimhood in the political arena, there is a striking lack of response to the immediate needs of victims and survivors of past crimes, and their voices and perspectives have largely been excluded from the current political debate on both regional and national levels.

In what follows, I shall focus on the survivors of the Anfal operations in Kurdistan in 1988, and especially on the large number of women among them, whose memories and narratives are competing with multiple other memories of suffering in Kurdistan and Iraq. I will look at the construction and transformation of individual and collective memories and narratives on the Anfal operations within the group of survivors, closely linked to and shaped by gender and social, economic, and political factors. I will show that the memories of survivors of the Anfal compete not only with conflicting memories on the national level, but also with the dominant narrative on the Anfal within Kurdish society. Since their claims and needs remain unaddressed and their voices are excluded from public discourse, they feel increasingly disappointed and alienated from both the Iraqi national and the Kurdish regional political process.

I will argue that, given the long term effects of traumatic experiences of violence and loss among substantial segments of the population, it is essential that Iraqi society should address the needs of victims of past crimes for evidence, justice, compensation and acknowledgement, and that the development of strategies for dealing with the past is a vital precondition for engaging the population in a national dialogue on conflicting and competing memories and narratives on past and present in order to avoid or arrest further fragmentation.

My observations are based on many years of practical work and psychological research with women survivors of the Anfal in the Germyan region in Iraqi Kurdistan since 1991, with reference to psychological concepts of individual and collective trauma and traumatic memory, and to the victim-centered psychological debate on reconciliation processes after violence, war and conflict.

Traumatic Memory, Fragmented Memory

Given that large parts of the Iraqi population have been exposed to experiences of massive violence and loss in the more and less recent past, and that Iraqi society has been pervaded by structural violence and the destruction of social textures, the notion of trauma is in my view an important category for understanding and analyzing current conflicts and social and political processes in Iraq. While critical of the inflated use of the concept of trauma in public debate, and in an increasing number of disciplines beside psychology, and of the widespread tendency to psychologize social and political processes and thus to pathologize whole populations as traumatized,[1] I am referring to a socially and politically contextualized concept of trauma. I approach it not as a purely individual experience, but as the destruction of individual and/or social and collective structures, considering the political and social context in which the violence occurred, as well as the impact of social, political, economic, and gender aspects on the coping strategies of survivors in the aftermath of violence.[2]

The concept of trauma describes an overwhelming experience of violence and loss, in which the victims suffer loss of control over their physical and psychological functions, feelings of complete powerlessness and the destruction of their physical and psychological integrity (Herman, 1992). Their concepts and assumptions about themselves and the world are deeply shattered. Shame and guilt are prominent feelings in the aftermath of violence: For the loss of control during the violence, for entering in a sort of relationship with the perpetrator, for not having been able to protect relatives or fellows and also for having survived while others have not.

Traumatic experiences have an especially strong impact on memory. Survivors of extreme violence continuously relive parts of the violent

---

[1]The prominent concept in public trauma discourse is Post Traumatic Stress Disorder (PTSD), a clinical approach defining the effects of a traumatic experience as a series of symptoms such as nightmares, flashbacks, dissociated memories, anxiety and depression. It gives little importance to the specific social and political circumstances of the particular type of violence experienced, and tends to equate different qualities of experience such as loss, shock, violence and disaster and to pathologize the victims (see Becker, 1997, 2006; Summerfield, 1997).

[2]This concept is largely informed by psychoanalytical theory and methodology and has been developed in research on Holocaust survivors, enriched by working with Vietnam Veterans, victims of torture in Latin America and victims of sexual abuse. For an overview see Becker, 1992; Herman, 1991; Lennertz, 2006; and the work of the International Trauma Research Network at <www.traumaresearch.net>.

experience, while other parts of the experience are repressed and often completely dissociated. They still persist in flashbacks, nightmares, or translate into psychosomatic symptoms. They might appear in the form of obsessive wishes to repeat the unbearable situation, or as a state of disorientation and the incapacity to distinguish between past and present. Dissociated or suppressed memories of traumatic experiences might be reactivated subsequently by further experiences of violence or humiliation after a period of latency. These parts of the individual's memory are not accessible to a narrative or autobiographic memory; they cannot be integrated in one's biography, exist in pieces without making sense and are not under the individual's control. Traumatic memory is fragmented memory, disrupted memory.

In order to define the impact of experiences of violence shared by a group of people, the term "collective trauma" is frequently used, not only in psychological debate but also in social and cultural sciences and historiography. While it seems strikingly evident at first sight that a traumatic experience shared by members of a group, collective or society will have a traumatic impact on the whole texture of society, the notion of collective trauma is as yet very sparsely conceptualized from a psychological point of view, and there is no evidence to suggest how psychological mechanisms occurring after an experience of extreme violence might be transferred from the individual psyche to a group, collective or even a nation.[3]

There is instead an evident correlation between individual traumatic experiences of violence and the impact of social, political, and economic factors on how individuals react to trauma and the various strategies they are able to develop in the aftermath to come to terms with their experience. Reconstructing fragmented traumatic memory, transforming it into a narrative sense-making memory and reintegrating the trauma into one's biography — thus also relating to life before the trauma — are important steps for coming to a point of closure with the past on an individual level and are largely dependent on external factors such as safety (in the

---

[3]More conceptual research exists on how the traumatic experiences of individual members of a group enter the collective memory and how members of a group often refer to traumatic experiences as constituent elements of group identities. These processes have been largely explored within the research on the long term and trans-generational impact of the Holocaust both on the victims' society and the perpetrators' society (Bar-On, 1989; Kestenberg, 1982; LaCapra, 1992). In *Trauma and Collective Memory* Angela Kühner summarizes attempts to conceptualize "collective trauma" both from the psychological trauma discourse and from interdisciplinary approaches to "collective memory". She suggests the use of the terms "collectivized trauma" or "symbol-mediated trauma" instead of collective trauma (Kühner, 2008).

sense of the sustainable absence of the perpetrator and the unlikelihood that the traumatic event will be repeated), as well as social and political acknowledgement of the suffering and forms of symbolic closures. While the impunity of perpetrators can prolong the individual suffering of the victim, punishment of the perpetrators can assist in the coping process (Rauchfuss, 2006). Symbolic closures such as memorials, ceremonies, apologies by the perpetrators and reparations can help victims to come to terms with the traumatic past and reintegrate into their present life. Acknowledgement and symbolic closure are especially important for relatives of disappeared persons, of whom there are many in Iraq, members of a number of different socio-political and religious groups (Hamber *et al.*, 2003).

"With our Husbands gone our Lives have Disappeared": Experiences, Memories and Narratives of Women Survivors of the Anfal in Germyan

My research is focused on the situation and perspectives of women survivors of the Anfal in the Germyan region of southeastern Kurdistan, which borders Kirkuk in the west and Iran in the east. I have shown in previous research how their strategies of coping with their experiences of violence and loss and their possibilities of developing new life perspectives are limited by social and economic factors and gender relations in the patriarchal and traditional context of Kurdish rural society, and how their individual suffering is being prolonged and reinforced by the lack of social and political acknowledgement, and the absence of institutional steps to bring past crimes to account on both the Kurdistan regional and Iraqi national levels (Mlodoch, 2000, 2009). The following observations are based on experiences working with women survivors and on systematic interviews between 1994 and 2008.[4]

---

[4]Between 1991 and 1995, I worked for the German NGO medico international in reconstruction programs for destroyed villages in Kurdistan-Iraq; since 1995 I been working with assistance programs for Anfal women survivors for the German NGO HAUKARI. I interviewed Anfal women survivors on their memories of the Anfal and their psychological situation in 1994–1995, 1999–2000 and 2003–2008. Specifically, one group of women survivors of the Anfal in Sumud/Rizgary has been interviewed in each of these time periods. Changes in their living situation and in their memories and narratives were observed over a period of some 15 years. Finally, the interviews with the daughters of women survivors of the Anfal in Sumud began in 2007.

The Germyan region was affected by what is widely regarded as the most savage Anfal operation, beginning in April 1988. After shelling villages and towns — some with poisonous gas — the Iraqi army, assisted by Kurdish militias cooperating with the Ba'th regime, destroyed houses and rural infrastructure and gathered the population in transitory camps. Here men between 15 and 60 years old and young women were separated and deported southwards. While the mass graves found along the deportation routes and the very few testimonies of survivors of the deportation suggest the systematic mass killing of the deportees, there is still no solid evidence about the individual fate of most of them. Kurdish sources estimate the number of disappeared and killed persons during the Anfal operations to be about 182,000, while the military commander directly responsible for the Anfal operations, 'Ali Hasan al-Majid, is reported to having confirmed "not more than 100,000 victims." Human Rights Watch has a list of 50,000 names that have been found in the regime's own documents (Ebdurrehman, 1995; Fischer-Tahir, 2003; Hiltermann, 2008; Middle East Watch, 1993, 1994).

Elderly people and women with children were brought to other transit camps and then to the notorious prisons of Dibs and Nugrat Salman in Southern Iraq. Here they were held for six to seven months and then released under an amnesty and transported to so called collective towns *(mujamma'at),* where they lived under the direct control of the perpetrators until 1991, restricted in their movements and without any possibility of going back to their villages or starting any productive activity.

In 1991, when large parts of Kurdistan gained provisional autonomy, the reconstruction of the destroyed villages began. While many families returned to the villages and restarted their agricultural life, other Anfal survivors stayed on in the *mujamma'at*, including a large group of women whose husbands, brothers, fathers, sons and daughters, sometimes numerous relatives, had disappeared during the Anfal. In the Kurdish society, they are referred to as *Bêwajin-î Enfal*, Anfal women without men. These women survivors have been reluctant to return to their original villages for all these years or to engage in other activities such as income-generating projects or education, living in precarious and provisional conditions in the collective towns of Shoresh and Sumud.

The very term *Bêwajin-î Enfal* — women without men — reveals how Kurdish society defines these women through the absence and loss of their husbands and male relatives. Most of the Anfal surviving women bear the physical and psychological scars of the massive violence they have experienced. They have suffered massive attacks on their physical and psychological integrity during the Anfal. Their daily lives were suddenly and brutally disrupted; they were separated from their husbands, brothers, fathers, sons, and daughters and most of them have not heard from any of them ever since. They were held prisoners for months and exposed to appalling atrocities during their imprisonment. They were kept without sanitation and little food and water in overcrowded halls, beaten up and tormented. Their parents and children died in their arms — survivors report dozens of prisoners dying daily — their corpses were thrown into the desert surrounding the prison, and the women witnessed the corpses of their loved ones being torn and eaten by wild dogs at night. The world and self-concepts of these women, defining their roles as caring mothers, wives and daughters, were deeply shattered. Recalling their "failure" to protect their parents and children produces strong feelings of guilt and shame. The women are struggling until today with the memory of these unbearable situations, for example not being able, or being forbidden, to cry after the death of a child (compare Hardi, 2006, 2008).

After their release from the detention camps, they spent years under the control of the perpetrators in the *mujamma'at*. When other families started to return to the rebuilt villages after 1991, they continued to wait for their lost loved ones in temporary accommodation, being confined by societal norms to the role of waiting women without men. Thus the loss of their husbands and male relatives and their uncertain destiny became the distinct experience and the dominating narrative and memory both in their own perception and in that of the rest of society, thus sidelining their own experiences of violence.

Today, 20 years after the Anfal, the memory of it is present everywhere in the Germyan region and is suspended over the people and the region like a big cloud. History is divided between the time before the Anfal and the time after the Anfal. The term Anfal has entered daily language, when people are talking about their disappeared relatives as "The Anfals" or when they simply say, "my husband was Anfal."[5] The *Bêwajin-î Enfal* dominate the landscape in the streets of the former *mujamma'at* like Sumud and Shoresh.

---

[5] As far as I know there has been no suggestion either from the survivors of the Anfal or in the political or academic circles in Kurdistan that the name "Anfal" which was given to the aggression by the perpetrators, should be dropped in favor of another term. The aggressor's nomenclature is being used by the survivors alongside other terms such as "genocide," and "*karesat*" (catastrophe, disaster). See Fischer-Tahir's contribution to this volume.

They wear dark traditional clothes, sit in front of their houses, and queue at water outlets and health centers. Many of them bear physical signs of the violence they have suffered. Anfal women talk easily and continuously about their experience. Their stories are full of details, the most appalling cruelties often told without visible emotion, but they are rarely specific in time and location, and often do not correspond to historically documented facts.

At times it is not easy to distinguish between individual memories lived through in the first person and the memories of others which have been integrated into an individual's own story. Thus many women will summarize their experience by saying: "Our children were eaten by black dogs." While this atrocity occurred in the prison of Nugrat Salman, it is also brought up by women who have been held in other prisons or camps. The experience became a synonym for the suffering during the Anfal.

Women survivors of the Anfal continuously construct and transform their individual memories in communication with other members of the group, interweaving their own memories with those of others to form a collective narrative of suffering. Their constantly flowing story-telling is not oriented towards dialog, but instead seems to erect a wall between their own world and that of other people. It reflects what Judith Herman calls the central dilemma of trauma: A permanent oscillation between the desire to speak out and the desire to deny (Herman, 1992).

The collective narrative of the Anfal both breaks the silence and maintains it at the same time, thus granting some anonymity and protection to the individual victim within the group. There is little purpose in looking at testimonies of Anfal survivors simply to search for historical facts. Instead, looking in detail at Anfal testimonies not only in terms of content, but also in terms of how they are narrated, which aspects they reveal and which they deny or hide, gives a complex picture of the lived experience of the Anfal and also of the needs and expectations of Anfal survivors which ought to be addressed today (compare Dori Laub and Shoshana Felman's extensive work on Holocaust testimonies, Felman *et al.*, 1992).

Anfal women relive the Anfal daily and recall their absent relatives. All of them recount years of daily listening at the door and asking questions: "What happened to them: Do they live, are they dead? Will I still be here when they come back?" of daily swings between desperation and hope. Even today, nine years after the fall of the regime in 2003, there is little evidence about the fate of individuals and thus little possibility of going through a process of mourning, of accepting loss and restarting life. Thus the women continue to wait, seemingly frozen in the past.

Research on the situation of relatives of disappeared persons in Chile, Argentina, Bosnia, and Nicaragua shows that this sense of "being frozen in the past" is characteristic of the situation of relatives of the disappeared across different cultural and social contexts. They suffer from permanent psychological stress, daily re-living the experience of loss. Attempts to reorganize the families, develop new relations and plans are felt to be a betrayal of the disappeared and are accompanied by strong feelings of guilt. They cannot go through a process of grieving, and they have no place to mourn. The uncertainty about the fate of their loved ones makes the survivors' own lives temporary and uncertain (Amnesty International, 1982, 1996; Becker, 1992; Lagos *et al.*, 1994; Meyer, 1981, 1994; Mupinda, 1995; Preitler, 2008; Quirk *et al.*, 1994; Tully, 1994).

While the specific stress symptoms of relatives of the disappeared have many resemblances in different cultural, social, and political contexts, ways of coping with the situation vary. In Zimbabwe, relatives of missing persons have organized symbolic funerals to appease anxious spirits they believe in and to put an end to uncertainty. The "Mothers of the Plaza de Mayo" in Argentina and the "Saturday mothers" of political prisoners in Turkey have given face and name to their missing sons and daughters during public demonstrations. Translating their suffering into activity for justice, they overcame paralysis and developed new energies and social networks. Especially for the women relatives of the disappeared, the possibility of reorganizing their lives depends largely on their social and political range of movement and their role within the society.

The Anfal operations in Iraqi Kurdistan hit a mostly rural, mostly illiterate population in remote and under-serviced areas. Social and gender relations in the Germyan area are still largely regulated by traditional patriarchal codes of morals and ethics, influenced by Islamic beliefs and tribal law (see also Qani'a, 1979; Qaradaghi, 1995). In the traditional understanding, women are subordinate to the men of their family. Their range of movement is limited by the concept of honor and shame and by a network of social control and sanctions. There is no socially accepted notion of women living without male breadwinners and protectors. In this context, social and cultural norms confine the women survivors of the Anfal whose husbands have disappeared to the only socially acceptable role, of waiting and mourning women.

The Anfal has destroyed the entire social and economic texture of the affected regions. There is hardly any family in Germyan who has not lost members during the Anfal; they now live in precarious family constellations, lacking income opportunities. The social and legal status of the *Bêwajin-î Enfal* within this disrupted texture is unclear. They are without men, but not widows. They have to defend the honor of their disappeared husbands and male relatives without enjoying their protection and provision. They cannot count on being maintained by their father's or husband's relatives who are themselves affected by the Anfal. Yet many Anfal women have been staying with relatives of their husbands, tolerated only because of their children. When returning to their father's relatives, the women risk losing the right to be with their children. Many women are furthermore bound by traditional marriage contracts such as *jin be jin* (two male friends marrying each other's sisters), risking large family conflicts if the agreement is disrupted. Remarriage has been legally possible but emotionally unthinkable for most of them due to feelings of guilt and, again, the fear of being separated from their children. Caught in this net of social rules, many Anfal women have been living in a depressing and unhappy family constellations, considered as an economic burden, unloved and often subject to domestic violence.

Those who have no relatives to fall back on have been living alone in provisional housing and extreme poverty for years, bringing up their children on their own by smuggling across the Kurdistan-Iraqi border, as day-laborers or beggars. These Anfal women have only received a pension from the Kurdistan Regional Government since 1999, and until recently this has not been sufficient to cover basic needs.

While — as outlined above — the women's own experience of violence is "hidden" behind the disappearance of their male relatives, society's imagination about what they have gone through, and especially the sexual violence to which they were assumed to have been subjected in the prisons, constitutes a taboo in Kurdish society. Thus the women themselves are stigmatized, since they constitute a challenge to the social concept of honor.

Because of the absence of their husbands, the Anfal women are subject to social control by their environment. They are considered "women at risk", and easily suspected of dishonorable behavior or prostitution when going out for work. While Anfal women do not enjoy any protection against domestic violence and sexual assaults during work, male relatives of their disappeared husbands and fathers control and sanction them when they have allegedly violated the code of honor.

Anfal women are expected to be women in grief. Indeed, they rarely participate in social activities apart from funerals. Sitting in groups at corners and in front of houses, they are like a public symbol of mourning. The consolation found in their children, most of whom have now grown up, is overshadowed by their worries about the children's fatherless childhood and youth. Daughters of Anfal women suffer from the same stigmatization as their mothers: Their fatherless youth is considered a stain on their virtue, and many find it difficult to find a spouse. Hence, gender and social norms and constraints reinforce these women's own perception that their lives have been lost with their husbands and male relatives, and keep them in the role of perpetual mourners, blocking them from developing new life perspectives.

This notion of helpless and weak women without men has generally been reproduced in Kurdish public discourse, including civil society and women's rights groups, whose main goal in the 1990s was to allow women survivors of the Anfal to remarry. This deeply offended many of them and indicated a lack of empathy for their situation.

The disappointment about the lack of social and political acknowledgement and of any concrete assistance within Kurdish society after 1991 added to the psychological suffering of the Anfal survivors, who felt increasingly bitter and marginalized. Their hope for change was directed almost exclusively towards the fall of the Ba'th regime and the eventual return of their male relatives. Yet within the limited range of movement conceded to them, they have shown strong agency: They survived and have managed to bring up their children despite many economic and social constraints. They have done all kinds of casual and manual work during the last 21 years and made creative use of the limited funds and assistance granted by the Kurdish government and local and international organizations. They have invested in the future of their children, and quite a number of their daughters and sons have finished secondary school or attend university and form a strong and conscious voice among the second generation of Anfal survivors.

The women survivors have formed informal networks, supporting and consoling each other. They have a strong sense of collective identity and are connected to each other by numerous and invisible channels of communication and information. Visitors coming to the former collective town of Sumud/Rizgary to talk to them need only approach one woman to have a group of 50 joining within minutes. Although most of them are illiterate, they are well informed about political and social developments and when given the opportunity of articulation in a public or semi-public space, they are clear in their claims and also fearless in discussions with political representatives.[6]

---

[6]Further comparative research would be needed (for example between women survivors of the Anfal in Germyan and women who have lived in urban centeres after the Anfal)

Hopes and Disappointments and the Transformation of Memories and Narratives after the Fall of the Ba'th Regime in 2003

For the women survivors of the Anfal in Germyan, the US-led intervention in Iraq in 2003 and the fall of the Ba'th regime marked a dramatic change, long desired and enthusiastically welcomed. Beside the relief and satisfaction they felt at the news and pictures of Saddam Husayn's fall, hope flourished anew that their missing relatives might return, and they entered into a state of excitement, some of them rushing to police stations, government offices and sites of mass graves to obtain definite evidence.

With the passage of time and the discovery of numerous mass graves throughout Iraq, the fate of those deported during the Anfal has become increasingly evident. Yet until now, due to the volatile security situation, only a few mass graves have actually been opened. The process of individual identification turns out to be problematic and only a few Anfal survivors have actually had information about the fate of their relatives. Many of them report that with the dashing of hopes combined with not having any certainty about the fate of individuals, and still having no place to mourn, they fell into a deeper depression than before.

With the social and political changes occurring in Iraq and Kurdistan, the survivors' memories and narratives are also undergoing transformation. After the fall of the Ba'th regime, the Kurdistan Regional Government has — although with some hesitation — invested in the infrastructure in the Anfal-affected regions and the former collective towns, where large numbers of women survivors live. The pensions of Anfal survivors were raised, and in 2008 many of them received funds to build houses. In the collective towns like Sumud (the Arabic name given it by the Ba'th regime — translated pride or steadfastness — has been replaced by the Kurdish name Rizgary — Freedom), water and sewage projects, health stations, schools and libraries have been constructed, thus creating jobs and income opportunities and generally improving the economic situation.

While the survivors' narratives were focused on their missing male relatives until 2003, now, with the lessening of economic pressure and the end of

---

to see how far access to cultural/social capital has helped them deal with their traumatic experiences by giving a broader sense to their tragedy and thus to foster their reintegration in life. My observations so far suggest that to the extent to which survivors engage in public discourse and articulate their experiences and claims, access to education is less significant for them than their partisan activities before and after the Anfal and the social networks and support around them.

any hope that their relatives will return, they are coming to focus increasingly on demands for evidence, justice, compensation and acknowledgement. At the same time, their own experiences during the Anfal and its aftermath have made them become more articulate in their narratives. They increasingly report about the violence and torture that they suffered in the detention camps and prisons. They also focus increasingly on their living situation in the aftermath of the Anfal, on their suffering, their bitterness about the lack of assistance and acknowledgment, but also stress their own strength both in surviving and having brought up their children without any economic or social support.

Their children, now grown up, play a major role in shifting the focus of the collective narratives in Germyan from the disappearance of the males to the fate of their mothers have during and in the aftermath of the Anfal. Many of the second generation of Anfal survivors have had access to education and — relating their own situation to the general economic upturn in Iraqi Kurdistan — express anger about the lack of assistance and the miserable situations their mothers have had to endure for so many years. They are also proud of their mothers' strength in having brought them up despite so many hardships and shortages. In particular, their daughters, who have suffered from the same kinds of social stigmatization as their mothers, are now very outspoken and clear in making demands for more assistance and social and political acknowledgement for their mothers and themselves, such as seeking special grants for students from Anfal families.

Another example of the transformation of narratives is the memory of sexual assaults and rape suffered by women and girls during Anfal. Since this has been a taboo for many years and is related to social stigmatization, the experience of sexual violence has until recently not been part of the narratives of the survivors. Indeed their experiences have been turned against the women as a stigma and did not feature in their narratives for many years. Only some of the older women, who have lost their fear of bad reputations, eventually talked about sexual violence, yet mostly in the form of hints and references to others, never in first person. "They took our beautiful girls at night," or "it was not good for a girl to be beautiful" were some of the euphemisms used to hint at the nightly selection of girls by Iraqi soldiers, who would then never be seen again. In 2005, during the proceedings of the Supreme Iraqi Criminal Tribunal on the Anfal operations against Saddam Husayn, 'Ali Hasan al-Majid and others, the public prosecutor explicitly denounced the systematic sexual violence against women during the Anfal. From then on this part of their experience was integrated more consistently into the narratives of the women survivors, and also began to be discussed in meetings and conferences.[7] Here the increasing development of a women's rights movement in Iraqi Kurdistan, which has broken with quite a number of previous taboos on issues such as social and domestic violence against women and honor killings, has also played a role. With the ending of the taboo of mentioning sexual violence in the camps, other shameful experiences such as giving birth to children without any sanitation, having to keep menstrual blood in one's clothes for months, the suspension of menstruation for a long period after release from prison etc. are also gradually being mentioned, even in public gatherings.

With the greater distancing from the perpetrators, another formerly repressed memory is becoming more articulated in the collective narrative of the survivors, the accounts of Kurdish militias collaborating with the Ba'th regime and being actively involved in the destruction of Kurdish villages and the deportation of their inhabitants. In many individual interviews I conducted in the 1990s, Anfal survivors frequently referred to this memory as a particularly dramatic form of betrayal by their "brothers" and neighbors. Yet the memory remained on an individual level without entering the collective narratives in the victims' community. There seems to have been an acute sensitivity to the fact that while the Iraqi regime was still in place and threatening the provisional autonomy of the Kurdish area, the debate on collaborators was too explosive to be bearable in the fragile state of Kurdish society. Only after the fall of the Ba'th regime and the establishment of Kurdistan as an autonomous region of a federal Iraq did the memory of Kurdish collaboration with the regime entered the collective narratives of Anfal survivors. Today one of the key claims of the Anfal survivors against the Kurdistan Regional Government is that the amnesty given to collaborators in 1991 should be revoked and that they should be brought to justice.

Representation of Anfal Survivors' Memories and Narratives in Public Discourse in Iraqi Kurdistan

The Anfal and the memory of the Anfal has a high importance for the Kurdish political elite and society in the process of legitimating their claims

---

[7]For example at the conference "Gewalt, Erinnerung und Aufarbeitung im Irak. 20 Jahre nach den Anfal Operationen in Kurdistan: Die Perspektive der Überlebenden" in Berlin, 17 April 2008, organized by HAUKARI e.V. and the ZMO Berlin.

for autonomy, for power sharing on a national level and for international guarantees of Kurdish rights. As with the chemical attack on Halabja in 1988, the Anfal operations are considered a "collective trauma" and a constitutive element of Kurdish national identity. As Andrea Fischer-Tahir has outlined in her contribution to this volume, the acknowledgement of the Anfal as a genocide on both the Iraqi and international level is accorded high significance, not only among the Kurdish political leadership, but also in academic and public discourse.

In the hegemonic discourse, the women survivors are represented as poor and helpless victims, weeping and grieving women without male breadwinners, symbolic of the suffering of the entire Kurdish nation. The identification of the survivors through the disappearance of their male relatives is being largely reproduced both by the Kurdish political elite and civil society groups in the public debate. Apart from the role attributed to them as national symbols of Kurdish victimhood, their concrete experiences of violence and loss, their testimonies, voices and claims have been hidden and largely excluded from public discourse. Instead, pictures of Anfal women dressed in black, carrying photos of their missing loved ones, weeping or screaming, frequently appear on television and in the newspapers. In commemorative ceremonies they appear as rows of mourning women, without ever giving speeches in first person. Apart from few prominent women who have entered the political sphere as a result of their own militancy and act as delegates of Anfal survivors in parliament or on public occasions, the majority of women survivors remain in the shadows and are excluded from political and public participation.

What are the reasons for this ongoing marginalization of women survivors of the Anfal and their exclusion from public discourse? On a more general level, the exclusion from public discourse in the aftermath of violence is an experience Anfal survivors share with survivors of genocide, war and violence in other cultural and political contexts. Their experience distinguishes them, but their survival stigmatizes them at the same time. They are living monuments of the past, an awkward reminder to society of the violence and conflict it would prefer to leave behind. Certainly, in the context of a society which is currently undergoing a process of attaining a form of autonomy sanctioned in the constitution, and of economic progress and modernization, there is a strong wish to leave conflict and violence behind and not to go too deep into the desperate situation of the survivors. Indeed statements like "the Anfal women should stop suffering and begin to live their lives again" are frequently heard.

Gender is an important category to consider. The representation of women among the Anfal survivors as symbols of grief and suffering, defining them through the absence of their male relatives and sidelining their concrete experiences and living situations, widely corresponds to the dominant patriarchal discourse among the Kurdish political elite.

There are class aspects to consider as well: Germyan remains a remote region in terms of infrastructure, social services, and education. Most of the Anfal survivors are villagers, the majority of the women are illiterate and adhere to traditional moral and religious codes of conduct. They speak the Germyan dialect, rather than the "pure Kurdish" promoted in political and academic fields. In addition to this, as described above, the memories and narratives of the Anfal survivors themselves come in fragmented form. In general, from the perspective of the Kurdish elite and academia, who are pushing the case of the Anfal in the political arena, these women do not seem to be qualified to act as bearers of testimonies which will advocate effectively for Kurdish rights and national interests.

Beyond this, there are some very concrete political issues that these women might bring into the political debate through their testimonies, which conflict with the hegemonic Kurdish narrative of the victimhood of the Kurdish nation as a whole. As mentioned previously, their testimonies will bring up the awkward issue of Kurdish collaborators and their role during the Anfal operations, and the high-ranking political positions of some of these former collaborators within the present Kurdish political elite. Similarly, these testimonies may also pose some embarrassing questions about the role of the Kurdish political parties currently in power, which are at times criticized for not having done enough to warn and protect civilians during the Anfal.

The dichotomy between the survivors and the hegemonic Kurdish national discourse being made here is certainly simplified and there are other more nuanced narratives of the Anfal within Kurdish society. Despite the limited possibilities for Anfal survivors to organize themselves and put their claims forward, their voices and testimonies are increasingly entering public space. Some members of the Kurdish parliament are themselves Anfal survivors or are originally from the regions affected by the Anfal, and have advocated for the survivors in the political arena. Also some civil society and women's rights groups and newly developing independent newspapers are giving space to the claims and voices of survivors or offer different interpretations of their role in the Kurdish society. Unease about corruption and the abuse of power on the part of the ruling Kurdish political parties is growing within Kurdish society, and critical voices against the Kurdistan regional government increasingly refer to the Anfal survivors as yet another example of how the Kurdish elite is neglecting the hopes and needs of the Kurdish people. In addition, women activists in the parliament or civil society groups refer to the survivors as strong women who have shown strength without male protection. Thus, while the overall tendency among all political and civil society actors is still to confine the role of these women to being symbols of grief without conceding them agency, the transforming testimonies and narratives of Anfal survivors are increasingly competing with and challenging the hegemonic Kurdish national narrative on the Anfal.

The conflict between the memories of the women survivors and the dominant discourse is also part of the debate on ceremonies and memorials in the Kurdish region. Official commemoration ceremonies usually take place in the urban centers, which are far from the affected regions, with only a few survivors participating. Kurdish government plans to construct central memorials as an expression of the dimensions of the national catastrophe, are in stark contrast to the need and claims of the survivors to have the graves of their loved ones near their homes and to have memory sites in their immediate neighborhoods as places for mourning and coming together. Recently an Anfal memorial has been built in Germyan in the form of a traditional shepherd's cloak. The survivors are indignant about this memorial, which, they complain, represents them as "remote and uneducated shepherds." They demand a memorial representing women and children, acknowledging not only their suffering but also their contribution to and sacrifice for the Kurdish cause.

The conflict between memories, narratives and claims of the Anfal survivors and the local hegemonic discourse tends to alienate the survivors from other Kurdish political process and contains the potential for future conflict on the regional level. In March 2005, the survivors of the chemical attack on Halabja expressed anger and bitterness about the lack of assistance by holding a demonstration against the official anniversary celebration, burning down the memorial of Halabja in the course of the protests, and much anger and bitterness is openly expressed by Anfal survivors in the Germyan region. In April 2009, the first 187 corpses of Anfal victims found in a mass grave in Najaf were buried in the city of Rizgary. During the ceremony, the survivors protested sharply against the absence of senior Kurdish politicians and criticized the political parties for not bringing the collaborators to justice.[8]

Delay and Hesitation in Dealing with the Past on the Iraqi National Level

The Anfal survivors are equally bitter that their claims for evidence, justice, and compensation against the Iraqi government in Baghdad remain unaddressed. In the first year after the fall of the regime, the debate on a transitional justice process for Iraq, including judicial measures, truth-finding instruments and compensation for victims was pushed forward not only by the US-led Coalition Provisional Authority (CPA) and the UN and other international organizations, but also by the former Iraqi opposition parties including the Kurdish parties. Yet the topic of developing strategies to deal with the past was soon pushed off the political agenda by the increasing violence, the deteriorating security situation and the growing conflicts between different ethnic and religious factions. For all the various factions, victimhood of past and present violence is significant for legitimating their power claims on the national level. None of these factions was ready to delegate the responsibility for a transitional justice process — and thus the power of interpretation of past and present — to the national level. National initiatives such as the setting up of a National Center for Missing Persons are still developing, but get little support on the local and regional level throughout Iraq (Mlodoch, 2003).

In this context the number, suffering, and situation of victims of past and current violence is largely debated in the political arena, while little attention is given to addressing their actual needs or their claims for evidence, justice and compensation. Thus instead of fostering dialog between different groups of victims, hierarchies and competition between different victim groups and between different victims of past and current violence are being reinforced.

I would like to share some observations from my work in an assistance center for victims of political violence in 2005/2006 in Tuz Khurmatu in Takrit governorate, a city with strong Arab, Turkmen and Kurdish communities, the latter widely affected by the Anfal operations. The center was set up by the German NGO HAUKARI to accompany survivors of past crimes

---

[8]My own observations during the ceremony, 14 April 2009.

in the process of opening mass graves, to identify and bury their relatives and to give effect to their voices in the course of a wider process of transitional justice which was expected to develop after 2003. The center was open to victims of violence from all ethnic and religious groups including victims of current violence such as imprisonment or raids by occupation forces. Yet as the transitional justice process became more and more delayed, the center's activities were soon reduced to granting psychosocial and educational assistance and encouraging dialog on the local level. The attempt to work with a multi-ethnic team to bring victims of past and current violence together soon turned out to be premature without being embedded in a wider transitional justice debate in Iraq. Sunni Arab members of the city council objected strongly to the center for addressing past crimes since they considered the US-led aggression against them was much more virulent. Kurdish women survivors would refuse to be assisted by Arab physicians. Turkmen staff members would remove the term "Anfal" from reports, substituting "military operation", because they did not consider the Kurdish case in any way specific, which deeply offended the survivors. Mistrust and conflicts between staff members from different ethnic groups were permanent and hampered the work of the center. In such circumstances, it became almost impossible to render adequate assistance to survivors of past and current violence. Working with survivors of trauma requires empathy with their unique experience of violence and a clear identification of victims and perpetrators in order to set up a relation of trust. Constant compromising between completely different and often contradictory claims and the needs of victims of past crimes and current violence and between different interpretations of past and current realities risked leading to fail to distinguish between different experiences of violence, thus undermining the confidence of the survivors in the assistance program. Indeed the center closed after only two years due to the deteriorating security situation and the conflicts described.

This experience showed how the absence of a debate on transitional justice and strategies for dealing with the past fosters hierarchies and competition between different groups of victims. So far the transitional justice process in Iraq has been reduced to a precipitate and subsequently revised de-Ba'thification law and the trials of Saddam Husayn, 'Ali Hasan al-Majid and a very few other senior Ba'thists by the Supreme Iraqi Criminal Tribunal (former Iraqi Special Tribunal).

The Tribunal has been heavily criticized on both the national and international level for the central involvement of the US government in its foundation, for disregarding international human rights and legal standards, for the rejection of international involvement in the Tribunal and for sentencing and — in case of Saddam Husayn — implementing the death penalty (Amnesty International, 2005). It has also been criticized for focusing purely on those which are judged as the most prominently responsible for the past crimes (Donovan, 2008).

Nevertheless, from the perspective of the Anfal survivors the Supreme Iraqi Criminal Tribunal's trial of Saddam Husayn and 'Ali Hasan al-Majid was an important milestone. The detailed narratives of the atrocities committed during the Anfal and their televised transmission throughout Iraq, were keenly followed by the women survivors, and were significant for them in terms of feeling acknowledged and considered. It was an especially important experience that some women survivors of the Anfal from Germyan gave their testimonies in person in front of Saddam Husayn.

As outlined above, the denunciation of systematic sexual violence against Anfal women prisoners by the public prosecutor opened a door, which might integrate the long hidden experiences of sexual violence into the individual and collective memory of the Anfal survivors. Yet at the same time, the premature and precipitate execution of Saddam Husayn for the massacre of 148 Shi'is in Dujayl before the Anfal trial had come to an end was a discouraging experience for them. They felt that with Saddam Husayn's death they were cut off from further information on the fate of their relatives and on other persons responsible for directing the Anfal, which he might have given. They also felt indignation that Saddam Husayn's execution should appear on the historical record as being the consequence of the massacres of Shi'is rather than of the Anfal.

They felt betrayed in their need for justice and left alone with strong feelings of vengeance. From their perspective Saddam Husayn had been granted rights and dignity through his imprisonment, which he had never granted to his victims. Indeed statements like "they should have given him to us, we would have cut him in pieces" are often heard. As for 'Ali Hasan al-Majid, whose death sentence has not yet been carried out because of the veto of President Jalal Talabani, some claim he should be brought to Halabja and killed there at the place of his crimes.

Women survivors of the Anfal also call for further steps to bring the perpetrators to justice, including the international companies which supported the Ba'th regime by supplying it with advanced technology. While the Iraqi National Assembly acknowledged the Anfal operations as genocide in April 2008, no apology for the Anfal has ever been made to the Kurds.

The women survivors demand such an apology as well as the rapid opening of mass graves and a program of giving reparations to the survivors.

The delay and hesitation of the Iraqi government in addressing the needs and claims of survivors of past crimes and the absence of a national debate on how to deal with the past has resulted in great bitterness and the prolongation of the suffering of the victims and survivors and more generally in alienating them from the broader national political process.

Conclusion

Twenty years after the Anfal operations, many Anfal survivors remain in a marginal situation, their suffering prolonged by the lack of evidence of the fate of their relatives. They ask for the opening of the mass graves and for evidence of what happened in the past, as well as for justice and compensation and the social and political acknowledgement of their distinct experience in order to come to a form of closure with the past and to develop new lives.

Currently they feel betrayed by the Iraqi government in their hope for evidence, justice and compensation. In addition, they feel bitter and used by the Kurdish national elite which gives strong political weight to the Anfal in the Iraqi national arena while sidelining the needs of the survivors and excluding their voices from the political debate. Their bitterness adds to their suffering and translates into alienation from both the Kurdish and the Iraqi political process and contains the potential for future conflicts.

The discrepancy between the individual needs and expectations of victims of extreme violence for justice, punishment of the perpetrators, for compensation and the acknowledgement of their specific experience on one hand, and the need for political reconciliation and compromise between victims and perpetrators on the other, is characteristic of many societies coming out of experiences of extreme violence. Even the South African reconciliation process via the Truth and Reconciliation Commission, often considered as a successful example of dealing with the past after extreme violence and conflict, could not adequately address the needs and claims of the survivors of violence for the punishment of the perpetrators and acknowledgement of their specific individual suffering (Hamber *et al.*, 1998; Merk, 2006).

While on a political level the objective of social peace and unification after conflict and violence might require a balance between remembering and forgetting and institutional forms of closure within a defined time frame, victims of extreme violence have to remember and to cope with the impact of violence and loss through their lifetimes. Institutional and juridical steps to deal with the past are important for creating public spaces and frameworks in which the diversity of competing and conflicting memories and narratives of past and present can be expressed and mediated.[9] Currently, the process of dealing with the past is hampered by the ongoing occupation, and continuing violence and fragmentation within Iraqi society. Regarding the political agenda, priority is being given to the process of national dialog and unification, while the debate on developing strategies for dealing with past crimes is being neglected.

I argue that on both national and regional levels the development of juridical and institutional instruments to deal with past atrocities and to address the needs of the victims of past crimes for evidence, justice, reparations, and an acknowledgement of their specific experiences, are essential for engaging them in the regional and national political discourse. At the same time, multiple social and public spaces will be required within Iraqi society where deeply contrasting and competing memories and narratives of past and present between victims of past crimes and victims of current violence can be expressed and discussed, in order to avoid further fragmentation.

Electronic references

Hardi, C (2006). *Breaking the Circle of Silence about Anfal Women.* Interviews with Anfal surviving women. Online. Available HTTP: <www.chomanhardi.com> (accessed 10 November 2009).

Lennertz, I (2006). Trauma-Modelle in Psychoanalyse und klinischerPsychologie. *TRN-Newsletter*, Special Issue 2006. Hamburg: Institute for Social Research. Online. Available HTTP: <www.traumaresearch.net/special2006/lennertz.htm> (accessed 10 November 2009).

---

[9]See Brandon Hamber's extensive comparative work on reconciliation processes after violence and conflict, Hamber, 1998; Hamber *et al.*, 2002; Hamber, 2003.

SEARCHING FOR SENSE: THE CONCEPT OF GENOCIDE AS PART OF KNOWLEDGE PRODUCTION IN IRAQI KURDISTAN

Andrea Fischer-Tahir

In Iraqi Kurdistan, most writing about the Anfal campaign mentions the word genocide, rendered in Kurdish by the transliteration *cînosayd*. Kurdish authors explain frankly why they have chosen this term. The academic lawyer Dr Maruf Omer Gull,[1] for example, states in his paper entitled "Anfal — a Stage of Practising Genocide," published in 2002 in the English edition of *Anfal — A Document & Research Magazine* (Gull, 2002, p. 50):

> Genocide is a new word in Kurdish encyclopedias and culture. In Kurdish language, we can say (*Kurd qran* — extermination of Kurds) for the genocide of the Kurdish people. But because the term genocide is more meaningful and powerful in the scientific area it is better to use genocide.[2]

It is not surprising that a jurist should deal with the issue of genocide. However, title and quotation refer to three different things: First, to historical periodization; second, to the indigenization of Western[3] concepts; and third, to frames of reference. This raises questions on the production

---

[1] Authors' names including academic titles as stated by the authors themselves in Kurdish, Arabic, and English, transcription from the Kurdish or from the Arabic. Names of well-known persons outside of Kurdistan are given in the versions in which they appear.

[2] Sequence as translated by Azad Jalal Hassan. Dr Maruf Omer Gull is also Dr Maruf 'Omer Gul', to be quoted later in this article as author of the Kurdish text.

[3] Terms such as Western (European) and Eastern (Oriental) in the context of social phenomena are used by the Kurdish agents themselves. Being aware of the "Orientalist trap", I put such terms tentatively into quotation marks.

of scientific knowledge concerning the genocidal persecution in Kurdistan: How is the Anfal being described and explained? Who is speaking and who is not? Where do the new terms arriving in Kurdistan come from? Why is some specific knowledge welcomed and some rejected? Our jurist refers to Kurdish terms to describe mass killing, justifying the preference for genocide as a more "meaningful and powerful" concept. What meaning does this concept convey? Whom does it empower, whose power does it legitimate, and whose power does it help to challenge?

In the recent Iraqi past, "al-Anfal" (*The Spoils of War*, Sura 8 of the Qur'an) was the name given to the eight military campaigns carried out by the Iraqi regime against the Kurdish resistance forces and their civilian supporters in the rural areas of Iraqi Kurdistan between February and September 1988. Shortly after the Kurdish uprising in the spring of 1991,[4] Kurdish politicians claimed that 182,000 people had "disappeared" during the Anfal.[5] From a sociological perspective and from the perspective of the UN Convention on the Prevention and Punishment of Genocide (1948), it is the definition of "the enemy" by the perpetrator's propaganda machine, the systematic use of chemical weapons, and the bureaucratically organized selection, deportation and annihilation of thousands of Kurds, that make these campaigns crimes of genocidal persecution.

However, as a Western researcher who relies on Western theories and certain academic debates, I do not want to discuss the Anfal campaign from a particular historiographical, legal, psychological, or sociological perspective. Rather, I want to take a closer look at the reception of the Anfal within the context of scientific knowledge production in the region of Iraqi Kurdistan itself.[6] On the basis of monographs, essays, articles and conference papers

---

[4]In the aftermath of the Kuwait war in 1991, people in many parts of Iraq rose up against the regime in Baghdad. The Kurdish uprising began on 5 March in the town of Raniya, next to the Iranian border, and was a joint effort on the part of civilians, *Peshmerga* and armed men who had previously been loyal to the Ba'th regime but who had changed sides. At the end of March the Iraqi regime started military actions to end the uprising and caused a human catastrophe in the border areas with Iran and Turkey, where most inhabitants had sought protection from persecution. In April 1991, the humanitarian intervention of the US-led alliance stopped the Iraqi army and paved the way for the independent development of Kurdistan (Keen, 1993; Cook, 1995; Laizer, 1996).

[5]See, for example, "Declaration of Federalism" by the Kurdistàn Parliament, 4 October 1992, documented in *Perleman* (The Parliament) 3/92: 4. See also Middle East Watch, 1993: xviii.

[6]The "Western" research: From a legal perspective see, in particular, Middle East Watch/Human Rights Watch, 1993; Middle East Watch and Physicians for Human

by Kurdish researchers, I examine the representations applied to describe mass killing. In doing so, I have to consider the distribution of capital and relations of power in the "scientific field" (Bourdieu, 1984, 1998). In consequence, writings on the Anfal have to be analyzed in the light of struggles for significance and power. For my paper, I have chosen about 50 texts written in Sorani Kurdish, Arabic and English, published since 1991,[7] although this is only a small selection from the vast amount of material available in Iraqi Kurdistan. In addition, many texts on the Anfal have been published by diaspora Kurds outside Kurdistan. But even though I am aware of the diaspora's influence on knowledge production,[8] I am trying to focus on texts written by those living and working inside the region. What I also want to state clearly is that I do not seek completeness or full representation. Instead, I want to identify *tendencies* in the current debate.

Who is Speaking?

During the 1990s the bookshops of Sulaimaniya, Erbil, and Dohuk displayed a proliferation of writings dedicated to the political history of Iraqi Kurdistan. Higher-ranking politicians competed in telling "true stories" about the liberation movement — often only in order either to legitimate or to question the new government established by the Kurdistan Democratic Party (KDP) and the Patriotic Union of Kurdistan (PUK).[9]

Rights, 1993; Human Rights Watch, 1994. From the perspective of Islamic Law, see Ofteringer (1999). From a historical perspective, see Saeedpour (1992); Bruinessen (1994); Hiltermann (2007). From a psychological perspective, see Mlodoch (2006), and from a sociological perspective Fischer-Tahir (2003: 152–181). For Iraqi authors with a Western frame of reference see Makiya (1993) and Hardi (2008) (also the interviews with survivors on her website www.chomanhardi.com).

[7]I collected most of the texts in 1999, 2001, 2005, and 2006. The texts published between 2007 and 2008 were sent to me from Sulaimaniya by my husband, Herish Tahir. I also want to express my gratitude to Andréa Vermeer for having sent me conference papers from Erbil.

[8]During the 1970s–1990s many Kurdish academics sought refuge in the "Western" world, or Kurdish refugees became academics. Several of them returned in recent years, in particular after April 2003, and some of them have either re-migrated again to the "West" or move regularly between Kurdistan and the diaspora. They have contributed enormously to new developments in Kurdish language, literature, social and natural sciences.

[9]In May 1992, the first elections to the Kurdistan Parliament took place and the winning parties, KDP and PUK formed a regional government. After the elections for a Kurdish parliament in 1992, the unity of the region was not to last — due to the political heritage

However, compared to the issues of party history, fighting between the
Iraqi regime and the *Peshmerga* (Kurdish fighters), and conflicts between
the different Kurdish parties, the subject of the Anfal campaign was
marginalized. Let me give three examples from the PUK: In his book
on the *Revolution of Kurdistan* (1993) Hikmet Mihemmed Kerîm (Mela
Bextiyar)[10] mentions the Anfal only in so far as "the Anfals" ("enfalekan,",
he uses the plural form) are "the most shameful and disastrous actions
in the history of the Iraqi regime," which marked the end of the "struggle of the mountains" (Kerîm, 1993, p. 253).[11] His opponent Newşîrwan
Mistefa Emîn[12] argues in a similar way in *Going around in Circles* (1999):
The Anfal is the end of the *New Revolution* that had begun in 1975.[13]
However, the author calls the Anfal campaign a "national catastrophe"
("karesatêk-î neteweyî") and a "genocide" ("cînosayd"), and he highlights
the joint responsibility of the Kurdish *jash*, that is, soldiers of the Iraqi
National Defense Battalions recruited by the regime in order to fight the
Peshmerga, and of the *misteşar*, that is, Kurdish "military counselors."
He also responds to reproaches of "intellectuals" ("roşinbîrîyekan"), as
he calls them in quotation marks and thus in a condescending manner, who blamed the Kurdish *Peshmerga* for having provoked the massacre of Halabja by cooperating with the Iranians when they moved
into the city in early March 1988, (Emîn, 1999, pp. 129–153). The third

---

of the Ba'th regime, old conflicts and the competition between the Kurdish parties, the
proximity of the Iraqi army and the continued existence of the regime in Baghdad, and
the lack of international recognition. In late 1993 a war between the militias of the various
parties began; in 1994 the regional government in Erbil collapsed, and KDP, PUK, and the
Islamic Movement in Kurdistan/Iraq (IMKI), the third most powerful faction since the
uprising in 1991, established separate administrations/governments in the areas controlled
by their respective armed forces (Gunter, 1996; Leezenberg, 1997; Stansfield, 2003). The
region became partly re-unified after April 2003 and more completely after the elections
for the Iraqi and the Kurdistan Parliaments in December 2005.

[10]Mela Bextîyar was an early activist of the Marxist-Leninist Komel'e, one of the founding
factions of the PUK, later considered as a "left-wing-apostate", then one of the leaders of
the Kurdistan Toilers' Party (*Zehmetkêşan*), and finally reintegrated into the PUK and a
leading politician today.

[11]All the translations of quotations from texts in Kurdish and Arabic are mine.

[12]In 1979, Newşîrvan Mistefa Emîn was appointed as head of the Komel'e and became
the second powerful man in the PUK. In 2007, he resigned from all party positions.

[13]The PUK history speaks of *New Revolution* (*Şoriş-î Nwê*), distinguishing the era after
1975 from the *September Revolution* (*Şoriş-î Aîlul*), the latter under the leadership of
the Kurdistan Democratic Party and its leader Mulla Mustafa Barzani between 1961 and
1975.

significant example comes from Hawrê Baxewan and his *Hawrêname* (1999), a historiography of Kurdistan, which is inspired by Sherefkhani Bitlisi's *Sherefname* (1597) and even dedicated to "the first Kurdish historiographer" (Baxewan, 1999, p. 3). Here, the Anfal appears as a series of military campaigns against the *Peshmerga* carried out by the "Iraqi occupiers" ("dagîrkeran-î 'Iraq"). But the Anfal is only one among many actions carried out by the occupiers in order to suppress the Kurdish nation (Baxewan, 1999, pp. 325–327). In all three examples, the noncombatants, in particular women and children as victims of the Anfal campaign are absent.

Having been the domain of politicians for about one decade, writing history has become much more democratized in recent years. There are academics and non-academics, writing inside and outside universities, quite a common mixture in the writing of political history. In fact, knowledge production in the humanities and social sciences attracts people from completely different educational and biographical backgrounds. Thus, apart from the younger generation, there are numerous men and women who had been prevented by the Ba'th regime from completing their studies or having an academic career, including former *Peshmerga* and members of the city-based resistance, who claim to be writing objectively. In some NGOs, which are committed to human rights and gender, research has accompanied social work. Sorani Kurdish distinguishes between *lêkol'înewe* (any kind of research) and *tojînewe* (scientific/academic research). Both concepts may refer to: Identifying the research subject, developing hypotheses and theses, working according to internationally recognized methods, and presenting new findings in monographs, essays, papers and lectures. The hierarchy of power in the "scientific field" determines whether a person is recognized as *zana* (scholar), or merely as *pispor* (expert), *mamosta* (teacher), or *nûser* (writer), the latter covering all kinds of writing including aesthetic literature, philosophy, and journalism. Academic title and a university position as professor greatly increase the possibilities of recognition and acceptance. However, this recognition also depends on age, gender and class of the "candidate".

In recent years, there has been an increasing interest in the Anfal campaign, partly because of the growing distance from 1988, the political climate after April 2003, and the trial of Saddam Husayn and other leaders. Interestingly, the scene is dominated by academics and non-academics using sociological and psychological approaches, or from the perspective of international law and Islamic Studies, and dominated by non-academics acting as historiographers. At the same time, professional historians are less visible. This might be related to the specific experience of historians during the Ba'th era when it was less dangerous to deal with earlier centuries. Once the more distant past had become the principal object of an individual's interest, it might be difficult to switch to completely different subjects and periods.

As for other topics of knowledge production, writing on the *Anfal* is also a matter of competition, and academic degrees and professional positions, where institutionalized academic capital is used in order to support one's statements. The importance of institutionalized capital is mirrored by the efforts of the media to offer space to men and women with higher degrees for publishing on the Anfal and to win well-known academics as members of editorial boards. The KDP-backed magazine *Hawar-î Enfal* (Call of the Anfal), for example, established in 2002 by the Erbil Anfal Centre and owned by the leading KDP-politician 'Arif Taîfur Serdar, names as editor-in-chief Prof Dr Şukrîye Resul, who obtained her doctorate in the Soviet Union and now teaches Kurdish folklore at Salahuddin University. The editorial and advisory boards consist of 13 members, six of them professors, two of them doctors. Despite their active role, non-academics are less visible at, or even not invited to, conferences organized by the political authorities. The authorities themselves, or more precisely, the KDP and the PUK, try to control the production and circulation of knowledge through their printing offices and publishing houses, and by the staffing policy in the higher education sector.[14] Those who have been most completely marginalized in writing the history of the Anfal are the villagers who have been most affected by it.

Who is being Quoted?

In any review of recently published texts on the Anfal, Middle East Watch's *Genocide in Iraq* (1993) is the most frequently quoted work of reference. The report is based on testimonial interviews, forensic research, and on documents seized by the *Peshmerga* during the uprising in 1991 and delivered to Middle East Watch in May 1992 (Middle East Watch/Human Rights Watch,

---

[14]However, there are other agents besides the dominant parties. Thus, the private company Awêna, which has published an independent weekly of the same name since 2006 published the Kurdish translation of Joost Hiltermann's *A Poisonous Affair* (2007).

1993, pp. xi–xxx). The report was translated into Sorani Kurdish in 1999 and 2000.[15] Kurdish authors tend to follow its organization in their own texts or in the historical contextualization and chronological description of the report, and reprint its maps, figures, and documents. They frequently refer to its *Introduction*, in particular to the report's reference to Raul Hilberg's work *The Destruction of the European Jews* (1985) and thus, to a certain paradigm of genocide: That of *definition* ("pênaskirdin") — *concentration* ("kokirdnewe") — *annihilation* ("labirdin") of "the enemy" (Middle East Watch, 1993, p. 7; Middle East Watch, 2000, p. 34).

One of the main Kurdish reference texts is Zîyad 'Ebdurrehman's *Fire Chamber of Death* (1995). This book presents original documents and also statistics of the Committee for the Defence of the Rights of the Victims of the Anfal (C.D.R.V.A.), a PUK-backed organization. However, when 'Ebdurrehman's text appeared for the first time, the experiment of Kurdish quasi-statehood was still in its infancy and the process of nation-building demanded "national unity". Thus, the acts of the former *jash* and *misteşar* had to be "forgotten" through an amnesty, offered by the *Peshmerga*-parties as early as January 1991 to gain the support of those Kurdish men carrying Iraqi guns for a possible Kurdish insurrection. In addition, the Kurdish experiment was endangered by the wars between the various Kurdish militias in the mid-1990s. At that time, several parties sought the support of former *jash* in order to win the struggle for power, resources, and revenues. Within this climate, 'Ebdurrehman's description of the "dozens of *misteşar* and thousands of *jash* who [...] participated massively in the Anfal attacks" ('Ebdurrahman, 1995, p. 9) could have been taken as a counter-narrative to the dominant nationalist narrative which posits *the whole Kurdish nation as a victim of the* Anfal. Thus, there was no public discussion of the book at that time.

Another important Kurdish text is Yusif Dizeyi's *Anfal. Catastrophe, Result and Methods*, a Master's thesis submitted at the Department of Sociology, Salahuddin University, Erbil, and published in 2001. The author is concerned with the social situation of the Anfal survivors, and concludes with recommendations addressed to the Kurdish government, the Kurdish public and the international public as well. However, what made Dizeyî a preferred source of reference is his theoretical discussion of the term

---

[15]By Siyamend Muftîzade, published 1999 by the PUK-associated media company Xak in Sulaimaniya, and by Cemal Mîrza 'Elî, published 2000 by Havîbûn, a cultural center for diaspora Kurds in Berlin.

genocide. Following Middle East Watch and using other references such as Frank Chalk and Kurt Jonassohn's *The History and Sociology of Genocide* (1990), he introduces Raphael Lemkin and describes the origins of the UN's Genocide Convention. He writes about the Armenian Catastrophe and the Shoah as the most important examples of *cînosayd*, a word he describes, in taking reference to another Kurdish author, as "a new concept for an old crime" (Dizeyî, 2001, p. 39).[16]

Another prominent text frequently to be found as reference is Kanan Makiya's *Cruelty and Silence* (in English, 1993, in Arabic, 1996). Two other texts have join the ranks of standard works despite the fact that they do not deal with the events of 1988: The first is Çiya (Mamosta Emîn)'s *Deportation, Arabization and Ba'thification* (1987), the second Dr Nuri Talabani's *Changing the National Identity of Kirkuk* (1999). Using figures and documents, both authors describe the regime's policies of internal displacement and deportation, and the suppression of the Kurdish resistance, particularly during the 1970s and 1980s. Talabani goes as far back as the early 1960s. The richness of the information and their careful historical contextualization probably account for the popularity of these two books,[17] which leads me to the arguments developed and presented in the academic debate on the Anfal in Kurdistan.

What do They Say About the *Anfal* Campaign?

There are two central and in a sense complementary arguments. First, that the term Anfal should not refer only to the military campaigns of 1988 but to a process that had already begun decades earlier. Second, that the Anfal is only the most recent of a long series of attempts to exterminate the Kurdish people.

In his book *Genocide of the Kurdish People* (1997), the jurist Marruf Omer Gull (Maruf 'Omer Gul') develops Ismail Beşikçi's notion of Kurdistan as an "international colony" (Beşikçi, 1997), and he states: "Genocide is an extensive and long-term program carried out by the occupying, neighboring regimes of Kurdistan" (Gul', 1997, p. 20). The author refers in particular

---

[16]The quote's reference is Baba 'Elî, 1999, p. 148.

[17]And not only among Iraqi Kurdish authors. I used both books for my PhD thesis, in particular Çiya, as references to describe Ba'th security policies in Iraqi Kurdistan during the 1980s (see Fischer-Tahir, 2003, pp. 74–84).

to the Turkish regimes that have ignored the Kurds as a nation, banned their language, suppressed their resistance and made them into "mountain Turks." From Gul's perspective, the Anfal in the sense of the military campaigns carried out between April 22 and September 6, 1988, was merely one genocidal act among many others in the history of the Kurdish nation. (Gul', 1997, p. 38).

Other authors focus only on the Iraqi Kurds. 'Arif Qurbani, for example, a non-academic poet and editor-in-chief of several magazines, is the editor of four volumes entitled *Witnesses of the Anfal*, in which, as well as documents and statistics, he presents a wide range of interviews with survivors and, moreover, with men and women as "witnesses of the Anfal from different perspectives" (Qurbani, 2007, p. 131). The author puts the Anfal into the context of Arabization, which he considers had already begun in the early 1930s (Qurbani, 2002, pp. 16–26). In the same way 'Ebdul'l'a Kerîm Mehmud, a PUK activist and a member of C.D.R.V.A., mentioned above, argues in *The Storm of Poison and the Anfal*, two volumes that present interviews with Anfal-survivors as well as documents provided by private persons and political organizations:

> The Anfal [...] was one of the strategic aims of Iraqi colonialism in order to destroy the Kurdish nation, to exterminate the roots of the Kurdish human beings in Southern Kurdistan, to disintegrate the nature of their homeland geographically, demographically and culturally, and to eliminate the danger of restarting the Kurdish national movement. [...] the Anfal has been [...] planned for thirty years (Mehmûd, 2002, p. 4).

Numerous authors name the year 1963 and the suppression of the Kurdish resistance after the first Ba'thist *coup d'état* as "the beginning of the war of extermination and of the Anfal" ("sereta-î ceng-î qiṟkirdin-u Enfal"), like Dr Refîq Şiwanî, Assistant Professor at Salahuddin University in Erbil, in a paper published in *Hawar-î Enfal* (Şiwanî, 2002, p. 9). The terror of 1963, the mass deportation of the Fa'ili Kurds in the 1970s and in 1980 (cf. Talabani, 1999; Vanly, 1988), the killing of thousands of Barzanis in 1983 (cf. Bruinessen, 1994, p. 156), and the bloody mass escape (*ko ṟaw*) after the failed uprising of 1991 are frequently listed as examples of genocide against the Iraqi Kurds (for example Mela Şaxî, 2001, p. 6; Mehmud, 2002, pp. 5–7; Salih, 2005, p. 77). These examples also describe the "linear progression" of the Iraqi–Arab regimes towards the Anfal campaign as the "final solution" (Ministry of Human Rights, Refugees and Anfal, 2002, p. 3). Sometimes, the words Anfal and/or *genocide* are even put into the plural. The sociologist

Mihemmed Re'uf 'Ezîz, for example, concludes in his book *Sociological Dimensions of the Anfal* that "the catastrophe (*karesat*) of Anfal [...] was a part of the genocides of the Kurds" ("cînosaydekan-î kurd") ('Ezîz, 2005, p. 179).[18] Most authors base their argument on the long-standing nature of the genocide and its relation to policies of Arabization with reference to the works of Çîya (Mamosta Emîn) and Dr Nuri Talabani.

In the texts on the Anfal two terms dominate: Catastrophe and genocide. The Kurdish term *karesat*, derived from the Arabic *karitha* (catastrophe), is used to describe the Anfal campaign as well as the use of poison gas in Halabja. The latter has often been combined with Hiroshima, for instance in the phrase: "Hel'ebce — Hîroşîma-î Kurdistan" ("Halabja is the Hiroshima of Kurdistan"), which can be traced back to the year 1988.[19] Zîyad 'Ebdurrehman and Yusif Dizeyî frequently use the term *karesat*, for example, as part of a genitive-compound "karesat-î Enfal" ("Anfal catastrophe"), as do many other authors. However, at least from the perspective of several authors the term *karesat* seems to be too weak, and thus they often combine it with *qiṛkirdin*, meaning to exterminate or extermination. Thus, for example, Dr Refiq Şiwanî writes of "the catastrophe of the extermination (genocide) of the Kurds" ("karesat-î qiṛkirdin-î [cînosayd] kurd") (Şiwanî, 2002, p. 12).

The concept of genocide was introduced into Soranî Kurdish in the early 1990s and translated as *cînosayd*. Many authors begin their discussion of the Anfal as genocide or as part of genocide by explaining the basic meaning of the word as deriving from Greek and Latin (*génos — caedere*), followed by some explanation about the Genocide Convention and by some definitions of genocide, and sometimes of kindred concepts such as ethnocide, ecocide, gendercide, ethnic cleansing, etc (for example, Gul', 1997, p. 9; Gull, 2002, p. 50; Dizeyî, 2001, p. 39; 'Ezîz, 2005, p. 33; Salih, 2008, p. 5; Herutî, 2008, p. 1). In this context but also elsewhere, authors tend to refer to the Shoah, as for example: "The Anfal must [...] be compared with the annihilation of the Jews by the German Nazis. Hitler managed to kill six million Jews, and Saddam had the same intention" (Qeredaxi, 2008, p. 1).

---

[18] For his study Mihemmed Re'uf 'Ezîz distributed a questionnaire among Anfal survivors in order to obtain data to describe their social situation. His sample consisted of 182 respondents, chosen according to the knowledge or the narrative of 182,000 Anfal victims.

[19] Its usage by Kurdish nationalists is well-known, but interestingly even Islamists quickly adopted the symbolic connection between Halabja and Hiroshima (Islamic Kurdish Army, 1988; Serdema Nû, 1988).

Or to the Shoah and the Armenian Catastrophe, as for example:

> The first massive crime of genocide was carried out by the Turks who killed three million Christian Armenians. The second massive crime of genocide was carried out [...] when Hitler became German chancellor, and it was the mass gassing of the Jews [...]. The third biggest example of crimes of genocide is the catastrophe of the genocidal crimes of the Anfal and the poisonous massacre of Halabja (Mehmud, 2007, pp. 41–42).

It is not clear where the process of *cînosayd* against the Kurds ends. For some authors, "the genozidation of the Kurds" ("cînosayd-kirdin-î kurd"), a compound created analogically to the "Anfalization of the Kurds" (*"enfal-kirdin-î kurd"*), came to an end with the uprising in 1991, while others argued that policies of ethnic cleansing in Kirkuk during the 1990s which ended in April 2003 should also be considered as "continued genocide." (Mehmud, 1993, p. 360; Qeredaxi, 2008, p. 1; Herûtî, 2008).

Interestingly, it seems to make a difference whether an author relies on (translated) Western expert literature or on other sources. Reference to Jews and Armenians is frequently made, and concerning the first, most authors speak of the "Nazis," or of "Hitler" in the context of Saddam Husayn. Marruf Omer Gull's (Maruf 'Omer Gul') book on *Genocide*, however, is a text, in which I found phrases such as: "in consequence of the crimes of the Fascists" (Gul', 1997, p. 9, 169). As a girl brought up in East Germany, this reminds me of what we were taught at school during the 1980s, when the term "Jews" was often modified to "innocent victims of Fascism". In his book, Gul' refers mostly to the texts of Soviet jurisprudence of the 1970s and 1980s. Either way, the author and his Kurdish colleagues use the term *cînosayd*, understood as the effective or the intended extermination (*qiɽkirdin*) or annihilation (*labirdin*) of a "race" (*regez*) or ethnic group/group of common origin (*grup-î etnikî or nejade*).

Within this context it is also necessary to take a look at concepts that have not yet been established, or maybe never will be. One of those concepts is *enfalizm* (Anfalism). Mela Ebubekrî Hemewendî argues in an article published in the PUK-backed magazine *Şehîd*,[20] that the Anfal has nothing to do with the religious meaning of the word as found in the Qur'an. Rather, the Anfal has to be analyzed in terms of totalitarianism and is comparable

---

[20] The magazine *Şehîd* is issued by the Centre Martyr Rêbaz in Sulaimaniya, named after the *Peshmerga* Rêbaz, one of the fighters who returned after "Anfal" to the "forbidden areas", and wrote a manual for other fighters (Rêbaz, 1988–1989).

to "the mentality and thought of Fascism and Stalinism." Consequently, the author suggests the addition of two new terms to the political dictionary: Firstly, "Anfalism — a cruel, political progression towards genocide and ethnic extermination which has been legitimized by the Qur'an and the [Ba'thist concept of] the eternal mission (*risala khalida*):"[21] second, "Anfalist (*enfalîst*) — all those having participated in the Anfal attacks, regardless of his place or person" (Hemewendî, 1999, p. 26). Other authors argue that "the Anfal is a form of Fascism" (Letîf, 2005), but even though terms such as totalitarianism are widespread in certain debates in Iraqi Kurdistan, the word *Anfalism* is not widely used, probably because it is weaker than *cînosayd*, and because it is too close to the "language of the enemy." Moreover, Mela Ebubekrî Hemewendî is neither an academic authority, nor a political figure with significant recognition.

A further suggestion to explain the Anfal comes from Abdulkhalegh Yaghoobi (2008) who prefers the word "natiocide". He states that the concept of genocide emphasizes the ethnic and religious differences between the perpetrator and the victim, as was the case with the Armenians and the European Jews. But the Kurdish case is different, he says, and the religious connotation of the term Anfal is completely misleading. The term "natiocide," however, reflects the real core of the matter, and the real core is the lasting confrontation between Arab nationalism as a force *in* power and Kurdish nationalism as a force *claiming* power. This confrontation, he argues, is most visible in the attempts of many Arab regimes to change the ethnic reality of Kirkuk. Yaghoobi's paper was presented in English at an International Anfal Conference organized by the Kurdistan Regional Government in Erbil in January 2008, which was attended by numerous Westerners and by Arab–Iraqi speakers and guests. This leads to the next question, which is:

Whom are the Texts Addressing?

The West

It is not surprising that papers on the Anfal presented at international conferences and texts published in English, primarily address "the West". Like politicians, the researchers tend to prefer "meaningful and powerful" terms

---

[21]On the Ba'th ideology, Anfal and the issues of *al-risala al-khalida*, of apostasy and of betrayal, see also Makiya, 1993: 90.

such as genocide.[22] This tendency reflects a number of aspirations: First, for the recognition of the suffering of the Kurds; second, for lasting international protection; and third, for the recognition of national rights such as the right to a nation state. The struggle for this right does not necessarily mean the demand for political representation at the United Nations, even though some political actors in Kurdistan consider Kurdish independence a strategic aim. However, in this view, the term *cînosayd* and references to the Armenians and, more frequently, to the European Jews make sense. The argument is as follows: The Jews suffered genocide, the whole world recognized their suffering, and consequently, they got their own nation state. Fascinatingly, there has been a recent increase of interest in Jewish history and culture (Qadir, 2007; Kurde, 2007). This practice also responds to the wish for powerful allies in the region, which is itself rooted in feelings of revenge, uncertainty, and fear. Thus, Shorsh Haji Resool writes in the *Anfal Magazine*: "Even if we assume that Saddam will be toppled, *can anyone predict the actions of Saddam's successor against the Kurds?* [author's emphasis]" (Resool, 2002, p. 22).[23]

The Iraqi Arabs

In texts directly addressing the Iraqi–Arab (academic and political) public, the Anfal campaign and the massacre of Halabja are described as *karitha* (catastrophe), *harb al-ibada* (war of annihilation), *'amliyyat al-ibada* (campaigns of annihilation) or as *al-ibada al-jama'iyya* (genocide) (for example, Salih, 2005; Khalid, 2005). In the texts of Kurdish authors two principal points emerge. First, the Kurdish sufferings from persecution by the former

---

[22] An early example is the scholar Kemal Mîrawdelî who alarmed the international public already in 1988: "All indications confirm that Iraq is persistent in its war of genocide against the people of Kurdistan turning it into a killing zone for experimentation with the most deadly modern weapons. [...] we can see that the tragedy of Armenia is being repeated in Kurdistan" (Meerawdeli, 1988, p. 8).

[23] *Anfal Magazine* (No. 2, 2002) is a good example of a publication that directly addresses "the West". It was issued when international debates on the war of the United States against Iraq arose and presents texts on Anfal and Arabization in Kurdistan by prominent politicians and academics such as Muhammed H. Tofiq (Tofiq, 2002), Dr Nuri Talabani (Talabani, 2002), Dr Khalid Salih (Salih, 2002) and Dr Maruf 'Omer Gul' (Omer Gull, 2002). The term Genocide appears in almost all their titles, the chief reference being the Middle East Watch report from 1993.

Iraqi regime and their claims to recognition as special victims (and consequently, the implied claim to political, cultural, and economic rights within the new Iraq). The second point is related to the actual or assumed effects of Iraqi propaganda before 2003. Kurdish authors argue that despite the religious meaning of the term al-Anfal, the Kurds were not singled out for extermination because they were nonbelievers or apostates. Thus, 'Adalat 'Abdullah (2005) argues in *Anfal Magazine* that "millions of Kurds [...] follow the same Islamic rites [as the Arabs] and the same *surāt* and *āyāt* of the Qur'an." So, the catastrophe of the Anfal had nothing to do with a "lack of faith." Instead, it was "a political and racist game" on the part of the regime ('Abdullah, 2005, p. 62, 65).

Several Kurdish authors argue in a similar manner when they address the Kurdish reader: They stress the loyalty of the Kurds to Islam, while arguing that it was the intention of the Ba'th regime to humiliate the Kurdish Muslims and to confuse the Arab and international public (Refiq, 2002; Dizeyî, 2001, p. 27; 'Ezîz, 2005, pp. 26–31). Interestingly, it was the Islamic Union in Kurdistan-Iraq which had already preferred the term *cînosayd* the late 1990s, and spoke of "killed," not of "anfalized people". They argued that the regime simply misused the Islamic religion for particularistic goals (Mihemmed, 1999, p. 74, 84). This aspect of the struggle for significance and meaning brings us back to the Kurds as readers.

The Iraqi Kurds

Certainly, the "meaningful and powerful" concept of genocide helps to explain a catastrophe that is perceived as unbelievable and overwhelming, and the concept obviously serves to legitimate nationalist claims towards "the others". It is also not surprising that researchers consider themselves agents with a mission and that knowledge production regarding the topic of the Anfal is both a result and a means of nation building in Iraqi Kurdistan. However, if academics can argue that the Anfal had been planned for several decades, and that the purpose of the regime was to exterminate the Kurdish nation, it follows that any resistance to the Anfal would necessarily have been futile. The concept of genocide helps to explain why the *Peshmerga* — despite their will, their self-image, and their brave and desperate acts — were incapable of protecting the Kurdish people in 1988. I interviewed some former *Peshmerga* with Anfal experience in 1999. All of them referred to or spoke directly about feelings of guilt towards the civilians they could not rescue from deportation and death (Fischer-Tahir,

2003, pp. 159–181). Many of the authors writing about the Anfal are former *Peshmerga* and political activists. For them, the term genocide may also offer a kind of relief, and maybe both their desperate resistance and their suffering makes more sense in the light of this "meaningful concept".

If the authors state that the regime's purpose was "to exterminate the Kurds" (Gull, 2002, p. 42) or to "to annihilate the Kurdish national group" (Salih, 2008, p. 5), it becomes easier to integrate the *jash* into the image of national suffering. During the 1990s, it was difficult even to speak about them in public. But this changed completely after the peace-agreements between the PUK and the KDP, and especially with the Tribunal of 2006–2007, when the Kurdish media allowed open discussions about the Anfal.[24] It changed also as a result of the work of those authors who had offered more space to survivors of the Anfal and their stories, which did not avoid the topic of the *jash*, although this was less true when former *Peshmerga* wrote about their personal experiences of those "who had sold themselves and lacked a [national] position" (Mehmud, 2002, p. 4). However some authors call for different ways of dealing with the *jash*. Thus, Latîf Fatih Ferec writes in *Heştawheşt*:

> We cannot look at the *jash* as if all of them were the same. [...] There were brutal and black *jash* [...] while others were forced to become *jash* [...]. There were *jash* who brought the heads of the *Pershmerga* to the Ba'th and attacked and destroyed villages even before the soldiers did [...] and there were those who became *jash* merely because of the situation.

He concludes that "there must be more research and studies about the *jash*" (Ferec, 2005, pp. 158, 160). Mehabad Qeradax̱î, a writer and feminist politician, believes in making such distinctions. Using certain psychological and sociological approaches, she explains that the actions of the *jash* were a normal reaction to their status as members of a suppressed nation: Their "mental state [was] weaker and therefore they earlier [fell] under the influence of [the occupiers]" (Qeredaxî, 2008, p. 8). The *jash* served the enemy in order to protect themselves. Qeredaxî refers to Abraham Maslow and speaks of "defense mechanisms." She also states that the Anfal has divided the Kurdish people into "anfalized people" and "un-anfalized people." Using interviews with un-anfalized men and women and discussions of the meaning

---

[24]The independent media played an important role in the discussions on the *jash*, in particular the weeklies *Awêne* and *Hawelatî*, and the radio channel *Newa* with its programme "Without censorship."

of the word Anfal and emotional reactions to the word and to stories told by survivors, for example on television, Qeredaxî proves her thesis that the whole Iraqi Kurdish nation is still suffering from the Anfal. Concerning the *jash* she suggests they should be treated psychologically "to bring them back into their own group."(Qeradaxî, 2008, p. 16).

A range of authors focus on the cruel experience and on the social and mental problems of the survivors of the Anfal campaign and make suggestions to the Kurdish government to improve their situation (Dizeyî, 2001; Salih, 2002; Resûl, 2002; 'Ezîz, 2005; Salih, 2008). But the survivors are dealt with only as victims; the survivors even seem to be newly discovered patients (especially 'Ezîz, 2005; Salih, 2008). Also women who disappeared or/and were killed during the Anfal tend to be considered as objects. Thus, Dr Refîq Şiwanî points out that the aggressors took away especially the "beautiful, gracious and attractive women" (Şiwanî, 2002, p. 12). What does this mean? Does sexual violence against women depend on the women's physical appearance? Of course, during the 1990s speaking about sexual violence during the Anfal campaign was taboo, and compared to the stories about male Kurdish heroes, the women of the Anfal were only rarely visible. Nowadays, they are visible, but most of the time they appear as harmed or lost female bodies.[25] However, a few authors criticize Kurdish society for having forgotten the Anfal-women or for marginalizing them. Already in 1999, on the basis of video material and articles from media belonging to the Kurdistan Communist Party, Teha Silêman published a book entitled *On the Edge of the Anfal*, which focuses on the everyday-life problems of survivors in the district of Germiyan. The author voices harsh criticism of those people spreading bad rumors about those Anfal-women who are obliged to leave home in order to find work and income (Silêman, 1999, p. 61). Also Yusif Dizeyî is very clear in his words when, addressing the Kurdish public, he writes: "Do not look at the children and Anfal-women in a humiliating way"

---

[25]This became particularly visible within the media debate about an Iraqi document from the Directory of the Intelligence Service of the Governorate of at-Ta'mīm, from December 1989, which speaks about sending 19 Kurdish females aged between 14 and 29 years to Egypt. This document appeared after 2003, and was published in various places (for example in Mehmud, 2003: 1171). In 2007 the weekly *Mîdiya* tried to profit from the debate, publishing a story suggesting that these women were still alive and waiting in Egypt for their release and return home. In the magazine *Heştawheşt* 'Omer Mehmud (2007) voiced harsh criticism of this and other stories playing with the feelings of the Anfal survivors.

(Dizeyî, 2001, p. 244). Dr Şukrîye Resûl, however, remains more careful. In *Hawar-î Enfal* she writes: "Even though these Anfal families suffer from so many problems, people look at them in a different way" (Resûl, 2002, p. 48).

Neglecting the survivors' capacity for agency makes it seem as if the group of "genocided Kurds" is imagined as being divided into two separate sub-groups: One consisting of well-educated middle- and upper-class agents capable of writing, lecturing, and explaining the world, and the other of those incapable of speaking for themselves. In this view, the production of scientific knowledge buttresses and confirms social hierarchies. Moreover, the argument that the Anfal has been only one genocidal act among many others means that the survivors are not considered special victims anymore, and thus do not need (or deserve) special attention. Instead, from the perspective of many of those who produce academic knowledge, the Anfal-survivors are what they have been before 1988: Lower-class rural people and — subalterns. However, even if Anfal-survivors lack economic, social and cultural capital, and even if they are — as Karin Mlodoch shows in this volume — "frozen in the Anfal", oppressed both by the hegemonic political discourse of national suffering and the social discourse of family honor, the subalterns struggle for their lives and they struggle to be heard and to gain representation (cf. Spivak, 1990).

In the dominant political discourse, the concept of genocide may not only give answers to questions of the past, but it may also serve as a means of interpreting the present and the future. The narrative of Kirkuk as a "predominantly Kurdish city that, due to the oil richness of the area, has always been the object of desire of the Arab regimes in Baghdad" is part of the "everyday knowledge" of Iraqi Kurds. The political discourse and academic writing on the Anfal campaign links the genocidal persecution of 1988 to the future of Kirkuk. However, from the perspective of the Kurdish political rulers it makes sense to connect Kirkuk with the Anfal, since "the people" have to be mobilized for Kirkuk! From the perspective of the Kurdish rulers, national unity and strong national feelings are more important than corruption, maladministration, or all the other "minor matters" that seem to concern the independent media. Any disunity or lack of national feelings might have harsh consequences, because "any Arab regime's purpose is to exterminate the Kurdish nation," one of the dominant narratives of Kurdish discourse. In this view, it also makes sense to teach "the people" what the word genocide basically means, where it comes from, and that in Kurdistan genocide is not only an experience situated in the past but a lasting (and continuing) threat.

THE 1991 *INTIFADA* IN THREE KEYS: WRITING THE HISTORY OF VIOLENCE

Dina Rizk Khoury

On June 1, 2007, Judge Ja'far al-Musawi notified the lawyers of the 15 men accused of committing "crimes against humanity" of their impending trial. The director of the district attorney's office in the High Iraqi Tribunal had now turned his attention to the Ba'thist leaders, including 'Ali Hasan al-Majid, who were responsible for the suppression of the popular uprising against the regime of Saddam Husayn in 1991. In his opening statement on 21 August, the attorney for the prosecution made the government's case. Saddam Husayn (now dead) and the leadership of the regime had initiated an illegal invasion of Kuwait and brought destruction to their country. In the wake of Saddam's unilateral order for withdrawal from Kuwait, exhausted and bedraggled soldiers and the hungry citizens of the South rose up against the regime. The leadership of the Republican Guard and the security forces reacted swiftly and brutally. More than 100,000 people were killed and tens of thousands fled their homes. Their actions in suppressing what was a legitimate rebellion against the regime represented a gross violation of human rights.[1]

The third in a series of trials meant to bring to justice members of the Ba'thist regime responsible for the death and/or ethnic cleansing of Iraqi citizens, the *Intifada Sha'baniyya* trial, so called after the month in the Muslim calendar during which the uprising took place, presented the court with a number of difficulties. The defendants were accused of crimes against humanity. To prove the guilt of the 15 men, the lawyers for the

---

[1] *al-Mada*, August 22, 2007. Available online: http://www.almadapaper.com/paper.php?source-akbar&mlf=interp (accessed June 4, 2008).

government had to gather testimonies that linked the defendants to the crimes. Collecting forensic and documentary evidence connecting the defendants to mass executions and inhumane treatment of detainees was a difficult and painstaking process. It was fraught with claims and counter-claims by victims and perpetrators and hampered by struggles over jurisdiction on the part of different institutions such as the various provincial offices of the Ministry of Human Rights and local Shi'i *waqf* officials. The trial was postponed several times in the course of the following months and reached a decision only in December 2008.[2] While human rights organizations and several observers have expressed deep ambivalence about this and other trials and objected to their political nature, the current Iraqi government and sections of Iraq's population have insisted that they do provide a legitimate venue for bringing the criminals of the old regime to justice.

Where do We Locate the "Truth"? The Problems of Sources and Evidence

The difficulties that have emerged with the trial of the *Intifada* are products of a lack of consensus among the different Iraqi constituencies about an "*Intifada* Story". There is no agreement about the nature of the *Intifada*. Was it a chaotic and destructive rebellion or a popular and legitimate uprising? Was it a sectarian uprising by a Shi'i majority against a Sunni dominated regime, as both the Ba'thists and some of their opponents maintain? While these questions inform the public debate about the uprising, that is to say, the way it was and continues to be discussed in the press

---

[2] *al-Mada*, March 17, 2008. Available online: http://www.almadapaper.com/paper.php?source-akbar&mlf=interp (accessed June 4, 2008). At one point, the defendants requested a postponement because their lawyers were too afraid to come to the court. At another time, a witness who had placed the main defendant, 'Ali Hasan al-Majid, in Basra at a certain date was quickly dismissed because al-Majid was in Kirkuk on that date. Calls were made by the court and by officials in the provinces of Maysan and Basra, the two provinces that were the focus of the investigations of the trial, for witnesses to come forward and for gravediggers not to disturb evidence of mass graves in the provinces. *al-Mada*, August 21, 2007. Available online: http://www.almadapaper.com/paper.php?source-akbar&mlf-interp (accessed June 4, 2008). Contaminated evidence was a continuous concern of the Ministry of Human Rights, the institution designated by the Parliament responsible for "mass graves" under Law of Protection of Mass Graves issued in May of 2006. *al-Mada*, August 7, 2007. Available online: http://www.almadapaper.com/paper.php?source=akbar&mlf-interp (accessed June 4, 2008). For Law see http://www.niqash.org/content.php?contentTypeID=276&id=1759.

and among the larger public, the trial of the *Intifada* frames the whole issue in the depoliticized language of human rights violations. These appear at first glance to be two radically different framings of the uprising, one highly political and embedded in narratives of memory and reconstructions of Iraqi communal and national identities and the other divorced from the specificity and passions of the political and dressed in the universal language of humanitarianism. While there have been denunciations of the politicization of the trials by human rights and other organizations, their arguments have been based on the assumption that there is a clear difference between a trial that is merely meant to punish old political foes (like the Mahdawi court under Qasim and the show trials during the Ba'th regimes), and a trial that is based on judicial procedure and rules of evidence that are considered legitimate by the international community. One is based on a political, that is to say ideological, reading of Iraqi history, while the other is based on forensic science that takes the body as the site of evidence for violations of human rights. It is true that the testimonies of witnesses and victims play an important part in the trial's proceedings, but these are often trumped by the physical evidence of mass graves, corporeal evidence of torture and a paper trail. The dichotomy is a result of how social scientists, legal experts and the interested parties categorize evidence.

On the one hand, physical evidence (bodily torture, mass graves) provides incontrovertible proof that violence has taken place, but does not inconclusively prove who committed that violence. Documentation from archival sources (usually police records or other government records) helps to determine who the perpetrators and victims were. These are usually regarded as stronger evidence that could be supplemented by the evidence of witnesses, relatives or victims. On the other hand, the memories of participants and witnesses provide crucial information not only as to why such violence occurs but also contextualizes it within a historical memory. Yet even that is subject to manipulation and forgetfulness and is very much part of the present. While it provides valuable insights into the subjectivity of participants and witnesses, its historical value for ascertaining "truth" remains suspect. Thus one tends to think that, on the one side, there is evidence and historical record "uncontaminated" by political passion and personal memories, and on the other, that there is data derived from testimonies and witnesses that, although important, are highly charged politically and hence unreliable (Fassin, 2008, pp. 531–558; Fassin and Halluin, 2005, pp. 597–608; Hesford, 2004, pp. 104–143; Feldman, 2004, pp. 163–201).

In this paper, I would like to explore the question of the context under which the different categories of evidence are collected. I do not plan to make an argument but rather to open up a debate on the problems we encounter as we try to put together a coherent narrative of an event as fraught with political meanings as the *Intifada*. For a historian writing the history of the recent past, this dichotomy between "strong" evidence and data and "weak" sources based on oral testimony and politicized narratives is questionable. It is often articulated as the difference between "reality" and "representations of reality". All records, however, are products of social and cultural processes through which "documentation" takes place. As such they are never "apolitical" or free from power relations. The historian's challenge lies in trying to locate these relations in the narratives of the different sources and set the sources against each other to arrive at a narrative that approximates to the complexity of the historical reality. I hope to do so in this chapter by examining the *Intifada* through three prisms: First through the documents of the Ba'th party issued during and directly after the uprising; Second, through the prism of publications and media that the Ba'thist government and the opposition produced in the 1990s; and finally, through oral interviews that I conducted with Iraqis in Jordan and Syria in the summer of 2007. I would like to focus in my analysis on the categories of perpetrator and victim/martyr. These were, and continue to be, the most contested categories in the struggle over the narrative of the *Intifada*. And they continue to shape the discourse of political organizations and NGOs that seek to organize the Iraqi population around the *Intifada*.[3] Who is the perpetrator? Is it a party, a community or foreign power? Or is it the individual, his family or clan? Is it the regime, or a particular individual or organization within the regime? Does the category of "victim" apply only to those who were killed fighting or does it extend to those who had merely been innocent bystanders caught in the cross-fire? Are those killed in 1991 because they were perceived by the rebels as Ba'thists considered victims, or are they part of the fallen regime?

---

[3]Hence, during the first election in 2005, the *"rabitat al-intifada al-sha'baniyya"* won 3,022 out of 71,327 votes in Basra. The demands of the *rabita* seem to be focused on entitlements for the martyrs of the *Intifada* and for preferential treatment for the families that had suffered at the hands of the Ba'th in employment. In Diwaniyya, on March 25, 2007, the United Front of the *Intifada* of Iraq organized a yearly celebration of the martyrs of mass graves of the *Intifada* in *"Intifada* Square". An *Intifada* operetta was performed written by poetess Fadila Zaydan. The secretary general of the Front is Dr. Tawfiq al-Yasiri from a tribe that had led the *Intifada* in the area. Commemorations also took place in Karbala.

The Ba'th Party Archival Record

The archival sources I draw on are the Ba'th Party Regional Command documents made available to me by the Iraq Memory Foundation in Washington DC. The story of the acquisition and the provenance of these documents has been controversial, and the controversy itself tells us much about the politics of memory and the role that archives play in the attempt to shape the debate on human rights violations, memory and the politics of transitional justice. They form an important chapter in the struggle over the memory of the Ba'th and the attempts to shape it by NGOs and the post-2003 regime.[4] My concern, however, is with what these documents tell us about the early phases of the *Intifada* and how the regime documented it. I have used two sets of documents. The first is a ledger of correspondence between the regional offices of organizations of the Ba'th party in various southern Iraqi cities and the secretariat of the regional offices of the Ba'th about the development of the *Intifada*.[5] The second set of documents is a ledger recording the victims or martyrs of the Ba'th party killed in the *Intifada*.[6] These were issued between March and November 1991, that is to say during the uprising itself and in the months immediately after it had been suppressed.

Reports on the nature of the uprising, its causes and its participants began to come into the Ba'th party Baghdad office (*tanzim* Baghdad) headed by Sa'd Mahdi Salih, later speaker of the Parliament, by 10 March 1991 and were issued by members of the Ba'th party in the various southern

---

[4]The Iraq Memory Foundation was founded by Kanan Makiya to collect testimonies and documents of the Ba'th regime. Its initial set of documents was obtained in 1991 from the Kurdish Autonomous region and they constitute the North Iraq Dataset (NDIS). The Foundation has also obtained the documents of the Ba'th Party Regional Command in 2003 and they now constitute the Ba'th Regional Command Collection (BRCC). All in all, the Foundation has nearly 13 million pages of documents of which a fraction has been digitized. In the spring of 2008, the Foundation, with the support of the Iraqi Government, signed an agreement with the Hoover Institute to move the documents to Palo Alto, which allows the Institute to hold them until the Iraqi government is ready to take them. The controversy over the documents erupted when the head of the Iraq National Library and Archives, Dr. Sa'd Eskandar, demanded that these documents be returned and be housed in the Library because they are part of the patrimony of the Iraqi state. For a background on this see the website of the American Association of Librarians and Archivists and MESA. The latest iteration of this controversy can be found on the Social Science Research Website at http://www.ssrc.org/essays/minerva/2008/10/29/eskandar. For the politics and collection of the Iraq Memory Foundation, see www.iraqmemory.org.
[5]Iraq Memory Foundation (MF), Ba'th Regional Command Collection (BRCC), 3455–02.
[6]MF, BRCC, 3134–0004.

provinces. Many had been written a few days after the outbreak of the Intifada and had been filed either when their authors had succeeded in flee-ing to Baghdad, or when they had found someone to forward the reports through the various party organizations. Except for the Ba'th party mid-Euphrates branch (Najaf and Karbala) which sent its report directly to the General Secretariat of the Ba'th in Baghdad, most of the information was sent to Salih's office and then forwarded by him, after the information had been reworked, to the Party secretariat, the security services and to the office of the President (to the secretariat). The last reports in the ledger were written in October 1991.[7]

Much of the reporting on the *Intifada* relies on the written testimonies of witnesses from the Ba'th party who acted as informants and who provided the names of the perpetrators and an assessment of what had happened. Thus, their reporting is colored by their politics as well as their vulnerable position as individuals and families targeted by the rebels. There are reports by party members who had had to flee for their lives, often on foot, and hide with relatives in the countryside. There is a report of one party member from Basra who was taken as a prisoner to Iran (to Dezful prison) and then released to his family that had camped in a refugee camp within the borders of Iran.[8] The other kind of correspondence in the ledger traces the early assessment of local party officials of the causes of the uprising and the most effective ways to locate and punish the perpetrators.

Two aspects of the reports on the events are important to highlight before moving into an analysis of the perpetrators and victims of the upris-ing. The first is the dominance of women as witnesses and informants. Most of these women were heads of local chapters of the Federation of Iraqi Women whose offices were targeted and who were forced to flee to relatives in neighboring areas or to Baghdad. They filed their reports to the central office of the Federation headed by Manal Yunis who then for-warded it to the local offices of the Federation or Professional and Labor Syndicates. These were then sent to the secretariat of the party or to the Baghdad branch and truncated versions were sent to the security apparatus and the presidential office. Of the 26 eye-witness reports sent by various Ba'th members and officials, nine were sent by women. Their reports were often long, laden with the moral language of good and evil and stressed

---

[7]MF, BRCC, 3455–0002–01.
[8]MF, BRCC, 3455–0002–0029.

the destructive aspects of the uprising, focusing on looting and pillage and occupation of government buildings. They also provided, whenever possible, detailed information about participants, their place of residence and their family affiliation.[9] The role of the woman as informant, as fighter, as victim and most important, as barometers for the morality or immorality of the perpetrators (whether Ba'thists or rebels) becomes central to all the narratives of the events that emerged in the 1990s.

The second aspect of the report is the centrality of the Ba'th party leadership at the provincial and national levels to the collection of information, the planning of responses and the assessment of damages. Despite the participation of Ba'th party rank and file in the rebellion, it appears that substantial sections of the leadership became the effective arm of the intelligence for the state. In part this can be explained by the wide-scale destruction of government offices including those of the intelligence and police. More significantly, I think, is the presence of Ba'th party leadership cadres at every level of society. As early as 14 March, for example, Sa'd Mahdi Salih, the head of the Baghdad organization of the party whose office became the central clearing house for reports from party officials in the provinces, forwarded a recommendation made by the leader of the Rashid branch of the party in Baghdad to the general secretariat of the party. He laid out the policy recommendations that seem to have been initiated by the regime.

It is quite clear, according to the author of the letter, that the rebellion was the result of the psychological disintegration of the armed forces in the South and the collapse of the party. He suggested that the mopping up operations by the Republican Guard be carried out with the help of cadres of the party who had worked in or were drawn from the targeted areas. Their knowledge of the topography, the situation of the towns and the reputation and allegiance of tribes and families was crucial for the success of the operation. At the same time, they would be able to re-affirm to the people in the provinces that the party and the "revolution" would remember

---

[9] See for example a report from a Ba'th party female member from the district of Shamiyya, written sometime before March 23. The woman names 29 participants, lists their employment and places of residence. When her house came under fire and her car (given to her by Saddam) was stolen, she fled to her parents' house. When that was attacked she carried her daughter on her shoulders and with her three children trailing behind, walked 3 km to her relatives' house in the countryside. When the rebels followed her there, she and her family dressed like peasants and fled to Baghdad. The part of the report that made it to the office of the president and the security services just mentioned the names of the 29 men involved in the uprising in her area. MF, BRCC, 3455–0002–0249, 0250, and 0251.

the loyalists in its reform and humanitarian initiatives and that its primary aim was not to target the whole of their communities, but to "cleanse our people from the criminal and traitorous elements."[10] On 20 March, Saʻd Mahdi Salih wrote to the general secretariat supporting a policy for dealing with the rebels. He recommended, at the suggestion of the head of the special security service of the party (*jihaz al-amn al-khass*), that anyone caught looting or in possession of government property be executed without recourse to the courts. He considered that this measure would give the citizens a sense of security and help to restore order.[11] While the letter does not specify whose prerogative it is to execute culprits, the security officers within the party or ordinary party members, it does indicate the basis for the criminalization of the participants in the uprising (they were thieves) as well as the extrajudicial power given to party members on the ground.

Who were the perpetrators of the uprising? On March 15, 1991, Saddam Hussein addressed the nation and declared the end of the uprising giving it its official name, "The Page of Betrayal and Treachery" (*safhat al-ghadr wa'l-khiyana*). It was portrayed as an Iranian attempt to control Iraq. The instigators were dismissed as saboteurs who came from "behind the border." No mention was made of the catastrophic occupation of Kuwait and the withdrawal of the Iraqi army. Nor was there any mention of the humiliating cease-fire agreement that had been signed in Safwan. By April 1991, when the Kurdish uprising had also been suppressed and Iraq was clearly losing sovereignty over its Kurdish areas, the government press and the Baʻthist newspaper *al-Thawra*, had spun the uprising as the work of *ghawgha'iyun* and saboteurs who were disloyal to Iraq and who were funded by the forces of imperialism, Zionism and Iran. In particular, the early press reports stressed the destructive nature of the uprising and the moral depravity of the rebels. In an infamous series of articles, *al-Thawra*, the organ of the party, maligned the populations of the South and spoke of the Shiʻis in sectarian terms and as constituting a fifth column in the heart of Iraq. This reading became the official version of the state and affected its policies in the South and mid-Euphrates regions of Iraq until its demise in 2003 (al-Salhi, 1998). The opposition's version of events painted another picture of the uprising.

---

[10]MF, BRCC, 3455–0002–0362, and 0363.
[11]MF, BRCC, 3455–0002–0335.

A series of reports and press releases issued by an opposition group in Damascus during the uprising portrays the government as engaged in horrific acts of violence and the rebels as forming a unified opposition seeking to establish a state that was not allied to Iran nor necessarily Islamic. From the beginning the opposition was well aware that the uprising was being interpreted in sectarian terms by the international media and by the Sunni Arab states. They were quite concerned that the uprising be regarded as a popular revolt supported by wide swaths of the Iraqi population. At the same time, the opposition tried to give a coherent narrative of the *Intifada* implying that there was a leadership and clearly defined objectives (Joint Committee of Iraqi Opposition Forces, 1991; al-Majid, 1991).[12] Yet, the reports written from the scene during and immediately after the uprising belie both the government's and the opposition's readings. Their reports vary as to the slogans espoused by the main figures. Some state clearly that some of the rebels had pictures of al-Hakim and Khomeini while others stress that role of the tribes and military in the uprising. Many simply allude to the rebels as the *mu'arada*, the opposition, although it is not clear who these were. To a great extent, their reports attest to the highly localized nature of the uprising and its leaders.[13] They also attest to the centrality of family and clan networks both in the mobilization for the *Intifada* and ultimately in the government's definition of the culpability of the perpetrators to include not only the individual rebel but also his or her whole family.

---

[12]al-Majid's book was issued in June of that year and it is clear that the information obtained by the author came from the opposition in Iraq, international press reports and the office of Ayatullah Muhammad Taqi al-Din al-Mudarrisi, who issued daily reports on the *Intifada*. Mudarrisi was in the leadership of the opposition based in Damascus and took part in the conference in Beirut organized by the opposition to look into the future of Iraq. Dar al-Wifaq was funded by his organization. See also the book issued by his organization, *al-Intifada al-sha'biyyah fi al-'Iraq: al-Asbab wa' al-nata'ij wa mustaqbaluha bi nadhar Ayatullah al-Sayyid Muhammad Taqi al-Din al-Mudarrisi* (The Intifada of Iraq: Its Causes, Consequences and Its Future in the View of Ayatullah al-Sayyid Muhammad al-Mudarrisi) in 1991.

[13]Thus in a report written by a witness from Basra, the *mu'arada* (opposition) rebels in Basra chanted anti-Saddam and pro-Baqir al-Hakim slogans. In 'Amara, the opposition headquarters was in a *husayniya* with pictures of Khomeini and Baqir al-Hakim. MF, BRCC, 3455–0002–0436 and 0437. However, in Qadisiyya province, and in particular in Diwaniyya, the uprising seemed to have been organized by retreating army officers and some tribal leaders and had very little commitment to an Islamic state or to the Shi'i opposition parties. One of the witnesses states that teenagers and youth were engaged in a *farhud*. MF, BRCC, 0053 and 0054.

The reports from Najaf, Qadisiyya and Dhi Qar provinces where the violence from both sides was most intense gives an idea of the diversity in the makeup of the participants of the *Intifada* as it also clues us into the manner in which the government created the category of perpetrator and classified the hierarchy of "crimes". In Najaf, as early as 10 March, the Ba'th party office reported to the Special Security Apparatus that the rebels were using loudspeakers to assure the citizens of the city that Ayatullah Khu'i was supporting the uprising.[14] A week later, a report from a Najaf security agent confirms that the leaders of the Najaf uprising, two of the Khu'i children and Hajj 'Abbas and his children, had escaped the city to the Rahiyya area outside Najaf. At the same time, the report allows us a glimpse into the leadership of the rebellion in Najaf, which included a security officer, an employee of the food warehouse, a communist deserter from the army and the director of the Najaf hospital.[15] Clearly, in the early days of the uprising the support of Ayatullah Khu'i was crucial for the rebels and while his children might have been involved, as were other *sayyids*, Khu'i confined himself to urging the rebels not to attack property and to bury the dead. He was soon called to Baghdad by Saddam Husayn and forced to describe the rebellion as *ghawgha'*, a term that the government had used to characterize the rebels (al-Shalhi, 1998). While the religious establishment in Najaf did form a central committee made up of minor clerics, it also had wide support from army officers who had deserted. In the rural areas around Najaf, army officers, shop owners, lower middle class state employees and relatives of individuals executed by the regime seem to have played an important role in the organization of the uprising.[16]

In Qadisiyya, long regarded by the Baghdad government as essential for the security of the capital, the uprising was instigated, according to the earliest report filed on 11 March, by returning soldiers and POWs who poured into Iraq from Iranian prisons in 1990, as part of a deal struck between the Iranian and Iraqi government in the wake of the occupation of Kuwait. The al-Yasiriyya clan played a leading role in mobilizing the rebels outside Diwaniyya.[17] Other tribes joined, including the head of the Khaza'il

---

[14]MF, BRCC, 3455–0002–0309.

[15]MF, BRCC, 3455–0002–0421.

[16]MF, BRCC, 3455–0002–0252. This is a report sent by a party member who was in the Shamiyya district when the party headquarters in Qa'qa' were destroyed.

[17]MF, BRCC, 3455–0002–0517 and 0518.

tribe who was a member of the national assembly.[18] Yet not all the tribes of the region supported the rebels. Early on, the head of a tribe in the Hamza region offered his men's services (some 170–200 tribesmen) to the state and provided a detailed list of those tribes that were leading the uprising.[19] The rebels were also supported by a substantial number of officials from the Baʻth party, a number of ex-communists and relatives of Daʻwa party members executed by the regime.[20] The alliance of soldiers, many of them officers from tribal backgrounds, made the uprising in Qadisiyya among the more organized in the southern and central Iraqi regions. It is also quite clear that the leaders of the uprising in the province had little idea, beyond unseating the Baʻth, of the form of government they wanted to institute.

Reports from the province of Dhi Qar are the richest in detail and the most abundant. American troops were still on the outskirts of the province and in some cases they were seen in Suq al-Shuyukh and in Nasiriyya. It was thus important for the government to gauge the extent of support that the Americans were giving to the rebels. The most comprehensive report comes from the president of the Dhi Qar branch of the Federation of Iraqi Women and covers Suq al-Shuyukh where the Intifada had started on 1 March and Nasiriyya where it had spread by 2 March.[21] The uprising was the most chaotic in Dhi Qar province. In Suq al-Shuykh, it was dominated by tribes but included former communists and Daʻwa party members who initiated contacts with the Americans; in Nasiriyya it was led by members of the opposition and army deserters. The reports stress the role played by soldiers who were stranded in Nasiriyya and the potential trouble they could wreak as they abandoned their weapons and tried to find food and money to get to their homes. Yet, unlike the rebels in Qadisiyya and Najaf, they were less organized and could not forge a disciplined leadership. Army officers do not seem to have played an important role in planning the rebellion. Like the rebels in other parts of Iraq, the Iraqis of Dhi Qar targeted government and party buildings, census bureaus and military recruitment bureaus.

It is clear from these reports that while the conduct of the uprising was a local affair, the main actors were the clans, tribes, soldiers (deserters and POWs) and some opposition parties long thought of by the regime as having been marginalized or destroyed (communists and Daʻwa). More

---

[18]MF, BRCC, 3455–0002–0352 and 0353.
[19]MF, BRCC, 3455–0002–0372.
[20]MF, BRCC, 3455–0002–0485 and 0486.
[21]MF, BRCC, 3455–0002–0337 to 0344.

significant for our purposes is the manner by which the various witnesses
and the party hierarchy assigned guilt. In many accounts by informants,
the name of one member of the family is listed along with a vague mention of his brothers, his children or his cousins. Thus it is hard to tell how
many members of his family were involved and who actually took part in
the rebellion. When tribes are mentioned, there are sometimes allusions to
the clan within the tribe that participated, thus condemning the whole clan.
At the same time, some reports were more precise about the specific participation of the rebels: For example, who killed Ba'th party members, who
manned silos, who drove a truck with rebels in it etc. Eventually, the level
of involvement in the *Intifada* would be used by the government to exact
punishment or to determine access to resources, rations under the sanction
regime and to various other entitlements to the shrinking resources available to the state in the 1990s. Guilt, innocence, or collaboration during the
Intifada constituted the cornerstone of a policy instituted in the 1990s that
had at its core the apparently contradictory trajectories of tribalization and
atomization that not only encompassed the realm of politics but also the
legal and social realms. Increasingly for Iraqis in the south, an individual's
daily existence was tied to the involvement of his family, clan, or town in
the uprising. But it also tied him or her separately to the state for access
to any kind of services. For the most part this is also the way in which the
post-2003 governments have chosen to assign guilt and distribute resources,
despite attempts to cloak their efforts in the language and procedure of
human rights.

As important as the category of perpetrator for the Ba'th party and the
government was the category of victim and/or martyr of the *Intifada*. Like
that of the perpetrator it held political, social and legal meanings. That this
was the case became evident soon after the suppression of the uprising. On
28 April, the secretariat of the Ba'th party wrote to the Basra branch seeking
clarification on a report it had received that those killed in the events of
the uprising were given certificates of martyrdom by the doctors at a Basra
hospital who were sympathetic to the rebels.[22] On 6 June, the secretariat
directed a request to the presidential office asking it to issue an order that
would consider those families who had died as the result of uprising as
martyrs, particularly those who had died fighting. The order should make
it clear that those certificates of martyrdom issued by doctors in hospitals

---

[22]MF, BRCC, 3455–0002–0102.

under the control of the rebels were void and that the families of those who died resisting the rebels during the *Intifada* should be duly compensated.[23] The conflict over certificates of martyrdom and the determination of who was a martyr was a reflection of the centrality of martyrdom as a category of citizenship in Iraq during the Iran–Iraq war, when close to 4% of the male population died and compensation to families of soldiers became an essential entitlement for large sections of the Iraqi population. Attempts on the part of the rebels to expand the category to include their allies among the dead during the *Intifada* challenged the Ba'thist version of martyrdom that had become central to the state. The party's quick response and the government's issuing of martyrdom certificates and their memorials to the Ba'thist victims of the Intifada in the ensuing months was an attempt to reassert control over the definition of victim and martyr. By August 1991 the Ba'th had issued and the government had approved 714 martyr's certificates to victims, most of whom belonged to the party.[24] Orders went out to various areas to organize memorials for the martyrs.

Witnessing the Uprising: Witnessing as Politics and Rhetoric

If eyewitness accounts formed the cornerstone of the intelligence gathered by the Ba'th during the uprising, then witnessing with its moral, religious, and psychological dimensions was central to the dissemination of the state's version of the events in the press and public discourse in the first three years after the *Intifada*. Such witnessing included accounts by victims of the *Intifada* who had been imprisoned or had been traumatized by the events. The form and tone of the testimonies was designed to de-politicize the uprising and place it in the realm of a cataclysmic event often articulated in religious and apocalyptic terms. Editorials in *al-Jumhuriyya* and *al-Qadisiyya* compared the *Intifada* to the *ridda* wars of early Islam when the tribes of Arabia declared their apostasy after the Prophet's death, or the battles in early Islamic history that took place between various areas of Iraq. The most potent analogy was the description of the *Intifada* in terms

---

[23] MF, BRCC, 3455–0002–0107.

[24] MF, BRCC, 3134–0004. Of these only 89 were issued to the Republican guard from the 15th and 17th division. See 0101–0106 of ledger.

of the Zanj revolt that had threatened the Abbasid state.[25] Needless to say, this kind of apocalyptic de-politicized language was designed to distract the Iraqi public from the actual reasons for the uprising, the catastrophe of the first Gulf war and the continuing sanctions against Iraq.

The testimony of 'Ali Haydar, a Ba'th party member imprisoned by rebels in Najaf, gives some sense of the mingling of the apocalyptic and the factual characteristic of a great deal of the telling of the *Intifada*. 'Ali Haydar was taken into a subterranean room where he was kept for seven days. The rebels abused people and executed those they deemed as collaborators. They were led by a *sayyid* who seemed to know Persian and a person who had been expelled from Iraq to Iran but had returned. A number of the rebels spoke Arabic with a Persian accent and were planning to install an Islamic government similar to the one that existed in Iran. At one point, the rebels claimed the Revolutionary Command Council was going to pardon all soldiers who had fled the war and cancel military service in the future. The rebels had burned down the directorate of military service and personnel affairs so that the government could no longer trace who was eligible for military service. Thus, despite the intimation that this was a foreign conspiracy, 'Ali Haydar was clear as to the real demands of the rebels. They wanted no more wars and they wanted the deserters to be pardoned. Yet, Haydar's narrative takes on a rhetorical flourish and apocalyptic tone when he discusses the role of women in the uprising. The *mujahidat* as they were called, were women who supported the rebels and hit the prisoners with their shoes and at some point bastinadoed some of the captives. Haydar compares them to prostitutes in Greek and Assyrian tragedies. The rebels' desecration of a holy place (Ali's mausoleum) which was now filled with dead bodies as well as prostitutes was similar to the use of pagan temples and evokes the days of the *jahiliyya*, before the advent of Islam.[26] The witnessing by victims and participants in the uprising continued to fill the pages of the press on the anniversary of the event until 1994, when the party had re-established control. As the event receded in memory, the language of the

---

[25] *al-Qadisiyya*, April 11, 1991, article by Safi 'Awdah, entitled "It is the *fitna* of the devil." See also an article by 'Ali Khayyun, in the same newspaper July 6, page 8 where the author compares the uprising to the *ridda* wars. July 16, page 8, 1991, has an article comparing the towns of Hayy and Muwafiqiyya during the *Intifada*, tracing the roots of betrayal by the former and loyalty of the latter to the times of the Abbasid Caliph al-Muwaffaq bi Illah.

[26] *al-Qadisiyya*, May 19, 1991.

witnessing became more formulaic and less specific and was meant to extol
the virtues of the leader and to point to the vices of the rebels.

For the opposition the audience was the international community that
should have intervened to prevent this gross violation of human rights. The
opposition in Damascus, for example, provided information to the international press based on testimonies of witnesses who had fled (al-Majid, 1991,
pp. 34–59). Few journalists were allowed into the affected areas immediately
after the suppression of the rebellion. For those who were, it was difficult to
sift through the information provided by the people they interviewed in the
presence of government minders and the physical evidence of destruction.
Nor were they able to tell the level of casualties, and figures of the victims
of the *Intifada* and its suppression continue to be rough estimates. Human
rights organizations, such as Human Rights Watch, interviewed witnesses
in refugee camps in Saudi Arabia and Iran, but were unable to corroborate
their testimonies with hard evidence such as mass graves. But the opposition played an important part in bringing to the fore a new discourse
about the regime which had at its heart the concept of humanitarianism
(Human Rights Watch, 1992); the regime needed to be removed or encir-
cled because of its crimes against humanity. Together with the witnessing by
refugees, the power of the visual media as a form of witnessing was part of
the attempts by the opposition to tell the story of the uprising. During the
suppression of the uprising in Dhi Qar province, the regime filmed Major
General Mustafa Kamal al-Tikriti ordering the security forces to arrest a
young man and to tie his body to two pick up trucks that then tore it in
two. Another scene shows Muhammad Hamza al-Zabidi ordering his troops
to destroy houses with RPGs and then shovel the rubble. The most troubling scene is of a Ba'thist woman informant, her face hidden behind a mask,
identifying young men who were taken part in the uprising.[27] The video was
made by the government but was soon used by the opposition to inform the
human rights community of the crimes committed by the regime. Another
video taken in Karbala by the rebels shows the last days of the *Intifada*
and its suppression by the Republican Guard. These videos are now part of
the various electronic sites of supporters of the *Intifada* and are often used
to position the rebellion as the first step towards the disintegration of the

---

[27]I have not been able to view the video but have been told about it by my informants
and it is cited by Najib al-Salhi, in *ZilZal*, his account of the uprising.

regime and to lay claim to the heroic resistance of the people of southern and central Iraq.[28]

The politics of witnessing that emerged after the *Intifada* had its roots in the Iraq–Iran war. The regime's cultural apparatus such as the Directorates of Political Indoctrination in various ministries and within the party (*dawa'ir al-tawjih al-siyasi*) and the various programs run by the Ministry of Culture and Information, relied on witnessing by soldiers, journalists, intellectuals, and victims of Iranian bombing to tell the story of the war. The rhetoric of witnessing was well entrenched in the public culture of Iraq by the time the first Gulf war took place. That rhetoric depended on certain rules in which the specificity of the personal experience was marginalized by the "truth" of the importance of a heroic and honorable stance in face of an enemy. And while later witnessing often addressed the misery and the wastefulness of war, it never challenged the war as a moral and national imperative or the legitimacy of the regime's decisions to go to war.[29] The first Gulf war and the ensuing uprising unsettled the rules of witnessing that had been established by the government during the Iran–Iraq war. The Anfal and Halabja atrocities were closely monitored by the regime as were the reports by human rights organizations on these atrocities. But it offered no attempt to counter the witnessing of the victims of these events. The problem with the uprising was that the enemy was more difficult to demonize and the victims of the regime's violence constituted large sections of the Iraqi population, including the figure of the soldier, which had been elevated to be the moral witness *par excellence* during the Iran–Iraq war. Thus, the perpetrators were described by the "official" witnessing in vague and generalized terms with religious overtones and the victims of the violence were confined to those Ba'th party members and the Republican Guard that had died during the suppression of the uprising.

Unlike the Iran–Iraq war, however, the uprising took place on the home front and exacted its toll among civilians. The language of witnessing was thus focused more on the "inhuman" behavior of the rebels, their irrationality and their practices that defied the "civilized" behavior governed

---

[28] Available online: http://www.youtube.com/watch?v=jDQ_EtpeNrY (accessed May 2, 2008). On the uprising in Karbala, see http://www.youtube.com/watch?v=5jF5-4kr2sQ& feature=related (accessed May 2, 2008).

[29] I am currently working on a book entitled "War, citizenship and remembrance in Iraq" which addresses some of these issues. It is due to be published by Cambridge University Press in 2012.

by norms of human rights. While accusations of treachery and sabotage remained the staple of the official commentary on the uprising, the language of witnessing employed both the norms of human rights and the apocalyptic imagery of the struggle between the forces of good and evil. This language of witnessing also permeated the accounts of the opposition forces, whether in its dissemination of the imagery of the suppression of the *Intifada*, or in its focus on the regime's "crimes against humanity". In the absence of "hard evidence" to help understand the *Intifada*, it now depended on the testimonies of witnesses as a cornerstone of the story that the different protagonists wanted to tell. In this telling, there were perpetrators and victims/martyrs but the stories of other Iraqis who fall outside this paradigm were seldom heard or told.

The "End of Days": Oral Histories of the *Intifada*

The oral interviews of witnesses of the *Intifada* belie the bifurcated classification of Iraqi's experience as divided between victims and perpetrators. Nor do they adhere to the sectarian division between Shi'i and Sunni, Ba'thist and rebel that is found in the sanctioned witnessing of both the government and the opposition. What all share, however, is the sense that the experience of the first Gulf war and the ensuing uprising created an atmosphere of chaos and violence of apocalyptic proportions. Two of the informants I discuss below had not as of yet processed either the meaning of the *Intifada* or its trauma. They spoke in a disjointed manner, often inflecting their narrative with details of daily life or mundane concerns. In so far as they had time to tell the story of the uprising, they seem to have not attempted to give it any specific political meaning beyond the personal. The third informant had thought about the uprising and had attempted to make sense of it and situate it within the current sectarian climate of Iraq. He spoke in a clear narrative, often using "high" Arabic (*fusha*) rather than Iraqi dialect, and attempted to impart his political reading of the uprising to me rather than his more subjective feelings during the event. All three interviews offer a glimpse into the promise and limitations of oral history.

The three interviews were conducted in Amman in July 2007 and were set up as conversations with participants and witnesses in the uprising from different cities and different social and economic backgrounds. The interviews were not designed to focus on the uprising but to explore the experience of the informants of the Iran–Iraq war and the first Gulf war. The purpose of the interviews was to get at the subjective experience of these Iraqis rather than to interrogate the truth or falsity of information about these events. The interview with the member of the Republican Guard division called "al-Madina al-Munawwara" (i.e., Medina) was conducted over four days and 10 hours of interview time at the informant's house in Mahatta in Amman. The interview with the physician was conducted in his place of work over two sessions that came to five hours of tape. Finally, the interview with the Iraqi intellectual who was a participant in the Najaf uprising was conducted in a café frequented by Iraqi intellectuals in Amman and took place over two sessions lasting four and half hours.

Abu Sayf fought on several fronts in the Iran–Iraq war as a member of the Republican Guard, and his experience in the fall of the Fao peninsula in 1986 and its liberation in 1988 had left an indelible mark on his psyche. He had a desk job that few of his colleagues envied. His duty was to visit the front at the end of each battle to assess the losses of human lives and equipment suffered at the end of each day. When the invasion of Kuwait commenced he found himself being asked to move towards the Saudi border without much direction or knowledge as to the purpose of such movement. In the final days of the ground war, he and his comrades were hungry, dirty and buried with their equipment in trenches dug underneath the sand. He and his comrades found out about the order to withdraw from Kuwait on 28 February, only when they heard the rumbling of tanks and military vehicles as they lay asleep in their trench. At dawn he woke up to find that soldiers were running barefoot in front of and alongside military vehicles driving towards the Iraqi border. They were running as if the "end of days" (*al-akhira*) had come or escaping from a cyclone (*i'sar*). He and his unit began their withdrawal until they reached Zubayr. They looked like monsters (*wuhush*); they were dirty, hungry, without shoes and with days-old beards (*multahin*). On their way from Zubayr to Basra, his unit was strafed by US planes and he could find very little to hide under. When they reached Khalid bridge between Zubayr and Basra, he found that it had been destroyed by the bombing and that a makeshift bridge had been erected to allow for transport of the military. It was at this point that Abu Sayf broke down, both in this interview and with his retreating comrades. He had a brother in the army in Kuwait and had hoped that he would see him among the army units now gathering around the bridge. Instead, he saw soldiers from the army dead in a pit underneath the bridge; they had been mowed down by enemy planes. As he climbed down the pit to look for his brother, he saw dogs eating the bodies of dead soldiers. He started crying and it took several of his friends to calm him down. He resolved to leave his unit and go into Basra to look for his uncle's family. He arrived at Sa'd Square on 1 March but found it empty and became suspicious that something was wrong. Returning to his unit, he and his division were ordered to march towards Qurna to continue their movement to the North. A day later, the leader of the Republican Guard, 'Iyad al-Rawi, visited their division and told them that a revolt had broken out in Basra and that its target was the government and the Republican Guard. He said that Saddam Husayn had issued orders to shell the districts of Sa'd Square, Jumhuriyya street and all other areas that the rebels had taken over. Abu Sayf's best friend in the unit was a Shi'i corporal whose family lived in Jumhuriyya and he did not know what to do. It is at this point that Abu Sayf expresses his consternation and the depth of his confusion:

> Frankly, I am not a politician and I do not know who is right and wrong and what the reality is. I was physically and psychologically exhausted and I could not understand what these orders meant. I was supposed as a soldier to fight the enemy. This is what I did in the Iran–Iraq war and this is what I did with the Americans. But I cannot now turn my weapons against Iraqis even though I could not understand why these Iraqis did not welcome me when I returned after I fought the enemy in Kuwait. This is police and security work; the army should not kill Iraqis. I just left. I found a person who was going to Kut and I said, just take me to Kut and I will find my way to Diyala where my family is. My wife is about to deliver and she has not heard from me in two months, she must think I am dead.[30]

Abu Sayf's division was dismantled in the aftermath of the *Intifada* because large numbers of its soldiers had surrendered their weapons. He never rejoined the Republican Guard and did not even claim retirement benefits, but attempted to make a life for himself, not too successfully, as a small businessman.

The story of Dr. Rafid of Nasiriyya, who was 16 years old at the time of the uprising echoes Abu Sayf's in its portrayal of the *Intifada* as a time of unprecedented violence when categories of victim and perpetrator were fluid. He spoke of the uprising as the *ridda*, one of the official names given to it by the regime, named after the early wars of tribes who had declared their apostasy after the Prophet's death. He was a member of a solid middle class family: A brother in medical school, a father who was an engineer working for the government and a mother who taught English in government schools.

---

[30]Interview with the author. Amman, July 7, 2007.

For him, the *Intifada* was the most traumatic event of his young life. A self-contained man, his voice rose to a pitch when he spoke of his fear and his experience during the *Intifada*.

Dr. Rafid remembers that two Iraqi soldiers knocked at their door requesting food and civilian clothing after the order came for the withdrawal of the Iraqi army from Kuwait. During the first two days there had been some shooting in the streets of the city in celebration of the end of the war. But on the third day, the situation began to change. His first inkling of trouble came when he saw a barefoot child a few years younger than himself, running towards the security directorate in their neighborhood and telling them that a rebellion was taking place. Dr. Rafid's description of the armed men echoes some of the other reports I heard from witnesses and some of the official accounts. The armed men had beards (*multahin*) indicating that they were religious (although most returning soldiers had beards because they had not bathed or shaved for weeks). Barefoot women and children were in the streets looting the government buildings that had fallen to the rebels. When he went to visit his aunt's house in the Sabaean quarter of the city (Dr. Rafed is Sabaean), he saw men wearing traditional dress (*dishdishas*) manning checkpoints and asking people for identity cards. They were looking for party members and let them go as soon as they found out they were Sabaean.

The city was under the control of the rebels for a number of days and was in a state of total chaos. Dr. Rafid and his family wanted the government to re-establish order. When they heard on the radio that the Republican Guard was on its way to establish order, his father sensed that the confrontation was going to be bloody. He decided to divide his family up to ensure that at least some of them remained alive. He sent Dr. Rafid and his brother to his aunt's house in the Sabaean quarter of the old city, while he, his wife and his daughters remained at home. But what was thought of as a safe haven ended up being a dangerous place. The Republican Guard bombarded the quarter for whole week destroying most of its buildings and killing a number of innocent civilians including two of the residents in his aunt's building. In the midst of all this five families were huddled together in one room, surviving on dry bread dunked in water and boiled eggs.

When Dr. Rafid and his brother ventured back to their home, they went through city streets strewn with bodies to find their house empty. His father had fled to the house of one of his employees in Suq al-Shuyukh. When the family was reunited his father told them how he had tried to return to the house only to be prevented by the army when they came to the Industrial quarter. There was a large crowd in the square. The army separated the men, young men and women into three groups. There was a woman wearing a black plastic bag on her head with two holes around the eyes who was pointing out the rebels to Muhammad Hamza al-Zabidi, then Prime Minister. His father would have perhaps suffered the fate of the rebels had he not indicated to one of Hamza's lieutenants that the two of them had crossed paths when he had been an engineer in Kirkuk in 1979 and Hamza was Minister of Development.

It is difficult to verify this last portion of the story since Hamza and the woman with the mask have become part of the lore of the suppression of the rebellion in Nasiriyya. What is clear, however, is that despite Dr. Rafid's use of the terminology of the Ba'th in his description of the rebels (strange clothes, barefoot and *murtaddun* from *ridda*), he and his family were victims of the suppression of the rebellion rather than the rebellion itself. His telling of the story focuses not only on the strangeness of the rebels but also on their class. They were tribesmen and poor people who had taken over the streets. It is this aspect of their identity that seems to hold most significance to him. The men who undertook the mopping up operation were, in his words all "fierce Tikritis with rippling muscles" that could crush the rabble that came from the countryside.[31]

H. S. is an Iraqi from Najaf, a prominent young intellectual who writes on the Iraqi political scene for Arab newspapers and is currently working at a research institute in Amman. A native of Najaf, he was in his twenties when the uprising took place. He remembers hearing that a revolt had begun in Basra, and rumors were circulating in Najaf on 3 March that something extraordinary was going to happen at 2:30 pm. His mother told all of them to go to her father's house in the old city before that time to avoid whatever was going to happen. At 2:10 pm, they heard gunshots. He left his grandfather's house to investigate and found a man wearing a black headdress (*kufiyya*) carrying a machine gun and chanting "Long Live Baqir al-Hakim." Later he saw pictures of Khomeini and wondered who was responsible for this and the chants he heard "There is no *wali* except 'Ali and we want a Ja'fari leader." H. S. joined the youth that flooded the streets for two days but then found himself outnumbered by those carrying signs with Shi'i slogans calling for the establishment of an Islamic republic. Like Dr. Rafid, H.S. expressed his concern about the rebels through comments on the contrast between the

---

[31]Interview with the author. Amman, July 1, 2007.

way he was dressed and clothing worn by the rebels. He said he had gone into the streets wearing a leather jacket that his father had brought for him from Germany and thought that he was very elegant and modern. Most of the rebels were wearing the Iraqi *dishdisha*, the traditional garb of the more conservative lower classes. The deciding moment for him came when one of the rebels climbed on the roof of the security building, tore down the Iraqi flag and replaced it with a green flag. While he was opposed to the kind of nationalism espoused by the Ba'th, he had no desire to see a theocratic state. He harbored resentments against the exclusion of Shi'is from positions of power in the Ba'thist regime, but felt that the *Intifada* should not be a Shi'i *Intifada*.[32]

The interviews provide no unified story of the experience of the uprising. More significantly, they blur the clear distinction between victim and perpetrator that the Ba'thists, the opposition and the current government of Iraq want to make. Most of the Iraqi population remained on the sidelines of the *Intifada* and suffered losses of life and property inflicted on them from both parties. At the same time, despite their explicit commitment to one party or the other, their telling of their stories attests to the ambiguity of their situation. Unlike the Palestinians of the camps who remember the 1948 *nakba*, they are still not able to integrate their memories into a national narrative of any sort. Like the Palestinians interviewed by Rosemary Sayigh, however, those among them with clear political views seem to have been able to relate to the uprising with more clarity and less personal anguish (Sayigh, 2007, pp. 135–158).

Conclusion

I would like to conclude by raising a series of questions about evidence and witnessing as cornerstones of writing the history of violent events. Among the Israeli "New Historians" who have re-written the history of 1948, it has become axiomatic that they have been able to revise the history of the *nakba* through their access to new materials in the Israeli archives. Much of their work has mined the correspondence and meetings in the interwar period as well as IDF archives to conclude that the expulsion of the Palestinians was a concerted policy based on a variety of strategies, including massacres, first

---

[32] Interview with the author. Amman, June 23, 2007.

by Zionist organizations and then by the Israeli state. Yet, relying on government archives as the sole source of incontrovertible truth has been questioned by both Palestinian historians and by post-Zionist academics. These
scholars question their colleagues on two issues: First whether this reliance
on government sources did not completely delegitimize other sources, particularly the testimonies of Palestinians who have long provided their own
story; and second, whether the act of dismissing oral history was not itself a
deliberate attempt at forgetfulness that is highly political in nature (Beinin,
2005, pp. 6–23; Sa'di and Abu Lughod, 2007). The debate among these
historians goes to the heart of the conundrum about the use of sources,
the political nature of their production and the writing of history. Among
those who write the history of Palestine/Israel, the debate is embedded in a
moral sensibility that seeks to redress wrong and establish justice. This, of
course, is also at the heart of the trial of the *Intifada* and the writing of its
history. Yet, one should ask at the same time, whether the work of the historian necessarily involves taking sides and whether the multi-dimensional
nature of the *Intifada* makes it possible to arrive at a clear definition of
who is victim and who is perpetrator. There is no doubt that the 15 men
who were tried for their connection to the suppression of the *Intifada* bear
a measure of responsibility for its execution. What is one to do, however,
with the countless individuals who performed criminal acts? Or the rebels
who executed Ba'thist officials without due process? What is the role of the
historian in all of this? Does if only complicate the picture by pointing out
the "contaminated" nature of *all* the sources used?

Electronic references

Human Rights Watch (1992). Endless Torment: The 1991 uprising in Iraq and its
    aftermath. Online. Available HTTP: <http://www.hrw.org/file://G:\Iraq926.htm>
    (accessed June 12, 2008).
al-Mada (17 March, 2 June, 7 August, 21 and 22 August 2007). Online. Available HTTP:
    <http://www.almadapaper.com/paper.php?source=akbar&mlf=interp> (accessed June
    4, 2008).
al-Salhi, N (1998). *Zilzal.* Online. Available HTTP: <http://www.Iraq4all.dk/Zlzal/Zm.
    htm> (accessed April 28, 2008).
Social Science Research Council (2008). Online. Available HTTP: <http://www.ssrc.org/
    essays/minerva/2008/10/29/eskandar> (accessed September 2, 2008).

QADISIYAT SADDAM: THE GAMBLE THAT DID NOT PAY OFF

Chérine Chams El Dine

After the Iranian Revolution of 1979, relations between the Iraqi regime and its Iranian counterpart gradually deteriorated. In Teheran's eyes, the "atheist" Iraqi regime was the embodiment of evil in the Persian Gulf. In contrast, for Saddam Husayn, the new Islamic Republic represented a source of grave danger for Iraq, notably because of its encouragement of the clandestine Shi'i opposition movements, among the most important of which were *al-Da'wa* (the Call), *Jund al-Imam* (the Army of the Imam) and *Munazamat al-'Amal al-Islami* (the Organization of Islamic Action, OIA). These groups had agreed on the necessity of initiating violent action against the Iraqi regime, and in April 1980, a member of OIA attempted to assassinate Tariq 'Aziz, the Deputy Prime Minister. This provoked an immediate reaction on the part of the Iraqi regime, namely the execution of one of the most influential Shi'i leaders, Ayatollah Baqir al-Sadr, an unofficial representative of Khomeini in Iraq, and of his sister, Bint al-Huda.

Moreover, after 1980, the Iraqi regime began massive deportations of Iraqi Shi'is supposedly "of Iranian origin" (40,000 individuals) and seized their possessions. While the new Islamic Republic certainly posed political problems for Saddam's regime, this cannot be the only explanation of the invasion of Iranian territory. Obviously other factors must be considered. In particular, the war against Iran embodied symbolic values, and Saddam reckoned on gaining political benefits from it, not only by strengthening his personal position but also by strengthening Iraqi national identity by binding it seamlessly to his own person.

Since the late 1970s, Saddam had wished to make Iraq a pivotal state, with himself as leader of the Arab world and defender of the Gulf Arab countries, whose regimes generally perceived the emergence of a radical Islamic Republic in Iran as a serious threat to their political stability. Therefore a "lightning war" would probably force Iran to make territorial concessions[1] and to recognize the pre-eminence of its Iraqi neighbor. Such a confirmation of Iraq's pivotal role in the region would have strengthened the image of himself that Saddam Husayn was trying to project as a historic Arab leader, and his newly established power in Iraq.

An even more important factor concerns the construction of an Iraqi national identity around the personality of Saddam Husayn. While recognising the plural character of the Iraqi population, Saddam wished to create a new national identity gathering the various ethnic and confessional groups into a unique community of which he claimed to be the only defender (Tripp, 2000, pp. 229–232). This new Iraqi national identity linked to his person was supposed to find its application during the war against Iran, which was immediately named "*Qadisiyat Saddam*".[2] This epithet was supposed to rally all Iraqis, regardless of their community of origin, and to emphasize the centrality of Saddam Husayn to this new identity.

Thus, in the Iraqi President's view, a limited and quick war that Iraq would of course win would force Iran to negotiate in a way favorable to him, and then to make territorial concessions. Nevertheless, these concessions were not the ultimate purpose of the campaign against Iran: As Saddam gave more importance to the symbolic value of the victory, it would have allowed him to strengthen not only the leadership of Iraq in the Arab world but also his own power within Iraq.

On September 22, 1980, Saddam announced the abrogation of the Algiers agreement of 1975. The Iraqi Revolutionary Command Council (RCC) gave the order to the armed forces to attack Iranian military positions and invade Iranian territory "to dissuade the racist Iranian regime from challenging Iraqi sovereignty" (Balta, 1989, p. 36). While some Iraqi military units targeted specific objectives, others simply received an order to invade Iranian territory and to occupy it as much as possible. Clearly, the war against Iran had no clearly defined operational objectives, and does not seem to have been the result of detailed planning. Saddam Husayn envisaged it rather

---

[1] These concessions concerned the redefinition of the Iraq–Iran borders, fixed in 1975 by the Algiers agreement. Iraq claimed sovereignty over the whole Shatt al-'Arab which marked the border between the two countries.

[2] Also known as "Second Qadisiyya", a reference to the Battle of Qadisiyya in 636 during which the Arab Muslims defeated the Persians, which began the Islamization of Iran.

as a "war of demonstration of Iraqi strength," (Tripp and Chubin, 1988, pp. 54–57) whose purpose was to strike fear in the minds of Iranian leaders and to face them with the dilemma of having to choose between military escalation and territorial concession. The issue of the war was only a question of time for Saddam, since the high human cost would soon force the Iranian leaders to give up.

But the very first days of the war proved the failure of Saddam's design. Not only had he overestimated the skills of the Iraqi army, but the Iranian government regarded the invasion of its territory as a kind of test for the revolution. The defense of Iranian territory and of the revolution was the occasion of a massive mobilization of the Iranian population around its regime. Hardly a week after the beginning of the war, on September 29, 1980, while none of the parties seemed able to take the lead over the other in the short term, Iran declared three conditions for the opening of negotiations with Iraq, the first being "the fall of the Iraqi regime," in other words the resignation of Saddam Husayn.[3] The call for his resignation as one of Iran's condition for ending the conflict echoed the rhetoric of the Iraqi leader himself, and thus did nothing but strengthen the association between the war and the person of the President. Ironically, this strategy aimed at linking the personality of Saddam Husayn to the war, positioning him as defender and "rallying point" of the Nation, was gradually to turn against him. This proved most sharply when the human and economic costs of the war[4] began to be felt, added to the refusal of any mediation on Teheran's part.[5]

---

[3]The other conditions were: (1) the occupation of Basra by Iran as a war indemnity and the implementation of a referendum in this town to allow the inhabitants to express their desire to remain under Iranian or Iraqi sovereignty, and (2) the organization of a referendum among the Iraqi Kurds on the choice between autonomy and joining Iran (Balta, 1989: 37).

[4]Iraqi oil income fell from $26 billion in 1980 to $9 billion in 1982, after the destruction of the Iraqi refinery at Fao and Syria's decision to stop pumping Iraqi oil through the Kirkuk–Banias pipeline in April 1982. Thus oil revenues could no longer compensate for increasing military expenditure. Later Iraq experienced a decline in its foreign currency reserves and an increase in its debts, which amounted to $25 billion in 1983 (Tripp, 2000: 235; and *Financial Times*, March 26, 1982). Moreover it is worth noting that after three years of war Saddam asked the citizens to donate their jewellery to the "war effort". In such ways every citizen was supposed to feel even more personally involved in the fight against "the Persian enemy". This campaign lasted for four months and is said to have collected between 50 and 100 tons of gold. *Le Monde*, October 23 and 24, 1983.

[5]Several attempts at mediation were made by the Organisation of the Islamic Conference (in October 1980), the NonAligned Movement and the Arab League.

Saddam Husayn's strategic misjudgment was best illustrated during the Iranian "reconquest" in May–June 1982 and the fall of Fao and Mehran in 1986. To secure the durability of his authority, Saddam implemented a series of changes in 1982 and then again in 1986–1987. Not only did he modify his rhetoric, but also the pattern(s) of management on the part of the ruling elite (in the Ba'th Party and the government), and he even introduced a process of economic and administrative reform. In other words, he ordered changes within the regime to avoid a change of regime. This study focuses on the repercussions of the Iraq–Iran war on the internal politics of Iraq through an analysis of the official discourse, the patterns of elite management[6] and the nature of the economic-administrative reforms. It examines the regime's strategies of survival in the aftermath of its consecutive military 'debacles' in 1982 and 1986, and it also highlights the measures taken by the Iraqi regime to overcome its defeats.

1982 Iraqi Withdrawal and Necessity of Internal Reshuffles

Between April 30 and May 24, 1982, Iran launched a counter-offensive in three phases to recapture the territories occupied by Iraq since the beginning of the confrontation. Basra was massively bombed between June 1 and 5, 1982, so that within a few days, Iran was successful in repelling the Iraqi army and in getting back most of the territories lost in 1980. The war then entered a second phase, during which it was no longer an Iraqi "demonstration of strength" but a "war of survival" (Tripp and Chubin, 1988, pp. 57–61) whose purpose was not only to defend Iraqi territory from "the hostility of the Persian enemy," but also to defend Saddam's leadership, weakened by the military reverses of 1982. Indeed, the events of May and June 1982 widely questioned Saddam's military and strategic calculations, and consequently his authority and skills as a leader — while Saddam had launched the war against Iran in September 1980 to strengthen his power both internally and in the region as a whole.

If the Iraqi president was able to isolate the population (except in Basra) from the consequences of the war for quite a long time — by maintaining,

---

[6]The analysis of the elite's reshuffling in 1982 and then in 1986–1987 is based on a study of the profiles of the Iraqi ruling elite under Saddam Husayn, the subject of the author's PhD dissertation.

at least during the first years of the conflict, the basic components of the welfare state (health, education, etc.) — members of the ruling elite, including those belonging to the circle closest to Saddam, quickly suffered from the political fallout of the war. Such individuals seem to have considered their political fate threatened in spring 1982, if Iraq did not reach a peace agreement with Iran. Some of them even suggested Saddam's resignation, at least temporarily, in favor of his predecessor Ahmad Hasan al-Bakr,[7] to satisfy Iran's conditions and stop the war.

The situation became alarming for the Iraqi President on June 9, 1982, when a joint extraordinary meeting gathering members of the Revolutionary Command Council (RCC),[8] Regional Command (RC), the National Command of Ba'th Party and the Iraqi Military Command, took place without him. At the conclusion of this meeting, a RCC statement proposed a cease-fire to Iran and a return to the *status quo ante bellum* — in other words, the withdrawal of all Iraqi troops from Iranian territory. At the origin of this proposition was the "necessity of concentrating the resources and the efforts [of both countries] to face the Zionist aggression[9] against the Arab Nation, in Palestine and Lebanon" (FBIS, 1982). This meeting without Saddam Husayn and the elaboration of a proposition of cease-fire with Iran without his signature was evidence of the existence of a major political crisis within the Iraqi ruling elite. The Iranian refusal to consider a unilateral cease-fire on 10 June allowed Saddam to reaffirm his power. Ironically, *a posteriori,* it thus seems clear that the political grip of the Iraqi President would have been greatly weakened if Iran had not rejected this proposition outright.

On June 20, 1982, he announced the unilateral withdrawal, within a period of 10 days, of all Iraqi troops from Iranian territory to the international border. A clear change of rhetoric can be observed, in this speech, especially the justification of the war against Iran. All Iraqi claims on Iranian

---

[7]Fortunately for Saddam, al-Bakr's unexpected death in October 1982 put an end to this plan.

[8]Theoretically, the Ba'th Party's highest executive authority was the National Command, which included representatives of the Ba'th Party from other Arab countries. In practice, however, the Regional Command (RC) in Iraq had the real authority. It had major responsibilities in running party affairs, but usually operated in the shadow of the Revolutionary Command Council (RCC). The latter was the supreme governing body in Ba'thist Iraq, and functioned as the supreme executive and legislative body until 2003.

[9]The Israeli army had entered southern Lebanon on June 6, 1982.

territories, which had allowed Saddam to justify the war, had been completely forgotten by June 1982. In his speech, he mentioned neither the liberation of Khuzistan (Arabistan), nor the restoration of Iraqi sovereignty over the Shatt al-'Arab. On the contrary, the war was presented as a "defensive" one, a battle the Iraqis had been forced into by attacks from Iran. Rewriting history, he even asserted that the war had begun on 4 September, and not on September 22, 1980 — the date mentioned in his previous speeches and in accordance with the facts. He explained, "when [the Iranians] began to bombard our cities on the border, on September 4, 1980, from Iraq territory that they occupied, and then closed our only maritime outlet to the world, at this moment, it was not possible to remain silent any more" (Husayn, 1982).

Saddam's speech also emphasized the victimization of Iraq, presented as suffering from the hostile front put up by the Zionists, the Iranians and their Syrian allies, and from the plot to mutilate the country, to divide its territory and to stir up conflicts between the citizens. Saddam never admitted military defeat; quite the contrary. According to him, Iraq was victorious; it had managed to reach "its defensive objectives," unlike Iran, which had experienced a "historic defeat" by failing to realize "its aggressive and expansionist objectives." Finally, Saddam tried to justify Iraq's withdrawal from Iranian territory by underlining that this decision was based on a sense of responsibility, to destroy the various pretexts Teheran could use to continue the war, and thus to thwart Iran's "obnoxious plot" against Iraq (Husayn, 1982).

On June 22, 1982, the President of the Iranian parliament, Hashemi-Rafsanjani, once again rejected this Iraqi proposal and declared, "the war will continue until Saddam's overthrow so that we will be able to pray in Karbala and Jerusalem." He added, "the road to Jerusalem passes through Karbala and the elimination of the Iraqi Ba'th" (Balta, 1989, p. 48). Paradoxically, Iran's obstinacy resulted once again in strengthening Saddam Husayn's power and made it unthinkable for members of the ruling elite to express dissent or to stop pursuing the war against Iran.

Three days later, Saddam convened the Ninth Congress of the Iraqi Ba'th Party. His objectives were clear: to rally party members, to muzzle criticism, to solve conflicts with the opponents within the party and, finally and especially, to legitimate his authority by displaying himself as *al-qa'id al-darura*, the indispensable leader. This Ninth Congress is especially interesting for two reasons. First of all, the political report was very different compared to former ones. Subjects rarely broached previously, like Islam, the superiority of Iraqi nationalism over Pan-Arabism, or even Saddam's role as the "ultimate arbiter of the party's ideology" (Tripp, 2000, p. 237) were mentioned prominently. In this report, Saddam appropriates Ba'thist ideology completely. The Iraqi president is presented as the one who had commanded the Ba'thist regime since its creation in 1968 and had acted as the supreme Ba'thist ideological guide since 1963. In this way Saddam obliterated the role of his predecessor Ahmad Hasan al-Bakr. The report went even farther by placing Saddam Husayn above the Ba'th founder, Michel 'Aflaq: It underlined that Ba'th ideology was failing until Saddam's arrival, and that he was the first in the history of the party to formulate a coherent Ba'thist action plan in different domains.

Moreover, during the keynote speech of the Congress, Saddam explained that the Revolution — in other words, the Ba'th — faced internal problems, such as deviations from the line or even "counter-revolutions." According to him, the main responsibility for these difficulties was to be laid at the door of some Ba'th members, accused of weakness, incompetence and lack of dedication to Ba'thist principles (*Hizb al-Ba'th*, 1983). Such changes paved the way for large-scale reorganizations[10] — in the RCC, the RC and the government — which happened only three days after this intervention.

An analysis of the reshuffles in the Ba'th command reveals the strategy adopted by Saddam Husayn towards the 1982 crisis. On June 28, 1982, the Ba'th Regional Command composed of 15 members, including Saddam, was reduced by half. Only seven members of the original "hard core" of the regime kept their positions: 'Izzat Ibrahim, Taha Yasin Ramadan, Tariq 'Aziz, 'Adnan Khayrallah, Sa'dun Shakir, Hasan 'Ali, and Na'im Haddad. Considered Saddam's closest associates, he had promoted all of them through the main Ba'th institutions at least since 1977.

As for the other half of the RC, the new members were relatively younger than the former. Born between 1938 and 1945,[11] they were between 37 and 44 years old when they were appointed to the RC. Four of them were Shi'i — while the majority of the dismissed members were Sunni (four out of seven) and natives of al-Anbar and Salah al-Din provinces (five out of seven). If the new members' regional origin varied widely, they were mainly from the South and the center of Iraq. They had all joined the Ba'th party in the 1950s when they were teenagers. These new RC members were approximately

---

[10]The main source for the 1982 reshuffles (within the RCC, the RC, and the government) is *al-Jumhuriyya*, 29 June 1982.

[11]The only exception was Sa'dun Hammadi, a Ba'th veteran born in 1930.

the same age as Saddam Husayn, and indeed some were some younger: They had grown politically in step with him, and owed him direct personal loyalty.

The changes within the RCC, the Iraqi regime's supreme institution, were even more significant. In June 1982, the number of RCC members decreased, for the first time since the major reorganization of September 1977, from 16 to nine members, including Saddam. With one exception, the RCC was composed of the seven dignitaries who had formed the "hard core" of the regime since 1979; in the popular perception, they were so much a part of Saddam's regime and so much involved in the regime decision-making that they represented absolutely no credible alternative to the current ruler, and thus could not work for his overthrow. In 1982, this "inner circle" thus represented the common denominator between the Iraqi regime's three authorities: RCC, RC, and the government.

Symbolically, Saddam completed the RCC by appointing Taha Muhyi al-Din Ma'ruf, a Kurd who enjoyed no popularity and was representative neither of the Kurdish resistance movement nor of the Kurdish population. On the other hand, his appointment showed the desire of the regime to give the population the feeling that the Kurds were represented within its highest echelons. Ma'ruf was a lawyer and had been vice-President since 1974, but he had never been influential in political decision-making, and his power was purely ceremonial and symbolic.

At the same time, Sa'dun Ghaydan was dismissed from all his functions in the RCC and the government on 28 June 1982. Although close to the Ba'th, Ghaydan and Ma'ruf had never been party members, despite their appointment to the RCC. After the Ba'thist Revolution of 1968, Ghaydan was appointed Commander of the Republican Guard and a member of the first RCC (in July 1968), a position he held until 1982. In addition, he had been successively Minister of Interior, of Communications and then Deputy Prime Minister. His departure from the RCC and the government seems highly significant as Sa'dun Ghaydan was the last member of the first RCC formed after the 1968 Revolution, but also the only high-ranking military officer in the Ba'th leadership apart from Saddam's cousin, 'Adnan Khayrallah.[12]

---

[12]Since 1979, 'Adnan Khayrallah had accumulated the positions of member of the RCC and RC, of Deputy Commander of the Armed Forces, of Minister of Defence and Deputy Prime Minister.

During the ministerial reshuffles of June 28, 1982, technical and economic portfolios (Local Administration, Health,[13] Youth, Transport, Planning, Industry, Agriculture and Oil) were involved. Given the deterioration of the economic situation during the war, the regime was anxious to isolate the civilian population from its effects by guaranteeing the functioning of the public sector. The ten new ministers were mostly technocrats, only half of them (five out of ten) belonging to the Ba'th. Three held postgraduate degrees, two of them obtained abroad (in Europe). These new ministers were born between 1931 and 1941 (and were thus between 41 and 51 in 1982), with the exception of 'Abd al-Jabbar al-Asadi, born in 1927, one of the few military officers in the 1982 government. Asadi had occupied several important positions in the army, and was appointed Minister of Transport and Communications in June 1982.

Finally, two structural changes happened in 1982; a new Ministry of Light Industry was created, while the position of adviser to the President with ministerial rank, established on this occasion, was given to six of the seven new RC members: Muhammad Hamza al-Zubaydi, 'Abd al-Ghani 'Abd al-Ghafur, Samir Muhammad 'Abd al-Wahhab al-Shaykhli, 'Abd al-Hasan Rahi Fir'awn, Sa'di Mahdi Salih and Mizban Khidr Hadi. If these positions were a material and symbolic reward for Saddam's new right-hand men, they indicated unambiguously that from this time all political decisions would be taken in the presidential palace.

Probably the most interesting feature of the reshuffle in 1982 was that the "hard core" of the regime — composed of Saddam's acolytes, who had already been with him in 1977, before his accession to power — remained intact. In addition, these men were involved in the three main organs of the Iraqi regime (RCC, RC, and government), a further indication of the concentration of power in the hands of a small circle of dignitaries loyal to the President. In other words, in the face of the political crisis of 1982, Saddam tightened the base of his power, by relying on a circle of trusted men whose political fate was indissolubly connected to him. The best indication of this strategy was given by the reshuffle of the RCC, which was now reduced to nine members.

---

[13]The outgoing Minister of Health, Riyadh Ibrahim Husayn, had been executed by Saddam Husayn in October 1982. He had suggested that Saddam Husayn should resign and end the war on the basis of Iran's proposed peace terms. In the official version, Riyadh Husayn was executed because of his involvement in corruption (MECS, 1982–1983, pp. 563–564).

In addition, these reshuffles signified Saddam's intention "to restore order" within the ruling elite. First, they were designed to prevent the formation of an opposition front composed of opponents of Saddam's policies (which some had considered strategic errors), including those who had asked for his resignation to stop the war against Iran. On the other hand, these changes conveniently created "scapegoats", who could be considered responsible for the mismanagement of internal affairs during the war.

Finally, in 1982, Saddam decided to inject some "fresh blood" in the RC, by allowing the entrance of new members who had made the proof of their loyalty and their efficiency, while dismissing those considered responsible for major failures. The cases of Burhan al-Din ʿAbd al-Rahman and ʿAbd Allah Fadhil, perceived by the regime as incapable of making Baʿth principles take root in the Kurdish provinces, are illustrations of this.

A similar scenario took place in 1986–1987, following the fall of the Iraqi port of Fao and the evacuation of the Iranian city of Mehran. While these events also led to a large-scale reshuffle, the technique used by the regime to deal with the crisis, in terms of its management of the ruling elite, differed sharply from the one in 1982.

"The cup drunk down to the last drop": the military collapse and the new crisis

On February 10, 1986, Iran launched its "Fajr VIII" offensive, which ended with its capturing of the port of Fao and taking 1,000 Iraqi prisoners of war. At once, Iraq launched a counter-offensive led by the Presidential Guard. This turned out to be a disaster, not only because of the failure to recapture Fao, but also because of the high human cost (10,000 Iraqi casualties). As commander-in-chief of the armed forces, Saddam had preferred a defensive strategy, contrary to the opinion of some of the members of his staff, who supported a massive attack, even a partial occupation of Iranian territory. For his part the Iraqi president wished to avoid losses at the front as much as possible, as well as Iranian reprisals against the Iraqi population, which would inevitably have repercussions upon his own political authority. The violent struggle to take Fao continued, but it was only at the end of March 1986 that Iraq admitted that its troops were surrounded (Balta, 1989, p. 81).

Facing the impossibility of re-taking Fao, Saddam approved an offensive strategy in April. For the first time since the Iraqi withdrawal in 1982, he decided to adopt the new tactic of occupying positions in Iranian territory; this became a reality on May 17, 1986 with the capture of the Iranian city of Mehran. Nevertheless, this success was quickly reversed, first after Tehran's refusal to exchange Mehran for Fao, as Iraq had proposed, and even more when Iranian troops retook Mehran some weeks later. On July 2, 1986, the Iranians pushed Iraqi troops back to the international border (Balta, 1989, p. 83), which led to an even more serious crisis of confidence within the Iraqi political leadership than the one after the fall of Fao some months earlier. After the fall of both Fao and Mehran, Saddam faced growing demands both from the military — seeking greater independence in commanding the operation — and the political elite — asking for more participation in the decision-making process.

Confrontation with the Iraqi Military Command

A victim of the old complex of the "civilian in military uniform", Saddam had always wanted to exert total control over the army, preventing it from being independent from the political authority and most relevantly from ever becoming powerful enough to overthrow the regime. This was in order to protect himself from the recurrent scenario of all the revolutions in the recent history of Iraq.[14] Not only had the political leadership decided the military strategy during the Iraq–Iran war, but Saddam Husayn did not allow contacts between the various sections of the army, as any military requests had to go through Baghdad. Nevertheless, after the defeats at Fao and Mehran, the Iraqi President faced the *esprit de corps*, or professional solidarity (Tripp, 2000, p. 241) of the senior military command, asking for greater operational freedom of action from the political leadership in order to respond more effectively to Iranian attacks without having to refer constantly to Baghdad. Confronted with this pressure, Saddam yielded to the demands of his military officers by establishing an implicit contract with them. He guaranteed them some decision-making autonomy on the front

---

[14]During the 1960s and 1970s, a confrontation had taken place within the Ba'th between the civil and military wings of the party, and the army had become effectively politicised.

and access to all the resources (money, provisions, equipment, etc.) they needed for continuing the fighting. In return, Saddam kept an eye on the army, thanks to the security apparatus and his network of patronage, i.e., by appointing relatives or clients in army headquarters.

After the fall of Fao, Saddam was obliged to adopt a series of face-saving measures. Given the necessity of identifying those responsible for this symbolically fundamental military defeat, he decided on a wide-scale reshuffle in the military command and executed a number of officers.[15] Among the prominent generals Saddam was to lean on during the Iraqi counter-offensive was Mahir 'Abd al-Rashid. Popular within the army, a native of the same village as Saddam, he was the father in law of Qusayy, Saddam's younger son. 'Abd al-Rashid was thus appointed military commander of the seventh armed force, responsible for the Iraqi counter-offensive to recapture Fao,[16] and then promoted to the rank of Lieutenant-General after the fall of Mehran.

'Abd al-Rashid's meteoric rise reflected a new tendency within the whole ruling elite (among the party leaders and within the government) since 1986; Saddam began to lean in a increasing way on relatives or persons to whom he was connected by "alliances" (such as General 'Abd al-Rashid), and not only, as had been the case since his coming to power, on henchmen or trusted individuals — an development which will now be analyzed in detail.

If Saddam was prepared to yield to pressure from his senior military officers by granting them greater independence and greater freedom of maneuver in military operations, it was unthinkable that a similar change should take place within the political leadership — that is, that he would make himself accountable to the political elite, or that he would allow the latter increased participation in the decision-making process. On the contrary, he further strengthened his influence over the leading institutions and began a widespread reshuffle, first of the Ba'th command (in July 1986), then of the cabinet (in 1987).

Essentially, Saddam repeated the scenario of June 1982. He convened an extraordinary Ba'th Congress, sent an open letter to the Iranian leaders

---

[15]The officers were executed because they were allegedly responsible for the military defeat (MECS, 1986: 366). Paul Balta has mentioned an attempted coup d'état against the regime in which these officers were said to be involved (Balta, 1989: 83).

[16]'Abd al-Rashid fell into disfavor after the failure of the Iraqi counter-offensive, but kept his position following the threats of his officers to resign if their commander was not maintained in his position (Tripp and Chubin, 1988: 118).

proposing an "honorable peace,"[17] and finally introduced an "administrative reform" accompanied by a ministerial reshuffle.

Extraordinary Ba'th Congress (July 10, 1986)

In circumstances similar to those of the Ninth Ba'th Congress (in June 1982), Saddam convened the members of the party for an extraordinary meeting. He wanted to be reelected as Ba'th Secretary General and thus to insure his legitimacy within the party and within the army, thereby remedying the destabilization of his political base after the military defeats of 1986. He opened the session with a speech[18] during which he did not mention either the political problems or the ideological line of the party; he concentrated on a unique subject: "the plot against the party and the Nation." Saddam used the word "plot" on 25 occasions to stress on his intention to be released from any responsibility either for the initiation of the war of for the way it had been conducted.

During this extraordinary congress, Saddam enlarged the Ba'th Regional Command from 15 to 17 members, to whom three new substitute members were added (FBIS, 1986a). The mandates of the individuals elected in June 1982 were renewed, except Na'im Haddad, who lost all his prerogatives in the Iraqi leadership. A Shi'i, Saddam's henchman and a Ba'th veteran,[19] Haddad had held the positions of President of the National Council (the Iraqi parliament) and Secretary-General of the Progressive National Front until October 1984.[20] He had also been a member of the RC (1974–19786) and the RCC (1977–1986). Following the reorganization of July 1986, Haddad was replaced in the RCC by Sa'dun Hammadi, also a Shi'i and the acting President of the National Council. Since Haddad's dismissal on July 16, 1986 was not justified officially, it is worth noting that this

---

[17]In his letter to the Iranian leaders, on August 2, 1986, Saddam proposed conditions which he considered would lead to an "honorable peace": (1) the complete and unconditional withdrawal of both armies to the international borders, (2) the exchange of all war prisoners, (3) the signature of a peace and nonaggression treaty, (4) nonintervention in the hope that Iran and Iraq contribute jointly to the stability and the security of the region, notably in the Gulf (FBIS, 1986b; *Libération*, August 4, 1986).

[18]*al-Jumhuriyya*, July 12, 1986.

[19]He had joined the party in 1956.

[20]Founded in 1973, this structure was officially the alliance of the Ba'th with the Iraqi Communist Party and the Democratic Party of Kurdistan, although it had long ceased to play any but a symbolic ride.

close associate of Saddam had begun to fall into disfavor in October 1984, when he was not reelected as President of the National Council. Criticism of the conduct of the war against Iran was said to have been the cause of his disappearance from the political stage (MECS, 1986, p. 368).

Even more important was the arrival within the RC of three new members (Latif Nasif Jasim, 'Ali Hasan al-Majid, and Kamil Yasin Rashid), and three substitutes. Let us begin with Latif Nasif Jasim. This protégé of Saddam, one of his closest associates, had been Minister of Culture and Information since July 1979, when Saddam came to power. Before the Ninth Party Congress, Jasim had been decorated by Saddam to honor the role which the media in general and Jasim in particular had played during the war against Iran, notably by working to raise the morale of the citizens and to cultivate the image of the President after the 1982 defeat.

Another Ba'thist to be added to the list of the RC members in 1986 was Kamil Yasin Rashid, who belonged to Saddam's tribe (Albu-Nasir) and was related by marriage to the President: His brother, Arshad Yasin, was the husband of Saddam's sister, Nawal. Finally, 'Ali Hasan al-Majid,[21] Saddam's first cousin and chief of national security (*al-amn al-'amm*), was appointed to the RC. The choice of members of the RC among the persons in charge of security also became a reality by the inclusion of another Takriti as substitute member: Fadhil al-Barrak, the head of intelligence at that time.

The "gradual" appointment of new elite members chosen from among Saddam's relatives and the heads of the various security apparatuses had been a general tendency since 1986, all evidence of Saddam's insecurity and the destabilization of his political base after the 1986 crisis. The President wished to tighten his grip on the state apparatus by appointing more protégés and relatives, considered personally loyal almost by definition. He also integrated individuals from the security apparatus into the party command to keep a firm control on his political circle and to avoid any subversive action against him.

al-Thawra al-Idariyya (The administrative revolution)

The continuation of the war against Iran, the reduction in Iraqi oil production,[22] the fall in oil prices and the accumulation of external debts all

---

[21] After this, 'Ali Hasan al-Majid and Latif Jasim attended Saddam's meetings with the military commanders.

[22] A large part of the oil infrastructure was not in working order, to the extent that it was estimated that production capacity had decreased by a million barrels per day. *Le Matin*, January 29, 1987.

contributed to the deterioration of the economic situation in Iraq. For a regime whose popularity rested largely on its capacity to redistribute at least some of the country's wealth, an economic crisis of this magnitude risked undermining its social base. Since the beginning of the conflict, Saddam had wanted to continue economic development in tandem with the war effort in order to maintain the living standards to which the population had grown accustomed. But there had been no development plan since 1986–1987, and the austerity measures taken by the authorities were beginning to have a significant effect on the standard of living of most Iraqis.[23] At this point Saddam began to mention an "administrative revolution" or even "a wide movement of reform affecting the totality of the structure of the Iraqi economy," to underline the necessity of taking advantage of "the positive aspects of the war to introduce reforms the people could accept at this stage, but not when the conflict would have come to an end."[24]

Following the example of the Egyptian President Sadat, who had launched a policy of *infitah* (economic open door) after the war of October 1973, Saddam recommended a reduction in government expenditure, decreasing the role of the public sector in the economy and favoring private initiative. He seems to have come to the conclusion that the commitment of the public sector to economic activity, and more generally the whole system of "state socialism", which had been adopted in Iraq until then, represented a major obstacle to the development of the Iraqi economy.

Certainly the decay of the economic situation and the incapacity of the public sector to cover all expenditures, in other words to provide both "guns and butter" at the same time[25] according to Latif Jasim, the Minister of Culture, provided the main motives for economic liberalization. This was perceived as necessary to stimulate economic performance, and thus strengthen Saddam's popularity and power. On the other hand, this reform was a clear rejection of "socialism", one of the main principles of Ba'th ideology. In this context, the war represented both the cause and the occasion for Saddam to introduce such reforms. Nevertheless, the latter, through the encouragement of the private sector, also allowed the President to shake the control of the Ba'th party and individual Ba'thists over the economy and to open the way for emergence of a group of businessmen who would be loyal to Saddam because they now had an interest in keeping him in power (Springborg, 1986, p. 34).

---

[23] *Le Monde*, October 15, 1986.
[24] *al-Thawra*, June 10, 1987.
[25] *Le Monde*, December 14, 1987.

Wide Ministerial Reshuffle (1987)

Together with the economic reform, a broad ministerial reshuffle took place in 1987, in three successive phases — March, August, and September.[26] It is clear that the main motivation for this series of reshuffles was to reduce government expenditure and to improve economic performance. Several ministries disappeared (like the Youth Ministry); others were merged (Agriculture and Irrigation were replaced by a larger Ministry of Agriculture). Finally the missions of others changed (the Ministries of Commerce and Minerals and of Light Industry became respectively the Ministries of Heavy Industry and of Industry). This hypothesis — that changes in the cabinet were primarily aimed at improving the economic situation and at implementing reforms — is confirmed by the fact that the reorganization was directed particularly at the technical and economic portfolios: Industry, Heavy Industry, Oil, Commerce, Agriculture, and Transport and Communications.

The new ministers were mostly technocrats who had already occupied positions in the economic organs of the state. Thus Qasim Ahmad Taqi had been an under-secretary in the Ministry of Commerce and Minerals, then Minister of Oil after 1982, while 'Isam al-Chalabi had been chairman of the Iraqi National Oil Company (INOC) and under-secretary at the Ministry of Oil. Three of them had been trained abroad (in Great Britain and the United States). Even more interesting, these new ministers were mostly not Ba'th members, which meant that professional skill and technical efficiency, rather than party membership, was the main criterion for their recruitment. At the same time, Hasan 'Ali, one of the Ba'th veterans who had been propelled into the limelight by Saddam in 1977, when he was appointed Minister of Trade and became member of both RC and RCC, was dismissed. Muhammad Mahdi Salih, a young economist with a PhD in planning from the University of Manchester, replaced him in 1987 as Minister of Trade. He was the head of the economic reforms inaugurated at the end of the 1980s. As head of the economic service in the presidential cabinet, then deputy head of this same cabinet, Muhammad Mahdi Salih maintained a direct relationship with the President and was thus answerable to Saddam himself, not to the Ba'th.

---

[26]The main sources for the RC and RCC reshuffles are *al-Jumhuriyya*, 24 March, 3 August, 7 August, 20 September, 23 and 29 September 1987.

The necessity of getting the country out of the economic crisis explains this trend of appointing competent professionals, especially since many of them were not Ba'th members, and thus were unlikely to oppose the implementation of such reforms on the grounds that they contradicted Ba'th principles. Moreover there was certainly the will to push aside the "old guard" of the Ba'th from the ministerial portfolios. Nevertheless Ba'thists kept three of them, including Interior, where Sa'dun Shakir was replaced by another Ba'th member, Samir 'Abd al-Wahhab, who then combined the positions of Minister of Interior and of Higher Education. On the other hand, the fact that Sa'dun Shakir and Hasan 'Ali, both Saddam's old companions, had left their positions seems more ambiguous; the only official justification of their dismissal was the necessity for them "to dedicate themselves to their party responsibilities"[27] — which meant, in Ba'th jargon, that they had fallen into disfavor. The other portfolios remaining in Ba'thist hands in 1987 were: Transport, headed by Muhammad Hamza al-Zubaydi; and Agriculture, chaired by Karim Hasan Ridha. Born in 1944 and 1945 respectively, neither Karim Ridha nor Samir 'Abd al-Wahhab were members of the Ba'th "old guard" and thus owed their political careers to Saddam personally.

A last remark concerns the abolition of the Ministry of Youth, officially to reduce the state bureaucracy, but in fact to facilitate the rise of 'Uday, Saddam Husayn's elder son, who was the head of the Iraqi Olympic Committee. Indeed, with the abolition of the Ministry of Youth, many of its prerogatives passed to the Olympic Committee.[28] Finally, another relative of Saddam was promoted in 1987 in the new cabinet. Hatim 'Abd al-Rashid, a member of Saddam's tribe but also the brother of General Mahir 'Abd al-Rashid, the father in law of Qusayy, was appointed Minister of Industry.

Thus, confronted with the military defeat of 1986 and the ensuing crisis, Saddam did not rely on the "inner circle" of old Ba'th companions, as he had done in 1982. On the contrary, he brought new members into the party's command (especially in the RC). These individuals belonged to Saddam's family ('Ali Hasan al-Majid, Kamil Yasin) or were protégés (Latif Jasim) as well as members of the security apparatus. Thus 1986–1987 showed the beginning of the rise of Saddam's relatives within the leading institutions — as was highlighted by the examples of 'Adnan Khayrallah,

---

[27] *al-Jumhuriyya*, August 3, 1987.
[28] *al-Jumhuriyya*, September 29, 1987.

Minister of Defense and a member of both the RCC and the RC; 'Ali Hasan al-Majid, head of General Security and a RC member; Kamil Yasin, a RC member; Hatim 'Abd al-Rashid, minister of Industry; and 'Udayy Saddam Husayn, head of the Olympic Committee. Nevertheless, it is not possible to assert that, when confronted with this crisis, Saddam "tightened up his control of the state apparatus [...] relying even more heavily on the narrow circle of kinsmen and associates, who formed the core of his regime." (Tripp, 2000, p. 242) Indeed, the Iraqi President did not rely on a narrow circle, but diversified and widened the base of his power by gradually integrating his relatives *alongside* his old Ba'th companions who had kept their influence within the party's leading institutions (RCC and RC) until then. The same tendency can be observed through the reorganization of the government, where we can notice the appointment of experienced technocrats, capable of implementing the economic reforms required to improve the economic situation and thus to strengthen Saddam's power. Of course this attempt at economic liberalization was in no way the beginning of political liberalization; on the contrary, it led to an inevitably 'timid' economic reform, considering the nature of the Iraqi political system which could neither allow the emergence of a "business culture,"[29] nor the blooming of the private sector.

By adopting quite different techniques of elite management in 1982 and then by changing his rhetoric, and even by initiating an economic reform in an attempt to enhance the regime's economic performance, in 1986–1987, Saddam attempted to distract attention from his military defeats. Moreover, the Iraq–Iran war was the first crisis to test Saddam's legitimacy and the regime's resilience and is fundamental to any understanding of Iraq's relations with Iran and its Gulf neighbors in the aftermath of the war and until the regime's collapse in 2003. It was the first of a series of crises which Saddam's regime managed to survive through the perpetuation of "changes within the regime" to avoid a "change of regime".

---

[29]See Michael Field, "A grip that strangles reform," *Financial Times*, December 5, 1988.

SHI'I ACTORS IN POST-SADDAM IRAQ: PARTISAN HISTORIOGRAPHY

Peter Sluglett

Introduction

In broad terms, the history of twelver Shi'ism in Iraq since the 18th century has become reasonably well known, largely from the writings of Juan Cole (1985, 1988), Pierre-Jean Luizard (1991), Chibli Mallat (1988, 1993), Yitzhak Nakash (1994) and Meir Litvak (1998). Juan Cole gives a highly nuanced account of the eventual "triumph of Usulism" (sc. over Akhbarism) in the eighteenth century: he shows how the Afghan conquest of Isfahan in 1722 caused many 'ulama families to flee from Iran to the Iraqi 'atabat. Most of them were Usulis, followers of an interpretation of Shi'i Islam which "legitimated an activist role[1] for the clergy as legal scholars in society" (1985, p. 5), in contrast to the 'ulama living in the Ottoman-controlled Iraqi shrine cities, many if not most of whom were Akhbaris. For a while, the newcomers were influenced by the Akhbarism they found in their new home, but in the 1760s, as Ottoman influence in the Holy Cities declined, and as the star of Karim Khan Zand, and later of the Qajars, began to rise in Iran, the Usulis, whose world view enabled them to interact more easily with a strong secular power, gradually became the mainstream element among the Shi'i clergy (both in Iran and in Iraq). The "triumph of Usulism" is associated with the long career of Muhammad Baqir Bibihani (1706–1792) (Heern, 2010).

Cole also underlines the more practical factors that influenced the rise of Usulism, factors which had little to do with religious conviction, in much the same way as doctrinal details were not always the decisive factor in pushing some German princes to choose to become Protestants and others to remain

---

[1] The distinction between "activist" and "quietist" 'ulama is one made by outside observers and is not part of any indigenous typology or usage.

Catholics.[2] In a relatively lawless society, or at least one in which the state and its representatives were often ineffectual and/or far away, and also in the absence of the Hidden Imam, it was highly desirable that a respected body of scholars (the *mujtahids*) could provide religious and moral guidance for the laity through the regular performance of *ijtihad*, independent reasoning, a major factor in accounting for the particular vitality of Shi'ism since the end of the eighteenth century (Enayat, 1991, p. 160). In contrast, "conservative Akhbarism, in which most state-related functions of Islamic government were considered lapsed in the absence of the Imam, could not fulfil state needs for legitimation nearly as well" (Cole, 1985, p. 27), nor, of course, were the Akhbaris able to give much in the way of practical advice to the faithful, since they held that no human agent could take the place of or deputise for the Hidden Imam. The "state needs" which Cole mentions were those of the Zands (1751–1794) and the Qajars (c. 1779–1925): The general weakness of the Ottoman state (in Iraq in particular) for much of the late 18th and the first half of the 19th centuries meant that there were few barriers to the continuous strengthening of ties between the clergy of the Holy Cities and the successive ruling dynasties in Iran.

The triangular relationship between the Ottomans, the Qajars, and the 'ulama of the *'atabat* in the latter part of the 19th century is discussed in the second half of Litvak's *Shi'i Scholars of Nineteenth Century Iraq* (1998). As already implied, the Qajars themselves (and the Pahlavis after them) could not and did not claim any religious legitimation and were thus ideologically dependent on the moral support of the Shi'i 'ulama "who firmly dominated the [Iranian] masses with [their] exclusive religious authority." (Arjomand, 1984, p. 219). Of course, this moral support could be withheld, as happened first in the Tobacco Rebellion in the early 1890s and then during much of the Constitutional Revolution. In contrast, although they rarely made the claim between the 16th and the 19th centuries,[3] the Ottomans based their own claim to legitimacy on the notion of a "donation" of spiritual power (however spurious) by the last 'Abbasid ruler in Egypt, al-Mutawakkil II, to Sultan Selim I in 1517, a kind of apostolic

---

[2]With the obvious difference that Akhbarism has largely died out; there is a small and apparently dwindling community in Bahrayn (Nasr, 2006: 69).

[3]i.e., between the reign of Sulayman I (1520–1566) and 'Abd al-Hamid II (1875–1909). The gradual (and uneven) adoption of Twelver Shi'ism on the part of the Safavid dynasty indicates that it is premature to present the 16th century in terms of a Sunni (=Ottoman) versus Shi'i (=Safavid) struggle: see Newman (2006).

succession from the early caliphate. Although there is a large amount of written evidence of "jurisprudential activism" on the part of many Sunni judges, muftis, and holders of the office of *shaykh al-Islam*, the "official" Ottoman Sunni 'ulama as a whole tended to rubber stamp what the state wanted (for instance in matters related to the succession, or the oath of office), and certainly never functioned as a political body either independent of or opposed to the state. In any case, any potential autonomy was eroded by the creation of a Department of Religious Foundations under Sultan Mahmud II in 1837 (which effectively relieved the 'ulama of their control of *awqaf*). Thus in the unique circumstances of Iraq, the Ottomans ruled a Shi'i majority whose clergy were at best indifferent (or at worst hostile) to the Ottoman state, whose nominal subjects they were, while at the same time acting as the legitimators of Qajar rule.

As far as the Ottomans were concerned the unsettling aspects of this situation were exacerbated by the almost wholesale conversion of the tribes of southern Iraq (most of whom had migrated out of the Arabian Peninsula) to Shi'ism in the second half of the 19th century (Nakash, 1994). For a while the Ottoman authorities tried to counter this trend by sending Sunni "missionaries" (Turkish *misyoner*) to Iraq to guide the faithful back to the true path, or by funding students to attend Sunni *madrasas*, who would then be educated enough to counter the Iranian and Indian money and Shi'i propaganda flooding into the Holy Cities (Deringil, 1990). Attempts were also made to ban the performance of *taziyas* in Iraq. None of this worked, but the adoption of these various counter-measures shows the extent of the state's concern. On the other hand, it was also the case that for much of the last decades of Ottoman rule the state either tended to give a wide berth to the religious authorities in the shrine cities, or, in accordance with 'Abd al-Hamid's pan-Islamism, made conciliatory gestures to the Shi'i 'ulama (such as gilding the minarets of the mosque over the tomb of 'Ali in Najaf). In fact, whatever their differences with the Ottoman state, the Shi'i *mujtahids* of Iraq issued an immediate call for a *jihad* against the foreigners (Ende, 1981) when the British landed in southern Iraq at the end of 1914.

Litvak shows that in contradistinction to their contemporaries in Iran itself, the 'ulama of the *'atabat* generally adopted a quietist attitude to Iranian politics, so that their much vaunted participation in the Tobacco Rebellion in 1891–1892 was (until that moment) a one-off and exceptional event. This caution began to evaporate only with the bankruptcy of the Iranian government (forcing it to borrow, mostly from Russia, which in return tried to control Iran's finances), and the economic depression of the first five years of the 20th century. This combination of fiscal and economic woes had an immediately negative effect on the fortunes of the "Iranian bazaar" (the major source of income for the *'atabat*), which encouraged the 'ulama to speak out, first on economic and then on socio-political issues.

In the course of the 19th century (certainly no earlier), something approaching a "clerical hierarchy" had developed in the Holy Cities, with figures such as Muhammad Hasan Najafi (d. 1848), Murtada Ansari (d. 1864), Mirza Hasan Shirazi (d. 1895) and (somewhat later) Taba'taba'i Yazdi (d. 1919) emerging as *maraji' taqlid*, sources of emulation. This designation has continued into more recent times, although it has proved sufficiently flexible to permit more than one *marja'* to function at the same time without splitting the community. Thus during the *marja'iyya* of the revered Iranian Husayn Burujirdi (c. 1946–1962), most Arab Shi'is (inside and outside Iraq) followed the Iraqi Muhsin al-Hakim (1889–1970). After his death al-Hakim was "succeeded" by another Iraqi, Abu'l Qasim al-Khu'i (1899–1992), who was generally recognized (by Shi'is everywhere) as "the" *marja'* in spite of the obviously greater prominence and profile of Ayatullah Khomeini. al-Khu'i in his turn was followed as *marja'* by his own most famous student 'Ali al-Husayni al-Sistani (born in Iran in 1930, and a resident of Najaf since 1951) whom Vali Nasr describes as "the undisputed leader of Iraq's Shias [after the death of al-Khu'i ... who] was quickly recognized as such by Shias from Lebanon to Iran to Pakistan." (Nasr, 2006, p. 171). The "chain" linking al-Hakim, al-Khu'i and al-Sistani (though the *hawza* of Najaf) is especially interesting: al-Hakim was active against Communism and secularism in the 1940s and 1950s, perhaps especially during the time of 'Abd al-Karim Qasim, who became president of Iraq after the revolution of 1958. al-Khu'i, who was generally regarded as a "quietist", rejected Khomeini's doctrine of *vilayet-i faqih*, but in March 1991, at the age of 92, was obliged by the Iraqi leadership to appear on television praising Saddam Husayn and the Ba'thist regime, and to call on Iraqi Shi'is to end the intifada which had followed the US invasion to restore the sovereignty of Kuwait (Nakash, 1994, p. 278). al-Sistani, who became *marja'* after his mentor's death in 1992, lived under a loose form of house arrest in Najaf between 1994 and 2003. In the course of his career he trained several prominent scholars now prominent in Iran, Iraq, and Lebanon. Since the US invasion he has played a key role both by urging Shi'is to participate in politics (by discussing issues and voting in elections) and not to retaliate against sectarian attacks by Sunnis.

Nakash emphasises both the recentness and the unique nature of Iraqi Shi'ism, noting particularly close relationships between the tribes and the *'atabat*. I am a little doubtful of what I understand to be his assertion that the coming of the British and the creation of an Iraqi state and an Iraqi monarchy somehow frustrated the formation of a *Shi'i state* (e.g., pp. 4–5, where the process of conversion in southern Iraq is compared with the Wahhabiyya, the Mahdiyya, and the Sanusiyya, while these other movements carried out their proselytizing by armed force). Nevertheless, his point that the creation of modern states in Iran by Reza Shah in Iran, and by the British and their Sunni partners in Iraq had very different effects on the Shi'i communities in each state is well taken. However much Reza Shah and his son tried to restrict the power of the clergy and generally to secularize the Iranian state, they could not, given the place of Twelver Shi'ism in Iranian society, make that power disappear entirely, and the symbiosis between Iranian-ness and Shi'i-ness, and the requirement that in order to be legitimate the regime should maintain some semblance of clerical support proved very resilient.[4] In Iraq, in contrast, while it is true that the founding fathers, who were all Sunnis, wanted to create a secular state (rather than a Sunni state), they and their British mentors were also extremely anxious to curtail the powers of the Shi'i 'ulama, whom, as will be explained, they regarded with extreme suspicion.

A few months after the end of the First World War, Ayatullahs Muhammad Taqi al-Shirazi and Shaykh al-Shari'a al-Isfahani, both resident in Najaf, wrote two letters to President Woodrow Wilson, seeking his aid against Britain and the British occupation of Iraq. The second letter, dated February 21, 1919, contains the following passage:

> The desire of all Iraqis, as [members of] a Muslim nation is that they should be given the liberty to choose a new independent Arab and Islamic state, with a Muslim king assisted by a national assembly. As far as the question of a protectorate [*wisaya*: This letter antedates the term mandate, *intidab*] is concerned, it should be up to the national assembly to accept it or reject it, after the convening of a peace conference.[5]

Similar sentiments were expressed in various petitions submitted to the British occupation authorities in the run up to what has become known in

---

[4] Ayatullah Khomeini's attacks on the Shah in the 1960s and 1970s struck home precisely because of the withdrawal of legitimacy that they implied.

[5] Quoted in Pierre-Jean Luizard (2003: 363–364, my translation of Luizard's French). See also Luizard (1991).

somewhat grandiose terms as "The Great Iraqi Revolution of 1920." The words "independent Arab and Islamic state" or "independent Islamic state" crop up again and again. For their part, British reports routinely portrayed the Shi'i *mujtahids* as extremists, fanatics, and reactionaries irrevocably opposed to progress, presumably in an attempt to deflect attention from the *mujtahids'* core (and ultimately unacceptable) demand for complete independence. Of course, given their previous linkages to the Ottoman state, it was almost inconceivable that members of the Sunni "aristocracy of service" should seriously have associated themselves with what they considered to be a Shi'i independence movement. If this were to succeed, it would almost certainly undermine the foundations of their own power. This explains the Sunni elite's eager alignment, almost immediately after the revolution of 1920, with the British mandatory authorities, its ready embrace of the ideology of Arab nationalism, and rather later, of the notion of a united Fertile Crescent under Hashemite rule.

In fact the short-lived "national unity" which supposedly came into being during 1920[6] was soon followed by a major confrontation between the state and the Shi'i 'ulama. In their defiance of the British mandate, some of the most prominent 'ulama (notably Abu'l-Hasan al-Isfahani, Mahdi al-Khalisi, and Muhammad Husayn Na'ini — the latter had played a particularly prominent role in the Iranian Constitutional Revolution some 15 years earlier) issued *fatwas* in November 1922 stating that participation in the elections to the Iraqi Constituent Assembly (which had been set up to deliberate and vote on the Iraqi constitution) was unlawful.[7] This led to a stalemate for several months, and eventually to the Iraqi government's decision to deport the *mujtahids* to Iran in June/July 1923. (Sluglett, 2007, pp. 42–64).

Further discussion of events in Iran lies outside the scope of the three papers under review, but it is of course important to stress that while Iraqi Shi'ism and Iranian Shi'ism developed along different trajectories, events in each country inevitably influenced events in the other. For example, the clampdown on the Iraqi shrine cities in the 1920s had its effects in Qum, in that a group of profoundly anti-imperialist activists, "refugees from Iraq",

---

[6]For a somewhat revisionist interpretation of the events of 1920, see Peter Sluglett (2007, pp. 43–45).

[7]It is a measure of the extent to which times have changed that in the context of the Iraqi elections of January 2005, al-Sistani emphasized that participation was a duty incumbent on all Muslims, both male and female.

spent several years there[8] at the time when the young Ruhallah Khomeini (b. 1900) was beginning his studies. It also had a long-term effect on student numbers. "In 1918, no fewer than 6,000 students attended the theological *madrasas* ... of Najaf. By 1957 student numbers had declined to 1,954, of whom only 326 were Iraqis" (Batatu, 1981, p. 586). Eighteen years later, Michael Fischer's tabulation of enrolments at Qum in 1975 (Fischer, 1980, p. 79) shows 6,414 students, of whom 780 came from Iraq, that is, more than twice the number enrolled in Najaf in 1957.[9] Many other cross-fertilizations could be mentioned, including, as has already been noted, the presence of several *mujtahids* and ayatullahs in Iraq who were highly respected in Iran, indeed sometimes more than their Iranian counterparts,[10] but the most obvious was the Iranian Revolution of 1979, which, at least in its initial manifestations, gave enormous hope to the "downtrodden Shi'i masses" suffering under the Ba'thist jackboot in Iraq.

The 1940s and 1950s marked a major expansion in educational facilities all over Iraq, particularly, of course, in the urban areas, which was accompanied by a degree of secularization of both political and social life. Although the proportion of Shi'is in government service (including the teaching profession) did increase gradually over these decades, and Salih Jabr became the first Shi'i Prime Minister between March 1947 and January 1948,[11] it remained far lower that the percentage of Shi'is in the population as a whole. Thus there was a general sense on the part of Iraqi Shi'is — noted by fairly shrewd foreign observers such as the US ambassador Loy Henderson and the veteran British adviser C. J. Edmonds — that the monarchy's unwritten "glass ceiling" policy of exclusion from high government service (and from the military and police academies) was causing mounting resentment (Nakash, 1994, pp. 125–138). The effects of this were twofold: The

---

[8]For the career of the son of Mahdi al-Khalisi (his father died in 1924), see Werner Ende (2007: 231–244). After 27 years in Qum, Khalisi returned to Iraq in 1949.

[9]In the same year (1975), there were 1,800 students studying in Mashhad, 500 in Tabriz, 250 in Shiraz and 300 in Yazd (Fischer, 1980: 77).

[10]For what it is worth, my not especially religious in-laws in Mashhad regularly sent their religious donations (=*sahm-i imam*) to the *madrasa of* Abu'l Qasim al-Khu'i in Najaf.

[11]Two other Shi'is served as Prime Minister in the last decade of the monarchy. Muhammad al-Sadr (b. 1882), who had been active in the revolution of 1920 and was often President of the Senate, served between January and June 1948; the American-educated Fadhil Jamali (b. 1903) served several times as Minister for Foreign Affairs and as Prime Minister between September 1953 and April 1954. Neither Jabr, nor Sadr, and especially not Jamali, who was a committed Pan-Arabist, could be said to have embodied (or claimed to embody) the political aspirations of their fellow Shi'is.

attraction of the Iraqi Communist Party for many Shi'is, both educated and uneducated, and the revival of Shi'i ideology, partly but not entirely in an effort to contain and constrain the former. Batatu's vast work (1978) shows the attraction of the Communist Party for the radical left of all sects, especially the Shi'is. It continued to wield extraordinary influence (out of all proportion to its numbers) until it cast in its lot with the Ba'th in the Patriotic National Front of July 1973, which caused many of its members to wonder why they had sacrificed so much over the previous decade. One major problem for the Communists was that (partly in order to win them over) Ba'thist socio-economic policies between the late 1960s and early 1970s seemed to be mimicking their own (for example, the Iraqi-Soviet Friendship Treaty of April 9, 1972, and the nationalization of the Iraq Petroleum Company a few weeks later, which the Communists had been advocating for years, and which would have been impossible without Soviet help). Another problem (see Franzén, 2011) was that they were being prodded into this position by the Communist Party of the Soviet Union, stuck in the heyday of its advocacy of the strangely aberrant theory of the 'non-capitalist road' (Farouk-Sluglett and Sluglett, 2001, pp. 141, 339, n. 99).

In the 1940s, the Shi'i clerical hierarchy of the Holy Cities had become extremely anxious about the inroads being made by the Communist Party. Various *mujtahids*, including the *marja'* Muhammad Kashif al-Ghita' (1877–1954) (see Naef, 1996), urged the British to cooperate with the *mujtahids* in their anti-Communist crusade, and in 1949 managed to convince the Iraqi government to allow Muhammad ibn Muhammad Mahdi al-Khalisi "to return to Iraq from his exile in Iran in order to preach against communism in his native city Kazimayn" (Nakash, 1994, p. 134). This rather hysterical attitude to communism and all its works persisted among the Shi'i hierarchy, now led by Ayatullah Muhsin al-Hakim, after the Revolution of July 14, 1958. In contrast to their broader minded predecessors in 1920, for whom anti-imperialism was the heart of the matter, the clerical hierarchy in the 1950s and 1960s seemed not to have regarded the fundamental anti-imperialism at the core of Communist ideology as particularly significant, concentrating instead on the evils of materialism, asserting that Communism was incompatible with Islam, most notably in a *fatwa* in February 1960 (Nakash, 1994, p. 135).

Between 1958 and 1968, the main right/left political struggle was between Ba'thism and Communism. After the events of the late 1950s and early 1960s, and what was and still is regarded as the fatal dithering of the Communist leadership at the time (Farouk-Sluglett and Sluglett, 2001, pp. 69–70, 74–76), many secular Shi'is came to despair of the Communists' capacity to deliver. On the other hand, few were attracted to Ba'thist pan-Arabism, which seemed to function as a vehicle for the maintenance of Sunni supremacy.[12] During this same period, Muhsin al-Hakim did not confine his strictures to the Communists. In addition to his disapproval of the overtly political position taken by Ayatullah Khomeini, al-Hakim was also extremely wary of *Hizb al-Da'wa* (see below), and eventually forbade both his sons and Muhammad Baqir al-Sadr to have anything to do with it, perhaps because of the danger it seemed to represent to the secular authorities in Iran, to whom al-Hakim was then closely connected, who were under serious challenge from Islamic activists (Luizard, 2002, p. 97).

In the last years of his life, al-Hakim also ran foul of the Ba'thists, who had become involved in quarrels with the Iranians over the boundary between the two states in the Shatt al-'Arab. In addition, the Ba'thists accused his son Mahdi of being a CIA agent, and the Iraqi regime was evidently becoming fearful of the growing organizational strength of what it seemed to regard as a kind of "Shi'i renaissance",[13] which was also affected by the presence of Ayatullah Khomeini in Najaf between 1964 and 1978. This led to the deportation of thousands of "Iraqis of Iranian origin", beginning in April 1969, the estrangement of the large and influential Hakim family from the Iraqi government, and eventually to the imprisonment and execution of many of Muhsin al-Hakim's sons and grandsons in the 1980s.

Let us return for a moment to the situation a little earlier.[14] Massive rural to urban migration, from 'Amara and other parts of the South, had created a large Shi'i underclass living mostly in slums on the outskirts of Baghdad. As we know, many of these individuals, and well as many much longer established urban Shi'is, had been attracted to the Communist Party. One reaction of the religious hierarchy had been simply to fulminate

---

[12] "Through association of control of the state with by a small Sunni Arab elite, Pan-Arabism became for many Iraqis a metaphor of the political, economic, and cultural exclusion of the bulk of the populace from public life" (Davis, 2005: 55).

[13] Other leading *mujtahids* in the Holy Cities at the time included the future Lebanese Hizbullah leader Muhammad Husayn Fadlallah (1935–2010), Muhsin al-Hakim's son Muhammad Baqir, (1939–2003), later President of SCIRI (see below), Muhammad Mahdi Shams al-Din (1936–2001), President of the Supreme Shi'i Council of Lebanon from 1978 until his death, etc.

[14] The information on Shi'i movements in Iraq between the 1950s and 1980 and on the career and influence of Muhammad Baqir al-Sadr has been summarized from Farouk-Sluglett and Sluglett (2001: 190–200).

against communism and materialism, but some subtler minds seem to have understood the limitations of this approach, and began to engage with Marxism as intellectuals rather than simply vilifying it. In the autumn of 1958, some of the leading 'ulama of Najaf took the unusual step of founding a political organization, *Jama'at al-'ulama' fi'l-Najaf al-Ashraf* (the Association of Najafi 'ulama), whose members formed the nucleus of what became *al-Da'wa al-Islamiyya* (the Islamic Call, or Mission) in 1968. The declared purpose of the Association was to raise the consciousness of the community and to combat atheism (=communism and Marxism). Since the Association was a secret society, there is little accurate information about its origins and membership, but Muhammad Baqir al-Sadr (b. 1935) played an important role in its activities, and was the author of many of its publications (Rieck, 1984, p. 45). Sadr published *Falsafatuna* (Our Philosophy) and *Iqtisaduna* (Our Economic System) in 1959 and 1961 respectively. *Falsafatuna* is a wide-ranging critique of European philosophy rather than an exposition of Islamic thought, and testifies to its author's breadth of reading and analytical skill; while *Iqtisaduna*, which has gone into at least 11 editions, is a book of some 700 pages containing a long discussion of European economic and social thought as well as an outline of the ideological foundations of an Islamic economic order. Almost a third of the text of *Iqtisaduna* is a critique of Marxism and dialectical materialism in what may be described as rational rather than religious terms, reflecting the concern of its author to try to produce convincing counter-arguments to the principal political current of the day. An important feature of all Sadr's major works is that they are addressed to *Muslims* in general rather than to Shi'is in particular, "advocating social change within an Islamic framework," obviously a crucial necessity if a religious revival was to be brought about in Iraq (Mallat, 1988, pp. 707, 713). In addition, although al-Sadr's books apparently do not contain a single reference to any work of Khomeini's, and the two do not seem to have been in particularly close contact with each other during the latter's exile in Najaf, their ideas on the proper form of the Islamic polity have many similarities, as became clear from al-Sadr's enthusiastic support for the Iranian Revolution in 1979.

Although opinions differ on the precise circumstances of the foundation of *al-Da'wa*, it seems that al-Sadr, who had himself attained the rank of *marja'* in the late 1960s, was the moving spirit behind its formation in 1968. Unlike the Association of 'ulama, *al-Da'wa*, although a clandestine organization, was aimed at a wider constituency. Its founders attempted to set up a secret network of members whose task was to assist in the creation of an

Islamic order along the lines proclaimed in the underground periodical *Sawt al-Da'wa*. As these activities became more widespread and gained increasing popular support, a separate branch of the Ba'thist *mukhabarat* was created to deal specifically with potential Shi'i opposition groups. In 1969, Ayatullah Muhsin al-Hakim had found it necessary to protest to the Ba'th against what he termed the "degradation of the religious leaders" in the Holy Cities, and the government's harassment of many Iranian residents (Akhavi, 1980, p. 131). However, the first widely reported indirect indication of the existence of Shi'i opposition groups was the execution, for reasons that were not made public at the time, of five 'ulama in December 1974. These exemplary sentences seem to have had the effect of dampening down the opposition from that quarter for some time, since there were no further signs of specifically Shi'i unrest over the next two years.

A much more ominous incident, indicating a far wider degree of public involvement, took place in February 1977, on the occasion of the *'Ashura* celebrations in Muharram, when thousands of pilgrims gather at the shrines of Karbala' and Najaf. On 5 and 6 February, members of the clergy appeared at the head of large demonstrations that seem to have taken the regime by surprise. Troops were dispatched to the Holy Cities, and a number of pilgrims were killed in the fighting that followed. Some 2,000 people were arrested, and a special court was set up to investigate these incidents: Eight 'ulama were executed and 15 sentenced to life imprisonment. After this, Muhammad Baqir al-Sadr gradually emerged as the main symbol of Shi'i opposition. An uneasy *modus vivendi* continued on both sides until the expulsion of Khomeini from Iraq in October 1978, and the inauguration of the Islamic Republic in Iran a few months later.

Particularly in its early stages, before it began to discredit itself with acts of wanton brutality and inhumanity, the Iranian Revolution engendered a tremendous sense of optimism and enthusiasm among a wide body of Muslim opinion. This atmosphere evidently encouraged *al-Da'wa* and its leaders to engage the Ba'th in open conflict, attacking party offices and police posts and making open declarations of their support for the Iranian Revolution. The Ba'th responded with its familiar carrot and stick tactics, first by making a series of apparently conciliatory gestures, including setting aside large grants for religious purposes, showing increasing deference to Islam in public statements, and by arranging televised visits by dignitaries to the Shi'i South and Madinat al-Thawra during which television sets and gifts of money were distributed in public, sometimes by Saddam Husayn in person. At the same time, a ferocious campaign was launched against *al-Da'wa* and its leaders. Large numbers of those suspected of being members of the organization were arrested, and actual membership was made punishable by death. al-Sadr himself was taken to Baghdad for interrogation; when he refused to make a public recantation of his position, he was put under house arrest in Najaf, with no contacts with the outside world after water, electricity, and the telephone were cut off. Eventually, he and his sister Bint Huda were taken to Baghdad, where they were executed by the Ba'th on 9 April 1979. The regime's ruthlessness seems to have been effective to the extent that no major Shi'i demonstrations were reported after al-Sadr's seclusion in 1979. Furthermore, to the Ba'th's inestimable advantage, the war with Iran pre-empted the possibility of any effective reformation of the movement in Iraq itself by creating a situation in which the idea of a "Shi'i polity" became synonymous with treason.

The Papers

As their titles indicate, the three papers in this section discuss various aspects of Iraqi Shi'i political organization and "political thought", mostly (the exception is Michaelle Browers) in the last few decades. Robert Riggs' "Partisan and global identity in the historiography of Iraqi religious institutions" is a study of the *hawza* of Najaf and more particularly of the career and activities of Ayatullah Sistani since the US invasion of Iraq in 2003. It is difficult not to be impressed by this courageous individual, who has stood up to the occupation authorities with much the same tenacity as he stood up to the regime of Saddam Husayn since the early 1990s, insisting on respect for the constitution and the rule of law. As we have seen, Sistani was born in Iran and settled permanently in Najaf in the early 1950s; he was evidently groomed for the succession by his mentor Abu'l-Qasim al-Khu'i, who died in 1992. His concerns have included giving practical answers to questions from Muslims living in the West and their concerns about working alongside non-Muslims, with whom he encourages Muslims to associate freely; he is generally averse to highly literal interpretations of particular verses of the Qur'an; he sees no reason which women should not have careers, or play political roles (such as becoming members of the Iraqi parliament). After the US invasion (although rarely before it), he issued many statements condemning US policy (especially his *fatwa* against the acceptance of the CPA's suggestion of an appointed rather than elected constituent assembly), as well as advocating cooperation among religious groups, the transcending of sectarian divisions and the protection of Christian minorities in Iraq: A degree of inclusiveness and pluralism, as Riggs says. He also asked for material aid from abroad (baby food, medical supplies) during the chaos and breakdown in public order in 2003–2005; such aid was distributed through his own liaison offices. In a brief section, Riggs discusses Sistani's general distaste for *vilayet-i faqih*: While the clergy should have an important advisory role in politics, there is no reason why they should themselves exercise political power. Riggs ends on a note of caution, wondering whether Sistani's pragmatism and moderation will survive his death (he was born in 1930, and is in indifferent health), or whether the more "activist" line adopted by Muqtada al-Sadr will not turn out to have greater influence.

Michaelle Browers' "Najaf and the (re)Birth of Arab Shi'i Political Thought" analyses the writings of three generations of Shi'i intellectuals trained in Najaf and working between Najaf and Lebanon. She follows a typology first introduced by Albert Hourani in *Arabic Thought in the Liberal Age*: A first generation who took up reformist themes, a second generation who engaged with modernists and secularists, and a third generation who came of age when the Arab regimes passed from colonial to independent rule. She aims to challenge both the privileging of Sunni over Shi'i intellectuals by most historians of intellectual trends, as well as the tendency to consider Iraqi and Lebanese intellectuals as part of Iranian political thought. In the 1920s, after the expulsion of many 'ulama from Iraq (see above), the "first generation", many of whom had been active in the Iranian Constitutional Revolution, became increasingly active politically, speaking out against British and French policies, participating in the Muslim Congress in Jerusalem in 1931. For all his "reactionary" stance, Kashif al-Ghita', whom we have already encountered, was, in his own words, "submerged in politics from head to toe", and advocated an Islamist vision of Arabism, which of course would require a Sunni-Shi'i rapprochement. His dislike of Communism was accompanied by some sort of understanding of why Communism might attract followers, although he feared the total marginalization of the clerical hierarchy if it were allowed to gain any sort of foothold. He thought that Iraqi sectarianism had been fashioned by the British to disenfranchise the Shi'is; there is *some* truth in this, but the reality is rather more nuanced.

Browers' second generation includes Muhsin Sharara, Muhammad Ridha al-Mudhaffar, and Husayn Muruwwa, none of whom were "clergy" (Muruwwa, who studied in Najaf in the late 1920s and early 1930s, eventually joined the Lebanese Communist party). They all deplored the lack of vitality of the *hawza* of Najaf, the decline in its educational activity, and the anti-reform attitudes of many members of the clergy; all were influenced by the (Sunni) Islamic modernism of Muhammad 'Abduh, and generally rejected Pan-Arabism because of its essentially Sunni undertones.

The major point of departure of the next generation, which included Muhammad Baqir al-Sadr, Musa al-Sadr, Muhammad Mahdi Shams al-Din, and Muhammad Husayn Fadlallah, was the articulation of "a modern revolutionary project within an Islamic framework". All of them were studying in Najaf during the formation of *al-Da'wa*, when the confrontation between communism/secularism and religion was at its height. As we have seen, Baqir al-Sadr tried to engage with communism in Islamic terms, stressing the flaws and failings inherent in both communism and capitalism in comparison with the virtues of Islam. Capitalism subordinates society to the individual, while communism subordinates the freedom of the individual to the needs of society: This cannot work because of the facts of human nature. He advocates securing the spiritual and material dignity of the individual, which he considers can only be done through religion; absolute sovereignty of "belongs only to God". Events in Iraq eventually led to Sadr's death, and the subsequent expulsion or departure of many Lebanese Shi'i students. While both Shams al-Din and Fadlallah (and Baqir al-Sadr in the brief time allowed to him) welcomed the Iranian Revolution, both the two Lebanese (in common, as we have seen, with Sistani) rejected the notion of *vilayet-i faqih*; in a late work, al-Sadr prefers the notion of *vilayet-i umma*, stressing a popular/democratic source for political authority. To some extent, this is a reflection of the fact that while the Shi'i communities of Iraq and Lebanon form major components of the population, the sensibilities of other social and religious groups have to be taken into account, but also of a broader conviction that a clerical monopoly of power is simply undesirable. Browers' brief intellectual history shows that the development of Shi'i thought has many parallels with the development of Sunni thought, although it is difficult to escape the conclusion that the former is inherently more interesting.

Finally, Elvire Corboz analyses the social and political history of the Supreme Assembly for the Islamic Revolution in Iraq (SAIRI), now known as ISCI, the Islamic Supreme Council of Iraq, an organization of the Iraqi (Shi'i) opposition set up in Teheran in November 1982, and headed, more or less since its inception, by members of the al-Hakim family ('Ammar al-Hakim, b. 1971, is its current leader). Since it has always been based in Iran, it has been accused of being a vehicle for Iranian interests, and its activities have certainly made a great deal of difference to the many Iraqi refugees and prisoners of war resident in Iran, in some cases for more than

30 years. The organization maintained its legitimacy by claiming to be an extension of the Najafi *marja'iyya* of Muhsin al-Hakim and Baqir al-Sadr, the latter being not only a *marja'* but also a martyr (*shahid*). Many members of the original leadership were part of al-Sadr's immediate circle in Iraq; it is suggested in some sources that they formed a deputy leadership, closely attached to *Hizb al-Da'wa*, nominated by al-Sadr himself, although membership of the group is not always consistent. The leadership rallied Iraqi refugees in Iran, toured refugee camps, opened schools (most refugee children did not know Persian), provided documentation enabling Iranians and Iraqis to marry, handed out financial and medical aid, gave political and religious speeches, and planned cultural events for Iraqis in Iran, as well as in Syria and the United Kingdom. It also established a system of allocations for the families of soldiers that had been killed in the war, emulating similar practices put in place by Baghdad.

SAIRI has defined itself as a popular movement rather than a political party; it will be remembered that Muhsin al-Hakim's own attitude towards *Hizb al-Da'wa* was quite ambiguous, reflecting his unease at any association of the *marja'iyya* with a body that was overtly political. It also emphasized the great sacrifices made by the al-Hakim family, many of whose members were executed by Saddam Husayn. Since no pictures of SAIRI gatherings were published it is difficult to estimate how many supporters the movement actually had. The movement also financed the Badr brigades, which (quite daringly) took up arms on the side of Iran against Iraq, both on the front and in guerrilla operations in Northern and Southern Iraq; altogether the Badr brigades had some 30,000–40,000 soldiers, the largest opposition militia. While Corboz does not take the story beyond 1992, the organization and activities of SAIRI have played a major role on the Iraqi political stage after 2003. Given the circumstances under which it operated, SAIRI was closely identified with the ideology of the regime of the Islamic Republic, (for instance in its support for *vilayet-i faqih*) and it was unable (and almost certainly did not want) to secularize its approach after the Iraqi regime was overthrown.

PARTISAN AND GLOBAL IDENTITY IN THE HISTORIOGRAPHY OF IRAQI RELIGIOUS INSTITUTIONS

Robert J. Riggs

The state of research on the role of the *hawzah 'ilmiyyah* (Shi'i religious learning centers) in Najaf, is limited primarily to historians of the Shi'is, who relegate the authorities located there to a partisan fold, primarily disinterested in directing political events in Iraq. Nevertheless, the US-led invasion of Iraq in 2003 has handed the reins of leadership in part to political parties who rely on constituencies in Najaf. This study will focus on Ayatollah Sistani (b. 1930), who has resided in Najaf since 1951. A living embodiment of the transnational religious figure, Sistani's authority and ideological viewpoint ranges across a wide spectrum of regions and ethnicities, through his writings and charitable associations. Sistani could be viewed as having positioned himself intentionally as an authority figure in an imagined religious community centered on the traditional pilgrimage sites of Shi'i Islam, but imbuing these sites with contemporary political and religious relevance. Sistani builds his constituencies through the proliferation of his messages using contemporary methods of communication such as the Internet, and gives tacit legitimacy to international political entities, such as the UN. In tandem with this internationalism, Sistani has consistently defended Iraqi nationalism and emphasized the importance of adherence to Iraqi state law, as enshrined in the constitution.

Rather than posit a static oppositional or cooperative stance for Sistani vis-à-vis the state and society in which he operates, this study will elucidate how he has sought to create a new Shi'i modernity predicated upon a delicate balance between Shi'i partisanship, pan-Islamic ideals, Iraqi nationalism and cosmopolitanism. Integrating recent theories of globalization with an understanding of the historical position of the ayatollah in the Shi'i communities allows for a more nuanced view of their role in an increasingly interconnected global system. By viewing the religious authorities in Iraq as part of an integrated societal structure, historians can develop a more balanced picture of the contemporary history of Iraq.

Biography of 'Ali Sistani

Grand Ayatollah Sayyid 'Ali al-Husayni al-Sistani was born on August 24, 1930 in the Shi'i shrine city of Mashhad,[1] and was raised in a family imbued in the Shi'i clerical tradition.[2] He began learning the Qur'an at the age of five after which he entered a religious center for reading, writing, and for learning basic mathematics and geography. In the beginning of 1941, he started studying Islamic legal and theological training. In 1948–1949, he migrated to Qum to complete his studies in *Fiqh* and *Usul*(Islamic legal jurisprudence and its rules of usage). In early 1951 or 1952, he left Qum for Najaf and reached Karbala on the occasion of the *Arba'in* commemoration of the martyrdom of Imam Husayn (al-Sistani, 2000, p. 3).

Ayatollah Sistani traveled back to his hometown, Mashhad, in 1960, where he expected to settle. However, during the same year, he was given formal permission to teach the curriculum of the *hawzah* by Ayatollah Khu'i and another by Shaykh Hilli, two highly esteemed Shi'i clerics of the time. These documents (*ijazat*) certified that he had attained the level of *mujtahid* (one qualified to deduce legal judgment in matters of religion using his reasoning capabilities) and are perhaps comparable to a doctorate. Having attained this status, he became qualified to issue a *fatwa* (a legal opinion based on an interpretation of Islamic jurisprudence). He returned to Najaf in 1961, and began to research and teach Islamic jurisprudence (al-Sistani, 2000, pp. 3–4).

Some clerics in the *hawzah* of Najaf have been quoted as saying that they advised the late Ayatollah Khu'i to groom someone for the office of supreme

---

[1]There is some debate as to the year of his birth. According to his official website: www.sistani.org, he was born on 9 Rabi' 'Awwal 1349 (August, 24, 1930), but a brief biography prefacing his work called *Rules Relating to the Deceased: Philosophy and Ahkam* states that he was born in 1346 A.H. (1928–29). This confusion is probably a clerical error on the part of the publishers.

[2]Ali al-Sistani, "Biography of Grand Ayatollah Sistani." See <http://www.sistani.org/> [cited under English, Biography].

religious authority and director of the religious centers there. Thus, after the brief accession of Ayatollah Golpaygani from 1992–1993, the choice fell on Sistani because of his merits, eligibility, knowledge, impeccable character and close relationship to his primary mentor, Khu'i. Accordingly, he started leading the prayer in the mosque adjacent to the tomb of 'Ali in Najaf, called *al-Khadra'*, at Khu'i's request in 1988. Later, he wrote a commentary on the *risalah* (a compendium of legal rulings that most leading Shi'i religious scholars publish) of Ayatollah Khu'i. After the death of Khu'i, Ayatollah Sistani was one of six high-ranking Shi'i religious leaders who participated in the funeral and Sistani performed the funeral prayers over Khu'i's body, a sign of his rising status and authority (al-Sistani, 2000, pp. 8–9). After Khu'i's death, Sistani became the primary *marja'* (religious authority, literature source of emulation in religious matters) in Shi'i Islam outside Iran (Mallat, 1993, p. 38).[3] He continued leading the prayers until Saddam Husayn closed the mosque in 1994[4] as part of a series of retributions enacted against Shi'is in the wake of the 1991 uprisings (Stoel, 1994).

In 1964, Sistani traveled to Mecca for his first pilgrimage, returning there for a second time in 1985 and for a third time in 1986. His students have recorded his lectures on many subjects since the death of Khu'i in 1992.[5] Sistani maintained a carefully-guarded stance towards the ruling regime throughout his time in Najaf leading up to the US-led invasion in 2003, preferring to focus on issuing legal rulings for Islamic practice and advising his constituency on political and social issues through personal meetings and statements. Within these rulings and statements, however, exists the key to understanding his sociopolitical philosophy and its potentially cosmopolitan import.

Sistani's Fatwas

Sistani has produced over 40 works on Islamic law and philosophy. One of the more telling examples of his practical stance on the application of

---

[3] Chibli Mallat writes "This body, *al-marja'iyya ad-diniyya al-'amma* (the general religious marja'iyya), represents the highest marja' of the Shi'is by giving out a monthly stipend to the students each according to his status (*tabaqat*)."

[4] Ali al-Sistani, "Biography of Grand Ayatollah Sistani." See <http://www.sistani.org/> [cited under English, Biography] (accessed 4 June 2005).

[5] Ibid.

Islamic Law in the context of Muslim emigration to the West lies in a compilation of his legal rulings entitled, *Islamic Law for those living in the West*(*Fiqh li'l-Mughtaribin*). In this volume, he discusses the practical questions that arise for Muslims living in non-Muslim societies. The book is organized under the traditional headings of prayer (*salah*), fasting (*sawm*), ritual purity and impurity (*tahirah wa al-najasah*), the pilgrimage (*hajj*), and burial rituals (*shu'un al-mayyit*), but it also contains practical guidance on living and working with non-Muslims. An example of this type of guidance states

> The people of the book (*ahl al-kitab*), i.e., the Jews, Christians, and Zoroastrians, are ritually pure, as long as you are not aware of any ritual impurities in them. You are able to work on this basis with them in your communities and to touch them (al-Sistani, 1998, p. 76).

While the concept of becoming "unclean" through touch is an alien concept in a secular Western context, this statement constitutes pragmatism within an Islamic legal context, given that it is obligatory for a Muslim to perform ritual cleansing before prayer and that ritual impurity can preclude one from participation in prescribed acts of worship. Rather than taking a rejectionist stance towards non-Muslims, Sistani offers a pragmatic solution when dealing with the issue of ritual purity in relation to non-Muslims. If a Muslim does not have an explicit reason for doubting the purity of a non-Muslim, he is allowed to associate with him in close proximity. This ruling allows Iraqi Shi'i Muslims to enter into business partnerships with non-Muslims and integrate fully into the society at large. By extension, the concept of participation in institutions that are not explicitly Islamic could encourage an active role in the growth of a pluralistic Iraqi civil society.

One contentious issue that often ignites tensions between Muslims and non-Muslims around the world is the issue of Islam's prohibition on alcohol consumption. Regarding ritual purity laws and alcohol, Sistani responds to several interlocutors that

> Alcohol in all of its forms, except that taken from timber or the like, is pure, not unclean. Medicines, perfumes, and foods prepared in alcohol are pure and you are able to use it and take it also if the amount of alcohol is less than 2% (al-Sistani, 1998, p. 76).

Ostensibly, his use of the word timber (*akhshab*) references alcohol distilled from plants, for use as a beverage. In light of this fact, one notices that rather than taking a simplistic stance on the prohibition on alcohol in

Islamic Law (i.e., alcohol is prohibited in all circumstances without exception), Sistani recognizes the licit usage of alcohol for medicinal purposes as well as in industry. He is also very precise in its legal usage, limiting alcohol as an ingredient to 2%.

As an Islamic legal scholar, Sistani focuses in his studies on the historical contextualization of sacred texts. Many Muslim jurists take historical texts literally, focusing minutely on their precise terminology. For instance, such jurists interpret the apparent meaning of the prophetic *hadith* prohibiting the early Muslims from eating the meat of domestic donkeys during the battle of Khaybar (629 A.D.), and deduce from this that eating donkey meat is prohibited in all circumstances. According to Sistani, however, jurists must grasp the universal meaning behind the words of the texts. He says that the Prophet wanted to utilize the few donkeys the Muslims had in the most efficient way. One of those ways was to carry arms and other important provisions for the Muslim army, since they were the only means of transport available. Hence Sistani believes that the prohibition must have been temporary and should not be understood as being permanent (al-Sistani, 2000, pp. 5–6). This seemingly esoteric hermeneutical debate can have far-reaching ramifications in contemporary Iraq. If the leading Shi'i religious authority in Iraq espouses a hermeneutical method that grounds Islam in its historical and cultural context, the interpretation of texts relating to the relationship between Muhammad and his enemies, be they Muslim or non-Muslim, could also be used to undermine more fundamentalist interpretations put forth by various Islamic groups.

In his book, *Islamic Legal Jurisprudence for Today (Fiqh al-Hadarah)*, Sistani writes in relation to women:

> It is necessary for them to cover their hair and their bodies except for their face and hands in front of anyone other than their husbands and close relatives. As for the hands and faces, show them except if you are in fear of falling into a state of ritual impurity [...] exception is made for older women who are beyond marrying age (al-Sistani, 2000b, p. 191).

Sistani seems to favor a conservative role for women in adhering to traditional Islamic codes of dress and practice. However, he does not mention any limitations for women in procuring certain vocations within the greater society. In fact, in response to a query regarding the role of women in the new Iraqi parliament after the fall of Saddam Husayn Sistani explicitly encourages women to play an active role in the new Iraqi government (al-Sistani, 2007, p. 213). His primary concern is with matters of personal purity and adherence to accepted roles within an Islamic religious milieu. While Sistani takes a conservative stand on the roles of men and women in Islamic social settings, he reinterprets the rulings in the light of situations in the 21st century. This pragmatism is also evident in his statements issued during and after the invasion and occupation of Iraq in 2003.

Sistani's Public Statements

Until the US invasion of Iraq in 2003, Sistani had not issued any explicitly political public statements with the exception of several statements condemning Israeli attacks on Qana, Lebanon in 1996 and a statement of solidarity with the Palestinians during the second *Intifada* in 2002.[6] The reasons for this lack of direct political involvement probably lie not in a static belief in political nonengagement on Sistani's part, but rather in a practical choice to avoid the imprisonment, torture, assassination and execution that many of his clerical colleagues faced in the 1990s for their alleged political activities against the regime. In Sistani's view, the role of a leading Shi'i authority is not circumscribed along a political/apolitical binary, but has to do with the organic connection between religion and state. Therefore, when the opportunity arose to engage in the political scene in Iraq after the invasion, Sistani was not reticent in issuing statements on matters that affected his constituency and Iraq in general. The question is not one of whether to engage in politics or not, but rather of the method and societal context of the engagement.

As Iraq descended into chaos in 2003, a statement was issued from Sistani's office in Najaf which placed responsibility for the lack of civil stability squarely on the coalition forces. This statement reflects a commitment to unifying society at a local level. Rather than encouraging sectarian divisions along religious or political lines, he emphasizes the need for cooperation to ensure stability and the revivification of civil society.[7]

---

[6] "The supreme religious authority of the Shia world, His Eminence Ayatullah Al-Udhma al-Sayyid al-Sistani (Dama Dhiluh), on the current situation in occupied Palestine." under "Statements" (2002) Online. Available HTTP: <http://www.sistani.org/> [cited 26 Muharram 1423 (9 April 2002)] (accessed 5 May 2005).

[7] Ali al-Sistani, "About His Eminence Ayatullah Al-Udhma al-Sayyid al-Sistani (Dama Dhiluh), during the current situation in Iraq" under "Statements" (2003, in Arabic). Online. Available HTTP: <http://www.sistani.org/> [cited 12 Safar 1424 (15 April 2003)]. <http://www.sistani.org/messages/message1-a.htm> (accessed 5 May 2005).

Shortly after this statement, another more explicit pronouncement was made through Sistani's London office, which exhibited an almost uncanny understanding of the need for cooperation among the various sectarian groups in Iraq in order to ensure a stable future for the country. He clearly condemned the continuing presence of an occupying force in Iraq and strove to mobilize Iraqis to organize themselves for self-protection. Showing a keen awareness of the need to preserve their historical heritage, al-Sistani denounced the looting and arson of the National Museum and National Library and demanded that all looted items should be returned to the Museum and Library via local mosques. He lucidly and unambiguously renounced any desire of his own for direct political leadership in a new Iraq and placed responsibility for the instability and power vacuum in Iraq squarely on the shoulders of the coalition forces for failing to prevent widespread looting and chaos. Sistani seemed to be planning to implement his stabilization strategy for Iraq through his representatives

----

The Statement reads:

> [...] In protest against the violation of the sanctity of the Mausoleum of 'Ali, the Commander of the Faithful, in Najaf, the breakdown of law and order and the anarchy still taking place in Najaf, His Eminence will continue to remain out of sight until the situation becomes normal again.
>
> In the meantime, His Eminence's advice is to save lives and properties, uphold law and order, join ranks, and reject sectarian and ethnic discords and conspiracies. He also expressed his utter disappointment with the looting and ransacking of many public properties and the homes of defenseless civilians.
>
> The active participation of the general population including honorable tribesmen, who devoted their noble efforts to extinguish the fire of conspiracy, clearly demonstrated their credibility and reflected the depth and strength of their relationship with their religious authorities.
>
> While once again we place the responsibility for the present state of anarchy gripping most of Iraq and Najaf in particular upon the coalition forces, we emphasize the sanctity of the Holy Shrines and the lives of eminent religious scholars and urge everyone to do their utmost to deter this great danger.
>
> We ask the Almighty to rid the population from distress and endear to them the religion and all noble and righteous values.

The Office of H. E. Grand Ayatollah Sistani (long may he live), 15 April 2003.

(*wukala'*) making announcements at the Friday prayer gatherings at local mosques.[8]

---

[8]Ali al-Sistani, "The communiqué issued by the supreme religious authority of the Shia world, His Eminence Ayatullah Al-Udhma al-Sayyid al-Sistani (Dama Dhiluh), on the current situation in Iraq" under "Statements" (2003). Online. Available HTTP: <http:// www.sistani.org/> [cited 15 Safar 1424 (18 April 2003)]. See also <http://www. najaf.org/all/view.asp?l=ARA&c=statement&t=STA&i=18042003>(Arabic) (accessed 5 May 2005).
The statement reads:

> [...] In these crucial times and in the absence of a central authority to govern the country — leading to widespread anarchy and breakdown in law and order — we urge the active participation of our pious brethren everywhere, including those living through the events unfolding in our beloved Iraq, to fill the current vacuum with suitable and devout people. To cooperate in resorting to law and order by establishing councils for each province [...] and district whereby well-known spiritual figures and committed older members of the community, heads of tribes and others can assist in organizing the affairs of the country and restore law and order to each area. The main priority of such councils has to be the removal of all weapons from the hands of the general public. The sight of armed men still terrifies everyone, because weapons in the hands of irresponsible people who do not adhere to religious or moral values are indeed a great danger to society. The supreme religious authority in Najaf has ordered all of its representatives throughout Iraq to implement this matter urgently before it is too late. It is everyone's responsibility with no room for excuses, no matter what the circumstances.

The Marja', H. E. Sayyid Sistani (long may he live) is closely monitoring the situation from the South to the North and the center of Iraq. Sunnis and Shi'is, Arabs or others are all equal in His Eminence's eyes. He believes the security of each and every Iraqi citizen, whoever they are, is his own security and their anxiety is his anxiety. The Marja'iyyah therefore underlines the following issues:

> Reject any foreign rule in Iraq. Emphasis is also made by His Eminence that he will not interfere in the type of government the Iraqi people wish to choose to govern the country, highlighting that Iraq is a Muslim country that draws its tenets, laws, values and education from Islam where Muslims and non-Muslims, whatever their religion may be, can live in peace and security. The new government must therefore recognize this point. His Eminence also points to the history of Shi'i scholars in Iraq, which, since the beginning of the last century has been confronting invading powers. Shi'i scholars and their sons were at the forefront of freedom fighters that faced the invading British forces despite the fact that they also endured the Ottoman invasion.
>
>   The supreme religious authority is by no means whatsoever looking to establish itself as a political authority in Iraq. Implement the principle

While such actions can be viewed as part of a straightforward strategy of self-preservation, there is cause to view Sistani as more than a mere pragmatic power broker. He exhibits an understanding of the need

---

of "enjoining good and discouraging evil" for this is the criterion in Islamic Law that safeguards Muslim society from going astray.

The supreme religous authority always transcends political parties and groups. It safeguards the interests of religion and guides those who distance themselves from the truth back to the right path.

One must be careful that former government staff and others who have tortured and persecuted people do not creep back into government posts. The coalition forces should be totally responsible for the insecurity in Iraq and for having allowed looting and ransacking to take place everywhere.

To activate the infrastructure of the country after the necessary repairs especially hospitals, medical centers, water and electricity generating plants, communication centers and other important services and needs such as food and medicine required by the general population inside as well as outside of Iraq.

Caring for the religious, scientific and historical Iraqi heritage and guarding religious sites, mosques, museums, public and private libraries and manuscripts centers from abusers and looters. If only one tank had guarded the National Museum and public libraries and manuscript centers — as it guarded the oil ministry — there would have been no arson or looting there.

Prohibiting acts of violence no matter what the motives may be, especially on the basis of difference in religion or faith because one of the intrinsic values of the supreme religious authority, particularly during such trying and decisive times, is to safeguard brotherly relationships and harmony among Muslims. We have also seen how the supreme religious authority in Najaf has personally contributed to the construction of Shi'i and Sunni mosques alike.

Just and reliable representatives must convene Friday prayers in all areas in accordance with Shari'ah standards and invite everyone to abandon violence and discord and search for secret prison sites and detention centers and return all looted goods and volunteer to serve society while relying on Almighty God for victory and support.

The supreme religious authority conveys its gratitude to the tribesmen and devout youth who sincerely volunteered to converge on Najaf from the North, South, and Central Iraq — offering to protect him and their great religious learning centers from irresponsible and reckless people. However, there remain many new and ongoing threats to the religious authorities in Najaf; as witnessed when the sanctity of the Mausoleum of 'Ali, the Commander of the Faithful was violated by the use of weapons inside and the shedding of blood on its doorstep [...].

The Liaison Office of Grand Ayatollah Sistani, London, 18 April 2003.

for cooperation among the various sectarian entities in Iraq in order to ensure the restoration of a stable infrastructure. His reluctance to make public proclamations in person distinguishes him from the religious leadership in Iran. Rather than assume a visible role in post-Saddam Iraq, he has remained above the political fray and seeks to motivate his constituency in a more broad-based manner. Nevertheless, it is incorrect to assume that his lack of willingness to engage in direct political activity in the new Iraq indicates any lack of interest in politics. On the contrary, in response to a question regarding his view of the role of religious authority figures in politics, he stated that he does not encourage religious scholars (*'ulama al-din*) to involve themselves in daily political affairs, but this does not preclude them from offering guidance and advice to politicians (al-Sistani, 2007, p. 219).

Sistani has also issued statements through his affiliated office in London to raise money and resources to alleviate the suffering caused by the breakdown in basic social services. The first of these statements asked were specifically for baby food and medical supplies.[9] This initial call for aid garnered a strong response and led to a second statement that explicitly listed contribution information, including bank accounts in various European and Middle Eastern cities.[10]

---

[9] Ali al-Sistani, "Iraq Relief" under "Statements" (2003). Online. Available HTTP: <http://www.najaf.org/> [cited 19 Safar 1424 (22 April 2003)] (accessed 5 May 2005).
[10] Ali al-Sistani, "Iraq Relief" under "Statements" (2003). Online. Available HTTP: <http://www.najaf.org/ > [cited 3 Rabi' al-Awwal 1424 (5 May 2003)] (accessed 5 May 2005).

The statement reads:

Dear Brothers

In response to the feedback we received from *hujjat al-Islam w'al-Muslimin* Sayyid Muhammad Rida al-Sistani (may Allah protect him); medical aid including medicines, medical equipment, and ambulances have been sent to Najaf where they will be distributed to other Iraqi towns. In conjunction with "The World Federation" the first consignment of aid has reached Kuwait en route to Iraq. The second consignment will reach Iraq next week. The Office of His Eminence in Qum has also sent a number of trucks loaded with different types of aid such as food and medicine to Iraq and was immediately distributed among the needy people. His Eminence Ayatollah Sistani (long may he live) has thanked the doctors and advisers in London for their support and their readiness to go to Iraq to treat the sick and wounded. His Eminence (long may he live) also greatly values the fact that such professionals have put themselves on standby for his instructions to go to Iraq at short notice — praying for their success in both worlds.

Sistani has used his network of liaison offices worldwide to gather the basic commodities necessary for his constituency, which shows the broad authority that he commands among Shi'is generally. After his call for assistance, aid poured in from various European and Middle Eastern countries, including Iran. Sistani welcomed assistance from any country or individual, regardless of religion or political persuasion. In the aftermath of infrastructural collapse, Sistani encouraged the development of local civil society by providing much needed social services.

Despite his concern for the provision of social services, conflict between Sistani and the subsequent Coalition Provisional Authority (CPA), came quickly as a plan was proposed by Paul Bremer to appoint members of a constitutional preparation assembly from various political and social groups within Iraq through a caucus system. Sistani issued a terse rebuttal in the name of the Almighty:

> Those forces have no jurisdiction whatsoever to appoint members of the preparatory Constitutional Assembly. Also there is no guarantee, either that this Assembly will prepare a constitution that serves the best interests of the Iraqi people, or express their national identity whose backbone is sound Islamic religion and noble social values. The said plan is unacceptable from the outset.
>
> First of all there must be a general election so that every Iraqi citizen who is eligible to vote can choose someone to represent him in a preparatory Constitutional Assembly. Then the draft Constitution can be put to a referendum.
>
> All believers must insist on the accomplishment of this crucial matter and contribute to achieving it in the best way possible.
>
> May Allah The Blessed Almighty guide everyone to that which is good and beneficial.
>
> Peace and Allah's love and blessings be upon you.
>
> Signed and Sealed

Believers all over the world have been constantly asking our offices about ways of assisting the Iraqi people and requesting bank account numbers in their respective countries so that everyone can have easy access to make financial contributions. Several reliable charitable organizations listed below have been kind enough to provide us with their account numbers to coordinate the sending of financial contributions through them and the main account in London. We also urge all Believers, if they can, to send their contributions/assistance directly to the required destination Iraq in order to save time [...] and whatever good you send before for yourselves, you shall find it with Allah. Surely Allah sees what you do (Qur'an 2:110). Lastly, we ask the Almighty to grant everyone success in both worlds, May 5, 2003.

Ali al-Husayni al-Sistani

June 26, 2003[11]

Sistani threw the CPA's plans into immediate disarray. Refusing to endorse the CPA's decision to appoint representatives, he chose to base the future leadership of Iraq on legitimately-held direct elections. When asked whether he desired a privileged position for the Shiʻis, Sistani replied that the future government of Iraq must respect Islamic principles and be formed in keeping with the principles of pluralism, equality, and justice (al-Sistani, 2007, p. 184). While the definition of "Islamic principles" evades simple definition, the significance of his choosing to pursue the option of democratic free elections in a sovereign Iraq leads to the question of how Sistani views the position of Iraq vis-à-vis the international community.

The Clerical Veto

In the UN report on the fact-finding mission of special envoy Lakhdar al-Ibrahimi to Iraq in February 2004, Sistani is mentioned in the context of the impending electoral and constitutional crises in Iraq:

> It should be recalled that the current political impasse originated in June 2003 with the controversy over the process through which the country's constitution would be drafted by a constitutional convention "selected" by the Coalition Provisional Authority: This led to Ayatollah Sistani issuing a "fatwa" calling for an elected constituent assembly to draft the country's constitution (al-Ibrahimi, 2004, p. 6).

This fatwa led to a direct confrontation between the CPA and Sistani's representatives over the nature of the provisional government to be formed in the wake of the fall of Saddam Husayn. Why was Sistani so vehemently opposed to the appointment of candidates for a transitional constitutional assembly? Perhaps the answer lies in his previous statement made on April 18, 2003, where he says, "Reject any foreign rule in Iraq." The Shiʻi political and religious authorities have always taken an extremely critical stance

---

[11] Ali al-Sistani, "The reply by Grand Ayatullah Sayyid Ali Al-Hussaini Al-Sistani in response to an inquiry made by a group of Iraqi people regarding the preparation of the next Iraqi Constitution" under "Statements" (2003). Online. Available HTTP: <http://www.sistani.org/> [cited 25 Rabiʻ al-Thani 1424 (26 June 2003)]. See also <http://www.sistani.org/messages/qanon-ara.htm>(arabic) (accessed 6 June 2005).

towards any external intervention in their affairs, going back to the British period in Iraq.

In *The Shi'ite Movement in Iraq*, Faleh Abdul Jabar cites five major issues that have played a historically pivotal role in Shi'i agitation. These included political under-representation, economic disenfranchisement, cultural encroachment through Arab nationalism, citizenship rights, and secularization (Jabar, 2003, pp. 67–71). It is not surprising, therefore, to see Sistani resisting any interference on the part of a foreign occupying force in the constitutional process. As frustrating as Sistani's intervention must have been to the CPA at the time, the effect was to reinvigorate the political process within the various Iraqi communities. Rather than attempting to impose clerical rule on society from the top down, as happened in Iran, Sistani chose to emphasize the right of Iraqis to self-determination through free elections.

The UN fact-finding report also explains the explicit nature of the disagreement:

> On November 15, 2003, the Coalition Provisional Authority and the Governing Council signed an Agreement on the political process to accelerate the transfer of sovereignty from the Coalition Provisional Authority to an Iraqi administration by the end of June 2004. The political developments arising from this Agreement provided the context in which the United Nations fact-finding mission took place. The 15 November Agreement set out the conditions for the dissolution of the Coalition Provisional Authority, with a new transitional assembly and provisional government assuming power. However, key Iraqi figures, including many members of the Governing Council itself, and a number of political and religious groups opposed the caucus-style process suggested as the basis for choosing the transitional assembly. Many, including Ayatollah Sistani, demanded direct general elections and claimed that it was possible to organize a reasonably credible election before June 30, 2004 (Jabar, 2003, p. 5).

Sistani repeatedly rejected the notion of caucuses in favor of general elections. Although the majority of Iraqis, and even those within the CPA, were confused as to the exact mechanism for choosing the representatives, Sistani understood the nature of a caucus-style election and viewed the process as a *carte blanche* for special interest groups and minorities to obtain a greater proportion of power than their percentage of the population warranted. He explicitly stated his guiding political philosophy on October 18, 2003:

> Differences of opinion and directions within the Shi'i arena are quite natural — just like any other arena — so there is no cause for concern. Normal dialog between the parties in question is the ideal way to solve

> any disputes. Respect for the majority's opinion by the minority without the majority trying to dominate and rule over the minority is the basis that has to be observed in politics.[12]

Sistani sees value in protecting minority rights, while also emphasizing the need for majority rule.

While emphasizing his authority as a guardian of the Islamic religion for all Muslims, Sistani has consistently shown respect for the authority of the United Nations. When making his case for the feasibility of holding general elections in Iraq, he cited the UN supervised elections in East Timor (al-Sistani, 2007, p. 36). He also suggested that the deployment of the Japanese army in Iraq could be beneficial if it came under the authority of the UN and helped to facilitate peaceful elections (al-Sistani, 2007, p. 42). By acknowledging an international governing body such as the United Nations, Sistani appears to cede political authority and lay the groundwork for a potential sea change in the nature of national sovereignty in Iraq.

Sistani also focuses his efforts on protecting minority religious communities within Iraq and issues a statement in reaction to attacks made on minority Christian communities in the nation:

> In The Name of Allah The Merciful The Most Compassionate
>
> As part of the cycle of criminal acts witnessed in beloved Iraq, targeting its unity, stability and independence, a number of Christian churches in Baghdad and Mosul were viciously attacked — leading to tens of innocent victims falling dead and wounded as well as the destruction of many public and private properties. We disapprove and condemn such abhorrent crimes and see the necessity to consolidate efforts and cooperation by everyone — government and people — in order to stop attacks against Iraqis and root out the attackers; we stress the need to respect the rights of Christians and other religious minorities. Among these rights are their right to live in their country, Iraq, in peace and security.
>
> We ask Allah The Almighty, The Omnipotent, to protect all Iraqis from harm and misfortune and to bless this beloved country with security and stability, He is All Hearing and [He] Answers Prayers.
>
> Office of Ayatollah Sistani — Najaf August 2, 2004[13]

---

[12]'Ali al-Sistani, "The Office of Ayatullah Sistani in Najaf Al-Ashraf to questions by Associated Press Release" under "Statements" (2003). Online. Available HTTP: <http://www.sistani.org/> [cited 21 Sha'ban 1424 (18 October 2003)]. See also <http://www.sistani.org/messages/name.htm> (arabic) (accessed 6 June 2005).

[13] Ali al-Sistani, "The Office of H. E. Grand Ayatullah Sistani in Najaf in condemnation of the abhorrent attacks against Christian churches in Iraq." under "Statements" (2004). Online. Available HTTP: <http://www.sistani.org/> [cited 15 Jumada al-Thani

This statement implies a level of inclusiveness and pluralism that places the rights of the citizen above the rights of a tribe or sect. Since Sistani had issued earlier rulings regarding the ritual purity of Christians, it is not surprising that he would condemn violence against them. Sistani's message has been consistent, albeit sometimes muted, throughout his career as the premier Shi'i cleric in Iraq.

Despite Sistani's push for general elections on June 30, 2004, the fact-finding mission of the UN found the situation on the ground in Iraq insufficiently prepared for the holding of undisputedly free elections. On June 28, 2004, Iyad Allawi took power as interim Prime Minister in a transitional government brokered by Lakhdar al-Ibrahimi and appointed by the CPA at the beginning of June. Sistani issued a statement in response to questioners that condemned the establishment of an un-elected body while simultaneously encouraging cooperation with the new government.[14]

1425 (2 August 2004)]. See also http://www.sistani.org/messages/najjaf.html (arabic) (accessed 6 June 2005).

[14] Ali al-Sistani, "The Office of H. E. Ayatullah Sistani in Najaf to an inquiry concerning the newly appointed government in Iraq." under "Statements" (2004). Online. Available HTTP: <http://www.sistani.org/> [cited 4 Rabi' al-Thani 1425 (3 June 2004)]. See also http://www.sistani.org/messages/bayyan.html (arabic) (accessed 6 June 2005). The statement reads:

In the Name of the Almighty

His Eminence has repeatedly emphasized the necessity of having an Iraqi sovereign government emanating from free and fair elections through the general participation of the Iraqi people. However, for many obvious reasons the election option was excluded — between delay and procrastination, objection, and scare-mongering. Thus, time ran out and the deadline of 30 June approached when the Iraqis were supposed to regain sovereignty over their country. So, a new government was appointed which lacked the legitimacy of elections as well as not properly representing all segments of Iraqi society and its political forces. Nonetheless, it is hoped that this government will prove its efficiency and integrity and carry out the mammoth task that rests on its shoulders as follows:

Obtain a clear resolution from the UN Security Council restoring sovereignty to the Iraqi people — a full and complete sovereignty in all its political, economic, and military and security forms and endeavor assiduously to erase all traces of the occupation.

Provide security in all sectors of the country and curb organized criminal activities and all other criminal acts.

Provide basic services to the citizens and alleviate the hardships they encounter in their daily lives. Carefully prepare for general elections adhering to its set time at the beginning of next year so that a national council may be formed that is not bound by any of the laws issued under occupation including the so-called administrative law for the transitional period.

The new government will not gain popular acceptance unless it proves through clear and practical steps that it diligently and honestly seeks to accomplish the aforementioned tasks. May Allah grant everyone success to achieve that which pleases and satisfies Him.

Through this statement, Sistani disapproved of the transitional process without supporting the insurgents. He denounced occupation while also promoting a political resolution to the power struggles in the post-Saddam polity. He issued a statement regarding the political process in Iraq during the preparations for the January 2005 elections for a Transitional National Assembly, which was charged with drafting a new Iraqi constitution.

> In The Name of The Almighty
>
> All citizens, male and female, who are eligible to vote must make sure that their names are properly registered on the electoral register. Whoever has not registered his name or has done so incorrectly must refer to the electoral committee in their area and provide the required documents for registration and/or amendments. Our legitimate and reliable representatives should form local committees in their areas to assist citizens in realizing this important goal so that everyone will be able to participate in the election which we hope will go ahead on the set date and it (the election) will be a free and fair one with the participation of all Iraqis. Success is from Allah.
>
> Seal of the Office of Ayatollah Sistani in Najaf, October 1, 2004.[15]

This statement illustrates the pragmatic nature of Sistani's leadership. Rather than resisting the occupying forces in ways which might end up sabotaging the nascent democratic process, he has encouraged his powerful constituency to participate in the process for the furtherance of its political aims and of the sovereignty of Iraq.

Conclusions

The aftermath of the invasion of Iraq on March 19, 2003 saw the dissolution of the bureaucratic infrastructure of the Ba'thist regime and the subsequent breakdown in the basic functions of civilian life. Crime increased exponentially and militias were formed to resist the occupying forces as well as to consolidate power under the control of local religious or political figures. As the leading Shi'i religious leader in Iraq, Sistani has remained above the prevailing social disorder and chaos and exercised his influence as a peacemaker in the emerging political process. In opposition to un-elected bodies,

---

Seal of the Office of Ayatollah Sistani in Najaf, June 3, 2004.

[15] Ali al-Sistani, "The latest statement concerning Iraq election." under "Statements" (2004). Online. Available HTTP: <http://www.sistani.org/> [cited 26 Sha'ban 1425 (1 October 2004)]. See also http://www.sistani.org/messages/entekhab01.html (arabic) (accessed 6 June 2005).

Sistani consistently pushed for general elections for a transitional body to draft the new constitution that would respect Islamic principles as a basis for law and society in a new Iraq.

Sistani's Iranian birth and the close collegial ties that he maintains with the Iranian Shiʻi clerical establishment, has led to him being accused of having secret sympathies for Iran and especially the concept of *wilayat al-faqih al-mutlaqah* (the absolute governance of the Islamic jurist), the concept popularized by Ayatollah Khumayni in the years leading up to the Iranian revolution of 1979. While Sistani commands authority among the Shiʻis of Iraq (as exhibited by the commanding victory of the Sistani-endorsed United Iraqi Alliance in the January 2005 elections), his relationship to the state remains ambiguous. He appears to desire a growth in stability and encourages civic duties, such as voting, as a means to further sovereign Iraqi interests. He clearly views Islam as the one true religion while also respecting the rights of minority religious groups within Iraq. It is clear that "Sistani's stance provides an alternative to Shiʻi Khomeinism and its messianic inclination for revolution" (Rahimi, 2004, p. 15). Howerver, it is unclear that his movement towards democratic government and civil society will survive after his death; he is at least 80 years old, and underwent angioplasty surgery in the UK in August 2004. Iraqis of various political and religious affiliations widely view Sistani as a moderating force, but Muqtada al-Sadr's movement may well eclipse Sistani's political influence. Additionally, the structure of Shiʻi religious authority structure militates against the consolidation of power in the hands of a single supreme leader, leading to a plethora of socio-political opinions emanating from various leaders.

The ascendance of ʻAli Sistani arose during a time of upheaval and iconoclasm in Iraqi society. His political activism within the context of nation-building has been tentative and cautious and the statements he has issued have combined the anti-occupation stance of the insurgency with encouragement for participation in a political process triggered by the invasion. While the intervention of an Ayatollah in political affairs appears diametrically opposed to the concept of religious and political pluralism, Sistani has continually positioned himself as a transnational, cosmopolitan religious figure, both in his *fatwas* and in recent political statements. With a keen understanding of global current affairs and political systems as well as local Iraqi politics, Sistani has appeared on the scene as a stabilizing force during a tumultuous period. By remaining within the boundaries of established Shiʻi legal precedent and authority structures, Sistani has increased his influence over his constituency in the Iraqi Shi'i community through strategic statements and aid distribution. He utilized his influence to unify rather than divide the country after the collapse of the Ba'th regime and his actions have allowed the nascent development of civil society in Iraq. Whether Sistani will continue to encourage cooperation with the UN and inclusion of the various ethnic and sectarian groups in the governance of Iraq in the future is an open question, but based upon the consistency of his statements issued both before and after the invasion, it is difficult to expect a less cosmopolitan identity for Iraq under his influence.

Electronic references

Rahimi, B (2004). Ayatollah Ali al-Sistani and the democratization of post-Saddam Iraq. *Middle East Review of International Affairs*, 8(4). Online. Available HTTP: <http://meria.idc.ac.il/> [cited December 2004] (accessed 5 May 2005).

Stoel, M. van der (1994). Situation of Human Rights in Iraq. United Nations General Assembly Report of the Special Rapporteur of the Commission on Human Rights, Section V:C:87, Online. Available HTTP: <http://www.unhchr.ch/Huridocda/Huridoca.nsf/TestFrame/4ca4ae2431b4edb880256708005c71fa?Opendocument> (acessed 4 April 2005).

NAJAF AND THE (RE)BIRTH
OF ARAB SHIʻI POLITICAL
THOUGHT[1]

Michaelle Browers

In his classic work *Arabic Thought in the Liberal Age* (1962) Albert Hourani examined four generations of intellectuals engaged in attempts to revive political thought and address challenges confronting contemporary Arab societies. The power of Hourani's narrative centers on the tensions between opposing strands of thought. The first generation he studied had borrowed fairly unproblematically from the West. A second generation, more aware of the threats posed by Europe, undertook the task of reinterpreting Islam along modern lines. Modernist and Islamic thought move farther apart in Hourani's third generation, as distinctly secular and Islamist trends emerged. In the fourth generation, Hourani identified three trends (Islamist, Arab socialist nationalist, and Pan-Arabist) that compete on an increasingly ideologized terrain.

Students of Shiʻi political thought and of Iraqi intellectual life will notice that Hourani's study remains short on both counts. That is, the classic account of Arab political thought is both short on consideration of intellectual trends emanating from Shiʻi schools and on consideration of Iraqi intellectuals. And the lack of study of the latter may be at least part of explanation for the lack of attention to the former. The recent history of

[1]Some of the ideas expressed in this chapter first appeared in Browers (2009). The author wishes to gratefully acknowledge research support from the Consortium of American Overseas Research Centers and The American Academic Research Institute in Iraq (TAARII) for this project.

Arab political thought, told from the perspective of Shi'i intellectuals in Najaf, reveals striking parallels with Hourani's narrative, which remains largely centered on Christian and Sunni intellectuals and on the circulation of ideas in Egypt and Lebanon. Without that perspective, much of the history of Arabic thought is incomplete, as much of what begins in Najaf has a significant impact on not only Iraq, but also on Hourani's own Lebanon. In what follows, I analyze three generations[2] of Shi'i intellectuals working in Najaf and between Iraq and Lebanon in order to offer a typology of sorts, which demonstrate some "family resemblances" to Hourani's second, third, and fourth generations: A first generation of leading clerics who took up reformist themes near the end of the *nahda* period; a second generation which engaged modernist and secularist writings; and a third post-*nahda* generation of political thinkers, who came of age during a time of great turmoil when competing political forces battled over the form that the region's newly independent states would take.

The analysis reveals rough similarities to the changes and continuities across the generations that Hourani identified. The thought and conduct of the first generation outlined here proved important in laying the foundation for the emergence of a new class of Shi'i intellectuals and political actors who, in a second generation, offered distinctly modernist visions of literature, philosophy, and society, as well as a third generation that proved crucial in developing an ideological understanding of Islam as a comprehensive vision for political life. Many from the middle generation later came to embrace other ways of thinking, particularly communism. However, it is only with the third generation that major efforts were put into creating modern Islamist movements and political parties that could compete with Arab nationalists, socialists, and communists.

While we should not be surprised to find such similar developments among Sunni and Shi'i intellectuals in Arab contexts, it is somewhat surprising to find these ideas developing within the traditional religious institution of the *hawza* (the Ikhwan did not develop out of al-Azhar, for example). It is also apparent that English language scholarship on modern Arab political thought gives less attention to these parallels than those Shi'i individuals

---

[2]By "generation," I mean what sociologists refer to as a "political generation." As Braungart and Braungart (1991, pp. 297, 299) argue: "an age group is transformed into a political generation when a bond is created among its members based on their unique growing-up experiences in society and a shared feeling that they have a mission to perform by changing [or resisting change to] the political status quo."

who express them in their attempt to forge movements aimed at reform, modernization, and revolution. In fact, in may be misleading to characterize Shiʻi intellectual trends as parallel to those Hourani studied. These were not isolated individuals, working on the margins of Arab political thought. Rather, these individuals were aware of, familiar with, and fully engaged in, debates taking place in intellectual circles outside the *hawza*.

My aim in highlighting this particular strand of intellectual activity is not to argue for its distinctiveness within Arabic thought but, rather, to challenge the dominant narrative of Arab political thought. Lack of attention to the role of Shiʻi intellectuals in Arab political thought feeds the all too common tendency to treat intellectual trends emerging from Iraqi and Lebanese Shiʻis as a subset of Iranian political thought. Like Nakash (2003), I maintain that Iraqi Shiʻism is generally distinct from its Iranian counterpart, offering, for example, a form of political Shiʻism different from that which developed in Iran around the institution of *wilayat al-faqih* (the rule of the jurist). However, whereas Nakash attributes the divergence primarily to tribal values and identities that the Shiʻis in southern Iraq maintained after their conversion from Sunni Islam in the 19th century, I shift emphasis to the role of Iraqi intellectuals and the impact of their political marginalization on their thinking. Outside Iran, the Shiʻis constitute national minorities, and even in Iraq and Lebanon, where the Shiʻi population outnumbers the Sunni, the political power of Shiʻis has been historically circumscribed. This was exacerbated by the fact that the Shiʻis constituted the underprivileged in most countries of the Middle East. In both Iraq and Lebanon, the formulation of political thought and practice had to be negotiated not only against sectarianism, but also against competing ideological discourses (nationalist, Arab nationalist, and socialist) aimed at transcending confession, sect and tribe.

The *nahda* from Najaf

Activism and quietism have long coexisted in a state of tension within Shiʻi religio-political discourses. For centuries the dominant image of Shiʻis was of fatalistic believers awaiting the return of the Mahdi. Quietism did not mean that Shiʻis have not engaged in political affairs. In fact, traditional quietism was often accompanied by a denial of the legitimacy of existing regimes, but it was only rarely associated with political activism, that is, with efforts aimed at removing illegitimate rulers and replacing them with rightful successors. This quietism was fed by the development of a hierarchical but decentralized structure of authority in which scholars ('ulama) acted as community leaders. In the absence of an Imam[3] (divinely guided descendent of 'Ali), the faithful are required to follow or imitate (*taqlid*) a *mujtahid* (one qualified to practice *ijtihad*, the interpretation of Islamic law) in the conduct of life. Most Shi'i clerics have remained focused on providing a means of accommodating *de facto* powers within the context of interpreting Islamic law.

However, before the Iranian revolution in 1979, discourses of reform and resistance had also become prevalent among Shi'i communities in Arab contexts, particularly in Iraq and Lebanon, first in communist and socialist guises,[4] and later, among religious scholars. Najaf has long constituted the principal seat of Shi'i religious learning: The first *hawza* was established there in the 11th century. While Najaf's religious establishment remained largely acquiescent at the beginning of the 20th century, there were a few brief exceptions: Perhaps most significantly, that of their emergence as a central point of resistance against the British in the early 1920s. After the "defeat" of the 'ulama in their confrontation with King Faysal and his British advisers, many of the main jurists went into exile and most of the rest returned to teaching and study and refrained from political activity and discussion. But a few prominent 'ulama developed increasingly political outlooks and took on increasingly political roles. Among the factors that may have contributed to a more engaged clerical class are: The revival of the Usuli legal school, which clarified some of the functions of the *mutjtahid*; the centralization of Shi'i leadership, facilitated by the introduction of telegraph lines between Iran and Iraq; and the spread of modernist ideas through such Islamic thinkers such as Tahtawi, Afghani, 'Abduh and Rida (Nakash, 2003, pp. 49–50). The politicized members of the generation that emerged after the turn of the century were certainly spurred by events such as the Iranian Constitutional Revolution of 1905–1911 and Young Turk Constitutional Revolution of 1908, which provided space for Shi'i 'ulama to develop an image of themselves as leaders of an Islamic opposition (Nakash, 2003, p. 54).

---

[3]The Shi'is believe that the Imamate ended when the 11th Imam died without leaving a son to act as 12th Imam. Different Shi'i factions have different explanations of this end. The largest Shi'i group, the twelvers, maintain that the 12th imam was born but went into occultation in 939.

[4]Pan-Arab ideas proved less appealing to Shi'is, who feared their distinctiveness as Shi'i Arabs would be lost in a larger Arab community.

The First Generation and the Call for Reform

Prominent figures in this first generation are Muhammad al-Husayn al-Kashif al-Ghita' (1877–1954), the Najafi cleric and reformist mujtahid, and 'Abd al-Husayn Sharaf al-Din Musawi (1872–1957), a Shi'i scholar from Jabal 'Amil, who completed his higher studies in Najaf between 1889 and 1903 before returning to Lebanon, settling in Tyre, and becoming the first leader of Lebanon's Shi'is. In 1920, Sharaf al-Din issued a fatwa legitimizing *jihad* (struggle) against the French. Kashif al-Ghita' and Sharaf al-Din both took part in the events of the 1920s against the Iraqi monarchy and its British sponsors. Both individuals also sought to situate the Shi'is within the framework of Islamic unity. To that end Kashif al-Ghita' attended the Muslim Congress in Jerusalem in 1931, visited Cairo and other Arab capitals during his lifetime, and maintained an important correspondence with Mahmud Shaltut prior to the latter's issuing of a fatwa declaring worship according to Twelver Shi'i doctrine to be valid and introducing the study of Shi'i jurisprudence into the curriculum of al-Azhar. Sharaf al-Din visited Egypt and met with Shaykh Salim al-Bishri, then the head of al-Azhar, and published a widely read Shi'i-Sunni dialog (2001).

In Najaf, Kashif al-Ghita' gained prominence for the extent and duration of his political activity, which spanned his entire life. He also challenged the withdrawal and abstention of the *marja'iyya* (the institution of the *marja'*, or religious authority) from political affairs. "I am," he declared, "submerged in politics head to toe. Politics is one of my essential duties that I am accountable for before God and my conscience" (1954, p. 86). As Nakash notes, "for Kashif al-Ghita', the revival of Islam could only be accomplished through the combination of education and action (*al-'ilm wa al-'amal*)" (2003, p. 54). As such, he sought to reform the *hawzas* of Najaf, to engage in correcting various misconceptions about Shi'i doctrine (on the part of both Sunnis and Shi'is), and to address the pressing political issues of his day.

Kashif al-Ghita' was also notably less rejectionist toward Arab nationalism than most Shi'i 'ulama, though he always insisted that Arabism be placed within an Islamic framework. In fact, among his publications is an "Arab National Covenant" (*al-mithaq al-'arabi al-watani*) (1935), in which he extolled the importance of the Arab language in uniting people of different faiths, nationalities, and races. It is interesting in this regard that the Iranian translator of *Shi'ism: Origin and Faith* felt obliged to provide a critique of Arab nationalism for the reader, since it was not to be found in Kashif al-Ghita's text: "conversion of Islamic Internationalism into Arab Nationalism is a great mistake and a sort of reaction and re-echo of the pre-Islamic age of ignorance which should be corrected as soon as possible" (1982, pp. 30–1, fn. 1).

So too, Kashif al-Ghita's writings demonstrate an understanding of the appeal of communism. When he met with the American and British ambassadors in Najaf he complained to them that their support for the Zionist presence in Palestine and their support of the corrupt regime in Baghdad provided fertile ground for communism (1987, p. 21). In a letter written to the American Friends of the Middle East in 1954, declining their invitation to attend a conference in Lebanon aimed at exploring potential common grounds between Islam and Christianity in order to combat communism, he points out to this group (whom he seems to have equated with the US government) that "as long as your behavior against the people of the world, and especially the Moslems, remains as it is, most people will say, 'A thousand regards to Communism!' Although we despise it and fight against its destructive principles with all our might, when we compare the deeds of both sides, tolerating communism becomes easy for us" (1987, p. 9). Here too, the "explanation" provided by Kashif al-Ghita's Iranian publisher of the English translation of this work is revealing:

> It may be in point to mention here that at the time the author [...] wrote his article the danger of Communism was not as apparent as it is today. As long as the slogans of the Communists were thought to be and had the appearance of being in the interests of the human race, Communism did not seem to be such a threat to the Islamic World. Hence the Allamah did not condemn strictly, or outright, Communism on Page 12 (*sic*) of this book.

"Publisher's note" aside, by the 1950s, the communist challenge had clearly made considerable inroads into the fabric of the 'ulama's traditional audience. Communism proved appealing, particularly among the more disenfranchised Shi'is. Kashif al-Ghita' noted the "wide nests" of "spirited and ardent young men" who had managed to penetrate even the holiest of cities "without logic or proof and unassisted by funds or patronage or dignity of rank" (1987, p. 5). The leaders of Najaf and Karbala faced complete marginalization, if not the risk of becoming obsolete. Anxious calls to reject the communist appeal emerged from members of the Najafi 'ulama.

In 1931, Kashif al-Ghita' was invited to the Pan-Islamic congress in Jerusalem, where he spoke at the opening session and again in the 12th session. In his remarks, he called for Islamic unity and emphasized the central place of Jerusalem in Islamic consciousness. In order to underline the message of unity, he led the Friday prayer at al-Aqsa. Among those who lined up behind him to pray were scores of prominent Sunni 'ulama, including Rashid Rida. The congress was important not only for transforming Palestine into a pan-Islamic issue, but also for publicly positioning the Shi'is within the circle of Islamic unity (Nafi, 1996, pp. 267–268). Kashif al-Ghita' was adamant about the need for unity and the dangers caused by discord. In responding to the Egyptian modernist Ahmad Amin (1886–1954), who described Shi'ism as "a refuge for those who wish to destroy Islam" (Amin, 1945, p. 33), Kashif al-Ghita' asserted that such ignorant prejudices are "a source of joy and a major weapon for the imperialists and atheists of our time" (Kashif al-Ghita', 1982). Inter-Islamic strife, he argued, is likely to invite outside interference to the detriment of all. However, he understood that unity was not necessarily at odds with difference. He maintained that the goal was not to eliminate differences among the schools of Islamic law but to abolish the sources of animosity between them, quoting the Qur'anic verse which explains that God could have made all of mankind one, but did not, because he asserts that differences are natural and even a healthy sign of intellectual activity. The goal is to affirm the basic brotherhood, friendship, and unity of all who believe in the *shahadatayn* (that God is one and that Muhammad is God's messenger). The argument that the "five madhhabs" constitute legitimate variations of Islam was championed by Sharaf al-Din and al-Ghita' and formalized in Shaltut's fatwa in 1958.

While at the international level Kashif al-Ghita' preached a pan-Islamic ideal based on rapprochement between Sunnis and Shi'is, in Iraq itself he expended much effort in uniting and mobilizing the Shi'is of Iraq to advance their rights. In a speech in 1934, he compared the situation of the Shi'is to a herd of domestic animals: "every day the butcher takes some of you while the rest continue to graze, unaware that they are next." He argues that "power lies in your unity" but that unity must be excised. "Rights," he argued, "are taken, not given" (1969, pp. 145–149). While calling for the Shi'is to unite and resist their government, Kashif al-Ghita' also criticized policies aimed at dividing Iraqis along sectarian lines. When he convened a conference in 1935 to discuss the "Arab National Covenant," a series of reforms that would be outlined and sent to King Ghazi bearing the signatures of 73 leaders of Iraq's Shi'i tribes, his main indictment of the Iraqi political system was what he identified as its sectarianism. Sectarianism, which he argued was formalized by the British, had impoverished and disenfranchised the Shi'is of Iraq. Kashif al-Ghita' argued for reforms that would spread power, resources and representation more equally for all of members of Iraqi society. The covenant called for such things as parliamentary representation in proportion to the Shi'i population, the inclusion of Shi'i judges in all sections of the courts, and a more equitable distribution of endowments to Islamic institutions and of health and educational institutions.

The negotiation of identity among Arab Shi'i intellectuals during this period took place in the context of developing national contexts in which Shi'is formed a political (if not always numerical) minority. Chalabi "reveals the extent to which Arab nationalism has been an expression of the ideological enframement of the Sunni majority. There is an implicit hierarchy in the Arab national community, the criteria for the top level being Arab, Sunni, and urban. The Shi'i community, lacking two of the three criteria, is explicitly patronized by Arab nationalist intellectual and politicians" (Chalabi, 2006, p. 6). In this sense, Arab nationalism often constituted a tool of political domination, rather than an ideology of opposition and empowerment, for Arab Shi'is. Kashif al-Ghita's hierarchy is rather different, as is revealed in the letter he wrote in 1954 to the American Friends of the Middle East: "Our only motive is to assure prosperity and greatness for our dear homeland, Iraq. Not only for Iraq, but also for our brother nations and for our neighbors Jordan, Kuwait, Saudi Arabia, Egypt, Yemen; and for all those distant lands with whom we share our religion, language, race, and our problems — Tunisia, Morocco, Algeria, and Libya; as well as other Islamic countries with whom we share not only our religion, but also our hardships and problems — Iran, Afghanistan, Pakistan, and Indonesia" (Kashif al-Ghita', 1982, p. 36). What is interesting is the way in which he reveals a series of shared interests and identities that prioritize (Iraqi) nationalist, then Arab-Islamic, and finally pan-Islamic concerns. And he does so in a non-sectarian way — that is, without reference to distinctions between Sunnis and Shi'is.

One finds within this first generation many themes which were further developed by subsequent generations: (1) the "renewal" of Islam within the context of the achievement of nationalist aims; (2) the necessity for Islamic unity and the desire for Sunni–Shi'i rapprochement (*taqrib* or *taqarrub*); and (3) the construction of an engaged rather than simply rejectionist critique of competing ideologies (communism, socialism, and Arab nationalism). While the later generations surpassed this first one in terms of political theorizing, the thought and actions of prominent later Shi'i figures reveal the distinctive influence of their forbears.

The Middle Generation and the Modernist Project

The first generation raised many of the issues that continued to be important throughout the 20th century, such as foreign intervention, the division and disunity of Muslims, and the marginalization of religious institutions in general and of the Shi'is in particular. Yet, the development of a modern and modernist political vocabulary is very much the project of the second generation of writers.

As some leading clerics, such as Grand Ayatollahs Muhsin al-Hakim and Abu'l-Qasim al-Khu'i were advising a quieter (and in the case of Khu'i, one might argue, quietist) approach to reform, journals such as *al-'Irfan* (published in Sidon) gave voice to the reformist ideas of individuals such as Muhsin Sharara (1901–1946), Muhammad Rida al-Muzaffar (b. 1904) and Husayn Muruwwa (1910–1987), among others. Sharara declared the need for a Shi'i Muhammad 'Abduh in the pages of *al-'Irfan*. Like many others of this generation who studied and lived in Najaf, Sharara was highly critical of what he saw as the sad state of intellectual and educational activity at the *hawza* and the reactionary fears of modern and scientific reform on the part of its 'ulama.[5] This generation was also tasked with responding to the educational policies and nationalist ideology set in place by Sati' al-Husri during his 20 years in Iraq (when he held such positions as director-general of education, 1923–1927),[6] which perpetuated the stereotype of the "ignorant and fanatical Shi'i," questioned the loyalty and ethnic origin of the Shi'is, and allocated insufficient resources for education in the Shi'i provinces (Nakash, 2003, p. 111). The space for this response was enhanced as Husri's Shi'i opponent, Muhammad Fadhil al-Jamali, began to play a greater role in shaping Iraq's educational system. It is during this period that Muzaffar and others established Muntada al-Nashr in 1935, which published modern books, created modern syllabi, and established a "reformed" religious school.

---

[5]See, for example, Zayn (1939). Despite his article's title — "Harbingers of Reform in the University of Najaf, or the Renaissance of Kashif al-Ghita' " — Zayn is more critical than approving of the current state of reform in Najaf. However, the use of the word *"buwadir"* (singular, *badira*) carries an ambiguity: Meaning alternatively harbingers or blunders. Sharara wrote similarly critical articles around the same time in the same magazine. Muruwwa wrote an open letter to Kashif al-Ghita' imploring him to lead the call for reform (1937).
[6]See his *Mudhakkirati* (1967–1968).

Muzaffar sought to reform education along the lines 'Abduh had planned for al-Azhar.

The generation coming of age in this period proved more radical in its critique than the first generation and much more willing to call upon "new," "modern," or "Western" intellectual traditions in articulating the changes they viewed as imperative. The pages of *al-'Irfan* carried poetry mocking backwardness and false piety; essays unselfconsciously discussing secularism, communism, and democracy; and translations of literature, philosophy, and political writings published in the United States and Europe. As a result of their writings, many of the second generation came under fire.[7] Some found they had no future among the clergy, and indeed some who studied at the *hawza* of Najaf went so far as to remove the turban (so to speak) and chose other paths. This is perhaps best epitomized by Muruwwa, who eschewed his father's dream that he would become a religious scholar and joined the Communist Party. Muruwwa, who studied in Najaf between 1924 and 1938, proclaimed in an article in 1984 that "Marx entered my life from Najaf (*min al-najaf dakhala hayati marx*)." His journal *al-Hatif* became an important forum for airing these more radical ideas. Certainly some of communism's appeal is related to the failure of Pan-Arabism to act as a unifying framework for Shi'is, while some of it is related to the lack of an Islamic alternative.

What Hourani says of the Arab intellectuals that he studied during this same period could certainly considered as relevant for these Shi'i intellectuals: The two strands of thought that *nahda* thinkers worked hard to keep together had begun to move farther apart after 1924 and the gap began to widen between those who held to the necessity of an Islamic basis for society and those who held that social life should be regulated by secular norms. Both the middle and the third generation were formed amidst great frustration with their exclusion from the political process. That frustration helps explain why many in the middle generation began to adhere to communism and to join the Iraqi Communist Party (Shi'is constituted the majority of the ICP's rank and file and dominated the party organizations). Yet it is only in the generation that follows that the project of articulating a modern revolutionary project within an Islamic framework is fully undertaken.

---

[7]See, for example, Ende (1997). Mervin (2001) also provides a rich account of this period of intellectual life.

The Third Generation: Toward a Revolutionary Islamism

The third generation were the graduates of the reformist schools set up by Kashif al-Ghita' and Muzaffar: Muhammad Baqir al-Sadr[8] (1935–1980), perhaps the central philosopher of the renewal of Shi'i Islamic political thought (Mallat, 1993); Musa al-Sadr (1928–1978) the founder of Lebanon's *Afwaj al-muqawama al-lubnaniyya* (Lebanese Resistance Detachments, better known by the acronym AMAL); Muhammad Mahdi Shams al-Din (1935–2001), who headed Lebanon's Higher Islamic Shi'i Council after Musa al-Sadr's disappearance; and Muhammad Husayn Fadlallah (1935–2010), in his lifetime Lebanon's most prominent Shi'i intellectual and the founder of numerous charitable and educational institutions in Lebanon, Syria, and elsewhere.

All these individuals were students in Najaf during the formation of the first revolutionary Shi'i Islamist party, *Hizb al-Da'wa al-Islamiyya* (around 1957 or 1958), for which Baqir al-Sadr is often cited as the central intellectual and political force. Shams al-Din and Fadlallah were born in Najaf and remained there until the ages of 33 and 31 respectively, while Musa al-Sadr's period of study was much briefer. However, according to Shams al-Din, the "new vision" present in Najaf in that period crystallized at precisely the time of Sadr's arrival. Fadlallah also notes the similarities between Musa al-Sadr and Muhammad Baqir al-Sadr's thinking in regard to the cultural and political atmosphere of the time (in Sharaf al-Din, 1996).[9] Both Shams al-Din's metaphor of shared vision and Fadlallah's metaphor of, in a sense, breathing the same air, point to the commonality among themselves and Musa Sadr and Baqir al-Sadr, which they associate with their generation and with Najaf.

The atmosphere described by Shams al-Din and Fadlallah is one dominated by communism and Arab nationalism, in which Islamic institutions and ways of thinking were increasingly marginalized. Anxious calls to reject the communist appeal came from members of the Najaf 'ulama, including Grand Mujtahid Muhsin al-Hakim and Baqir al-Sadr's uncle, Murtada al-Yasin. Thus, this generation's worldview was formed in the midst of a confrontation between the 'ulama of Najaf, with its traditional education

---

[8]Throughout this paper, Muhammad Baqir al-Sadr will be referred to as Baqir al-Sadr, to distinguish him from Musa al-Sadr.

[9]Husayn Sharaf al-Din's 1996 study includes interviews with both Fadlallah and Shams al-Din about their memories of Musa al-Sadr and Najaf.

and strict hierarchical structure, and the Communists, whose message was spreading and gaining ground the Middle East. Fadlallah describes a kind of intellectual terrorism (*irhab*) in this period against anything Islamic (in Sharaf al-Din, 1996, p. 110). It was against this trend — and in a manner reminiscent of Kashif al-Ghita' — that Shams al-Din began to insist that the very purpose of *ijtihad* (independent reasoning) is to apply Islamic theory to all spheres of human life (Shams al-Din, 1990, p. 49) and that Fadlallah began to preach that the jurist who removes himself from contemporary politics risks losing his function as a *marji'* (authority) in other realms of life (Fadlallah and Hasani, 1993, p. 103). Of course, some of the anti-communist activity was undertaken with the sanction of traditional religious forces higher up in the hierarchy. Muhsin al-Hakim and the Society of 'Ulama in Najaf (*jama'at al-'ulama fi'l-najaf al-ashraf*) was at the forefront of these activities. Some of the younger members of the latter organization formed the nucleus of what would become the Da'wa party.

The Da'wa was described as *haraka taghyiriyya* — a movement for change — that is, change that is *inqilabi* (revolutionary) rather than *islahi* (reformist), although the term *inqilabi* (which was also used by the Ba'th) — used in contradistinction to the communist-circulated word (*thawri*) — was dropped in the late 1960s, in favor of *thawri* (Jabar, 2003). This third generation not only took up the challenges first of the communists and then of the Arab nationalists and Ba'thists, but also translated the issues and rhetoric of these ideologies into Islamic categories. It is in this spirit that Baqir al-Sadr takes up the "social issue" in his 1959 work, *Our Philosophy* (*Falsafatuna*), which he defines as the broaching of the following question: "Which system is best for human beings and provides them with a happy social life?" (Baqir al-Sadr, 1987, p. 5). *Our Philosophy* was followed in 1961 by *Our Economy* (*Iqtisaduna*), which attempted to counter the communist appeal toward redressing the "social balance" and communist criticisms that Islam lacked solutions to contemporary problems.[10] One of the main claims in Baqir al-Sadr's contribution to this genre is that neither communism nor

---

[10]Baqir al-Sadr intended these books to form part of a series. A third manuscript in the series, entitled *Our Society* (*Mujtama'na*), was never published. We know that the volume was planned, since Sadr refers to it on several occasions in other works, including in *Our Philosophy*, but whether parts or all of it were written and that it was seized when he was arrested by the Iraqi regime in 1980, cannot be confirmed. We do, however, have a volume called *Our Message* (*Risalatuna*), which contains a number of articles on social themes collected from Baqir al-Sadr's contributions to *al-Adwa'*.

capitalism (which he views as the two chief ideological rivals in the modern world) can offer real fulfillment to human beings, as he details what he takes to be the flaws and shortcomings of each, in contrast to the truths and benefits of Islam.[11] In Lebanon, Musa al-Sadr stated that "we are neither of the right or the left, but follow the just path (*al-sirah al-mustaqim*)" (cited in Norton, 1994, p. 199).

While Baqir al-Sadr views capitalism and communism as the two main ideologies that "divide the world today" — and while his main concern is to criticize communism, which he perceived as the most immediate threat in Iraq in the 1950s — he identifies four competing schools of thought that attempt to address social issues in contemporary politics: Capitalist democracy, socialism, communism, and the Islamic system. His distinction between socialism and communism is based on the idea that the former is the precursor of the latter. Since he argues that the world is largely divided between capitalist and communist systems, we must take him to mean that those parts of the world today choosing the communist option have not yet reached their goal of a classless society where all property is held in common, but remain in a socialist (pre-communist) stage. Communism, like the Islamic system, Baqir al-Sadr notes, is "in actuality purely ideological," by which he means that each offers a comprehensive worldview that is sought, but not fully realized, in the present (Baqir al-Sadr, 1987, p. 6).

With regard to democratic capitalism, Baqir al-Sadr argues that though this system may offer respect for the freedom and interests of the individual, it offers no moral center and is ultimately prey to an extreme form of materialism. He maintains that while democratic capitalism is not based on a detailed materialistic philosophical notion of life, the historical conditions of its emergence, which included spiritual doubt and confusion, as well as outright anger against institutionalized religion, precluded any goal beyond individual interests and always subordinated society to the interests of individuals (1987, pp. 9–11). It is this materialist philosophy that, he argues, results in the "chain of social tragedies" that accompany the capitalist system. The first "neglect of human dignity" arises when a majority of interests tyrannizes minority interests. The second occurs when a minority of capitalists attains wealth and are able to use their power to advance their interests

---

[11]Many looked to the figure of Abu Dharr, an early Muslim convert whom Shi'is revere for his support of 'Ali and whose opposition to the nepotism and coveting of luxuries that took place while 'Uthman was Caliph is recounted to demonstrate the existence of egalitarian and socialist thought in Islam.

at the expense of the rest (workers). Baqir al-Sadr's final critique moves from a Marxist critique of capitalism to a Leninist critique, as the need for new markets "provides a justification or a logical formula for assaulting and dishonoring peaceful countries, in order to control their fate and their large natural resources, and to exploit their wealth to promote surplus products" (1987, p. 14). All the "calamities of this system" he attributes to its "materialistic spirit" which provides the individual with "no purpose other than his personal interests."

While capitalism subordinates society to the individual, communism makes the opposite error in completely subordinating the freedom of the individual to the needs of society. Baqir al-Sadr rejects the notion that individual freedom is the price that must be paid in order to establish the ideal society. The fundamental error of communism — and the reason communists have found it impossible to move from a socialist to a communist society — is that it fails to take into account human nature as it actually is. Human nature did not change under socialism or under the iron hand of the dictatorship of the proletariat, so that "personal interests and individual considerations" were "replaced by a social mentality and social inclinations" and individuals "would think only of social welfare, and would be motivated only for its sake" (1987, p. 16). Baqir al-Sadr does not accept the Marxist conviction that, if the social and economic structure is changed, human nature will change. Rather, what takes place — and this is confirmed, he argues, in the practice of contemporary socialist societies — is that the creative powers of individuals are stunted and they come to neglect their social duty, beyond what is required of them by a dictatorial state: "why should he be motivated to make happiness available to others, and to bring comfort to them by his own sweat and tears and by the sap of his life and capacities, as long as he does not believe in any values other than those that are purely materialistic?" (1987, p. 16). The primary character of human nature, the individual's "natural reality," according to Baqir al-Sadr, remains "self-love, which we express by our yearning for pleasure and hatred of pain" (1987, pp. 21–22). Thus, the most communism can do is deliver the individual from the greed of the capitalists into the hands of communist leaders who will inevitably subordinate society to their own interests (1987, p. 26). While Marxists are right to criticize capitalism, the problem with capitalism is not simply private property, but materialism: "if the self [...] is an expression of a limited material power, and if pleasure is an expression of the delights and joys that matter makes available, than it is natural for people to feel that their opportunity for profits is limited, and that the race for their goal is short, and that their goal in the race is to acquire a certain amount of material pleasure" (1987, p. 22). In short, what capitalism, socialism, and communism suffer from is the absence of moral principles to guide society.

So, what are these new principles? Baqir al-Sadr suggests they must be found in "a system in which the individual is not considered as a mechanical tool in the social system, and where society as an organization is not established for the sake of the individual." Instead, the principles must secure for "each — the individual and society — their rights" and provide "for the individual both his spiritual and material dignity." The means of eradicating materialism "in a manner harmonious with human nature" (1987, p. 26) lie in religion: "religion unifies the natural criterion of action and life — this criterion being self-love — and the criterion that must be laid down for action and life" (1987, p. 28). It does so, he argues, in two ways by providing a spiritual explanation of human life and a mode of moral education (1987, pp. 28–30).

The Islamic alternative to materialism, whether in its Marxist or capitalist form, is understood by Baqir al-Sadr to respect the legitimate self-interest of the individual while subordinating this to the traditional Islamic proposition that "absolute sovereignty belongs to God," that God is the source of all power over all the earth and that human beings owe homage to God alone. Baqir al-Sadr asserts this as the basis of human freedom, rather than its antithesis: "The sovereignty of Allah means that man is free. Neither any individual, nor any class or group possesses a supreme power and authority over him [...] This principle does away with every kind of oppression and one man's exploitation by another man" (Baqir al-Sadr, 1982a, p. 75).[12] Human beings must understand that their fulfillment is dependent upon the extent to which they satisfy God. Individual self-love must be conditioned by the awareness of the existence of rewards and punishments in the afterlife and an extension of the individual's concern for their well being in the present and future. "Muslims must convert their faith into a constructive activity" in the present, striving to do good and avoiding evil, and "straining every nerve" to overcome "backwardness." At the same time they must recognize that "the world is a prelude, not a goal, and a means, not an end" (1982a,

---

[12]Hanna Batatu recognizes this element in Baqir al-Sadr's thought: "at bottom the call for a return to Islam [in Baqir al-Sadr's thought] is a call for a return to God's dispensation and necessitates a 'social revolution' against 'injustice' and 'exploitation,' but it is a revolution which has a 'universal' rather than a 'class' character and one in which the virtuous rich and the virtuous poor stand shoulder to shoulder" (Batatu, 1981: 579).

pp. 18, 27). Comprehension of substantive movement reveals that human agency, rather than being episodic and epiphenomenal, constitutes a way of life. Islamic society, in turn, must create conditions that foster that knowledge through education and the enforcement of society's legitimate claims on the individual.

This third generation perceived its revolutionary project in multiple stages: (1) the intellectual stage (*al-marhala al-fikriyya*), where the intellectuals of the movement consolidate and Islamist ideas are formulated and disseminated; (2) the political stage (*al-marhala al-siyasiyya*), where the struggle develops a mass base and shifts to a struggle for power; (3) the revolutionary stage (*al-marhala al-thawriyya*), where focus is on removing un-Islamic ruling elites from power; and (4) the governmental phase (*al-marhala al-hukumiya*), where the ideal Islamic polity is constructed (Jabar, 2003, p. 81). Nonetheless, with only a few exceptions, the intellectuals of this generation did not progress far beyond the first stage. Baqir al-Sadr, for example, was reportedly pressured by senior members of the *hawza* to cease his involvement in the party as early as 1961. This indicates that at least part of the reason is that they were forced to fight a generational struggle within the *hawza* before they could take the struggle to the next phase, as Fadlallah (1982) noted in his introduction to Baqir al-Sadr's *Risalatuna*, where he reflected on the role of the short lived publication *al-Adhwa'*. In addition to the pressures to suspend or quit their party membership, many of the leading ideologues of this new Islamism were forced to leave Iraq, Muhammad Baqir al-Sadr was killed, and others, such Fadlallah and Shams al-Din, played occasional and marginal or indirect roles in politics thereafter, even occasionally shunning party politics as such.

While the establishment of the Islamic Republic of Iran in 1979 offered a prototype of the Islamic polity for Shi'is in general, and while all of those individuals discussed here who lived to see it established voiced support for it and for Khomeini as its leader, none of these individuals posits the rule of the jurist (*wilaya al-faqih*) as the basis of their views of just government. One of Baqir al-Sadr's later works, *Introduction to the Islamic Political System*, contains a discussion of the Islamic Republic in Iran in response to a question put to him by Lebanese religious scholars: "what is the intellectual basis of the Islamic republic [in Iran]? (1982a, p. 69). He prefaces his remarks on the latter by affirming that "absolute sovereignty belongs to God" and saying that man is free, since, no "individual, nor any class or group possesses a supreme power and authority over him [...] This principle does away with every kind of oppression and one man's exploitation by another man" (1982a, p. 75). Baqir al-Sadr argued that Islamic rule embodied not only God's sovereignty on the basis of Islamic law, but also the principle that, while the clerics had religious authority, human beings in general represent God's vicegerents on earth and are entrusted with legislative and executive powers. In political terms, Baqir al-Sadr argues for a moderate supervisory role for the clergy in judicial matters and retained a broader vision of involvement in politics on the part of the community. Rather than *wilayat al-faqih*, he puts forth the concept of *wilayat al-umma*, recognizing the popular basis of political authority. We see this difference of opinion even in Baqir al-Sadr's justification of Khomeini's rule. He does not use Khomeini's argument to justify his authority. Rather, he argues that Khomeini's authority is "religious" and his eligibility to hold the position of the supreme representative of Islamic government is based on several qualifications: he is a *mujtahid* of first rank, that his religious authority is in accordance with the shariʻa, that he has the support of the majority of the members of the consultative council, and that the people, as the "rightful bearers of the trust of government" possess the right to vote and take part in politics (1982a, p. 79).

Shams al-Din (1992) maintains that, in the absence of the Imam and his divinely mandated authority, *wilayah* of the *umma* reverts to the *umma* itself. Since no authoritative text dictates that the *umma* should be under one single political power, Shams al-Din argues that this trusteeship may be exercised differently and by different sources in different national contexts. His assessment of the Islamic Revolution in Iran is that it represented an expression of popular will, and he supported the right of the Iranians as a national community to submit to it. However, he also argues that Iran's *wilayat al-faqih* cannot be binding on those outside its borders. It is the prerogative of any Muslim community to choose its form of government and he advises that Shiʻis should continue to promote an understanding of just governance in ways that are consistent with loyalty to the nation-state. We see this idea developed by Shams al-Din in the 1980s, as he puts forth the concept of a "civil state" as an alternative to both the confessional state and to a secular state. While the civil state would have no declared religion, it would be based on a return to the shared religious sentiments of both Christianity and Islam, within "pluralism" or *al-ʻadadiyya*. This civil state was to affirm religion along "the general lines of the system of a pluralist democracy" and "based on the principle of consultation." In his *Wasaya* (2008), he clarifies that this model of pluralist democracy would not be government by the majority, but would require a renegotiated system of allocation of representation for the Christian community in Lebanon.

The national state frames the political projects of this generation, which indicates its members' willingness to share power and governance with non-Shi'i groups. However, in the view of many scholars, the primary legacy of the third generation in particular lies in the various Shi'i Islamist movements that currently animate politics in Iraq and Lebanon. Certainly there is a later generation, which includes the leadership of Hizbullah, such as Abbas al-Musawi (1952–1992) and Hasan Nasrallah (1960–), and various past and present leaders of Iraq's Da'wa party, such as Ibrahim al-Ja'fari (b. 1947) and Nuri al-Maliki (b. 1950). While much of the credit (or blame, as the case may be) for developing distinctly Shi'i modes of engaging and competing in national political processes certainly lies with this generation, members of the third generation often seek to retain their distinctiveness. For example, they tend to characterize the generation after themselves as one of pragmatic political thinkers, rather than Islamic intellectuals as such. Explanations of generational differences may point to the fact that many from the fourth generation had their period of study in Najaf cut short by the Ba'thists' expulsion of foreign students from Najaf in 1978, or, for those who remained in Iraq, had their political activity curtailed by Saddam Husayn. Or they may indicate a more general preference for direct action over intellectual work on the part of this fourth generation. Others point to the different environment in which each generation came of age. For example, as Jihad al-Zayn, a writer for *al-Nahar* and descendent of Ahmad 'Arif al-Zayn, has described it, the "new Mullah" of the earlier generation emerged out of an ideologically and intellectually mixed milieu, while the generation of Nasrallah was "born completely Islamist."[13] However, here too, we find that the development of the thinking of Arab Shi'is is not unlike other trends in Arab political thought.

Electronic reference

Hakim, MB (2004). Hiwar fi al-marja'iyya al-fiqhiyya wa al-marja'iyya al-siyasiyya. Online. Available HTTP: <http://www.al-hakim.com/estfta.htm> (accessed 10 November 2009).

---

[13] Interview with author. Beirut, January 30, 2009.

BETWEEN ACTION AND SYMBOLS: THE SUPREME ASSEMBLY FOR THE ISLAMIC REVOLUTION IN IRAQ AND ITS BID FOR POLITICAL LEADERSHIP

Elvire Corboz

The nature of the Supreme Assembly for the Islamic Revolution in Iraq (SAIRI) has been a matter of debate since its creation in November 1982.[1] From the first days of its existence, SAIRI has been perceived as an Iranian puppet. With its headquarters in Tehran, it was set up under Ayatullah Khomeini's patronage to act as an umbrella organization for the various non-Iranian Islamic opposition groups active in the Islamic Republic. Iran's territorial gains in its war with Iraq during the summer of 1982 and its anticipation of Saddam Husayn's fall required, more than before, the establishment of a body representing the Iraqi opposition that would, in turn, become Tehran's legitimate interlocutor.

In this chapter, I propose to shift the perspective from SAIRI's relationship to its Iranian host to its ties with its popular constituency. Like other exile organizations, SAIRI depended on the support of its fellow-citizens to legitimize its political and military activities against the regime at home. To turn its situation of exile into an advantage it tried to connect with the Iraqi people and mobilize them. While the organization never gave up its

---

[1] The Supreme Assembly for the Islamic Revolution in Iraq (SAIRI) — a body also commonly called the Supreme Council for the Islamic Revolution in Iraq (SCIRI) — has been known since 2007 as the Islamic Supreme Council of Iraq (ISCI). In this chapter, since I examine the organization in the pre-2003 period, I will therefore use its former name and its acronym SAIRI.

efforts to reach out to its potential constituency inside Iraq and for some time actually gained access to the south of the country, its leadership found it much easier to establish ties with Iraqis who had left home. This is why the Tehran-based organization sought to build upon its physical proximity to the community of Iraqi refugees and prisoners-of-war based in the Islamic Republic of Iran — and to a lesser extent in other countries — in order to attract potential followers.[2]

Looking into the nature of the relationship between SAIRI and its base during the 1980s, I will argue that the clergy-run organization capitalized on the symbolic attractiveness of themes borrowed from the contemporary history of Iraqi Shi'ism as a way of gaining legitimacy as representative of the Iraqi people. One should note that SAIRI also insisted that it represented all Iraqis, regardless of their ethnicity or religion. It is beyond the scope of this paper to discuss the veracity of this claim; here I will only consider this organization in its relationship to the Iraqi Shi'is.

To illustrate my argument, I will analyze two themes that SAIRI imported from Iraq to use trans-nationally for popular mobilization. First, its clerical leadership capitalized on the idea of the Najaf-based *marja'iyya*. In particular, the organization tried to derive legitimacy from two major Iraqi religious figures who had reached the status of *marja'* (source of emulation) in the second part of the twentieth century, namely Ayatullah Muhsin al-Hakim (d. 1970) and Ayatullah Muhammad Baqir al-Sadr (d. 1980). Taking the legitimacy of their *marja'iyya* as a given, I analyze the strategies elaborated by SAIRI to keep the legacy of al-Hakim and al-Sadr alive and transfer their religious and social prestige to itself. Since it was geographically distant from the Iraqi shrines and centers of learning, it was crucial for the organization to present itself to the community not as an alternative to the traditional religious institution of the *marja'iyya*, but rather as an extension of it.

Second, SAIRI built upon the idea that Islam was under threat in Iraq to convince the people of the righteousness of its opposition to the regime of Saddam Husayn and to enjoin them to join the struggle. In order to do so, it turned the persecution and martyrdom of religious figures into a strong mobilizing symbol to which Iraqis could relate because of their own suffering at the hands of the Ba'th regime. The symbolic power of Muhammad Baqir

---

[2]SAIRI had representatives working in all refugee camps for Iraqis in Iran and probably in the cultural committees established in the POW camps. The organization also opened offices in Damascus, London, Geneva, and Vienna in the late 1980s and early 1990s.

al-Sadr was once again central in the exploitation of this theme, as he not only represented the traditional religious leadership as a *marja'*, but was also the figurehead of the contemporary Iraqi Islamic movement and its most emblematic *shahid* (martyr). Other clerical figures, among them members of the al-Hakim family who had been imprisoned or executed in Iraq, also became central in SAIRI's treatment of this theme.

In the following sections, I will look at three domains where the *marja'iyya* and the idea of martyrdom have been used in practice to create and sustain ties between SAIRI and the Iraqi refugees. The first domain is the composition of SAIRI's leadership, and here I will show that the clerics heading the organization gained prestige in the eyes of their constituency precisely because of their personal links with contemporary Iraqi *maraji'*. Then I will move on to analyze the symbolic dimension of SAIRI's philanthropic services for the community, and document how symbols gave additional meaning to the organization's social performance in the Islamic Republic of Iran. Finally, I will look at SAIRI's use of mass politics and discuss its strategies to encourage the participation of Iraqi refugees and POWs in popular demonstrations.

The Internal Organization of SAIRI's Leadership: Replicating Interpersonal Ties with the Iraqi *marja'iyya*

Looking at the composition of SAIRI's leadership provides the first indication that the organization was constructed in exile as a continuum of the Najaf-based *marja'iyya*. In particular, most of the clerical personalities who founded and headed the organization in the early 1980s were, members of Muhammad Baqir al-Sadr's entourage during their time in Iraq. Their interpersonal relations with al-Sadr took on meaning trans-nationally in becoming the main organizing principle of SAIRI's internal structure and in helping its leaders gain access to their constituency outside Iraq.

Born in 1935 in the shrine city of Kazimayn and educated in the seminaries of Najaf, Muhammad Baqir al-Sadr emerged in the 1970s as a prominent member of Najaf's community of learning and as a possible successor to the *marja'* of the time, Abu'l-Qasim al-Khu'i. In addition to his scholarly activities, the Iraqi *mujtahid* became politically active in the late 1950s. His role in the creation of the Iraqi Hizb al-Da'wa (*al-Da'wa* Party) as well as his political writings made him the figurehead of the Iraqi Islamic movement. In 1979, he began to be called the future Khomeini of Iraq (Aziz, 1993, p. 207).

Fearful of al-Sadr's political and religious influence, the Ba'th regime executed him on April 8, 1980.

Before his death, al-Sadr is said to have designated four or five clerics to form a *qiyada al-na'iba* (vice-leadership) and head the Islamic movement in the event of his death. The identity of the clerics selected for this collective leadership is slightly at variance in the literature, apparently because al-Sadr was adding some names while removing others (al-Mu'min, 2004, p. 331). The names of Mahdi al-Hakim, Muhammad Baqir al-Hakim, Mahmud al-Hashimi, Kazim al-Ha'iri, and Murtada al-'Askari have appeared in one source or another (al-Mu'min, 2004, p. 331; Jabar, 2003, p. 142; Wiley, 1992, p. 60; al-Asadi *et al.*, 1984, p. 98). The background of these clerics suggests that both the traditional teacher–student relationship and religiously oriented political activism were decisive criteria in al-Sadr's selection of members of the *qiyada al-na'iba*.

With the exception of al-'Askari, all the appointees to the vice-leadership had attended al-Sadr's classes in the seminaries of Najaf. Some of them also assisted their mentor in his scholarly work. For instance, al-Hashimi co-authored with him a multi-volume study entitled *Buhuth fi Sharh al-'Urwa al-Wuthqa* (1971) (Studies on the Interpretation of *al-'Urwa al-Wuthqa*) (Mallat, 1988, p. 720). For his part, Muhammad Baqir al-Hakim assumed the editing and printing of al-Sadr's seminal work, *Falsafatuna* (1959) (Our Philosophy) (al-Hakim, 2005b, p. 78). Finally, al-Ha'iri assisted his teacher in the writing of *al-Asas al-Mantiqiyya li'l-Istiqra'* (1972) (The Logical Bases of Induction). In addition to their scholarly ties with Ayatullah al-Sadr, the clerics designated for the *qiyada al-na'iba* had a record as political activists in the Iraqi Islamic movement. The two al-Hakim brothers, al-Ha'iri and al-'Askari were all, at one point or another, involved in Hizb al-Da'wa.

In Iran, al-Hashimi, Muhammad Baqir al-Hakim and al-Ha'iri lived up to their moral responsibility towards their martyred teacher and started to organize collective action against the Iraqi regime. With Ayatullah Khomeini's support and blessing, they cooperated with other clerical activists to form the *Jama'at al-'Ulama' al-Mujahidin fi'l-'Iraq* (the Society of Militant 'Ulama in Iraq) in late 1980.[3] Modeled on the *Jama'at al-'Ulama*

---

[3]Two other short-lived organizations predated the creation of this society. The first was the Assembly of "Ulama" for the Islamic Revolution in Iraq (Majlis al-"Ulama" li'l-Thawra al-Islamiyya fi'l-'Iraq) which was presided over by Murtada al-'Askari. It was abandoned because it lacked Khomeini's support. The second attempt was the Islamic Revolutionary

that had been established in Najaf's clerical milieus in 1959, this society concentrated its activities on *tabligh* (propaganda). In 1981, tensions over the society's leadership prompted Muhammad Baqir al-Hakim to set up the *Maktab li'l-Thawra al-Islamiyya fi'l-'Iraq* (Bureau of the Islamic Revolution in Iraq). This organization was short-lived and was soon replaced by SAIRI.

At the time of its creation in 1982, SAIRI was headed by a *majlis al-shura* or central committee composed of 16 dedicated activists (Ra'uf, 2000, p. 312). The membership of this committee increased to 17 in the following year and reached 32 in 1985 (Jabar, 2003, p. 240). Mahmud al-Hashimi was the organization's chairman and al-Hakim its spokesman.[4] The internal structure of SAIRI underwent important changes in January 1986 with the creation of a general assembly (*hay'a 'amma* or *jam'iyya 'umumiyya*) with about 80 delegates. This body was formed to extend the reach of the organization to include a broader palette of groups, in particular Kurdish, Sunni and other Islamic entities.[5] On 9 January, the general assembly elected a new *majlis al-shura* of eleven members — in subsequent years their number varied between 11 and 15. It was also at that time that al-Hashimi and al-Hakim swapped their positions of chairman and spokesman.

SAIRI's central committees contained both clerical and lay activists with a larger representation of the former. The founding statement of the organization expressed the leading role the clerics played: "The line of the 'ulama is the main line which controls the action of the assembly [i.e., SAIRI] and the presence of the 'ulama in the assembly manifests their real existence in terms of number and influence." (SAIRI, 1983, p. 21, my translation) The composition of the first *majlis al-shura* indicates that the clerical group was largely constituted of clerics who had studied with Muhammad Baqir al-Sadr in Iraq.[6] In addition to al-Hashimi, Muhammad Baqir

---

Army for the Liberation of Iraq (al-Jaysh al-Islami li-Tahrir al-'Iraq) which aimed at mobilizing Iraqi refugees for the armed struggle against the Iraqi regime: Internal factionalism within its leadership led to its dismissal (Mallat, 1988: 81; Jabar, 2003: 236; al-Asadi *et al.* 1984: 101–103).

[4] For a brief period 'Ali al-Ha'iri, another former student of Muhammad Baqir al-Sadr', replaced al-Hashimi as chairman of SAIRI (al-Mu'min, 2004: 342; interview with Ghanim Jawad. London, March 2009).

[5] *al-Shahada*, January 21, 1986.

[6] It is worth remembering that the educational system in the seminaries promotes the mobility of students by allowing them to attend the classes of different teachers. In practice it means that, while these clerics had built ties with al-Sadr, some of them had also attended the classes of apolitical *maraji'*, such as Ayatullah Abu al-Qasim al-Khu'i.

al-Hakim, and al-Ha'iri, to whom reference has already been made, there was Muhammad Baqir al-Muhri, Muhammad al-Haydari, Muhammad Mahdi al-Asifi, Muhammad Baqir al-Nasiri, Husayn al-Sadr, and 'Abd al-'Aziz al-Hakim.

From the perspective of their long-standing scholarly and interpersonal ties with Muhammad Baqir al-Sadr, SAIRI's leaders had a solid base of legitimacy to help them reach out to the Iraqi community in Iran. Thus their connection to the figurehead of the Islamic movement was publicized in the opposition press through pictures showing them posing with him.[7] Building upon the charismatic legacy of their mentor, these personalities developed a public presence: They headed SAIRI-sponsored marches and demonstrations, gave religious and political speeches on numerous occasions, and frequently toured refugee and POW camps. This was especially the case of Muhammad Baqir al-Hakim, SAIRI's first spokesman and the only personality whose identity was known to the public during the first years of the organization's existence.[8]

A number of al-Sadr's prominent students were dropped when a new central committee was formed in the beginning of 1986, including Kazim al-Ha'iri and Husayn al-Sadr. Similarly, Muhammad Baqir al-Nasiri, the acting president of SAIRI's general assembly, left the organization in December 1986. Although these personalities were replaced by other clerical activists, the newcomers had lower religious credentials than their predecessors. This may have signified an attempt on the part of al-Hakim and his supporters to curb the influence of senior figures — in terms of age and religious status — and to promote younger, less experienced and more compliant members (Jabar, 2003, p. 241). A couple of years later it was Mahmud al-Hashimi's turn to leave the organization. One view holds that he was dropped from the movement because he had more academic credentials than Muhammad Baqir al-Hakim. By way of contrast, SAIRI's official discourse explains that al-Hashimi became disillusioned with the world of oppositional politics and felt that he should concentrate on studying and teaching in order to keep the scholarly heritage of Ayatullah al-Sadr alive. In

---

[7]For example *Liwa' al-Sadr*, April 8, 1984.

[8]It was initially agreed that the names of the activists involved in the movement would not be disclosed out of fear of reprisals against their families left behind in Iraq (SAIRI, 1983: 24).

other words, he believed that he could be more useful in the *hawza* than in SAIRI.[9]

With the departure of these clerical activists — and with greater powers vested in the office of chairman after Muhammad Baqir al-Hakim rose to this position in 1986 — SAIRI became increasingly associated with the al-Hakim current. In addition to his scholarly and personal ties with Ayatullah al-Sadr, SAIRI's head could build his prestige upon the "sacredness" of his own family history. He was the son of a most revered *marja'*, Muhsin al-Hakim, who was the most widely followed religious authority between 1961 and 1970. His family's reputation gave him an advantage over others (such as al-Hashimi) to strengthen his leadership among ordinary Shi'is. Another important explanation for the rise of Muhammad Baqir al-Hakim was the privileged relationship that the Iraqi cleric maintained with the Iranian revolutionary regime. His candidacy for SAIRI's chairmanship in 1986 was backed by Khomeini who, according to one of the ayatullah's close associates, gave his assent to every appointment made in the organization and had already suggested in 1982 that al-Hakim should act as its chairman.[10]

Social Services: Operational and Symbolic Performance

From the early days of their Iranian exile, SAIRI's leaders established many social and educational services. In distributing patronage, the Tehran-based organization gave a clear sign to Iraqis that it cared about them and deserved their trust, loyalty, and support. To put it crudely, social services were material rewards to be dispensed in exchange for popular recognition. Improving living conditions for the Iraqi refugees and POWs in Iran was also crucial in ensuring that they would not return home until the overthrow of the Ba'th regime. The Islamic opposition needed them to stay in Iran to avoid losing access to its popular base.[11] Finally, patronage was a means for clerical

---

[9]Interview with Hamid al-Bayati. New York, May 2007.

[10]Interview with Hasan Bujnurdi. Tehran, November 2006.

[11]More than once, SAIRI advised Iraqi refugees and POWs against returning to Iraq when they had the possibility to do so. Shortly after Iran's acceptance of a cease-fire with Iraq in July 1988, for instance, al-Hakim explained his views about the repatriation of Iraqi POWs. The cleric claimed that returning captives were likely to face death and persecution back in Iraq, explaining that several prisoners who went home during the war had reportedly been executed. Therefore he advised POWs to seek asylum in the Islamic Republic of Iran (*Liwa' al-Sadr*, August 28, 1988; *al-Shahada*, August 30, 1988). Similarly, SAIRI clearly did not want refugees to return to Iraq. In June 1999, Baghdad

exiles to give confirmation that they were working through a continuation of the *marja'iyya*, thus fulfilling the same social and educational mission.

SAIRI's leaders maintained a high degree of visibility as providers for their fellow-citizens in Iran. They regularly toured the refugee camps, inspecting the facilities and listening to people's views about their living conditions.[12] Muhammad Baqir al-Hakim also dedicated time every Wednesday evening to receive written and oral complaints in his office from those who hoped that he could find solutions to their problems (al-Jayashi, 2006, p. 139). In addition, the cleric and his associates developed a large network of philanthropic institutions that provided services ranging from the distribution of financial and material assistance to the refugees in need, the creation of housing units in refugee-populated Iranian cities, and the provision of free medical services.[13]

Over the years, SAIRI also opened 18 primary and secondary schools throughout Iran to provide for the children's educational needs (SAIRI, 1994/5, pp. 26, 33). Iraqi pupils could not easily join Iranian governmental schools because they were required to take an entry exam in Persian, which most of them did not know. To some extent, Iran's strict requirements for the enrolment of Iraqi children in the governmental educational system gave an opportunity for SAIRI to attract these pupils to its own schools, and hence promote the name of the organization among the younger generation of refugees and their parents. One Iraqi father explained:

> The education of my daughters was ruined by deportation. They had almost completed their secondary studies... When we were deported to Iran, they entered the Iraqi school established by the Imam martyr al-Sadr foundation. I think that it is the Supreme Council for the Islamic Revolution which administers it. They have succeeded [...]
>
> (cited in Babakhan, 1994, pp. 136–137, my translation).

---

unexpectedly announced its readiness to issue passports to all Iran-based exiles, regardless of their political affiliations, in order to allow them to return to Iraq or travel to a third country. SAIRI warned the people not to be fooled by Iraqi propaganda, trying to convince them that Baghdad's offer could in no way erase its long history of oppression against the Iraqi people and that tyranny was not coming to the end in Iraq. SAIRI's arguments did not carry much weight and thousands of Iraqis returned back home with their new passports (Luizard, 2002: 274; *Mideast Mirror*, September 10, 1999).

[12]See for example *Liwa' al-Sadr*, May 19, 1982; *Liwa' al-Sadr*, November 19, 1983; FBIS, NES-91-068, 9 April 1991: 75.

[13]Interview with Hamid al-Bayati. New York, May 2007; interview with Sahib al-Hariri. Tehran, March 2008; see also *Liwa' al-Sadr*, October 17, 1984; *Liwa' al-Sadr*, November 28, 1984; *Liwa' al-Sadr*, January 3, 1985; *Liwa' al-Sadr*, March 6, 1985.

Furthermore, SAIRI's leaders regularly interceded with the Iranian authorities to have them ease the restrictions imposed on Iraqi refugees with regard to work, travel, marriage, and application for asylum. For instance, conditions to settle outside the refugee camps were eventually relaxed in 1987 — refugees were previously required to find an Iranian citizen ready to act as their guarantor. The revised law allowed SAIRI members, as well as certain categories of Iraqi residents in Iran, to vouch for those wishing to leave the camps.[14] SAIRI's legitimacy was enhanced because the organization had solved a problem that, according to Babakhan's study, ranked high on the list of the refugees' preoccupations (Babakhan, 1994, p. 133). Among other positive achievements were changes made to facilitate marriage between Iraqi and Iranian nationals. The law asked a foreigner wishing to take an Iranian spouse to get legal documents for the marriage from his/her embassy. With no diplomatic representation in Tehran, Iraqi citizens could not comply with this requirement. In 1988, Iran's Interior Ministry eventually allowed Muhammad Baqir al-Hakim and his Shahid al-Sadr Foundation to issue documents instead of the Iraqi authorities (Sande, 2000, appendix 3). As SAIRI is known to have encouraged Iraqi POWs to take an Iranian wife and start a family in their host country instead of returning back home, this compromise was an important achievement for the Iraqi opposition leadership (International Crisis Group [ICG], 2007, p.4).

Clearly, SAIRI was profoundly concerned to better the life of the Iraqi people in Iran. Yet, one can legitimately suspect that there was more to its social role than the genuine fulfillment of humanitarian duty. Patronage was a means for the organization to distribute collective symbols of solidarity in order to create emotional ties with its popular base. SAIRI stressed its Islamic nature when it named several of its social projects after the 12 Shi'i imams — a practice traditionally used in the projects of the *marja'iyya*. In this regard, one can mention the Imam 'Ali Benevolent Clinic, the Imam al-Murtada Foundation for Medical and Philanthropic Assistance, as well as the Imam Husayn, Imam Reza, Imam Sadiq, and Imam Baqir schools, to name a few of these projects. SAIRI also tried to capitalize on the power of Shi'i rituals when, for example, it distributed special gifts to Iraqi refugees and POWs during the month of Ramadan.

More significant were the symbols that referred to the heritage of the Iraqi Islamic political movement and to its martyrs. The memory of the

---

[14] *Liwa' al-Sadr*, January 29, 1987.

religious figures who had fallen for the sake of the Iraqi cause was revived through the names given to SAIRI's charitable projects in Iran. Ayatullah Muhammad Baqir al-Sadr became the most recurrent symbol and several clinics, schools, and other institutions were named after him. The legacy of the Iraqi martyr was also symbolically transferred to SAIRI's social projects when inauguration ceremonies for these projects were scheduled during the "Week of al-Shahid al-Sadr," a special week organized every year in April to commemorate the killing of the ayatullah in 1980.[15] Using the name of al-Sadr had the double advantage of giving visibility to SAIRI's ties to the most emblematic martyr of the Islamic movement in Iraq, and also to an important *marja'* of contemporary Iraqi Shi'ism.

The memory of other figures who had been martyred by the Ba'th regime was also kept alive through several social institutions. This was the case for example of Bint al-Huda, the sister of Muhammad Baqir al-Sadr, who met the same tragic fate as her brother; her name was used for a school established in the camp of Shushtar in Iranian Khuzestan for Iraqi girls. Similarly, one of SAIRI's schools for boys in the city of Dezful was named after Mahdi al-Hakim, a brother of Muhammad Baqir al-Hakim and a charismatic opposition figure assassinated in 1988 by Iraqi security agents in Sudan. Over the years, new symbols from the recent history of Iraq were added to SAIRI's narrative. For example the organization paid tribute to the revolutionary spirit of the Iraqi people and to their sacrifices when it named two of its schools "al-Intifada school", in reference to the popular uprising that spread throughout Iraq in March 1991 and was violently crushed by Saddam Husayn's Republican Guard.

In linking its social services to the legacy of the martyrs of the Islamic movement, the Iraqi opposition not only aimed to honor their name, but it also hoped to promote the idea of noble self-sacrifice among different layers of the refugee community. SAIRI distributed social rewards to those who had shown their readiness to fight and die for the cause. Its Unit of Social Services provided special treatment to the families of those fighting in the Badr Corps, SAIRI's military force. The organization also opened a Section for the Martyrs (also called the Martyrs Foundation of the Islamic Revolution in Iraq) to assist the families of those who were killed in the struggle against the Iraqi regime.[16] Working in close collaboration with the

---

[15] *Liwa' al-Sadr*, April 16, 1987.
[16] *al-Shahada*, August 22, 1989.

Iranian Martyrs Foundation, this office distributed monthly emoluments to its beneficiaries.[17] It also organized special activities, such as trips to the shrine of Sayyidatna Zaynab in Damascus, for "the recreation of these families which offered the most valuable of their possessions in the path of Islam."[18]

In addition to infusing revolutionary spirit in the hearts of the people, these rewards were to some extent a means for SAIRI to compete with the Ba'th regime over the distribution of compensation honoring the name of Iraqi martyrs. As Dina Khoury explains in this volume, Baghdad ran a system of allocations for the families of its many soldiers who died in the war with Iran. Through its own services, SAIRI showed that it was not a lesser provider to the families of its own martyrs than the Iraqi regime, proving to its supporters that they had been right to turn against Saddam Husayn and his clique.

Mass Politics and Armed Struggle: The Mobilizing Power of Shi'i Iraqi Themes

From its creation, SAIRI has defined itself as a popular movement "resembling the movement of the religious *marja'iyya* in the *umma*" (Bayati, 2004, p. 170, my translation). It has always strongly contested the label of a Western-style party and preferred the appellation "umbrella organization". It had member organizations, officials with functions inside its apparatus, but did not establish a formal system of membership for its grass-roots followers. The organization stood as the representative of all the Iraqi people and, as one observer perceptively explained:

> "The choice of inclusive supporter status rather than exclusive membership gives the SCIRI [i.e., SAIRI] similar opportunities as those the marja'iyya benefits from when addressing the people. Without the boundaries of party organization that separates the party from the people, it can evade the distinction between 'them' and 'us', relying on choice, appeal and religious obligation rather than command and instruction."
>
> (Sande, 2000, p. 65)

SAIRI's inclusive nature found its origin in the *marja'iyya*'s own long-standing hesitation over formal association with party politics. Muhammad

---

[17]Ibid.

[18]*al-Shahada*, November 7, 1989, my translation.

Baqir al-Hakim's father, Ayatullah Muhsin al-Hakim, had already made this clear in the early 1960s when he instructed two of his sons to leave *Hizb al-Da'wa*. The *marja'* had approved the creation of this group a few years before, but came to realize that the participation of his sons in its activities would not reflect well on the institution of the *marja'iyya* and might even weaken it (Louër, 2008, p. 21). Muhsin al-Hakim believed that his role was to defend public affairs without restriction and preserve the independence of his office (al-Hakim, 1999, p. 95). For his part, Muhammad Baqir al-Sadr understood that his involvement in *al-Da'wa* would compromise his rise in the *hawza* because the community of learning "would not accept an active *mujtahid* for the position of grand *marja'*, at least not a member of a political party" (Aziz, 1993, p. 210).

Therefore, SAIRI gave priority to mass mobilization through popular gatherings instead of establishing a formal system of membership. The organization was able to legitimize its approach to mass politics with a practice that became commonplace in the contemporary history of "high Shi'ism" in Iraq, starting with Muhsin al-Hakim's *marja'iyya* when religious events increasingly took on a political bent under the patronage of the religious establishment in Najaf. Furthermore, SAIRI's leadership could profit from its own experience in the general mobilization of the masses within the framework of the *marja'iyya* in Iraq. For instance in the 1960s and 1970s Muhammad Baqir al-Hakim had frequently organized ceremonies during the numerous religious festivals that mark the Shi'i calendar in which he explained the political stance of Muhsin al-Hakim and later of Muhammad Baqir al-Sadr with regard to the governments ruling in Baghdad. Strong from his experience "in the field" while he was still in Iraq, the cleric was ready to engage in similar activities in Iran and elsewhere for the mobilization of refugees and POWs.

In SAIRI's view, mass politics had several advantages. First, popular participation was a clear sign that the Iraqi people regarded the Islamic opposition as legitimate. It proved that SAIRI "had deep roots in the *umma*"[19] and presented the organization as a viable alternative to Saddam Husayn and his clique, should they be overthrown. Second, mass politics helped create and strengthen solidarity within the whole community, even across national borders. Popular events were generally organized simultaneously in various countries, each of them being thoroughly detailed in the opposition

---

[19] *al-Muntalaq* (April/May 1981, p. 29), my translation.

press.[20] Those who read these accounts were left with a feeling that SAIRI encompassed a broad transnational community. Third, the events sponsored by SAIRI or other institutions close to the movement were a good opportunity to collect individual donations in support of the organization's social, political, and military activities.[21]

To put its strategy of mass politics into practice, SAIRI had a "special committee for celebrations" in charge of planning events for Iraqis living in Iran with the stated objective of attracting "the largest possible number of Iraqis" (SAIRI, 1994/5, p. 61). Forthcoming events were publicized in the mosques and *husayniyyat* (Shi'i places of worship), as well as on the Iraqi opposition's radio programs. SAIRI's cultural officers in the POW camps regularly encouraged Iraqi captives to participate in demonstrations, especially when local or foreign visitors were touring the detention facilities.[22] The organization also tried to reach out to Iraqis outside Iran. For instance, its delegates always arranged a time to meet the refugees living in the countries they visited. After SAIRI set up its offices in Damascus and London, popular events were scheduled more regularly in the Syrian and British capitals. Islamic activists and 'ulama close to SAIRI organized similar activities in their places of residence.

The ratio of Iraqis participating in SAIRI-sponsored events in Iran is difficult to establish. Reporting in the opposition's weekly press was elusive; it generally talked of "a number of" Iraqis, rarely mentioning barely more precise figures such as "hundreds" or "thousands" of people. Similarly, *Liwa' al-Sadr* and *Shahada* did not publish pictures taken during demonstrations, which might have given a sense of the size of the gatherings. The only source providing an estimated figure in this regard was a report of a UN fact-finding mission to Iran's POW camps stating that "[a]bout 50% of the POWs in the camps visited took part in [anti-Iraq] demonstrations, shouting slogans; but many of them were clearly under the influence of a minority of perhaps 10% or 20%" (UN, 1988, p. 14).

More instructive than the actual number of participants whom SAIRI succeeded in attracting to its events is the strategy that the organization used to rally them around its political movement. To mobilize the community politically, SAIRI capitalized on the Shi'i narrative. The singularity of its approach was that it sought to reinforce the meaning of traditional

---

[20]For example *Liwa' al-Sadr*, May 27, 1986; *Liwa' al-Sadr*, April 16, 1987.
[21]For example *Liwa' al-Sadr*, November 21, 1987; *al-Shahada*, June 21, 1988.
[22]For example *Liwa' al-Sadr*, August 12, 1982.

religious celebrations (such as the birth and death of the Prophet and the 12 imams) with the commemoration of religious figures who had influenced the recent history of Iraqi Shi'ism.

The figure of Ayatullah Muhsin al-Hakim was a case in point. SAIRI organized yearly gatherings to commemorate his death in order to keep alive the devotion that people felt towards him when he was their *marja'*.[23] Speeches given on these occasions reminded the audience that the late ayatullah had engaged in political action throughout his life.[24] The most common references were his participation in the jihad against British occupation troops during World War I, his opposition to the successive despotic regimes that had ruled over Iraq since independence and, more importantly, his open confrontation with the Ba'th regime during the last years of his life. The organization also liked to remind the people of al-Hakim's quote that he felt like Imam Husayn on his way to Karbala' when he personally traveled from Najaf to Baghdad in 1969 in protest against the Iraqi regime (al-Hakim, 2005a, pp. 23–24). This somewhat exaggerated portrayal of Ayatullah al-Hakim's political role allowed SAIRI's leadership to create symbolic "approval" for the organization's own activities against the regime many years after al-Hakim's own death. It also proved to be a strong appeal to the people to take on the moral responsibility of following the path of the *marja'* and hence of supporting SAIRI in its political mission.

In addition, and more significantly, SAIRI sought to generate emotional ties between the Iraqi Shi'is and the religious figures who had been persecuted and martyred in Iraq. In the organization's narrative the traditional martyr figure of Imam Husayn gave room to the 'ulama who had fallen under Saddam's hand. Ayatullah al-Sadr was one such figure. His mobilizing power had already been tested during the Rajab Intifada of 1979 when people came out on the streets to protest the arrest of the cleric and forced the Iraqi authorities to release him. Speaking about this event, Muhammad Baqir al-Hakim acclaimed: "The masses had the power when they managed to save the life of al-Sayyid al-Shahid [al-Sadr]."[25] To foment political fervor in support of its activities, SAIRI cultivated the deep attachment that

---

[23] For example *Liwa' al-Sadr*, November 21, 1987; *al-Shahada*, November 11, 1988.

[24] It is worth noting that the Iraqi Islamic opposition has systematically emphasized Muhsin al-Hakim's political role in its publications, while underplaying the theological sphere of his *marja'iyya*.

[25] *Liwa' al-Sadr*, April 17, 1984, my translation.

the people felt for al-Sadr, never failing to display pictures of the martyred ayatullah in its processions and demonstrations.

Alongside the emblematic figure of Muhammad Baqir al-Sadr, the al-Hakim family became another strong rallying force in SAIRI's political movement. In May 1983, the Iraqi regime arrested 90 members of the family, killing a group of six people shortly afterwards, keeping the others in prison. Ten additional members of this family were executed two years later. In January 1988, it was Mahdi al-Hakim's turn to be assassinated in Sudan. The fate of the al-Hakim family had an important mobilizing potential that SAIRI was ready to exploit. To this end, the organization created a cult of commemoration around the figures who had been killed, publishing their pictures and biographies in its newspapers and staging yearly gatherings to commemorate their death.[26]

These events provided an opportunity for the leadership of SAIRI to tell the people that the killing of these persons was not a matter concerning the al-Hakim family only, but the community as a whole for at least three reasons (al-Hakim, 1984, pp. 74–76). First, the regime in Iraq intended to destroy Islam. In targeting a *sayyid* family and the relatives of a most revered *marja'*, Baghdad had committed a crime against the prophet and against the religious institution of Shi'ism. Second, the arrest and execution of Ayatullah Muhsin al-Hakim's sons and grandsons was described by SAIRI's leadership as an act of revenge against the late ayatullah who had stood in defense of the common good against the Ba'th regime after it came to power in 1968. For their part, the al-Hakim family members who had been arrested and killed in Iraq were apolitical members of Najaf's community. Their persecution proved that aloofness from politics did not provide a guarantee against the regime's actions; this provided grounds for the people to engage actively in opposition. Third, Muhammad Baqir al-Hakim's insistence on opposing the regime in spite of the risk that this posed to his family was a clear signal to the Iraqi masses that SAIRI's leader was willing to make sacrifices for the cause. He was a model to emulate.

The persecution of the al-Hakim family attested to the fact that ordinary Iraqis shared a common destiny with their leadership in exile. In the words of Muhammad Baqir: "The al-Hakim family is just one section of the suffering Iraqi people. I do not want to talk about a specific family, but about my

---

[26]For example *Liwa' al-Sadr*, May 15, 1984; *Liwa' al-Sadr*, July 10, 1985; *Liwa' al-Sadr*, May 20, 1986; FBIS, NES-91-057, 25 March 1991: 9.

big family."[27] SAIRI symbolically tried to reinforce this sense of common suffering when it proclaimed the anniversary of the killing of al-Hakim family members a day of solidarity with the Iraqi people detained in Iraq — many refugees had relatives left behind in Iraq who faced persecution (Babakhan, 1994, pp. 129–130). 'Abd al-'Aziz al-Hakim explained in an interview that it was natural to choose this date because: "We all remember our fathers, mothers, brothers, sisters, and children detained in Iraq; we remember their miseries and what they endure under the hand of Iraq's tyrant Saddam."[28] To mark this day of solidarity, SAIRI organized demonstrations in front of the UN office in Tehran and demanded that "the silence be broken" about the human rights situation in Iraq.[29]

SAIRI did not only expect its supporters to actively participate in its political events but also hoped to mobilize them militarily. Named the Badr Corps — a reference to a battle fought by the Prophet Muhammad and his companions in 624 against the pagan merchants in Mecca — SAIRI's armed force fought for the first time on the side of Iranian troops during the July–August 1983 operations code-named Fajr II in northeast Iraq (al-Jayashi, 2006, p. 175; ICG, 2007, p. 5; al-Mu'min, 2004, p. 482). In addition to participating in military operations on the front, the Badr Corps conducted independent guerrilla-type operations in the South and in the North of Iraq (al-Mu'min, 2004, p. 482).

SAIRI's decision to take up arms on the side of Iran against Iraq represented a serious challenge to perceptions about the organization's national loyalty (Shain, 2005, p. 130). In response to this challenge, SAIRI justified the creation of the Badr Corps and its participation in the Iran–Iraq war as part of the history of the Iraqi Islamic movement's armed struggle against the Ba'th regime. According to the Islamic opposition's narrative, the movement reached a turning point in July 1979 when Muhammad Baqir al-Sadr, then placed under house arrest, issued a verbal fatwa enjoining:

> [e]very Muslim in Iraq and every Iraqi outside of Iraq to do whatever he can, even if it costs him his life, to continue the jihad and struggle in order to remove this nightmare from the land of the beloved Iraq, liberate themselves from this inhuman gang, and establish a righteous, respectable and honorable rule based on Islam.
>
> (al-Bayati, 2004, p. 190, my translation)

---

[27] FBIS, NES-95-061, 30 March 1995: 54.
[28] *Liwa' al-Sadr*, May 20, 1986, my translation.
[29] For example *al-Shahada*, May 23, 1989.

According to Wiley, the removal of Hasan al-Bakr and the concentration of power in Saddam Husayn's hands had made interactions between the Islamists and the regime impossible (Wiley, 1992, p. 53). al-Sadr's fatwa led to the creation of armed cells inside Iraq, some of which were later integrated into the Badr Corps.

For Muhammad Baqir al-Hakim, the Iraqi people had "the ability and responsibility to engage in jihad in the path of Allah, the path of the nation and the path of the people" (al-Bayati, 2004, p. 169, my translation).[30] Refugees became the main target group for the opposition's mobilization campaigns. For the first time in July 1983 (probably as a result of the successful Fajr II operations), SAIRI issued a joint communiqué with the Islamic Revolutionary Guard Corps announcing that volunteers should register in SAIRI's military centers.[31] Rapidly the organization opened bureaus for mobilization in most of Iran's refugee camps.[32] Iraqi POWs became another source of SAIRI's fighters in 1986 when Khomeini gave the green light to the opposition to integrate POW volunteers in a special brigade attached to SAIRI (al-Mu'min, 2004, p. 431). The captives joined the Badr Corps as *tawwabin* (penitents), after receiving an amnesty from Muhammad Baqir al-Hakim or another religious authority for their previous participation in Saddam Husayn's army (Jabar, 2003, p. 253).[33]

In the years immediately before 2003 the strength of the Badr Corps was estimated between 30,000 and 40,000 soldiers, making it the Iraqi opposition's largest militia (Luizard, 2002, p. 191).[34] To convince its followers to take up arms against their home country, SAIRI used both symbolic and material arguments. To a large extent, the organization resorted to the same religious symbols as those used to attract the Iraqi masses to its political gatherings. The notion of martyrdom was again particularly present in SAIRI's discourse because of its mobilizing power in the context of jihad. The figure of Imam Husayn contained symbolic appeal for the contemporary struggle against tyranny: "Oh brothers in Iraq you should be convinced that the path of Husayn, the path of sacrifice, is the way through which we will

---

[30]Khomeini echoed this view when he said: "The Iraqi people will deal the deadliest blows against that regime as much as they can, just as they have already dealt it blows strong enough to knock that regime senseless." (FBIS, SOA-VIII-083, 28 April 1983, I1).

[31]FBIS, SOA-VIII-145, 27 July 1983, I5.

[32]*Liwa' al-Sadr*, October 23, 1985; *Liwa al-Sadr*, December 26, 1987.

[33]*Tawwabin* refers to the Muslims who fought Imam Husayn in Karbala in 680 and later repented.

[34]FBIS, NES, 9 February 1999; Radio Free Europe, 6(13), 24 March 2003.

realize our objectives," al-Hakim said in a speech (al-Hakim, 198?, p. 20). Iraqis had the moral and legal responsibility to avenge by force the blood of Imam Husayn's successors, above all Ayatullah al-Sadr and the al-Hakim martyrs. Their participation in the jihad would prove to Saddam Husayn that his crimes did not undermine the people's will (al-Hakim, 198?, p. 26). SAIRI's rhetoric was expected to intensify the rage and thirst for revenge that already fuelled the hearts of many Iraqi refugees because of their own experience of deportation, dispossession, and violence at the hands of the Ba'th regime.

While a number of volunteers joined the Badr Corps out of ideological commitment, others did it for material reasons. Iraqi recruits received a modest salary for their engagement and gifts on special occasions,[35] probably sufficient incentive for young Iraqis without work prospects in the refugee camps to enroll in SAIRI's military force (Babakhan, 1994, p. 111). Finally, not all Iraqi POWs were truly "volunteers". According to the testimonies of former prisoners collected by the International Crisis Group, SAIRI exerted moral and physical pressure on prisoners to recruit them (ICG, 2007, pp. 4–5).

Conclusion

The legitimation of Shi'i groups established outside Iraq in the Saddam Husayn era still has repercussions on contemporary Iraqi politics. In this chapter, I have taken a few steps back in time in order to address the question of the legitimacy of an exile organization, the Supreme Assembly for the Islamic Revolution in Iraq, during the first decade that followed its creation in November 1982.

Headquartered in Tehran, SAIRI had direct access to large numbers of Iraqis living in the Islamic Republic — to its potential popular base if you will. However, its presence in Iran meant physical distance from the home country and a possible setback for its bid for legitimate leadership. To connect with the refugees and POWs and secure their support for its opposition to Saddam Husayn's regime, SAIRI kept the idea of Iraq's religious legacy alive, integrating Shi'i symbols in its social, political and military activities. The organization proposed a vision of its mission as the representative

---

[35] Interview with Ihsan al-Hakim. London, March 2009.

of the Iraqi people that stressed the endurance of Muhsin al-Hakim's and Muhammad Baqir al-Sadr's *marja'iyyat* over time and space. At the same time, SAIRI nourished and exploited the long-standing emotional power that its potential constituency felt for religious figures who were persecuted and had died under the dictator's hand in Iraq. Like most liberation movements in the Middle East and elsewhere, the Iraqi Islamic opposition turned its martyrs into national heroes and presented them as models to emulate.

Trying to clarify the historical record of an important actor in the Iraqi Islamic opposition movement, I have shown that SAIRI was a more complex organization than has been generally acknowledged. Its activities in Iran showed that the organization remained, at least symbolically, attached to the home country. Suffering from negative perceptions about its loyalty to the Iraqi state because of Iranian patronage, SAIRI stressed its Iraqi identity through the distribution of symbols emanating from home and by connecting exclusively to the Iraqi people — for instance the Iranian poor were not recipients of its patronage. Yet, it remains clear that the Tehran-based organization acted with the approval of the Iranian authorities, as the revolutionary regime was also keen on providing proof of the Iraqi Islamic opposition's independence whenever it suited Iran's interests.

In 2003, the leaders of SAIRI returned to Iraq with the intention of participating in the post-Saddam political order. The shift from opposition politics in exile to running for elections at home forced the organization to adapt to new conditions. There has been continuity in its strategies to connect with the Iraqi people, however. To win over their electorate SAIRI's leaders have persisted in capitalizing on Iraqi Shi'i symbols. As they did it in exile, they have insisted on their loyalty to the *marja'iyya* in Najaf, using the powerful imagery of Ayatullah Muhsin al-Hakim but also trying to develop and publicize ties to the highest contemporary religious authority, Ayatullah 'Ali al-Sistani (ICG, 2007, pp. 9, 11–12). Similarly, martyrdom has remained central to SAIRI's political activities in Iraq. Adding his name to the long list of the al-Hakim *shuhada'*, Muhammad Baqir al-Hakim emerged as a new mobilizing symbol after his assassination in August 2003. Headed by 'Ammar al-Hakim (Muhammad Baqir's nephew and SAIRI's vice chairman), the Najaf-based Mu'assasat Shahid al-Mihrab (Martyr of the Pulpit Foundation) kept the religious, social and political legacy of SAIRI's martyred leader alive through the provision of philanthropic services in Iraq. Overall, SAIRI's profoundly religious nature and its constant use of Shi'i symbols would not allow its leaders to secularize their approach to politics in post-2003 Iraq. While this did not prevent the organization's candidates from doing well in the 2005 elections, it clearly cost them many votes in the provincial elections of January 2009.

Electronic reference

ICG (2007). Shiite politics in Iraq: The role of the Supreme Council. *Middle East Report*, 70, Online. Available HTTP: <http://www.crisisgroup.org/home/index.cfm?id=5158> (accessed 20 November 2007).

THE POLITICS OF POPULATION MOVEMENTS IN CONTEMPORARY IRAQ: A RESEARCH AGENDA

Géraldine Chatelard[1]

A significant blind spot in the historiography of contemporary Iraq is the question of the recurrence and durability of population displacement and forced migration.[2] Whereas a large body of research has been devoted to Palestinian displacement, to the point of constituting an area of scholarship of its own within the broader field of Palestinian studies, displacement and other forms of involuntary migration in and from Iraq have largely escaped academic interest as topics in their own right. Recent trends of involuntary migration taking place in the wake of the change of regime in 2003 — particularly the sectarian-based displacement which erupted on a large scale after the al-'Askari shrine bombing in Samarra' in 2006 — have spurred a new policy interest for those Iraqis defined by international law and humanitarian organizations as refugees when they have crossed international boundaries and as internally displaced persons (IDPs) when they have fled from their homes but remained inside their country. As seems invariably to be the case

---

[1]The author would like to thank Hamit Bozarslan, Peter Harling, Riccardo Bocco, and Peter Sluglett for their suggestions on previous versions of this chapter.
[2]There is considerable debate in the overlapping fields of forced migration and refugee studies with regard to terminology and typologies. Hence, I use *displacement* when migration takes place under direct compulsion, whereas I reserve *forced migration* for cases where compulsion exists but is indirect and the scope for deciding to migrate is wider. I use *involuntary migration*, or *involuntary population movements*, to encompass both instances. I do not deny that subjects have the capacity to exert their agency and make migration decisions even under severe compulsion, but it is not my aim in this essay to discuss the perspective and experience of the migrants themselves.

with 'hot' issues on international humanitarian and policy agendas, a growing number of researchers — particularly doctoral students affiliated with Western European and North American universities — are focusing on the post-2003 displacement.[3] Several publications attempt to provide documentary or analytical views of the most recent trends in internal displacement and refugee migration since the regime of Saddam Husayn was brought to an end.[4] These works, published or in progress, are dominated by the approach of refugee studies and are concerned mostly with the anthropological, sociological, humanitarian, or policy dimensions of involuntary migration from Iraq to foreign countries. First-hand empirically based academic research on the dynamics, politics and socioeconomic effects of involuntary migration *inside* Iraq is conspicuously lacking, most likely because of the tense security situation which is not conducive to research. On the other hand, there might also be a more structural reason for this near absence of research on involuntary migration inside Iraq: The tendency of refugee studies to focus on the same issues, populations and geographical areas as those of concern to institutional actors within the international refugee regime whose mandate has traditionally emphasized the protection of refugees in host countries.

The focus on current trends, and on refugee experiences and institutional policies outside Iraq has had at least two important disadvantages. On the one hand, it leads to disregarding historical continuities in the phenomenon of involuntary migration in/from Iraq. On the other hand, the causes of internal displacement and refugee movements are widely attributed to generalized violence and inter-sectarian conflict ensuing from the security void created by a weak state after regime change in 2003. In this vision, which appears to be the one most generally shared by humanitarian actors and Western governments with a stake in Iraq, the restoration of state authority — expected to guarantee overall security and re-start economic

---

[3]Personal observations and communications with over forty mostly US and Western European researchers since 2007.

[4]Since 2007, advocacy and humanitarian organizations have produced dozens of reports on Iraqi refugees abroad and IDPs inside Iraq. Since 2008, media coverage, especially in the US and UK press, has been significant. A number of documentary films and book essays, mostly by journalists, have also been devoted to Iraqi refugees. A new but growing trend is that of memoirs written by Iraqis who recount their experiences of exile. Published academic or para-academic production is still limited, but also growing (see, in particular, Marfleet, 2007; Shoeb *et al.*, 2007; International Crisis Group, 2008; Leenders, 2008; Sassoon, 2008; Doraï, 2009; Chatelard, 2010).

development[5] — is seen as the ideal solution which will curb further involuntary migration and lay the ground for the return of the refugees and those internally displaced. For those acquainted with the modern history of Iraq, maybe the most problematic aspect of this faith in the role of the state to solve the current "Iraq displacement crisis" and prevent new involuntary population movements is that it is precisely the Iraqi state, in its various guises between 1920 and 2003, that has been principally responsible for instigating involuntary migration inside and outside the country. Furthermore the Iraqi state, especially under Saddam Husayn, also displayed remarkable tenacity in keeping many Iraqis inside the country against their will,[6] and in confining certain populations to specific areas of Iraq. Without seeming excessively pessimistic about the type of regime that will emerge from the eventual consolidation of the new Iraqi state, it is worthwhile reflecting upon the fact that government stability and economic prosperity in Iraq — both of which existed to some extent, however briefly, under the rule of the Ba'th — have not previously been synonymous with the principle of freedom of movement. Although I will not address the issue here, I would argue that it is useful to consider recent trends in displacement and forced migration in the light of previous episodes and ask in precisely which ways the post-Saddam Husayn trends differ from previous ones while still displaying several similar characteristics.

No general historical work on modern Iraq fails to mention the episodes of mass displacement or forced migration to which Assyrians, Kurds of all persuasions, Turkmen, Jews, individuals deemed of Iranian descent, and Shi'i Arabs from the South have been subjected. In the same books, readers will find accounts of the emigration (by eviction or voluntary exile) of political opponents or irredentist populations, such as the Kurds and Yazidis, a trend that dates back to the British mandate era (1920–1932). Most of

---

[5]Economic factors have been identified by Philip Marfleet (2007) as one major cause of departure from Iraq in the post-2003 period.

[6]Alan Dowty, who surveyed emigration policies worldwide in the 1980s, placed Iraq on a list of 21 states imposing severe restrictions on the ability of their citizens to leave the country of their own free will. The most obvious common denominator among these states was not the level of economic development, nor the threat of brain drain, but the nature of the regime: all were heavily ideologized one-party states. Iraq stood out, together with Burma and Somalia, as an exception in that, contrary to the 18 other states, it was not a self-defined Marxist-Leninist regime. Dowty notes that: "Although large numbers [of people] may occasionally leave such states, legal exit is basically viewed as a privilege to be granted by the government rather than a right to be exercised" (1988, p. 90).

the instances of displacement, forced and political migration listed above have also been documented, often in great detail and using original sources, in scholarly monographs devoted to particular ethnicities, displacement episodes, political parties or historical periods. Iraqi historians writing from the perspective of Arab nationalism or official Ba'thist history are no more prone than their colleagues with different outlooks to gloss over involuntary migration and political emigration. They simply place them in a different interpretive framework and couch them in other terms.

In addition to scholarly works, involuntary migration features largely in the apologetic writings dealing with, and often produced by, politicized intellectuals among Iraqi Shi'is, Kurds, Turkmen and Assyrians, and in the advocacy literature of human rights and refugee organizations. It would be surprising if published or unpublished memoirs, essays and pamphlets by members of opposition parties in Iraq overlooked these issues. Here too the selection of facts, interpretation and terminology are likely to differ from the ones adopted by historians trained in Western academia. Most certainly, such accounts must stand in sharp ideological contrast to those written by pan-Arab or Ba'thist historians.

What seems to be lacking, therefore, is not historical and empirical material — necessarily varied in nature and perspective — but rather any conceptual attempt to link various types and episodes of involuntary migration together to try to make sense either of the recurrence of the phenomenon or of a certain regularity in the ways it occurs. This is what I propose to attempt in this essay by broadening the perspective to discuss the politics of population movements from the inception of the modern Iraqi state to the present. In addition to what is classically subsumed under the phrase involuntary migration, this problematization will lead me to consider other types of population movements affected by the state and by other political actors.

Nation Building and State Control over Population Movements

State and conflict-induced population displacements and migration have a long history in the Middle East, going back to the Ottoman empire and beyond to the Byzantine era. Such population movements have had a broad regional scope and their effects are felt in most of the modern states previously under Ottoman rule (Shami, 1996). In the introduction to her recent historical and ethnographic study, *Displacement and Dispossession in the*

Modern Middle East, Dawn Chatty notes that "The Middle East in particular has been the scene of continuous forced migration over the past 150 years" and that dispossession of people in the region should be located "as part of the policy of empire, carried further by the colonial encounter and then revitalized in the Arab socialist awakening of the mid-twentieth century" (2010, pp. 1–2).

There are several possible frameworks through which to interpret the complexity and durability of involuntary population movements in Iraq. However, the overarching one is likely to remain the process of nation building. Modern Iraq indeed appears as a classical case of 20th century post-imperial nation-state formation of the type that the prominent refugee studies scholar Aristide Zolberg analyzed in his seminal 1983 article on "The Formation of New States as a Refugee-Generating Process". Population displacements in Iraq were intrinsically linked to the creation of a nation state seeking to homogenize populations, assert sovereignty over territories contested by other nationalist claims, silence domestic political opposition, and perform population engineering as part of policies of modernization and development. Successive Iraqi regimes have exerted control over population movements both by limiting the mobility of certain categories of the population inside the national territory and across borders, and by forcibly displacing other categories internally or outside the national space under a variety of policies and legitimization exercises. While displacement took place under direct compulsion exerted by state authorities or because of conflict, forced migration for its part was usually the uncontrolled result of policies of political engineering or modernization, particularly mass migration from rural to urban areas. Other trends of emigration under various levels of constraint were the consequences of crises of the political system or political decisions taken by governments. This was the case with the departure of families who were members of the elite under the monarchy after the 1958 revolution. It was also the case with the economic migration of the middle class under the international embargo imposed on Iraq in 1991 as a result of the invasion of Kuwait, and, arguably, with the exodus of the Christians over the same period. Each of these emigrant groups were driven by a set of dynamics that cannot be reduced to their relations with the state, but in each instance, state policies were a determining factor that indirectly impacted their decision to leave Iraq.

Recasting displacement as a form of state control over population entails considering the phenomenon in correlation with policies restricting the mobility of people or forcing their emplacement and confinement in certain locations. Through systems of identification that formed the basis for practices of exclusion and inclusion, successive political powers have defined the boundaries of the nation and created different categories of subjects. These categories ranged from those fully admitted into the national body to those considered alien to it and susceptible to physical expulsion from the country. Several groups fell into intermediate categories: They were the primary targets of population engineering by the state, particularly mass relocation from one area to another inside the country or forced confinement. Some also ran the risk of being downgraded to non-nationals.[7] Furthermore, other types of manifestations of authoritarian governance have to be considered as regards the effects of state policies over human mobility, or as particular forms of exclusion from the allocation of economic resources under developmental regimes.

At another level, and more obliquely, practices of control over population movements represent an angle from which to understand the durability of violence as a means of exercising and accessing power. Examining the multiple effects of governmentality on human mobility and immobility allows a possible and more inclusive reading of the way in which certain practices of power and certain political identities have been historically encoded, leading to patterns of reproduction of violence.[8] Looking at the nexus between state policies and population movements/mobility has the potential to illuminate a series of extremely important historical phenomena in contemporary Iraq. On the one hand, it may help understand how, in the process of construction of a post-imperial, post-colonial, self-declared progressive and

---

[7]By degrees, during the last phases of the Anfal campaign, such sanctification of national identity and exclusionary policies laid the ground for justifying the mass physical elimination of those rural Kurds who resisted relocation from their villages in areas where Kurdish guerrillas were active (the so-called "prohibited areas"), and who did not register in the 1987 national census as residents of designated towns or residential complexes under government control. These Kurds lost their Iraqi citizenship and were presented by the official rhetoric not only as traitors and saboteurs, but also as having excluded themselves voluntary from the national ranks. Families of "unrepentant saboteurs" were physically removed from government-controlled areas and forced to join their kin in the prohibited areas. This mass deprivation of citizenship seems to have been a necessary step in convincing local commanders loyal to the central Iraqi regime to enforce a directive ordering armed forces to kill all living beings, human or animal, within the prohibited areas (see Human Rights Watch, 1993, Chapter 2).

[8]I draw theoretically on the concept of governmentality developed by the philosopher Michel Foucault and on the work of the political scientist John Torpey on the monopoly claimed by modern states on the legitimate means of circulation (Torpey, 1988; Caplan and Torpey, 2001).

developmentalist nation-state — where the public discourse of nationalism and modernization has generally dominated — a set of social, religious and cultural identities have continued to be primordialized and have acquired (or at least have not lost) political and conflictual dimensions. Furthermore, looking at the movements of population throughout the modern history of Iraq identifies some of the continuities that have existed in the exercise of power under successive regimes — monarchical, republican, military — all autocratic or authoritarian in varying degrees. Finally, an examination of control over population movements across time might reveal the sociological continuum that exists between states and would-be-states, that is the actors who project themselves from exile or from inside Iraq as potential states. Population movements should therefore be read as a factor structuring political identities and the reproduction of political violence.

One important premise guides my argument: The rejection of essentializing analyses of violence and political instability in Iraq as being embedded *intrinsically* in the fragmentary nature of the society as a consequence of supposedly incompatible religious, ethnic or tribal identities. These approaches are problematic from an epistemological as well as a moral point of view. Morally, they justify authoritarianism and state coercion[9] as necessary modes of governance to "hold together" groups between which no social contract is alleged to be possible. Alternatively, they have come to inspire the political project of territorial-based ethnic and confessional federalism promoted and implemented in post-Ba'thist Iraq at various times both by the US administration and by a number of local political actors. Epistemologically, I share the hypothesis put forth by several scholars of Iraq that political identities based on 'primordial' affiliations are largely historical constructs.[10] They have developed in a dialectical relation between state power (colonial rulers, Iraqi national governments, or governments of neighboring countries) and local leaderships: The latter have been cast by state rhetoric and actions as ethnic or religious leaders; at other times, ethnic or religious identity politics has proven more efficient to access resources and power. Note should also be taken of the works of scholars who have shown that this dynamic has coexisted with the development of other nonsectarian and nonethnic political ideologies, from pan-Arabist and communist to Iraqi

---

[9]I take coercion as a category of political violence exerted on populations by states or other political organisations (parties, militias, etc.).
[10]In particular, see Peter Harling's contribution to this volume.

nationalism.[11] Others have underlined one particularly striking feature of modern Iraq: the coexistence, within the authoritarian state, of modernization policies expressed through development projects and the allocation of resources.[12] What follows should be taken as a thesis in progress and a research agenda that offers hypotheses and tries to open up a number of conceptual pathways in the hope that some will be tested and others contested by scholars of contemporary Iraq.

Control over Mobility and Political Coercion

Although the volume of the various displacement episodes taking place in Iraq since the 1920s has been variable, one constant has been their collective nature: The displaced have been members of social groups identified by various political regimes as sharing an identity both cohesive and primordialized (ethnic, confessional, ethno-confessional, or ethno-national, but also based on kinship ties within a patriarchal system) deemed incompatible with and/or a threat to some notion of Iraqi national order. Several episodes have been massive, with people displaced by the tens and even hundreds of thousands. Others affected only members of the religious or political elites of specific groups. Displacement was induced directly by state policies of deportation usually following denial of citizenship or denationalization. This was the case as early as 1923, with a handful of prominent Shi'i clerics who were also political leaders opposed to the British mandate whose Iraqi nationality was contested or in some cases taken away by the government before they were deported to Iran (Nakash, 1994; Luizard, 1996). In the early years of the Ba'thist takeover, this line of thinking re-emerged with great vigor: The same accusations of collusion with Iran and betrayal of Iraqi national interests were made against Shi'is deemed of Iranian descent who were deported in very large numbers in the 1970s and 1980s (Nakash, 1994; Babakhan, 1994a). Through a series of discriminatory measures, executions, and accusations of Zionism, almost all the Jewish population of Iraq was obliged to relinquish Iraqi citizenship and emigrate between 1950 and the early 1970s (Shiblak, 1986). In all instances, it was in the name of defending Arab nationalism that numerically significant groups of the

---

[11]Especially Hanna Batatu (1978), Sami Zubaida (2003), and Eric Davis (2005).
[12]Such as, but not limited to, Marion Farouk-Sluglett and Peter Sluglett (1983), and Habib Ishow (1996).

population were denied national status and consequently expelled from the Iraqi national body.

Armed conflicts, domestic or international, have also provided direct or indirect inducements for forced population movements, especially those that erupted in connection with Kurdish and Assyrian nationalist claims as early as the 1930s. Kurdish displacement continued for decades, peaking in the 1980s during the eight-year war with Iran. Revolts against the Ba'thist regime, particularly the 1991 uprising in the South and North of the country, were other occasions for large-scale displacement inside Iraq or to neighboring countries (Yacoub, 1986; Babakhan, 1994a; Babakhan, 1994b; Fuccaro, 1997; Alborzi, 2006). Whereas some populations were forced out of specific spaces (rural, regional, or national), the Ba'thist regime in parallel pursued policies of population redistribution and demographic engineering combining the relocation of some ethnic groups (particularly the Kurds and the Turkmen) and importing Arabs, the so-called policy of Arabization of the oil-producing regions of Kirkuk and Mosul (Hilterman, 2007). Most of these displacements were linked to one another: The settlement of Arabs led to the displacement of Kurds and Turkmen through different administrative techniques entitling the former to food distribution, land and house ownership while depriving the others of those same entitlements (Romano, 2005).

In contrast with liberal states, successive Iraqi regimes have not enshrined the principle of the free circulation of their nationals in law. The granting of travel documents has been restricted from the time of the British mandate until the post-Ba'thist era under various types of legitimation and using various administrative practices. Under the Ba'th, passports were delivered on the basis of individual and family loyalty or at least individual compliance with the regime, while the post-2003 government introduced new control mechanisms on issuing passports shortly after it came to power.[13] In both cases, national security has been used as the principal justification for checking the political loyalties of those allowed mobility across borders. More recently, a new mechanism has been put in place to control the exit of nationals by proxy. At the request of the Iraqi government, Syria and Jordan, whose regulations had previously permitted the free entry of Iraqis, introduced visas in 2007. Those wanting to leave Iraq now have to undergo a double process of screening by the Iraqi authorities and those of Syria or

---

[13] Author's interviews with Iraqi migrants and refugees who left Iraq during the embargo and after the 2003 change of regime.

Jordan (Chatelard and Doraï, forthcoming). This is not to say that Iraqis have not been able to bypass the various control mechanisms imposed on their movements, in particular by resorting to irregular practices (bribes, forged documents, etc.) or by activating patronage ties. However this has financial and social costs that act as selection mechanisms in themselves on would-be migrants, including those fleeing violence (Chatelard, 2010).

Other types of mass population movements have been approached from the perspective of control over land ownership and production and the enhanced socio-economic role of the landlords. Alternatively, they have been analyzed from the perspective of social, economic, and political history. They can also be read more systematically as displacement phenomena resulting, often unintentionally, from the application of authoritarian policies in the rural areas. In successive historical periods, land or agricultural policies in rural Iraq have been motivated by a national political agenda. This was the case when the monarchy sought to reinforce the economic base and the allegiance to the regime of a Kurdish and Arab landowning elite (Farouk-Sluglett and Sluglett, 1983). After the 1958 military coup, the state's new agrarian policies were aimed at undermining the power of that elite and ensuring state control over land (Ishow, 1996). Although policies shifted radically between the monarchy and the various post-1958 regimes, the various land-tenure or agrarian reforms correlated directly with the massive migration (amounting to several millions) of peasants to urban centers, particularly Baghdad and Basra, between the late 1920s and the 1970s. This large-scale internal migration had long-term repercussions on the economic and socio-political fabric of the country. The concept of "development-induced displacement" might be adequate if it did not usually fail to qualify the context within which development decisions are taken, which usually served to conceal the inequalities of power and coercion mechanisms in society.

Highly authoritarian measures to maintain the rural labor-force in the countryside proved largely counter-productive. In order to contain the massive potential migration of impoverished peasants to the cities under the monarchy, a law was passed in 1933 (the Law Governing the Rights and Duties of Cultivators) about which Marion Farouk-Sluglett and Peter Sluglett wrote: "One of the most important features of the law was that *fallahin* indebted to the landowner were not permitted to leave his employment until the debts were paid off. As the vast majority were permanently indebted, the only way to break the circle was to run away from the land" (Farouk-Sluglett and Sluglett, 1983, p. 500). After 1958, the republican and military regimes attempted to nationalize arable lands within a socialist ideological frame, prioritizing state planning and the collectivization of the means of production, and later, at the time of the Iran–Iraq war, presiding over the (re)privatization of these state-owned lands to wealthy individuals (Ishow, 1996, p. 195). All these measures failed either to increase agricultural production substantially or to keep peasants in the countryside. The latter move, in correlation with the drafting of Iraqi men to be sent to the Iranian front, created the conditions for another massive population movement, the migration to Iraq of almost half a million Egyptian agricultural laborers (Ishow, 1996, p. 194).

Habib Ishow identifies the principle of state property over lands as bearing heavily upon the rural communities by legitimizing the *de jure* and *de facto* abuse of authority on the part of central governments (Ishow, 1996, p. 192). In addition to the poor performance of the agricultural sector and the creation of food insecurity, it resulted in the destruction of many rural communities and much of the tribal system. In the cities it brought about new class distinctions and new dynamics of economic, social and spatial marginalization and eventually mobilization and violent claims against the regime. The term *shruqi* became a stigmatizing social category originally used by Baghdadi urbanites to qualify the new migrants of rural background settled in slums on the periphery of the city, especially the area that became integrated into the urban fabric as a poor city neighborhood, called Madinat al-Thawra in 1958, then Madinat Saddam, and finally Madinat al-Sadr after the fall of the Baʻth. At this juncture, the term came to be used in a derogatory manner by those castigating poor militant Shiʻis. The further swelling of impoverished marginal neighborhoods in the cities of the South and center in the 1990s resulted also in part from state policies depriving noncompliant social groups of access to vital resources. The draining of the marshes in the early 1990s led to the destruction of the habitat and livelihoods of a marginal rural Shiʻi population that had largely managed to evade the control of the regime. The number of *shruqi*-s kept growing in the cities and, at least in the imagination of those who have been casting them as barbarian Others, now form the majority of the recruits of the Jaysh al-Mahdi militia, one of the would-be-state organizations that carried out new forms of violence and sectarian cleansing in several major urban centers between 2006 and 2008.

In combination with control over the international movement of nationals, various legal or administrative measures have aimed at confining populations to specific spaces inside Iraq. This was the case with the settlement policies of tribespeople on agricultural estates owned by landlords and control of the crossborder movement of Bedouin tribes aiming at settling populations, containing them within national boundaries and making them obedient and productive subjects (Toth, 2006, p. 70). Already under the monarchy, civil status registration in one's place of residence was used as a means of population control and of coercing peasants to remain as debt-bonded laborers on the landowners' estates (Ishow, 1996, p. 118). Here again, fugitives to the cities tried to escape coercion by avoiding registration. The system remained in place throughout subsequent decades until the food distribution system introduced during the Iran–Iraq war, which was maintained in place during the economic embargo starting in 1991, became a more effective tool of population surveillance and control since ration cards had to be renewed annually and change of residence without re-registration would entail the loss of entitlements (von Sponeck, 2006, p. 35). The vast number of fugitives and displaced during the last period of Ba'thist rule were *de facto* deprived of access to important food resources. In other instances, the confiscation of ration cards was used by the government's coercive apparatus as a means of forcing people to move. The ration card system, which has remained in place under the post-Ba'thist regime, continues to be used by various authorities as a means of inducing people either to move or to remain where they are. More than in the past, the cards have become a tool of population engineering, ensuring the ethnic, sectarian or tribal homogeneity of entire areas, and the forming of electoral constituencies now that the same system serves as the basis for voter registration. The situation of those displaced in the previous period or under the new regime, the so-called IDPs, is critical in this regard (Romano, 2005, p. 438). Today, a number of other administrative measures imposed by the central government as well as by the Kurdish Regional Government (KRG) impede mobility between areas inside the country: In addition to ration cards that cannot be easily transferred between administrative areas, non-Kurdish Iraqis residing in the centre or south of the country who want to enter the Kurdish autonomous region must find a legal guarantor who is a civil servant in the administration of the KRG.

The modalities of repression via state or other control over the mobility of political opponents have varied, and have been devised in relation to the way regimes have qualified the nature of oppositions, rather than in relation to the way these oppositions have expressed and identified themselves. On the one hand, the various regimes have constantly tried to "purify" Iraq from those recalcitrant social elements whose ethnic or confessional identities were considered part of non-Iraqi or non-Arab identities (such as

Assyrian, Jews, Iranian, Kurds, or Turkmen). However, even between categories of non-Arabs, the political grammar of Arabism in Iraq has operated a distinction between the Jew/Zionist, and Kurdish or Persian/Iranian. Since the creation of the state of Israel, the former has implied an absolute disqualification and separation from Arabism, whereas the latter two have generally been allowed certain forms of inclusion. On the other hand, regimes have tried to discipline and punish oppositions within the national space expressed in the idioms of nationalist or internationalist political ideologies (Communism, pan-Arabism, Syrian Ba'thist in particular) that are generally not totally incompatible with the versions of Arabism sponsored by Iraqi governments.

Political repression was translated into various modes of control over mobility, from expulsion and deportation to confinement — including house arrest and incarceration. In all cases, however, this control represented one particular form of coercion accompanied by other forms of violence, including the physical elimination of individuals as members of social groups redefined as political groups. All possible manner of violence was applied, ranging from torture and individual executions, to collective assassinations and mass killings. In several instances, mass crimes, in particular against the Kurds (Babakhan, 1994b; Hilterman, 2007), also caused large-scale displacement inside or outside the country. In other instances, the deliberate deprivation of access to resources vital for the security of individuals (land, water, food, shelter, access to employment in the public sector, citizenship) compelled large numbers of the categories targeted to migrate to other areas where alternative resources or security were available. Finally, individuals have sought to protect themselves from coercion by withdrawing within infra-state social units (whether religious community, tribe, family, domestic space), not necessarily implying physical but social, symbolic, and psychological displacement (Bozarslan, 2003, p. 32).

Under all the different political regimes in Iraq, and in various ways, the state has placed entire categories of the population in situations of great insecurity through actions in different spheres (legal, administrative, economic, political, security, military etc.) but whose commonality is that they were expressions of a sovereignty that did not seek legitimation through the rule of law, universal suffrage or the people's exercise of democratic choice. For the individuals or the groups targeted by coercion, spatial mobility has represented an answer, reactive or planned, to recover security, inviting in turn new responses from the state in its aim to maintain control over individuals and populations.

A vast research agenda can be envisaged that would allow the identification of the trajectories of the changes — emergence, amplifications, or decline — in coercive practices and methods. A major question is the recurrence of several of these practices under different political regimes, a phenomenon that calls for interrogating how various security agencies have endowed coercive practices with different meanings and have embedded them in difference systems of legitimation. New ideological frames of reference, new emergencies, new historical contingencies, have all provided new interpretive frameworks and vocabularies justifying coercion and the control of mobility, and new types of social group to whom to apply this control. The content and meaning of such notions as treason and enmity in particular have shifted over time. This leads to questioning the production of discourse and symbols by state authorities, along the lines of Eric Davis' work (2005) on historical memory and authoritarian rule under the Ba'th. While expanding an examination of official narratives and representations to the monarchy, republican and post-Ba'thist periods, there should be a particular focus on the elaboration and dissemination of discourses justifying control over population movements: Imaginations of the nation and of the threats allegedly bearing down upon it, territorial borders and internal social and spatial boundaries, security and protection, enmity and treason, and images and sources of inspiration regarding sovereignty and its performance are all themes that should be traced, unpacked and studied in connection with the power practices they justified.

Other items on a research agenda would be the structures put in place for the identification and categorization of individuals necessary to control their mobility. Here again, time frames should be delineated and their coincidence with ruptures in political history should be verified. The example of the food distribution system that has been carried over from the Ba'thist to the post-Ba'thist era is a case in point. Another one is the mention of religious or tribal affiliation on identity cards: In which contexts were various items and categories introduced or removed? Still another one is the presence or absence in censuses of questions on ethno-national affiliation, particularly Turkish (for the Turkmen) or Kurdish and the implications for individuals of registering as such.[14] One objective would be to identify spheres of action

---

[14]It is unclear from the literature when and in which regions certain categories were used, and also if published census results reflected the questions asked when the censuses were actually taken. For Kurds in the 1987 census, see Human Rights Watch (1993) and also Michiel Leezenberg (1997) for the case of the Shabak, a small syncretistic religious

(legal or administrative), methods or techniques (such as censuses), and technologies (such as statistics or computerization) that have been used by successive regimes and non-state political actors today to objectify individuals through practices of identification and identity categories, in particular as members of a biological group (the patriarchal family, the tribe) or of a community (an ethnicity, a religious group, a national body).

A rich area of research concerns the actors who imagined and developed the categories of identification together with policies and measures of confinement, exclusion or expulsion. What are their backgrounds? What were their models, their inspirations at difference periods? How was the Indian colonial model adapted to the Iraqi theater by the mandate administration and how was it contested or implemented by high-level civil servants under the monarchy? Similar questions could be asked about the adoption of a Stalinist model by Saddam Husayn, and an Israeli model for the US occupying power. What models do today's militias use to categorize individuals and to operate ethnic or sectarian cleansing? What about the KRG? An as a corollary, how have individuals strived to evade the stigmas attached to certain identifications and the resulting threats to their security? Identity concealment, formal religious conversion (empirical evidence suggests that both were adopted by a number of Iraqi Jews in order to remain in Iraq), the recourse to patronage in rural and urban contexts, attempts to secure alternative identity documents by bribing civil servants or acquiring them on the false identity market, as well as migration itself, have all been strategies to evade the ascriptive dimension of identity categorization and its effects.

Political Migration and the Reversal of Violence

Especially since the revolution that overthrew the monarchy in 1958, a considerable number of Iraqis have attempted to escape direct political repression or limitations on their individual freedom by leaving the country. This politically motivated emigration, in conjunction with successive waves of displacement resulting from violence and conflict, has led to the formation of sizable exile communities of Iraqis in several Middle Eastern countries (Iran, Saudi Arabia and the Gulf, Jordan, Syria, Yemen and, to a

---

community in Northern Iraq, who were displaced as a result of their being registered as Kurds.

lesser extent, Turkey) and beyond (Great Britain and a number of other Western European states, the countries of the former Eastern bloc, the USA, Canada, Australia etc.) (Cigerli, 1998; Al-Rasheed, 1998; Vanly, 2002; Fattah, 2007; Shoeb *et al.*, 2007; Chatelard, 2010). At times, these "exits" from the national and political space have taken place despite measures put in place by the state security apparatus to control the movements of opponents beyond national boundaries. At other times, they have been the result of deportations carried out by the state authorities.

From a historical perspective, spatial mobility cannot be considered anomalous in the Middle East (Shami, 1996; Chatty, 2010). In the Iraqi context in particular, the Ottoman legacy calls for a re-examination in relation to more recent trends of emigration. Modern Iraqi society inherited from the Ottoman era vast and complex social networks based on the free circulation of people, goods, money, and ideas extending far beyond what became the frontier of the modern state. Pastoral herders, tribal leaders, traders, Shi'i pilgrims, religious students or clerics, members of Sunni Sufi orders, Kurdish nationalist elites, members of extended families and of certain ethnic or ethno-religious communities (Assyrians and Chaldeans, Turkmen etc.), those influenced by Turkish and Iranian intellectual movements, activists in modern political parties (like the Syrian Ba'th) etc., have all circulated within and exchanged across ecological, social, religious, political and economic spaces whose boundaries did not necessarily coincide with those of states. People of all social classes and ethnicities have therefore been mobile and, for those who were not, their social world was shaped and influenced by the mobility of others who belonged to their tribal, familial, intellectual, political or religious group. Territoriality and identity as defined by the practices and subjectivities of these social groups have differed markedly from those defined by the national order that colonial and post-colonial states have striven to create and secure. Places of deportation or emigration outside Iraq can therefore at times be conceptualized as spaces of belonging and familiarity rather than spaces of exile and alienation, especially if they provide security and access to material, social and/or symbolic resources.

As for political migration, its "identity cycle" in space and time and within changing political and ideological contexts should be considered to understand how particular identities, claimed or ascribed in Iraq, have been maintained or reshaped in migration and mobilized to contest regimes in power in Iraq and, eventually, to take power through violence. How has the context of the countries of emigration provided the resources to claim political power in Iraq? In which rhetoric have these claims been voiced: As victims, minorities, as pan-Arabists, pan-Turkists, as Assyrian or Kurdish nationalists, as communists, internationalists, revolutionaries, in the vocabulary of political Islam, in sectarian terms etc.? What types of mobilizations have been available (armed, militant, diplomatic, intellectual etc.)? A particularly important question to be asked is why, unlike the nationalist momentum of the 1970s — early 1990s within the Palestinian refugee diaspora which was similarly scattered between several countries and split into numerous political currents, Iraqi political exiles and refugees did not develop a largely unified discourse and practices of resistance. What historical factors and local dynamics have maintained the fragmentation of the discourse, of the actions and of the identities of Iraqi exiles?

Together with the above, another set of questions regards the production of antagonistic group memories as victims of competing visions of an Iraqi political project. What are the experiences and idealized frames of reference that have come to shape the collective imaginations of the exiles? How have those who have escaped violence through emigration integrated into their subjectivities and projects the experiences of those members of their groups who have suffered torture, assassination, displacement etc.? What role do the ideas of return and revenge play in these imaginations and projects?

When the international balance of power allowed political groups from the diaspora to participate on the Iraqi national stage in 2003, violence was first turned against the individuals who had contributed to the maintenance of the Ba'thist regime. Eventually violence was also aimed at a whole series of social groups, negating their right of existence in a unified political community on the basis of their "difference". The theme of "insiders" versus "outsiders", of exile and return, initially restructured the political arena and that of violence. However, the process of "othering" shifted quickly to take on sectarian overtones. The groups and factions competing for power in the new Iraqi political order took over the monopoly of the exercise of violence (Al-Rachid and Méténier, 2007, p. 115) and also appropriated another former monopoly of the Ba'thist state: The means and modalities of control over population movements. In the last few years, a multiplicity of collective actors has directed violence against the confessional, ethnic and class composition of entire urban and rural areas, displacing populations inside and outside the country, and forcing others to be immobilized. Many members of the Ba'thist political, military and bureaucratic elite have been compelled to emigrate, mostly to other Arab countries, from where some have attempted to mobilize resources to support the resistance undertaken by neo-Ba'thist insurgents inside Iraq. Violence and vexations exerted against secular intellectuals and members of certain professional groups, and against women who refuse to conform to norms of public behavior deemed Islamic have all been incitements to remain within restricted domestic or social spaces or, conversely, to leave Iraq for neighboring countries or the West, or to take refuge in the "pacified" Kurdish autonomous region. Iraq today is characterized by an uneven socio-spatial distribution of human security: Human mobility is restricted due to the fragmentation of the Iraqi national space into sub-units under different kinds of sovereignty, and to the insecurity attached to the expression or presumption of certain group identities in specific areas. On the one hand, the sorting out of population on ethnic, communal and class grounds is outliving the rule of the militias and other armed groups who initiated the process. Relative social homogeneity is now maintained through other economic and psychological mechanisms (such as livelihoods found in new areas of residence, the fear of moving back to former neighborhoods, internalization of the ethno-sectarian territorial divide etc.) and, arguably, due to government policies to maintain displaced populations in the areas to which they have been directed or displaced. On the other hand, the Iraqi government and the occupation forces have developed measures to contain population movements between neighborhoods and regions (security barriers and walls, check-points, registration systems etc.) while exit from central and southern Iraq towards the Kurdish north or neighboring countries is impeded in various ways both by the Iraqi authorities and by those of neighboring political entities. This is despite the fact that the uneven socio-spatial distribution of security inside Iraq still makes mobility a security strategy for many individuals and collectivities.

One possible reading of the reluctance of Premier Nuri al-Maliki and most members of his government — the majority of whom lived in exile in Iran, Syria and elsewhere, some of them since as long ago as the 1970s — to take any meaningful step towards engaging with those who have taken refuge abroad since 2003 is their belief that forced exile is a deserved punishment or, alternatively, that refugees are traitors who refuse to adhere to the political project of the so-called new Iraq.[15] In this conceptualization, those newly exiled are paying the price for having caused — if only by having failed to be sufficiently active in their opposition to Saddam Husayn — the exile

---

[15] Several public statements by members of the Maliki government support this conclusion.

of those who are in power today. Similar remarks can be made regarding practices on the ground and official policies aimed at reversing the demographic balance that resulted from the Arabization campaign in the areas disputed between the KRG and the Baghdad government. For the political leadership, in Baghdad as well as in the KRG, "a displacement for a displacement" is therefore a just form of retribution in a vision of justice where the punishment of the perpetrators must somehow equate to the wrong they have committed, but also where whole social groups can be made responsible for the doings of one or some of their members. Whatever the cultural (some would say tribal and Islamic) legitimation of this juridical ethos, it is a matter of particular concern that far from trying to playing a mediating role by sponsoring processes of reconciliation between different groups and generations of exiled and internally displaced persons, the new Iraqi authorities are themselves partisan actors justifying, if not actively promoting, revenge through involuntary migration. Let us note here that although the Iraqi state today is no longer the proximate cause of forced migration, there is a remarkable continuity in the conception of retributive justice and the moral economy of displacement shared by the ruling elites.

Many of those working in humanitarian organizations wonder about the possible return of recent exiles said to belong in their vast majority to the educated and secular middle class. Others have discussed the effects of the most recent brain drain that entails loss of competence and human capital but also jeopardizes the bases on which a pluralistic civil society might be constructed in the new Iraq.[16] Might the current ruling powers be convinced by these arguments and finally pursue a pro-active policy to regain the confidence of the exiles and promote their return? Or rather, might we see a repetition of the period between the 1950s and the 1980s when the economic void created by the involuntary emigration of Jews, Fa'ili Kurds and other Shi'is — who also formed a large part of the economic, professional, and intellectual elite — was rapidly filled by an emerging middle class trained and employed in government institutions, who became the new clients of the state? Several testimonies from recent exiles who have tried to regain their positions as civil servants point to the fact that posts have been filled by a new generation of graduates whose allegiance to one or the other faction in the new government is assured, and who are overwhelmingly

---

[16]See Joseph Sassoon's contribution to this volume.

Shi'is, many from lower middle class backgrounds.[17] The vast program of 10,000 scholarships launched by Premier al-Maliki to support the education of postgraduates in all disciplines in the best foreign universities is also already starting to produce a new cohort that is taking over from those who have fled the country. The socio-economic background, sectarian affiliation and political leaning of the majority of the grantees are anyone's guess.

In this context, despite the radical rupture in the Iraqi political order in 2003, the continuities with previous periods need to be highlighted. This item on a research agenda centered on the nexus between violence, human mobility and identity politics will require in depth exploration of the actors who have redistributed between themselves the means of control over population movements, their modalities of action, and the effects of the latter on individual experiences of violence and collective identities. In post-Ba'thist Iraq, notions of territoriality and sovereignty have been profoundly altered. The state lost, and is trying to regain, the monopoly over coercive violence and over its technologies. It also lost the monopoly over the symbolic resources needed to exert and legitimize this violence. How the relations between violence and population movements are being reconfigured today is a crucial question.

What therefore could be concluded from a systematic study of the politics of population movements is that, beyond the numerous and brutal ruptures in Iraqi political history, governmentality in modern Iraq can be analyzed along the paradigms of the developmental and the authoritarian state. Both models are adopted concomitantly by ruling powers to exert their sovereignty over population by sorting out individuals along naturalized identity categories, each the object of different treatment. In modern Iraq, it is the state (and would-be states) which appears as the principal instrument of the fragmentation of the social and the political by categorizing people not as individual citizens but as members of quasi-biologized collectivities. The result is that Iraqis today do not see themselves as citizens, but as members of particular social groups that have been victimized by one or (several) other groups. Many, including those at the highest levels of the political apparatus, are locked in mindsets and imaginations that make them incapable of reversing patterns of social fragmentation and political violence, of which displacement and forced migration are only some of the negative consequences.

---

[17] Author's interviews with Iraqis in Amman and Damascus in 2009–2010.

THE BRAIN DRAIN IN IRAQ AFTER THE 2003 INVASION

Joseph Sassoon

In the aftermath of the 1968 *coup d'état* that brought Saddam and the Ba'th party to power, an initial brain drain began. During the 1970s and 1980s, the government began to focus on attracting Iraqis back, and incentives were introduced to revive the private sector of the economy. Emphasis was placed on improving education, and laws were passed to enhance women's rights and encourage them to study. The urban professional middle class was growing. But after the 1991 Gulf War, which had come so soon after the 1980–1988 Iran-Iraq war, a second wave of Iraqis began to leave as they realized that with two wars almost back-to-back, the opportunities for professionals would dwindle dramatically. The fabric of Iraqi society began to unravel during the 1990s, aggravated by hyperinflation and the collapse of the Iraqi dinar. This was truly the beginning of the demise of the middle class. By the time of the 2003 invasion, estimates of Iraqi exiles ranged from two to four million people. Whatever the statistics are, there is no doubt that Iraq under Saddam had suffered an enormous brain drain, with many exiles settling in Arab countries and the West.

The US Invasion and its Aftermath

In 2003, after two wars, many years of sanctions and the increasing economic autonomy of Kurdistan, the Iraqi economy was highly fragmented and there was little in the way of a national macroeconomic policy. Iraq had faced one economic and political crisis after another since 1980, and "normal" circumstances did not exist. The country's dependence on its relatively huge oil revenues since the early 1950s culminating in the late 1970s and early

379

1980s turned Iraq into a classic case of rentierism.[1] Thus Iraq's economy was severely weakened in every area; foreign reserves were depleted, development planning had virtually ceased, the infrastructure was severely damaged and the vast majority of the population was impoverished.[2] In spite of the shattered economy and weak institutional organization, the Iraqi state functioned and essential services were provided to the population. However, with the fall of Baghdad, the state collapsed and there was nothing to take its place. All the government's ministers, deputy ministers and thousands of top Ba'thists had fled the country.[3] The US Office of Reconstruction and Humanitarian Assistance (ORHA) set up only seven weeks before the war under General Jay Garner to "manage" Iraq after the war, was not intended to fill the gap; its involvement in running the country and its economy was rudimentary, since its emphasis was to be on refugee work and oil field repair. As it happened, there was neither a refugee problem nor oil field fires. In other words, ORHA's planning for the post-war period was based on a set of assumptions that proved to be wrong (Phillips, 2005, p. 131). Garner himself admitted to Congress that "this is an ad hoc operation, glued together over about four or five weeks' time", and added that his team "did not really have enough time to plan".[4]

The dire economic situation was further exacerbated by massive looting that took place throughout the country. In effect, 17 out of 23 ministry buildings were destroyed and looters dismantled the electricity grid, thus creating power shortages (Phillips, 2005, pp. 134–135). There is no doubt that the looting also had a devastating effect on the post-war administration. American officials estimated the cost of looting in the early weeks after the end of the war to be around $12 billion (Packer, 2005, p. 139).

As violence spread in Iraq and ethnic cleansing began in earnest following the Samarra' bombing of February 2006, the emigration of highly skilled Iraqis intensified. Apart from insecurity and violence, a combination of other factors led to new waves of brain drain: Low levels of services (electricity,

---

[1]For a detailed analysis of rentierism in Iraq, see al-Khafaji, 2003: 77–92.

[2]For a review of the impact of wars and sanctions, see Alnasrawi, 2002b: 343–348.

[3]Within a week of his arrival, the American administrator in charge of overseeing the Coalition Provisional Authority (CPA) issued the decree mandating de-Ba'thification. Overnight, almost 30,000 Iraqis were dismissed from their job (see the papers of Peter Harling and Fanny Lafourcade). For Bremer's point of view, see Bremer, 2006: 39–42, 343–344.

[4]Schmidt, E and DE Sanger. "Reconstruction Policy: Looting Disrupts Detailed US Plan to Restore Iraq". *The New York Times*, May 19, 2003.

water, sewage, etc.); high levels of unemployment and inflation; and pervasive corruption (Merza, 2007, p. 173). The internal displacement in which more than 2.7 million lost their homes created another "push" factor for the brain drain.

Academics and doctors who were, even remotely, associated with the Ba'th party were targeted. The scope of the targeting soon expanded and a combination of militias and criminal gangs began killing or kidnapping professionals and their families. In addition, in spite of the large numbers of professionals who left Iraq the opportunities for those who stayed behind were rather slim, forcing many to move to the calmer region of Kurdistan in search of better opportunities.

As of 2008, estimates for unemployment ranged from 25% to 40%, which even at the lower rate is socially and economically destabilizing.[5] Employment (or lack of it) continues to be a serious problem for Iraq. Under Saddam's regime, employment was a political tool and after 2003 continued to be so: Herring and Rangwala have referred to "employment brokerage" by the different political parties (Herring and Rangwala, 2006, p. 131).

Bremer's dissolution of the Iraqi Army, which had employed between 400,000 and 500,000 people (some 7% of the labor force), coupled with de-Ba'thification, added something like 8–10% to unemployment, especially among Sunnis. High rates of unemployment damaged the social fabric by depriving families of economic security. The unemployment crisis also threatened the gains that had been made by women in Iraq during the 1960s and the following two decades. Unemployment among women was estimated at 70% in 2004, and professional females have been obliged to seek employment as housekeepers and in other domestic work (WILPF, 2006).

What is important from the point of view of brain drain is the unemployment among the highly skilled. A survey conducted in 2004 by the United Nations Development Program (UNDP) and the Iraqi Ministry of Planning showed that unemployment reached an astonishing 37.2% among young men with secondary or higher education (UNDP, 2005, p. 133). Iraqi economists have been warning that unemployment is a time bomb and that the major reason for its spread is the "impairment of the economic basis" of the country following the invasion.[6]

---

[5]The Brookings Institution, *Iraq Index*, 31 March 2008. Online. Available HTTP: <www.brookings.edu/saban/iraq-index.aspx> (accessed 16 February 2009).
[6]*al-Hayat*, 23 July 2004.

Another economic problem contributing to the exodus of professionals was inflation. Again, this problem has been recurrent in Iraq. As a result of the invasion of Kuwait and the UN sanctions, hyperinflation became a structural problem (Alnasrawi, 2002a, p. 104). Consequently, people were forced to liquidate their assets and huge disparities in income between the rich and the poor were created (al-Shabibi, 2002, pp. 24–25). This signaled the weakening of the middle class, which gathered momentum after the 2003 invasion.

After the collapse of Saddam's regime inflation stabilized at around 32% to 34% per annum. However, inflation began to rise sharply in late 2005 due to increased violence, the fallout from state control, corruption, higher wages, the increased cost of house rentals, and the rise of fuel prices.[7] Supply shortages and the weakness of the distribution system exacerbated the problem (Merza, 2008, pp. 8–9).

In addition to the economic problems that plagued the country, corruption has become endemic. Corruption was prevalent during Saddam's time, but after the invasion it became integral to the way the government ran the country. Nuri al-Maliki's government has been systematically dismissing the oversight officials who were installed to fight corruption in Iraqi ministries.[8] Corruption can be identified in four major areas: Oil production, public contracts, government services and employment (Merza, 2007, pp. 22–23). The last three have a direct impact on the brain drain.

Hence, corruption and wasteful reconstruction efforts have dominated the management of Iraq's economy since 2003. Five years after the war, and with $117 billion spent on reconstruction, the rebuilding effort had achieved little more than restoring what was destroyed during the invasion and the looting that followed.[9]

The Spread of Violence

As the country plunged into a state of violence, and economic problems mounted by the day, targeted attacks on academics gathered momentum in 2006 as part of the more general spread of violence. The dividing lines

---

[7] *al-Zaman*, 20 November 2006.

[8] *The New York Times*, 18 November 2008.

[9] See the history of the American-led reconstruction of Iraq: Office of the Special Inspector General for Iraq Reconstruction, "Hard Lessons: The Iraq Reconstruction Experience," February 2009. A draft appeared in *The New York Times*, 14 December 2008.

between insurgency and mafia-style gangs became blurred. For example, some kidnappings were sectarian, while others were carried out purely for ransom. The gangs believed professionals were an excellent target due to their position in society and their potential earning power. In January 2004, there were about two kidnappings per day in Baghdad, but by mid-2006 the number had risen to 30 (al-Khalidi, Hoffman and Tanner, 2007, p. 7). Iraq became a "killing field" for academics.

Although there are no accurate statistics on the number of Iraqi academics and doctors who fled the country, one rough estimate suggested that 1,500 Iraqi academics are living in Syria, Jordan, and Egypt. Presumably a number have also gone further afield. Estimates of the number of doctors who have left Iraq since 2003 vary widely, from 3,000 to 17,000. What is clear, however, is that Iraq lost a large percentage of its medical specialists (some say 70%) and probably 25–35% of its overall medical staff. These are massive numbers, especially since the majority of this exodus took place over just 18 months.

Data on academics and professionals who were assassinated are more accurate. The Brussels Tribunal compiled a list of 350 names of professionals (the vast majority being PhD holders) who were murdered.[10] The Iraqi Lawyers Association published a list of 210 lawyers and judges killed since the invasion and said that the number of lawyers in Iraq had decreased by 40%.[11] Thus hundreds of Iraq's finest minds were left with no option but to flee the engulfing flames of sectarian hatred and pervasive violence that dominated every aspect of life and threatened themselves and their families. It should be pointed out that another reason for the exodus of skilled professionals is the encroachment of religion and the Shi'i militias into day-to-day academic life, which makes it impossible to write freely or express secular or opposing views.

The implications for Iraq of this brain drain are extensive and far-reaching. However, there are three significant areas where it has been felt particularly deeply — economy, health, and education. The emigration of professionals has constrained the ability of the civil service to execute and plan the policies needed for the revival of the Iraqi economy. In the health and educational sectors, the *crème de la crème* of their cadres has been lost, thus leaving a huge hole.

---

[10] See: <www.Brusselstribunal.org/academicsList.htm> (accessed 16 February 2009).

[11] *Integrated Regional Information Networks (IRIN)*, "Iraq: Justice delayed as lawyers live under threat," 30 April 2007.

With regard to management skills, a report by the US Government Accountability Office (GAO) concluded that "the central ministries had spent only 4.4% of their investment budget, as of August 2007". GAO attributed this, *inter alia*, to the fact that recent refugee outflows and de-Ba'thification had reduced the number of skilled workers (GAO, 2008).

The impact of the brain drain on the health sector was severe. Doctors and medical workers were specifically targeted. Unlike Saddam's era when doctors left Iraq because they were individual victims of the regime, in post-2003 Iraq doctors became a target as a group. They were kidnapped for ransom and were tortured and killed to disrupt the basics of civil society. As they had to move around in public in and out of clinics and hospitals, they became an easy and soft target for their attackers. Nurses were also a target: Between 2003 and at the end of 2006, it was estimated that 160 had been murdered and more than 400 wounded.[12]

According to one estimate, 23% of all academics murdered in Iraq were doctors, 90% of whom were medical doctors, 6% veterinary surgeons, 2% dentists and 2% pharmacists. Almost 50% of those murdered were specialists, 14% being surgeons. The vast majority (98%) were Muslims (no identification of Sunni or Shi'i but one could assume a high percentage of the former) from the Baghdad region.[13]

As mentioned before, there are no official or accurate statistics about the number of doctors who left the country. Whatever the number of those who left and those who are still working, two points are clear: First, Iraq lost thousands of its physicians and with them the country lost a wealth of experience. Second, Iraq's health system has crumbled, and the health conditions (physical and mental) of Iraqis have deteriorated dramatically in the five-year period following the invasion.

The implications of this brain drain for all patients in Iraq were severe. Two Iraqi doctors from Diwaniya and Kufa colleges of medicine wrote in the *British Medical Journal* that:

> Medical staff working in emergency departments admit that more than half of those killed could have been saved if trained and experienced staff were available. Our experience has taught us that poor emergency medicine services are more disastrous than the disaster itself (Al-Sheibani, Hadi and Hasoon, 2006, p. 847).

---

[12] *IRIN*, "Iraq: Neglected nurses fight their own war," 19 November 2006.
[13] Jalili, I., "Plight of Iraqi Academics," presentation to the Madrid International Conference on the Assassinations of Iraqi Academics, 23–24 April 2006. The data was updated by Dr Jalili in May 2006. See: <www.iraqis.org.uk/contents> (accessed 16 February 2009).

The Iraqi health system was no longer able to give proper care to victims of violence, particularly those with severe burns or in need of prosthetic surgery.

As for education, the quality of higher education and research has been steadily deteriorating since the late 1980s. The real decline was in the 1990s during a major brain drain; in addition the research community suffered from being totally isolated from the international academic community.

Thus it is important to keep in mind that Iraq's higher education has been on a slippery slope since the early 1990s. In the immediate aftermath of the 2003 invasion, universities were among the first institutions to face looting. By summer 2003, almost none had escaped: From the veterinary college in Abu Ghraib that lost all its equipment to the faculty of education in Waziriya, a suburb of Baghdad, which was raided daily for two weeks (Munthe, 2003). Two years after the end of Saddam's regime, a report by the United Nations University stated that 84% of Iraq's higher education institutions had been burnt, looted or destroyed. According to the report, the infrastructure that survived mostly had unreliable water or electricity supplies, was badly equipped and lacked computer facilities. Overall, the teaching staff was under-qualified; 33% held only Bachelor degrees despite rules requiring a minimum of a Master degree, 30% held Master degrees and only 28% of the teaching staff had PhDs (UNU, 2005). Students complained that Iraq's university system had significantly declined, dragged down by chronic cancellations of lectures and decrepit equipment.[14]

At the same time, the atmosphere of terror and violence began dominating the campuses and the day-to-day lives of all academics. Like the doctors, lecturers and university staff were being targeted. Scores of Iraq's best minds were exiting the country, running away not just from the violence but from the creeping control of the religious parties, through their militias, over the lives of the universities. In Basra, the militias forced segregation between males and females in classes. As a result, many academics fled to Northern Iraq, and Kurdistan is providing a haven for them. According to the Kurdish Regional Government's figures, about 1,900 university lecturers from outside Kurdistan have joined universities in the Kurdish area, and more than 3,700 students from Baghdad and Mosul study in Kurdish universities.[15]

---

[14]Cave, D. "Cheated of Future, Iraqi Graduates want to Flee." *The New York Times,* 4 June 2007.

[15]Kurdish Regional Government (KRG), 20 November 2008. See: www.krg.org.

The Loss of the Middle Class

Can Iraq's brain drain be reversed, how does it compare with the experiences of other countries, and what are the long-term implications for the country? As has been mentioned, such brain drains are observable in several other places in the world. In Iraq, however, it took place over a relatively short time span (2006–2007) and, unlike some other countries, Iraq is not being compensated for the loss of its human capital by the exiles' remittances. This is a critical point when one looks, for example, at the brain drain from Lebanon, Egypt or India. In many countries remittances are an important source of foreign exchange for the country and income to their families at home.[16] Very few Iraqis are working abroad and earning enough to remit back a portion of their income. On the contrary, there has been a process of reverse remittance, whereby refugees rely on their own savings in Iraq or remittances from their families to support them because of the lack of employment opportunities in the host countries.

With its loss of human capital, Iraq lost its middle class. Two economists who researched the middle class have reached the conclusion that the middle class is the driver of democratization and has a crucial role in consolidating democracy (Acemoğlu and Robinson, 2006, pp. 38–43). After the invasion and the violence, the weakness of Iraq's middle class meant that its private sector also faltered. Hampered by a decimated infrastructure, the lack of foreign investment and a flood of imports that undercut local businesses, the private sector has failed to flourish. US efforts to develop the sector did not materialize and the Iraqi government "has been sustaining the economy in the way it always has: by putting citizens on its payroll".[17]

The USA, which invaded Iraq to create democracy, did not take enough steps to protect and expand the middle class, thus losing the major contributor to, and beneficiary of, a democratic state. In fact, it is interesting to note that while the US media highlights the number of casualties among US troops, it rarely mentions the number of Iraqis killed or maimed, except for occasional reports of death tolls as a result of large scale attacks. "Rarely, if ever, do they mention such disparate issues as the massive brain drain that has taken place in Iraq, the staggeringly high

---

[16]In 2006, migrants from poor countries worldwide sent home $300 billion, about three times the world's foreign aid budgets combined. See Deparle, J. "Western Union as a player in immigration debates". *International Herald Tribune*, 22 November 2007.

[17] *The New York Times*, 11 August 2008.

unemployment rates, or the growing destitution of Iraqi refugees in Syria."
(Ferris, 2008, p. ix).

One final aspect in considering the brain drain is to examine the reactions
of the Iraqi government to this crisis. A tragic but critical point from the
end of the 2003 war is that the Iraqi authorities are reluctant to recognize
and admit that there is indeed a humanitarian crisis, and do so only under
pressure from international organizations and media.[18] Even in September
2007, *al-Zaman* newspaper accused the government of being "in total denial
about the daily killings, the uprooting of millions of Iraqis [...] and even
the imminent imploding of a whole nation."[19]

If violence comes to a halt or ebbs, would these professionals return to
their country? It seems very doubtful that many of those who have managed
to get to the West (top specialists and members of the different minorities)
will return to Iraq. Research done worldwide indicates clearly that only a
relatively small percentage of educated skilled professionals return to their
home countries, even when political and economic conditions ameliorate.
Also, the longer these professionals stay abroad, the less likely they are to
return to their home countries.[20] The difference in Iraq's case is that some
of the academics and doctors have been unable to find suitable jobs in their
host countries — a situation defined by economists as brain waste (Özden
and Schiff, 2006, pp. 227–244) — particularly in Syria and Jordan. As many
of those professionals have not managed to get jobs that meet their qualifications, a large number feel frustrated with their professional life. But even
for them, a number of basic conditions would have to be in place before large
numbers head home. Apart from the reduction or cessation of violence, ethnicity and sectarianism have to retreat significantly from daily life. Those in
exile will consider employment opportunities and would need to be confident
that jobs and opportunities would be given on merit rather than according to
affiliation to the right party and clan. Other considerations would be access
to essential services (water, electricity, etc.) and quality education for their
children. Another critical factor is property rights and the ability to return
home. Needless to say, this assumes that the refugees will return due to
'pull' factors in Iraq rather than "push" factors in their refugee countries.

---

[18]Oxfam, *Rising to the Humanitarian Challenge in Iraq*, 30 July 2007. See: <www.oxfam.
org.uk> (accessed 16 February 2009).
[19]*Azzaman*, 6 September 2007.
[20]Shinn, D "Reversing the Brain Drain in Ethiopia," a lecture delivered to the Ethiopian
North American Health Professionals Association, 23 November 2002.

Five years after the war, the level of oil production in Iraq is unchanged (revenues are five times the pre-war level, but that is only due to the dramatic increase in oil prices in the first nine months of 2008), and the electricity supply is not back to the pre-2003 level, although it improved towards the end of 2007 after severe shortages between 2004 and mid-2007. No major industries have sprung up, and an analysis of Iraq's economy would indicate that oil price hikes, from $25 to $30 per barrel in 2003 to a peak of $147 per barrel in July 2008, actually masked the government's incompetent management and the corrosive corruption. One could argue that the country would have probably imploded if oil prices had not gone to $100 and above, and had the US presence not supported the Iraqi government in spite of all its shortcomings. Hence the rentier nature of the economy has not changed in the last five years. Thus, Iraq's reliance on its oil and the lack of development of new industries will not spur employment, which means fewer "pull" factors to attract back the professionally skilled emigrants who fled their country. This became even more true at the end of 2008, when oil prices plummeted to $40. The Iraqi government will face tough times balancing its budget and creating employment opportunities.

The emigration of the highly skilled is not always a brain drain for their home countries. In certain cases, countries benefit from more investment in education as a result of the emigration; in other circumstances remittances become an important factor in the home economy. In other cases, emigration is only temporary and the professionals return having gained new skills in jobs overseas. In Iraq's case, the exodus has been a net brain drain and the emigration of so many skilled professionals has irreparably harmed the basic needs of the country (Lucas, 2005, pp. 103–144).

In the long term, the brain drain issue must be addressed since Iraq's oil wealth and US investments will not be able to compensate for the loss of human capital. Apart from paying lip service, the government has to launch the right projects to attract Iraqi talent back from abroad. This will happen only if violence ebbs and professionals living in exile feel they could return to work in a safe environment and without undue pressure from militia groups and religious fanaticism. Overseas governments and international organizations must be involved, as "Iraqis need training for civil servants, scholarships and agreements with foreign universities."[21]

---

[21] Malley, R. Testimony to the Senate Armed Services Committee. 9 April 2008.

From the point of view of this book, one final point needs to be raised about writing of the history of Iraq. It is too early to gauge the impact that the brain drain is having on academics and teachers involved in writing the history of Iraq. On the one hand, there is, undoubtedly, more freedom to write different aspects of Iraq's history from a wide spectrum of views; on the other hand, many Iraqi historians have left their country and are thus far away from the sources that they need to write its history.

Electronic references

Munthe, T (2003). Will harsh weed-out allow Iraqi academia to flower? *The Times Higher Education Supplement*. Online. Available HTTP: <http://www.thes.co.uk> (accessed 16 February 2009).

al-Sheibani, BIM, NR Hadi and T Hasoon (2006). Iraq lacks facilities and expertise in emergency medicine. *British Medical Journal*, No. 333. Online. Available HTTP: <http://www.BMJ.com> (accessed 16 February 2009).

United Nations University (2005). *UNU calls for World Help to Repair System*. Online. Available HTTP: <http://www.unu.edu> (accessed 16 February 2009).

Women's International League for Peace and Freedom (2006). *Iraq: Unemployment Forces Female Professionals Into Domestic Work*. Online. Available HTTP: <http://www.peacewomen.org> (accessed 16 February 2009).

COSMOPOLITANISM AND IRAQI MIGRATION: ARTISTS AND INTELLECTUALS FROM THE "SIXTIES AND SEVENTIES GENERATIONS" IN EXILE[1]

Diane Duclos

Edward Said (2000, p. 173) defines exile as "the unhealable rift forced between a human being and a native place, between the self and its true home: its essential sadness can never be surmounted." It is challenging to discuss complex migration routes and processes without systematically attributing a positive or negative value to the contrasting experiences characterizing them. Indeed, the multitude of elements wrapped up within migration studies — losses from the country of origin, encounters and exchanges as well as the creation of new combined identities — makes the design of an analytical framework challenging for scholars. This paper tries to show how these difficulties can be tackled by adopting a biographical perspective, leading the researcher to consider a plurality of "belongings", with the migrant clinging to a sense of belonging to country of origin and to destination and transit countries, as well as potential forms of hybrid identities. The case of artists and intellectuals who left Iraq during the 1960s and

---

[1]This paper presents the preliminary results of ongoing doctoral research initiated in 2008 at the Graduate Institute of International and Development Studies (Geneva) under the supervision of Professor Riccardo Bocco. Qualitative interviews have been conducted to date in Damascus, Beirut, Geneva, Paris and London. Further fieldwork in Amman is planned for the year 2011. The author would like to thank Riccardo Bocco, Jordi Tejel and Peter Sluglett for their useful comments on previous versions of this text, and Silvia Naef for her support in the research. She is also very grateful to Jabr Alwan, Hoshang Waziri and all the other persons who kindly agreed to take part in this research.

1970s illustrates the existence of transnational collective dynamics in exile. By generating and analyzing life stories among those migrants, this study aims to explore the notion of cosmopolitanism as an analytical tool (Beck, 2004), a set of practices and values and an *imaginaire*. This may enable the researcher to transcend the communitarian focus that sometimes seems "natural" when regarding Iraqi society.

Iraqi Migration: The Case of Artists and Intellectuals

Long overlooked in migration studies, Iraq has attracted increasing academic attention since 2003. Until the late 1980s, Iraq was regarded primarily as an immigrant destination, attracting laborers from several countries in the region. Since the 1940s, however, internal politics and unrest, among other factors, have led large numbers of Iraqi nationals to emigrate.

Linking departures from Iraq to specific violent periods, such as the 2003 war, should not prevent scholars from examining former displacements. The long history of Iraqi emigration and the "multipolarity" of the "Iraqi migration system" (Chatelard, 2005) enlighten us on the strategies of migrants on both regional and global scales. By raising spatial and temporal issues, the Iraqi case questions the individual and collective dynamics of migrants in exile — from the existence of collective coping strategies outside Iraq to potential practical or symbolic relationships linking migrants to their homeland:

> For decades, Iraq has not only existed inside the territorial boundaries of the nation-state but has also stayed alive within the numerous migrant and exile communities dispersed throughout the world. Iraq has been living in the hearts of diaspora Iraqis and has filled their imaginations. Alienation, nostalgia and depression are chronic and widespread amongst Iraqis abroad, whether living in one of the neighboring countries in the Middle East or further away, in Europe, the Americas, Australia or the Far East; speaking to them one often senses a great sadness. Yet, diasporic communities have also been great sources of hope, of political mobilization, of humanitarian and financial assistance as well as creative synergies (al-Ali, 2007, p. 14).

It is interesting to note that many of the Iraqi artists and intellectuals who left their country between the 1940s and 1970s are considered to be pioneers who opened the road to exile for other Iraqis. Simultaneously, their work produced outside Iraq, like the poetry of Sa'di Yusif and Mudhaffar al-Nawwab, often explores the idea of being far from home.

Artists and Intellectuals: "Generations" of Migrants

As early as the 1930s, artistic life in Baghdad was characterized by international exchanges, particularly through scholarships that enabled Iraqi students, like the famous painter Jawad Salim, to obtain a European education. A handful of artists, such as the Polish painter Roman Artymowski in the 1960s, visited the Baghdad Fine Arts Institute (Naef, 1996, p. 260). Exchanges among the artists favored the circulation of ideas that deeply influenced the theorization of visual art in Baghdad. These artistic debates somehow generated discussions about Iraqi society in general, gathering large ranges of artists and intellectuals in the numerous literary *cafés* of the capital. A great number of these artists and intellectuals were members or sympathizers of the Iraqi Communist Party (ICP), which was very influential in Iraq between its creation in 1934 and the 1970s. In fact, many of these leftist artists and intellectuals were among the first to emigrate. The repressions of 1978 and 1979 only combined to accelerate the exodus, giving rise to a specific generation of migrants:

> The generation of Iraqi intellectuals to which I belong is probably the first which had no longer been able to meet those from that wave of intellectuals who had left Iraq after the massacres committed against the Communists in 1979 by Saddam Hussein. They called themselves the 'sixties generation' (Bader, 2007, p. 39).

It is important to consider the migratory trajectories of these individuals from a sociological or anthropological perspective, as this approach will reveal both personal and collective dynamics of migration that often go beyond the bounds of confessions. Today, such "sixties and seventies generations" Iraqis are spread all over the world, and many of them have obtained citizenship outside Iraq, in spite of still being connected to each other and, to a lesser extent, to Iraq. Studying their trajectories contributes both to the shaping of a certain cultural history of Iraq and to our understanding of Iraqi migration networks. At this stage it will be important to define what is intended by the constant references to "artists and intellectuals." In this research, the challenges associated with names and categorizations are paramount. Indeed, the usual categories of networks used in migration studies in the Middle East — confessional, tribal, familial or professional — cannot be applied to this case. During the fieldwork research undertaken to date, interlocutors have often defined themselves in Arabic as *muthaqqafin*, coming from *thaqafa*, meaning "culture." Acknowledging the diversity of these men and women is a central aspect of the research, and vital for any valid investigation of the collective dynamics that gather diverse individuals together.

Appealing to Life Stories in Migration Studies

In order to "give a face" to Iraqi society (Luizard, 1999, p. 6) and to understand migration processes, we must be willing to listen to what witnesses have to tell, and to accept the various contradictions and paradoxes conveyed in their narratives. From this perspective, life stories are certainly an important resource in helping to contextualize the experience of migration within an entire life, and to express the pains and joys wrapped up in the journey.

Life Stories as a Methodology

I have so far highlighted the lack of academic knowledge of Iraqi society, which has often been reduced to focusing on some sort of violent practices. Placing the exchanges between artists and intellectuals in exile at the heart of my research appeals to the testimonies formulated by the migrants themselves. Descriptions produced through narratives play an essential role in drawing a portrait of Iraqi society, complete with its diversity. Along this vein, Nuha al-Radi's *Baghdad Diaries* (2003) evocatively describes the city of Baghdad under sanctions, as well as the pragmatic aspects of its author's daily life in exile.

In this perspective, a biographical approach provides a useful means of understanding the dynamics of exile. "Oral histories allow for a holistic approach to the past and the present by allowing people not only to provide accounts of specific events, but also reflect on their own roles, their interpretations of events and their emotions" (al-Ali, 2007, p. 9) The use of life stories enables the researcher to integrate the representations of exile from the protagonists' perspective, and somehow to accept the complexity and the contradictions of exile. However, as Plummer points out, the collection of life stories does not necessarily lead to a revelation of truth: "life story work involves recollecting, remembering and rediscovering, along with the active processes of memorializing and constructing history" (Plummer, 2001, p. 233). The transition from oral interviews to written accounts — from transcription, to editing and publishing — is a co-construction involving the researcher and the interviewee(s) (Jones,

2004), a process which is challenging and requires time. Even after time, life stories do not reveal the intricate details of daily lives situated outside formal institutions or power struggles (Robin, 1986). Nevertheless, we can agree with Elizabeth Tonkin (1995) that memory in the narratives is an intermediary between the individual and the society. Memory is also an intermediary between the past and the present. The wording that recounts individual experiences of exile reconstructs life stories and forms part of the shaping of history. While Iraq faces a current, crucial period of historiographical issues, the inclusion of migrant perspectives is all the more important. Exploratory biographical interviews conducted with Iraqi artists in Damascus in 2008 have shed light on innovative topics such as the generational division among Iraqis, because, as Haleh Ghorashi (2007, p. 130) stated in her life stories-based study with Iranian refugee women, "room was created to go beyond the assumptions prior to the research and to incorporate the dynamic of the conversations into gaining new insights into the life experiences."

Interdisciplinarity at Stake

This research has been guided by a series of anthropological studies on mobility, movement and migration (Auge, 2009; Fresia, 2007; Monsutti, 2004; Tarrius, 2000; Malkki, 1995). These scholars have adopted an approach that contrasts with state centered analyses, while simultaneously suggesting an original interpretation of what constitutes a "border." From this perspective, while keeping some distance from the exclusively political and legal analyses of human movement, my research aims to place migrants, their strategies and representations at the centre of migration issues. In this perspective, I prefer the terms "migrant" and "exile" to the term "refugee", which I use only in a legal sense. This terminological discussion is significant in the field, where I am alert to the vocabulary used by the migrants both in English and Arabic. Given the fact that "many stories and histories simply cannot be told when the social frameworks are not there" (Plummer, 2001, p. 235), it remains essential to assemble historical and political knowledge in order to complete oral narratives through documentary research. My approach thereby aims to provide an account of the social processes of migration starting with the individual and his representations. The collection and analysis of narratives is not generalized, but rather contextualized through the use and consideration of other sources. Even though presenting a social anthropological approach to migration, this research still appeals to other disciplines. For instance, an historical perspective is needed to embed the notion of cosmopolitanism in the Middle East, or to place the construction of the Iraqi state within a temporal dimension, as well as to analyze the narratives formulated by my interlocutors. I also appeal to the discipline of political science through my enquiry into the state-system in which these various population movements are occurring. The disciplines of human and social geography are useful for the consideration of migration within an urban context. Finally, the understanding of cosmopolitanism and its development needs some crucial philosophical inputs.

Multi-sited Fieldwork

The multipolarity of the "Iraqi migration system" (Chatelard, 2005) in general, and of the particular trajectories of the artists and intellectuals I am working with, has led to the adoption of a multi-sited fieldwork. The field is being shaped according to the social networks of my interlocutors, and has so far driven the research from Geneva to Damascus, Beirut, Paris and London, and, in the near future, to Amman. However, data collected in such diverse locations constitutes a coherent field through its generational and urban aspects. Each site remains specific regarding its geographical, cultural and political situation as well as its creative atmosphere. In addition to the cities where the field is actually situated, narratives of Iraqi cities like Baghdad, Kirkuk, Erbil, Karbala, Basra, or Najaf are present in this work through accurate descriptions often related to the childhood and youth of my interlocutors. Therefore, these cities influence the content of my interviews and contribute to the cosmopolitan aspect of this study, becoming actors in the research.

The Contribution of Cosmopolitanism to the Iraqi Migration Studies

Transnational exchanges between Iraqi urban migrants, as well as literary and artistic work produced by "Iraqis from outside" question a notion that has been increasingly used as an analytical tool in migration studies — cosmopolitanism. The historicity of cosmopolitan cities in the Middle East emphasizes the relevance of this notion regarding Iraqi regional and transcontinental migrations.

Cosmopolitanism in Dimension(s)

I am tackling the idea of cosmopolitanism through the experiences of Iraqi artists and intellectuals and through their own problematization of exile. Cosmopolitanism can signify different things, depending on whether it is considered from a philosophical, sociological or political standpoint. It can be viewed as a project, an ideal, a doctrine or a set of practices. According to Steven Vertovec and Robin Cohen:

> Cosmopolitanism suggests something that simultaneously: (a) transcends the seemingly exhausted nation-state model; (b) is able to mediate actions and ideals oriented both to the universal and the particular, the global and the local; (c) is culturally anti-essentialist; and (d) is capable of representing variously complex repertoires of allegiance, identity and interest (Vertovec and Cohen, 2003, p. 4).

Alain Tarrius defines a new form of cosmopolitanism, suggesting that it is no longer a "juxtaposition of foreign groups" but rather a "synergy of circulations and encounters of differences" (Tarrius, 2000, p. 8). In their book titled *Cosmopolitanism in practice*, sociologists Magdalena Nowicka and Maria Rovisco ask: "But how are cosmopolitan ideas, narrative and values, which are institutionally-embedded, shaping every day life experiences and practices? How are ordinary individuals and groups 'cosmopolitan'?" (Novicka and Rovisco, 2009, p. 1). Within the social sciences, the meaning of this concept has evolved in recent years — from a non-state-related cosmopolitanism to a transnational one; and from a kind of elitist cosmopolitanism to one that affects every layer of society. Gerard Delanty mentions a cosmopolitan turn in social sciences:

> While cosmopolitanism has become influential within normative political theory, it has been taken up in a different guise in disciplines such as history, sociology, anthropology, and cultural studies where the tendency has been toward a more situated or rooted understanding of cosmopolitanism as always contextualized (Delanty, 2009, p. 3).

This important move in social sciences has shed light on transnational spaces, questioning borders in a globalized world. However, according to Gerard Delanty's notion of *cosmopolitan imagination*, we can argue that cosmopolitanism should not be reduced to transnational experiences. In other words, it is important to analyze cosmopolitanism through concrete practices, without rejecting its normative dimension:

> Transnational movement, cultural diversity and hybrid cultures do not in themselves constitute cosmopolitanism, although they are undoubtedly important preconditions for cosmopolitanism. [...] Without mutual

> criticism and self-problematization, cosmopolitanism loses its force and become reduced to the mere condition of diversity (Delanty, 2009, p. 16).

The tension between a universal reading of cosmopolitanism and a situated one appears to be a strength rather than a contradiction in the light of the migratory trajectories of Iraqi artists and intellectuals. The claim for universal values is often embedded in the accounts of specific experiences inside Iraq and in exile. As Plummer states (2001, p. 262) "This human being that life stories aim to describe is always an embedded, dialogic, contingent, embodied, universal self with a moral (and political) character." This study does not aim to redefine the concept but rather strives to highlight its appropriation in the field of migration studies through practices, representations and values conveyed by Iraqi artists and intellectuals who have settled abroad. For this purpose I am paying particular attention to the relational aspects of cosmopolitanism. In other words, what matters are the interactions between entities, however bounded (for example as states, cities, communities, generations, individuals, viewpoints, etc). Through this specific focus we may be able to grasp the dynamic and constructed aspect of the processes.

Cosmopolitanism and Migration

For more than 20 years, the notion of transnationalism has been gradually gaining space within migration studies: "transmigrants are immigrants whose daily lives depend on multiple and constant interconnections across international borders and whose public identities are configured in relationship to more than one nation-state" (Glick *et al.*, 1995, p. 48). This notion, when regarded as an analytical tool, has enabled researchers to look beyond the categories of "integration", "assimilation" and "uprooting" in order to acknowledge the numerous belongings and connections surrounding processes of migration. Nevertheless, transnational theories seem to focus on the spatial side of migration. The key point of analysis, even though contested, remains where the border is drawn. Yet, migration processes are embedded in space as well as in time. Introducing cosmopolitanism to migration studies complements the geographical perspective of human displacement by contributing a memorial and discursive thrust. Even though the advent of nation states seems to have generated the fall of cosmopolitan cities in the Middle East, I put forward the hypothesis that Iraqis in exile, (re)constitute, through their practices, exchanges and discourses, a new form of cosmopolitan space. The Iraqi case, largely analyzed to date in terms of a fragmented and violent society, is all the more interesting to examine in the light of cosmopolitanism.

Remembering Cosmopolitan Baghdad from Outside: Nostalgia within Narratives

A specific use of "cosmopolitanism" emerged from my readings and interviews when referring to the Baghdad of the past. Interestingly, the image of the Iraqi capital in the 1960s, as conveyed by a discourse enunciated exclusively from outside, tends to depict a period of peaceful cohabitation between all the components of the society in an effervescent cultural life. Both the city and the atmosphere are described as "cosmopolitan." Therefore, the adjective "cosmopolitan" evokes both "peace" and a certain sense of "creativity". During my fieldwork in Damascus, I conducted interviews with the Iraqi-Italian painter Jabr Alwan. Remembering his youth in Baghdad when he was studying at the Institute of Fine Arts, he described a multicultural society. According to him, the teachers in the Institute of Fine Arts had been exposed to different cultures and influences, having traveled a lot. Some of them had studied in Paris, Rome, Moscow or London. There were some positive struggles towards cultural development at the end of the sixties "After the class in the Institute, we went every day to *Umm Kalthum* café where poets and painters were meeting. Later in the evening, we went to Abu Nawas Street." In 1972, Jabr Alwan settled in Rome and finally obtained Italian citizenship in 1995:

> Today, he lives between Damascus and Rome. He chose to spend time in Damascus for cultural reasons, feeling he was forgetting a lot of his memories. He feels the atmosphere in Damascus close to that of Baghdad. Until now, he refuses to go back to Iraq: "I have beautiful memories of Baghdad, the river full of fish, an active cultural life. I am afraid to go back to Iraq and not find these memories [...] I do not want to go back because I want to keep my memories."[2]

I encountered comparable portraits of lost Baghdad in many narratives, with constant references to the existence of mixed neighborhoods, literary cafés where leftist ideas were circulating, books were discussed and exchanged and where Iraqi art was in search of an identity. This city, is

---

[2]Excerpts from an interview with Jabr Alwan (Damascus, January 2010).

it a *souvenir*? A ghost? A dream? A project? These moving testimonies must be understood both in the light of the personal experiences of the persons enunciating them and of the increasing categorization of Iraqi society in terms of violent oppositions between "communities", "confessions", or "ethnic groups". In other words, taking into account a certain feeling of nostalgia is crucial to understand these narratives. The reconstitution of cosmopolitan Baghdad echoes the distance and time that separate these men and women from the beloved city. The writer and journalist Husayn al-Mozani, who left Iraq in 1978 and who is currently living in Berlin, relates his *Last Trip to Baghdad* in 2008, providing the reader with contrasting descriptions between the Iraqi streets he left and the one he found after thirty years of absence. According to him Baghdad "has become a non place, represented by concrete walls" (Al Mozany, 2010, p. 14). In his narrative, the tone is raw, straightforward and somehow emotional:

> So this is Rashid street: its corners have crumbled, its pavements have been upturned, its columns dirtied, their paint peeling off and their capitals crumbling. It appears loud and uproarious, but it is lifeless, no longer appealing to suicide bombers. This street, that some used to call Iraq's aorta, has committed suicide, and now all that remains is its long corpse stretched out among the scattered, blackened shops that mourn a street which bid its people farewell and then killed itself. (Al Mozany, 2010, p. 18)

The city seems to bleed like a human body. The deliquescence of Rashid Street might be a metonym for the whole country. However, the violence of the images conveyed by this narrative makes me think that there is no such thing as resilience. In the light of this testimony, reminiscences of a cosmopolitan Baghdad from "the good old days" can be viewed as a proposition for openness and diversity.

Disengaging from Confessional Approaches in Iraqi Studies?

Without denying that confessional dynamics exist in Iraqi society, this study suggests that other categories can be taken into account to analyze Iraq. Among them, we have underlined the importance of "generations". Given the wide interest in the confessional dynamics of Iraqi society, a cosmopolitan approach to the topic in itself may constitute an innovative choice:

> Precisely because of this prevalent preoccupation with clash, it becomes morally imperative to underline the other, more common but unnoticed

and inaudible processes of human conduct, to show how people belonging to different cultural groupings can transcend their immediate selves
by intensely interacting in their life-worlds with members of other ethnic
or religious collectives. Would we still imagine today's Iraq as the "natural" embodiment of sharp ethnic and religious boundaries (because
the "nation" was no more than an artificial and imposed construct), if
only we knew how twentieth century Iraq was replete with instances of
individuals, families, and neighborhoods from Sunni, Shi'i, Jewish, and
Christian communities engaged in interactions and shared lives? (Bayat,
2008, p. 5)

This research does not strive to deny or contradict potential confessional
dynamics that guide certain steps of my interlocutors' journeys, but instead
it strives to promote an alternative reading of this society that will enable
us to uncover other forms of collective dynamics.

REPRESENTING IRAQ HISTORY
THROUGH THE ARTS

Hamit Bozarslan

Over the decades, artistic creation in Iraq has been heavily influenced by the country's political conditions, which have had their efforts on forms and styles. Perhaps paradoxically, it has also managed to preserve some marginal, and thus autonomous, forms of expression. Thus, in spite of intense control on the part of the regime, the Ba'thist period did not constitute a moment of total discontinuity, at least from that point of view. One should not be surprised by such a statement: Under totalitarian regimes, political discourse is under constant surveillance, but this does not always extend to nondissident forms of artistic discourse, which can sometimes become expressions of passive resistance. For instance, Shostakovich could produce a highly subversive and almost openly critical *Lady Macbeth* under a massively totalitarian regime; his opera was eventually banned, although this was many months after its first presentation and only when Stalin himself came to see it.

For understandable reasons, artistic and literary creation in Iraq has been little explored by scholars. Given the current state of the art, it will be difficult to elaborate sociological profiles of successive generations of Iraqi artists, writers and filmmakers throughout the second half of the twentieth century (Naef, 1996). On the basis of available knowledge in the main European languages, however, one can conclude there are both continuities and tremendous differences between engaged and contesting forms of art in the 1940s and 1950s, the subordinated arts of the 1970–1990s and the fragmented and sceptical arts of the 2000s. The first period was heavily militant, and as Leslie Tramontini's contribution shows, at least to some extent bore the burden of radical ideologies, including social-Darwinism and the cult of blood; but in contrast with these ideological barriers, the art of this period is a voluble expression of the dreams of politicized generations and evinces real autonomy, not simply *vis-à-vis* political actors, but also towards the state. Under the Ba'th regime (and this was also true to some extent under Qasim and the 'Arif brothers), the artistic domain had a rather reduced space of autonomy; the state could not entirely control artistic and literary creation, but this was one of the main instruments of production of a cult of personality as well as of pride in being a citizen of Ba'thist Iraq. No wonder, then, that poetry, or the modern *qasida* glorifying the *ra'is*, became a widespread literary genre. During this period, however, the language of abstract art became an instrument of the construction of an internal space of exile, allowing the preservation of limited personal autonomy for artists. The artists also tried to have some circles of socialization and to use official institutions as spaces where they could testify their loyalty to the regime, but this ceremonial allegiance should be considered, at least in some cases, as the *sine qua non* of the negotiation of some degree of autonomy rather than an act of voluntary submission (Shabout, 2004). In some cases, as in Kurdistan, the "folklorization" of minority cultures also gave artists and authors the possibility of inventing semi-autonomous spaces and of expressing the aspirations of their ethnic groups. In the post-Saddam period, Iraqi art and literature has largely freed itself from state control; as, elsewhere in the Middle East (and many other non-Western countries), post-modern forms of expression have become the chosen means of artistic and literary production.

Obviously, some themes, such as the Arab national question or the idea of self-sacrifice for the nation, are present in Iraqi art throughout all three periods. But this continuity is not necessarily a decisive feature of the artistic and literary landscape, nor does it mean that the creative artists of the various periods have mobilized similar resources or have common aspirations. For instance, in the first period, the artist as an individual creator, i.e., subject, renounces his/her individuality in order to defend the collective entity of Iraqi society or the Arab nation; the dissolution of individuality is seen as the condition for the emergence of the nation as a historical project. In the second period, the artist is constrained to serve a regime that obliges him to glorify the spirit of self-sacrifice in the name of the nation and of the ruler who incarnates it; but this national/institutional and coercive obligation that he/she has to fulfil also reminds him/her of the necessity to remain an autonomous and reflective subject. In the third period, that of deceptions and sceptical glimpses of a fragmented Iraqi society, a defeated Middle East and a tragic world, the artist claims his/her rights to be an ironical, violent, or in any case, critical, voice towards his/her society. Even the idea of sacrifice wins a new meaning: It is not accepted as a national or social duty, but as a response to the absurdity of the world. Hence the discontinuities, which are perhaps more significant in Iraq than any other place in the Middle East, are not only generational; they also concern the reading of the world.

The evolution of the arts and literature in Iraq clearly testifies to the internal paradoxes of the country, but these paradoxes are the common heritage of many countries in the Middle East. For instance, one observes a gap between political evolution and syntax, which is marked by coercion, violence, and ideological engagements, on one hand, and the language of artistic creation on the other. Of course, in Iraq, as in the rest of the Middle East and the world in general, poetry has been used as a privileged genre in order to evoke emotions, affiliations, and slogans and to boost the cult of personality. But apart from this very specific usage, we observe that it is almost impossible to translate radical commitments into artistic language. Many politically committed artists, in fact, have been deeply scarred by their own experience — while their ideological and political commitments may have pushed them to celebrate an unfolding world of heroism and self-sacrifice, their artistic being has pushed them towards a cruel description of their society, their marginality, and a world in decline.

Similarly, literature and art in Iraq, as elsewhere in the Middle East, have become fields of expression of what society cannot confess to itself, phenomena of coercion, violence, self-destruction, and radicalism, but also processes of alienation. Political language has always tried to explain these phenomena either in terms of the presence of internal and external enemies or of nationalist, leftist or Islamist teleological readings; it has posited a temporal separation between the current slavery of the nation and its future deliverance, which requires sacrifices in the present. In contrast with these premises and promises, some artists have either opted for an *intimiste* narrative, or adopted dynamic, tension-filled styles of creation, or chosen irony or the theatre of the absurd. The remarkable analysis of *Baba Sartre* by Sami Zubaida definitely fits into this category. This style, which can take a rather cruel form, is also the most appropriate means of depicting the condition of victimhood and the dreams of individuals in a society where the "individual scale" becomes the only meaningful one. No wonder then, that in Iraq as elsewhere in the Middle East, a not necessarily reflective postmodernism has become the language of describing, rather than denouncing the human condition.

In Iraq, art and literature have been in the service of a failed nation-building process; but at least at the margins, they have also reflected the plurality of society. As in other Middle Eastern cases, the Iraqi case also shows that the centuries-long imperial legacy did not disappear with the creation of new states in the 1920s (and the radical re-foundation of Turkey on a nationalist basis in the 1910s and 1920s). Obviously, the Ottoman Empire came to an end in the aftermath of World War I, but some cities remained imperial, thanks to their multi-ethnic and multi-religious texture, the visibility of different ethnic and linguistic communities in the urban landscape, and to their complex and multiple affiliations. Even under very harsh dictatorships, these urban spaces remained theatres of communal solidarities and networks, but also of horizontal forms of solidarities and even social and political mobilization. Cities like Istanbul, Aleppo, Jerusalem, Kirkuk or Baghdad can be defined as imperial not because they were necessarily prestigious imperial cities, but because they perpetuated parts of the imperial tradition of coexistence and by their calm vitality, challenged dominant nationalist ideologies and showed other possible political formulae. As discussed in this chapter, they can also become important places of artistic creation.

One last point: As Nicolas Masson shows, since the 2003 War, which turned out to be a war of American deception and self-doubt, Iraq has become a reservoir of images and clichés of a brutal exoticism. Following Pierre Hassner, we can say that the "Western bourgeois" defined the territory of the city (and the civilization) and acted as a "barbarian" outside this territory (Hassner, 2004). In this circle of alienation, the main question that concerns the "bourgeois" is not the fate of the victims, but his own transformation into a "barbarian". Will American movie-makers be able to go beyond this *déchirure* and also reflect Iraqi experiences, sufferings, and expectations? Will Iraqi artistic narratives, particularly the cinematographic ones analyzed by Lucia Sorbera, make contact with these external narratives and adopt new artistic styles in order to describe their own experiences? Will the new artistic expressions emerging out of crosscutting and reflective readings of the war be able to use the artistic exhibitions studied by Silvia Naef to send new messages to a wider public? Only the future will be able to answer these questions.

LITERARY GLIMPSES OF MODERN IRAQI HISTORY AND SOCIETY

Sami Zubaida

The literary production of the twentieth century has played a crucial role in the imagining of Iraq as a country and a nation. This was most famously accomplished in poetry. The birth of the nation and the contentions over its shape and destiny were prominently recorded in the poetry of Jamil al-Zahawi and Ma'ruf al-Risafi (Rusafi). The politics and the tribulations of the twentieth century were recorded and dramatized by the leading poet of Iraq, Muhammad Mahdi al-Jawahiri, whose life coincided with the century: Badr Shakir al-Sayyab and 'Abd al-Wahhab al-Bayati, both innovators and modernists in the forms and styles of Arabic poetry, participated in the images and contentions of the country. Politics, society, sentiment, nature, love, were all interwoven into these poetic imaginations, but also satire and fun. The world of music, song and the demimonde of cabarets and courtesans featured prominently in the poetic commentaries. al-Jawahiri celebrated the renowned beauties, dancers and singers of his time in memorable lines. Mulla 'Abbud al-Karkhi (1861–1946) had a sharp tongue satirizing and ridiculing all levels of Baghdadi society in his colloquial poetry, which often got him into trouble. His famous poem *al-Mahalat* (The Impossibles) rhymed on the impossibility of donkey men coming from London and him assuming the post of minister of the interior, of the moon rising at midday, and the names of 'Aisha and 'Umar among the Ma'dan (the Shi'i marsh dwellers): *"yesir bil-ma'dan isim 'aisha w-'umar/yesir bin-har al-dhuhur yetla' al-gumar"* (Karkhi, 1933, 284–292). His obscene elegy on the death of a famous pimp, Da'ud al-Lampachy, drew a comic picture of the then licensed brothel quarter of Baghdad, and led to his receiving a beating from a famous lady inhabitant, Maryam al-Kurdiya who was included in the satire and took her revenge when the poet was pointed out to her

in *Suq al-Haraj*. While not included in Karkhi's *diwan*, this poem continues to be chanted (after Yusuf 'Umar, the prominent *maqam* singer of the
twentieth century) at drinking parties of older Baghdadis. All these different kinds of poetic production have not only portrayed and commented on
Iraqi politics and society, but have also shaped the collective memory and
imagination of the country and the culture as shared realities.

Unlike poetry, the literary form at which Arabs and Iraqis excelled, fiction is a relative newcomer. It took some time for modern Iraq to produce
the novelists who would record and imagine the tangle of its social relations
and the corners of its urban spaces. Here I will examine three novels, each
focussing on a particular aspect of Iraqi life in the second half of the twentieth century. The three are quite different and disparate, and the choice
may appear arbitrary. But the contrast of style and content may in itself be
illuminating.

Fu'ad al-Takarli, al-Raj' al-Ba'id (The Long Way Back)

Fu'ad al-Takarli was a lawyer and judge for 35 years. He resigned in 1983
to write full time and moved to live in Tunis. He had spent a study leave
in Paris in the 1960s. He started writing in the 1950s, but his major novels
were published in the 1970s. He finished *al-Raj'* in Paris in 1966, which
was published later in Beirut in the 1970s, and then brought to Baghdad.
It is said that the Iraqi censors refused to permit the novel unless one of the
main characters, 'Adnan, a thug and a Ba'thist, was written out, which the
author refused to do. The events are set in 1962, the last difficult days of
the Qasim regime, culminating in the Ba'thist coup in 1963.

The style of the novel is "modernist", in that it employs different narrative voices, and the narrative moves back and forth in time. Some of
the voices speak in a "stream of consciousness" style. The narrative voice
is in *fusha*, standard Arabic, while the (extensive) dialog is in colloquial
Baghdadi. For the Iraqi reader the language of the dialog is highly evocative, with close attention to the vocabulary and the rhythm of Baghdadi
voices, nuanced by the characteristic speech of the different genders and
generations. This has the effect of identifying and reinforcing Iraqi com-
munalities and the "imagination" of the nation. In his seminal *Imagined
Communities*, Benedict Anderson has pointed to the novel as the modern
medium *par excellence* which facilitates that imagining.

al-Raj' al-Ba'id is a family saga, set in a lower middle class household in Bab al-Shaykh, a popular quarter of central Baghdad around the shrine and mosque of 'Abd al-Qadir al-Gaylani (the Shaykh of the Bab, although this fact is of no significance for the novel). The family lives in an old traditional house, with a long corridor entrance, a central courtyard, a tree and a small pond, with rooms around on two floors and a flat roof, where the family sleeps during the summer months, and a small *sardab*, a cellar, cool and dark for siestas. These two features, the roof and the *sardab*, are highly evocative for Iraqis and the stuff of nostalgia for expatriates and exiles. Like all good narratives, much of the action is portrayed through these spaces.

The *Dramatis Personae*: The head of the household is Abu Midhat, a functionary in the customs administration, elderly and frail, kind and mild. His two sons: Midhat is a law graduate and a government functionary, Karim, frail and troubled, is struggling through college and failing exams repeatedly and his nervous disposition brings him close to breakdown after witnessing the death of a close friend in an accident. Their mother, Umm Midhat is the mainstay of the household, aided by her daughter Madiha, a teacher. Madiha is separated from her husband, Hasan, a bank functionary, who "dropped out," leaving his job and family and taken to drinking, lodging in a poky and malodorous room in his aged aunt's house in Hayy al-Akrad, close to Bab al-Shaykh, a particularly poor neighborhood, so called because it was the abode of mostly Fa'ili Kurds (of little significance in the book). Madiha has two young daughters, who play an important part in the narrative. Then there are two old ladies who share a room in the house, one the grandmother and the other the unmarried sister of Abu Midhat, referred to as *'Ammat* Midhat (paternal aunt). The two old ladies (*al-'ajayiz*) provide a comic chorus commenting on people and events, forever moaning and complaining, in a particularly colorful vocabulary and idiom.

Added to this multigenerational household are two resident relatives: Umm Midhat's sister, Umm Munira, and Munira herself. Munira is a beautiful young woman, with what seems an unexplained sadness. We learn she is a schoolteacher who left her job in Ba'quba in a hurry and after some kind of setback. She and her mother were living there with another sister and her family. Munira is waiting for an order from the Ministry of Education transferring her to a Baghdad school. Munira's presence and beauty become a cause of infatuation and tension for the two young men of the family, with the emerging presumption that she may marry Midhat. But there seems to be a shadow over her past that inhibits her attitude and conduct. We soon learn that this shadow is to do with 'Adnan, the son of her Ba'quba sister, a young man in his late teens who dropped out of school and worked in his father's greengrocery business. This family is set in contrast to Abu Midhat's honorable and educated but poor household. 'Adnan's father was a bare-foot (*hafi*) peasant, who has mysteriously acquired wealth. His son is a thug and a bully, who is in charge of the family car and drives between Ba'quba and Baghdad. We eventually learn that he raped his aunt Munira, which accounts for her plight and the shadow over her affairs. 'Adnan keeps badgering Munira, calling at Abu Midhat's house with menaces and messages. But her ordeal is kept secret from the household and only partially unfolds after her disastrous marriage to Midhat towards the end.

The urban petty functionaries were living through interesting times in the 1950s and 1960s. Abu Midhat, Midhat, Karim, Madiha and Munira — all have government positions, *wadhifa*, by virtue of literacy, education, and a diploma. They see themselves as "modern". There is little religiosity in the family, confined to fasting during Ramadhan for some, and celebrating the Eid: No one, not even the old ladies, seems to observe the daily prayers. Drinking beer and arak seem to be unexceptional for the men, and the errant husband Hasan is an alcoholic. This neglect of religious observance was not unusual or remarkable in the Baghdad of those days. Yet, familiar patriarchal gender roles and relations seem to belie this modernity. Though a teacher and an earner, Madiha remains the domestic manager coordinating the other women. Munira's disgrace remains unspoken and secret. Her loss of virginity through rape proves to be a disaster when discovered by her modern-educated bridegroom, who responds by absconding from home, then drifting with the destitute Hasan between the *maykhana* and the lowly lodgings till his death. The two old ladies, the *'ajayiz*, occasionally mention "tradition", sometimes to censor Munira and her mother, but more insistently to invoke respect for their old age, and particularly on the duty to supply them with food. They are constantly complaining of hunger and having to wait for their meals, speaking comic dialogs on all the fine meats they are missing: Kebabs, lamb shank stew, and *tashrib*, broth with bread. These demands contrast sadly with the egg and spinach of the normal family meals of the hand to mouth lower middle class. Kebab only appears at one Ramadan *iftar*.

The narrative takes place largely within domestic spaces and the surrounding streets and markets. The nearest it comes to public locations is the not so public space of the arak shop. Penniless Hasan, forever begging and sponging on his relatives, is to be found on evenings at the backyard of Awanees' (an Armenian name) drink shop in Bab al-Sharqi. Hasan explains to Midhat: "the neighborhood is not classy, but this Abu Kamal (Awanees), charges low prices for the drinks, there is no better place in the area" (Takarli, 1981, p. 101). In fact the owner is not licensed to run a bar, but puts a few tables with stools and barrels in his backyard, where Hasan drinks in the company of other marginal characters drawn from all corners of Iraqi society, who provide a commentary on people and events and get into quarrels. Midhat goes there to see Hasan and gets drawn into the conversations. Adnan, too, comes to drink and see Hasan, probably to get news of Munira. He is an outspoken contributor to the drunken conversations, and to the alarm of the drinkers and landlord, spouts dissident politics. This is 1962, a year of increasing discontent with Qasim's indecisive and crippled government, which did not please any of the contending forces. Ba'thists and Arabists were particularly vocal in denouncing the "Sole Leader", who was considered by his opponents to be unhinged and unpredictable. 'Adnan, the spoiled, thuggish youth was clearly a Ba'thist.

Politics intrude only obliquely into the family saga, but ultimately determine its fate. The lower middle class family of functionaries did not include political actors, but it was the victim of political transformations in which it played no part. The Ba'thist coup of February 1963 sees Midhat, destitute, having abandoned his bride and his family, living in an alcoholic mist in Hasan's lowly lodgings in Hayy al-Akrad, with Hasan's aunt and her demented old husband spouting military jargon in Turkish. As we know, Hayy al-Akrad became the center of popular resistance to the Ba'thist coup, led by communists. It resisted for three days and was ultimately bombed into submission, with many casualties. Midhat meets his death not as a participant in the resistance, but as a bystander. Confirmation of his death is brought to the family by 'Adnan, now in uniform (presumably of the National Guard), and the now rehabilitated Hasan, apparently with the Ba'th. The novel ends with a prospective reconciliation between Hasan, now recovering in a clinic, and his wife Madiha. Munira is sad, near collapse, but pours out her fury on the infatuated younger brother Karim, denouncing Midhat and the family for running away and not facing up to the dilemmas of their strained existence and the contradictory attitudes.

In their small and apolitical way, members of the Midhat family are the seeds of the emergent national class: Products of the national educational system, functionaries of the national government, the spaces of the modern nation defining their horizons and aspirations, subject to the vagaries of its shaky politics. They appear to be de-tribalized and non-sectarian — religion hardly plays any role in their life. The Baʻquba family of ʻAdnan's parents provide a contrast: An illiterate peasant who becomes a shady entrepreneur; a spoiled son who drops out of school, a thug and a rapist. He is the budding Baʻthist, and a type that would come to prominence in the later decades of Baʻth rule. After a brief period of limited prosperity in the mid-1970s, the national class of the salaried and the professionals become increasingly subordinated and impoverished, in favor of the political class and its dependents.

Ali Badr, *Baba Sartre*

This is a surrealist novel, totally different from the modernist realism of the previous book. It is "realist", however, in its drawing of the topography and the landmarks of Baghdad in the 1960s, with occasional glimpses of Paris. The characters and events are exaggerated caricatures, enacting a comic commentary on society and culture. The inhabitants of this novel's Baghdad are far from Takarli's families and their habitats, all Muslims and Arabs (with the exception of the Armenian tavern keeper), though not overtly religious. Badr paints a picture of cosmopolitan Baghdad, which has many Christian characters and some Jewish ones too, with the occasional foreigner. Its spaces oscillate between grand palaces and hovels, with some landmarks of real cafés and bookshops thrown in. Takarli's narrative occurs in domestic spaces, Badr's in surreal public spaces.

The narrator is hired by a dubious and bizarre couple (Christians) to research and write the life and (mysterious) death of the "philosopher of Sadria" (a central Baghdad neighborhood and market). The narrative then unfolds, backward and forward in time, between Baghdad and Paris, showing episodes of the philosopher's family and childhood, time in Paris, and as a celebrity in Baghdad as the Arab Sartre.

The main character is Abd al-Rahman, the son of a rich family, of aristocratic, Ottoman descent, which lost some of its wealth and privilege in the "Revolution" (i.e., of 1958, the nearest the novel comes to mentioning political events). This spoilt only child is sent to France to study philosophy. During one of his holidays in Baghdad (in the 1950s), his father takes him to meet Nuri al-Saʻid with the prospect of employing him as a philosophical consultant to the cabinet. In Paris, Abd al-Rahman does not perform well in his studies, and fails to master the French language beyond simple exchanges. However, he nurtures a deep attachment to Sartre (who he has never met, but shakes with apprehension when the great man is nearby in Montparnasse). Abd al-Rahman discovers that he has a physical resemblance to the philosopher and tries to imitate (the philosopher) by copying his hairstyle and sense of dressing. He regrets his healthy eyes, and wears spectacles similar to Sartre's, and, in Baghdad, envies and berates a poor vegetable seller, Jasib al-A'war, for being one-eyed (*a'war*). We discover that he barely understands existentialism beyond stock phrases, "Being in itself and for itself," and, above all, the state of "Nausea," *ghuthian*, a concept and a recurrent state which he preached to all his confrères, who embraced it as a philosophical feeling. Ideas of freedom and the lack of meaning are bandied as conditions of loose living and aimlessness. In Paris, Abd al-Rahman marries a poor and plain-looking blonde girl and takes her to Baghdad and introduces her as Sartre's maternal cousin. This is a commentary on a common phenomenon of those years: The Iraqi student in Europe or America who fails in his studies, and brings home a blonde wife instead of a diploma. Thus, Abd al-Rahman "appropriated" France and its philosophy by acquiring a French wife. He shunned high society as well as intellectual circles in Baghdad, expressly out of existentialist contempt, but the author suggests the real reason is that those circles would laugh at his existentialist posturing. The philosopher, Abd al-Rahman, seeks disciples and followers among the low life, including the stars of a cabaret on Rashid Street, whose owner, Dalal, happily accepts him as *maître*, indulges in nausea, as do her star artistes, mostly in response to his money and custom. A large portrait of Sartre hangs in the main salon of the cabaret, and its stars assume suitable titles, like one Virgin of Existentialism (*'athra' al-wujudiya*). His main disciple and a key character is Isma'il Hadub, also known as Ismail Falsafa.

Isma'il hails from the lowest depths of Iraqi society. During his growing years, he was a petty thief, pimp and seller of dirty postcards. He lodges in a filthy *khan*, alongside *hammals* (porters) and thugs, among open sewers and rats. One of his clients for dirty pictures is Shaul, a Jewish merchant in the Sadriya market. Shaul turns out to be a kind of Utopian socialist who seeks suitable disciples, and after sacking his Jewish servant for theft, adopts Isma'il as a suitable replacement. He cleans up the lad and installs him in his own luxurious palace by the Tigris as servant, factotum and disciple. Shaul is also a patron of intellectuals and artists and hosts a weekly salon for them (with named real characters of that world). Gradually, Ismail imbibes all sorts of notions and vocabularies. Shaul is an improbable character — it is difficult to imagine any other shopkeeper in Sadria with such a fabulous fortune as Shaul; it would probably only have been possible (to amass this sort of a fortune) by a financier or an import-export merchant or a car import agent (like the real Lawi [Levy] brothers who are mentioned). Intellectual ambitions seem to be out of place with his other traits. In any case, Shaul takes a dislike to the philosopher of Sadria and is highly critical of his existentialism; he prompts market characters like Jasib al-A'war to repeat slogans against that philosophy and hurl obscene curses against Suhayl Idris, then the main Arab exponent of Sartre (Abd al-Rahman, though, fulminates against him as the rival Arab Sartre). Feeling trapped in Shaul's clutches, Isma'il turns to the existentialist philosopher and becomes his companion and disciple with much greater scope for fun, drink, cabarets, whores and the intellectual ambience. His aspiration to philosophy leads him to fornicate with Abd al-Rahman's French wife, thus taking a share of Sartre's charisma through possessing his supposed cousin. Germaine, the wife is fed up with her pretentious husband, who in any case stays away most nights with his cabaret mistresses. The affair is discovered in a bizarre episode in which the Imam of the adjoining mosque observes, from the minaret, the naked lovers having intercourse on the roof at dawn. He then catches Ismail stealing apples from a tree in the garden in the mosque, and ties him naked to the tree and invites people to come and ridicule the *zani*, adulterer. It is suggested that Abd al-Rahman's death soon thereafter was suicide at the humiliation of the scandal. It would appear that Isma'il was deliberately complicit in the exposure and the scandal in order to bring about the demise of the philosopher, and that he did so at the instigation and with some payment from another quarter, another sub-plot in this complicated narrative.

The other set of characters is the Christian family of Khadduri and their beautiful daughter Nadia, who works at the Mackenzie English bookshop on Rashid Street (a real establishment, and a prominent cultural monument in Baghdad). The Khadduris are rich, and Nadia is admired and courted by a cousin, Edmond, later known as Edmond Trotsky. His shift to militancy is occasioned by Nadia's attraction to Abd al-Rahman, on one of his visits to Baghdad from Paris. In addition to her beauty, the philosopher was attracted by her apparent knowledge of Sartre's books: She knew the location of their shelving at Mackenzie's, as well as their prices. While enjoying the philosopher's company and his love talk, she resists his physical advances: Like Munira in the previous story, Nadia was hiding a secret. She had been raped as a young girl by the Jewish accountant at her father's business, a wicked and devious man — now deported from the country — who had wormed his way into the family's gratitude by arranging, through a subterfuge, the agreement to the marriage of an uncle to a Jewish beauty, by persuading the Jewish family that the uncle was an undercover Jew (a most unlikely tale).

In what seems to be an open intellectual and even Bohemian milieu it would seem that the loss of virginity still weighs heavily on a girl, and Abd al-Rahman is finally dissuaded from pursuing the affair, we later learn, because she told him about it in a letter. When Edmond finally weds Nadia, he is devastated to discover that she is not a virgin, and blames Abd al-Rahman, despite her denials. Enraged by the saga, the Khadduri family instigates a plot with Isma'il (by offering a hefty bribe) to expose the adultery of Abd al-Rahman's French wife, which humiliates him and finally drives him to suicide. The tale becomes even more complicated and bizarre when we discover that one of the characters commissioning the narrator to research the life and death of the philosopher, a rich and elegant man with the name of Sadiqzadeh, is none other than a metamorphosis of Isma'il. In the closing scene, the narrator, having been cheated of his fee, is then invited to meet another character, Michel, with the first woman contact, the louche Nunu Bahar. Michel turns out to be yet another incarnation of Isma'il, now with a shaved head and square metal spectacles, standing under a portrait of Michel Foucault, and proposing to the narrator that he would ghost-write a book on the History of Madness in the Arab world. Sartre is *passé*, Foucault is the new vogue, and Isma'il /Michel wants to be the structuralist (*bunyawi*) of the Waziriya (the posh Baghdad suburb which he now inhabits). It is not clear whether the misconception about Foucault being a structuralist is Isma'il's or the author's.

Having narrated this strange tale, I am now at a loss as to how to justify including it in a paper on history through literature. What is it satirizing? Certainly not the main intellectual and cultural scenes in Baghdad of the 1960s, which boasted of many interesting and creative intellectuals, poets and artists, many of whom are mentioned by name, in passing, in the novel. Politics only come into the novel in comic contexts, and there is no hint of the political currents, violence and oppression of that decade, and nothing about the Communist Party, which provided the frame for much intellectual activity. There is no mention of government or police or censorship. In short, the novel is not about real history. So why do we bother with it, and why does it hold such fascination for many Iraqi readers? Perhaps the reason is that the novel reveals many of the attitudes and personalities common among the educated and semi-educated people of those times. The novel delves deep into the fascination with Europe, studying there even if it is only to secure a diploma, the posturing of those who have been there, and the blonde foreign wife as the appropriation of a chunk of Europe (especially Sartre's cousin!). There is also a real stratum of café intellectuals and literati who discourse at length on books of which they only know the titles, and of ideas that are acquired from gossip. The milieu of jealous personal relations, gossip and back-stabbing, is skilfully satirized in the novel.

However, despite its fantasy, the novel does point to important realities of Iraqi society during those decades. One is the topography of Baghdad, and the character of various neighborhoods. Cultural Baghdad around Rashid Street features some the landmarks of the time: Mackenzie's bookshop, the café milieu of the literary world, the Brazilian and the Swiss cafés, the Waq Waq, Sharif wa-Haddad bar. It draws interesting sketches of the neighborhoods, markets, and particularly of slums (including the *sarayif*, hovels, in al-'Asima, the shanty town of rural migrants from the south and their buffaloes, later to become successively Madinat al-Thawra, Madinat Saddam, Madinat al-Sadr). More important, the novel tries to evoke a cosmopolitan Baghdad, featuring the Christians, the Jews and an Europeanized milieu (but not Shi'is and Sunnis!). It is a de-tribalized, non-sectarian Baghdad, where religion enters only fleetingly, and in comic contexts. The characters, as we saw, are not entirely credible, and the Christian and Jewish accents of Baghdadi speech are not always accurate. Yet, the atmosphere of a now forgotten pluralist Baghdad is well evoked. It is, perhaps, part of the wave of nostalgia for the cosmopolitan which we now find in intellectual milieus from Istanbul to Alexandria to Beirut: The attempt to recapture a romanticized past while facing the rampant waves of sectarian religiosity and xenophobia of the present.

Hayat Sharara, *Idha al-Ayamu Aghsaqat* (When Darkness Fell)

This is a transparently autobiographical novel, recounting the life of university academics in the 1980s and 1990s, during the Iran war, then the Kuwait war, and the years of sanctions. Those were decades of catastrophic decline in Iraqi economy and society, and of ever more repressive and arbitrary measures by the regime. It is the period of impoverishment, subordination and humiliation of the educated and professional middle classes. Hayat Sharara, a professor of Russian literature at Baghdad University, and a writer and a translator, committed suicide in 1997. This book was published posthumously. She was from a renowned intellectual Iraqi-Lebanese family, and her father was a writer and teacher with known communist affiliations. She left the communist party after a while and was politically independent. She refused to join the Ba'th Party, and was one of the few academics that remained outside. Because of her refusal to join the Party, she was transferred to work as a translator in the Ministry of Industry, but eventually returned to the University. During the 1990s, she suffered huge hardships and harassment in her profession. Her husband, a surgeon, also suffered discrimination for being an ex-communist and for refusing to join the Ba'th. He died of a stroke in 1982, leaving Hayat with two daughters.

The novel is written in the style of a documentary and is considered stark and transparent. It is narrated in first person by a male professor, also on the point of applying for retirement, and surveying his career in the university and the day-to-day events at the end of his working life in the 1990s. Along with other members of this middle class, the professors are beset by poverty and the constant struggle for the basics of life, but also by oppressive and arbitrary harassment at work and by the petty controls imposed on them. The sense that comes out of these events is that of constant humiliation, a narrative of petty surveillance, accusations and disciplinary measures against the professors. This sense of hopelessness stems from the bitter truth that the personnel in top positions, such as Dean and Head of Department, have reached these positions not on the basis of merit and professional competence but because of their rank in the Party and the security apparatus. They are resentful of colleagues with any claim to scholarly distinction, and ever jealous to assert their authority. The Dean is a bully, always bad- tempered and anxious to find fault with the professors and issuing arbitrary penalties. He stands at the entrance to the college in the mornings to catch professors who may arrive late. He harangues and humiliates the narrator, a distinguished senior professor. The staff members are also subject to regulations and controls from security personnel: For example, entering the photocopying room requires security clearance and express permission from the officer-in-charge. An angry and threatening security officer confronts a professor ignorant of this new regulation. Students with Party rank are admitted without the necessary qualifications. The professor is confronted with a demand from the Head of Department to pass a student who did not attend classes or submit any of the required course work, and threatened with dire consequences when he demurs. The most vulnerable group are the female teaching assistants, recent graduates with high honors who are appointed to these posts while preparing for doctorates. They are mainly female because their male equivalents have been conscripted into the army. They are expected to be at the beck and call of the senior authority figures, making tea and performing menial services. They are harassed and exploited, and any protest or complaint can lead to dismissal or worse.

The professional associations, such as the professors' union or the historians' society, are all incorporated into the Party, and rather than affording their members protection, actually act as disciplinary organs. This is an example of how the most basic units of "civil society" are colonized and incorporated into the Party and the regime. The culture of surveillance and accusation is illustrated by the plight of one of the professors, Badri, whose cousin, a cloth merchant in the Shi'i shrine city of Karbala, is arrested and convicted of "sabotaging the national economy" and sentenced to ten years in prison. As a result, all his family members come under suspicion. Badri is called and interrogated by college security, and his protests that he had no connection to his cousin do not protect him from repeated questioning and suspicion. Periodically, all professors were required to answer a questionnaire about their own activities and associations, past and present, and also about members of their family and kinship group to the fourth degree: Their residence and work, whether they had participated in the war with Iran, and which of them were killed, wounded or taken prisoner, or traitors who were imprisoned or executed. If a relative had been so indicted then the respondent is under further suspicion: Guilt by kinship or association. These responses are then checked for accuracy and any evasive response pursued with further questioning. In this case Badri was repeatedly harassed and threatened until he agreed to turn spy and informer on his colleagues and students.

In 1986, during the war with Iran, all university students and staff under the age of 45 were required to "volunteer" for military training. No exceptions were allowed, even on grounds of health and disability. Even the spastic and the blind were taken. All were taken in buses and lorries to desert camps, where they spent months in the middle of the burning Iraqi summer. Some were injured or fell ill, and there were a few deaths too. That exercise made no serious contribution to the military effort; its function was the mobilization of the educated elites and their subordination to military discipline and regime control, yet another method of imposing fear and subordination.

The general sense of helplessness, fear and humiliation on the part of the middle classes after 1990 was reinforced and exacerbated by the constant struggle for material necessities, primarily for food. Food of all kinds was plentiful in the shops, but the prices were far beyond the means of those earning inflation-hit public sector salaries. Meat became a rare luxury for these families, and their diet depended primarily on cheap seasonal vegetables and pulses, with occasional dairy products. Public sector functionaries, including professors, were granted certain privileges, such as subsidized food from cooperative societies specific to their institutions. For our professors, the cooperative society shop provided some food items, mainly pulses and basic vegetables like onions, and occasionally yoghurt or cream. However, many of these provisions were stolen by the shop assistants to sell on the open market. The professors were exposed to further hardship and humiliation as they elbowed one another in long queues waiting for the doors to open and pushing to the front to get the most desirable items before they ran out. On one such occasion our protagonist only managed a tub of yoghurt and small pack of cream.

A further "perk" was a monthly cash grant for writers, intellectuals and journalists. The amount varied according to one of four ranks of merit into which the recipients were placed. The ranking was, apparently, arbitrary, and some senior academics found themselves in the lower orders. The petty rivalries so generated were further avenues of humiliation. The grants were eroded by inflation and became nearly worthless. But the recipients were compelled to receive them, on one appointed day per month, when they had to crowd into an office and wait for long periods. So, rather than a privilege, the grant became yet another burden, and the compulsory wait for it another avenue of humiliation.

The most novel episode of harassment and humiliation, however, was that of body weight control for public sector functionaries, starting the late 1980s, then at yearly intervals into the 1990s. An order came from the Presidency that all public servants should keep their body weight within certain limits, determined by age, sex, and height. A healthy and elegant appearance was required of all state functionaries, and excess weight in its servants was considered to diminish the dignity of the state. Hence a date was set for the personnel of each sector to present themselves for weighing, and if found overweight, they would be subjected to penalties of demotion and cuts in salary. There is a description of the great hardships suffered by all these middle-aged professors on strict diets. The Iraqi middle classes were, as a rule, fond of drink, especially ice-cold beer in the middle of a hot summer day, and abstention from this pleasure was a great deprivation. As the fateful day approached, those with excess weight had to intensify their diet, many fasting for a week and taking small amounts of fluids. The ultimate hardship was on the day itself, when a large crowd of professors waited in line for many hours in the heat, only to encounter added bureaucracy, requiring each to answer a questionnaire, but without enough copies to go round.

The clinic was narrow, badly organized and unprepared to cope with the great numbers, with the result of a crush of anxious and angry academics trying to elbow their way in, then unable to get out because of the crush outside, and many resorting to squeezing in and out through a street window. It is a comic scene, but one which underlines the abjection to which intellectuals and professionals were subjected, proclaiming the regime's control over their bodies as well as their souls. The regime intruded into their professional lives, censored and dictated what they researched, taught and wrote, mobilized them for its political and military functions, subjected them to constant suspicion, surveillance and investigation, and ultimately sought to attack their well-being and dignity with these harsh and humiliating rituals.

Material hardships inevitably affected relations between staff and students. Realizing the poverty of their teachers, students sought to bribe them for higher grades. The higher the teacher in the regime hierarchy, the more confident were students in offering such bribes, of items of food, drink (especially whisky), tobacco, car spare parts and domestic implements. Girls were exploited by some of them for sexual favors. Hardship also drove female students to genteel prostitution.

In short, the regime pampered the intelligentsia, or those of them who had survived the campaigns of repression and arbitrary punishment in the heyday of prosperity in the 1970s, providing them with incentives for allegiance and active support. But when resources declined, they were diverted more exclusively to the benefit of the ruling cliques and the circles charged with their security. The intelligentsia were then subordinated and controlled by direct surveillance and arbitrary discipline, always reminding them of their vulnerable and subordinate position.

As a documentary novel, this narrative does not have much of a developing plot, just the episodes illustrating the impoverishment and humiliation of the university community and its ever more abject subordination to the ruling cliques and their security apparatus.

Conclusion

I have surveyed three rather different and disparate books. Each gives a glimpse of some aspect of Iraqi society during the second half of the twentieth century. The main subject is the intelligentsia and the educated middle class, although the lower middle class of functionaries and teachers are the subjects of Takarli's novel. Genteel poverty and decent living, the voices of different genders and generations, torn between modern careers and education on the one side and traditional gender roles and notions of honor on the other, finally subject to the vagaries of political upheaval and violence. Badr's satire is of another sector of the intelligentsia, constructing a rickety imaginary world of Bohemian indulgence, picking crumbs of ideas and slogans from European philosophies. At the same time it reminds the reader of a cosmopolitan and pluralist Baghdad in which tribe and religion play little or no part. It was written in the 1990s when tribe and religion had come to the fore. The intelligentsia and the educated professional classes had by then been marginalized, impoverished, and subordinated. Sharara's novel traces the brutal contours of that decline. The aftermath of the American invasion encouraged the rise of tribalism, religious authority, and sectarianism. All these had been nurtured by the Saddam regime, but were given free rein with the collapse of government and any vestiges of civil society. The essentially "national" class has been driven underground and into exile.

HISTORY AND FICTION
IN THE NEW IRAQI CINEMA

Lucia Sorbera

The close relationship between cinema and history represents a challenging field for historians. Since its inception, cinema has drawn from history, and the history of cinema is therefore the history of its bond with human history. Cinema has been a source for historians, as historical writing, as the agent of history,[1] as a tool to collect data and to bear witness; the relationship between the two has always been contentious and it continues to rack the brains of historians.[2]

The earliest commentators to theorize on the use of feature films as historical sources were Marc Ferro and Pierre Sorlin in the 1970s. Until then, historians had been very cautious, almost suspicious, about using audiovisual sources, and when they were used, they were almost always documentaries.[3] The new lease of life initiated — albeit with different accents and nuances — by Ferro and Sorlin had been one of the legacies of the *nouvelle histoire*. In fact, the lesson given by the *Annales* was seminal

---

[1]The notion of cinema as an agent of history was introduced by Marc Ferro (1977). It implies that cinema influences the evolution of society. The most obvious case is propaganda, where a certain vision of the world is also imposed through films. But even in nondictatorial contexts, cinema makes a contribution to the building of the imaginary of an epoch.

[2]For a survey of the debate see Pithon (1995, pp. 5–13) and Lagny (2001: 265–291).

[3]In the introduction to *The Film in History. Restaging the Past*, Pierre Sorlin underlines that, in fact British scholars used films to teach history much more than their French colleagues, but they favor documentaries over fiction films. To give some example of this trend, Pierre Sorlin quotes *The Birth of the Movies* (Wenden, 1975), *The Historian and Film* (London and Smith, 1976). At the time when Sorlin was writing (1980), the issue was significant. Today, historians and filmmakers dispute the border between fiction and documentary as well.

in shifting the notion of "historical source," acknowledging that every object, material or immaterial, if adequately questioned, can become an historical source, and that every human cultural and material expression has the potential to be a source for the historian (Le Goff and Nora, 1974/1981, pp. vii–xii).

Ferro and Sorlin pay attention to the analysis of both film and production, considering that both aspects are strictly correlated in the historical process. According to Ferro, films enlighten what remain hidden memories in official texts. Sorlin asserts that fiction films are sources for social history, and he suggests a method of analysis which blends a sociological approach (grounded in the study of the cinema as an unity of production founded on the division of the work) with a semiotic one, according to which cinema is a system of signs. Sorlin invites us to search into the cinema, to look for what is before everyone's eyes, but which no-one can see: Representations and self-representations, which constitute the essential part of the history of mentalities (Sorlin, 1979, p. 69).

Thirty years of studies, publications and debates could not arrive at a solution, but at least all this activity has brought scholars a series of new theoretical questions. During a brief survey of studies of this intricate issue since the 1970s, I have found important suggestions in a series of questions proposed in a recent work by Michèle Lagny. Under what conditions can we use cinema for historical research? What objectives can historians achieve by using cinema as a source? What is the bond between filmic representation and memory or collective mentalities? Can the cinema serve to build critical history? (Lagny, 2001, p. 267). I have approached contemporary Iraqi cinematographic production with this set of questions in mind.

In Iraq, as in many other parts of the world, cinema has a long tradition. Throughout this period, the Iraqi dream factory went through different stages, in which periods of growth alternated with periods of stagnation. The years immediately following the fall of Saddam Husayn's regime stand out as one of the brightest for Iraqi cinema, in particular for independent productions, which seem to be having some success in the cultural panorama of the country after decades of state hegemony and violent censorship. In the aftermath of the fall of the regime, several Iraqi intellectuals, both resident and expatriate, are involved in cinema production. Participating in a general mood of confidence in the new cultural atmosphere, Iraqi filmmakers of several generations are engaging in a lively creation of audiovisual productions.

An important part of this activity is simply to document what is going on in the country under occupation. Indeed, film makers express varying attitudes toward the present condition of the country: A plethora of emotions, ranging from hope to despair, from confidence to fear, from happiness to powerlessness, make their way in what may be called the new Iraqi cinema.

In recent years, interest in new Iraqi cinema production and in its predecessors has gone beyond the borders of the Middle East. The seventh edition of the *Biénnale des Cinémas Arabes* (Paris, 2004) dedicated a section to Iraqi cinema where 20 Iraqi movies (feature films, short films, documentaries) were screened. The overview ranged from the classics to the cinema of the *mahjar*, to the new productions. Between 2006 and 2008 several cultural cooperation projects have resulted in many festivals dedicated to new Iraqi cinema. On the one hand, it is a consequence of the sad reality of the country, while on the other, it is the first sign of an interest that goes beyond politics to embrace artistic developments.

Given this general context, this paper has two main goals. The first is to situate these new productions within the wider context of Iraqi cinematic history, looking at linkages with contemporary international productions and finding out frames of reference as well as principal trends. The second is to make a contribution to the contemporary debate about the rebuilding — or reshaping — of Iraqi memory and history, trying to shed light on the elements of this new cinema which might help historians in understanding and writing the past.

After a short historical account, where the most important directors, titles and genres will be mentioned, I will focus on the films made immediately after the fall of Saddam Husayn's regime, in order to show the main trends and the principal topics as well as the daily problems faced by Iraqi filmmakers today. The corpus of work to which I am referring includes feature films, short films and documentaries. The majority of these works are concerned with contemporary realities, while others focus on collective memory. My general aim is to show how, in the hands of the historian, they can also function as documents and historical accounts.

One Century of Iraqi Cinema and Beyond

The first screening in Baghdad took place in the Dar al-Shifé Café, on July 26, 1909. Until the end of the 1940s, all films viewed in Baghdadi theatres and cafés were imported from abroad, mostly from Britain, France, and Egypt. *Cairo-Baghdad* by Ahmad Badrakhan (1945) and *Ibn al-Sharq* by Niyazi Mustapha (1946) inaugurated the trend of Egyptian-Iraqi co-production. In that period, "Iraqi" movies were directed by Egyptian film-makers, filmed in Baghdad and Cairo studios, and acted by Egyptian and Iraqi actors.

In 1948, Baghdad Studio, run by Iraqi producers, had fairly sophisticated equipment, but its life was fated to be short. Some of its founders, who were Jewish businessmen, were accused of being Zionist spies and the Studio was forced to close. One of the most beloved films in the history of Iraqi cinema was shot in a Baghdad Studio: *'Aliya wa 'Isam* (1948), by the French director André Shatan. Freely inspired by Romeo and Juliet, the film tells the story of a young Bedouin, 'Isam,.who falls in love with 'Aliya. Their two families, in conflict because of a history of tribal revenge, are opposed to the match; indeed, 'Isam is murdered and 'Aliya commits suicide. On the set, we can see some of the stars-to-be of Iraqi cinema for the first time, among them the much loved Ja'far al-Sa'di and Salima Murad.

New attempts to create Iraqi cinema productions were made in the 1950s, when the two actors Yas 'Ali al-Nasir and Salah al-Din al-Badri founded *Dunya al-Fann*, and produced *Fitna wa Hasan* (1954). The romantic topic of *'Aliya wa 'Isam* was taken up, and the Bedouin setting, which was very popular at the time (in Iraq, but also in Egypt) explains much of the film's popularity. Among the fairly forgettable films shot in the 1950s, only two stand out: *Man al-Mas'ul?* (Who is Responsible? 1956) by 'Abd al-Jabbar al-Wali, and *Sa'id Effendi* (1957) by Kamran Husni. The two directors, just back from studying cinema in the United States, aimed to lay down the foundations of an Iraqi realist cinema, and they achieved their ambition.

Man al-Mas'ul? is the story of a young lower-class woman who is raped by a middle-class man. She does not reveal this and marries a man from her own class background. But, on the first night of their marriage, the groom discovers that she is not a virgin. When she tells him her story, and convinces him that she is a victim, he decides to keep her. Later on, she gets sick and, before she dies, she reveals to her husband that the doctor who is healing her is also her rapist. After the woman's death, the husband decides to avenge her honor by killing the doctor and, in consequence, is condemned to spend the rest of his life in prison.

This film was the first appearance of Nahida al-Rammah, a star of Iraqi realist cinema. She would later be forced to flee from Iraq to Europe, and her biography has been recently narrated in a documentary by the director

Qutayba al-Janabi: *Wasteland, Between London and Baghdad* (London, 1998).

Sa'id Effendi was based on a book by Edmond Sabri, a famous Iraqi writer of the first half of the twentieth century. It is the story of an old employee of the Ottoman administration, who is losing his privileges in a changing world. The film was meant as a criticism of the monarchy and adopted a realist style. It was presented at the Moscow film festival in 1958, the year of the July revolution.

Until the late fifties, several documentaries were made by the Iraq Petroleum Company (IPC), which produced *Baladna*, a cine-news series screened before the main movie. Most of the cameramen were British, working in the cinema department of the company. The only exception was Majid Kamil, who would later become a famous Iraqi cameraman.

The Iraqi government took control of cinema production soon after the 1958 revolution. The General Department for Cinema and Theatre was created in 1959, under the Ministry of Culture. In that period several patriotic movies were produced, like as *Iradat al-Sha'b* (The Will of the People, 1959), and *Ana al-'Iraq* (I am Iraq, 1960) by Burhan al-Din Jasim. Nevertheless, Iraqi production remained weak. Viola Shafik reminds us that only 99 films were produced between 1946 and 2003, less than two a year. There were few productions, and they were generally controlled by the government, whose policies exhibited various degrees of discontinuity. In fact, one-third of these 99 films were released between 1959 and 1977, and after 1991 production was reduced to a few TV series (Shafik, 2007, p. 41).

Hence about 30 films were produced between 1959 and 1977 — patriotic and historical films, but also comedies, westerns, *noirs* and melodramas: *Nabuchadnezar* (1962), directed by Kamil al-'Azzawi; *Qitar al-Sa'a Saba'a* (The Seven o'clock Train, 1963) directed by Hikmat Labib, who tried to replicate American suspense movies after his stay in the United States; *Na'ima* (1962) directed by 'Abd al-Jabbar Wali, a comedy set in the countryside. *Abu Hilla* (Hilla's Father, 1962), directed by Muhammad Shukri Jamil and Yusuf Girgis, portrays the generational gap among the young of the 1960s and their parents, in a movie where the older characters are ridiculed, while *Basrah Sa'a ahad-'ashara* (Eleven o'clock in Basra, 1965), by William Simon is inspired by the American police genre.

After the *coup d'état* of February 8, 1963, cinema production experienced the waves of fear prevalent throughout the country. *Awraq al-kharif* (Autumn Leaves, 1963) by Hikmat Labib played in almost empty cinemas. *al-Haris* (The Night Watchman, 1968), by Khalil Shawqi, marks a second important stage in the history of Iraqi cinema. It tells the story of a night watchman who fall in love with a widow. When she refuses him and marries someone else, he steals the portraits that another admirer, a painter, had made of her. Produced by *Aflam al-Yawm* the film had a great success (90,000 viewers in two weeks) and in 1968 it won the Silver Tanit at the Carthage Film Festival, the first for an Iraqi film.

After the *coup d'état* that brought it to power in 1968, the Ba'th Party started a program of cultural nationalization. After that, filmmaking became quite dangerous, since the directors were required to be loyal and not create problems for the regime. The situation became even worse after Saddam Husayn's seizure of power. Several ideological films were produced in this period, including *al-Zami'un* (The Thirsty, 1972), *al-Aswar* (The Wall, 1979) and *al-Mas'ala al-Kubra* (The Great Question, 1983), all by Muhammad Shukri Jamil. *al-Ra's* (The Head, 1976) and *al-Nahar* (The River, 1977) were directed by Faysal al-Yasiri.

During these years, many Egyptian directors worked for the Iraqi Film and Theatre Organization. *al-Qadisiya* (1981), by Salah Abu Sayf, recalls the battle for the conquest of Iraq from the Sasanians. Like several of the movies made in under the Ba'th, *al-Qadisiya* is a typical example of what Sorlin teaches about historical fiction: "a historical film reorganizing the present on the pretext of the past" (Sorlin, 1980/84, p. 75). In the context of the time it was propaganda aimed at mobilizing people in favor of the war against Iran.

In 1980, *al-Ayyam al-Tawila* (The Long Days), by Salih Tawfiq, tells the story of the group which attempted to assassinate 'Abd al-Karim Qasim in 1959. The attempt failed and the would-be assassins (who of course included Saddam Husayn) are forced to flee to the desert. *al-Malik Ghazi* (King Ghazi, 1993), by Muhammad Shukri Jamil, was the regime's last big production, another national epic, this time to justify the invasion of Kuwait.

These first decades bear out at least two of the axioms taught by the scholars who explored the connection between cinema and social history. The first is that films, with their imaginary stories, occasionally reveal the problems that the authorities try to conceal (Sorlin, 1980/84, p. 73). At first glance historians might be tempted to reject them out of hand, on the grounds that they are simply "propaganda" and that, as falsifications of reality, they cannot be useful sources of investigation. On the contrary, if subjected to rigorous investigation, they can yield important information. Of course the questions will not be concerned with the historical tales the films pretend to tell, but with the time at which and the context in which they were made.

Second, these films do not give us a direct understanding of the political history of the period (in this case, the political history of Saddam Husayn's regime). They ask the historian to change his questions and to shift from political history to the history of mentalities. Indeed, they can open a window on the collective imaginary of the Iraqi people at the time, permitting a kind of historical anthropology. Given the proper questions, any film can became a source in spite of itself.

The history of cinema has a complex character, which allows a wide perspective on reality. This is because cinema is a privileged historical observatory. It develops many histories and it appears like a privileged *topos* from which complexity can be challenged (Brunetta, 2001, p. 196). After the earlier productions, à la Hollywood-on-the-Nile, with popular love stories and musicals, and after the subsequent trend of the realist-oriented and socially committed films of the late 1950s and 1960s, Saddam Husayn's regime represented a period of extreme difficulty for the development of Iraqi cinema. In this field, as in other cultural fields, the regime used culture and arts to promote its goals. The state presented itself as the main promoter of culture, and, in doing so, it financed the work of selected directors. But the lack of a coherent cultural policy was not without its harmful effects. After the 1980s, cinema productions and equipment deteriorated, and many master tapes were destroyed, due either to military operations during the war against Iran or to the embargo.

The situation began to change somewhat in Kurdistan in the 1990s where the greater autonomy gained as a result of American military operations also affected cinema production. In fact, the Iraqi-Kurdish film *Narjis, Bride of Kurdistan* by Ja'far 'Ali was released in Arbil in 1991, and a number of films have appeared in Kurdistan since 2003: *Kilometre Zero* by Hiner Salem (2005); *Zaman al-Narjis* (Narcissus Blossom, 2005) by Mas'ud 'Arif Salih; *Parinawa la Ghobar* (Crossing the Dust) by Shawkat Amin Korki; and *Makaab Shaab* (The Rebirth of the Citizen). These movies narrated the sufferings imposed by Saddam's regime on the Kurdish people. None of them were screened in Baghdad until the most recent *al-Mada* cultural festival in May 2008. Meanwhile, thousands of Iraqi intellectuals and artists, including many filmmakers and technicians, had been forced to leave the country. Beirut was their first destination, then Europe and the United States. Thus the history of Iraqi cinema in the *mahjar* began.

Being a Filmmaker after the Fall

The growth of Iraqi cinema has been marked by domestic and international troubles since its early stages. In the 1990s, political tyranny and the UN sanctions constrained freedom of artistic expression and compelled many filmmakers to flee the country. Today the situation is completely different, but it would be unrealistic to claim that all the problems have disappeared. In what follows, I will examine the complex situation that affects cinema and the arts in general today, trying to look at the situation from the artists' point of view. For this purpose, an overview of the leitmotifs of cinematographic discourse since 2003 will be useful.

"Baghdad, open city," was the subheading of the two stories narrated in *Underexposure*, and *Ahlam*, the first feature films shot in Iraq after the Anglo–American invasion. The crew working on these two movies were professional volunteers, while the post-production took place in Europe (Germany and UK), because after thirteen years of embargo and three wars there are no film labs in Iraq. The two films were shot outdoors, and the helicopters and tanks of the occupying forces continuously crossed the sets. Meanwhile, the focus on private, individual stories allows the directors to elaborate the present-day condition of artists in the country. The dramatic expedient used by the authors was to overturn the topic of heroism often at the core of the narrative genre that, more than any other, narrates war: the epic.[4] In doing so, they might seem to be paying homage to some Italian neorealist's *chef d'oeuvre*, in which the occupation of Rome was narrated through the eyes of the citizens. However, the comparison is only partially accurate, since Rossellini's war trilogy does not privilege anti-heroism, but instead, the heroism of ordinary people. The reverse of the traditional canons of narration is typical of contemporary productions. In fact, there are also examples of anti-heroism in contemporary Middle Eastern cinematography, particularly in recent Lebanese and Palestinian films.[5] Certainly, this way of narrating the war represents a clear discontinuity from the Iraqi cinema of the 1980s, in which, as we have seen, cultural production was largely aimed at mobilizing the population in support of the war. The discontinuity from the previous Iraqi school is underlined by 'Udayy Rashid when he remembers the time that he left the Baghdad Academy of Fine Arts, feeling

---

[4]For the representation of war in Western literature see Scurati (2007).
[5]See, for example, Viola Shafik's comments about *West Beirut* by Ziad Doueiri, in Shafik (2007: 229–231).

uncomfortable with the traditional way of teaching, preferring to find his own way.[6] 'Udayy Rashid was born in 1973 and belongs to a generation that, thanks to Saddam regime and UN sanctions, was kept out of international cultural life for more than a decade. In 1991, he was one of the founders of *al-Najin*, the survivors, a group of artists, writers, poets, and directors whose mission was, in his words: "an emotional and cultural reaction to what was happening." Before 2003, the group performed its projects underground to avoid censorship. After the Anglo–American invasion, the artists of *al-Najin* appeared in public with a series of notable performances.[7] One of the main assertions of this young generation is the creation of a clear discontinuity from the recent past. Meanwhile, they call for a deep re-examination of the Iraqi artistic heritage, taking into account the dialectic between specificity and entanglements with other cultural contexts. Again, 'Udayy Rashid underlines that:

> "Baghdad used to be the cultural center of the Arab world. While I am talking about Baghdad, I am talking about hundreds of years. After 30 years of dictatorship, three wars, 13 years of sanctions, we need to rebuild our minds, not just the buildings. Until today, we suffered the censorship of the regime. Today, we suffer the censorship of sectarianism and fundamentalism."

Underexposure was filmed between November 2003 and April 2004, but the crew could not stay on the set more than 30 days because of worsening security conditions. The title refers to the material used in a masterly fashion by the director of photography Ziyad Turki — old 35 mm films that had been abandoned in a storehouse since the time of the embargo. "It was the first time that Ziyad worked with 35 mm films," says Rashid. At the same time, the title is also a metaphor for the condition of Iraqi artists. In fact, Rashid explains that: "underexposed are the lives that we lived from Saddam Husayn to now." Behind the main character of the story, a filmmaker named Hasan, wandering in the ruins of the city, hides the director of the film himself, his questions, his doubts, and his fears. Hasan is the alter ego of the director and, maybe, of all his companions, when he says, "I am a

---

[6]This and other biographical information about Udayy Rashid's work and poetry comes an interview with the director, made by the author on October 7, 2007 in Hamburg.

[7] *They Passed by Here*, a play written and directed by Basim al-Hajar, was performed on Sunday May 4, 2003 at al-Rashid theater, the most famous Iraqi theater, which was bombed in 2003; the building of a statue in Fardous Square, where Saddam's statue previously stood. The monument of al-Najin was built by the sculptor Basim Hamad and was unveiled on May 29, 2003.

survivor." 'Udayy Rashid defines his film as a sort of "visual diary," and he asserts the willingness to "rebuild our memory archive." Even if the general idea had been in his mind since the beginning, the script was written day by day in collaboration with the poet Faris Harram.

Underexposure is a film about Baghdad during the war. The story of the city reflects the condition of the artist who resists violence. It is both a claim to the right to produce culture and beauty, and a declaration of love for the masters of *neorealismo* and *nouvelle vague*. We can add that it is a film made out of the ashes of war and occupation, but in which war and occupation are also objects of narration. The war is a metaphor representing the difficulty of living an ordinary everyday life, the complexity of growing up and being considered to have come of age as an artist, and the difficulty of being free and of expressing oneself.

Ahlam was directed by Muhammad al-Daradji and, like *Underexposure*, was filmed in the aftermath of 2003. In the classic war film — as in the epic narrative — the hero is a man, or, to make the point, a soldier. In *Ahlam* the main character is a young woman, who becomes insane and is recovering in a psychiatric hospital after the killing of her husband on their wedding day. During a bombing, the psychiatric hospital in which Ahlam has been confined is hit, and all the patients, herself included, run away.[8] In *Ahlam*, war does not produce heroes, only armies of mad ghosts roaming in the city under occupation (helicopters and tanks are always on the ground) in desperate and vain attempts to regain it. Ahlam seems to be a cinematographic transposition of a post-modern knight errant, a sort of contemporary Orlando. Rambling in the city wearing her wedding dress, she is naïve, vulnerable and hallucinating. The destiny of Ahlam is interwoven with that of the former soldier — and deserter — 'Ali, and of Dr. Mahdi, in a sort of picaresque novel, where it is not clear whether madness is inside or outside the walls of the hospital, and where it is not obvious who is Don Quixote, or

---

[8]As very often in contemporary in Iraqi cinema, the story was inspired by real events. In the aftermath of the Anglo–American invasion, the marines came through the gates of the al-Rashid psychiatric hospital in Baghdad and knocked down the walls with their tanks. Waves of looters came in with them and stole everything. Chronicles of the time describe the hundreds of fugitives and the destruction of the hospital. See Patrick E. Tyler, "Aftereffects: The Psychiatric Hospital in Baghdad's Anarchy, the Insane Went Free," *New York Times*, May 12, 2003; Christine Aziz, "Al Rashid psychiatric hospital, Baghdad," *The Magazine of the Red Cross and Red Crescent Movement*, 2003; Andrew Buncombe, "Psychiatric hospital in chaos amid claim that patients were raped by looters," *The Independent*, April 19, 2003.

Sancho Panza, or Dulcinea. In this feature film, as in the first one, the reverse of the canons of war narration is the most interesting element. Less convincing, and not really corresponding to present day social realities, is the use of the woman as a metaphor of the raped, occupied nation.[9]

To stage the anti-hero is the only way to tell the war without indulging in the rhetoric of nostalgia, of liberation or of patriotism (all clichés present in the "regime cinema" of the 1980s, but also in some American films set in contemporary Iraq). Madness, the second key element in *Underexposure* and *Ahlam*, is the only way that the characters of the films can survive the realm of the chaos in the city. Ahlam, who loses her sense of the pain inflicted by the regime, will not come to her senses after the "liberation." Bombs can break the walls of the madhouse, but they cannot give back the lost years to its mad inhabitants. The young director seems to suggest that there cannot be any liberation for people that have suffered so much. On another level, entrusting the view of the city in flames to such characters, who have always been emblematic of alienation from historical time, could be a way of suspending judgment on present day realities.

The Iraqi cinema of today has been compared to Italian neo-realism, and the youngest directors try to pay explicit homage to the masters of this cinematographic genre. In Iraq, the renaissance of cinema took place, as in the Italian case, after the fall of a dictatorial regime. But more than 50 years have passed, and the Iraqi scene today is completely different from that of Italy after the Second World War. The various legacies and identities emerging from these films seem plural and fragmented, which makes any true comparison difficult. It may be that the neo-realist lesson learned by these directors is an attempt to render the atmosphere of the end of the regime and of the war through the dramas and problems of everyday life. From this point of view, there is a common thread running through the feature films and documentaries produced in Iraq since 2003: the compelling need to bear witness.[10]

---

[9]Of course, it is possible that the rape of Ahlam is not intended to be a metaphor, but simply an account of what actually happened in those days to many women patients at the hospital. If it is the case, the episode has to be read as a denunciation, uncovering a social problem that strongly affects the Iraqi people today. For a more general examination of gender and violence issues in Iraq under occupation see Al-Ali (2007: 214–259); Al-Ali and Pratt (2009: 75–80).

[10]As observed by Michèle Lagny with regard to Italian neorealism, the distinction proposed by Marc Ferro between "cinema as a witness" and "cinema as an agent" needs to be nuanced. In fact the two functions tend to fuse together. All witnessing seeks to be efficacious, and no action can be sustained without witnessing (Lagny, 2001: 277).

Novels of Everyday Life as Told
by the "Embargo Generation"

In the audiovisual panorama in Iraq today, the border between fiction and documentary is blurred. As we saw above, reality tends to blend with fiction, while some elements of fiction become introduced into the documentary. As Rancière has remarked "documentary is the cinema par excellence" (Rancière, 1998, p. 57).

Soon after the fall of Baghdad, the occupation became the principal reality affecting the everyday lives of ordinary people. This experience became the focus of many films. In particular, telling stories about everyday life and the longing for "normality" seems to be the task of the rising generation of younger Iraqi filmmakers, who are mostly under 30. This so-called "embargo generation," which grew up in the 1990s, is mostly active in making short films. Everyday life is explored in all its aspects: private and public, work and love, family and friendship, homesickness and fears. They are backed by older Iraqi filmmakers and teachers, mainly expatriates, who run training programs for them. I refer in particular to two examples: The Independent Film and TV College of Baghdad (IFTVC), headed by Maysoon Pachachi and Qasim 'Abid, and the project Hometown Baghdad, coproduced by the New York based Chat the Planet (a global youth dialog company) and directed by Ziyad Turki.[11]

The first four documentaries made by students of the IFTVC in Baghdad were shot between the end of 2004 and October 2005. "Each opens a window into the life of ordinary Iraqis in this extraordinary time. Elections were held in January 2005 and there was a referendum on the constitution in October; the films reflect the confusion between distrust and hope felt by many Iraqis at the time."[12] Maysoon Pachachi says that the courses were held in very challenging and dangerous circumstances. She adds:

> Over a period of two months, two of the students had relatives kidnapped, one had a cousin badly injured by a bomb and one had an uncle killed in an explosion. The disruptions and violence in Baghdad often meant students had difficulty getting into the colleges or were unable to shoot. Several times, they had to rethink their projects and start again. However, their commitment never wavered and they tried to do their work in any way that they could.[13]

---

[11]See HTTP: <http://chattheplanet.com/index.php?page=videos&v=38> and <http://www.iftvc.org/> (accessed 14 November 2009).

[12]See HTTP: <http://www.iftvc.org/> (accessed 14 November 2009).

[13]From the presentation on the IFTV college made by Maysoon Pachachi in Hamburg, October 2007.

One of the most appreciated IFTVC productions is *Baghdad Days* by Hiba Bassam. Already acclaimed at the Rotterdam Arab Film Festival in 2006, where she won the Golden Award, and at the al-Jazira Film Festival in Doha in 2006, where she received the Horizon Silver Award, it is still screened regularly all over the world.[14] Hiba Bassam, a young woman from Kirkuk, documents her return to Baghdad after the war to finish her studies at the Academy of Fine Arts. In a visual diary, she documents her attempts to find a job and a place to live. She documents her graduation from college, how she deals with family problems and struggles to come to terms with her position as a woman working in the media, which she depicts as "still a male-dominated environment."[15]

Hiwar, directed by Kifaya Salih, documents the activities of a cultural center opened in 1992 by a group of artists headed by Qasim Sabti. The difficult experiences of Iraqi in the 1980s and the 1990s are recalled through the story of this meeting place. Qasim Sabti remembers that the war against Iran was supposed to last for two or three years but instead it lasted for nine. He declares that during the war he found his social role, and the importance of bearing witness.

'Umar is my Friend, by Munaf Shakir, tells the story of a student at Baghdad University who works as a taxi driver. The camera follows the taxi driver in a tour of the city, and registers the many daily problems that he faces: The presence of American soldiers in the streets, check-points and closed roads, the lack of petrol. In spite of all these difficulties, the young man, who has four daughters, is still hopeful for the future: "when I have my university degree, I will find a better job in my field." Six months later, the director films him again, and he says, in resigned tones, "in this situation all my studies were of no value."[16] *Let the Show Begin*, by Dhafir Talib, weaves the history of Iraqi cinema into the experience of the International Iraqi Short Film Festival, held in Baghdad in extremely difficult circumstances in September 2005.

Between 2006 and 2007 a second documentary course was held, and six new films were produced. *A Candle for Café Shahbandar*, by 'Imad 'Ali, is extremely moving, thanks to its capacity to combine the café's 90 year history (1917–2007) with the lives of the people who hang out in it now; the main story is told in documentary form through the director's own experience while he was filming. Café Shahbandar was a magnet for Iraqi

---

[14]HTTP: <http://www.iftvc.org/> (accessed 14 November 2009).
[15]*Baghdad Days*, by Hiba Bassam, Iraq, 2005.
[16]*'Umar is My Friend*, by Munaf Shakir, Iraq, 2005 (15 mins.)

intellectuals; founded in 1917 in al-Mutanabbi Street, in the heart of the old center of Baghdad, it was a place where generations of Iraqis came to discuss and debate literature and politics. 'Imad 'Ali had shot most of his film by the end of 2006, but in March 2007, a massive car bomb destroyed the café and all the bookshops on al-Mutanabbi Street, and killed and wounded scores of people. Days later, Baghdad's poets and artists held a walk in the ruins of the street they loved so much and 'Imad took a small camera and went back to film. As he was leaving, he was attacked, his camera was stolen and he was shot in the legs and chest. His own story is an epilogue to his film about the Café Shahbandar and al-Mutanabbi Street before and after they were destroyed.

A Stranger in His Own Country, by Hasanayn al-Hani, recounts the difficult situation in which thousands of displaced people are living in Iraq. The witness is Abu Hali, a refugee from Kirkuk in Karbala'. Abu Hali deplores the "sectarian violence" that forces people to leave their houses. "It has nothing to do with religion [...] they are terrorists."[17] *Leaving*, by Bahram al-Zuhairi, portrays the journey of a Mandaean family from Baghdad, where they had lived for more than thirty years, to Damascus. Again, a story of displaced people, narrated in the first person.

Dr. Nabil, by Ahmad Jabbar tells the story of a surgeon who works at a small understaffed Baghdad hospital, suffering from lack of equipment and medicines. Unlike many other doctors who have been killed or have fled the country in fear of their lives, Dr. Nabil has decided to remain in Baghdad. *Documentary Course March 2006*, by Ahmad Kamal, documents the lives of his fellow students at the IFTVC in Baghdad as they try to get to class, find subjects for the films they want to make and deal with the difficulties of trying to film in Iraq at the moment. In the end, the college has to close down when two people are abducted from the building and an explosion in the street below shatters all its windows. Violence, displacements, sectarianism, explosions and abductions are some of the most current words and themes in these documentaries. These are only a selection of the films that have been produced in Iraq between 2004 and 2008 but, as far as I know, production is still in progress.

The extensive interest in people that we find in Iraqi films and documentaries is expressed at many levels. Some documentaries explicitly address social issues, like, for example *In the Department of Security* (Iraq, 2005)

---

[17] *A Stranger in his own country*, by Hasanayn al-Hani, Iraq, 2007.

and *The Night of the Gipsy Descent* (Iraq, 2006), both by Hadi Mahud. The filmmaker, who is originally from Samarra, lived in Australia for ten years and returned to the country after 2003.[18] Hadi Mahud carries his camera on his own back and engages in direct dialog with people on the road, focusing on marginal districts. The result is the revealing of a subaltern, hidden history, a history of a people with no voice.

Like fiction and all other artistic work, documentaries are not straightforward reflections of reality. On the contrary, they are the artist's interpretation of reality, just as history is the historian's interpretation of the past. It would be very naïve to assert that these works give an accurate portrait of present day Iraq. It is even doubtful whether they can give a picture of the representation of Iraq by Iraqi artists today. In other words, they can inform us about the cultural imaginaries about the present, the past and the future in Iraq today.

Indeed, in looking at these films, we need to remember that the cinema's peculiarity is to present major historical turning points not only through events and the principal actors in them, but also through the everyday behavior of ordinary people. Cinema is particularly well-equipped to record the dialectic between the individual and the flow of history.

The Return to the Homeland and Memories

Soon after the fall of Baghdad, many filmmakers based abroad came back to the country for a variety of reasons: The need to observe what was going on in person, the wish to make their own peaceful contribution to the reshaping of the nation, or simply homesickness. *Return to the Land of Wonders* by Maysoon Pachachi, *Where is Iraq* by Baz Sham'un, *The Dreams of Sparrows* by Haydar Daffar, *The Song of the Missing Men* by Layth 'Abd al-Amir, *About Baghdad* by Sinan Antun, *Life after the Fall*, by Qasim 'Abid are some of the films that tell the story of the return to the homeland.

Dialectic between exile and homeland is not new in Iraqi expatriate filmmakers. Maysoon Pachachi had approached the issue earlier in 1994 with *Iraqi Women — Voices from Exile* (UK, 1994); Qutayba al-Janabi in 1998 with *Wasteland-Between London and Baghdad* (UK, 1998). In 1991 Qasim 'Abid portrayed the lives and work of four Iraqi artists leaving in Italy (*Amid the Alien Corn*, UK, 1991); in 2002 Samir documented the stories

---

[18]Interview with Hadi Mahud in Hamburg, October 9, 2008.

of Iraqi Jews who had fled from Iraq after the 1950s, through the lives of many intellectuals (*Forget Baghdad*, Switzerland/Germany, 2002); 'Abbas Fadhil documented his return to Iraq in 2002 with *A'ada ila Babil* (2002) and in 2004 with *Nahnu al-'Iraqiyyun*, as well at Tariq Hashim in 2002 with *16 Sa'a fi Baghdad.*

Talking to people on the road and asking them about their past, their present life and their hopes and wishes for the future, is the most common theme of the work of these expatriate filmmakers. They present themselves as Iraqis living abroad and engage in a close debate with people, some of whom criticise them for having lived abroad during the years of the regime and the sanctions. Some of these directors observe with sadness that it is difficult to deconstruct the myth of the "ivory tower" in which émigré artists sometimes find themselves.[19]

Maysoon Pachachi's camera films the experience of her father 'Adnan, who returned to the country after a long exile to draft Iraq's temporary constitution in 2004. During her journey, she talks with ordinary people about their present situation and about their aspirations for the future, about the different but mirror image experiences of exiles and Iraqis living in Iraq, in a sophisticated weaving together of private and public. She is not new to this kind of subtlety; as I have mentioned above, another of her numerous documentaries, *Iraqi Women: Voices from the Exile*, is dedicated to Iraq. It was filmed in the aftermath of the 1991 Gulf War and the subsequent embargo. While the world was looking at Iraq as the field of a virtual war, represented like a tragic video-game, Maysoon Pachachi focused on women's voices, telling the history of their exile and their nostalgia for their lost country. With rare sensitivity, she collected the private and hidden memories of Iraqi women living in Britain, showing, through her fascinated but discreet gaze, the intersection between private and public histories, individual and collective fates.

The confrontation between the narration of the Gulf War emerging from the video interviews made by Maysoon Pachachi and the television images broadcast during the same period, testify that images are less about facts than about witnessing the perceptions that we have or wish to have at a certain moment. Maysoon Pachachi's most recent production, *Our Feelings Took the Pictures: Open Shutters Iraq*, is another chapter of Iraqi history narrated through women's eyes and words. The documentary films

---

[19] *Return to the Land of Wonders*, by Maysoon Pachachi, Iraq/UK, 2004.

12 women from five cities in Iraq, who are gathering in Damascus to take part in a workshop led by the photographer Eugénie Dolberg and by the Iraqi project manager Irada Zaydan. Living together in a traditional court-yard, they learn photography and tell each other their 'life map'. When they come back to their own cities, they try to write a photo-story of what they see. Again, the director takes the spectator on a journey into memory and, once more, the private merges with the public, the individual with the collective, in women's experience. The workshops changed the way the par-ticipants looked at reality. At the same time, the vision of the documentary changes the way the spectator thinks about the recent history of Iraq.

Qasim 'Abid left Iraq in 1974 and returned for the first time in October 2003. *Life After the Fall* starts with the images of his journey home and the welcome from his family: "three generations of my large family were there to welcome me. They were close, and yet they were strangers."[20] He approaches his family and his country with the tool with which he is most familiar, the camera. He films between October 2003 and April 2007. The involvement of his whole family in the project allows him to shoot a wide range of different attitudes toward present realities, according to gender and age. This film is an example of the connections between the everyday lives of ordinary people and major historical events, between individual stories and history.

The first months after the fall of the regime were marked by a certain degree of optimism. Qasim's brothers and sisters remembered when people were terrified of the *mukhabarat*; now they hoped that the country would be free. In December 2003, when the media announced the capture of Saddam Husayn, people were very happy. In 2004, for the first time since 1991, Shi'is could celebrate Ashura, and people considered this as a sign of slow return to normalcy and freedom. But one year after the fall, on April 9, words like poverty, unemployment, and despair were being mentioned more and more frequently. Qasim 'Abid films an artistic performance called "pave-ment newspaper," where people asked for the armies to leave Iraq. In the background, a handwritten sign on the wall reads: *man al-mas'ul?*

In October 2005, Saddam Husayn was put on trial and on October 10, the Constitution was voted. The girls of the family were opposed to a con-stitution that, according to them, does not give proper representation to women. In December 2005, people voted in the elections. At the end of

---

[20] *Life After the Fall*, Qasim Abid, Iraq/UK, 2008.

the year, the filming of the celebrations alternated with interviews in which people expressed increasing fears. In April 2006, three years after the fall of the Ba'th regime, the Qasim brothers and sisters appeared psychologically exhausted, depressed, comparing their situation to being in jail, that they fear everything. Every day is worse than the previous one. The country is hostage to gangs who are killing journalists, physicians, and professors. In July 2006, Qasim's brother 'Ali is abducted from his shop. His family looks for him for days and days, until they discover that he has already been assassinated and buried. Qasim's film is dedicated to his memory and to the memory of all the Iraqis who have been murdered in this way.

Hidden and contested memories are at the core of almost all contemporary Iraqi audiovisual productions. The way the artists approach the issue is varied. In *Under the Ashes*, photographer and director Ziyad Turki follows the writer 'Ali Badr[21] on his return to Iraq from Jordan (where he lives), to attend the al-Mada cultural festival in Arbil, in April 2006. 'Ali Badr talks with writers and thinkers at the conference about the role of intellectuals in contemporary Iraqi society, raising crucial topics like sectarianism and contested memories, and cultural perspectives in the country. According to its director, this documentary is a chapter of a visual archive of memory of the twentieth century. It is a courageous and original approach, in a time and a place when being able to remember is not without risk. The documentary, funded by UNESCO, engages a discourse fixed on people, not on objects. It focuses on the importance that widespread awareness of a shared cultural heritage will assume in the reshaping of Iraq. Perhaps resorting to some hyperbole, it seems to suggest that heritage is not made by old stones (the ancient treasures of Iraq) but by old stones impressed in people's memories and bodies. The minds of intellectuals are the real treasure of the country.

The Problems of Iraqi Cinema Today

Until the end of 2007 all directors cited, more or less explicitly, the lack of security as the main problem in doing cinema in Iraq today. Most of the films and documentaries made in Iraq were shot between 2003 and 2004. Security was such a big problem that it actually became the subject of many documentaries.[22]

---

[21] Sami Zubaida's paper in this volume discusses Ali Badr's novel *Baba Sartre*.

[22] See, for example, *Baghdadi Correspondent. The Story of Jawad Khadom*, by Qutayba al-Janabi, and *Trip of Dreams*, by Muhammad al-Daradji.

In the context of serious security problems, the situation of women working in the audio visual field was full of contradictions. On one side, they evidently benefited from the increasing television market. After 2003, many Iraqi TV channels were established, while before they were only two, both under strict government control. Today, there are a whole host of TV channels, most of them private, employing a number of technicians, directors and producers, many of whom are women. Women involved in the field think that, in spite of the difficult security situation, artists, both men and women, have better chances today than before 2003.

However, it is also undeniable that in what has become a far more religiously oriented society, the presence of women on the screen is seen as subversive, and as breaking old/new taboos of the visibility of women in public space. In *Baghdad Days*, Hiba Bassam expresses her unease as a woman working on a TV crew, still very much a male-dominated environment. One of the participants in the project *Open Shutters Iraq* has been assassinated. Qasim 'Abid's nephew tells how attitudes toward women changed during the time of the sanctions, when economic difficulties made people more and more conservative. This trend is confirmed by many studies in the field (al-Ali, 2003, pp. 233–246; Kamp, 2009, pp. 194–216). It is important to underline that, notwithstanding severe difficulties, these young artists are emerging and gaining their space.

Lack of funding is another major problem mentioned by many artists. The Iraqi regime used to finance cultural production for its own propaganda, although at the price of freedom of expression. After the collapse of the state institutions, artists hoped to regain freedom of expression, but they very quickly became aware that there were no new democratic institutions to finance the production of culture, art and knowledge. At the same time, economic and political insecurity discouraged private producers from investing.

Problems engender problems: For example, the lack of funding has led filmmakers to develop a sort of self-sufficiency. In Iraq the filmmaker is often also producer, writer, photographer, and distributor. The director is hyper-represented in the film, and is also often the main character.

Lack of funding and of equipment, the brain drain — which has affected the country since the 1970s — and the consequent shortage of skills are real problems. Given this overall situation, is it correct to say that this is not the best time to make films in Iraq? I do not think so. But if we want to have a wider picture of contemporary Iraqi production, we cannot restrict our analysis to 35 mm films or to film made specifically for cinema. On the contrary, we need to broaden the scope to other audiovisual arts, including television and the Internet. If we take these productions into account as well, we will find hundreds of films, facing a multitude of issues and spanning many genres. One the one hand, all this activity reveals specific local problems (the legacy of the politics of the regime, the sanctions, and war), while on the other it reflects a global trend, of greater ease of access to new technologies.

Conclusions

This overview of contemporary Iraqi cinema raises a series of questions of great interest for historians. The first of these relates to the shift from classic cinema, made by feature films shot in 35 mm, to new contemporary genres. This shift has both poetic and technological aspects. The narrative of Iraqi cinema today is characterized by the irruption of reality into the world of fiction. The few feature films that have been analyzed are very much grounded in reality, and the space for the authors' fantasy is quite restricted. Indeed, most productions are documentaries or docu-fictions.

In view of this, the historian should not be concerned about the reliability of audiovisual narrations. As the studies on cinema and historiography quoted above have argued, this is not the issue. Rather, the historian should investigate the reasons for this trend and the representations of itself that Iraqi society wants to produce as a result.

The filmmaker's principal commitment seems to be his or her duty to bear witness to what is going on in the country. In a continuous interplay between the continuity from Iraq's distinguished cultural heritage and discontinuity from the recent political order, filmmakers are also introducing new languages and new tools of expression, like beta cam or DVD.

The reshaping of Iraq's audiovisual panorama today involves many cultural actors: Filmmakers from the homeland and expatriates, Iraqi and foreign producers, artists and organizers of cultural events. Narrating the country, its everyday reality, its history, and its people, is a game with high stakes, and in spite of the immense problems that they face, Iraqi artists want to take charge of the narration and to tell their own history to the world.

Even if we have just passed the celebrations of the centenary of the showing of the first film in Baghdad, and despite the lively cultural panorama that has continuously characterized Iraq ever since, the harsh conditions in which Iraqi artists are forced to work definitely restrict the dynamism of production. The artists are profoundly aware of the high cultural tradition that they have inherited and, at the same time, they draw insights from a broader global heritage. Living abroad has made them cosmopolitan, citizens of the world; however, the predominance of political themes and the duty to testify sometimes diverts space and attention from artistic discourse. This is at least one of the reasons why there is a preponderance of documentaries instead of fiction and, in the fiction, a substantial absence of the dimension of dreams and "unreality", the elements that make up so much cinema. Instead, most contemporary Iraqi films are testimonies.

Here historians will raise a second issue. If audiovisual productions are historical sources, then they should surely be collected in archives. Given the difficulties of preservation in the Iraqi context, this has already become a vexed topic. Many of the masterworks of Iraqi cinema were damaged because of a lack of funds during the sanctions and the bombings during the various wars over the last thirty years. With more recent productions, it is difficult to collect them because they are scattered, and sometimes only the director/producer actually owns them. Anyway, if we assume that audiovisual sources are a vital part of the location of historical memory, historians, filmmakers and producers must collaborate in collecting and studying them; to some extent, this has already taken place.

And now for a last question: Can we talk about a renaissance of Iraqi cinema today? Maybe it is a little premature, although the audiovisual productions of this period certainly deserve careful attention. Apart from the quantitative aspects, there is a discursive element to take into consideration, the ways in which cultural actors (producers, organizers of events, artists) represent contemporary phenomena and how they represent themselves. In fact, their way of presenting their cultural activities illustrates their efforts to claim both discontinuity with the system of production before 2003, and continuity with the masters of the history of Iraqi and world cinema.

The Italian historian of cinema G.P. Brunetta wrote that "cinema was — among many other things — a privileged ritual-lay space, where twentieth century man accumulated and transformed the light of the screen and communion with the images into emotional, social and ideological energy" (Brunetta, 2001, p. 210). There is no better framework of meaning to describe the series of events that have been organized between 2004 and 2008, in spite of the harsh conditions in Iraq. Here I refer in particular to the Iraqi Festival of Short Films (Baghdad, 2005) and al-Mada Cultural Festival, an event that took place for the first time in Arbil (2006) and then in Baghdad (2008).

It is evident that there is a conscious, coherent, concrete desire to make the Iraqi cinematographic industry flourish again. The determination with which filmmakers are still producing films, in spite of economic and security worries, and the audience's persistence in taking part in cultural events, embodies the evidence of a real commitment on the part of civil society to establish a "normal" way of life in the country. The importance of Iraqi cinema today is due to the fact that it exists and that it is made up of artists from different generations, plural cultural backgrounds, and multiple expressive and stylistic references.

In that sense, contemporary cinema and art have assumed a double value: On the one hand they represent reality, while simultaneously contributing to the creation of that reality. In the cinematographic product, the function of testimony has tended to prevail, but cultural events (festivals, screenings), mark the assertion of existence by a civil society that dreaming of a cultivated, rich and pluralistic country. In Iraq, cinema today does not simply reproduce reality; it is a reality that may help in understanding the past and shaping the future.

WAR, CRIMES AND VIDEO TAPES: CONFLICTING MEMORIES IN FILMS ON IRAQ

Nicolas Masson

This article analyses how films can address the complex challenge of narrating the recent and earlier history of Iraq. In times in which images have become the prevalent medium through which historical events are received, perceived, and assimilated by Western and Middle Eastern audiences alike, films can provide meaningful interpretations of what happened in post-2003 Iraq. The dominant role of the Western film industry in formulating cinematic war narratives does not undermine the capacity of Iraqi filmmakers and media practitioners to develop their own visual recollections of events that marked the history of their country.

The year 2007 represented a crucial moment in American and British war film productions on Iraq. The four films released that year had very similar rationales, all attempting to account for real war crimes committed by coalition soldiers in Iraq. *In the Valley of Elah* (Paul Haggis, USA) related the murder of Specialist Richard Davis by his platoon comrades in 2003. *The Mark of Cain* (Marc Munden, UK) referred to the scandal which 18 year-old Fusilier Gary Bartlam provoked after developing pictures of abused Iraqi prisoners while on leave in the UK in 2003. *Battle for Haditha* (Nick Broomfield, UK) was a re-enactment of an incident in which one US Marine and 24 Iraqi civilians were allegedly killed on 19 November 2005 in the Iraqi town of Haditha. Finally, *Redacted* (Brian de Palma, USA) described the rape of a 14 year-old Iraqi girl, 'Abir Qasim Hamza, and the subsequent murder of her family, perpetrated in March 2006 by a group of five US Army soldiers.

Carrying explicit or implicit anti-war messages, these films have signally failed to attract large audiences, let alone rally public opinion against the war. Several reasons have been offered for this failure, including the poor quality of the films, their criticism of the war effort in Iraq and the perception that their release during the ongoing war would affect the morale of troops and viewers alike.

The indisputably Western-oriented approach of the films and their omission of Iraqi viewpoints on the war might explain why they did not succeed in generating major attention or in provoking debate in Iraq and the broader Middle East. Yet, Western and Iraqi memories of war are interconnected in a continuum of violence and trauma which determines both sides' visual and historical perspectives. The appropriations by Western filmmakers of Iraqi traumatic memories and their insertion within long-term eschatological readings have prompted Iraqi directors to reclaim ownership of their own history. During "Operation Iraqi Freedom", certain aspects of the ground military operations and situations of urban combat recalled some of the practices of repression performed in the early stages of the Baʻth regime. This led Iraqi filmmakers to propose their visual narrations of the most painful aspects of their recent past. Thereby, they acknowledged the increasing importance of filmic narrations in recounting the events that have marked their collective memory.

Shifting Visual Representations of Iraq

The outbreak of the war created the conditions for a "media boom", which was announced as finally allowing the world to see what had happened, and was happening, in Iraq. By the time Muhammad Saʻid Sahhaf, the Iraqi Information Minister, declared at a press conference, on April 7, 2003, that the "soldiers of Saddam Husayn gave [American troops] a great lesson that history will not forget" (Ricks, 2006, pp. 133–134), an estimated 3,000 international journalists, including 700 embedded correspondents, the "largest media war force ever assembled" (Ramesh, 2003, p. 254), were already deployed on the ground filming and reporting the "fall of Baghdad". The former practices of strict media control by the Baʻth regime were overturned by a suddenly overwhelming media presence and activity in the country. The rapid expansion of digital imagery and the diversification of information sources — further enhanced by the emergence of Arab and Iraqi news platforms — raised the prospect for unprecedented visual accounts of the country's political and historical destiny.

However, since July 2003, deteriorating security conditions on the ground have added to the difficulties of Iraqi and foreign media practitioners and directors elaborating on these early visual narratives of the war. The lack of access for journalists and cameramen to sensitive combat or urban zones in Iraq and the targeting of the media by insurgents and coalition forces alike, strongly limited the possibility of producing independent and reliable filmic accounts of the situation. In addition, the US military and the Coalition Provisional Authority imposed strict controls over information concerning certain operations conducted by coalition troops. Military censorship and the practice of embedding journalists in coalition battalions helped to prevent the release of accurate and balanced media reports.

This situation led key actors in the war to use individual internet and media platforms in order to make their voices heard and communicate with the outside world: Iraqi civilians increasingly described their war experiences in weblogs; Iraqi insurgents used the internet to upload their political messages, and coalition soldiers transmitted digital pictures or short movies to their relatives in their countries of origin.

In Brian de Palma's *Redacted*, the director uses these phenomena of diverse media technologies to explore ways to rewrite historical events through filmic scenarios. In this film, the reality of the war in Iraq is recounted through the collage of a variety of seemingly real media accounts: Soldier video diaries, surveillance recordings, *jihadi* propaganda websites and American anti-war blogs, *You Tube* videos, *Skype* conversations, US and Iraqi TV news reports, representing the plethora of new visual modes of sharing the war experiences.

In *Redacted*, Brian de Palma questions the very possibility of filmmakers operating in contemporary war contexts such as Iraq. While filmmakers were at the forefront of the production of imaged narratives of combat and ground operations during the Vietnam War, the Iraq war marginalized their role by making the individual use of internet and pocket cameras sources of visual information. For de Palma, the apparent diversification and democratization of technical media resources do not guarantee the accuracy of the visual statements produced on the war in Iraq and on the country's history. Modern war coverage is shown as a superimposition of equally ambiguous data made freely available on the web or on TV without distance or discrimination. *Redacted* suggests that instead of offering an opportunity for the interpretation and the consolidation of historical meaning, the multiplication of sources of information leads to its dilution. In his film, de Palma denounces the fact that even the most despicable war crimes, such as the rape of an Iraqi civilian or the beheading of a soldier by insurgents, can nowadays be consumed indiscriminately by web-pornography and Internet snuff-movie viewers.[1]

Rather than revealing unknown and unseen events, *Redacted* and the three other war films released in 2007 can also be seen as attempts to safeguard the memory of what happened in the early phases of the war. Dramatic political and volatile security developments in Iraq only underscore the necessity of keeping a record of all previous phases of the war that could have implications for a future peace settlement. In a context where written historical and archival documentation is missing, films might play a crucial role.

Changing Strategic Spaces

Since the First Gulf war and throughout the 1990s, "techno-war" and satellite imagery has continuously determined the collective mental image of Iraq and its people. Hollywood blockbusters like *Courage under Fire* (Edward Zwick, USA, 1996) and *Three Kings* (David O. Russell, USA, 1999) conveyed heavily mediated, hazy pictures of Iraq. They presented Iraq's desert landscape, and made Iraq's ruler Saddam Husayn the sole cause of the Iraqi people's misery. The media recounted the repeated US military interventions in Iraq through video-game animations and satellite pictures of bombed warehouses empty of human beings. US soldiers were rarely shown in any sort of contact with Iraqi civilians. When a GI shoots at a faceless and nameless Iraqi in the first scene of *Three Kings*, his mate congratulates him: "You got yourself a raghead. I did not think I would get to see anyone shot in this war!"

The films released in 2007 underscore the sudden physical proximity between the soldiers and the Iraqi civilians as the war was transformed from the aerial campaigns of the First Gulf War to the land invasion of "Operation Iraqi Freedom". Nick Broomfield's *Battle for Haditha* highlights this major change of strategic combat spaces. At first, the mid-sized Iraqi town of Haditha is shown in the frame of a satellite map hanging on the walls of US military headquarters. The bombing of the city from the air

---

[1] A snuff-movie is a short amateur motion picture showing the supposedly real or even actual murder of a human being or of an animal, generally preceded by pornographic acts.

recalls the previous video-game imagery of Iraq during the 1991 Gulf War. Yet, the Olympian American domination over the town, depicted through traditional Hollywood imagery of the "panoramic gaze objectifying the landscape through the imperial power and authority of an external observer" (Khatib, 2006, p. 33) proves tactically unproductive and unsuccessful for the US forces. Military success depends on the penetration of the urban jungle and its pacification. Overlapping houses and narrow alleys are the new locations where combat occurs.

Battle for Haditha, like the other war films released in 2007, created a new visual identity for Iraq. The décor now consisted of the "concrete jungle" of the "cramped" and "crowded Arab city", the "rubble, shabbily veiled women, sandbags, bombed buildings, checkpoints and exploded cars" (Khatib, 2006, p. 25), as opposed to the previously dominant images of empty Arabian desert steppes or the mountains of Kurdistan. A significant implication was that media observers of Middle Eastern wars were forced to acknowledge the sudden remarkable resemblance between these images of the war in Iraq and the images of the Israeli offensive in Lebanon in the summer of 2006. The similarities in the media representations of both contexts were striking for Iraqi media observers who were discovering the images from Lebanon on their TV screens in Iraq:

> I woke up this morning to scenes of carnage and destruction on the television and for the briefest of moments, I thought it was footage of Iraq. It took me a few seconds to realize it was actually Qana in Lebanon. (Riverbend, 2006)

Unlike the Lebanese example, this urban Iraqi décor was a reconstructed visual statement of the situation on the ground. In reality, the war films released in 2007 were all shot in other Arab countries, such as Jordan (*Battle for Haditha, Redacted*). Insecurity and threats to production teams in Iraq led filmmakers to take advantage of the flow of Iraqi refugees into Jordan to recruit actors and extras. Real-life refugees suddenly played the role of armed insurgents, worried mothers and hopeless children, all expressing their fears and hopes in Iraqi dialect.

A central element of the new visual representations of Iraq became the family home. In the four films released in 2007, private houses are shown as the constitutive place of Iraqi identity, at the very heart of the concentric circles encompassing "childhood, the family, the neighborhood, the village, confessional and ethnical belonging" (Luizard, 1999, p. 6) of the people. The Iraqi family home appears as the space given to Iraqi actors — mainly women — to express themselves in vernacular speech about the war.

The soldiers' violent irruption into this private, intimate space appears as a violation of a fragile sphere where Iraqi civilians are trapped and terrorized.

In contrast to the former techno-war imagery that dominated cinematic representations of Iraq in the 1990s, the new war films use urban landscapes and family homes as showplaces where Iraqi actors and coalition soldiers violently interact and where war crimes are committed. These scenic elements form the background for the soldiers' photographs and their video accounts of the war. The overlap of functions served by the soldiers-photographers, between warriors and reporters, puts into question the ability of their visual accounts to contribute to balanced history writing on Iraq. "What do you all think is going to be the first casualty of this entire conflict?" one soldier asks ironically in front of his video camera in *Redacted*. "It's gonna be truth."

Digital Pictures as "Transition Structures"

In May 2004, photographs of Iraqi detainees tortured by American soldiers were published in the international media. The Abu Ghraib images became the sickening icons of the war, the "defining association of people everywhere with the war" (Sontag, 2004) in Iraq.

It took more than three years for filmmakers to put forward interpretations of the so-called "trophy pictures" taken by American and British soldiers and their role in shaping shared mental and visual recollections of the war in Iraq. The war films released in 2007 underline the mediating function of digital war images and videotapes as "transition structures" (Ricoeur, 1998, p. 23) between the soldiers' fragmented memories and the collective memory of their societies as a whole. The narrative film techniques used to perform this transition process are recurrent flashbacks, "movies-within-movies," collages of scattered images stored in soldiers' cell phones and the re-assembly of scrambled computer files. The films suggest deciphering the soldiers' visual material as a memory healing method from which historical meaning and moral lessons are extracted. Thus the films' narratives fulfil the function of reorganizing the traumatic individual experiences of the soldiers and delineate ways of addressing actual war crimes committed in Iraq. They build a coherent historical discourse about the meaning of these crimes for Western societies at war.

In the Valley of Elah provides a good example in which digital pictures deal as "transition structures" between the reality of the war and the way American society receives and understands it. The narrative shows the father of a dead soldier gradually discovering the war crimes committed by his son in Iraq as he decodes the images stored in his son's cell phone. This damaged video material from Iraq is sent fragment by fragment to the father by a hacker. Torture and murder scenes are reassembled and finally become clear — to the father and viewers alike — only at the end of the film. This memory rehabilitation process follows the lines of history-writing: facts are gathered, reassembled in a coherent narrative discourse and proposed for interpretation. From the particular experience of the dead soldier and of his father seeking the truth, filmmaker Paul Haggis invites the audiences to recollect their memories of images of the two US-led military operations in Fallujah (April 2004, and November-December 2004), which constitute the historical setting of the film.

The technique of striking a balance between storytelling focused on individual facts and the need to question the acts and values of nations at war in Iraq is a common feature of the other war films released in 2007. The depiction of the soldiers who commit war crimes as familiar products of American or British middle and working-class societies participates in the transition process from individual to collective memory. As presented in these films, soldiers in Iraq are made to stand symbolically for the societies who decided to invade Iraq. They serve as storytellers who transmit their vision of the war back to their societies through the use of their commercial pocket cameras or camera-phones. Cameras and cell-phones are constitutive elements of these soldiers almost as much as their rifles: "If you can't shoot with your rifle, you shoot with your camera," soldier Shane says in *The Mark of Cain*, where British soldiers take scandalous "trophy pictures" of abused detainees. "While I am over here, I'm gonna be shooting whatever [...] goes on," states soldier Salazar in the introduction to his video war diary in *Redacted*.

At the receiving end of the images and videotapes recorded and sent by the soldiers are the families and societies who first refuse to see and accept this reality. Once collected, reassembled and released, the pictures taken by the soldiers become pieces of evidence upon which the healing process of collective memory is launched. At this stage, the psychological debriefing of the soldiers and the military court hearings constitute the ultimate steps before the start of a shared reconciliation process. In *The Mark of Cain* and *Battle for Haditha*, the courts martial where the perpetrators of abuses are tried and sentenced pave the way for crimes committed in Iraq to be acknowledged and judged by society as a whole. The courts morally engage the nation by symbolically addressing the question of shared responsibility and reparation for the abuses. In *The Mark of Cain*, the names of the tortured prisoners are invoked during the military trial as a sign of moral rehabilitation: "Sa'id, Ahmad, Abdallah, Omar. The people we did it to. Innocent." In *In the Valley of Elah*, the American flag is raised upside-down to mark the start of a national mourning process.

Appropriating Iraq's Traumatic History

The processes of transition from individual grievance and trauma to collective reconciliation described in the 2007 war films are Western-oriented and primarily concern American and British societies. The films focus on soldiers from the US and the UK and describe the ways in which their societies learn to come to terms with what happened in Iraq. Yet, these films fail to address the war traumas experienced by the Iraqis other than through allusion. With very few exceptions, Iraqi standpoints on the war are left unexpressed.

There are a number of reasons for this omission. First, the war films on Iraq are consistent with the traditional Hollywood war-film genre. The US soldiers involved in Iraq, like Vietnam GIs, remain "characters who lack knowledge and control of their environment, their activities, their enemies and their fates" (Neale, 2006, p. 24). The filmmakers' choice not to represent Iraqi perspectives of the war, and its abuses, can be seen as an implicit acknowledgment — or denunciation — of dominant western-oriented interpretations and a broad ignorance of the country's identity, history, main language and social codes.

A second reason for omitting Iraqi standpoints is the directors' underscoring of the conscious and abusive appropriation of Iraq's traumatic past by the occupiers. Major events in Iraq's past history are reinterpreted by coalition soldiers in order to justify new abuses. In *The Mark of Cain* for instance, a British officer motivates his troops to torture Iraqi suspects by referring to the practice of "prison cleansing" allegedly conducted by Saddam Husayn at Abu Ghraib:

> One day before Saddam's birthday, he ordered for two thousand prisoners to be killed at Abu Ghraib. This is what I read, right! And during one day. Officers said it could not be done, but he did it within fifteen hours. He used one bullet on everybody instead of three [...] Fifteen hours, two thousand men, that is about one every thirty seconds. Now, am I supposed to respect that human rights thing? [...] We have got six of them, and we are not supposed to even question them!

In Brian de Palma's *Redacted*, the abuses committed against Iraqi civilians are justified through the soldiers' groundless search for weapons of mass destruction: "We are here and we are gonna [...] find these [...] weapons. We are searching for evidence. We are looking for weapons of mass destruction," one of the four-gang rapists says once in the house of his victim. The underlying lie upon which the entire military engagement was based is voluntarily shown as leading to serious war crimes committed by frustrated and disoriented soldiers.

Another form of abuse of Iraq's memory in these war films consists in situating the soldiers' crimes and civilians' sufferings in a deeply rooted chain of guilt and collective moral responsibility. Appropriations of ancient folktales from Iraqi and Middle Eastern legends are performed in a rather dubious attempt to create a fateful link between the violence affecting the Iraqi population and the country's ancient mythic past.

Among the platoon of soldiers in *Redacted* who will be found guilty of rape and murder of civilians, one soldier is shown reading a novel by British novelist John O'Hara, *Appointment in Samarra* (1934). The novel's title is a reference to W. Somerset Maugham's 1933 retelling of an ancient Arabian Sufi folktale, itself allegedly inspired by a Talmudic legend. In the tale, a servant is threatened by Death in a market place in Baghdad. The servant's master lends a horse to his servant for him to escape Baghdad and find refuge in Samarra the same night. The master himself encounters Death and asks her why she had threatened his servant that morning at the marketplace. Death responds: "It was only a start of surprise. I was astonished to see him in Bagdad (*sic*), for I had an appointment with him tonight in Samarra'." The fateful "encounter" with, and the actual rape of, the 14 year-old girl which takes place shortly after the reference to this folktale is presented as a moral sin from which the soldiers and their societies cannot escape.

Similar appropriations of ancient moral legends are also made in the other war films, which also draw explicit comparisons between the war in Iraq and ancient Middle Eastern myths. For instance, both *In the Valley of Elah* and *The Mark of Cain* refer to Old Testament stories. The valley of Elah is the location where the Philistines sent Goliath to terrify the Israelites, and where young David felled the giant with his slingshot. Iraq's rebellion against the invaders is thereby explained as the revolt of the weak and anticipates their ultimate moral victory against the overwhelming power of the coalition forces. As for the mark of Cain, reference is made to the mark that God put upon Cain as a sign of protection from his enemies after he killed Abel. In Marc Munden's film, the mark of Cain appears as a curse that soldiers found guilty of war crimes will carry until their eventual trial or death.

These references to moral and religious traditions, appropriated by the filmmakers as Western cultural producers, situate the violence perpetrated in Iraq in a larger historical and moral continuum. Iraq is associated with the mythical genesis of times where original conflicts and traumas determined history and shaped values of guilt and redemption. This accentuates the feeling of culpability felt by the soldiers since their acts seem to reproduce crimes punished by God. The films draw a moral link between the most recent history of Iraq and myths that have marked Western collective memory. They offer a partial treatment of the history of Iraq that needs to be linked with the mythical and religious narratives that are well known to them in order to be understood by Western audiences.

Given these appropriations by foreign filmmakers of ancient Middle Eastern myths, historians are left wondering how far past historical traumas have shaped and still influence Iraq's collective memory. Films like *In the Valley of Elah* and the *Mark of Cain* encourage historians to investigate what kind of mental images the 2003 invasion actually stimulated among Iraqis. Did this invasion encourage them to try and regain ownership over their past? In what traumatic continuum did they situate the occupation of their country? Did they explore the possibility of using visual representations as "transition structures" in order to come to terms with their history?

The Return of "Abu Tabar"

If the 2003 invasion radically changed the parameters of visual representations of Iraq in American films, it also transformed the Iraqi approach to cinematic recounting of their history. Before the war, filmic representations of the situation in Iraq were inevitably influenced by the regime's strict control over national media and cultural production. The Iraqi film industry had become almost non-existent due to the extent to which it was curtailed and controlled under Ba'thist censorship.

Iraqi post-war film productions have attested the willingness of Iraqi directors to retell the history of Iraq. The post-2003 traumas could not help but establish direct mental connections between the practices of their old and new rulers. The torture and abuses committed by coalition soldiers at precisely the same symbolic locations where Saddam Husayn used to detain his opponents, such as Abu Ghraib prison, encouraged them to revisit events in their recent history.

The fall of Saddam Husayn, his arrest, and his execution in 2006, as well as the continuous internecine violence that has marked the years since the invasion in 2003, have brought Iraqi directors and media practitioners to recount the early phases of the Ba'th regime. Persistent feelings of fear and insecurity, and the failure of the occupying powers to establish functional and stable transition institutions led them to revisit the mythical narratives which had strongly influenced their relationship to political and military power.

Among the most famous mythical narrations, which marked Iraq's recent history, the story of "Abu Tabar" was well known to many Iraqis who had experienced the early phase of the Ba'th regime in the beginning of the 1970s. While the Ba'th Party was gradually accumulating power in Iraq, the mysterious character of "Abu Tabar" spread terror and fear in the streets of Baghdad. Abu Tabar — literally "father of the axe" — sneaked from one area to the other at night, broke into houses and slaughtered all innocent family members living there. For some months, Baghdad lived in fear and panic. Finally, Abu Tabar, a mentally ill criminal, was arrested and Iraqis witnessed his trial live on their TV screens. For many Iraqis, however, Abu Tabar was merely an urban legend created by the Iraqi security apparatus to cover up a real campaign of assassinations being conducted against supposedly dangerous opponents of the Ba'th regime.

In 2008, the Cairo-based Iraqi Satellite TV channel *al-Baghdadia* decided to re-enact the Abu Tabar legend in a 30-hour TV series, whose production started in November of that year and is still to be screened. According to the screenwriter, the Iraqi writer 'Ali Husayn, this TV series was a "social endeavor which dealt with the life of Iraqis in that period, their hopes, fears, and expectations." He described the aim of the re-enactment of the Abu Tabar legend in a TV series as an opportunity "to reflect on an important historical phase in contemporary Iraq" (*al-Mada*).

In the same year, *The Aboo-Tobar Returns* (sic), by Iraqi artist Ayad Jihad, was uploaded on *You Tube* in four parts. Considered to be "the first Iraqi animation film," the film starts with a flashback of the court hearing of the presumed criminal and his sentence to death according to the Iraqi penal code. This first scene is strongly reminiscent of the images of Saddam Husayn's trial. The visual connection between the court hearings of the former Iraqi president and the trial of Abu Tabar calls for a historical process of exploring and judging the acts of the Ba'th regime. What is striking about *The Aboo-Tobar Returns* is the graphic depiction of Baghdad as a city built upon a grid plan and the depiction of the heroes as Westernized characters speaking Arabic. The film adopts urban imagery directly borrowed from Hollywood and is evocative of Manhattan gangster movies. In this case, the authentic fascination for American imagery is not perceived as an obstacle for the expression of issues that concern Iraqi identity. It results from another type of appropriation process, different from the one referred to in *Redacted*, *In the Valley of Elah* and *The Mark of Cain*. Here, instead of Middle Eastern legends serving contemporary Western narrations, Western technical means and imagery serve as visual support for Iraqi-owned narratives.

The "return" of the Abu Tabar legend was understood by the Iraqi film-makers and producers as an attempt to repossess Iraq's traumatic past. The revival of the legend was deemed a useful tool to revisit the early phases of the Ba'th regime, but also to shed light on the immediate effects of the 2003 invasion. For some analysts, the indiscriminate violence of Abu Tabar was revived in the sectarian killings and mass 'cleansings' that have occurred in Iraq since 2003. For them, this violence represented "a severe moral crisis for society and for the Iraqi soul in general" (al-Anbari, 2007, pp. 17–19). But the legend of Abu Tabar was also used to denounce the practices of the occupying forces. Iraqi observers accused the US-led coalition forces of exploiting the mass media and creating "Hollywood-like scenarios" in order to spread fear and panic among the Iraqi people. Communication campaigns driven by the Coalition Provisional Authority and the US military were compared with the practices used by Saddam's security forces at the beginning of his rule. According to these readings, the repeated exploitation by international media of characters like Abu Mus'ab al-Zarqawi, al-Qa'ida's alleged chief representative in Iraq, who was killed in 2006, served the coalition forces as much as the character of Abu Tabar had served the Ba'th in establishing its hegemony in Iraq (Mesh'al).

The revival of the Abu Tabar legend confirmed that Iraqis had a clear understanding of how visual narratives could play a determining role in reinforcing executive power and justifying repressive methods. It also proved their capacity to revisit their past through original filmic techniques in an attempt to respond to the overwhelming foreign imposition of visual parameters and narratives of their country's history.

Conclusion

Caught between the quickly vanishing traces of their ancient past, symbolized by the sacking of the Iraq Museum in April 2003, Iraqi people helplessly witnessed the rapid construction of a visual "Western memory museum" (Sontag, 2004) over which suddenly no one had any control. The Abu Ghraib photographs and the American and British war films released during the war revealed the enormous gap between the way Iraqis traditionally represented themselves and the way they came to be represented by their invaders and the broader world.

The tension between the hyper-volatility and immediacy of mass media war footage on the one hand, and the country's long-term historical substance on the other, characterized Iraq as a battleground for conflicting memories both in reality and in the virtual world. In a global context where images play a determining role in shaping collective memories of historical events, the war films released in 2007 attempt to elaborate meaningful historical discourse out of an expanding diversity of visual material indiscriminately displayed on TV and on the internet. Building on the mental image of chaos prevailing in Western perceptions of Iraq, the films perpetuate Western-oriented interpretations of events that have deeply marked post-2003 Iraq.

Focused on the soldiers' traumas, these films generally fail to give voice to Iraqi standpoints on the war and the broader history of the country. Through the assemblage of scattered images, which serve as "transition structures" between the soldiers' traumatic experiences and the collective memory, they draw the lines for a historical reconciliation process that primarily concerns the Western societies actively engaged in the war. The current history of Iraq and its present turmoil are put into a moral continuum with myths and legends of the ancient orient. Iraq's past is thereby appropriated by external storytellers who perpetrate Western clichés about the Middle East. Western feelings of guilt, redemption and justice are shown as emanating from tales and legends belonging to the heritage of this invaded and violated country.

For Iraqi filmmakers, the challenges of producing visual interpretations of their country's history are manifold. The invasion of Iraq in 2003, which resulted in the implosion of the previously monolithic management of news and images, has offered them unprecedented access to platforms of visual expression. It has also allowed them to revisit the most traumatic events of their recent history and to interpret them through cinematic discourse.

The revival of the Abu Tabar legend through TV series and animation movies marks an early stage in this process. Revisiting the early Ba'th era appears necessary both to provide rational explanations for the ongoing violence and to come to terms with a 30-year historical period on which written and archival material is severely defective.

The dramatic character of the events that have marked this period and their persisting presence in the Iraqi collective memory will inevitably engender more attempts to rewrite the history of Iraq through visual means. The role of Iraqi filmmakers in producing cinematic narratives of their country's history can therefore be expected to grow in the coming years.

Electronic references

al-Mada (undated). al-akhira: Abu Tabar ya'ud ila Baghdad. Online. Available HTTP <http://www.almadapaper.net/paper.php?source=akbar&mlf=interpage&sid=50736> (accessed 15 May 2009).

Mesh'al, S (undated). Siyasat al-khawf min 'Abu Tabar' ila al-Zarqawi. Online. Available HTTP <http://www.alsabaah.com/paper.php?source=akbar&mlf=interpage&sid=21967> (accessed 15 May 2009).

Riverbend (2006). Qana massacre... Online. Available HTTP: <http://riverbendblog.blogspot.com/2006_07_01_riverbendblog_archive.html#115428447775330815#115428-447775330815> (accessed 15 May 2009).

Sontag, S (2004). Regarding the Torture of Others. Online. Available HTTP: <http://www.nytimes.com/2004/05/23/magazine/23PRISONS.html> (accessed 15 May 2009).

POETRY IN THE SERVICE OF NATION BUILDING? POLITICAL COMMITMENT AND SELF-ASSERTION IN MODERN IRAQI POETRY

Leslie Tramontini

I have discussed the Iraqi poetry of the 1920s and 1980s elsewhere (Tramontini, 2002–2003, p. 161–186; 2006, pp. 247–257; 2009): in this paper I would like to draw on some of the insights gained in these earlier studies, and to question the role of poets in nation building through the development of strategies of self-assertion to foster national identity. My hypothesis is that poets contribute to nation building by forming national consciousness, although in many cases they were not able to live up to their own political aspirations. They either succumbed to their own ambitions or let themselves become the instruments of political ideologies.

The political situation, cultural context and challenges of the periods compared differ; the whole global context was different, although both periods were times of major political and societal transition. In the 1920s, "the nation" served as a marker of identity, a newly fashioned term that could be filled with different meanings. In the 1980s Iraq had started a war with Iran, risking (and actually losing) much of the wealth it gained in the 1970s. In both cases, the construction of a [new] identity required a new reading of history, and the reconstruction of the past found its best expression in the nation. But who forms the nation?

The Concept of the Nation

After the fall of the old multi-ethnic empires in Europe and Asia, together with the proclamation of Woodrow Wilson's Fourteen Points in 1918, aspirations towards nation, national autonomy and self-determination became the principal political ideals. Iraq was no longer under Ottoman hegemony but immediately came under British occupation (British troops had landed in southern Iraq in 1914), and the direct confrontation with European colonialism led to increased levels of national consciousness. Iraqi authors indicated that the condition for the formation of Iraqi nationalism was the colonial creation of Iraq within its modern borders (Jabar, 2003, p. 53; Zubaida, 2002, p. 206). A country like Iraq allowed for multiple identities; hence the early idea of national identity — not yet strictly defined and still quite fluid — found expression in the term *watan*, indicating a homeland with borders not yet drawn and open to all possible options. This notion rapidly became politicized[1] and served as part of an integrative ideology that allowed for the development of national identity, an essential feature of successful nation building.[2]

In the early days of Iraqi nationhood, there were competing and at times overlapping claims to identity: Ottomanism, promoted by the Ottomans with the aim of unifying their Empire against threats from the West: pan-Islamism, essentially the creation of Sultan 'Abd al-Hamid II (1876–1909) in an attempt to reinvent the caliphate as the symbol of the unity of the Muslim world under his leadership: pan-Arab Nationalism, triggered by the Arab Revolt led by the sons of Sharif Husayn, which passed almost seamlessly into the concept of Arab unity, as adumbrated by Sati' al-Husri in the 1920s and 1930s, and Iraqi nationalism, which concentrated on Iraq alone. These visions were not yet well defined; in particular, the differences between Iraqi nationalism and pan-Arabism took some time to become clear-cut, and both visions of the future often incorporated Islamic themes. Of course, after the break up of the Ottoman Empire, it became clear that neither

---

[1]Thus losing the apolitical connotations it had for centuries: see Haarmann (2002: 174f.); also Dawn (1991, pp. 3–30); Hobsbawm (1992: 46).

[2]I will use the term nation-building here in the context of a fragmented society where it indicates a socio-political process of development that tries to forge a national state out of disparate communities. See Hippler (2003).

Ottomanism nor pan-Islamism had any chance against Arab nationalisms of any kind.[3]

The absent "United Arab Nation" was compensated for by a growing nationalist rhetoric: Like the idea of the nation that developed in German romanticism, nationalism in the Arab context served as a substitute for the "as yet" nonexistent nation.[4] Arab nationalism strove for the cultural rebirth of the Arab nation without taking any account of a genuine local Iraqi identity. This was inserted more or less by default in the early period, but at least since the revolution of 1963 and especially after the Ba'th take-over 1968, this view was officially encouraged and promoted.[5]

Strategies of Self-Assertion: The Early Years

In Iraq, it has generally been acknowledged that literature — and especially poetry — not only reflects society but also plays an important role in forming it, as well as voicing aspirations for social or political change. In twentieth century Iraq, this innate function of poetry may occasionally have declined and retreated to the background, but it was always subconsciously present. It was brought to perfection with the Tammuz poets of the 1950s: The poet-as-leader emerged as both engaged and committed to the cause of the nation. Within this long history of commitment (which informs the peculiarities of modern and post-modern Arabic literature, in comparison with Western literature), even decidedly apolitical authors acknowledge the political impact of their creative work. Poetry was and very much still is the vehicle for circulating ideas, slogans, and political aims; it is, in fact, an ideological intervention reaching out to reality (Klemm, 1998, p. 72f; Pflitsch, 2004, p. 17).

---

[3] Although several Iraqi poets remained loyal to the Empire even after its break up. For a discussion of the "ideologies of integration," see Gencer (2008), Reinkowski (2006), and also Davis (2005, pp. 176–199).

[4] Compare the interesting findings by Brunotte (2008, p. 104).

[5] In Iraq, the somewhat vague notion of pan-Arab Nationalism spread mostly among the lower and middle class Sunni population of Baghdad and the small towns of western Iraq: it remained part of the ideology of Sunni domination throughout the modern history of Iraq (Davis, 2005, pp. 176–199; Hourani, 1983, pp. 260–291; Rohde, 2003, p. 175). See Fouad Ajami: "[...] the forbidden secret of Arab nationalism: It was Sunni dominion dressed in secular garb" (1998, p. 133).

There are many possible reasons for this, probably the most important being the power of the word and of language.[6] The anti-colonial power struggle for self-affirmation and the instability that has followed led to a reassessment of personal heritage, and language became the unifying bond, the most important symbol of Arab national identity. Poets gave new readings of history as well as the will to create a new identity; confidence in the power of language to change the world made poetry political. Poetry served as a political tool from the very beginnings of the anti-colonial struggle; through the commitment of the poets a new political vision was promoted, modelled on the past and its glories. Recourse to the traditional authority and insight of the poet was an attempt to make the classical conventions of poetry relevant to modern times, and as such it can be considered a deliberate move of self-assertion. In this so-called neo-classical poetry, the poet could tackle modern problems and speak out freely, transforming the poems into vibrant emotional support for the new political consciousness. Poetry helped create "public opinion" by mobilizing the masses and spreading nationalist language, terms, and ideas.[7] This process of the politicization of the poetic self led to the identification of the self with the nation; private and national self-realization became identical. So, national identity served not simply as a political alternative to European colonialism, but was the only available option, the only reality for the individual self (Noorani, 1999, p. 238). The aim of poetry was to implant similar structures of identification in the minds of its audience.

In the framework of the new reading of history and of the past, resistance against colonial endeavors became common at quite an early stage. At the turn of the century, during the critical debates on reform within the Ottoman Empire, with the first direct encounters with the West some years in the future (the Italian invasion of Tripoli in 1911, the Balkan wars 1912/13, the outbreak of World War I), Iraqi poets tended to stress the need for reform and development. They issued a committed call to combat

---

[6]The notion of *I'jaz al-Qur'an*, the inimitability of the Qur'an in form and content, substantiated the prominent position of Arabic language that had long been a characteristic of the pre-Islamic poetry to which the poets of the early 1920s referred (von Grunebaum, 1971, p. 1018ff.).

[7]See Talib Mushtaq's account of the awakening of national feeling during the turbulent days of the 1920 Revolution: "All the speeches and recitals of poems fuelled the enthusiasm of the people and instilled in them feelings of pride and dignity. They inspired people with their demands for freedom and independence" (1989, p. 83). On the didactic role and the commitment of poetry to public life see Jayyusi (1975, pp. 188–189).

ignorance, which was often quite self-critical. Rafa'il Butti's compilation, *al-Adab al-'asri fi'l-'Iraq al-'arabi* (1923) shows the deep commitment of the various poets, the keywords being reform, education, science, progress, and pride in history and past achievements. At that stage, poets firmly believed that it was possible to bridge the distance and catch up with the West.

During the anti-colonial struggle in the early decades of the twentieth century, the *watan* — however unclear its geographical boundaries — came to bear a double meaning: first as the locus of a lost past which was better than the present, and therefore evoking a nostalgic yearning, and then, since the future has to be built on the past, the foundations of a new and better world. Poetry elaborated this idea and in search of a new identity fashioned against the West, which combined both national and religious feelings, pushed the audience towards the same goals that the poet himself internalized: The identification of self and the nation, and hence the necessity for political action. The impact of this amalgamation between private and national self-realization led to the transformation of the confessional credo into a credo in or for the *watan*. The most extreme example of this attitude is the poet Muhammad Hasan Abu'l-Mahasin (1876–1926),[8] who says, in a close adaptation of a famous verse by Kumayt, one of the best known Shi'i poets of the Umayyad period: "*wa-ma liya illa majdi qawmiya ghayatun/wa-ma liya illa salihi l-qawmi salihu* [I have no other aim than the glory of my nation/and no other interest than my people]."[9]

Similar sentiments were expressed by Jamil Sidqi al-Zahawi[10] (1863–1936), one of most famous poets of his time. As early as 1908, shortly before the restoration of the Ottoman constitution, he complained about the failure of the Ottoman Empire to implement reform and then criticized

---

[8]See Tamimi (1991, pp. 322–325); Wa'ili (1968, pp. 105–108); he later became minister of education.

[9]al-Kumayt b. Zayd al-Asadi (680–743); the original verse is: *wa-ma liya illa ali ahmadi shi'atun/wa-ma liya illa madhhabi l-haqqi madhhabu* (*tawil*). See Ya'qubi (1963, p. 37); also quoted in Wa'ili (1968, p. 106).

[10]Zahawi, who was of Kurdish origin, was born in Baghdad and held numerous positions first in the Ottoman administration and then in the Iraqi state: He was a teacher, writer, professor and a member of the Ottoman parliament in Istanbul. An early advocate for women's rights, he lost his job at the Baghdad law school in 1910 after publishing an article on this matter. After the British occupation of Iraq he became a member of the Education Council and cooperated with the new regime. See Walther (1994, pp. 430–450). For a contemporary view, see Widmer (1935, pp. 1–79).

increasing Western aggression:

> Enough, O West, with your boasting of being a developed nation/living in luxury with your fortune!
>
> Owning an enormous army/and an equally strong navy!
>
> You are developed, but with your strength came arrogance/You have enraged the Orient, but he concealed his anger!
>
> For a long time he stayed silent when his rights/were disregarded, as if the Orient hadn't a mouth!
>
> O West, so self-absorbed!/Slowly! What kind of reproachful infatuation!
>
> Hasn't it been the Orient who walked in front of you centuries ago/your great master who taught you!
>
> There was a time of knowledge in whose light the Orient/blossomed while the West lay in the dark [...]
>
> Do you believe that the Orient will remain abject/and occupied while you remain the noble one
>
> Dominating him/sucking his blood and violating him! [...]
>
> The countries of the Orient will rise after the times of decadence/if only its children awoke and learned!
>
> Its backwardness will totally vanish/if only the governments of its countries were functioning! (*Diwan*, 1979, p. 302f)

Composed in the tradition of a defamatory poem, this poem recognizes Western supremacy but also the greatness of the writer's own heritage: the last two verses breathe a prudent optimism. The anti-colonial counter-discourse of Zahawi rejects any conventional belief in European superiority and the *mission civilisatrice* of bringing civilization and modernity to the colonized who is not capable of self-expression. The "Orient" (*al-sharq*) is a still undefined territory that could refer to the Ottoman Empire as well as to some kind of (united) Arab nation, although it is defined in contrast to the colonial Other. Benedict Anderson's framework provides useful support here. His theory may not be fully applicable in the Iraqi context since Islam — contrary to Anderson's theorizing — has always been an active element in giving identity to newly developing nationalisms, but his definition of the nation as an imagined community (Anderson, 1986, pp. 6–7) helps understand the Iraqi case. To perceive of oneself as an entity, as "one", borders must be drawn against the external or foreign "Other". Each developing identity needs a counterpart, which is excluded. In the Iraqi case there was a choice of many 'others', but the colonial West was the most dangerous.

The verse *ka'anna l-sharqa laysa lahu fam*, which seems to have been taken straight out of an anthology of *postcolonial studies* ("The subaltern cannot speak") is less explosive if Zahawi's later works are taken into account. In the wake of World War I and the British occupation of Iraq, Zahawi switched sides in a 180°-turn, from a clear anti-colonial stance to complete collaboration with the British. Iraqi authors call this switching of sides *taqallub*. In the notorious poem *'ud li'l-'Iraq* the poet welcomes the British High Commissioner Sir Percy Cox back to Iraq after the suppression of the 1920-Revolution:

> Return to Iraq and repair what was broken/Install justice and grant the people a carefree life!
>
> Iraq is most happy to see him/as father, coming from a country of justice!
>
> Have mercy on a nation that was stirred up by unjust oppressors/The people did not want that!
>
> They believed it to be guidance what those others did/but sometimes what you take for guidance can lead you astray
>
> They thought that the nation will become happy/through its revolution. But the people didn't become happy![11]

'Ali al-Wardi (1913–1995),[12] one of Iraq's most renowned and acknowledged sociologists, ridicules the poets' claim to be leading the nation along the path of resistance. Uncompromisingly, he accuses the literati of pursuing their own interests and concludes his criticism with the verdict that since its very beginnings poetry has been the "opiate of the people," distracting them from pressing social and political injustices (Wardi, V.1, 44; VI.1, 253, and more frequently). Wardi's favorite example of such *taqallub* is Zahawi, but Rusafi and other poets are also not immune from his criticism (Wardi, IV, 373, 379; V.1, 43).

Faced with a common enemy there was unity among the different sections of Iraqi society, at least for the short period after World War I and before the installation of the monarchy by the British in 1921. The Shi'is, Sunnis, Christians and Jews were incorporated into the ideal of an independent and free Iraq. Many Iraqi poets actively contributed to this call for unity. Thus Khayri al-Hindawi (1885–1957), an employee of the British administration in Hilla, was exiled to the barren island of Hinjam in the Strait of Hormuz for writing this *qasida:*

---

[11] Quoted in Wardi (1969–1976, VI.1, 15f.); see also 'Abd al-Razzaq al-Hilali who notes that Zahawi has included this poem in his Diwan without mentioning the name of the honoured person, Sir Percy Cox; *Diwan* p. R, poem 330.

[12] On his work and research, see Ibrahim al-Haydari (2006) and Orit Bashkin's article in this volume.

> Tell the people that they broke their promise/and the contract. So get up and fly up high
>
> Pour down on them firmness and great courage/bombard them with true opinion and thoughts!
>
> Kiss the brother Jew in friendship/and publicly embrace the patriarch!
>
> Would that one day I could see/the banner of Husayn's son fluttering here![13]

In the year 1921, shortly before his coronation as the first King of Iraq, Faysal I said, echoing the rhetoric of 1920: "I do not want to hear the word Muslim, Christian, or Jew any more, because Iraq is the homeland of nationalism (*watan al-qawmiyya*). There exists only one thing here: everybody is Iraqi" (Wardi, VI.1/102). This was a conscious and deliberate attempt to include all ethnic and confessional segments of Iraqi society into the new *watan*. But who defines who the nation is? Ma'ruf al-Rusafi (1875–1945)[14] also takes the new historical awareness as a strategy of self-assertion, but in contrast to Zahawi he does not elaborate it in a triumphal and optimistic way but in a resigned and pessimistic manner. Rusafi, a free spirit and humanist who worked for social justice and peace, is regarded as one of *the* national poets. However, he had been affiliated with the liberal forces in the Ottoman Empire and never quite came to accept the new Iraqi regime. During World War I, he had angered the Hashemite family with his harsh criticism of the Arab Revolt against the Ottomans, and all his life he wavered between support for and rejection of the new Iraq.

Shortly after the 1920 Revolution against the British (in which he did not participate), Rusafi let loose his frustration about the way Iraq had been constructed in a poem dedicated to the Lebanese poet and traveller Amin al-Rayhani (1876–1940). Even if "[t]here is no indication [...] that the demise of the Ottoman *watan* was followed by a smooth transference of the idea of *watan* to the newly created state of Iraq" (Kadhim, 2004, p. 96), in this poem *watan* surely indicates Iraq:

> If you ask someone who studies the glory [of Iraq]/it is as if you would lament the remains of the abandoned campground!
>
> So weep like the sad one trying to hold back his tears/his teardrops pass beside his handkerchief

---

[13]Quoted in Nadhmi (1985, p. 376) (*khafif*). Later on he became a provincial governor: 'Abbasi (n.d.: 86). For more of his poetry see Butti (1923, p. 161–86).

[14]See the excellent chapter on him in Kadhim (2004, pp. 85–130). Also Moreh (1991, pp. 614–617); Khulusi (1950, pp. 616–626).

> The old glory of the country is gone/Destiny pulled a veil of lethargy over it [...]
>
> In religious affairs it is like this: If one of the Qur'an experts makes a statement/an expert in the gospels puts forward objections
>
> And if one capable of interpreting analyses their talk/attention is diverted by the allegation that he is an infidel (*bit-takfir*)
>
> And if educated men talk about their affairs/they protect knowledge by declaring him ignorant [...]
>
> But ignorance won't stay close to its masters/just like the sword doesn't feel mercy with the one it is about to kill
>
> O Amin don't be angry with me because/I don't claim anything without proof
>
> From where to hope for progress for Iraq/if the way of its rulers (*mumtalakihi*) is not his own?
>
> There is no good in a fatherland whose sword is with the coward/and whose fortune with the avaricious
>
> Whose wisdom is with the expelled (*taridihi*), whose knowledge is with the stranger (*gharibihi*)/and whose power is with the usurper (*dakhilihi*)
> (Butti, 1923, pp. 91–93).

By using the traditional *topos* of old Arabic poetry (weeping at the *atlal*, the remains of the camp ground), Rusafi succeeds in drawing a parallel to the current situation in Iraq and hinting at the irrevocability of past glory. The status quo is characterized in negative terms: the absence of independence, the absence of political decision-making, the absence of autonomy in important fields in social and political life like education, science, technology, and progress. An enlightened scholar and politician, Rusafi struggles against the confessional problems of Iraq, the superiority assumed by the conservative religious class, the enslavement of science and knowledge and the British presence in the country. Self-assertion is aimed both towards the inside and the outside: towards society itself (against ignorance and arrogance) and towards the external threat (the colonial power). Combining freedom and independence with *taqaddum* (progress) indicates the wide circulation of democratic thought and political commitment. However, these verses breathe resignation and pessimism.

The last three verses quoted are noteworthy for the negative definition of *watan*: In strict parallelism and repetition, Rusafi juxtaposes a positive value (like army, fortune, knowledge, science, power) with a negative value indicating the actual status quo (coward, avaricious, expelled, stranger, usurper). The positive values include the whole social and political domain, and by negating them all he makes a severe and scathing criticism of political life in Iraq. *Mumtalakihi* aims at the British colonial power; *tarid* is a subtle allusion to the Shiʻi men of religion who continued their political opposition after the 1920 Revolution and thus aroused the resentment of Faysal and the British, eventually being thrown out of Iraq in 1923 under the pretext of not being Iraqis but Iranians (Wardi, VI.1, 247ff.). Depicting Faysal and his government as *dakhil* (usurper, non-Iraqi) was an offense against the king.[15] The absolute negation (*la khayra*), which introduces the parallelisms of the verses denotes *watan* as a corrupted ideal. Unlike the brisk self-assertion of his contemporary Zahawi, Rusafi here dwells in resignation and hopelessness.

Strategies of Self-Assertion in the War Poetry of the 1980s

By the 1980s, Arab nationalism (as defined by the regime) had established itself more or less as the official ideology of the Iraqi Baʻthist state, relating to Iraq as a *"qutr"* (region) within the wider framework of the *"umma ʻarabiya"* (Arab nation).[16] However the definition of Arab nationalism under the Baʻth was coupled with Iraq's claim to lead the Arab world as well as with an attempt to harness Iraq's Mesopotamian heritage. Claiming Iraqi leadership of the "Arab nation", Saddam Husayn had already postulated at the end of the 1970s: "As long as we place Iraq at the core of the Arab nation, we are not afraid that strengthening Iraqi identification would occur at the expense of the Arab nation, much as we talk, with great pride, of Iraq's present, past and future" (quoted in Tripp, 2002, p. 108).

The Iran–Iraq war was described not only as threat to Iraq but to the Arab world as a whole. When it became clear that the war would not be won easily, the propaganda machine invented *Qadisiyat Saddam*, a reference to the battle in 637. Embedding a modern war in a historical framework was a conscious effort to shape the popular perception of history, and to appropriate the past into the national narrative, exploiting the associative power

---

[15]Compare to the findings of Kadhim (2004, p. 111, footnote 53). As a Hashemite from the Hijaz, Faysal was not interested in a narrowly defined Iraqi nationalism and preferred a more pan-Arab emphasis in his national education policies. However, he was quite conscious of the alienation of certain segments of Iraqi society — most of all the Shiʻis — who were not adequately integrated into the new state: see al-Hasani (1988, vol. III, 317).

[16]"*Umma ʻarabiya wahida dhat risala khalida*" was the slogan attached to every government building in Iraq, postulating the eternal validity of the united Arab nation. See Bengio (1998, p. 35–37).

of metaphor.[17] Qadisiya had occurred before the split between Sunnis and Shi'is, and could therefore be depicted in semi-secular terms as inter-ethnic, the natural outcome of an essentialist and "centuries-old" enmity between Arabs and Iranians, a historical continuity that made Iraq an eternal potential victim of external and internal threats (Davis, 2005, p. 184ff).[18] This interpretation of history ensured a hegemonic collective understanding of the past in which present enemies, whoever they were, could be depicted as foreigners, dangerous, and unauthentic.

In the course of the war, Saddam reacted to the unexpectedly resilient Iranian resistance — and even advance — by introducing Islamic rhetoric into his speeches, presenting himself and the Iraqi nation as defenders not only of the Iraqi–Arab cause but also of Islam. Avoiding the delicate subject of the confessional divisions in Iraqi society, the Iraqis were displayed as "Muslims" while the Iranians remained the infidels: "It is impossible for us to surrender Iraq, and we cannot allow ourselves to be the gate which collapses, causing Arab and Islamic territory to fall into Khomeini's hands. We are confident of God's help." This Islamic rhetoric was not only a concession to the enemy but a consciously elaborated move, in an attempt to anticipate Shi'i unease by stressing the Islamic credentials of the Iraqi cause.[19]

---

[17]Compare the use of heroic battles like Dhu Qar in 604, Yarmuk in 636, Qadisiya in 637 and Hittin in 1187 in the context of the Palestinian resistance, Khalili (2007, p. 152.)

[18]A similar line of argument was set in motion on the Iranian side: in contrast to the Iraqi attempt to play the ethnic card, the Khomeini regime played the religious one — quite successfully. Clothing the war in religious terms, and depicting Iraq as *Yazid* (the Umayyad ruler who had killed Husayn ibn 'Ali), aroused resistance and hate against the Iraqis. The seminal writings of Ali Shariati, one of the masterminds of the Iranian Revolution, concerning the symbolism of the sacrificial death of Husayn, opened the way for his reinvention as revolutionary and martyr: "Being Husayn makes it his responsibility to perform the jihad against all that is corrupt and cruel. He has no other means at his disposal for his jihad but his own death [...] It is in this way that the dying of a human being guarantees the life of a nation" [quoted in Donohue and Esposito, 2007, p. 364]. This reinvention constituted one of the incentives that made waves of young boys advance over the minefields to clear the way, — their death being equal to what had happened to Husayn 1400 years before (Cook, 2007, pp. 155, 140; Schmucker, 1987, pp. 185–249; especially 240 on the importance of martyrdom for the success of the revolution).

[19]"Our legitimate defense was not merely the defense of Iraq but also of the Arab nation. It was not merely defense of the process of building and development but also defense of Islam and its sacred things" (Hussein, 1986, pp. 24, 43).

Consistent with the general consensus that literature plays an important role in creating identity and shaping the conscience of society, the Ba'th tried to control Iraqi cultural production. The revival of the annual Mirbad poetry festival[20] in the 1970s is a good example of such control. A fashionable and respectable festival in which renowned poets from all over the world took part, these meetings became increasingly dominated by propaganda. The Ministry of Information and Culture tied it to the Iraqi–Arab cause and sought to foster support for the Iran war and the *Qadisiyat Saddam*.[21] Since the old Mesopotamian civilizations were all considered Iraqi, the past and the present could be established as an uninterrupted continuum, and the war as the outcome of an eternal static enmity. The opening speech of the Minister of Culture and Information Latif Nusayyif Jasim at the 1985 Mirbad is telling:

> Greetings to all of you, o poets, thinkers and artists, to you, my beloved poets of Iraq, poets of the Qadisiya, poets of the Fighting Word (*al-kalima al-muqatila*) [...] God is witness that you did not recite poetry but rather shed your blood during the years of war! Greetings to every writer, thinker and artist who participates in the battle of Qadisiya (*malhamat al-qadisiya*)![22]

The use of *malhama*, which fuses the meaning of battle and of great epic-writing is deliberate. This intentional doubling of literature and war was a strategy forced upon the poets from above, by a dictatorial regime whose

---

[20] *Mirbad* had been a center for trade and commerce in Basra in the seventh and eighth centuries which developed into a cultural meeting of poets, intellectuals, and grammarians, leading to the foundation of the "Arab Humanities" there (Pellat, 1993: 113f). In the 1970s this tradition was revived and institutionalized.

[21] Quite successfully: the power of the official Iraqi pan-Arab discourse left its impact beyond the borders of Iraq. The Iran–Iraq war was perceived as threat to Iraqi–Arab hegemony — one of the fundamental beliefs of Ba'thi ideology — which had to be defended. This defense became the duty of the poets, too. See the poem by the Kuwaiti poetess Su'ad al-Sabah "Qasidat hubb ila sayf 'iraqi", recited in 1985 at Mirbad: "I am a woman who has decided to love Iraq [...] Since I was little I blackened my eyes with the nights of Iraq/and colored my hands red with the clay of Iraq/and let my hair grow long to resemble the palm trees of Iraq! [...] I want to marry a sword/Millions of palm trees/My wedding night was the battle of/Qadisiya taking place in the shade of swords and in the light of torches [...]" (Salim, 1986: 49–53). For a slightly different version see the compilation *Li-madina nughani...* (1986, vol. 1: 331–337). In the introduction to her *diwan*, Saddam Hussein said: "Thanks to the poets and artists who sing for the battle. Their words have the power of flaming bombs. Thanks to the poets and artists who – by defending the Iraqi cause — defend the Arab cause! Thanks to them from the Iraqi people!" (Salim, 1986: 7).

[22] *Li-madina nughani* (1986, vol. 1: 9).

influence extended over all fields of public and private life. It was taken up by the war poets of the 1980s more or less willingly and elaborated further. This collective coercion, which left no free artistic space, constitutes a major departure from the patriotic poetry of the early years. Even if early poets like Zahawi and Rusafi can be accused of *taqallub* and of political naivety, they did not experience such pressure from above as the poets of the 1980s.

I have chosen Sami Mahdi,[23] a famous poet of the 1980s, as example of the Iraqi war poetry of that era.[24] Sami Mahdi held public office and exerted a great influence over the Iraqi media; — in contrast to the two earlier poets however, he actively and consciously adopted, even shaped, official Ba'thi discourse. Mahdi picks up the motif of literature and war, embedding it in the Mesopotamian mythology. In the post-Sayyab era, both sacrifice *fi sabil al-watan* (for the sake of the nation) and the use of myths in literature were well-established literary devices. In his long poem *Ra'aytu ma ra'aytu* he describes his experiences as head of a unit of the People's Army (*al-jaysh al-sha'bi*) and praises the idea of self sacrifice:

> Who are these, who?
> Men who wear the skin of Gilgamesh
> or Gilgamesh in each man?
> How did they know that the secret is here,
> the herb of life here? [...]
> Ishtar hears the tread of your steps
> And Tammuz knows you [...]
> Sihan is a virgin, men!
> Desired by Zara
> Zara wants her as slave in his temple [...]
> Sihan ... Sihan
> This is Sihan, comrades!
> This is the meeting point
> Here is the herb we want
> Let's spread its dew over our bodies
> And set free our minds in its gardens.
> This is Sihan, comrades!

---

[23]Born in 1940 in Baghdad, he was editor in chief of the daily *al-Jumhuriyya* until 1991, then became director of the TV and broadcasting corporation, and later editor in chief of *al-Thawra*. After 2003 he went into exile, and now writes for different Arab papers and journals. His new poems have been discussed quite controversially in various Internet sites (Laibi, 2008; Sabri, 2006).

[24]For other war poets like Yusuf al-Sayigh and Hamid Sa'id see Tramontini (2009).

Leave behind the elegies of Ur
Let us sing the songs of Baghdad
Let us start...
Let us start time from anew
Let us start from Dilmun
And pass through to tomorrow's sun!
The thread is weak, comrades
Death belongs to the notion of life
Death is the end of form
And life is its renewal.
So let us start
Let us start together the celebration of the renewal of form! [...]
Rain ... rain...
And the rain falls down.
This is the wedding of the night, comrade!
This is the wedding of blood!
Carry your blood sacrifice and walk in the vanguard
I know you are a poet
But it's not necessary to get old
And senile like Aragon.
I know you are sad
But it's stupid to commit suicide like Mayakovski
Don't think of the two, and not of anyone else!
Don't even think of Lorca
Because he was much too kind
He was kind
And was killed before he could fight.
That's life!
Or: That's how the enemy wants it.
So fight before you get killed
And carry your blood sacrifice and walk in the vanguard! (*al-A'mal al-shi'riyah*, 1986, pp. 313–335).

The poem resounds with allusions to Sayyab, both formally and stylistically (repetition of *matar*, breaking up of lines, the use of *Tammuz* and *Ishtar*, the call for self-sacrifice — all well established in the post-Sayyab era). A popular theme of the official Ba'th rewriting of history was the presentation of Mesopotamian culture as "Iraqi", thus viewing the present and the past as an uninterrupted continuum. The motif of sacrifice for the sake of the nation sets the land (*Sihan*) as eternal and quasi-sacred (the land itself holds the secret of life, the herb of Gilgamesh), and the relation of poet and land is one of love. If however, in Ba'th discourse, war poetry is equated with love poetry, then the motif of (self-) sacrifice becomes corrupt, since it is forced upon the poets from above. Turad al-Kubaysi, former director of the state-owned journal *Afaq 'Arabiya*, notes in his study on Iraqi war poetry (1986, vol. 1, pp. 7–8) that writing war poems is like writing love poems and continues: "The war poem is like the political poem or the love poem: it enriches our knowledge and our consciousness of love since it is in some way the embodiment of our historical consciousness." So the fusion of love and war seems to be the culmination of historical conscience, and the poets have to follow this way of interpreting past and present. *Sihan* is a virgin, who has to be protected from *Zara*, a terrible heathen creature that threatens both land and love. Both are consigned to eternal envy and threats, and to protect both, sacrifices have to be made, — even of one's own blood. References to Western poets like Louis Aragon, Vladimir Mayakovsky and Federico García Lorca illustrate the impossibility of following their example: they are not fit to guide since they were weak and failed. They were poets of resistance, fighting for political and social change, poets with a recognized claim to political authority, something with which Mahdi most probably would credit himself — but he demands more: The unconditional commitment to war which none of the three other poets seems to have made.

Conclusion

At the beginning of the twentieth century, there were different competing offers of identity, and it remains the case that in spite of 80–90 years of Iraq as a state and 50 years of *de facto* independence, national identity is still very much contested. It was neither Ottomanism, nor pan-Islamism, nor Iraqi nationalism but a form of pan-Arab nationalism that in the end was asserted by the regime as the dominant ideology in the modern history of Iraq. However, during and especially after the Iran–Iraq war it was thoroughly corroded and corrupted by Saddam's increasingly repressive system.

The question of the political commitment of the poets discussed here is difficult to answer. Both Zahawi and Rusafi have been considered the fieriest nationalist poets of their time (together with Muhammad Mahdi al-Jawahiri, 1900–1997), but their poetical oeuvres demonstrate a huge range of different, often contradictory, political affiliations, wavering between praise and rejection of the authorities. Their ideological grounding and their political insights seem to have been rather simple and naïve, and the fact that they were generally active in public life (from the Ottoman period to the monarchy), holding or seeking to hold public office, very often led them to make contradictory statements in their poems. It seems to me that the inner yearning for the nation as felt and expressed in poetry could not save them falling prey to their own ambitions. The fact that both poets are still — until now — held in high esteem is because both were free spirits, introducing new themes in poetry and a new commitment to social and political change, a commitment to reform, rationality, secularism, and progress. Notwithstanding their political unsteadiness, they succeeded in initiating a new kind of artistic commitment that left a deep impact on the development of Iraqi poetry.

This link between poetry and official authority in the early decades of the twentieth century can safely be said to have been re-established and reinforced under the Ba'th in the 1980s and after. However, if art or any cultural production is tied to high authority or state-given parameters, then it is will be deprived of its most vital and relevant function: to act as counter discourse, as dissociating from power. Confronted with the dominant state ideology that infiltrated and dominated culture, poetry in the 1980s more often than not was doomed to reproducing the hegemonic discourse. The war poetry as exemplified in the poem of Sami Mahdi was part of a dominant ideology to which many poets actively contributed and from which they profited.

The invasion of 2003 has set free centrifugal powers, which once more struggle for the nation, and try to redefine it. The question in search of a response is much the same as the one posed in the 1920s: "What kind of Iraq do we want to have? What do we have to do to achieve it?" It remains to be seen how the poets of the new generation will answer this question, which ideal of the nation they will call upon, and which strategies of self-assertion they will follow.

Electronic references

Hippler, J (2003). Nation-building: Begriff und Konzepte. Online. Available HTTP: <www.jochen-hippler.de/Aufsatze/Nation-Building_Einleitung> (accessed 10 October 2008).

Reinkowski, M (2006). Das Osmanische Reich: ein antikoloniales Imperium?. Zeithistorische Forschungen/Studies in Contemporary History, Online. Available HTTP: <www.zeithistorische-forschungen.de/16126041-Reinkowski-1-2006> (accessed 10 October 2008).

Sabri, F (2006). Qutlat al-ibda'. Sami Mahdi numudhajan. Online. Available HTTP: <www.aaramnews.com/website/22188NewsArticle.html> (accessed 10 October 2008).

NOT JUST "FOR ART'S SAKE": EXHIBITING IRAQI ART IN THE WEST AFTER 2003

Silvia Naef

It is generally admitted that the 1989 Paris exhibition *Les Magiciens de la terre* at the Centre Georges Pompidou constituted a breakthrough. For the first time, non-Westerners were shown as *artists* rather than craftsmen in a major Western contemporary art institution (Millet, 2006, pp. 93–95; Belting, 2003, pp. 67–68; Herzog, 2006, p. 565). Although the exhibition itself could not entirely escape from paternalism — as both the title of the exhibition itself and the admitted ignorance of the non-Western art scene on the part of the curators proved (Baykam, 1994, pp. 49–61) — it opened the doors for artists from the "outside". Since the mid-1990s, no major art event like the documenta or the Venice Biennale can conceive of itself without this presence, and among many others, artists with Middle Eastern backgrounds have benefited from it. Artists from Iraq have been absent from this 'globalization' of the international art scene for some time, although the country has been one of the most productive in the region since the 1950s.

The situation has changed since 2003. Although only rarely shown in the most prestigious art institutions, the work of Iraqi artists has circulated in France, Britain, Germany, Spain, Sweden, the United States, and elsewhere. This article will explore the history of these exhibitions and try to analyze the reasons behind them. In order to contextualize the topic, it will first give a general overview of the emergence of modern art in Iraq, concentrating on the most significant movements, before reviewing the various exhibitions and scrutinizing their place within the global art scene.

Modern Art in Iraq — The Emergence of a Local Art Scene[1]

Modern art (*al-fann al-hadith*, or, often less distinctly, *al-fann al-mu'asir*), by which we mean an art form inspired by Western models, started later in what was to become Iraq than in neighboring Arab countries like Egypt, Syria, and Lebanon. The three Ottoman provinces of Baghdad, Basra and Mosul were far away from the capital and the modernization process, to which the production of Western-style art was strongly tied, started later. Direct contacts with Europe were rare, as were European expatriates or tourists — including painters — in the region. As the British archaeologist H. Valentine Geere wrote in 1904:

> "I have no desire to compare the two countries and their antiquities; however, all that I wish to do is to point out that whereas Egypt enjoys a high degree of popularity, her poor sister [Mesopotamia] is treated with an indifference that I find it hard to understand" (quoted in Naef, 1996, p. 212).

In Ottoman times, modernization and Western influence came mainly through the mediation of the capital, Istanbul; and the first 'Iraqis' to paint in Western style, 'Abd al-Qadir al-Rassam (1882–1952), Muhammad Salih Zaki (1888–1974), Muhammad Salim (precise dates unknown) and his contemporary 'Asim Hafiz (1889–1976) had acquired their skills while studying at the Military Academy in Istanbul, where drawing and painting were part of the curriculum.

After World War I, the newly created Iraqi state caught up quickly. With the success of the art exhibition set up at the Industrial and Agricultural Fair in Baghdad in 1931, young students were sent to study art in Europe: Akram Shukri to Britain in 1931, Fa'iq Hasan to Paris in 1935, 'Ata Sabri and Hafiz al-Durubi to Rome, and Jawad Salim to Paris in 1939. World War II forced the expatriates to come back and, in 1939, a painting section opened at the Music Institute in Baghdad, and in 1941, an Institute of Fine Arts was created, directed by Fa'iq Hasan.

World War II led to a second British occupation of the country. Among these troops there were Polish volunteers, a few of whom were professional painters, including Joseph Czapski and Feliks Topolski. In contrast with

---

[1]For a more detailed account, see Naef (1996: 197–296) or Khamis (2001: 21–32). In Arabic, the two-volume study by Shakir Hasan al-Sa'id still constitutes a valuable source for the period under consideration (al-Sa'id, 1983, 1988).

the more academic teachers with whom the young Iraqi artists had studied in Europe, they had integrated the main lessons of modernity. 'Ata' Sabri, Fa'iq Hasan and Jawad Salim met them and discussed art with them in the cafés of Baghdad. For some of the young artists, this was the first contact with 'modern art' in the proper sense, although Iraqi art historians differ over whether these encounters were or were not decisive in the development of modern Iraqi art (Naef, 1996, pp. 225–228).

A modern art scene came into life in the 1950s, when three groups of artists formed: the Pioneers' Group (*Jama'at al-Ruwwad*) (1950), led by Fa'iq Hasan, the Baghdad Group for Modern Art (*Jama'at Baghdad li'l-Fann al-Hadith*), under the leadership of Jawad Salim and the Impressionists' Group (*Jama'at al-Intiba'iyyin*, 1953), which gathered around Hafiz al-Durubi. The Baghdad Group for Modern Art published two manifestoes, in 1951, and in 1955, and theorized what would become a central issue in Iraqi art: the reference to the "local character" (*al-tabi' al-mahalli*), later on referred to as "heritage" (*turath*). For the authors of the manifesto, this reference to local traditions was thought to confer an international relevance on Iraqi art by giving it a specific flair [*Illustration 1: Rasha al-Husayni*].

In the 1960s several younger artists went into abstract art; at the end of the decade, after the defeat in the Six Day War, committed art (*al-fann al-multazim*) started to play a bigger role [*Illustration 2: Sa'd Shakir*]. The group Toward a New Vision (*Nahwa al-ru'iya al-jadida*) was founded in 1969 in order to react against the intellectual attitude of hopelessness induced by the defeat. The Ba'th, which seized power in 1968, benefited from this "revolutionary" state of mind. Elias Farah, one of the party's thinkers, advocated "nationalist realism," stylistically unbounded but devoted to the nation. For Muhammad al-Jaza'iri, author of a book on committed art published in 1977 on the occasion of the 30th anniversary of the foundation of the Ba'th Party, art had to support the Arab question (*qadiya*) and should therefore be "readable" by everybody; abstraction, considered a mere bourgeois phenomenon, had to be avoided (Naef, 1996, pp. 281–283). The regime invested into the art scene by founding new museums and exhibition spaces and by expanding the existing ones. Culture, as defined in the report of the Eighth Regional Congress of the Arab Ba'th Socialist Party, was part of the development strategy of the Party and therefore, of the Iraqi government (El-Basri, 1980, p. 12). Writers, artists, intellectuals and journalists were to be attracted to the Revolution, in order to help spreading its goals (Arab Ba'th Socialist Party, 1974, p. 256). Cultural centers were opened abroad, in London and Paris for instance. The Iraqi Cultural Center in London was especially proactive: besides numerous exhibitions, it issued a lavish periodical, *Ur*, dedicated to the arts and literature, edited by the renowned artist Dhia Azzawi. In 1976, an exhibition of contemporary Iraqi art was shown in Paris, at the Musée d'art moderne de la ville de Paris (*Art irakien contemporain*, 1976). Publications on the arts were also promoted: a book, written by Nizar Salim, and published in several languages, retold the history of Iraqi art (Salim, 1977).[2] The al-Wasiti festival, hold for the first time in 1972, celebrated visual arts and literature; in 1973 Baghdad hosted the first Congress of Arab Artists, and the first Arab Biennale the following year. Other international events were the International Poster Exhibition (1979) and the First Arab Graphic Exhibition, held in London and Baghdad in 1978. A first wave of public sculptures, celebrating personalities of the Iraqi past or representing 'local' literary characters from the *Arabian Nights*, started to fill the streets of the capital (Baram, 1991, p. 77; Amanat al-'Asima, 1977).

After the dissolution of the National Front in 1978, which included the communists and the Kurdish parties, many Iraqi intellectuals, and among them numerous artists, left the country, mainly for Europe, where the majority had to give up the dream of living as artists, a story that has still to be written. The war against Iran in the 1980s reinforced emigration. Nevertheless, supported by the oil monarchies and the West, Iraq continued to promote its artistic production, although on a lesser level: the London produced *Ur* was replaced by *Gilgamesh*, printed in Iraq. In *La Lettre de Bagdad*, published by the Iraqi Embassy in Paris, Jamil Hamoudi, the founding father of the alphabetical art movement (*hurufiyya*), praised the generosity of the regime in the field of the visual arts (Naef, 1996, p. 295). The Iran–Iraq war was visually supported by the erection of majestic public monuments, as the 1983 *Martyr's Monument* by Ismail Fattah, the *Victory Arch* (1989), anticipating the victory over Iran (al-Khalil, 1991), or the 80 life-size statues of deceased officers erected in 1989 on the Shatt al-'Arab in Basra (al-Khalil, 1991, pp. 29–31).

The strong presence of Mesopotamian themes in Iraqi art during the decade, reflecting Saddam's desire to be recognized as a new Nebuchadnezzar, resulted not only from official pressures, but from a

---

[2] As well as the Arabic original, there were translations into English, French, Spanish, and Italian.

development proper to Iraqi art since the 1950s, as Amatzia Baram perti-
nently remarks (Baram, 1991, p. 80). He speaks of the co-optation of artists
by the regime, whereas Muhsin al-Musawi, describing the situation of the
Iraqi intelligentsia more generally, affirms that they resisted total allegiance
to the regime's propaganda culture and found subtle ways of resistance
(Musawi, 2006, pp. 86–87). Hana' Malallah depicts the choice that young
artists of the Eighties generation had in these terms: exile or isolation, especially from the West, which had been so influential to their art. She speaks
of a "consciousness of isolation" for those who remained in the country (Mal
Allah, 2001, p. 63), and sees the reference to Mesopotamian heritage as a
result of this. Wafaa Bilal, who was a student then, reports having painted
canvases that were critical of the regime (Bilal and Lydersen, 2008, p. 64).

Without the Kuwait war, the regime would probably have continued
its monumental plans, erecting statues of all the "kings and caliphs who
ruled Iraq before Islam and after it" (Baram, 1991, p. 82). With the sanctions hanging over the country after 1991, creativity became more difficult.
Materials were rare and expensive; artists had to find alternative solutions.[3]
Baghdad became a blank zone on the world map and therefore, international curators — who had started to look for talent outside the West in
these years — did not even think of it. Those Iraqi artists who had travelled
around the world and had largely benefited from the largesse of the regime,
were now obliged to stay home or took refuge in Amman, which became
the focal point for Iraqi artists in the 1990s (Maffi, 2006, pp. 317–318).
Paradoxically, the art market boomed in the country itself, as artists were
selling to international embassy and NGO employees. Qasim al-Sibti, the
founder of the Hewar Gallery, refers having had 100 commercial shows during this time (Vincent, 2004) [*Illustration* 3: *Qasim al-Sibti*]; 'Isam Pasha
reports having sold his pieces for $200 to United Nations personnel (*Taipei
Times*, 2006). Several galleries opened during this decade: Hewar which has
already been mentioned, in 1992, Athar, owned by Muhammad Znad, in
1996, and Dijla, owned by Zainab Mahdi, in 1997.

For the American art critic Steven Vincent, who had visited the country twice in 2003 and 2004 before being killed there, the selling of art to
Western expatriates resulted in what he defined as a "tourist" style, with
an Orientalist bias (Vincent, 2004). New trends, techniques and ways of

---

[3]For a detailed description of an artist's life in Baghdad during this decade, see al-Radi
(2003).

exhibiting that became popular throughout the region during the 1990s, did not touch Iraq, cut off from the flux of ideas and commodities, as was apparent in an Iraqi art exhibition shown at the Mairie du 9ᵉ Arrondissement in Paris in 2000. In spite of the quality of many exhibited works, they often seemed to be 'out of time', even by regional standards.[4]

Since 2003, the instability of the country has worsened the situation. More artists than ever — between 75 and 90 per cent according to different sources quoted on the Internet — emigrated. Vincent found that art students were producing only "tepid, unadventurous abstraction and portraiture." In addition, in April 2003, at the same time as the Iraqi Museum was looted, the Museum of Modern Art, which had a fairly representative collection of modern Iraqi art, was also plundered. Since this museum had no catalog or archives, it has become extremely difficult to recover the stolen goods, although many of the paintings were openly on sale elsewhere in the Middle East. The Iraqi Museum reopened in February 2009; at present there are no concrete plans for the Museum of Modern Art, although several private initiatives are trying to reconstitute the collection.

Exhibiting Iraqi Art: European Initiatives

The AyaGallery, London

Although it predates 2003, it seems useful to mention here the work done by the AyaGallery in London, because it has many points in common with later projects. Founded in 2002 and managed by the Iraqi architect Ali Mousawi and his wife, the artist Maysalun Faraj, its aim is to "exhibit and promote art predominantly from Iraq."[5] It owns a collection of works by Iraqi artists, from the early twentieth century to the present. Maysalun Faraj was the initiator, in 1995, of *Strokes of Genius*, originally a database on Iraqi art, together with Ulrike Khamis, an Islamic art historian and Rashad Selim, an Iraqi artist. They wanted to bring the "largely unrecognized artistic achievements" of Iraqis to the attention of the Western public (Faraj, 2001b, p. 16). After its first presentation at the Brunei Gallery in London in 2000, it toured to other locations in Britain and the United States

---

[4] "Exposition de peintres iraquiens," Mairie de Paris, 9ᵉᵐᵉ arrondissement, 22 June–1 July 2000, no catalog.
[5] See AyaGallery, <http://www.ayagallery.co.uk/>.

(before the war), mostly in university galleries.[6] *Strokes of Genius* transformed into iNCiA (International Network for Contemporary Iraqi Artists), whose purpose was to advance Iraqi art and public education in Iraqi art as an integral part of world art. A book, entitled *Strokes of Genius*, intended as a "reference work" (Faraj, 2001b, p. 15) was published in 2001: It included a general introduction to art in Iraq and articles by contemporary Iraqi artists, as well as reproductions of the works shown at the exhibition (Faraj, 2001a). iNCiA plans to publish a dictionary of Iraqi art and artists.

"Baghdad Renaissance", Galerie M, Paris, 2003

American troops had barely entered Baghdad and overthrown Saddam Husayn when two French women, Meriem Lequesne, owner of Galerie M in Paris and Caecilia Pieri, a publisher, left for Baghdad on June 15, 2003, in order to see what had happened to the visual arts inside Iraq, after "30 years of dictatorship [sic] and wars, not to mention the twelve years of generalized indigence" (*Bagdad Renaissance*, 2003, p. 8).

Their trip to Baghdad, where they stayed for ten days, was a revelation: where they had expected to find artists "buried alive" (*Bagdad Renaissance*, 2003, p. 8), they discovered a lively art scene. Some encounters were deeply moving, like their meeting with the 78 year old Nuri al-Rawi, an artist already active in the 1960s and author of one of the first books on modern Iraqi art, who recounted his life story to them. At Hewar Gallery they met Qasim al-Sibti, who had recovered twenty of the paintings looted from the Museum of Modern Art; they went to the ruined Academy of Fine Arts, where they discovered the first painting done by the students after the fall of Saddam, the *Painting of Liberty*, a group composition, which they took to Paris for the exhibition, together with some 70 other pieces of art.

The exhibition was well visited and all the works were sold to individuals or institutions: The *Painting of Liberty* was acquired by the Musée d'Histoire Contemporaine in Paris (formerly War Museum); media coverage

---

[6]Exeter University, Institute of Arab and Islamic Studies, 1 April–15 July 2001; Hotbath Gallery, Bath, UK, 8 August–13 September 2001; Faulconer Gallery, Grinnell College, Grinnell, Iowa, 29 January–15 March 2002; "Iraqi Art Today — Looking Out, Looking In," DePaul University, Lake Forest, Illinois, 10 January–16 March 2003.

was fair.[7] In consequence, a second exhibition, called "Painting in Iraq Today" followed a year later, displaying the work of eleven artists that Lequesne and Pieri had gathered during the trips they made to Iraq in 2004 (R.B., 2004).[8] It was less successful than the previous one, most probably, as some of the exhibitors expressed to me in interviews, because the wave of empathy for the Iraqi people had begun to die down.

An 80-page catalog, in French and English, entitled *Bagdad Renaissance*, was published with the first exhibition. According to the authors, it was the first printed source on modern art in Iraq to appear for a long time. It gives the reader some valuable historical information on the Iraqi art scene, but its main focus is on the present situation. Each artist is presented, and his/her struggle in a city so ravaged by events is described with much compassion; the exceptional quality of these artists, who continued to create in an extremely difficult situation, is highlighted. The catalog constitutes a precious snapshot of the immediate post-war situation and gives an insight into artistic life in Iraq under the sanctions.

"Baghdad–Paris", Musée du Montparnasse, Paris, 2005/6

The other major Paris initiative was "Baghdad–Paris, Artists from Iraq", held in 2005/06 at the Musée du Montparnasse.[9] The exhibition was sponsored by *Marianne*, the French news magazine, and Bernard Krief Capital, an international consulting firm. *Marianne* had been one of the rare Western media to report about the consequences of the looting of the Museum of Modern Art in Baghdad, in April 2003, and about the attempts to reconstitute a new collection of modern Iraqi art. It wrote about the efforts made by Muhammad Znad, the owner of the Baghdad Athar Gallery, who had been able to collect 800 works of art during the 1990s, and who intended to found a new museum of modern art (Gozlan, 2003).

The idea behind the exhibition was to show the development of modern Iraqi art and its strong ties to the French capital; hence the title, referring to major modern art exhibitions held at the Centre Georges Pompidou and illustrating the relations between Paris and other metropolises of modern

---

[7]Participating artists [spelling according to the catalogue]: Noori Al Rawi, Qassim Al Sabti, Fakher Mohammed, Jaafar Mohammed Khader, Falah Al Anee, Mohammed Jassim Al Zubaidi, Sat'ar Darwich, Ahmed Noussaïef, Hadi Mahood, Thikra Sarsam.

[8]"Peindre en Irak aujourd'hui," 22 September–8 October 2004.

[9]23 November 2005–19 February 2006.

art.[10] A total of 90 works by 42 artists were showcased, covering the whole history of Iraqi painting, with a focus on more recent creations, although there were also a few works by the pioneers of the art movement, as 'Abd al-Qadir al-Rassam, 'Asim Hafiz, Jawad Salim and Fa'iq Hasan. In the words of Znad, it was the first time, since the looting of the Museum of Modern Art, that such a "panorama" of Iraqi art had been exhibited in public (*Bagdad–Paris*, 2005, p. 10).

In the catalog, an article entitled "Art as survival" retraces the history of art in Iraq and the making of the exhibition (Seurel, 2005). It is written quite dramatically, emphasizing chaos, despair, and bloodshed, but also the hope represented by art and the courage of people like Muhammad Znad, who had run his gallery since 1996 and continued to do so, in spite of occupation and terror. It remembers how the organization of exhibitions, after 2003, represented "at the same time an existence detached from the horror that surrounds it, and an integral part of the country's drama" (Seurel, 2005, p. 6). In the same catalog, in a brief presentation text, the director of *Marianne*, Jean-François Kahn, said:

> An astonishing message has come to us from Iraq. It has moved the journalists at *Marianne*. In a country seized by chaos, artists continue to create. In spite of destruction and death, they organize exhibitions, try to keep ties to the outside world and continue to affirm the vitality and originality of Iraqi art (*Bagdad–Paris*, 2005, p. 8).

And Eric Vinassac, CEO of Bernard Krief Capital, underlined that the exhibition is a "symbol of what men and women, united beyond borders, can overcome in the service of a project, vital for the culture of a country which is a victim of war and terror" (*Bagdad–Paris*, 2005, p. 9).[11] This was also the tone of the news report on the opening night of the exhibition on the French TV channel TF1: The well-known reporter Marine Jacquemin commented on the exhibition saying that "art is stronger than weapons" and that "in the heart of the capital of suffering [Baghdad], dream and beauty survive[d] against everything." In an interview, Martine Gozlan affirmed that producing art in Iraq, in the present circumstances, was "a real insurrection against death."[12]

---

[10]Paris–New York (1977); Paris–Berlin (1978); Paris–Moscou (1979).

[11]The translations of the citations are my own.

[12]TF1, "Bagdad–Paris". See <http://tf1.lci.fr/infos/france/2005/0,,3266066,00-bagdad-paris-exposition-comme-autres-muse-montparnasse-paris-.html> (accessed 16 March 2009).

The exhibition thus resulted from a convergence between anti-war positions and the desire to denounce the loss of the Iraqi artistic heritage, as was confirmed in the course of a conversation I had with Muhammad Znad in Paris. Znad was also concerned about finding a safe place to store his collection, which he feared having to take back to Iraq. The political relevance of the exhibition was confirmed by research for media reactions on the web, including the website of the French Ministry of Foreign Affairs. In a press briefing that took place on the occasion of the visit of the Iraqi Foreign Minister Hoshyar Zibari on November 28/29, 2005, stressing French efforts to build a cultural presence in Iraq and to reinforce cultural ties, the Ministry's spokesperson affirmed that he had visited the exhibition and encouraged others to do so.[13]

Iraqi art, with works by Isma'il al-Shaykhli, Shakir Hasan al-Sa'id and from the collection of the Museum of Modern Art in Baghdad, was on display in Paris again during Iraqi cultural week, held at the UNESCO Palace in November 2007.[14] The exhibition was the result of collaboration between the UNESCO Office for Iraq, and the Ministries of Culture and of Tourism and Antiquities of Iraq. The Director General of UNESCO, Koïchiro Matsuura, declared: "it is a message of hope and support aiming to reinstate culture at the heart of the political process of dialog, peace, and reconciliation."[15]

Solidarity with the Iraqi people was also the motor behind the 2008 London exhibition "Riding on Fire: Iraqi Art under Occupation," held at Artiquea Gallery.[16] The gallery, which specializes in art and antiques, "the most enjoyable investment you can have," has a collection of "the best artists" in the Middle East.[17] The exhibition, showcasing works by 42 artists produced after the American occupation, had been organized in cooperation with the Stop the War Coalition.[18] Again in London, to accompany its

---

[13] French Ministry of Foreign Affairs, Press briefing, 25 November 2005: <https://pastel. diplomatie. gouv.fr/editorial/actual/ael2/pointpresse.asp?liste=20051125.html&submit. x=8&submit.y=13#Chapitre3> (accessed 16 March 2009).

[14] 12–21 November 2007.

[15] A brochure has been published, but was not available to us. For Matsuura's statement, see UNESCO, "Semaine culturelle irakienne": <http://portal.unesco.org/en/ ev.php-URL_ID=41232&URL_DO=DO_TOPIC&URL_SECTION=201.html> (accessed 16 March 2009).

[16] 19 September–31 October 2008.

[17] Artiquea, "Riding on Fire, Iraqi Art Under Occupation": <http://www.artiquea.co.uk/ index.php?main_page=index&cPath=1_22> (accessed 29 March 2009).

[18] "Riding On Fire: Iraqi Art Under Occupation," *Socialist Worker* 2120: <http://www. socialistworker.co.uk/art.php?id=16004> (accessed 29 March 2009).

exhibition "Babylon: Myth and Reality" (2008–2009), the British Museum showed the works of eleven modern artists — ten of whom were Iraqis — who took inspiration from ancient Mesopotamian cultures. The online brochure commented on their work, saying that besides reminding us of the millennia of Iraqi cultural history, they "lament[ed] the continued destruction of our shared heritage through war and neglect."[19]

"The Iraqi Equation"

"The Iraqi Equation" was first shown in Berlin in 2005–2006, at the Kunst Werke, then in Barcelona, at the Fundació Antoni Tàpies (2006), and in finally in Umeå, in Northern Sweden, at the BildMuseet (2006–2007), and has thus had a wider resonance than the other exhibitions discussed so far. Its high visibility is due to its organizer, the Frenchwoman Catherine David, the curator of documenta X (1997), one of the main figures on the European art scene. In 2002, she launched "Contemporary Arab Representations," a long-term project including seminars, exhibitions and discussions with those working in the arts, literature, and architecture. According to David, because of its great complexity, the Arab world can function as a laboratory for the whole planet and can help understanding contemporary culture in a time of globalization (*Tamáss*, 2002, pp. 10–11). She considers that the project is not only of an aesthetic nature, but subsumes a political posture. "Contemporary Arab Representations 1" in 2002 was dedicated to Beirut, Nr. 2 (2003) to Cairo; both were shown at the Fundació Antoni Tàpies in Barcelona, the Witte de With in Rotterdam and the BildMuseet in Umeå, Sweden and, for Cairo, at the Centro José Guerrero in Granada; a publication with critical texts accompanied the events (*Tamáss*, 2002, 2004). In 2007–2008, David organized "Di/Visions," a cultural and documentary project of "talks, discussions and screenings," at the House of World Cultures in Berlin. She has been chosen as the curator of Abu Dhabi's first exhibition pavilion at the Venice Biennale in 2009. Her involvement with the Arab world is strong and it is thus not surprising that the third part of "Contemporary Arab Representations" was dedicated to Iraq, especially since in 2003, when re-presenting "Contemporary Arab Representations/Beirut" at the Venice Biennale, David commented: "The consolidation and promotion of major works of contemporary Arab

---

[19] "Iraq's Past Speaks to the Present," British Museum, Room 34, 10 November 2008–15 March 2009.

culture has become even more urgent with the worsening situation after the violent and cynically premeditated dismantling of Iraq and the emergence of another colonial occupation in the region."[20]

"The Iraqi Equation" was conceived more as a "platform" than as an exhibition, since, for David, it was preferable to speak of "representations of a certain place and time" than to fall into the trap of making misrepresentations of globalized culture which would consist of searching for contemporary art in today's Iraq (Hurtado, 2006, pp. 7–8). In this sense, Catherine David was going back to the method she had adopted for the documenta X, where she had stated that "the pertinence, excellence and radicality of contemporary non-Western expressions often finds its privileged avenues in music, oral and written language [...] and cinema" (David, 1997, p. 11). It is also a formula that she would apply again for "Di/Visions", organized in Berlin in 2008, which, she explained, was "a complex format with different types of events, a movie program and interviews with different personalities form the Middle East, as well as a week-end of conferences and debates, [...] a virtual agora" (Wittmann, 2008). David herself had not been in Iraq before the exhibition (Grau, 2006); she mainly gave space to exile artists, because they had had more freedom for expressing themselves (Hurtado, 2006, p. 7). The exhibition was conceived as an "inventory" of Iraqi culture after thirty years of dictatorship, sanctions and occupation; it was supposed to challenge the TV images that invade our homes almost daily (Bax, 2006).[21]

The exhibition showcased only four visual art works, by Samir, Faisal Laibi Sahi, Talal Refit, and Nedim Kufi. The Iraqi-Swiss Samir, better known as a movie director (born 1955 and living in Zurich), had produced a video installation dealing with the changing image of Iraqis in Western representations, comparing shots from the 1924 Hollywood movie *The Thief of Baghdad* with photographs of a Baghdadi middle class family and with present-day TV reports (Mirza, 2006). Laibi's work was an enlarged reproduction of his 1984 painting *Coffeehouse in Baghdad*, a work considered as representative by many Iraqis, since its offers a critical look on their society. Laibi was born in Basra in 1945 and has lived in exile since 1974.

---

[20]Witte de With, Venice Biennale 2003: <www.wdw.nl/ENG/projects/arab_venice/index.htlm> (accessed 22 March 2009).

[21]14 pictures of the exhibition, including the works discussed here, can be seen on <http://www.universes-in-universe.de/islam/eng/2006/003/fotos.html> (accessed 20 March 2009).

Talal Refit (born in Kirkuk and living in Germany since 1985) exhibited a coffee house bench and gave it the title *Democracy* (2005). Nedim Kufi, born in Baghdad in 1962 and living between Cairo and Holland displayed text and image scrolls on a wall, texts and images that he has published on his Internet diary *Daftar* since 2004. A documentary by Sawsan Darwaza, entitled *An Artist with a View*, presented different figures in the intellectual and artistic life of Baghdad to the public; Samir's documentary movie *Forget Baghdad* (2003) gave an account of the country's Jewish heritage; and photographs lent by the Arab Image Foundation showed life in Iraq between the 1930s and the 1970s, including pictures from the 1960s by Latif al-Ani; TV-screens, showing news channels, were in another room (Mirza, 2006).

While the creative work was mostly by those who had long lived in exile, and the photographs and movies revived the memory of a country that had long disappeared, the TV channels showed daily life in present-day Iraq. Reactions were mixed. The hybrid composition of "The Iraqi Equation," situated somewhere between a museum exhibit and a documentary festival, irritated some reporters who did not know if they should consider it a testimony of solidarity with the people of Iraq, a way of attracting attention to the country's intellectual and artistic situation, or an art exhibition. The opinion-making newsmagazine *Der Spiegel* reportedly accused the exhibition of fostering anti-American feelings, an accusation David rejected (Grau, 2006). *Tageszeitung* journalist Daniel Bax criticized the omnipresence of screens in an exhibition that claimed to provide an alternative image to the televisual one; for him, "The Iraqi Equation" was more of "a multimedia installation," "a documentary film festival" than an exhibition, although he admitted that it did enrich the visitor's view of Iraqi culture to some extent. An article in the Berlin daily *Tagesspiegel*, entitled "Baghdad lies in agony," concentrated on the dire situation of culture in present-day Iraq (Naoum, 2006). Another author underlined how for most Iraqi exiles the situation in their countries of exile had become a central point of their work (Mirza, 2006). A Moroccan author commenting on the Barcelona exhibition shared this view, stressing that the war situation had forced the organizer to concentrate on artists and intellectuals living outside the country (Karroum, 2006). For him, the exhibition was a testimony, but it had not succeeded in solving the "Iraqi Equation;" he hoped in future that such an exhibition could relate something other than "facts."

However, this was one of its stated purposes: In an interview, David declared that she wanted to show artists whose work was tied closely to the contemporary situation (Grau, 2006) and which was also politically significant. Her project was meant to be an intellectual forum of resistance, a value she assigns to the arts.

Exhibitions in the United States

Exhibitions of Iraqi art in the United States started later, for both political and cultural reasons. With support for the war reaching 75% and public opinion often linking Iraq with 9/11, any presentation of the country under a different light would have been unpopular in the beginning. Culturally speaking, interest in non-European cultures had originated in the United States during the Civil Rights movement in the 1960s and sprang from the effort of ethnic minorities to be recognized by mainstream culture. Cultural institutions based on ethnic criteria were founded in order to give a presence to these minorities within the national landscape (Pett, 2002, pp. 43–52); examples of this are the Studio Museum in Harlem or the Arab American National Museum in Dearborn, Michigan. Thus the cultures of the "subaltern" are considered from a "domestic" rather than from a geopolitical perspective. With the absence of a large and influential (or concentrated) Arab diaspora community, things Middle Eastern — raï music, Oriental dance or Lebanese cuisine — have not generally become part of broader popular culture. And the visual arts even less: the first exhibition labelled "art from the Islamic world" was "Without Boundary, Seventeen Ways of Looking," shown in 2006 at the Museum of Modern Art in New York, displaying the works of 17 artists with an Islamic background, mostly living in the West (Daftari, 2006).

Not surprisingly thus, there were no exhibitions of Iraqi art before the end of 2005, when opponents of the war outnumbered supporters for the first time.[22] Although a direct correlation cannot be established, the opening of the debate about the war in Iraq coincided with an increasing number of exhibitions of Iraqi art throughout the country.

Iraqi Book Art or "Dafatir"

The first show of Iraqi art in the United States after the beginning of the war in 2003 was "Dafatir, Contemporary Iraqi Book Art," curated by Nada Shabout, a professor of art history at the University of North Texas in

---

[22]See <http://pewresearch.org/pubs/770/iraq-war-five-year-anniversary>

Dallas, herself of Iraqi origin. Since 2005, the show has circulated in university art galleries all over the country.[23] A 96-page catalog was published in 2008. The show consisted of 15 to 17 notebooks (*dafatir*), painted by different artists and belonging to the collection of London-based Iraqi artist Dhia Azzawi;[24] all of these artists had works in the looted Museum of Modern Art in Baghdad. The destruction of Iraq's cultural heritage was a theme of many of the works, for instance in Nazar Yahya's *Baghdad Day of Destruction* (2003) or in Azzawi's *Book of Shame: the Destruction of the Iraqi Museum*. The notebooks had been presented within the larger context of an Arabic–Islamic book painting tradition, symbolized by a facsimile of Hariri's *Maqamat*, a text illustrated in the thirteenth century by the Mesopotamian artist Yahya al-Wasiti. The University of North Texas website indicates that the exhibition showcased different generations of Iraqi artists with their varied experiences, adding that: "It [would] also bring contemporary Iraqi art to Texas at a crucial historical moment, to show a different face of a nation that is currently part of our daily news." Reactions insisted on the fact that the exhibition gave another view of Iraq, as an open-minded country where modern culture is at home. The educational aspect of the exhibition is often put in the foreground, for instance in an article published in the *Dallas Observer* which comments that the show "disabus[es] you of any misconceptions you might have had about Iraqi culture" (Dallas Observer, 2005). The gallery director at Carleton College, Laurel Bradley declared: "This exhibition demonstrates that artists will be artists even in adverse circumstances" (Lamb, 2005). Or, as Venetia Porter, the curator of Islamic art at the British Museum, writes in the catalog, the exhibition is a way of looking at Iraq's present situation through art, of seeing history through these artists' eyes.[25] In most cases, panel discussions and debates about the situation in Iraq accompanied the exhibition.

---

[23] University of North Texas, Dallas, 17 October–22 November 2005; University of Texas at El Paso, 7 April–10 June 2006; Carleton College, Northfield, Minnesota, with Minnesota Center for Book Arts 6, January–12 February 2006; Center for Book Arts, New York, 19 February–31 March 2007; Denison University, Granville, Ohio, 30 November 2007–7 March 2008; Arthur & Mata Jaffe Center for Book Arts, Florida Atlantic University, Boca Raton, Florida, November 2008.

[24] Dia al-Azzawi, Rafa al-Nasiri, Mahmud al-Obidi, Mohammed al-Shammarey, Sadig Kwaish Alfraji, Ammar Dawod, Mohammad Fakher, Ismail Fattah, Ghassan Gha'eb, Shakir Hassan Al Said, Nedim Kufi, Hana' Malallah, Moaid Nama, Ibrahim Rashied, Kareem Rissan, Samar Usama, Nazar Yahya [spelling according to website].

[25] Arthur and Mata Jaffe Center for Book Arts, "Dafatir": <http://www.library.fau.edu/depts/spc/JaffeCenter/jaffe.dafatir.htm> (accessed 29 March 2009).

Similar priorities were in the foreground for *Modernism and Iraq*, which Shabout co-curated with Zainab Bahrani, a professor of Ancient Near Eastern Archaeology and Art History at Columbia University in New York, where the exhibition was held in early 2009.[26] Created in collaboration with the Arab Museum of Modern Art in Doha, it displayed several works from its collection, as well as some paintings recovered from the looted Museum of Modern Art in Baghdad, as well as the notebooks exhibited previously.

The Pomegranate Gallery — Iraqi Art in SoHo

Pomegranate Gallery, located in SoHo, New York, in the middle of the city's art scene, was founded by Oded Halahmy and is funded by the Oded Halahmy Foundation for the Arts which he created in 2001 in order "to promote the work of Iraqi artists and writers" (Morad *et al.*, 2008, p. 56).[27] The Foundation strives for peace in Iraq, the Middle East and the world.[28] Born in Baghdad in 1938, Halahmy moved to Israel in 1951, studied art in London and lived for a short time in Toronto before settling permanently in New York in 1971. His sculptures have been acquired by many public and private collectors, mostly in the United States and Israel and find their inspiration in his Middle Eastern roots (Morad, 2008, p. 55). Halahmy, who defines himself an "Iraqi American sculptor," still has strong spiritual bonds with Iraq, which he visited in 2004 and which he perceives as "the [real] land of milk and honey" (Morad, 2008, p. 55). His concern for peace goes back many years, as some of his works prove (Henry, 1998, p. 136); he conceives of Pomegranate as a place where political controversy should be avoided and where "artists, musicians, poets and others from different background can come together in peace" (Lebowitz, 2006, p. 192). Through the gallery, he wishes to "awaken American consciousness of Baghdad's leading role in fine arts from the Arab world," thus opening the eyes of American collectors who, he thinks are insufficiently curious about of the international art world.[29] As an artist born in Baghdad, he says he is proud to present Iraqi artists in New York, his adopted city.

---

[26] Miriam and Ira D. Wallach Art Gallery, 28 January–28 March 2009.

[27] Its website indicates that its aim is to promote a better knowledge of the arts of the Middle East.

[28] Oded Halahmy Foundation for the Arts: <http://www.odedhalahmy.com/history.shtml>

[29] Pomegranate Gallery: http://www.pomgallery.com/.

The opening exhibition, "Ashes to Art: the Iraqi Phoenix," was curated by art advisor and publisher Peter Hastings Falk. It showcased Qasim al-Sibti, Mohammed Al Shammarey, Hana' Malallah, Nazar Yahya and Esam Pasha (Davis, 2006), all five members of the Iraqi Phoenix Group, which has ten members and was put together for the show.[30] Esam Pasha, a former translator for the US Army and a supporter of the US intervention, gave Falk the idea of an Iraqi art exhibition: When he heard that Pasha had over-painted a Saddam portrait, he was intrigued by it and contacted him (Beith, 2006).

"Ashes to Art" received good media coverage, from al-Jazeera to local news stations like NY1 to art magazines like *artnet* or the prestigious *Art in America*. *Newsweek* reported on it and even the *Taipei Times* published the AP press release. The location of the gallery in SoHo and the fact that the initiator and the curator are well-known personalities, most likely contributed to this. Even if the artists participating in the show did not want to make political statements (Beith, 2006), their works were largely read that way.

The Pomegranate has featured other exhibitions of Iraqi art, solo and collective: in March 2009, the US-based Iraqi artist Thamir Da'ud curated "Iraqi Mosaic: New Works by Iraqi Artists;" in spring–summer 2007, the gallery showed "Contemporary Iraqi Art," with works by Hana' Malallah, Qasim al-Sibti, and others; in May–June 2008, "Oil on Landscape: Art from Wartime Contemporaries of Baghdad" followed, featuring artists presently living in Iraq.

"Iraqi Artists in Exile", The Station Museum of Contemporary Art, Houston, 2008–2009

The Station Museum of Contemporary Art, Houston, was created by James Harithas and his wife Ann in 2001, with the goal of showing artists and art movements that are rarely exhibited elsewhere. Harithas, whose mother is Greek and who lived in post-war Germany as a child and in a number of other countries as an adult, has been a curator of many museum institutions around the United States, including the Corcoran Gallery of Art. He is known for featuring unknown or politically committed artists: he was one of the first to display works by Yoko Ono and Nam June Paik in the 1970s.

---

[30] A second exhibition with the same title followed in February 2006, showcasing other artists.

He thinks that most museums in the US are too much New York and Europe-focussed, and wishes to offer another perspective. For him exhibiting art is an aspect of his political activism and Houston, with its mixed population, is an ideal location, being more liberal than other cities. Before opening the Station Museum, which has devoted exhibitions to Palestinian, Mexican and Colombian modern art, he founded the ArtCar Museum in 1998, intended to be a museum accessible to popular audiences, as for him, "museums have failed to reach most of the people."

"Iraqi Artists in Exile," curated by Alan Schnitger, who had been in charge of previous shows at the Station Museum, showcased 15 artists,[31] and consisted of two parts, one dedicated to paintings, the other to note-books. Harithas had travelled to the Middle East to prepare the exhibition, as he had done for other shows of artists from war-torn countries (Rubinstein, 2006). Works of recognized artists of the older generation like Shakir Hasan al-Sa'id, Rafi' al-Nasiri, or Dhia Azzawi hung besides those by Hana' Malallah, Muhammad al-Shammarey or Karim Risn; artists who lived in exile during the heyday of the Saddam regime, like Faisel Laibi Sahi, were also represented, and internationally renowned contemporary artists, like the London based Jananne al-Ani, participated. As in "Dafatir," most of the works referred to Iraq's current situation and to the loss of its cultural values, as in Malallah's *Looting of a Baghdadi Manuscript*, al-Sa'id's *Tamziq Nr.* 1 (Dismemberment) or Karim Risn's *Uranium Civilization*. The museum's website emphasizes two aspects: The contribution of Iraq to contemporary art and the destruction brought by the war and occupation that forced numerous artists to leave the country. It compares Iraq with Vietnam and concludes by saying, "will the world ever forgive the United States for the genocide and the destruction of Iraq?" An article published by the *Houston Press*, claims that these works are witnesses of "the terrible devastation brought by the US war and occupation of Iraq, its people and culture" and of the "never-ending and incomprehensible havoc wreaked upon their land" (Secor, 2009). Another article mentioned that the exhibition had succeeded in being more than an anti-war show, since it connected the works with modernism and the Iraqi art tradition (Britt, 2008).

---

[31] 1 November 2008–1 February 2009. Participating artists: Sadik Kwaish Alraji, Himat, Ayad Alkadhi, Ali Talib Alkayali, Dia Azzawi, Jannane Al Ani, Mahmud Al Obaidi, Shakir Hasan Al Said, Mohammed Al Shammarey, Abdel Karim Khalil, Nedim Kufi, Hanaa Malallah, Rafa Nasiri, Kareem Risan, Faisel Laibi Sahi [spelling according to website].

"It is What It Is: Conversations About Iraq", The New Museum, New York, 2009

If not Iraqi art, Iraq as a discussion topic entered one of the most prestigious contemporary New York art spaces, the New Museum, in 2009.[32] Initiated by British artist Jeremy Deller, "It is What It Is: Conversations About Iraq," was an attempt to encourage public discussion on the country's situation with contributions from experts, Iraqis or Americans, who had either been there recently or whose work dealt with Iraq. After the New Museum, it circulated for three weeks in different towns throughout the country, before being performed at the Hammer Museum in Los Angeles and at the Museum of Contemporary Art in Chicago.[33] Three artefacts were displayed: the wreck of a car destroyed by an explosion on Mutanabbi Street in Baghdad in 2007, killing 30 people, a handmade banner by Ed Hall, and a wall graphic juxtaposing the maps of Iraq and of the United States. Iraqi art was represented through the presence, in the debates, of artist Esam Pasha, who had moved to the United States in the meantime. Its format recalls Catherine David's "Iraqi Equation," although it was even less an exhibit of visual works. Deller wanted the project to go beyond the images broadcast on TV, and beyond protest art, while of course being deeply political. It was intended to fill what Deller perceived as a media void in which the Iraq war was no longer a part of the public debate (Salisbury, 2009).

Iraqi Art Exhibitions between Politics and Art History

Is it possible to find a common thread between these different events? Two basic issues can be discerned running through all of them as a kind of "subtext": On the one hand, there is a generic solidarity with the Iraqi people, and a concomitant opposition to the war. On the other, Iraqi art is presented as making a contribution to the global visual arts movement, which ought to be included in any art historical discourse and recognized as contemporary. In other words: An art historical intent has been combined with a series of political statements.

---

[32] 11 February–22 March 2009.

[33] These museums have collaborated with the New Museum in the Three M Project since 2004, which aims at exhibiting at a national level and at acquiring works of art by artists that have not yet been sufficiently recognized.

Art Against War

To varying degrees, all the exhibitions adopt a political posture against the war or, at least, a manifestation of solidarity with the Iraqi people, as the exhibitors' statements express and media reviews reflect. However, behind this apparent commonality, the differences are strong. "The Iraqi Equation" and "It Is What it Is: Conversations About Iraq" are, from their basic conception, discussions about culture in Iraq in the broad sense. "Baghdad–Paris," "Dafatir" or "Iraqi Artists in Exile" have stressed the destruction of the modern Iraqi heritage under American occupation, whereas "Baghdad Renaissance," although expressing concern for the consequences of war and repression, focussed on the possibilities that might result from the fall of Saddam's regime (Bagdad Renaissance, 2003, p. 67), an attitude that can be attributed to the fact that the exhibition was held in June 2003, before the situation worsened. A similar position — although stemming from different considerations and coming chronologically later — is to be found in the exhibitions organized by the Pomegranate Gallery in New York.

Whether in Europe or the United States, the political stance is generally against the war and the destruction it has brought. A deeper reflection on the status of art in repressive regimes, or how creativity can be disrupted by war and forced exile, is often missing or mentioned only superficially. With the war still ongoing, current events have tended to prevail over history.

This becomes evident when looking at the notion of "exile," which appears in most of the exhibitions. In some cases — as in "The Iraqi Equation" — a definition was given. In other exhibitions, the term is used in a generic way to define the condition of Iraqi artists today as a whole, without specific hints to the historical background. Although exile reflects the present situation of a majority of Iraqi artists, not differentiating between the various waves of emigration, between those who left the country when Saddam Husayn was in power — after 1978, during the war against Iran, or after the first Gulf War and the crushing of the Shi'i *intifada* — and those who left after the American occupation in 2003, seems rather problematic. Uniting everyone under the label of victims of war and occupation, without distinction between those who had sometimes benefited — especially in earlier decades — from the regime's generosity and those who had to flee from it, or between those who, although staying in the country, were skilled enough to take advantage of the situation and those who found ways of not having to commit themselves, is inaccurate, or at least misleading, although this may be unintentional. In order to write the art history of Iraq, and eventually to inscribe it within a larger world art history, the question of the artists' political positioning cannot and should not be avoided, even if this causes pain and conflict. To do so would not imply any legitimization of the American occupation: on the contrary.

The Place of Iraqi Art on the Global Art Scene

Since Charles Taylor and other culturalists began showing that modernity itself is a cultural construct, stemming from particular conditions within Western civilization since the Enlightenment (Taylor, 2001), it is no longer viewed as "one and irradiating from the West," as Baudrillard defined it in 1989 (Baudrillard, 1989, p. 552), but is referred to in the plural. Postcolonial studies have postulated that, even if modernity originates in the West, it has been appropriated in other areas of the world and that local forms of 'modernities', adapted to their particular contexts, have been created. Although different from the (original) Western form, they have their own legitimacy and have to be considered as fully modern in the context that produced them.

In the art historical field this concept is beginning to be promulgated, especially by curators and art historians coming from non-Western countries. In a text published in 2000, the Turkish curator Vasif Kortun argued that an artwork that was modern in Cairo at some epoch ought not to be modern in Paris at the same time; yet, its modernity in Cairo could not be denied (Kortun, 2000). Mari Carmen Ramirez, curator of Latin American modern art at the Houston Fine Arts Museum, advocates Latin America's contribution to visual modernity as equivalent to that of the West. She highlighted the avant-garde dimension in an exhibition in 2004 showing a panorama encompassing the whole subcontinent, while excluding the ethnicizing experiences mostly known in the West, like as those of Frieda Kahlo or Diego Rivera (Ramirez, 2004).

This purpose was intelligible in all the exhibitions of Iraqi art, and constituted an important aim, together with the political statements. However, visitors and critics seldom perceive the modernity of Iraqi art. Reviews generally interpret the existence of art as a form of resistance to a situation of destruction and war. Artists are thus presented as the 'better Iraqis', as those who prefer to take a paintbrush in their hands rather than a gun. To Western audiences, they have to make clear that Iraq is not only violence, bloodshed and religious fanaticism. Empathy with the suffering of Iraqis prevails over other, art historical, considerations.

In addition, recognizing the "modernity" of Iraqi art within a world art narrative might be difficult because, as Hans Belting observed, art history as we know it today originated within the framework of European culture. He considers that because of its peculiar European (and Western) origin, art history as written nowadays would simply disappear if extended to include non-Western narratives — to do this, he argues, art history would need "structural changes [...] and cannot simply be exported as it is to other parts of the world" (Belting, 2003, p. 64). James Elkins puts forward an alternative vision: For him, art history has already become global, since non-Westerners have adopted Western categories of thought in the field (Elkins, 2007, pp. 19–21).

Beyond the more theoretical art historical purpose of the exhibitions, there is another, which aims to include Iraqi production into the globalized scene of contemporary art, in which some artists from Middle Eastern backgrounds have become successful over the last two decades. This leads to posing another question, which might be formulated by paraphrasing Gayatri Spivak: Can the "subalterns" speak their own language in a globalized art world?

To answer this question, let us start with this observation: The only two exhibitions that took place in contemporary art institutions, "The Iraqi Equation" and "It is What It Is: Conversations About Iraq," showed very few art works or none at all. This has largely to do with the definition of what contemporary art ought to be. In a seminal article, Alain Quemin has demonstrated convincingly that in spite of a largely accepted discourse arguing that the art scene has become multipolar, the dominant countries are still the US and Germany, followed by Switzerland, and, to a lesser extent, the UK, France and Italy (Quemin, 2006). Here are the most important galleries, the most renowned and expensive artists, and the big players in the field. These centers dictate the rules and prescribe what contemporary art is. The cooption of some artists from non-Western countries does not change the picture, particularly since most of them live in the West in any case. The dominant visual language is still created by the West (or in the West); and the language of communication and in which the often-conceptual artworks have to be conceived is English (Wright, 2006, p. 52; Mosquera, 2003, p. 18). Only artists who learn to express themselves within this given frame have a chance of being admitted to the "globalized" contemporary art scene. Even though a precise definition is lacking, and there is no pre-defined style to be followed or medium to be used, there are implicit expectations of what makes a work contemporary or not. Not every work of art produced today is considered "contemporary". Or, as a museum director answered in a survey quoted by Catherine Millet, "A traditional art work, even if new, could only be qualified with something like 'contemporary in a traditional style'" (Millet, 2006, p. 9).

In the Middle East in general and in Iraq in particular there is artistic production, an art-appreciating public and an art market that has grown exponentially in recent years, which does not speak the language of (Western) contemporary art. In Iraq for instance, the language used might well express concerns that are fully contemporary for Iraqi society, but this language is not compatible with the exigencies of an international globalized art scene that integrates other visual experiences only marginally. The power relations between center and periphery are revealed in this equation: The periphery cannot impose its conditions, its own visions and forms of imagination, on the center, unless they are filtered through the language created by the center. The enrichment of the center's art scene by experiences coming from elsewhere is thus a one-way street, since the criteria of the periphery are not given equal weight. If the work of Iraqi artists is

Illustration 1.   Rasha 'Adnan al-Husayni, from the Exhibition "Salute to Jawad Salim". Ceramic reproduction of Jawad Salim's painting *The Caliph's Gathering*. Al-Husayni is Iraqi, born in 1983. She created this tribute to Jawad Salim while studying at the Sharjah Art Institute, in the UAE, where her work was exhibited in 2008. A small catalogue was published.
Photo: Silvia Naef, Sharjah, 2008.

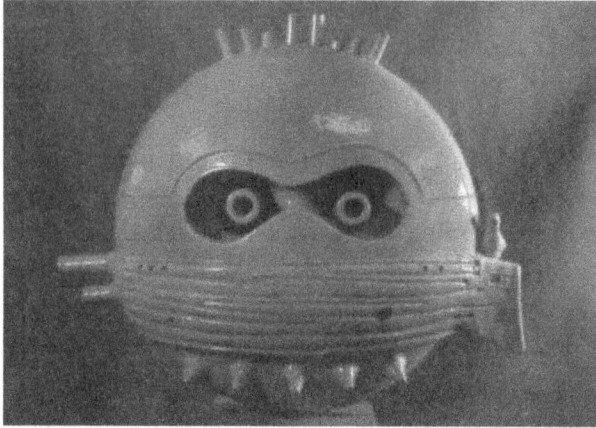

Illustration 2.   Sa'd Shakir, *Fedayee*, Ceramic, 1970s. Sa'd Shakir, born 1935, is a ceramist who works in different styles. *Fedayee* is typical of a period when many Iraqi artists felt strongly committed, namely to the Palestinian issue.

Illustration 3.   Qasim al-Sibti, *Baghdad*, Etching, 8/20, 1999. From the exhibition "Exposition de peintres iraquiens", Mairie de Paris, 9eme arrondissement, 22 June-1 July 2000.
Photo: Silvia Naef, June 2000.

not displayed in spaces consecrated specifically to contemporary art, it is not because their works are intrinsically not valid, but because they speak another language than the one used on the contemporary global art scene. Compared to mainstream art, they appear "old fashioned", as if the idea of "avant-garde", which has been declared dead since the 1980s, should somehow still determine the status of a work of art. Therefore, it seems legitimate to observe that — for the moment — the concept of equally valid although different "modernities" (or "contemporaneities") has not transcended the theoretical frame in the visual arts. For this reason, Rasheed Araeen suggests that non-Western artists should legitimate themselves instead of resorting to Western form of discourse which, in his view, is unable to "think of an agency outside of European society" (Araeen, 2003, p. 154).

Electronic references

AyaGallery. Online. Available HTTP: <http://www.ayagallery.co.uk/>.

Bax, D (2006). Blackbox Baghdad. Jan. 06, *Universes in Universe/Nafas. Art Magazine/ Iraqi Equation.* Online. Available HTTP: <www-universes-in-universe.de/islam/eng/ 2006/003/index-print.html> (accessed 7 March 2009). [English translation of an article published on 21 December 2005 in *Die Tageszeitung*].

Beith, M (2006). Post-Saddam art, painting and sculpture from today's Iraq reflect chaos, paradox and hope. *Newsweek*. Online. Available HTTP: <www. newsweek. com/ id/47323> (accessed 21 March 2009).

British Museum. Iraq's past speaks to the present. Online. Available HTTP: <http://www.britishmuseum.org/explore/galleries/middle_east/room_34_the_islamic_ world/iraq%E2%80%99s_past.aspx> (accessed 3 April 2009).

Britt, D (2008). Iraqi artists explore the tragedy of war. *Houston Chronicle*, 18 November 2008. Online. Available HTTP: <www.chron.com/fdcp?1237745307203> (accessed 22 March 2009).

Dallas Observer (2005). Dafatir: Contemporary Iraqi book art. 10 November 2005. Online. Available HTTP: <www.dallasobserver/com/content/printVersion/286912> (accessed 29 March 2009).

Davis, B (2006). Return fire. Artnet Magazine. Online. Available HTTP: <www. artnet.com/magazineus/reviews/davis2-9-06.asp?print=1> (accessed 21 March 2009).

Gozlan, M (2003). Ces artistes qui veulent ressusciter un siècle d'art moderne à Bagdad. *Marianne*, 14 July 2003. Online. Available HTTP: <www.marianne2.fr/Ces-artistes-qui-veulent-ressusciter-un-siècle> (accessed 10 March 2009).

Grau, TH (2006). "Die Medien reproduzieren Klischees," *Taz-Online*. Online. Available HTTP: <http://www.taz.de/index.php?id=archivseite&dig=2006/04/12/a0190&> (accessed 9 March 2009).

Karroum, A (2006). Contemporary Arab Representations, Act III (The Iraqi Equation). *L'Appartement 22*, 6 June 2006. Online. Available HTTP: <www.appartement22. com/?Contemporary-Arabic> (accessed 7 March 2009)

Kortun, V (2000). Türkei," in Museum für Gegenwartskunst Basel (ed.). Online. Available HTTP: <*Umgang mit nichtwestlicher Kunst*, Basel, Christoph-Merian-Verlag>

Lamb, L (2005). Contemporary Iraqi art exhibit to open. *Carleton News*, 21 December 2005. Online. Available HTTP: <http://apps.carleton.edu/news/?story_id=170441> (accessed 29 March 2009).

Mirza, A (2006). Kunst zwischen exil und existenznot. *Deutsche Welle*, 8 February 2006. Online. Available HTTP: <www.dw.-world.de/dw/article/0,,1893903,00.html> (accessed 9 March 2009).

Naoum, J (2006). Bagdad liegt in Agonie, Ein Treffen von Exil-Irakern in Berlin," *Der Tagesspiegel*, 1 March 2006. Online. Available HTTP: <www.tagesspiegel.de/kultur/art772,1905761> (accessed 9 March 09).

R.B. (2004). Artistes irakiens à Paris. *Le Nouvel Observateur*, 30 September 2004. Online. Available HTTP: <http://hebdo.nouvelobs.com/hebdo/parution/p2082/articles/a250318-etrangères.htm> (accessed 7 March 2009).

Rubinstein, R (2008). James Harithas with Raphael Rubinstein. *The Brooklyn Rail*, June 2008. Online. Available HTTP: <www.brooklynrail.org/2008/06/art/james-harithas-with-raphael-rubinstein> (accessed 22 March 2009).

Salisbury, S (2009). Personal views on the war in Iraq, in national exhibition, conversation is what it's all about. *The Philadelphia Inquirer*, 28 March 2009. Online. Available HTTP: <www.philly.com/inquier/local/pa/20090328_Personal_views_of_the_war_in_Iraq.html> (accessed 29 March 2009).

Secor, B (2009). 'Iraqi artists in exile' showcase their haunting works, cut and shot. *Houston Press*, 15 January 2009. Online. Available HTTP: <www.houstonpress.com/content/printVersion/1070794> (accessed 10 March 2009).

Taipei Times (2006). Shock and Awe in Store, Charred Elements Are a Common Strand in the Work of Iraqi Artists Who Are Exhibiting in New York, 19 January 2006. Online. Available HTTP: <www.taipeitimes.com/News/feat/archives/2006/01/19/2003289756> (accessed 21 March 2009).

The New Museum. It is what it is: Conversations about Iraq. Online. Available HTTP: <http://www.newmuseum.org/exhibitions/408> (accessed 29 March 2009).

The Station Museum of Contemporary Art. Iraqi Artists in Exile. Online. Available HTTP: <http://www.stationmuseum.com//index.php?option=com_content&task=view&id=103&Itemid=31> (accessed 10 March 2009).

University of North Texas. Dafatir. Online. Available HTTP: <http://unt.wampa.net/showexhibit.php?exid=37> (accessed 29 March 2009).

Vincent, S (2004). Art against the odds: On two recent trips to Iraq, the author found that artists are continuing to make work despite the massive upheaval in their country (report from Baghdad). *Art in America*, 92 (6). Expanded Academic ASAP. Gale. UNIVERSITY OF TORONTO (accessed 21 March 2009).

Wittmann, M (2008). Wir wollten keine Kunstwerke zeigen, Interview mit Catherine David. *Artnet*, 18 January 2008. Online. Available HTTP: <www.artnet.de/features/wittmann/wittmann01-18-09.asp> (accessed 9 March 2009).

Wright, S (2006). Whose Door? Whose Alien?. *Art Criticism & Curatorial Practices in Marginal Contexts, Addis Ababa, Three-Day Combined Seminar and Workshop, Organized by the International Association of Art Critics (AICA) Paris, and Zoma Contemporary Art Center, 26–8 January 2006*. Online. Available HTTP: <http://www.aica-int.org/spip.php?article638> (accessed 1 April 2009).

STATE OF THE ART ON IRAQI STUDIES: A BIBLIOGRAPHICAL SURVEY OF ENGLISH AND FRENCH SOURCES[1]

Hamit Bozarslan and Jordi Tejel

Until quite recently, the absence of a structured field has been a major obstacle confronting Iraqi studies. Among the three main reasons for this absence, one can first mention the general inaccessibility of the country. In fact, since the 1968 military coup (and even earlier), Iraq has been either "closed" to researchers or admitted them only under strict supervision, making it almost impossible to consult archival material or conduct fieldwork (Iraqi Kurdistan since 1991 has been an exception). The second reason is linked to the tragic marginality of "dissident Iraqi research", during the 1970s and 1980s. The available knowledge on Iraq testifies that the "long-distance research" on Iraq conducted in Europe or in the United States, was largely based on trustworthy data. But dissident researchers have often been accused of either exaggerating the evil nature of the regime or of being far too "radical"; their work was not always taken seriously and they had no proper resources to carry out long-lasting scholarly investigations. Many of them devoted a great deal of time to carry out what they regarded as the essential task of providing the most precise information possible on human rights violations in Iraq. Of course, one should not forget that for many decades a shamefully large number of European observers considered the Ba'th regime as progressive,

---

[1] An earlier version of this bibliography was published as "Revue bibliographique" in a special issue of *Critique Internationale* on Iraq (No. 34, 2007, pp. 79–86). For an earlier and highly comprehensive bibliographical survey of more than 6,500 books and articles on Iraq published between the 1900s and 2003, see Bleaney and Roper (2004), which has an introduction by Peter Sluglett.

or at least, secular. Thus, many Iraqi intellectuals in exile were obliged to use pamphlets as a means of communication with European public opinion at the expense of more fundamental and/or better problematised research (e.g., CARDRI, 1989).

Finally, one should mention the consequences of the 1991 War, which projected Iraq firmly onto the international stage, but also led to its further academic marginalization. The war largely "congealed" and/or essentialized available analytical knowledge on Iraq or transformed it into operational and therefore militarily useful knowledge. Thus Iraq's internal plurality was reduced to being synonymous with the existence of three homogenous blocs: Sunnis, Shi'is, and Kurds: The concept of the "Sunni Triangle" gave birth to the perception of the Sunnis as the organic basis of the power of Saddam Husayn and the Ba'th party, while tribal organization has been considered as *the* basic timeless social unit around which the majority of Iraqis frame their lives.

During the 2003 Iraq War, the political and military decision-makers used academic research as operational knowledge without taking into account the necessity of "methodological doubts" or internal contradictions in order to gain a better understanding of the history and politics of Iraq. This peculiar use of analytical knowledge as militarily useful knowledge goes a long way to explain the disastrous decisions taken after the war, such as the indiscriminate repression in those Sunni areas which were considered to constitute the social base of Ba'thism: "de-Ba'thification", which was conceived on the model of de-Nazification: the dissolution of the Iraqi army on the grounds that it was both "Sunni" and "Ba'thist", which pushed many former officers to join the armed insurrection, and the erroneous perception of the Shi'i community as a homogenous bloc, a perception that made it almost impossible to understand the dynamics of the Sadrist phenomenon. Everyone agrees today that the cost of such decisions and misperceptions has been very high, mainly for the Iraqis, but also for the coalition forces.

As the contributions to the present volume show, a specific field of Iraqi studies, bringing together scholars from different disciplines, countries, and generations, has emerged since the war. The improvement in access (at least for a brief period after 2003) and demands on various levels for a better understanding of the Iraqi situation have encouraged this new momentum for Iraqi studies. Still, only a dozen volumes out of about a hundred published on Iraq since 2003 have lasting academic value. The others either belong to the category of "War history", or are highly speculative in their conception and presentation, or elaborate an essentialized and rigidified knowledge, which may constitute the basis of a new "militarily useful knowledge" in the future.

The Period of Foundation and Consolidation

The absence of field research on Iraq for many long decades and the difficulties in carrying out research at the moment does not mean that we are facing a *terra incognita*. Readers have a number of major works at their disposal which allow them to understand the dynamics of continuity (such as the Kurdish issue or the progressive subordination of the Shi'i community in the 20th century), as well as the times and locations of the often brutal discontinuities which have shaped Iraqi history (the "revolution" of 1920, the Assyrian massacre of 1933 which took place in the immediate aftermath of independence, the 1958 "revolution", the Ba'thist coup of 1968). Edmund Ghareeb's historical dictionary (2004) does not give a particularly clear picture of the turmoil of the 1990s and early 200s, but gives much valuable information on the principal landmarks in Iraqi history. In spite of their limited size, the surveys by Charles Tripp (2007), Pierre-Jean Luizard (2002), and Phebe Marr (2004) highlight the main historical events of the 20th century. Although very conservative in its perceptions and methods, Stephen Longrigg's dated book (1956) is still useful for the inside information obtained through the author's employment in Iraqi government service during the 1920s and 1930s and subsequently in the Iraq Petroleum Company. For the "British foundations" of Iraq, Peter Sluglett's seminal work (2007, first published in 1976) remains the most important reference. In spite of their shortcomings, the first two volumes of Majid Khadduri's trilogy (1960; 1969; the third, *Socialist Iraq* [1978] is so adulatory of the Ba'th to be almost worthless) place Iraqi history in its post-Ottoman context without ignoring the country's own historicity. The contributions to the special issue of *REMMM* on Iraq (2007) offer some transversal glimpses of Iraqi history in the 20th century. Finally, Nadje al-Ali's work (2007) not only introduces gender into Iraqi studies but also makes a valuable broader contribution to the social history of Iraq.

Beyond these global historical accounts, one should mention the enduring importance of the *magnum opus* of Hanna Batatu (1978) on Iraq's "old social classes and revolutionary movements." Through the meticulous exploration of an enormous quantity of very rich material, Batatu gives a fascinating picture of the various transformations of Iraqi society between the 1920s and 1958. He also shows how a new country constructed on the basis of a hegemonic bloc of members of the former Ottoman elite, with the aid of a "foreign" king, some tribes and some sectors of the mercantile bourgeoisie, gradually transformed itself into a viable entity, although the price of this viability was a revolutionary contest inspired by both Arab nationalism and radical ideologies, propelled by an alliance between some sections of the intelligentsia and a younger generation of military officers which eventually overthrew the monarchy in 1958.

Although limited almost exclusively to an analysis of the Shi'i community, Pierre-Jean Luizard's masterly study (1991) of the formation of the Iraqi state contains very rich material; he suggests that the end of the Ottoman Empire brought new measures of exclusion, subordination, and domination to this community. Toby Dodge's highly sophisticated work (2003) creates problems for the central issues of coercion and symbolic violence during the period of formation of the Iraqi state. It shows convincingly that the 1920 Revolt, which mobilized sections of the population well beyond the Shi'i community, was as much a popular rejection of the Iraqi state created by the mandatory power as the founding act of Iraqi society on the part of a population which would henceforth be confined within new political and military frontiers. Orit Bashkin's book (2009) goes well beyond the promise of its title and gives an original reading of the intellectual milieus and militancy under the monarchy. Peter Wien's work (2006) on right-wing radicalism during the first decade of independence is also an important reference both for a better understanding of this period and for its genealogical perspective on the history of Iraqi radicalisms. The books of both Bashkin and Wien stress the significance of the generational factor in accounting for some of the major social and political transformations during the interwar period. Finally, one should warmly recommend Méouchy and Sluglett's remarkable volume (2004) on the British and French mandates in the Middle East, which, in a sense, constitutes the founding *manifesto* of "mandate studies". Through an intelligent combination of micro and macro levels of analysis, this huge volume invites readers to compare the Iraqi case on the one hand, and the Syrian, Jordanian, Lebanese, and Palestinian experiences on the other.

The Decades of "Revolutions" and Tyranny

Khadduri's (1969) and Dann's (1969) books are the principal references for the period between 1958 and 1968. However, Salih (1996) and Simon (2004) underline the central role played by the army, namely by the young nationalist officers in pre-1958 Iraq and during the 1958–1968 period. Farouk-Sluglett and Sluglett's important reference (3rd edition, 2001) analyses the passage from the somewhat classical nationalist and populist military regime of 1958 to the rule of the Ba'th, under which the army became progressively marginalized and the *de facto* single party itself became an empty shell. The accession of Saddam Husayn to the presidency, which was followed by the execution of one-third of the highest ranking Ba'th dignitaries and what turned out to be the permanent rupture of diplomatic relations with Syria, has been carefully analyzed by Eberhard Kienle (1990).

It is no surprise that Saddam Husayn, his reign of terror, and his security organs have been widely discussed over the past two decades. Notable here are Aburish's biography of the *ra'is* (2000), CARDRI's very well documented and still important work of reference (1989), the Human Rights Watch report (1993) based on Ba'th party archives captured after the 1991 War, Amatzia Baram's study on ideological discourse (1991), Eric Davis' book (2005) on identity politics and historical narratives and of course, Samir al-Khalil/Kanaan Makiya)'s seminal work, The *Republic of Fair* (1989). The volume edited by Chris Kutschera (2005) is probably the most exhaustive account of Saddam Husayn's repressive policies in the 1980s and 1990s so far. In contrast with the attention given to the repression exercised by the regime, the important transformations that Iraqi society underwent during the First Gulf War (1980–1988, the cause of an estimated 300,000 deaths on the Iraqi side alone) have not yet been sufficiently analyzed. This long war, as well the Second Gulf War, has mostly been studied from the perspective of military history (although, on the Second Gulf War, see the important volume of Sifry and Cerf, 1991).

Three volumes offer an insightful analysis of Iraq between 1991 and 2003. Based on quantitative and qualitative data, Graham-Brown's book (1999) gives a very rich analysis of the transformations of Iraqi society and power structures under the embargo: Retribalization, with the informal economy and smuggling as rent-creating resources, and the politics of surveillance through redistribution. David Baran (2004) studies the political engineering carried out after 1991 by Saddam Husayn, whom these events somehow liberated from any previous ideological commitment. With the survival of his regime as his sole objective, he could develop a subtle balance between outright theft, coercion and over-investment in some strategic domains. The more recent collection edited by Sifry and Cerf (2003) brings together a series of articles and documents mainly on the repression after the 1991 Intifada and the evolution of Iraqi society throughout this decade, and Peter Sluglett has written a brief narrative history of the period between 1990 and 2003 (2010).

After the 2003 War

In spite of abundant material, most writing about post-2003 Iraq has been mainly rather speculative (although for two academic counter-examples, see Lafourcade (2007), and Stansfield (2007), and for non-academic but highly sophisticated testimonies see Herring and Rangwala (2006), Allawi (2007), and Fergusson (2008)). Still, thanks to Mark Etherington (2005) and Peter Harling (2006) of the International Crisis Group and Patrick Cockburn (2007), readers have access to a nuanced sociological analysis of the Sadrist movement. These works allow us to understand that on one hand "Sadrism" reactivates a version of a group's historical affiliation to its "ancestors", while on the other, by its very existence, it testifies to the centrality of class differences and although to a less extent) generational discontinuities within the Shia community. The impressive volume of Ahmed Hashim (2006), a professor at the US Naval War College in Rhode Island, offers a complex picture of the insurrection within the Sunni community. His careful readings of the strategy of the former Ba'thists and the rise and growth of an Islamist guerilla movement makes Hashim's book the best account of post-2003 Iraq.

Ethnic and Sectarian Communities and Tribalism

It would be impossible to conclude this short biography without mentioning some "serious issues", for which there is scant analytical information. For instance, we know little about the bi-sectarian (i.e., both Sunni and Shi'i) Turcoman and Christian communities throughout the 20th century. We also have very little reliable information on the Fa'ilis or on the heterodox Kurdish communities (although see Rahe, 2005, pp. 255–267). In contrast with these insufficiently studied groups, there are several monographs and edited volumes on the Kurds (Ahmed (2005, 2007); Fuccaro (1999); Ghareeb (1981); Lawrence (2008); O'Leary *et al.* (2005); Picard (1991); Romano (2006); Stansfield (2003); Yildiz (2007)).

Similarly, thanks to the persistence of two authors, Faleh A. Jabar/Falih 'Abd al Jabbar (2002, 2003) and Yitzhak Nakash (1993, 2006), our "Iraqi library" has four important references, which add considerably to our knowledge and understanding of the Iraqi Shi'i community. Their books enable us to understand how this community, mostly formed during the 18th century, developed multiple strategies, including occasional cooperation with the central power, and how it was constantly re-shaped by its internal differentiations and its interactions with Sunnism and other Middle Eastern Shi'i communities, a process also analyzed in a comparative perspective by Nasr (2007) and Louër (2009). On another level, the study of Reidar Visser (2007) on "separatism" in Basra during the mandate sheds light on the local fragmentation and dynamics of "Shi'i politics". Finally, we should mention Jabar (2001) and Jabar and Dawod's edited volume (2003); both books remind us that the "tribal presence" observable in the 1990s and 2000s has to be read within a broader, social, and political framework. In general, scholars must be aware that it is vital to focus careful attention on the conflicting relations between the state and the tribes in order to explain the cycles of de- and re-tribalization in Iraq and elsewhere in the Middle East.

NOTES ON CONTRIBUTORS

About the Editors

Riccardo Bocco, PhD in Political Science, Sciences Po, Paris. Professor Bocco's main geographical area of fieldwork for the last 30 years has been the Near East with a particular focus on Jordan and Palestine. Three main research topics have successively shaped his work: Tribes, nationalism, development policies, and state-building; refugees, humanitarian policies, and Palestinian identity in the Near East; and the role of international aid in conflict and post-conflict contexts. He teaches at the Graduate Institute of International and Development Studies in Geneva.

Hamit Bozarslan obtained his PhD degrees in history in 1992 and in political science in 1994. He teaches at École des Hautes Études en Sciences Sociales. He has recently published *Une histoire de la violence au Moyen-Orient* (Paris, La Découverte, 2008) and *Le Conflit Kurde* (Paris, Autrement, 2009). He is currently working on the political and historical sociology of the Middle East.

Peter Sluglett is Professor of Middle Eastern History at the University of Utah, Salt Lake City. Among his publications are *Britain in Iraq: Contriving King and Country* (2007), and (with Marion Farouk-Sluglett) *Iraq since 1958; from Revolution to Dictatorship* (3rd ed., 2001). He is currently Visiting Research Professor at the Middle East Institute, National University of Singapore.

Jordi Tejel is a Research Professor of International History at the Graduate Institute of International and Development Studies in Geneva. His recent books include *Irak, chronique d'un chaos annoncé* (LaVauzelle, 2006), *Le mouvement kurde de Turquie en exil. Continuités et discontinuités du* *nationalisme kurde sous le mandat français en Syrie et au Liban (1925–1946)* (Peter Lang, 2007), and *Syria's Kurds. History, Politics and Society* (Routledge, 2009).

About the Authors

Orit Bashkin is an Associate Professor at the Department of Near Eastern languages and Civilizations at the University of Chicago. Her research interests include Arab intellectual history, modern Iraqi history and the history of Arab–Jews in Iraq and Israel. Her book *The Other Iraq; Pluralism and Culture in Hashemite Iraq, 1921–1958* was published in 2009 by Stanford University Press (paperback, 2010). She is currently working on a book project studying the history of Iraqi Jews in Hashemite Iraq.

Magnus T. Bernhardsson teaches Middle Eastern history at Williams College in Massachusetts. He received his BA from the University of Iceland and his PhD in Middle Eastern history from Yale University in 1999. He is the author of *Reclaiming a Plundered Past. Archaeology and Nation Building in Modern Iraq* (University of Texas Press, 2005) and has edited a number of volumes. He is currently working on a history of Baghdad in the 1950s.

Michaelle Browers is Associate Professor of political science at Wake Forest University, where she teaches courses in the history of political thought. She has authored two books: *Political Ideology in the Arab World: Accommodation and Transformation* (Cambridge University Press, 2009) and *Democracy and Civil Society in Arab Political Thought: Transcultural Possibilities* (Syracuse University Press, 2006). Browers was awarded a fellowship from the National Endowment for the Humanities for 2010–2011 to complete work on a manuscript, entitled "Arab Shi'i Political Thought since 1958."

Chérine Chams el Dine is a lecturer at the University of Exeter. In December 2007, she received her PhD degree in social and political science from the European University Institute (Florence), where she defended a thesis entitled "Survival strategies of authoritarian regimes: Management of the ruling elite in Iraq under Saddam Hussein."

Géraldine Chatelard is an Associate Researcher at the Institut français du Proche-Orient (Ifpo) in Amman. She graduated from the Institut national des langues et civilization orientales (INALCO) in Paris with a degree in Arabic, and completed a Doctorate in History a the École des hautes études en sciences sociales (EHESS), also in Paris. Her book *Briser la mosaïque* (CNRS Editions, 2004) revisited traditional paradigms applied to Christians in Muslim-majority societies with a focus on Jordan.

Elvire Corboz's principal research interests focus on transnational political Shi'ism and Iraqi exile organizations in the Saddam Hussein era. She obtained a D.Phil in Oriental Studies from the University of Oxford for her doctoral thesis entitled "Negotiating Loyalty Across the Shi'i World: The Transnational Authority of the al-Hakim and al-Khu'i Families." She is currently a Postdoctoral Associate at the Department of Near Eastern Studies, Princeton University.

Diane Duclos is a PhD candidate and a teaching assistant at The Graduate Institute of International and Development Studies, (GIIDS, Geneva, Switzerland). She graduated from the Institute of Political Sciences of Toulouse (France), and holds a Master's degree in Development Studies (GIIDS, Geneva).

Hala Fattah received her PhD from UCLA in the history of the modern Middle East in 1986. She has since authored two books (*The Politics of Regional Trade in Iraq, Arabia and the Gulf, 1750–1900*, 1997 and *A Brief History of Iraq*, 2008) and various articles on late Ottoman and independent Iraq. Hala Fattah is now an independent scholar and consultant in Amman.

Andrea Fischer-Tahir studied Arabic Language and Oriental Philology, Social Anthropology, and the History of Religions at the University of Leipzig. Her PhD thesis discussed experiences of resistance against the Ba'th regime and collective identity in Iraqi Kurdistan. Currently she is a researcher at the Zentrum Moderner Orient (ZMO) in Berlin, working on the topic of Identity Politics in the Changing Societies of Morocco and of Iraq. She has published *Brave men, nice women? Gender and symbolic violence in Iraqi-Kurdish urban society*, Berlin: EZKS (2009).

Johan Franzén is a Lecturer in Middle East Politics at the University of East Anglia in the United Kingdom. He holds a PhD from the School of Oriental and African Studies, University of London. He is the author of *Red Star Over Iraq: Iraqi Communism Before Saddam* (Hurst, 2011) and *A Modern History of Iraq* (forthcoming with Hurst). He has published widely on the topic of Iraqi history.

Peter Harling lived part time in Baghdad from 1998 to 2004. He toured the country both to conduct academic research and in his capacity as a freelance consultant with the French public and private sector. He first worked with the International Crisis Group as a consultant, in 2004, before joining the organization's permanent staff a year later. He established himself in Beirut and in 2006 moved to Damascus, where he currently resides. He has published extensively on Iraq, Syria and Lebanon.

Dina Rizk Khoury is an Associate Professor of History and International Affairs at George Washington University. She has written on Ottoman Iraq. Her book *State and Provincial Society in the Ottoman Empire: Mosul 1540–1834* (Cambridge University Press, 1997) won two prizes. She is currently working on a book entitled *War, Citizenship and Memory in Iraq* to be published by Cambridge University Press. The article in this volume is based on her research for that project.

Fanny Lafourcade wrote her doctoral thesis on the Iraqi political leadership after 2003. She carried out extensive field research in Baghdad, Erbil, Amman, Damascus, Washington, and Paris between 2001 and 2008. She has worked as well as a policy advisor for several NGOs in Iraq between 2003 and 2005. She is now in charge of academic and institutional cooperation at the French Consulate in Jerusalem.

Nicolas A. Masson graduated in 2002 with a Master's degree from the Graduate Institute of International and Development Studies in Geneva. He obtained a degree in Arabic language and history at the Institut français du Proche-Orient (Ifpo) in Damascus. Since 2008 he has worked for the Africa and Middle East Division at the Geneva Center for the Democratic Control of Armed Forces (DCAF). He has led development and research projects in the Palestinian Territories in the field of security sector reform (SSR).

Karin Mlodoch is a psychologist who has worked on humanitarian and psychosocial projects in Kurdistan-Iraq and Afghanistan. She is currently a research fellow at the Zentrum Moderner Orient in Berlin with a research project on "Violence, Memory and Dealing with the Past in Iraq: The Perspectives of Women Survivors of the Anfal in Iraqi Kurdistan" and preparing her doctoral thesis at the Institute of Social Psychology, Ethnopsychoanalysis and Psychotraumatology at the University of Klagenfurt/Austria.

Silvia Naef, Professor in the Arabic Studies Section of the University of Geneva, teaches the cultural history of the Arab world. She has been a visiting professor at the University of Toronto (2007–2009), lecturing on the modern art of the Middle East, and has taught in Basel and Tübingen (1995–2000). She has published mainly on modern and contemporary art in the Arab world and on images and representations in Islam.

Sara Pursley obtained her PhD in Middle Eastern History from the City University of New York in 2012; she is currently associate editor of the *International Journal of Middle East Studies.* Her dissertation is entitled "Race against Time: Governing Femininity and Reproducing the Future in Revolutionary Iraq."

Robert Riggs' primary research focuses on the construction and maintenance of socio-political and religious authority in the Arabic-speaking Shi'i communities of the Middle East. He has taught a variety of courses in Arabic language, Arabic literature and Middle Eastern history at Hofstra University, Brooklyn College (CUNY), Queens College (CUNY) and Franklin and Marshall College. He is currently an Assistant Professor at the University of Bridgeport, Connecticut.

Achim Rohde, PhD, is currently a research fellow at the Georg-Eckert-Institute for International Textbook Research, Germany, and a lecturer at the Asia-Africa-Institute of Hamburg University. Rohde is the author of *State-Society-Relations in Ba'thist Iraq: Facing Dictatorship* (Routledge, 2010), and co-editor (together with Amatzia Baram and Ronen Zeidel) of *Iraq Between Occupations. Perspectives From 1920 to the Present* (Palgrave Macmillan, 2010).

Joseph Sassoon is an Adjunct Professor at Georgetown University and Public Policy Fellow at the Woodrow Wilson Center in Washington, D.C. He is also a Senior Associate Member at St Antony's College, Oxford. Among his publications are: *Saddam Hussein's Ba'th Party: Inside an Authoritarian Regime* (Cambridge, 2012); *The Iraqi Refugees: The New Crisis in the Middle East* (I.B. Tauris, 2009) and *Economic Policy in Iraq, 1932–1950* (Frank Cass, 1987).

Lucia Sorbera has studied Arabic language and modern Middle Eastern culture at various Italian universities. She is currently a lecturer in Arabic, Islamic, and Middle East Studies at the University of Sydney. Her interests cover gender issues and feminist movements in the Arab World and among Muslim diasporas, modernization and secularization in the Arab World (especially Egypt and Lebanon), and cultural production and the role of intellectuals in war and post-conflict situations (Palestine, Lebanon, and Iraq).

Leslie Tramontini is currently working at the Center for Near and Middle Eastern Studies in Marburg University. Her research interests focus on literature and politics. She studied Arabic and Islamic Studies, Semitic Languages, and Philosophy at Westfälische Wilhelms-Universität Münster, Kuwait University and Baghdad University and specialized in modern Iraqi poetry with a PhD thesis on Badr Shakir al-Sayyab. As well as her academic work, she translates modern Arab poetry into German and is also a member of the editorial board of *Lisan* magazine for modern Arab literature (Basel). She is co-editor (with Stephan Milich and Friederike Pannewick, of *Conflicting Narratives: War, Violence and Memory in Iraqi Culture* (in press).

Reidar Visser is a research fellow at the Norwegian Institute of International Affairs. He has a background in history and comparative politics and holds a doctorate in Middle Eastern studies from the University of Oxford. He has published extensively on the history of Southern Iraq and the issues of decentralization and federalism, including three books: *Basra, the Failed Gulf State: Separatism and Nationalism in Southern Iraq* (2005) and (edited with Gareth Stansfield) *An Iraq of Its Regions: Cornerstones of a Federal Democracy?* (2007), and *A responsible end? the United States and the Iraqi Transition, 2005–2010* (2010) Many of his writings are available on his Iraq website, www.historiae.org

Peter Wien teaches Modern Middle Eastern History at the University of Maryland, College Park. He holds degrees from the Universities of Bonn, Oxford, and Heidelberg. He previously taught at al-Akhawayn University in Ifrane, Morocco, and was a fellow of the Center for Modern Oriental Studies in Berlin. In 2006, Routledge published his book *Iraqi Arab Nationalism: Authoritarian, Totalitarian and Pro-Fascist Inclinations, 1932–1941*.

Sami Zubaida is Emeritus Professor of Politics and Sociology at Birkbeck College, University of London, and Research Associate of the London Middle East Institute at SOAS. He has held visiting positions in Cairo, Istanbul, Beirut, Aix-en-Provence, Paris, Berkeley CA, and NYU Law School. His work is on religion, culture, law and politics in the Middle East, with comparative interest in Egypt, Iran, Iraq, and Turkey, and in food and culture. His main books are: *Islam, the People and the State* (3rd Ed., 2009); *A Taste of Thyme: Culinary Cultures of the Middle East,* (2nd Ed., 2001, co-edited with Richard Tapper); *Law and Power in the Islamic World* (2003); *Beyond Islam,* (2011), and articles on those themes, including many on Iraq.

BIBLIOGRAPHY

'Abbasi, K. al- (n.d.) *Shu'ara' al-thawra al-'iraqiya ithna' al-ihtilal al-britani f'il-'Iraq*, [Poets of the Iraqi Revolution during the British Occupation] Baghdad: Dar al-Ma'arifa.

'Abd al-Jabbar, F. (1992) *Ma'alim al-'aqlaniya w'al-khurafa fi'l-fikr al-siyasi al-'Arabi* [Signs of rationality and irrationality in Arab political thought], London.
See also Jabar, F. A., and Jaber, F. A.

——— (ed.) (2002) *Ayatullahs, Sufis and Ideologues; State, Religion and Social Movements in Iraq*, London: Saqi Books.

——— (2002) *al-Dimuqratiya al-mustahila, al-dimuqratiya al-mumkina: namudhaj al-'Iraq* [Impossible democracy, possible democracy; the example of Iraq], Damascus.

'Abd al-Jabbar, F. (ed. with Hoshem Dawod) (2003) *Tribes and Power: Nationalism and Ethnicity in the Middle East*, London: Saqi Books.

'Abd ar-Rahman, Z. (1995) *Tûn-î Merg. Hêrišekan-î Enfal*, Suleymaniyya: n.p.

Abdi, K. (2008) "From Pan-Arabism to Saddam Hussein's cult of personality: Ancient Mesopotamia and Iraqi national ideology," *Journal of Social Archaeology*, 8 (3): 3–36.

'Abdullah, 'A. (2005) "al-Anfal wa'l-Islam fi thuna'iyyat al-dhat wa'l-akhir" [Anfal and Islam in the dualism of the self and the other], *al-Anfal*, (7): 60–5.

Abdullah, T. (2006) *Dictatorship, Imperialism and Chaos: Iraq since 1989*, London and New York: Zed Books.

'Abir, A. (1942) "Hal yakhtalif manhaj al-'ulum li'l-bint 'an li'l-walad? [Should the girls' science curriculum be different from the boys'?]," *al-Mu'allim al-Jadid*, 7 (6): 512–20.

'Aboud, S. (2002) *Thaqafa al-'unf fi'l-'Iraq*, [The culture of violence in Iraq] Köln: Al-Kamel.

Abrash, B. and Walkowitz, D. (1995) "Narration cinématographique et narration historique. La sub(version) de l'histoire," *Vingtième siècle. Revue d'histoire*, (46): 14–25.

Abu Khalil, A. (1993) "Arab Intellectuals on Trial," *Middle East Journal*, (47), 4: 695–706.

——— (2004) "The Islam Industry and Scholarship," *Middle East Journal*, (58), 1: 130–7.

Aburish, S. K. (2000) *Saddam Hussein. The Politics of Revenge*, New York and London: Bloomsbury.

Acemoğlu, D. and Robinson, J. A. (2006) *Economic Origins of Dictatorship and Democracy*, New York: Cambridge University Press.

Agamben, G. (1998) *Homo Sacer: Sovereign Power and Bare Life*, London and Chicago: Stanford University Press.

——— (2005) *State of Exception*, Chicago: University of Chicago Press.

Ahmad, E. (1993) "The Question of Iraq," *The Nation*, August 9–16: 178–9.

Ahmed, M. M. A. and Gunter, M. M. (eds.) (2005) *The Kurdish Question and the 2003 Iraqi War*, Costa Mesa: Mazda.

Ahmed, M. M. A. and Olson, R. (eds.) (2007) *The Evolution of Kurdish Nationalism*, Costa Mesa: Mazda.

Ajami, F. (1999) *The Dream Palace of the Arabs; a Generation's Odyssey*, 2nd edn, New York: Vintage Books.

Akhavi, S. (1980) *Religion and Politics in Contemporary Iran: Clergy-State Relations in the Pahlavi Period*, Albany: State University of New York Press.

'Alawi, H. al- (1973) *Fi'l-din wa'l-turath*, [On religion and heritage] Beirut.

———— (1974) *Fi'l-siyasa al-islamiya*, [On Islamic politics] Beirut.

———— (1983), *al-Mu'jam al-'Arabi al-jadid*, [The new Arabic lexicon] Latakia.

———— (1998) *al-Mar'i wa'l-la-mar'i fi'l-adab wa'l-siyasa*, [The visible and the invisible in poetry and politics] Beirut.

Alborzi, M. R. (2006) *Evaluating the Effectiveness of International Refugee Law: The Protection of Iraqi Refugees*, Leiden: Martinus Nijhoff Publishers.

Ali, N. S. al- (2003) "Women, Gender Relations, and Sanctions in Iraq," in S. Inati (ed.) *Iraq: Its History, People and Politics*, Amherst: Humanity.

———— (2007) *Iraqi Women. Untold Histories from 1948 to the Present*, London and New York: Zed Books.

Ali, N. S. al-, and Pratt, N. (2009) *What Kind of Liberation? Women and the Occupation of Iraq*, Berkeley, Los Angeles and London: University of California Press.

Allawi, A. A. (2007) *The Occupation of Iraq. Winning the War, Losing the Peace*, New Haven & London: Yale University Press.

Alnasrawi, A. (2002a) *Iraq's Burdens: Oil, Sanctions and Underdevelopment*, Connecticut: Greenwood Press.

———— (2002b) "Long-term Consequences of War and Sanctions," in K. A. Mahdi (ed.) *Iraq's Economic Predicament*, Reading: Ithaca Press.

Al Rasheed, M. (1998) *Iraqi Assyrian Christians in London: The Construction of Ethnicity*. Lewiston, N.Y: The Edwin Mellen Press.

'Alwan, A. (n.d.) *Tatawwur al-shi'r al-'arabi al-hadith fi'l-'Iraq*, [The development of modern Arabic poetry in Iraq] Baghdad: Dar al-Shu'un al-Thaqafiya al-'Amma.

Amanat al-'Asima (1977) *Min ajl Baghdad ajmal, al-tamathil wa'l-ansab*, [For a more beautiful Baghdad: statues and monuments] Baghdad.

Amin, A. (1945) *Fajr al-Islam*, [The Dawn of Islam] 5th edn, Cairo: Matba'at Lajnat al-Ta'lif wa'l-Tarjamah wa'l-Nashr.

Amnesty International (1982) *Nicht die Erde hat sie verschluckt*, [The earth did not swallow them up] Frankfurt/Main: Fischer.

———— (1996) *Bosnia-Herzegovina: 'To bury my brother's bones'*, Amnesty International, Index: EUR 63/15/96.

———— (2005) *Iraq: Iraqi Special Tribunal. Fair Trials not Guaranteed*, Amnesty International Reports INDEX Nr. MDE 14/007/2005.

Anbari, S. al- (2007) *Thaqafa did al-'unf. Itlala 'ala 'iraq ma ba'd al-harb*, [Culture versus violence; Iraq in the aftermath of the war] Baghdad: Ma'had li'l-Dirasat al-Istratijiyya.

Anderson, B. (1986) *Imagined Communities. Reflections on the Origin and Spread of Nationalism*, London: Verso.

Anderson, L. (1999) "The State in the Middle East and North Africa," in T. Niblock and R. Wilson (eds.) *The Political Economy of the Middle East, Vol 5: The Role of the State*, Cheltenham, Northampton: Edward Elgar.

Ansari, B. al- (1979) 'al-Thawra: Quartier de Bagdad', thèse du troisième cycle, École des Hautes Études en Sciences Sociales, Paris.

'Aqrawi [Akrawi], M. (1942) "Curriculum construction in the public primary schools of Iraq in the light of a study of the political, economic, social, hygienic and educational conditions and problems of the country, with some reference to the education of teachers," unpublished thesis, Teachers' College, Columbia University.

Arab Ba'th Socialist Party (1974) *Revolutionary Iraq 1968–73, The Political Report Adopted by the Eighth Regional Congress of the Arab Ba'th Socialist Party-Iraq, January 1974*, Baghdad.

Araeen, R. (2003) "Come What May, Beyond the Emperor's New Clothes," in N. Papastergiadis (ed.) *Complex Entanglements, Art, Globalisation and Cultural Difference*, London/Sydney/Chicago: Rivers Oram Press.

Arendt, H. (2002) *Les Origines du Totalitarisme, Suivi de Eichmann à Jérusalem*, Paris: Gallimard.

Arjomand, S. A. (1984) *The Shadow of God and the Hidden Imam*, Chicago: University of Chicago Press.

Art irakien contemporain (1976) Paris: Musée d'Art Moderne de la Ville de Paris.

Asadi, al-, *et al.* (1984) *Dima' al-'Ulama' fi Tariq al-Jihad*, [The blood of the 'ulama on the road to jihad] SAIRI.

Auge, M. (2009) *Pour une Anthropologie de la Mobilité*, Paris: Payot.

'Awwad, K. (1969) *Mu'jam al-mu'allifin al-'Iraqiyin fi'l-qarnain at-tasi' 'ashar wa'l-'ishrin: 1800–1969*, [Directory of Iraqi authors of the nineteenth and twentieth centuries] Vol. 3, Bagdad.

Ayubi, N. N. (1995) *Overstating the Arab State: Politics and Society in the Middle East*, London: Tauris.

Aziz, T. M. (1993) "The Role of Muhammad Baqir al-Sadr in Shi'i Political Activism in Iraq from 1958 to 1980," *International Journal of Middle East Studies*, (25): 207–22.

Baba 'Elî, G. (1999) "Cînosaydêk le aîyin-da bo rewayetî degerêt" [A genocide returns from religion to legitimization], *Rehend*, 7: 148.

Babakhan, A. (1994) *L'Irak, 1970–90: déportation des chiites*, Paris: A. Babakhan.

―――― (1994b) *Les Kurdes d'Irak. Leur histoire et leur déportation par le régime de Saddam Hussein*, Paris: A. Babakhan.

Bader, A. (2007) "Iraq: A Long Phantasmagorical Dream," in A. Wollenberg and K. Glenewinkel (eds.), *Shahadat, Witnessing Iraq's Transformation after 2003*, Berlin: Friedrich Ebert Foundation.

Badr, A. (2001) *Baba Sartre*, Beirut: Riyadh al-Rayyis Books.

Bagdad Renaissance (2003) *Art Contemporain en Irak/Contemporary Art in Iraq*, Paris: Galerie M/Jean-Michel Place.

Bagdad–Paris (2005) *Artistes d'Irak, Musée du Montparnasse, 23 novembre 2005–15 janvier 2006*, Paris: Musée du Montparnasse.

Bahrani, Z. (1998) "Conjuring Mesopotamia. Imaginative Geography and a World Past," in L. Meskell (ed.) *Archaeology Under Fire. Nationalism, Politics and Heritage in the Eastern Mediterranean and Middle East*, London: Routledge.

―――― (2004) "Lawless in Mesopotamia," *Natural History*, 113 (2): 44–9.

Bailey, F. G. (1996) *The Culture of Indifference; on Domesticating Ethnicity*, Ithaca and London: Cornell University Press.

Balibar, E. (2004) *We, the People of Europe? Reflections on Transnational Citizenship*, Princeton NJ: Princeton Univ. Press.

Balta, P. (ed.) (1989) "Le conflit Irak–Iran 1979–89," *Notes et Études Documentaires*, Paris: La Documentation française, 4889.

Baqir, T. (1986) *Muqaddimah fi ta'rikh al-hadarat al-qadimah*, [Introduction to the history of ancient civilisation] Baghdad: Dar al-Shu'un al-Thaqafiyah al-'Ammah, Afaq 'Arabiyah.

Baram, A. (1989) "The ruling political elite in Ba'thi Iraq, 1968–86; the changing features of a collective profile," *International Journal of Middle East Studies*, (21): 447–93.

Baram, A. (1991) *Culture, History and Ideology in the Formation of Ba'thist Iraq, 1968–89*, New York: St. Martin's Press.

―――― (1994) "A Case of Imported Identity: The Modernizing Secular Ruling Elites of Iraq and the Concept of Mesopotamian-Inspired Territorial Nationalism, 1922–92," *Poetics Today*, 15 (2): 279–319.

―――― (1997) "Neo-Tribalism in Iraq: Saddam Hussein's Tribal Policies 1991–6," *International Journal of Middle East Studies*, 29 (1): 1–31.

Baran, D. (2003) "La guerre d'Irak: la stratégie du faible face à la puissance américaine," *Politique étrangère*, 2: 395–408.

―――― (2004) *Vivre la Tyrannie et lui Survivre: L'Irak en Transition*, Paris: Mille et Une Nuits.

Bar-On, Dan (1989) *The Legacy of Silence. Encounters with Children of the Third Reich*, Cambridge: Harvard University Press.

Bashkin, O. (2006) "Looking Forward to the Past: Nahda, Revolution, and the Early Ba'th in Iraq," in B. Deen Schildgen, Gang Zhou and S. L. Gilman (eds.) *Other Renaissances: New Approaches to World Literature*, New York: Palgrave.

―――― (2008) *The Other Iraq, Pluralism and Culture in Hashemite Iraq*, Stanford: Stanford University Press.

Basmachi, F. (1972) *Kunuz al-mathaf al-'Iraqi*, [Treasures of the Baghdad Museum] Baghdad: Wizarat al-Islam, Mudiriyat al-Athar al-'Ammah.

Batatu, H. (1978) *The Old Social Classes and the Revolutionary Movements in Iraq. A Study of Iraq's Old Landed and Commercial Classes and of its Communists, Ba'thists and Free Officers*, Princeton NJ: Princeton University Press.

―――― (1981) "Iraq's Underground Shi'a Movements: Characteristics, Causes and Prospects," Middle East Journal, 35 (4): 578–94.

Baudrillard, J. (1989) "Modernité," in *Encyclopaedia Universalis*, Vol. 15, Paris.

Bauer, Y. (2001) *Rethinking the Holocaust*, New Haven CT: Yale University Press.

Baxewan, H. (1999) *Hawrêname bo mêjû-î Kurdistan-u kurd*, [Hawrêname of the History of Kurdistan and the Kurds] Sulaimaniya: Serdem & Rûn.

Bayat, A. (2008) "Everyday Cosmopolitanism," *ISIM*, 22: 5.

Bayati, H. al- (2004) *Rub' Qarn ma' al-Shahid Muhammad Baqir al-Hakim*, [A quarter of a century with the martyr Muhammad Baqir al-Hakim] Baghdad: Mu'assasat Shahid al-Mihrab l'il-Tabligh al-Islami.

Baykam, B. (1994) *Monkey's Right to Paint and the Post-Duchamp Crisis, The Fight of a Cultural Guerrilla for the Rights of Non-Western Artists and the Empty World of the Neo-Ready-Mades*, Istanbul: Literatür.

Bayly, C. A. (1983) *Rulers, Townsmen and Bazaars: North Indian Society in the Age of British Expansion, 1770–1870*, Cambridge: Cambridge University Press.

Bazzaz, A. R. (1953) "Tathqif al-Mar'a", [Women's education] *al-Mu'allim al-Jadid*, 17(1–2): 40–9.

Beaudin-Saeedpour, V. (1992) "Establishing State Motives for Genocide: Iraq and the Kurds," in H. Fein (ed.) *Genocide Watch*, Yale: Yale University Press.

Beck, U. (2004) *Qu'est-ce que le Cosmopolitisme?* Paris: Éditions Aubier.

Becker, D. (1992) *Ohne Haß keine Versöhnung*, [Without hatred there can be no reconciliation] Freiburg i. Br.: Kore Verlag.

―――― (1997) "Prüfstempel PTSD ― Einwände gegen das herrschende 'Trauma' ― Konzept," [Evidence of PTSD: challenges to conventional notions of 'trauma'] in Medico International (ed.) *Medico Report 20, Schnelle Eingreiftruppe "Seele,"* Frankfurt/Main: Verlag Medico International.

―――― (2006) *Die Erfindung des Traumas.* [The invention of trauma] Verflochtene Geschichten, Berlin: Edition Freitag.

Bédarida, F. (1997) "La mémoire contre l'histoire," *Esprit*, 193: 7–13.

Beinin, J. (2005) "Forgetfulness for memory: The limits of the new Israeli history," *Journal of Palestine Studies* (34): 6–23.

Belting, H. (2003) *Art History After Modernism*, Chicago and London: University of Chicago Press.

Bengio, O. (1998) *Saddam's Word. Political Discourse in Iraq*, New York and Oxford: Oxford University Press.

―――― (1999) "Nation Building in Multi-ethnic States: The Case of Iraq," in O. Bengio and G. Ben-Dor (eds.) *Minorities and the State in the Arab World*, Boulder: Lynne Rienner.

Bennani-Chraïbi, M. and Fillieule, O. (eds.) (2003) *Résistances et Protestations Dans Les Sociétés Musulmanes*, Paris: Presses de Sciences Po.

Bernhardsson, M. (2005) *Reclaiming a Plundered Past. Archaeology and Nation Building in Modern Iraq*, Austin: University of Texas Press.

―――― (2007) "The Sense of Belonging. The Politics of Archaeology in Modern Iraq," in P. L. Kohl, M. Kozelsky, and N. Ben-Yehuda (eds.), *Selective Remembrances. Archaeology in the Construction, Commemoration, and Consecration of National Pasts*, Chicago: The University of Chicago Press.

Beşikçi, I. (2004) *International Colony Kurdistan*, London: Taderon Press.

Bigo, D. and Tsoukala, A. (eds.) (2008) *Terror, Insecurity and Liberty. Illiberal Practices of Liberal Regimes after 9/11*, London and New York: Routledge.

Bilal, W. and Lydersen, K. (2008) *Shoot An Iraqi. Art, Life and Resistance Under the Gun*, San Francisco: City Lights.

Black, J. (2008) "Contesting the Past," *History*, (93): 224–54.

Blackwell, S. (2005) "Review Article: Between Tradition and Transition: State Building, Society and Security in the Old and New Iraq," *Middle Eastern Studies*, 41 (3): 445–52.

Bleaney, C. H. and Roper, G. J. (eds.) (2004) *Iraq: A Bibliographical Guide*, Leiden: Brill.

Bogdanos, M. (2005) *Thieves of Baghdad: One Marine's Passion for Ancient Civilizations and the Journey to Recover the World's Greatest Stolen Treasures*, New York: Bloomsbury.

Bourdieu, P. (1984) *Homo Academicus*, Paris: Minuit.

―――― (1998) *Les Usages Sociaux de la Science. Pour une Sociologie Clinique du Champ Scientifique: Une Conférence-débat*, Paris: Minuit.

Bouzid, N. (1995) "Neo-Realism in Arab Cinema: The Defeat-Conscious Cinema," *Alif: Journal of Comparative Poetics*, 15: 242–50.

Bozarslan, H. (1997) *La Question Kurde. États et Minorités au Moyen-Orient*, Paris: Presses de Sciences Po.

―――― (2003) "Pouvoir et violence dans l'Irak de Saddam Hussein," in H. Dawod and H. Bozarslan (eds.), *La société irakienne. Communautés, pouvoirs et violences*, Paris: Karthala.

―――― (2007) "Revue bibliographique," *Critique Internationale*, (34): 79–86.

———— (2007) "Introduction," *REMMM*, 117–118: 13–29.

Bozarslan, H. and Harling, P. (2007) "L'Irak: violence et incertitudes," *Critique Internationale*, (34): 9–15.

Braungart, M. M. and Braungart, R. G. (1991) "The Effects of the 1960s Political Generation on Former Left-and Right-Wing Youth Activist Leaders," *Social Problems*, 38 (3): 297–315.

Bremer, L. P. (2006) *My Year in Iraq: The Struggle to Build a Future of Hope*, New York: Simon & Schuster.

Brodie, J. B. (1954) *Report to the Government of Iraq on Home Economics in Queen Aliya College*, Rome: Food and Agriculture Organization of the United Nations, FAO Report No. 320.

Broszat, M. (ed.) (1977–83) *Bayern in der NS-Zeit*, [Bavaria in the Nazi period] 6 Vol., Munich: Oldenbourg.

Browers, M. (2009) "Between Najaf and Jabal 'Amil: Three Generations of Shi'i Intellectuals," *TAARII Newsletter* 4(1): 6–9. Also Online. Available HTTP: <http://www.taarii.org/newsletters>.

Brown, K. L. (ed.) (2004) *L'Irak de la crise au chaos: chroniques d'une invasion*, Paris: Ibis Press.

Bruinessen, M. van (1994) "Genocide in Kurdistan? The Suppression of the Dersim Rebellion in Turkey (1937–8) and the Chemical War Against the Iraqi Kurds (1988)," in G. J. Andreopoulos (ed.) *Genocide*, Philadelphia: University of Pennsylvania Press.

Brunetta, G. P. (2001) "Storia e storiografia del cinema," [The history and historiography of cinema] in G. P. Brunetta (ed.) *Storia del cinema mondiale*, Milan: Einaudi.

Brunotte, U. (2008) "Martyrium, Vaterland und der Kult der toten Krieger", [Martyrdom, Fatherland, and the Cult of the Dead Warrior] in Andreas Krass and Thomas Frank (eds.) *Tinte und Blut. Politik, Erotik und Poetik des Martyriums*, Frankfurt: Fischer.

Burleigh, M. and Wippermann, W. (1991) *The Racial State. Germany, 1933–45*, Cambridge: Cambridge University Press.

Butti, R. (1923) *al-Adab al-'asri fi'l-'Iraq al-'arabi*, [Contemporary literature in (Arab) Iraq] Cairo: al-Maktaba al-Salafiyya.

Caplan, J. and Torpey, J. (eds.) (2001) *Documenting Individual Identity: The Development of State Practices in the Modern World*, Princeton, N. J.: Princeton University Press.

CARDI (Committee against Repression and for Democratic Rights in Iraq) (1989) *Saddam's Iraq: Revolution or Reaction?* London: Zed Press.

Ceram, C. W. (1967) *Gods, Graves and Scholars*, New York: Alfred A. Knopf.

Certeau, M. de (1990) *L'invention du quotidien, Vol. 1: Arts de faire*, Paris: Gallimard.

Chalabi, T. (2006) *The Shi'is of Jabal 'Amil and the New Lebanon*, New York: Palgrave Macmillan.

Chalk, F. and Jonassohn, K. (1990) *The History and Sociology of Genocide. Analyses and Case Studies*, New Haven: Yale University Press.

Chandhoke, N. (1995) *State and Civil Society: Explorations in Political Theory*, New Delhi: Sage.

Chatelard, G. (2005) "Un Système en Reconfiguration: l'Emigration des Irakiens de la Guerre du Golfe à la Guerre d'Irak (1990–2003)," in H. Jaber and F. Métral (eds.) *Mondes en Mouvements: Migrants et Migrations au Moyen-Orient au Tournant du XXIe Siècle*, Beirut: IFPO.

———— (2009) "Deferred Involvement: Memories and Praxes of Iraqi Intellectuals as Civil-Society Activists between Iraq, Jordan and Syria," prepared remarks at a conference at the University of Maryland, 1 and 2 May 2009.

——— (2010) "What visibility conceals. Re-embedding refugee migration from Iraq." in D. Chatty and B. Finlayson (eds.) *Dispossession and Displacement: Forced Migration in the Middle East and North Africa*, New York: Oxford University Press.

Chatelard, G. and Doraï, M. K. (forthcoming) "Les Irakiens en Jordanie et en Syrie: régime d'entrée et de séjour et effets sur les configurations migratoires," in Ch. Lequesnes (ed.) *L'Enjeu mondial. Spécial frontières*, Paris: CERI-Sciences Po.

Chatty, D. (2010) *Displacement and Dispossession in the Modern Middle East*, New York: Cambridge University Press.

Chaudhry, K. A. (1991) "On the Way to Market. Economic Liberalization and Iraq's Invasion of Kuwait," *Middle East Report*, 170: 14–23.

Chaumont, J.-M. (1997) *La concurrence des victimes. Génocide, identité, reconnaissance*, Paris: La Découverte.

Childress, F. J. (2008) "Creating the 'New Woman' in Early Republican Turkey: The Contributions of the American Collegiate Institute and the American College for Girls," *Middle Eastern Studies*, 44(4): 553–69.

Cicognetti, L., Servetti, L., and Sorlin, P. (2008) *Che storia siamo noi? Le interviste e i racconti personali al cinema e in televisione*, [What History are we? Interviews and personal accounts on film and television] Venice: Marsilio.

Cigerli, S. (1998) *Les réfugiés kurdes d'Irak en Turquie*, Paris: L'Harmattan.

Çîya (Mamosta Emîn) (1987) *Emin-î stratîcî-u sê koçke-î be'sîyan: terhîl, te'rîb, teb'îs*, [*Strategic Security and the Three Ba'thist Pillars: Deportation, Arabization and Ba'thification*] Qandil: Patriotic Union of Kurdistan.

Cleveland, W. L. (1971) *The Making of an Arab Nationalist; Ottomanism and Arabism in the Life and Thought of Sati' al-Husri*, Princeton: Princeton University Press.

Cockburn, P. (2008) *Muqtada: Muqtada al-Sadr, the Shia Revival and the Struggle for Iraq*, New York: Scribnor.

Cole, J. (1985) "Shi'i Clerics in Iraq and Iran 1722–80: The Akhbari-Usuli Conflict Reconsidered," *Iranian Studies*, XVIII: 3–34.

——— (1988) *Roots of North Indian Shi'ism in Iran and Iraq: Religion and State in Awadh, 1722–1859*, Berkeley and Los Angeles: University of California Press.

Colla, E. (2007) *Conflicted Antiquities. Egyptology, Egyptomania, Egyptian Modernity*, Durham: Duke University Press.

Cook, D. (2007) *Martyrdom in Islam*, Cambridge: Cambridge University Press.

Cook, H. (1995) *The Safe Haven in Northern Iraq. International Responsibility for Iraqi Kurdistan*, Colchester: Human Rights Centre.

cooke, m. (2007) *Dissident Syria. Making Oppositional Arts Official*, Durham and London: Duke University Press.

Cronin, S. (ed.) (2008) *Subalterns and Social Protest. History from Below in the Middle East and North Africa*, New York: Routledge.

Daftari, F. (2006) (ed.) *Without Boundary: Seventeen Ways of Looking*, New York: Museum of Modern Art.

Daloz, P. (1999) *Africa Works: Disorder as Political Instrument*, Bloomington: Indiana University Press.

Dann, U. (1969) *Iraq Under Qassem: A Political History, 1958–63*, New York: Praeger.

Dar al-Shu'un al-Thaqafiya al-'amma (ed.) (1986) *Li-madina nughanni ... li-mustaqbalina nutliq al-kalima*, [We sing for our past ... for our future we utter the word] 2 Vols, Baghdad: Dar al-Shu'un al-Thaqafiya al-'Amma.

Darle, P. (2003) *Saddam Hussein maître des mots: Du langage de la tyrannie à la tyrannie du langage*, Paris: L'Harmattan.

David, C. (1997) "Introduction," in F. Joly (ed.) *Documenta X, short Guide*, Ostfildern: Cantz.

Davis, E. (1991) "Theorizing Statecraft and Social Change in Arab Oil-Producing Countries," in E. Davis and N. Gavrielides (eds.) *Statecraft in the Middle East. Oil, Historical Memory, and Popular Culture*, Miami: Florida International University Press.

────── (1994) "The Museum and the Politics of Social Control in Modern Iraq," in J. R. Gillis (ed.), *Commemorations. The Politics of National Identity*, Princeton: Princeton University Press.

────── (2005) *Memories of State: Politics, History, and Collective Identity in Modern Iraq*, Berkeley: University of California Press.

Dawisha, A. (2009) *Iraq: A Political History from Independence to Occupation*, Princeton and Oxford: Princeton University Press.

Dawn, C. E. (1991) "The origins of Arab nationalism," in R. Khalidi *et al.* (eds.) *The Origins of Arab Nationalism*, New York: Columbia University Press.

Dean, M. (1999) *Govermentality. Power and Rule in Modern Society*, London: Sage.

Delacroix, C., Dosse, F., Garcia, P. (2009) (eds.) *Historicités*, Paris: La Découverte.

Delage, C. (1995) "Temps de l'histoire, temps du cinema," *Vingtième siècle. Revue d'histoire*, (46): 25–36.

Delanty, G. (2009) *The Cosmopolitan Imagination*, Cambridge: Cambridge University Press.

Deringil, S. (1990) "The Struggle against Shiism in Hamidian Iraq: A Study in Ottoman Counter-Propaganda," *Die Welt des Islams*, (30): 45–62.

Dizeyî, Y. (2001) *Enfal. Karesat, encam-u rehendekanî*, [Anfal. Catastrophe, Results and Methods] Erbil: Ministry of Education.

Dodge, T. (2003) *Inventing Iraq. The Failure of Nation Building and a History Denied*, New York: Columbia University Press.

────── (2008) "Iraq and the Next American President," *Survival*, (5): 37–60.

Donohue, J. and Esposito, J. (eds.) (2007) *Islam in Transition. Muslim Perspectives*, 2nd edn, New York/Oxford: Oxford University Press.

Donovan, N. (2008) "Improving the prospects of apprehending and prosecuting 'mid-level' al-Anfal perpetrators," in *International Conference on Genocide Against the Kurdish People*, Erbil: Arras.

Dorai, M. K. (2009). L 'Exil irakien à Damas: modes d'insertion urbaine et reconfiguration des réseaux migratoires. *Echobéo*, 8: <http://echogeo.revues.org/index 10976.html>

Dowty, Alan (1988) "The Assault on Freedom of Emigration," *World Affairs*, (151), 2: 85–92.

Ebdurrehman, Z. (1995) *Tûn-î merg. Hêrişekan-î Enfal le bel'genamekan-î rijêm-da*, [*Fire Chamber of Death. The Anfal Attacks in the Documents of the Iraqi Regime*] Tewrêz.

El Shakry, O. (2001) *The Great Social Laboratory, Subjects of Knowledge in Colonial and Postcolonial Egypt*, Stanford: Stanford University Press.

El-Basri, A. D. (1980) *Aspects of Iraqi Cultural Policy*, Paris: Unesco.

Eley, G. and Suny, R. G. (1996) *Becoming National: A Reader*, New York and Oxford.

Elias, M. J. (2008) *Stir It Up: Home Economics in American Culture*, Philadelphia: University of Pennsylvania.

Elkins, J. (2007) "Art History as A Global Discipline," in J. Elkins (ed.) *Is Art History Global?* New York & London: Routledge.

Emberling, G. and Hanson, K. (2008) *Catastrophe! The Looting and Destruction of Iraq's Past*, Chicago: The Oriental Institute Museum of the University of Chicago.

Emîn, N. M. (1999) *Xûlanewe naw bazîne-da. Dîwe-î nawewe-î rûdawekan-î Kurdistan-î' Iraq, 1984–8*, [Going round in circles. The inside story of events in Iraqi Kurdistan, 1984–8] Berlin: Awdani.

Enayat, H. (1991) *Modern Islamic Political Thought*, 3rd edn, Austin, TX: University of Texas Press.

Ende, W. (1981) "Iraq in World War I; the Turks, the Germans and the Shi'ite *mujtahids'* call for *jihad*," in R. Peters (ed.) *Proceedings of the Ninth Congress of the Union Européenne des Arabisants et Islamisants, Amsterdam, 1978*, Leiden: Brill.

—— (1997) "From Revolt to Resignation: The Life of Shaykh Muhsin Sharara." in A. Afsaruddin and A. H. Mathias Zahniser (eds.) *Humanism, Culture, and Language in the Near East: Studies in Honor of Georg Krotkoff*, Winona Lake, Ind.: Eisenbrauns.

—— (2007) "Success and failure of a Shiite Modernist: Muhammad ibn Muhammad al-Khalisi (1890–1963)," in A. Monsutti, S. Naef and F. Sabahi (eds.) *The Other Shiites: From the Mediterranean to Central Asia*, Bern: Peter Lang.

Eppel, M. (1998) "The Elite, the Effendiyya, and the Growth of Nationalism and Pan-Arabism in Hashemite Iraq, 1921–58," *International Journal of Middle East Studies*, 30 (2): 227–50.

Etherington, M. (2005) *Revolt on the Tigris: The Al-Sadr Uprising and the Governing of Iraq*, NY Ithaca: Cornell University Press.

'Ezîz, M. R. (2005) *Enfal-u rehende sosiyolocîyekan*, [The Anfal and sociological method] Sulaimaniya: Tîşk.

Fadlallah, M. H. (1982) "Introduction," in M. Baqir al-Sadr, *Risalatuna*, 2nd edn, Tehran: Maktaba al-Naja.

Fadlallah, M. H. and Hasani, S. (1993) *al-Ma'alim al-jadida li'l-marja'iyya al-shi'iyya: dirasa wa hiwar ma' al-sayyid Muhammad Husayn Fadlallah*, [New features of the Shi'i *marja'iyya*; a study and a discussion with Sayyid Muhammad Husayn Fadlallah] Beirut: Dar al-Malak.

Fagan, B. (1979) *Return to Babylon: Travelers, Archaeologists, and Monuments in Mesopotamia*, Boston: Little Brown Co.

Fakhir, W. (2004) "Der Schlächter und das Schweigen der Lämmer. Der Terror des Ba'th Regimes und die internationale Öffentlichkeit", [The butcher and the silence of the lambs: Ba'thist terror and international public opinon] in M. Kreutzer and T. Schmidinger (eds.) *Irak. Von der Republik der Angst zur bürgerlichen Demokratie?*, Freiburg: ça ira-Verlag.

Faraj, M. (2001a) (ed.) *Strokes of Genius, Contemporary Iraqi Art*, London: Saqi Books.

—— (2001b) "Preface," in M. Faraj (ed.) *Strokes of Genius, Contemporary Iraqi Art*, London: Saqi Books.

Farouk-Sluglett, M. and Sluglett, P. (1983) "The Transformation of Land Tenure and Rural Social Structure in Central and Southern Iraq, c. 1870–1958," *International Journal of Middle East Studies*, (15), 4: 491–505.

—— (1991) "The historiography of modern Iraq," *American Historical Review*, (96), 5: 1408–21.

—— (2001) *Iraq Since 1958: From Revolution to Dictatorship*, 3rd edn, London: I. B. Tauris.

Fassin, D. (2008) "The humanitarian politics of testimony: Subjectification through trauma in the Israeli-Palestinian Conflict," *Cultural Anthropology*, (23): 531–58.

Fassin, D. and Halluin, E. de (2005) "The truth from the body: Medical certificates as the ultimate evidence of asylum seekers," *American Anthropologist*, (107), 44: 597–608.

Fattah, H. (2007) "Les autres Irakiens: émigrés et exilés d'avant 2003 en Jordanie et leurs récits d'appartenance," *Revue des mondes musulmans et de la Méditerranée*, (117–18): 127–36.

Feldman, A. (2004) "Memory theaters, virtual witnessing and the trauma aesthetic," *Biography*, (27): 163–201.

Feldman, N. (2004) *What We Owe Iraq. War and the Ethics of Nation Building*, Princeton NJ: Princeton University Press.

Felman, S. and Laub, D. (1992) *Crises of Witnessing in Literature, Psychoanalysis, and History*, New York: Routledge.

Ferec, L. F. (2005) "Rol'-î caş le Enfal, [The Role of the Jash in the Anfal]" *Heştawheşt*, (4): 157–60.

Ferguson, C. H. (2008) *No end in Sight. Iraq's Descent into Chaos*, New York: BBS Public Affairs.

Fernea, R. A. (1970) *Shaykh and Effendi: Changing Patterns of Authority among the El Shabana of Southern Iraq*, Cambridge MA: Harvard University Press.

Fernea, R. and Louis, W. R. (1991) *The Iraqi Revolution of 1958: The Old Social Classes Revisited*, London: I.B. Tauris.

Ferris, E. G. (2008) *The Looming Crisis: Displacement and Security in Iraq*, Policy Paper: Brookings Institution.

Ferro, M. (1974) "Le film: une contre-analyse de la société," in J. Le Goff and P. Nora (eds.) *Faire de l'Histoire, III. Nouveaux objets*, Paris: Gallimard.

———— (1975) *Analyse de Film, Analyse de sociétés: Une Source Nouvelle Pour l'Histoire*, Paris: Hachette.

———— (1977) *Cinéma et Histoire*, Paris: Denoël and Gonthier.

Fink, G (1982) "Essere o essere stati: il film italiano, il tempo, la storia," [Being or states of being: Italian film, time, history] in G. Gori (ed.) *Passato ridotto*, Florence: La Casa Usher.

Fischer, M. J. (1980) *Iran: From Religious Dispute to Revolution*, Cambridge, MA, and London: Harvard University Press.

Fischer-Tahir, A. (2003) *"Wir gaben viele Märtyrer." Widerstand und Identitätspolitik in Irakisch-Kurdistan*, [We sacrified many martyrs: resistance and identity politics in Iraqi Kurdistan] Münster: Unrast.

Forgacs, D. (ed.) (2000) *Gramsci Reader: Selected Writings, 1916–35*, New York: New York University Press.

Foster, B., Foster, K. and Gerstenblith, S. (2005) *Iraq Beyond the Headlines. History, Archaeology and War*, New York: World Scientific Publishing Company.

Foucault, M. (1975) *Surveiller et Punir. La Naissance de la Prison*, Paris: Gallimard.

———— (1976) *Histoire de la Sexualité 1: La Volonté de Savoir*, Paris: Gallimard.

———— (1984) "Truth and Power," in P. Rabinow (ed.) *The Foucault Reader*, New York: Pantheon Books.

———— (1991) "Governmentality," in G. Burchell, C. Gordon and P. Miller (eds.) *The Foucault Effect: Studies in Governmentality*, London: Harvester Wheatsheaf.

Franzén, J. (2008) "Education and the radicalization of Iraqi Politics: Britain, the Iraqi Communist Party, and the 'Russian Link', 1941–9," *International Journal of Contemporary Iraqi Studies*, (2), 1: 99–113.

———— (2011) *Red Star over Iraq*, London: C. Hurst.

Fresia, M. (2007) "Les réfugiés comme objet d'étude pour l'anthropologie: enjeux et perspectives," *Refugee Survey Quarterly*, (26), 3: 100–18.

Friedländer, S. (1997) *Nazi Germany and the Jews. Vol. 1: The Years of Persecution, 1933–9*, New York: Harper Collins.

Friedrich, C. J. and Brzezinski, Z. (1965) *Totalitarian Dictatorship and Autocracy*, 2nd edn, Cambridge: Harvard University Press.

Fuccaro, N. (1997) "Ethnicity, State Formation, and Conscription in Postcolonial Iraq: The Case of the Yazidi Kurds of Jabal Sinjar," *International Journal of Middle East Studies*, (29), 4: 559–80.

–––––– (1999) *The Other Kurds. Yazidis in Colonial Iraq*, London and New York: I.B. Tauris.

–––––– (2004) "Minorities and Ethnic Mobilisation: The Kurds in Northern Iraq and Syria," in N. Méouchy and P. Sluglett (eds.) *The British and French Mandates in Comparative Perspectives/Les mandats français et britannique dans une perspective comparative*, Leiden: Brill.

Galbraith, P. (2006) *The End of Iraq: How American Incompetence Created a War without End*, New York: Simon and Schuster.

–––––– (2008) *Unintended Consequences: How War in Iraq Strengthened America's Enemies*, New York: Simon & Schuster.

Gallerano, N. (1995) (ed.) *L'uso pubblico della storia*, [The Public Usage of History] Milan: Franco Angeli.

Gannet Foundation, The (1991) *The Media at War: The Press and the Persian Gulf Conflict*, New York: Columbia University Press.

GAO (2008) *Iraq Reconstruction: Better Data Needed to Assess Iraq's Budget Execution*, Report to Congressional Committees.

Gellately, R. and Kiernan, B. (eds.) (2003) *The Spectre of Genocide: Mass Murder in Historical Perspective*, Cambridge: Cambridge University Press.

Gelvin, J. L. (1998) *Divided Loyalties. Nationalism and Mass Politics in Syria at the Close of Empire*, Berkeley and Los Angeles: University of California Press.

Gencer, M. (2008) "Zwischen Osmanismus und Panislamismus: Das Osmanische Reich unter Abdülhamid II. (1876–1909)," [Between Ottomanism and Pan-Islamism; the Ottoman Empire under 'Abd al-Hamid II (1876–1909)] paper presented at the DAVO-congress, October 2008.

Ghareeb, E. (1981) *The Kurdish Question in Iraq*, Syracuse NY: Syracuse University Press.

–––––– (2004) *Historical Dictionary of Iraq*, Lanham MD: Scarecrow.

Gharib, H. K. (2008) *Tadmir turath al-'Iraq wa-tasfiyat 'ulama'ihi*, [The destruction of Iraq's cultural heritage and the liquidation of its 'ulama] Beirut: Dar al-Tali'ah.

Ghorashi, H. (2008) "Giving Silence a Chance: The Importance of Life Stories for Research on Refugees," *Journal of Refugee Studies*, (21), 1: 117–32.

Gibson, McG. (2003) "Fate of Iraqi Archaeology," *Science*, 299, 5614: 1848–9.

Gleave, R. (2007) "Conceptions of Authority in Iraqi Shi'ism: Baqir al-Hakim, Ha'iri and Sistani on *Ijtihad*, *Taqlid* and *Marja'iyya*," *Theory, Culture & Society*, (24), 2: 69–78.

Glick Schiller, N., Basch, L., and Blanc-Szanton, C. (1995) "From Immigrant to Transmigrant: Theorizing Transnational Migration," *Anthropological Quarterly*, (68), 1: 48–63.

Goode, J. (2007) *Negotiating for the Past. Archaeology, Nationalism, and Diplomacy in the Middle East, 1919–41*, Austin: University of Texas Press.

Graham-Brown, S. (1999) *Sanctioning Saddam. The Politics of Intervention in Iraq*, London and New York: I.B. Tauris.

Gramsci, A. (1971) *Selections from the Prison Notebooks*, London: Lawrence and Wishart.

Grandin, G. (2005) "The Instruction of Great Catastrophe: Truth Commissions, National History and State Formation in Argentina, Chile and Guatemala," *American Historical Review*, (110), 1: 46–67.

Grobba, F. (1967) *Männer und Mächte im Orient. 25 Jahre diplomatischer Tätigkeit im Orient*, [Personalites and powers in the Orient; twenty-five years of diplomatic service] Zürich, Berlin and Frankfurt a. M.: Masterschmidt.

Gros, F. (2005) *Etats de violence. Essai sur la fin de la guerre*, Paris: Gallimard.

von Grunebaum, G. (1971) "Idjaz," *Encyclopedia Islamica*, Vol. III, Leiden, 1018ff.

Guha, R. (1996) "The Small Voice of History," in S. Amin and D. Chakrabarty (eds.) *Subaltern Studies* IX, Oxford: Oxford University Press.

Gul', M. 'O. (1997) *Cînosayd-î gel-î kurd leber roşnayî-î yasa-î taze-î nêwdewl'eta-da*, [The genocide of the Kurdish people in the light of new international law] Amsterdam: Mîdiya.

———— (2002) "A Stage of Practising Genocide," *Anfal*, 2: 42–54.

Gunter, M. M. (1996) "The KDP-PUK Conflict in Northern Iraq," *Middle East Journal*, (50), 2: 225–41.

Haarmann, U. (2002) "Watan," *Encyclopedia Islamica*, Vol. XI, Leiden, 174f.

Habermas, J. (1989) *The Structural Transformation of the Public Sphere: An Inquiry into a Category of Bourgeois Society*, Cambridge: MIT Press.

Haddad, U. K. (1950) *Harakat Rashid 'Ali al-Kailani sanat 1941*, [The movement of Rashid 'Ali in 1941] Saida/Sidon: The Modern Library.

Hafez, K. and Schäbler, B. (eds.) (2003) *Der Irak, Land zwischen Krieg und Frieden*, [Iraq; a Land between War and Peace] Heidelberg: Palmyra.

Haj, S. (1997) *The Making of Iraq 1900–63: Capital, Power and Ideology*, Albany: State University of New York.

Hakim, M. B. al- (1984) *Qatl al-'ulama' fi'l-'Iraq: yujasidu al-zahira al-Fir'awniyya*, [The killing of the Iraqi 'ulama: an example of Pharaonic practice] Tehran: Maktab al-Sayyid al-Hakim (Qism al-I'lam).

———— (1989) *al-Jihad, al-Hijra, al-Shahada: fi'l-dhikra al-sanawiyya li istishhad al-'allama al-mujahid al-sayyid Muhammad Mahdi al-Hakim*, [Jihad, hijra and Martyrdom; the annual commemoration of the martyrdom of the *mujahid* Muhammad Mahdi al-Hakim]; Qum: SAIRI (Qism al-A'lam, al-Wahda al-'Askariyya).

—— (1999) "La Résistance d'une famille religieuse," *Monde arabe Maghreb-Machrek*, 163: 93–111.

—— (2005a) *al-Marja'iyya al-Diniyya*, [The religious *marja'iyya*] Najaf: Mu'assasat Turath al-Shahid al-Hakim.

—— (2005b) *al-Shahid al-Sadr: qira'a tahliliyya fi'l-sira al-dhatiyya*, [An analytical reading of the autobiography of the martyr al-Sadr] Najaf: Mu'assasat Turath al-Shahid al-Hakim.

Hamber, B. (ed.) (1998) *Past Imperfect: Dealing with the Past in Northern Ireland and Countries in Transition*, INCORE/University of Ulster: Derry/Londonderry.

———— (2003) "Healing," in: *Reconciliation after Violent Conflict: A Handbook*, Stockholm: International Institute for Democracy and Electoral Assistance.

Hamber, B. and Wilson, R. (2003) "Symbolic closure through Memory, Reparation and Revenge in Post-conflict Societies," *Journal of Human Rights*, (1), 1: 35–53.

Hamber, B., Maepa, T., Mofokeng, T., and van der Merwe, H. (1998) *Survivors' Perceptions of the Truth and Reconciliation Commission and Suggestions for the Final Report. Submission to the Truth and Reconciliation Commission.* Johannesburg: Centre for the Study of Violence and Reconciliation.

Hardi, C. (2008) "Female victims and survivors of the Anfal campaign," paper presented at the Expert Meeting 'Gewalt, Erinnerung und Aufarbeitung im Irak: 20 Jahre nach den Anfal-Operationen in Kurdistan-Irak; die Perspektive der Überlebenden', HAUKARI e.V and Zentrum Moderner Orient, Berlin, April 2008 (unpublished).

Harling, P. (2000) *Bagdad Chrétienne à l'heure du Ba'th Saddamien: Exil, action et Passion des Chaldéens*, unpublished study.

―――― (2006) "The Falluja Syndrome: Taking the Fight to the Enemy that Wasn't," *Campaigning Journal*, 4: 26–30.

―――― (2007a) "Les dynamiques du conflit irakien," *Critique Internationale*, (34): 29–43.

―――― (2007b) "Saddam Hussein et la débâcle triomphante. Les ressources insoupçonnées de Umm al-Ma'arik," *Revue d'Etudes des Mondes Musulmans et Méditerranéens*, (117–118): 157–78.

Harling, P. and Nasser, H. Y. (2006) "Unité de façade des shiites irakiens," *Le Monde Diplomatique*, September: 16–17.

―――― (2007) "La mouvance Sadriste en Iraq: lutte de classes, millénarisme et *Fitna*," in S. Mervin (ed.) *Les mondes chiites et l'Iran*, Paris: Karthala.

Hartog, F. (2000) "Le témoin et l'historien," *Gradhiva*, (27): 1–14.

―――― (2003) *Régimes d'historicité. Présentisme et expériences du temps*, Paris: Seuil.

Hartog, F. and Revel, J. (2001) "Note de conjoncture historiographique," in F. Hartog and J. Revel (eds.) *Les usages politiques du passé*, Paris: EHESS.

Hasan, A. M. (1957) "Dawr 'idad al-mu'allimat fi'l-'Iraq [The Role of Women's Teacher Training in Iraq]," *al-Mu'allim al-Jadid*, (20), 3: 305–10.

al-Hasani, 'A. (1988) *Ta'rikh al-wizarat al-'iraqiya*, [History of the Iraqi ministries] 10 vols, 7th edn, Baghdad: Dar al-Shu'un al-Thaqafiya al-'Amma.

Hashim, A. S. (2006) *Insurgency and Counter-Insurgency in Iraq*, Ithaca, NY: Cornell University Press.

Hassner, Pierre (2006) *La revanche des passions*. Paris: Société des amis de François Furet.

Hauck, G. (2004) "Schwache Staaten? Überlegungen zu einer fragwürdigen entwicklungspolitischen Kategorie," [Weak states; considerations on a questionable category in development politics] *Peripherie*, 24 (96): 409–27.

Haugbolle, S. (2010) *War and Memory in Lebanon*, Cambridge: Cambridge University Press.

al-Haydari, I. (2006) *'Ali al-Wardi — shakhsiyatuhu wa-manhajuhu wa-afkaruhu al-ijtima'iya*, [Ali al-Wardi; his personality, his methodolgy and his social thought] Cologne: al-Jamal.

Hawal, K. (2004) "Regard sur le cinéma irakien," *7ème Biennale des cinémas arabes à Paris*, Paris: Institut du Monde Arabe.

Heern, Z. (2011) "Usuli Shi'ism: The Emergence of an Islamic Movement in Early Modern Iraq and Iran," Ph. D dissertation, University of Utah.

Helms, C. M. (1984) *Iraq, Eastern Flank of the Arab World*, Washington: Brookings Institution.

Hemewendî, M. E. (1999) "Enfal le twê-î ferheng-î sîyasî-da [Anfal in the political dictionary]," *Şehîd*, 5: 26.

Henry, G. (1998) "Oded Halahmy," *ARTnews* 97.

Herman, J. L. (1992) *Trauma and Recovery. The Aftermath of Violence. From Domestic Abuse to Political Terror*, New York: Basic Books.

Herring, E. and Rangwala, G. (2006) *Iraq in Fragments. The Occupation and its Legacy*, London: Hurst and Company.

Herutî, S. 'O. (2008) "Sîyaset-î paktaw-î ŗegez-î kurd le Kerkuk le şal'an-î dwaî ŗapeŗîn-da [The policy of Kurdish ethnic cleansing in Kirkuk after the uprising]," paper presented at the "International Conference on Genocide against the Kurdish People," Erbil, 26–8 January 2008.

Herzog, S. (2006) "Art global-perception locale", in J. Dakhlia *et al.* (eds.) *Créations artistiques contemporaines en pays d'Islam: des arts en tension*, Paris: Editions Kimé.

Hesford, W. S. (2004) "Documenting violations: Rhetorical witnessing and the spectacle of distant suffering," *Biography* 27: 104–43.

Hilali, A. R. (1946) "al-Madrasa wa atharuha f'il-'idad al-jil [The school and its influence in preparing the (new) generation]," *al-Mu'allim al-Jadid*, 10(6): 306–8.

Hilberg, R. (1985) *The Destruction of the European Jews*, New York: Holmes and Meier.

Hildbrand, K. (2003) *Das Dritte Reich*, 6th edn., Munich: Oldenbourg Verlag.

Hiltermann, J. (1999) "Clipped wings, sharp claws: Iraq in the 1990s," *Middle East Report*, 212: 58–60.

———— (2007) *A Poisonous Affair: America, Iraq and the Gassing of Halabja*, Cambridge: Cambridge University Press.

———— (2008) "The 1988 Anfal Campaign in Iraqi Kurdistan," in *International Conference on Genocide Against the Kurdish People*, Erbil: Arras.

Hobsbawm, E. J. (1990, 1992) *Nations and Nationalism since 1780: Programme, Myth, Reality*, Cambridge: Cambridge University Press.

Hourani, A. (1962) *Arabic Thought in the Liberal Age, 1798–1939*, Oxford: Oxford University Press.

———— (1983) *Arabic Thought in the Liberal Age*, Cambridge: Cambridge University Press.

———— (1990) "Conclusion: Tribes and States in Islamic History," in P. S. Khoury & J. Kostiner (eds.) *Tribes and State Formation in the Middle East*, Berkeley: University of California Press.

Humadi, Z. (1995) "Civil Society under the Ba'th in Iraq," in J. Schwedler (ed.) *Toward Civil Society in the Middle East? A Primer*, Boulder: Lynne Rienner.

Human Rights Watch (1993) *Genocide in Iraq: The Anfal Campaign Against the Kurds*, New York: Human Rights Watch.

———— (1994) *Bureaucracy and Repression*, New York: Human Rights Watch.

———— (1995) *Iraq's Crime of Genocide. The Anfal Campaign Against the Kurds*, New Haven and London: Yale University Press.

Hurtado, J. (2006) "Representacions àrabs contemporànies. L'equació iraquiana", [Contemporary Arab representations: the Iraqi equation] *Parachute* 125, Suppl., 7–8.

Husayn, S. (1982) *Hawl insihab al-quwwat al-'iraqiya min al-aradi al-iraniya* [On the withdrawal of Iraqi troops from Iranian territories], Baghdad: Dar al-Ma'mun, Ministry of Culture and Information.

Husayn, T. (1926) *Fi'l-shi'r al-jahili,* [The poetry of the *Jahiliyya*] Cairo: Matba'at dar al-kutub al-Misriyya.

———— (1927) *Fi'l-adab al-jahili,* [The literature of the *Jahiliyya*] Cairo: Matba'at al-i'timad.

Husri, S. al- (1962) *Ahadith fi'l-tarbiyya wa-ijtima,'* [Debates on education and society] Beirut: Dar al-'Ilm.

———— (1967) *Mudhakkirati fi'l-'Iraq, 1921–41* [My memoirs in Iraq 1921–41], vol. 2, Beirut: Dar al-Tali'ah.

—— (1974) " 'Awamil al-Qawmiyyah," [Factors in nationalism] a lecture given in 1928 at Nadi al-Mu'allimin in Baghdad), in S. al-Husri, *Abhath mukhtarah fi al-qawmiyyah al-'Arabiyyah 1923–63*, vol. 1, Beirut: Dar al-Quds.

Hussein, S. (1986) *Islam's Verdict on Iran's Aggression*, Baghdad: Dar al-Ma'mun.

Ibrahimi, L. al- (2004) *The Political Transition in Iraq: Report of the Fact-Finding Mission*, United Nations News Service.

Institute for War and Peace Reporting (2005a) "Iraq Crisis Report," 30 January.

—— (2005b) "Iraqi Press Monitor," 252.

International Bank for Reconstruction and Development (1952) *The Economic Development of Iraq*. Baltimore: Johns Hopkins Press.

International Center for Transitional Justice (2008) "Iraq's New 'Accountability and Justice' Law."

International Crisis Group (2006) *Iraq's Moqtada al-Sadr: Spoiler or Stabiliser?* Brussels and Beirut.

—— (2008) *Failed responsibility: Iraqi refugees in Syria, Jordan and Lebanon*, Middle East Report, 77, 10 July 2008.

Ishow, H. (1996) *L'Irak. Paysanneries, politiques agraires et industrielles au XXe siècle. Contribution à la réflexion sur le développement*, Paris: Publisud.

Islamic Kurdish Army (1988) *Ma'sāt Halabğa* (Hīrošīma Kurdistān) [The tragedy of Halabja. The Kurdistan Hiroshima], (n.p.).

Ismael, T. (2001) *Middle East Politics Today; Government and Civil Society*, Gainesville: University of Florida Press.

—— (2008) *The Rise and Fall of the Communist Party of Iraq*, Cambridge: Cambridge University Press.

Ismael, T. Y. and Fuller, M. (2009) "The Disintegration of Iraq: The Manufacturing and Politicization of Sectarianism," *International Journal of Contemporary Iraqi Studies*, (3): 443–73.

'Izz ad-Din, Y. (1977) *al-Shi'r al-'Iraqi al-hadith wa'l-tayyarat al-siyasiya wa'l-ijtima'iya*, [Modern Iraq poetry; political and social aspects] Cairo: Dar al-Ma'arif.

Jabar, F. A. (ed.) [Falih 'Abd al-Jabbar] (1997) *Post-Marxism and the Middle East*, London: Saqi Books.

—— (2001) "State and Society in Iraq: A Totalitarian State in the Twilight of Totalitarianism," *al-Huquqi* (1), 6: 14–31.

—— (2003) *The Shi'ite Movement in Iraq*, London: Saqi Books.

—— (2003) "Patrimonial Totalitarianism in Iraq, 1968–98," in F. A. Jabar and H. Dawod (eds.) *Tribes and Power. Nationalism and Ethnicity in the Middle East*, London: al-Saqi.

Jabar, F. A. and Dawod, H. (2003) *Tribes and Power: Nationalism and Ethnicity in the Middle East*, London: Saqi Books.

Jaber, F. A. (2002) *Ayatollahs, Sufis and Ideologues: State, Religion and Social Movements in Iraq*, London: al-Saqi.

Jaber, H. and Métral, F. (eds.) (2005) *Mondes en mouvements, Migrants et migrations au Moyen-Orient au tournant du XXIe siècle*, Beirut: Institut français du Proche Orient.

Jabra, J. I. (1980) "Modern Arabic Literature and the West," in I. J. Boullata (ed.) *Critical Perspectives on Modern Arabic Literature*, Washington, DC: Three Continents Press.

—— (2005) *Princesses' Street: Baghdad Memories*, Fayetteville: University of Arkansas Press.

Jamali, M. F. (1934) *The New Iraq: Its Problem of Bedouin Education*, New York: Bureau of Publications, Teachers College, Columbia University.

—— (1938) "al-Tifl wa'l-Umma" [The child and the nation], *al-Mu'allim al-Jadid*, (3), 3: 166–9.

—— (1960) "The Theological Colleges of Najaf," *The Muslim World*, (59): 15–22.

Jamil, H. (1983) *al-Hayat al-niyabiyya fi'l-'Iraq, 1925–46: mawaqif jama'at al-ahali minha*, [*Jama'at al-Ahali*'s views on parliamentary life in Iraq, 1925–46] Baghdad: Maktabat al-muthanna.

Jayashi, W. J. al- (2006) *Min al-Najaf ila al-Najaf: faqaha, jihad, shahada*, [From Najaf to Najaf: Understanding, *Jihad*, martyrdom] Najaf: Mu'assasat Turath al-Shahid al-Hakim.

Jayyusi, S. K. (1975) *Trends and Movements in Modern Arabic Literature*, 2 vols, Leiden: Brill.

Joint Committee of Iraqi Opposition Forces (1991) *Watha'iq mu'tamar al-'amm li qiwa al-mu'arada al-'Iraqiyya* [documents of the congress of Iraqi opposition forces], Beirut.

Jones, A. (2006) *Genocide. A Comprehensive Introduction*, London and New York: Routledge.

Jones, R. (2004) "Crafting a Narrative from Oral History Interviews," *The Oral History Review*, (33), 1: 23–42.

Joseph, J. (1983) *Muslim–Christian Relations and Inter-Christian Rivalries in the Middle East: The Case of the Jacobites in an Age of Transition*, Albany: State University of New York Press.

Kadhim, H. N. (2001) "'Abd al-Wahhab al-Bayati's 'Odes to Jaffa'," *Journal of Arabic Literature*, (32), 2: 86–106.

—— (2004) *The Poetics of Anti-Colonialism in the Arabic Qasidah*, Leiden: Brill.

Kadry, H. T. (1958) *Women's Education in Iraq*, Washington, D.C.: Office of the Cultural Attaché, Embassy of Iraq.

Kamp, M. (2009) "Fragmented Citizenship," in N. S. al-Ali and N. Pratt (eds.) *Women and War in the Middle East*, London and New York: Zed Books.

Karkhi, 'A. al- (1933) *Diwan al-Karkhi*, [The collected poetry of al-Karkhi] Volume 1, Baghdad: Matba'at al-Karkh.

Kashif al-Ghita', M. H. (1913) *al-Muraja'at al-Rayhaniyya*, [The revisions of al-Rayhani] 2 vols, Beirut: al-Matba'a al-Ahliyya.

—— (1954) *al-Muthul al-'ulya fi'l-Islam la fi Bhamdun*. [The lofty ideals of Islam will not be found in Bhamdun] Najaf: al-Matba'a al-Haydariyya.

—— (1969) *Qadiya filastin al-kubra*, [The great matter of Palestine] Najaf: Dar al-Nu'man.

—— (1982) *The Shia: Origin and Faith*. Accra: Islamic Seminary. Translation of *Asl al-shi'a wa usuluha* (First published 1931).

—— (1987) *Islamic Anti-Imperialism: Three Works*, Tehran: Islamic Propagation Organization.

Kayssi, R. al- (2000) "Sanctions in the Service of Tyranny and Dictatorship," *al-Huquqi*, (1), 1: 31–9.

Keen, D. (1993) *The Kurds in Iraq: How safe is their haven now?* London: Save the Children.

Kerîm, H. M. (1993) *Şoriş-î Kurdistan-u goṛankarîyekan-î serdem. Xebat şaxekan yan ṛapeṛîn-î şarekan?* [The revolution of Kurdistan and contemporary changes. Struggle in the mountains or rebellion in the cities?], Sweden (no publisher).

Kershaw, I. (2004) "Hitler and the Uniqueness of Nazism," *Journal of Contemporary History* (39), 2: 239–54.

Kestenberg, J. (1982) "Survivor parents and their children," in M. S. Bergmann and
M. E. Jucovy (eds.), *Generations of the Holocaust*. New York: Basis books.

Khalid, K. Y. (2005) "al-Anfal wa Halabja – bidayat al-sahwa al-kurdistaniyya, [The Anfal
and Halabja- the beginning of Kurdish awakening]" *al-Anfal*, (7): 68–9.

Khalidi, A. al-, Hoffman, S. and Tanner, V. (2007) *Iraqi Refugees in The Syrian Arab
Republic: A Field-Based Snapshot*, The Brookings Institute/University of Bern Project
on Internal Displacement.

Khalidi, R. (1991) "Arab Nationalism: Historical Problems in the Literature," *American
Historical Review*, (96), 5: 1363–73.

Khadduri, M. (1960) *Independent Iraq 1932–1958: A Study in Iraq Politics*, 2nd revised
edn., London: Oxford University Press.

————— (1969) *Republican Iraq: A Study in Iraqi Politics since the Revolution of 1958*,
London and New York: Oxford University Press.

————— (1978) *Socialist Iraq: A Study in Iraqi Politics since 1968*, Washington DC: The
Middle East Institute.

Khafaji, 'I. al- (1983) *Dawra al-tatawwur al-ra'smali fi'l-Iraq, 1968–78*, [The role of capitalist development in Iraq, 1968–78], Cairo: United Nations University.

————— (2000) "War as a Vehicle for the Rise and Demise of a State-Controlled Society,"
in S. Heydemann (ed.) *War, Institutions, and Social Change in the Middle East*,
Berkeley: University of California Press.

————— (2003) "A Few Days After: State and society in a post-Saddam Iraq," in T. Dodge
and S. Simon (eds.) *Iraq at the Crossroads: State and Security in the Shadow of Regime
Change*, London: Adelphi Papers.

————— (2004) *Tormented Births. Passages to Modernity in Europe and the Middle East*,
London: I. B. Tauris.

Khalil, S. al- (1989) *Republic of Fear. The Politics of Modern Iraq*, Berkeley: University
of California Press.

————— (1991) *Irak, la machine infernale, politique de l'Irak moderne*, Paris: JCL.

————— (1991) *The Monument, Vulgarity and Responsibility in Iraq*, London: Andre
Deutsch.

Khalili, L. (2007) *Heroes and Martyrs of Palestine. The Politics of National
Commemoration*, Cambridge: Cambridge University Press.

Khamis, U. (2001) "An Historical Overview, 1900s–1990s," in M. Faraj (ed.) *Strokes of
Genius, Contemporary Iraqi Art*, London: Saqi Books.

Khatib, L. (2006) *Filming the Modern Middle East. Politics in the Cinemas of Hollywood
and the Arab World*, London: I.B. Tauris.

Khayri, S. (1976) "The Battle of the Iraqi Working Class," *al-Thaqafa al-Jadida*, (85):
46–52.

Khulusi, S. A. (1950) "Ma'ruf ar-Rusafi, 1875–1945", *BSOAS*, (13), 3: 616–26.

————— (1953) "Tawhid aw ikhtilaf manahij al-ta'lim bayn al-banin wa'l-banat",
[Standardization or differentiation of the school curriculum for boys and girls] *al-
Mu'allim al-Jadid*, (17), 1–2: 61–4.

Kienle, E. (1990) *Ba'th versus Ba'th: The Conflict Between Syria and Iraq 1968–89*,
London: I.B. Tauris.

Kieser, H-L. and Schaller, D. J. (eds.) (2002) *Der Völkermord an den Armeniern und die
Shoa*, [The Armenian genocide and the Shoah] Zürich: Chronos Verlag.

Klemm, V. (1998) *Literarisches Engagement im arabischen Nahen Osten. Konzepte und
Debatten*, [Literary Engagement in the Arab Middle East: Concepts and Debates]
Würzburg: Reichert Verlag.

Kohl, P. and Fawcett, C. (eds.) (1995) *Nationalism, Politics, and the Practice of Archaeology*, Cambridge: Cambridge University Press.

Kohl, P., Kozelsky, M. and Ben-Yehuda, N. (eds.) (2007) *Selective Remembrances. Archaeology in the Construction, Commemoration, and Consecration of National Pasts*, Chicago: University of Chicago Press.

Kortun, V. (2000) "Die anderen Modernen," [The other moderns] in Museum für Gegenwartskunst Basel (ed.) *Totalglobal: Umgang mit nichtwestlicher Kunst*, Basel: Christoph-Merian-Verlag.

Kraushaar, W. (1993) "Sich aufs Eis wagen. Plädoyer für eine Auseinandersetzung mit der Totalitarismustheorie", [Walking on thin ice: A plea for a debate on the theory of totalitarianism] *Mittelweg, (36)*, 2: 6–29.

Kubaysi, T. al- (1986) *Qasidat al-harb al-haditha fi'l-'Iraq – dirasa wa-mukhtarat*, [Contemporary war poetry from Iraq: A study with selected poems] 2 vols, Baghdad: Dar al-Shu'un al-Thaqafiya al-'amma.

Kubie, N. (1964) *Road to Nineveh: The Adventures and Excavations of Sir Austen Henry Layard*, Garden City, N.Y.: Doubleday.

Kühner, A. (2008) *Trauma und kollektives Gedächtnis* [Trauma and collective consciousness], Gießen: Psychosozial-Verlag.

Kuklick, B. (1996) *Puritans in Babylon. The Ancient Near East and American Intellectual Life*, Princeton: Princeton University Press.

Kurde, B. E. (2007) *Culekan-î şar-î Slêmanî* [The Jews of the City of Sulaimaniya], Sulaimaniya: Rûn.

Kutschera, C. (ed.) (2005) *Le livre noir de Saddam Hussein*, Paris: *Oh!* Editions.

Labelle, M., Antonius, R. and Leroux, G., (eds.) (2005) *Le devoir de mémoire et les politiques du pardon*, Sainte-Foy: Presses de l'Université du Québec.

LaCapra, D. (1991) *Writing history, Writing Trauma*, Baltimore: John Hopkins University Press.

Lafourcade, F. (2001) "Stratégies de survie en Irak: l'exemple de l'institution universitaire," Institut d'Etudes Politiques de Paris.

———— (2007) *Le chaos irakien*, Paris: La Découverte.

Lagny, M. (2001) "Il cinema come fonte di storia" [The cinema as historical source material], in G. P. Brunetta (ed.) *Storia del cinema mondiale*, Milan: Einaudi.

Lagos, D. et al. (1994) *Argentina: Our experience in rehabilitation work with relatives of desaparecidos and other victims of political repression*, Working Paper EATIP, Equipo Argentina de Trabajo, Buenos Aires: Investigacion Psicosocial.

Laizer, S. (1996) *Martyrs, Traitors and Patriots. Kurdistan after the Gulf War*, London: Zed.

Larsen, M. T. (1996) *The Conquest of Assyria*, London: Routledge.

Lawrence, P. K. (1997) *Modernity and War. The Creed of Absolute Violence*, London and New York: MacMillan and St. Martin's Press.

Lawrence, Q. (2008) *Invisible Nation. How the Kurds' Quest for Statehood is Shaping Iraq and the Middle East*, New York: Walker Company.

Lawson, F. H. (2005) "Economic Liberalization and the Reconfiguration of Authoritarianism in the Arab Gulf States," *Orient*, (46), 1: 19–43.

Le Goff, J and Nora, P. (1974) *Faire de l'Histoire*, (trans. I. Mariani (1981) *Fare storia. Temi e metodi della nuova storiografia*, Turin: Einaudi).

Le Vine, M. (2006) "Chaos, Globalization, and the Public Sphere: Political Struggle in Iraq and Palestine," *Middle East Journal* (60), 3: 467–92.

Leach, E. R. (1940) *Social and Economic Organisation of the Rowanduz Kurds*, London: Athlone Press.

Lebowitz, C. (2006) "'Ashes to Art' at Pomegranate", *Art in America* (94/6), 191–2.

Leca, J. (1984) "L'hypothèse totalitaire dans le Tiers Monde: les pays arabo-islamiques," in G. Hermet, P. Hassner and J. Rupnik (eds.) *Totalitarisme*, Paris: Economica.

Leenders, R. (2008) "Iraqi Refugees in Syria: Causing a spillover of the Iraqi conflict?" *Third World Quarterly* (29), 8:1563–84.

Leezenberg, M. (1997) "Between Assimilation and Deportation: The Shabak and the Kakais in Northern Iraq," in K. Kehl-Bodrogi, B. Kellner-Heinkele and A. Otter-Beaujean (eds.) *Syncretistic Religious Communities in the Near East*, Leiden: Brill.

―――― (1997) "Irakisch-Kurdistan seit dem Zweiten Golfkrieg," [Iraqi Kurdistan since the second Gulf War] in C. Borck *et al.* (eds.) *Ethnizität, Nationalismus, Religion und Politik in Kurdistan*, Münster: Lit (Kurdologie).

Lenin, V. I. (1963) *What Is To Be Done?* trans. S. V. Utechin and Patricia Utechin; S. V. Utechin (ed.), Oxford: Clarendon Press.

Letîf, Y. (2005) "Enfalekan şêwazêk le Faşism. Yadewer-î bîr-î bal'a-yî nasiyonal — mezheb-î Be'sizm [The Anfal as a form of Fascism. Remembering the idea of national greatness of the Ba'th faction]," *Heştawheşt*, 4: 161–8.

Levene, M. and Roberts, P. (1999) (eds.) *The Massacre in History*, New York and Oxford: Berghahn Books.

Litvak, M. (1998) *Shi'i Scholars of Nineteenth-Century Iraq: the 'Ulama' of Najaf and Karbala'*, Cambridge: Cambridge University Press.

Lloyd, S. (1947) *Foundations in the Dust: The Story of Mesopotamian Exploration*, Oxford: Oxford University Press.

Lockman, Z. (1996) *Comrades and Enemies: Arab and Jewish Workers in Palestine, 1906–48*, Berkeley and Los Angeles: University of California Press.

Longrigg, S. H. (1925) *Four Centuries of Modern Iraq*, Oxford: The Clarendon Press.

―――― (1956) *Iraq, 1900 to 1950. A Political, Social and Economic History*, Oxford: University of Oxford.

Louër, L. (2008) *Chiisme et politique au Moyen-Orient: Iran, Irak, Liban, monarchies du Golfe*, Paris: Autrement.

Lucas, R. E. B. (2005) *International Migration and Economic Development, Lessons from Low-Income Countries*, Cheltenham: Edward Elgar.

Luizard, P.-J. (1991) *La formation de l'Irak contemporain. Le rôle des ulemas chiites à la fin de la domination ottomane et au moment de la création de l'Etat irakien*, Paris: CNRS.

―――― (1994) "Baghdad: une métropole moderne et tribale, siège de gouvernements assiégés," *Maghreb-Machrek*, 1: 225–42.

―――― (1995) "'Ali al-Wardi (1913–95) à la recherche de l'identité irakienne," *Monde Arabe Maghreb-Machrek*, 150: 120–6.

―――― (1996) "Iraniens d'Irak, une élite religieuse chiite face à un état Sunnite," *Cemoti*, (22): 163–90.

―――― (1999) "Mémoires d'Irakiens: à la découverte d'une société vaincue," *Maghreb-Machrek*, 163: 1–246.

―――― (2002) *La question irakienne*, Paris: Fayard.

―――― (2002) "The Nature of the Confrontation between the State and Marja'ism; Grand Ayatullah Muhsin al-Hakim and the Ba'th," in F. Abdul-Jabar (ed.) *Ayatollahs, Sufis and Ideologues: State, Religion and Social Movements in Iraq*, London: Saqi Books.

———— (2003) "Le mandat britannique en Irak: une rencontre entre plusieurs projets politiques," in N. Méouchy and P. Sluglett (eds.) *The British and French mandates in comparative perspectives/Les mandats français et anglais dans une perspective comparative*, Brill: Leiden.

———— (2009) *Comment est né l'Irak moderne?* Paris: CNRS.

Lukitz, L. (1995) *Iraq: the Search for National Identity*, London: Frank Cass.

Lutfi, 'A. M. (1944) *Qalb umm*, [A Mother's Heart] Baghdad: Matba'at al-Sabah.

Maffi, I. (2006) "Idées pour une recherche sur la formation du milieu artistique en Jordanie," in J. Dakhlia *et al.* (eds.), *Créations artistiques contemporaines en pays d'Islam: des arts en tension*, Paris: Editions Kimé.

Mahdi, S. (1986) *al-A'mal al-shi'riyah 1965–85*, [Collected Poetry 1965-85] Baghdad: Dar al-Shu'un al-Thaqafiya al-'Amma.

———— (2001) *Nahad al-Takarli: ra'id al-naqd al-adabi al-hadith fi'l-'Iraq*, [Nahad al-Takarli: A leading critic of modern Iraqi literature] Baghdad: Dar al-Shu'un al-Thaqafiyya al-'Amma.

Mahdi, U. (2004) "Tahawara mudir 'amm fi hayat ijtithath al-Ba'th fi'l-'Iraq," [Conversations with a general director in the course of the de-Ba'thification campaign in Iraq] *Elaph.*

Maier, H. and Schäfer, M. (eds.) (1996–2003) *'Totalitarismus' und 'Politische Religionen'. Konzepte des Diktaturvergleichs*, [Totalitarianism and political religion: Notions of comparative dictatorship] 3 vols., Paderborn: Schöningh.

Majid, M. al- (1991) *Intifadat al-Sha'b al-'Iraqi* [The uprising of the Iraqi people], Beirut: Dar al-Wifaq.

Makiya, Kanaan, (1993) *Cruelty and Silence. War, Tyranny, Uprising and the Arab World*, New York and London: W.W. Norton & Company.

———— (1996) *al-Qaswa wa'l-samat* [Cruelty and silence]' Erbil: Hay'at Irsal al-'Iraqiyya.

Malallah, H. (2001) "Consciousness of Isolation," in M. Faraj (ed.) *Strokes of Genius, Contemporary Iraqi Art*, London: Saqi Books.

Malkki, L. (1995) "Refugees and Exile: From Refugee Studies to the National Order of Things," *Annual Review of Anthropology*, (24): 495–523.

Mallat, C. (1988) "Religious Militancy in contemporary Iraq: Muhammad Baqer as-Sadr and the Sunni-Shia paradigm," *Third World Quarterly*, (10), 2: 699–729.

———— (1993) *The Renewal of Islamic Law: Muhammad Baqer as-Sadr, Najaf and the Shi'i International*, New York: Cambridge University Press.

Mallowan, M. (1959) *Twenty-Five Years of Mesopotamian Discovery, 1932–56*, London: British School of Archaeology in Iraq.

Marfleet, P. (2007) "Iraq's Refugees: 'Exit' from the State," *International Journal of Contemporary Iraqi Studies*, (1), 3: 397–419.

Marashi, I. al-, and Keskin, A. (2008) "Reconciliation Dilemmas in Post-Ba'athist Iraq: Truth Commissions, Media and Ethno-sectarian Conflicts," *Mediterranean Politics* (13), 2: 243–59.

Marr, P. (2004) *The Modern History of Iraq*, 2nd edn., Boulder: Westview.

Marrou, H.-I. (1954) *De la connaissance historique*, Paris: Seuil.

Masliyah, S. (1996) "Zahawi: A Muslim Pioneer of Women's Liberation," *Middle Eastern Studies*, (32), 3: 161–7.

Matlub, A. (1968) *al-Naqd al-adabi al-hadith fi'l-'Iraq*, [Contemporary literary criticism in Iraq] Cairo: Ma'had al-Buhuth wa'l- Dirasat al-'Arabiyya.

Matthews, R. (2003) *Archaeology of Mesopotamia: Theory and Practice*, London: Routledge.

Matthews, R. D. and Akrawi, M. (1949) *Education in Arab Countries of the Near East*, Washington, D.C.: American Council on Education.

Meerawdeli, K. (1988) "Halabja and the Days After," *Serdema Nû*, (3): 8–11.

Mehmud, 'E. K. (1993) *Unknown Destiny. Some Scenes from the Anfal*, in 'E. Kerîm Mehmud (2003) *Reşeba-î jehr-u Enfal. [The Storm of Poison and Anfal]* Volume II, Erbil/Sulaimaniya: Ministry of Culture.

———— (2002) *Reşeba-î jehr-u Enfal*. Volume I, Erbil/Sulaimaniya: Ministry of Culture.

———— (2003) *Reşeba-î jehr-u Enfal*. Volume II, Erbil/Sulaimaniya: Ministry of Culture.

———— (2007) "Enfal-u Hel'ebce, sêyemîn tawan-î cînosayd-î le cîhan-da [Anfal and Halabja, the third genocide in the world]," *Heştawheşt*, (7–8): 40–8.

Mehmud, 'O. (2007) "Kiçe enfalkrawekanman le Misr natwanin bibine semakar", [The girls of the Anfal in Egypt cannot dance] *Heştawheşt*, (7–8): 49–64.

Mela Şaxî (2001) *Enfal-î Xal'xalan* [The Anfal of Xal'xalan], Sulaimaniya: Danaz.

Méouchy, N. (ed.) (2002) *France, Syrie et Liban, 1918–46. Les ambiguïtés et les dynamiques de la relation mandataire*, Damas: IFEAD.

Méouchy N. and Sluglett P. (eds.) (2004) *The British and French Mandates in Comparative Perspectives/Les mandats français et britannique dans une perspective comparative*, Leiden: Brill.

Merk, U. (2006) "Jenseits der Wahrheitskommission auf der Suche nach Formen der Bewältigung von Gewalterfahrungen in Südafrika," [Beyond the Truth Commission: In search of ways of coping with violence in South Africa] *Zeitschrift für Politische Psychologie*, (14), 1-2: 49–64.

Mervin, S. (2001) "The Clerics of Jabal 'Amil and the Reform of Religious Teaching in Najaf Since the Beginning of the Twentieth Century," in R. Brunner and W. Ende (eds.) *The Twelver Shia in Modern Times*, Leiden: Brill.

Merza, A. (2007) 'Iraq: Reconstruction under uncertainty', *International Journal of Contemporary Iraqi Studies* (1), 2: 173–212.

———— (2008) *Political, Economic and Social Trends in Iraq: 2003–7*, paper presented to the International Association of Contemporary Iraqi Studies, 3rd Annual Conference 16-17 July, University of London: SOAS.

Méténier, E. (2006) "L'historiographie irakienne contemporaine est-elle réductible à un simple discours idéologique?," in G. D. Khoury and N. Méouchy (eds.) *Etats et sociétés de l'Orient arabe en quête d'avenir, 1945–2005*, Vol. I, Paris: Geuthner.

Meyer, J. E. (1981) "Über das Trauern um Vermißte. Eine Befragung von Ehefrauen, Kindern und Geschwistern," [Mourning for the disappeared; questions for wives, children and siblings] *Archiv für Psychiatrie und Nervenkrankheiten*, (230): 91–101.

———— (1994) "Trauerreaktionen," [Ways of mourning] in G. Rudolf and N. Leygraf (eds.) *Psychiatrie heute. Aspekte und Perspektiven*. Festschrift zum 60. Geburtstag von Reinhard Toelle. Munich: Urban und Schwarzenberg.

Middle East Watch (1993) *Genocide in Iraq, the Anfal Campaign Against Kurds*, New York, Los Angeles and London: Middle East Watch.

———— (1994) *Bureaucracy of Repression. The Iraqi Government in its Own Words*, Washington, New York: Middle East Watch.

———— (2000) *'Iraq-u tawan-î cînosayd. Şal'aw-î Enfal dijî kurd.* [Iraq and the Anfal campaigns against the Kurds]; trans. Jemal Mirza 'Ezîz, Berlin: Havîbun.

Middle East Watch and Physicians For Human Rights (1993) *The Anfal Campaign in Iraqi Kurdistan. The Destruction of Koreme*. New York: Human Rights Watch.

Migdal, J. S. (2001) *State in Society. Studying How States and Societies Transform and Constitute One Another*, Cambridge: Cambridge University Press.

Mihemmed, O. E. (1999) *Tirs le Islam le nêwan wehm-u rastî-da* [The fear of Islam; between madness and reality], Sulaimaniya: Islamic Union in Kurdistan-Iraq.

Milam, A. (1952) *Report to the Government of Iraq on Home Economics*, Rome: Food and Agriculture Organization of the United Nations, FAO Report No. 48.

Milam Clark, A. (1969) *Adventures of a Home Economist*, Corvallis: Oregon State University Press.

Millet, C. (2006) *L'art contemporain, Histoire et géographie*, Paris: Flammarion.

Ministry of Education (1952) "Manahij al-funun al-baytiyya", [The Home Economics Curriculum] *al-Mu'allim al-Jadid*, (15), 5: 434.

Ministry of Human Rights, Refugees and Anfal (2002) "The Crime of the Iraqi Regime against the Kurdish People that comes under the Category of Genocide," *Anfal*, (2): 2–5.

Mitchell, T. (1991) "The Limits of the State: Beyond Statist Approaches and their Critics," *American Political Science Review*, (85), 1: 77–96.

Mitchell, W. J. T. (ed.) (1981) *On Narrative*, Chicago and London: University of Chicago Press.

Mizrahi, J-D. (2003) *Genèse de l'Etat mandataire. Service des Renseignements et bandes armées en Syrie et au Liban dans les années 1920*, Paris: Publications de la Sorbonne.

Mlodoch, K. (2000) "Mit Anfal ist auch unser Leben verschwunden. Zur psychosozialen Situation Anfal überlebender Frauen in Kurdistan-Irak," [Our lives came to an end with the Anfal: On the psycho-social situation of women survivors of the Anfal] unpublished diploma dissertation, Berlin, Freie Universität.

―――― (2003) "Lange Schatten der Vergangenheit," [The long shadows of the past] *AI-Journal*, 3. Bonn: Amnesty International.

―――― (2006) "Iraq: The situation of *Anfal* women in the Germyan area and key experiences of the Counseling Centre for Victims of Political Violence in Tuz Khurmatu," paper presented at the Conference: "Trauma, Stigma and Distinction: Social Ambivalences in the Face of Extreme Suffering," St Moritz, Switzerland.

―――― (2009) *Iraq: The Situation of Anfal Surviving Women and Key Experiences of the Counselling Centre for Victims of Political Violence in Tuz Khurmatu*, revised edition of a paper presented at the 3rd International Trauma Research Net Conference 'Trauma, Stigma and Distinction. Social Ambivalences in the Face of Extreme Suffering', St. Moritz Switzerland, September 2006.

Monroe, P. (ed.) (1932) *Report of the Educational Inquiry Commission*, Baghdad: Government Press.

Monsutti, A. (2005) *War and Migration, Social Networks and Economic Strategies of the Hazaras of Afghanistan*, London: Routledge.

Morad, T., Shasha, D. and Shasha, R. (eds.) (2008) *Iraq's Last Jews, Stories of Daily Life, Upheaval, and Escape from Modern Babylon*, New York: Palgrave Macmillan.

Moreh, S. (1991) "Ma'ruf al-Rusafi," *Encyclopedia Islamica*, vol. VI, Leiden, 614–17.

Mozany, H. al- (2010) "The Last Trip to Baghdad," *Banipal*, (37): 6–19.

Mosquero, G. (2003) "Alien-Own/Own-Alien, Notes on Globalisation and Cultural Difference," in N. Papastergiadis (ed.) *Complex Entanglements, Art, Globalisation and Cultural Difference*, London/Sydney/Chicago: Rivers Oram Press.

Mu'min, A. al- (2004) *Sanawat al-Jamr: masirat al-haraka al-islamiyya fi'l-'Iraq, 1957–86*, [The years of burning coals; the experience of the Islamic movement in Iraq, 1957–86] Beirut: Markaz al-Islami al-Mu'asir.

Munazamat al-'Amal al-Islami (1991) *al-Intifada al-sha'biyyah fi'l-'Iraq: al-Asbab w'al-nata'ij wa mustaqbaluha bi nadhar Ayatullah al-Sayyid Muhammad Taqi al-Din al-Mudarrisi,* [The popular uprising in Iraq: Its causes, consequences and future in the view of Ayatullah al-Sayyid Muhammad Taqi al-Din al-Mudarrisi] Beirut: Dar al-Wifaq.

Munthe, T. (ed.) (2002) *The Saddam Hussein Reader, Selections from Leading Writers on Iraq,* New York.

Mupinda, M. (1995) "Loss and Grief among the Shona: The meaning of disappearances," paper presented at the VIIth International Symposium on Torture as a Challenge to the Medical Profession, Cape Town.

Muruwwa, H. (1937) "Kalima sariha ila maqam al-za'im al-muslih al-kabir al-imam Kashif al-Ghita," [The frank words of his Holiness Imam Kashif al Ghita'] *al-Hatif,* (64): 4–5.

———— (1984) "Min al-Najaf dakhala hayati Marx," [In Najaf, Marx Entered my Life] *al-Tariq* (June): 172–83.

Musa, S. (1956) *al-Adab li'l-sha'b,* [Culture for the People] Cairo: Salama Musa.

Musawi, M. J. al- (2006) *Reading Iraq. Culture and Power in Conflict,* London and New York: I.B. Tauris.

Mushtaq, T. (1989) *Awraq ayyami, Baghdad wa'l-'Iraq wa'l-watan al-'arabi 1900-1958,* [Pages of my life: Baghdad and the Arab homeland] Baghdad: Dar al-Tali'a li'l-Tiba'a wa'l-Nashr.

Nadhmi, W. J. O. al- (1985) *Thawrat 1920 — al-judhur al-siyasiya wa'l-fikriya wa'l-ijtima'iya li'l-haraka al-qawmiya al-'arabiya al-istiqlaliya fi'l-'Iraq,* [The Revolution of 1920; the political, philosophical, and social roots of the Arab national independence movement in Iraq] Baghdad: al-Maktaba al-'Alamiya.

Naef, S. (1996) "Un reformist chiite — Muhammad Husayn Āl Kashif al-Ghita," *Die Welt des Orients,* (26): 51–86.

———— (1996) *A la recherche d'une modernité arabe, L'évolution des arts plastiques en Egypte, au Liban et en Irak,* Geneva: Slatkine.

———— (2001) "*Shi'i/shuyu'i* or How to Become a Communist in Najaf," in R. Brunner and W. Ende (eds.) *The Twelver Shia in Modern Times: Religious Culture and Political Culture,* Leiden: Brill.

—— (forthcoming) "'Hidden Treasures'? Museum Collections of Modern Art from the Arab World," in I. Maffi and R. Daher (eds.) *Practices of Patrimonialization in the Arab World: 'Positioning the Material Past in Contemporary Societies,* London: I.B. Tauris.

Nafi, B. M. (1996) "The General Islamic Congress of Jerusalem Reconsidered," *The Muslim World,* (86), 3–4: 243–72.

Nakash, Y. (1994, 1996, 2nd edn., 2003) *The Shi'is of Iraq,* Princeton NJ: Princeton University Press.

———— (2006) *Reaching for Power: The Shi'a in the Modern Arab World,* Princeton NJ: Princeton University Press.

Nasr, V. (2006) *The Shia Revival: How Conflicts Within Islam Will Shape the Future,* New York and London: Norton.

Neale, S. (2006) "War Films," in J. D. Slocum (ed.) *Hollywood and War. The Film Reader,* New York: Routledge.

Neocleous, M. (1996) *Administering Civil Society. Towards a Theory of State Power,* London: Macmillan.

Newman, A. J. (2006) *Safavid Iran: Rebirth of a Persian Empire,* London, I. B. Tauris.

Niblock, T. (1993) "International and Domestic Factors in the Economic Liberalisation Process in Arab Countries," in T. Niblock and E. Murphy (eds.) *Economic and Political Liberalisation in the Middle East*, London: Tauris.

—— (1998) "Democratisation: A Theoretical and Practical Debate", *British Journal of Middle Eastern Studies* (25), 2: 221–33.

Nichols, B. (1991) *Representing Reality*, Bloomington and Indianapolis: Indiana University Press.

Noakes, J. (2004) "Leaders of the People? The Nazi Party and German Society," *Journal of Contemporary History*, (39), 2: 189–212.

Noorani, Y. (1999) "The Lost Garden of al-Andalus: Islamic Spain and the Poetic Inversion of Colonialism," *International Journal of Middle East Studies*, (31): 237–54.

Nora, P. (1996) "General Introduction: Between Memory and History," in P. Nora and L. Kritzman (eds.) *Realms of memory: Rethinking the French Past*, New York: Columbia University Press.

Norton, A. R. (1994) "Musa al-Sadr," in 'A. Rahnama (ed.) *Pioneers of Islamic Revival*, London: Zed Books.

—— (ed.) (1995) *Civil Society in the Middle East*, Leiden: Brill.

Nowicka, M. and Rovisco, M. (eds.) (2009) *Cosmopolitanism in practice*, Surrey, UK and Burlington VT: Ashgate.

O'Leary, B., McGarry, J. and Salih K. (eds.) (2005) *The future of Kurdistan in Iraq*, Philadelphia: University of Pennsylvania Press.

'Omer, 'E. (Salih, 'E. O.) (2002) "Prose-î Enfal-u karîgerîyekanî leser bar-î komel'ayetî-î afret-î kurd-da [The Anfal process and its impact of the social situation of women]," *Hawar-î Enfal*, (1): 51–60.

Ofteringer, R. (1999) *al-Anfal — schrankenlose staatliche Gewalt und ihre Legitimierung durch Verweise auf das islamische Kriegsrecht im Irak der 80er Jahre*, [al-Anfal: unfettered state violence and its legitimation with reference to the Islamic law of war in 1980s Iraq] M.A. thesis, Berlin, Freie Universität.

—— (2003) "Edward Saids Kontroverse mit Kanan Makiya," [Edward Said's debate with Kanan Makiya] *inamo*, (9), 36: 50–3.

Ortoleva, P. (1984) "Presentazione," [Presentations] in P. Sorlin (ed.) *La storia nei film. Interpretazioni del passato*, [History in film; interpretations of the past] Florence: La Nuova Italia.

Özden, Ç. and Schiff, M. (eds.) (2006) *International Migration, Remittances & The Brain Drain*, Washington DC: World Bank and Palgrave McMillan.

Packer, G. (2005) *The Assassins' Gate*, New York: Farrar, Straus and Giroux.

Pandey, G. (1989) "The Colonial Construction of Communalism," in R. Guha (ed.) *Subaltern Studies* VI, Oxford: Oxford University Press.

Papastergiadis, N. (2003) (ed.) *Complex Entanglements, Art, Globalisation and Cultural Difference*, London/Sydney/Chicago: Rivers Oram Press.

Pawelka, P. (2000) "Politische Systeme im Vorderen Orient: Analysekonzepte und Forschungs-strategien," [Political systems in the Middle East: Concepts of analysis and strategies for research] *Orient* (41), 3: 389–413.

Paxton, R. O. (2006) *The Anatomy of Fascism*, London and New York: Penguin.

Pellat, C. (1993) "al-Mirbad," in *Encyclopedia Islamica*, VII, Leiden, 113f.

Pett, I. (2002) *Annäherungen an den "Rest der Welt," Probleme und Strategien im Umgang mit "fremder" zeitgenössischer Kunst*, [Getting closer to the rest of the world: Problems and possibilities in the discussion of 'foreign' contemporary art] Münster/Hamburg/London: LIT.

Pflitsch, A. (2004) "Das Ende der Illusionen zur arabischen Postmoderne," [The end of illusions about the Arab post-modern] in A. Neuwirth, A. Pflitsch and B. Winckler (eds.) *Arabische Literatur, postmodern*, Munich: edition text + kritik.

Pflitsch, A. and Winckler, B. (eds.) (2006) *Poetry's Voice. Society's Norms*, Wiesbaden: Reichert Verlag.

Phillips, D. L. (2005) *Losing Iraq. Inside the Postwar Reconstruction Fiasco*, Boulder, CO: Westview.

Picard, E. (ed.) (1991) *La question kurde*, Bruxelles: Complexe.

Pingel, F. (2008) "Can Truth Be Negotiated? History Textbook Revision as a Means to Reconciliation," *Annals of the American Academy of Political and Social Science*, (617): 181–98.

Pithon, R. (1995) "Cinéma et histoire: bilan historiographique," *Vingtième siècle. Revue d'histoire*, (46): 5–14.

Plummer, K. (2001) *Documents of life 2*, London: Sage.

Polk, M. and Schuster, A. (eds.) (2005) *The Looting of the Iraq Museum, Baghdad*, New York: Harry N. Abrams.

Popkewitz, T. S. (ed.) (2005) *Inventing the Modern Self and John Dewey: Modernities and the Traveling of Pragmatism in Education*, New York: Palgrave Macmillan.

Post, J. M. and Baram, A. (2003) "'Saddam is Iraq: Iraq is Saddam' (Until Operation Iraqi Freedom)," in B. Schneider and J. M. Post (eds.) *Know Thy Enemy: Profiles of Adversary Leaders and Their Strategic Cultures*, 2nd edn, Maxwell Airforce Base, Alabama: USAF Counter-proliferation Center.

Postone, M. and Santner, E. (eds.) (2003) *Catastrophe and Meaning: The Holocaust and the Twentieth Century*, Chicago: University of Chicago Press.

Posusney, M. P. and Angrist, M. P. (eds.) (2005) *Authoritarianism in the Middle East: Regimes and Resistances*, Boulder and London: Lynne Rienner.

Poznanski, K. Z. (1992) *Constructing Capitalism. The Reemergence of Civil Society and Liberal Economy in the Post-Communist World*, Boulder: Westview Press.

Pratt, N. (2007) *Democracy and Authoritarianism in the Arab World*, Boulder and London: Lynne Rienner.

Preitler, B. (2006) *Ohne jede Spur: psychotherapeutische Arbeit mit Angehörigen 'verschwundener Personen,'* [Without a trace: the practice of psychotherapy with relatives of the 'disappeared'] Gießen: Psychosozial-Verlag.

Provence, M. (2005) *The Great Syrian Revolt and the Rise of Arab Nationalism*, Austin: University of Texas Press.

Pyta, W. (2006) "Die Herausforderungen der neueren Holocaustforschung für die Totalitarismustheorie," [The challenges of new Holocaust research for theories of totalitarianism] *Zeitschrift für internationale Diktatur- und Freiheitsforschung*, 3(1): 141–56.

Qadir, H. 'O. (2007) *Yahud Kurdistan* [The Jews of Kurdistan], Erbil: Hemdî.

Qani'a, B. (1979) *Bincîne komalayetiyakan-î afret-î ladeyî nişn-î kurdewarî* [Social Aspects of Kurdish Rural Women], Baghdad: Irshad.

Qaradaghi, M. (1995) *Le Penaw-î jiyanewe-î afret* [To revive women], Stockholm: Nawroz.

Qaysi, M. (1984) *Youth Education in Iraq and Egypt 1920–80: A contribution to comparative education within the Arab region*, The Hague: Helicon.

Qaysi, N. al- (1979) *al-Adib w'al-iltizam*, [Commitment and the intellectual] Baghdad: Jam'ia Baghdād.

Qeredaxî, M. (2008) "Karesat-î Enfal-u karîgerîye derûnîyekan-î leser komel'ge-î kurd [The Anfal catastrophe and its psychological effects on Kurdish society]," paper presented at the "International Conference on the Genocide against the Kurdish People," Erbil, 26–8 January 2008.

Quemin, A. (2006) "Globalization and Mixing in the Visual Arts, An Empirical Survey of 'High Culture' and Globalization," *International Sociology*, (21), 4: 522–50.

Quirk, G. J. and Casco, L. (1994) "Stress disorders of families of the disappeared: A controlled study in Honduras," *Social Sciences and Medicine*, (39), 12: 1675–9.

Qurbani, 'A. (2002) *Şayethal'ekan-î Enfal*. Volume I, Sulaimaniya: Asa.

––––––– (2007) *Şayethal'ekan-î Enfal*, Volume IV. Sulaimaniya: Asa.

Rachid, L. al- and E. Méténier (2007) "À propos de la violence irakienne. Quelques éléments de réflexion sur un lieu commun," *A contrario*, (2), 5: 114–33.

Radi, N. al- (2003) *Baghdad Diaries 1991–2002*, London: Saqi Books.

Rabinow, P. (ed.) (1984) *The Foucault Reader*, New York: Pantheon Books.

Rahe, J.-U. (2005) 'La déportation des chiites en Irak' in C. Kutschera (ed.) (2005) *Le livre noir de Saddam Hussein*, Paris: *Oh!* Editions.

Ramesh, R. (ed.) (2003) *The War We Could Not Stop. The Real Story of the Battle for Iraq*, London: Guardian Newspapers Ltd.

Ramírez, M. C. (2004) "A Highly Topical Utopia. Some Outstanding Features of the Avant-Garde in Latin America," in M. C. Ramírez and H. Olea *Inverted Utopias, Avant-Garde Art in Latin America*, New Haven and London: Yale University Press and The Museum of Fine Arts (Houston).

Rancière, J. (1998) "L'historicité du cinéma," A. de Baecque and C. Delage (eds.) *De l'histoire au cinéma*, Bruxells: Complexe.

Raphaeli, N. (2004) "The De-Ba'thification of Iraq — Pros and Cons," *Inquiry and Analysis Series* (The Middle East Media and Research Institute),no. 176.

Rauchfuss, K. (2006) "Gerechtigkeit heilt. Zur Bedeutung des Kampfes gegen Straflosigkeit für die Stabilisierungsprognose bei Überlebenden schwerer Menschenrechtsverletzungen," [Justice heals; on the significance of the struggle against giving amnesty for positive outcomes for survivors of serious human rights abuses] *Zeitschrift für Politische Psychologie*, (14), 1–2: 65–94.

Ra'uf, A. (2000) *al-'Amal al-Islami fi'l-'Iraq, bayna al-Marja'iyya w'al-Hizbiyya: qira'a naqdiyya li masira nisf qarn (1950–2000)*, [Islamic political activism in Iraq between party membership and the *marja'iyya*; a critical view of activity over half a century (1950–2000)] Damascus: al-Markaz al-'Iraqi li'l-I'lan wa'l-Dirasa.

Rayhani, A. al- (1935) *Qalb al-'Iraq; kitab siyaha wa-siyasa wa-adab wa-tarikh*, [The Heart of Iraq: Travel, Politics, Literature and History] Beirut: Matba'at Sadir.

Rawi, N. (1948) "Kalima tawjihiyya [Guiding remarks]," *al-Mu'allim al-Jadid*, (12), 1: 3–4.

Rêbaz (1989/1990) *Şe-î partisan le Kurdistan-da* [Partisan Struggle in Kurdistan], Patriotic Union of Kurdistan.

Reid, D. M. (2002) *Whose Pharaohs? Archaeology, Museums, and Egyptian National Identity from Napoleon to World War I*, Berkeley: University of California Press.

REMMM (2007) "Iraq en perspective," Special issue, No. 117–8.

Renan, E. (1882) *Qu'est-ce qu'une nation? Conference faite en Sorbonne le 11 mars 1882*, Paris: C. Lévy.

Resool, S. H. (2002) "The *Anfal* Campaign and the Kurds in Iraq," *Anfal*, (2): 17–22.

Resûl, Ş. (2002) "Hel'weşandin-î xêzan-î kurd le nêwan desel'at-î Be's-u maf-î mirov [The disintegration of the Kurdish family between Ba'thist rule and human rights]," *Hawar-î Enfal*, (1): 28–50.

Richards, A. (1993) "Economic Imperatives and Political Systems," *Middle East Journal*, (47), 2: 217–27.

Ricks, T. E. (2006) *Fiasco. The American Military Adventure in Iraq*, New York: Penguin Books.

Ricoeur, P. (1998) "Histoire et mémoire," in A. de Baecque, C. Delage (eds.) *De l'histoire au cinéma*, Paris: Editions Complexe.

Rieck, A. (ed. and trans.) (1984) *"Unsere Wirtschaft." Eine gekürzte kommentierte Ubersetzung des Buches 'Iqtisaduna' von Muhammad Baqir as-Sadr*, ['Our Economic System'; an annotated and abridged translation of *Iqtisaduna* by Muhammad Baqir al-Sadr] Berlin: Klaus Schwarz.

Rigaud, F. (2003) "Irak: l'impossible mouvement de l'intérieur?," in M. Bennani-Chraïbi, and O. Fillieule (eds.) *Résistances et protestations dans les sociétés musulmanes*, Paris: Presses de Sciences Po.

Robin, R. (1986) "Récit de vie, discours social et parole vraie," *Vingtième siècle*, (10): 103–10.

Rohde, A. (2003) "Von Kaisers Kleider: Wechselfälle des Nationalismus im Irak," [The emperor's new clothes; the changing nature of nationalism in Iraq] in K. Hafez and B. Schäbler (eds.) *Der Irak, Land zwischen Krieg und Frieden*, Heidelberg: Palmyra.

―――― (2010) *State-Society Relations in Ba'thist Iraq: Facing Dictatorship*, London and New York: Routledge.

Romano, D. (2005) "Whose House is this Anyway? IDP and Refugee Return in Post-Saddam Iraq," *Journal of Refugee Studies*, (18), 4: 430–53.

―――― (2006) *The Kurdish Nationalist Movement. Opportunity, Mobilization and Identity*, Cambridge: Cambridge University Press.

Rosenstone, R. A. (1995) "Like writing history with lighting. Film historique/vérité historique," *Vingtième siècle. Revue d'histoire*, (46): 162–76.

Rossi, P. (1958) "La Culture Nouvelle, mouvement révolutionnaire des intellectuels irakiens," *L'Orient*, (2), 8: 61–5.

Rothfield, L. (ed.) (2008) *Antiquities under Siege: Cultural Heritage Protection after the Iraq war*, Lanham: AltaMira Press.

―――― (2009) *Rape of Mesopotamia: Behind the Looting of the Iraq Museum*, Chicago: University of Chicago Press.

Rousso, H. (1998) *La hantise du passé*, Paris: Ed. Textuel.

―――― (2009) "Les dilemmes d'une mémoire européenne," in C. Delacroix, F. Dosse, and P. Garcia (eds.) *Historicités*, Paris: La Découverte.

Roux, G. (1980) *Ancient Iraq*, New York: Penguin.

Russell, J. M. (1997) *From Nineveh to New York*, New Haven: Yale University Press.

―――― (2001) "Robbing the Archaeological Cradle," *Natural History*, (110), 1: 44–56.

Sabbagh, S. al- (1956) *Mudhakkirat al-shahid al-'aqid al-rukn Salah al-Din al-Sabbagh: Fursan al-'uruba fi'l-'Iraq*, [The memoirs of the Martyr Staff Colonel Salah al-Din al-Sabbagh; Knights of Arabism in Iraq] Damascus (2nd edn., Baghdad: Dar al-Hurriya li'l-Tiba'a, 1983).

Sa'di, A. al-, and Abu Lughod, L. (2007) *Nakba, Palestine, 1948 and the Claims of Memory*, New York: Columbia University Press.

Sadr, M. Baqir al- (1961) *Iqtisaduna*, [Our economic system] 2 volumes, Najaf: Matba'at al-Nu'man.

―――― (1982a) *Introduction to the Islamic Political System*, Karachi: Islamic Seminary. Contains translated excerpts from *Manabi' al-qudra fi al-dawla al-islamiyya* [Sources of power in the Islamic state] (Beirut: Dar al-Ta'arif li'l-Matbu'at, 1979) and *Lamha tamhidiyya 'an mashru' dustur al-jumhuriyyat al-islamiyya* [A glimpse of the project of the Islamic Republic] (Beirut: Dar al-Ta'ruf li'l-Matbu'at, 1979).

———— (1982b) *Risalatuna,* [Our Message] 2nd edn, Tehran: Maktaba al-Naja.

Safar, F. (1974) *al-Hadar, madinat al-shams,* [al-Hadar, Sun City] Baghdad: Wizarat al-I'lam, Mudiriyat al-Athar al-?Ammah.

Saghieh, H. (2007) "The Life and Death of De-Baathification," *REMMM,* (117–18): 203–23.

Sa'id, A. (1949) "al-Ta'lim al-niswi [Female Education]," *al-Mu'allim al-Jadid,* (12), 5–6: 473–6.

Said, E. W. (1991) "The Intellectuals and the War," *MERIP Reports,* (171): 15–20.

———— (1996) *Representations of the Intellectual: The 1993 Reith Lectures,* New York: Vintage Books.

———— (2000) "Reflections on exile," in E.W. Said (ed.) *Reflections on exile and other essays,* Cambridge Massachusetts: Harvard University Press.

Sa'id, S. H. al- (1983, 1988) *Fusul min ta'rikh al-haraka al-tashkiliyya fi'l-'Iraq,* [Chapters from the History of Formalism in Iraq] vol. I, Baghdad: Wizarat al-Thaqafa wa'l-I'lam; vol. II, Baghdad: Dar al-shu'un al-thaqafiyya al-'amma.

SAIRI (1983) *al-Muntalaqat wa'l-Ahdaf,* [Initiatives and objectives] Tehran: SAIRI (Maktab al-Natiq al-Rasmi).

———— (1994/5) *Maktab Shu'un al-Muballighin wa Shu'un al-Jamahir,* [The office of the preachers and the masses] Qum: SAIRI (Maktab Shu'un al-Muballighin).

Sakai, K. (2001) "Modernity and Tradition in the Islamic Movements of Iraq: Continuity and Discontinuity in the Role of the *'Ulama' ",* *Arab Studies Quarterly,* (23), 1: 37–53.

Sakai, K. (2003) "Tribalisation as a tool of state control in Iraq: Observations on the Army, the Cabinets and the National Assembly," in F.A Jabar and H. Dawod (eds.) *Tribes and Power. Nationalism and Ethnicity in the Middle East,* London: al-Saqi.

Saleh, T. A. al- (2001) "Baghdad's Regime and the Legislative Process," *al-Huquqi* (1), 4: 5–49.

Salih, 'E. (Omer, 'E.) (2008) "Şal'aw-î Enfal-u karîger-î leser bar-î abûrî-u derûn-î-u komel'ayetî-î afret-î becêmaw-î Enfal [The Anfal campaigns and their impact on the economic, mental and social situation of Anfal women]," paper presented at the "International Conference on the Genocide against the Kurdish People," Erbil, 26–8 January 2008.

Salih, K. (1995) "Anfal: The Kurdish Genocide in Iraq," *Digest of Middle East Studies,* (4), 2: 24–39.

———— (1996) *State-Making, Nation-Building and the Military. Iraq 1941–58,* Göteborg: Göteborg University.

———— (2002) "Anfal. The Kurdish Genocide in Iraq," *Anfal,* (2): 30–41.

Salih, M. (2005) "Ibadat al-kurd fi watha'iq hizb al-Ba'th [The extermination of the Kurds in the documents of the Ba'th Party]," *al-Anfal,* (7): 77–93.

Salim, N. (1977) *Iraq Contemporary Art, vol. I, Painting,* Lausanne: Sartec.

Salim, S. M. (1962) *Marsh Dwellers of the Euphrates Delta,* London: Athlone Press.

Salim, Y. al- (1986) *al-Duktura Su'ad al-Sabah al-ittijah al-qawimi fi-shi'riha,* [Dr Su'ad al-Sabah; Arab Nationalism in her Poetry] Baghdad: Matba'at al-Diwani.

Sande, H. (2000) "The Supreme Council for the Islamic Revolution in Iraq: background, organisation and development, 1982–95," unpublished thesis, University of Bergen.

Sartre, J. P. (1988) *What is Literature? and Other Essays,* Cambridge, Mass: Harvard University Press.

Sassoon, J. (2008) *The Iraqi Refugees: The New Crisis in the Middle East*, London: I. B. Tauris.

Sayigh, R. (2007) "Women's Nakba stories: Between being and knowing," in A. al-Sa'di and L. Abu Lughod (eds.) *Nakba, Palestine, 1948 and the Claims of Memory*, New York: Columbia University Press.

Sayyid, M. A. al- (1978) *al-A'mal al-kamila li Mahmud Ahmad al-Sayyid*, [The Complete Works of Mahmud Ahmad al-Sayyid] Baghdad: Dar al-Hurriyya.

Schaebler, B. (1999) "Coming to Terms with Failed Revolutions: Historiography in Syria, Germany and France," *Middle Eastern Studies* (35), 1: 17–44.

Schaller, D. J. *et al.* (eds.) (2004) *Enteignet — Vertrieben — Ermordet. Beiträge zur Genozidforschung*, [Dispossessed — Expelled — Murdered. Papers on Genocide research] Zürich: Chronos Verlag.

Schmucker, W. (1987) "Iranische Märtyrertestamente", [Testamentary Statements of Iranian Martyrs] *Die Welt des Islams*, (27), 4: 185–249.

Schulze, R. (2000) *A Modern History of the Islamic World*, New York: New York University Press.

Scurati, A. (2007) *Guerra. Narrazioni e culture nella tradizione occidentale*, [War, narration and culture in the western tradition] 2nd edn, Milan: Donzelli.

Semah, D. (1974) *Four Egyptian Literary Critics*, Leiden: Brill.

Serdema Nû (1988) "The Kurdish Hiroshima & the United Nation," *Serdema Nû*, (3): 12–13.

Seurel, R. (2005) "L'art comme survie," in Bagdad-Paris *Artistes d'Irak, Musée du Montparnasse, 23 Novembre 2005–15 janvier 2006*, Paris: Musée du Montparnasse.

Shabibi, S. al- (2002) "An Economic Agenda For a Future Iraq", *Studies on the Iraqi Economy*, Iraqi Economic Forum: 24–5.

Shabout, N. (2006) "The Forgotten Era: Modern and Contemporary Iraqi Art," in J. Dakhlia (ed.) *Créations artistiques contemporaines en pays d'Islam; des arts en tensions.* Paris: Kimé.

—— (2007) *Modern Arab Art*, Gainesville: University of Florida Press.

Shafik, V. (2007) *Arab Cinema: History and Cultural Identity*, Cairo: American University in Cairo Press.

Shahir, S. 'A. al- (1978) "On the Role of the Party in Iraqi Literature," *al-Thaqafa al-Jadida*, (103): 96–101.

Shain, Y. (2005) *The Frontier of Loyalty: political exiles in the age of the nation-state*, Ann Arbor: The University of Michigan Press.

Shakir, N. (1986) *A la recherche du cinéma irakien, 1945–85*, Paris: L'Harmattan.

Shami, S. (1996) "Transnationalism and Refugee Studies: Rethinking Forced Migration and Identity in the Middle East," *Journal of Refugee Studies*, (9), 1: 3–26.

Shams al-Din, M. M. (1955) *Nizam al-hukm wa idara fi'-Islam*, [The system of governance and administration in Islam] Beirut: Dar Hamd.

Sharaf al-Din (al-Musawi), 'A. (2001) *al-Muraja'at: A Shi'i Sunni Dialogue*. Qum: Ansariyan Publications (First published in Arabic in 1936).

Sharaf al-Din, H. (1996) *al-Imam al-sayyid Musa al-Sadr: mahatat tarikhiyya Iran, al-Najaf, Lubnan*, [Imam Musa Sadr: his life in Iran, Najaf and Lebanon] Beirut: Markaz al-Imam Sadr.

Sharara, H. (2000) *Idha al-Ayyam Aghsaqat*, [When the days dawn] Beirut: al-Mu'assasa al-'Arabiyya li'l-Dirasat wa'l-Nashr.

Shawkat, S. (1939) *Hadhihi ahdafuna*, [These are our aims], Baghdad: Majjalat al-Mu'allim al-Jadid.

Shiblak, A. (1986) *The Lure of Zion: The Case of the Iraqi Jews,* London: Saqi Books.

Shils, E. (1958–9) "The Intellectual and the Powers: Some perspectives for Comparative Analysis," *Comparative Studies in Society and History,* (1): 5–22.

Shoeb, M., Weinstein, H., and Halpern, J. (2007) "Living in Religious Time and Space: Iraqi Refugees in Dearborn, Michigan," *Journal of Refugee Studies,* (20), 3: 441–60.

Short, K.R.M. (1981) *Feature Films as History,* London: Croom Helm.

Sifry, M. L. and Cerf, C. (eds.) (1991) *The Gulf War Reader. History, Documents, Opinions,* New York and Toronto: Times Books.

———— (eds.) (2003) *The Iraq War Reader. History, Documents, Opinions,* New York: Touchstone.

Silêman, T. (1999) *Le perawêz-î Enfal-da* [On the edge of the Anfal], Sulaimaniya: Asa.

Simon, R. (1997) "The Imposition of Nationalism on a Non-Nation-State: The Case of Iraq During the Interwar Period, 1921–41," in J. Jankowski and I. Gershoni (eds.) *Rethinking Nationalism in the Arab Middle East,* New York: Columbia University Press.

———— (2004) *Iraq Between the two World Wars. The Militarist Origins of Tyranny,* New York: Columbia University Press.

Sistani, A. al- (1998) *Fiqh al-Mughtaribin,* [Islamic Jurisprudence for Immigrants] London: Mu'assasat al-Imam Ali.

—— (2000a) *Rules Relating to the Deceased: Philosophy and Aḥkām.* Trans. Saleem Bhimji, Kitchener, Ontario: Islamic Humanitarian Service.

—— (2000b) *Fiqh al-Hadarah,* [Understanding Civilisation] Beirut: Dar al-Mu'arrikh al-'Arabī.

—— (2007) *al-Nuṣuṣ al-Ṣadirah 'an Samahat al-Sayyid al-Sistani fi'l-Masa'il al-'Iraqiyyah* [Texts issued by His Eminence Sayyid Sistani on Iraqi issues] Ed. Hamid al-Khafaf, Beirut: Dar al-Mu'arrikh al-'Arabi.

Şiwanî, R. (2002) "Zarawe-î Enfal-u Enfal-î kurd-u karîgerîyekan [The Anfal concept, the Anfalization of the Kurds and its effects]," *Hawar-î Enfal,* (1): 7–17.

Sluglett, P. (2004) "Les Mandats/The Mandates: Some Reflections on the Nature of the British Presence in Iraq and the French Presence in Syria," in N. Méouchy and P. Sluglett (eds.) *The British and French Mandates in Comparative Perspectives/Les mandats britanniques et français dans une perspective comparative,* Leiden: Brill.

———— (2004) "Introduction" to C. H. Bleaney and G. J. Roper (compilers) *Iraq: a Bibliographical Guide,* Leiden: Brill.

———— (2006) "The Blunder Books: Iraq Since Saddam," *Middle East Journal,* (60), 2: 361–8.

———— (2007) *Britain in Iraq. Contriving King and Country,* New York: Columbia University Press.

———— (2007a) "The Implications of Sectarianism in Iraq," *Journal of Middle Eastern Geopolitics,* (2), 10: 45–53.

———— (2010) "Iraq under Siege: Politics, Economy and Society, 1990–2003," in M. Lamani and B. Momani (eds.) *From Desolation to Reconstruction: Iraq's Troubled Journey,* Waterloo, ON: Wilfrid Laurier University Press.

———— (2011) "Hanna Batatu and the Historiography of Modern Iraq," in C. Toensing and M. Kirk (eds.) *Uncovering Iraq: Trajectories of Disintegration and Transformation,* Washington DC, Center for Contemporary Arab Studies: Georgetown University.

Sluglett, P. (compiler) (1983) *Theses on Islam, the Middle East and North-West Africa 1880–1978 accepted by Universities in the United Kingdom and Ireland,* London: Mansell.

Sluglett, P., Farouk-Sluglett, M. and Stork, J. (1984) "Not quite Armageddon: Impact of the war on Iraq," *MERIP Reports*, 125–6: 22–30.

Smith, P. (1976) *The Historian and Film*, Cambridge and London: Cambridge University Press.

Söllner, A. *et al.* (eds.) (1997) *Totalitarismus. Eine Ideengeschichte des 20. Jahrhunderts*, [Totalitarianism: a history of the idea in the twentieth century] Berlin: Akademie Verlag.

Sorlin, P. (1977) *Sociologie du cinéma: ouverture pour l'histoire de demain*; trans. L. S. Budini (1979) *Sociologia del cinema*, Milan: Garzanti.

—— (1980) *The Film in History. Restaging the Past*; trans. G. Gori (1984) *La storia nei film. Interpretazioni del passato*, Florence: La Nuova Italia.

Sousa, A. (1982) "The Eradication of Illiteracy in Iraq," in T. Niblock (ed.) *Iraq: The Contemporary State*, New York: St. Martin's Press.

Spivak, G. C. (1988) "Can The Subaltern Speak?" in C. Nelson and L. Grossberg, (eds.) *Marxism and the Interpretation of Culture*, Urbana: University of Illinois Press.

von Sponeck, H.C. (2006) *A different kind of war: The UN sanctions regime in Iraq*, Oxford: Berghahn Books.

Springborg, R. (1986) "Iraqi Infitah: Agrarian transformation and the growth of the private sector," *Middle East Journal*, 40(1): 33–52.

Stansfield, G. (2003) *Iraqi Kurdistan: Political Development and Emergent Democracy*, London: Routledge Curzon.

—— (2007) *Iraq. People, History, Politics*, Cambridge: Polity.

Steavenson, W. (2009) *The Weight of a Mustard Seed: The Intimate Story of an Iraqi General and his Family during Thirty Years of Tyranny*, London: Collins.

Steiner-Khamsi, G. (ed.) (2004) *The Global Politics of Educational Borrowing and Lending*, New York: Teachers College, Columbia University.

Stoler, A. L. (1995) *Race and the Education of Desire*, Durham, NC: Duke University Press.

Stone, P. G. and Bajjaly, J. F. (2008) *The Destruction of Cultural Heritage in Iraq*, Woodbridge, Suffolk : Boydell Press.

Stover, E., Sissons, M., Pham, P., *et al.* (2008) "Justice on hold: Accountability and social reconstruction in Iraq," *International Review of the Red Cross*, 90: 869.

Summerfield, D. (1997) "Das Hilfsbusiness mit dem Trauma," [The aid business and trauma] in Medico International (ed.) *medico report 20, Schnelle Eingreiftruppe 'Seele'*, Frankfurt/M.: Verlag medico international.

Takarli, Fu'ad al- (1980) *al-Raji' al-Ba'id*, [The Long Way Back] Beirut: Dar Ibn-Rushd.

—— (2001) *The Long Way Back*, translated by Catherine Cobham, Cairo and New York: American University in Cairo Press.

Takriti, S. 'A. al- (1990) *al-Asira raqm 93: Mudhakkirat Madiha al-Salman zawjat al-shahid Mahmud Salman*, [Prisoner No. 93; the Memoirs of Madiha al-Salman, wife of the Martyr Mahmud Salman] Baghdad.

Tamimi, J. al- (1991) *Mu'jam al-shu'ara' al-'iraqiyun*, [Encyclopedia of Iraqi Poets] Baghdad: Sharikat al-Ma'rifa.

Tamimi, K. al- (1996) *Muhammad Ja'far Abu'l-Timman: Dirasa fi al-Za'ama al-Siyasiya al-'Iraqiyya*, [Muhammad Ja'far Abu'l-Timman; a Study in Iraqi Political Leadership] Damascus: Dar al-Warraq.

Talabani, N. (1999) *Mintaqat Kirkuk wa muhawalat taghrir waqi'ataha al-qawmi* [The Region of Kirkuk and Attempts to Change its National Identity], (n.p.).

—— (2002) "Iraqi Regime's Crimes against Kurdish people enter into the concept of Genocide Crimes," *Anfal*, 2: 23–9.

Tamáss (2002) *Beirut Lebanon 1*, Barcelona: Fundació Antoni Tàpies.

—— (2004) *Contemporary Arab Representations: Cairo 2*, Barcelona/Rotterdam: Fundació Antoni Tàpies and Witte de With Center for Contemporary Art.

Tarrius, A. (2000) *Les Nouveaux Cosmopolitismes: mobilités, identités, territoires*, La Tour d'Aigues: Éditions de l'aube.

Tatchjian, V. (2004) *La France en Cilicie et en Haute-Mésopotamie. Aux confins de la Turquie, de la Syrie et de l'Irak*, Paris: Karthala.

Taylor, C. (2001) "Two Theories of Modernity," in D. P. Gaonkar (ed.) *Alternative Modernities*, Durham & London: Duke University Press.

Tejel, J. (2008) "Urban Mobilization in Iraqi Kurdistan during the British Mandate: Sulaimaniya 1918–30," *Middle Eastern Studies*, 44(4): 537–52.

Tibi, B. (1981) *Arab Nationalism: A Critical Enquiry*; trans. M. Farouk-Sluglett and P. Sluglett, New York: St. Martin's Press.

Tikriti, N. Al- (2005) "From Showcase to Basket Case. Education in Iraq," *ISIM*, 15: 25.

Todorov, T. (1995) *Les abus de la mémoire*, Paris: Arléa.

Tofiq, M. H. (Hama Tawfiq) (2002) "The Chronology of the Military Campaign of the Anfal," *Anfal*, 2: 6–16.

Tonkin, E. (1995) *Narrating Our Pasts: The Social Construction of Oral History*, Cambridge: Cambridge University Press.

Torpey, J. (1988) "Coming and Going: On the State Monopolization of the Legitimate 'Means of Movement'," *Sociological Theory*, 16(3): 239–59.

Torsti, P. (2007) "How to Deal with a Difficult Past? History Textbooks Supporting Enemy Images in Post-war Bosnia and Herzegovina," *Journal of Curriculum Studies*, 39(1): 77–96.

Toth, A. B. (2006) "Last Battles of the Bedouin and the Rise of the Modern State in Northern Arabia: 1850–1950," in D. Chatty, (ed.) *Nomadic societies in the Middle East and North Africa: entering the 21st century*, Leiden: Brill.

Trabulsi, F. (1994) "On Being Silent. A Response to Kanan Makiya," *Middle East Report* 24: 61–3.

Tramontini, L. (2002–3) " 'Fatherland, if ever I betrayed you...' Reflections on Nationalist Iraqi Poetry of *thawrat al-'ishrin*," *al-Abhath*, 50–1: 161–86.

—— (2006) " 'Wenn je dein Himmel mich einengte, o Vaterland...' Nationalistische Dichter im revolutionären Irak 1920," [If your skies should ever confine me, o Fatherland; nationalist poets in revolutionary Iraq, 1920] in A. Pflitsch and B. Winckler (eds). *Poetry's Voice — Society's Norms*, Wiesbaden: Reichert Verlag.

—— (forthcoming) "Poetry Post-Sayyab: Designing the truth in Iraqi war poetry of the 1980s", Beirut: AUB.

Trigger, B. (2006) *A History of Archaeological Thought*, Cambridge: Cambridge University Press.

Tripp, C. (2000) *A History of Iraq*, Cambridge: Cambridge University Press.

—— (2002) "The Iran–Iraq War and the Iraqi State," in T. Munthe (ed.) *The Saddam Hussein Reader, Selections from Leading Writers on Iraq*, New York: Basic Books.

—— (2007) *A History of Iraq*, 3rd edn, Cambridge: University Press.

Tripp, C. and Chubin, S. (1988) *Iran and Iraq at War*, Boulder: Westview Press.

Tully, S. R. (1995) "A painful purgatory: Grief and the Nicaraguan mothers of the disappeared," *Social Sciences and Medicine*, 40(12): 1597–1610.

United Nations Development Programme (2005) *Iraq Living Conditions Survey 2004*, Vol. II, Baghdad: Ministry of Planning and Development Cooperation.

United Nations Security Council (13 July 1988) "Report of the mission dispatched by the secretary-general on the situation of prisoners of war in the Islamic Republic of Iran and Iraq," S/20147.

van der Stoel, M. (1992) *Questions relatives aux Droits de l'Homme: Situations relatives aux Droits de l'Homme et rapport des rapporteurs et représentants spéciaux. Situation des droits de l'homme en Iraq, Rapport de M. Max van der Stoel*, Nations Unies, Assemblée générale, Distr. Générale, A/471367/Add.l.

Vanly, I. C. (1988) "Kurdistan im Irak," in G. Chaliand (ed.) *Kurdistan und die Kurden*. Vol. 1, Göttingen: Gesellschaft für bedrohte Völker.

_____ (2002) "The Forgotten Feili Kurds of Iraq," in M. Ahmed and M. Gunter (eds.) *Kurdish Exodus: From Internal Displacement to Diaspora*, Sharon, Mass: Ahmed Foundation for Kurdish Studies.

Vertovec, S. and Cohen, R. (eds.) (2003) *Conceiving Cosmopolitanism: Theory, Context and Practice*, Oxford: Oxford University Press.

Vincent, M-B. (2008) "Punir et rééduquer: le processus de dénazification (1945–9)," in M.-B. Vincent (ed.) *La dénazification*, Paris: Perrin.

Visser, R. (2005) *Basra, the Failed Gulf State: Separatism and Nationalism in Southern Iraq*, Münster: LIT Verlag.

_____ (2007) "Ethnicity, federalism and the idea of sectarian citizenship in Iraq: A Critique," *International Review of the Red Cross*, (89), 868: 801–22.

—— (2008) "The Western Imposition of Sectarianism on Iraqi Politics," *Arab Studies Journal*, (14–16) 1–2: 83–99.

_____ (2009) "Proto-political conceptions of 'Iraq' in late Ottoman times," *International Journal of Contemporary Iraqi Studies*, (3), 3: 143–54.

Volk, L. (2010) *Memorials and Martyrs in Modern Lebanon*, Bloomington and Indianapolis: Indiana University Press.

Wa'ili, I. al- (1968) *Thawrat al-'ishrīn fi'l-shi'r al-'iraqi*, [The Revolution of 1920 in Iraqi poetry] Baghdad: Matba'at al-Iman.

Wakil, F. H. al- (1980) *Jam'iyyat al-ahali fi'l-'iraq 1932–37*, [Popular associations in Iraq, 1932–37] Baghdad: al-Jumhuriyya al-'Iraqiyya, Wizarat al-Thaqafa wa'l-I'lam.

Walther, W. (1994) "Camil Sidqi az-Zahawi: Ein Irakischer Zindiq im ersten Drittel des Jahrhunderts," [Jamil Sidqi al-Zahawi: an Iraqi Heretic in the first Third of the Century] *Oriens*, (34): 430–50.

_____ (1996) "From Women's Problems to Women as Images in Modern Iraqi Poetry," *Die Welt des Islams*, (36), 2: 219–41.

Wang, T. (2005) "Rewriting the Textbooks: Education Policy in Post-Hussein Iraq," *Harvard International Review*, 26.

Wardi, 'A. al- (1957) *Usturat al-adab al-rafi'*, [The myth of elite literature] Baghdad: Matba'at al-Rabita.

Wardi, A. al- (1969–76) *Lamahat ijtima'iya min ta'rikh al-'Iraq al-hadith*, [Aspects of the social history of modern Iraq] 7 vols, Baghdad.

Watenpaugh, K. (2006) *Being Modern in the Middle East, Revolution, Nationalism, Colonialism, and the Arab Middle Class*, Princeton: Princeton University Press.

Watenpaugh, K., Méténier, E., Hanssen, J., and Fattah, H. (2003) "Opening the Doors: Intellectual Life and Academic Conditions in Post-War Baghdad," *The Iraqi Observatory*: 1–29.

Wedeen, L. (1999) *Ambiguities of Domination: Politics, Rhetoric, and Symbols in Contemporary Syria*, Chicago: University of Chicago Press.

Weitz, E. D. (2003) *A Century of Genocide: Utopias of Race and Nation*, Princeton: Princeton University Press.

Widmer, G. (1935) "Übertragungen aus der neuarabischen Literatur II: Der iraqische Dichter Gamil Sidqi az-Zahawi aus Baghdad," [Contributions to modern Arabic literature; the Baghdadi poet Jamil Sidqi al-Zahawi] *Die Welt des Islams*, (17): 1–79.

Wien, P. (2006) *Iraqi Arab Nationalism: Authoritarian, Totalitarian and Pro-Fascist Inclinations, 1932–41*, London: Routledge.

Wild, S. (1982) "Der Generalsekretär und die Geschichtsschreibung: Saddam Husayn und die irakische Geschichtswissenschaft," [The Secretary-General and the Writing of History; Saddam Husayn and Iraqi Historiography] in I. A. El-Sheikh *et al.* (eds.), *The Challenge of the Middle East. Middle Eastern Studies at the University of Amsterdam*, Amsterdam: University of Amsterdam.

Wiley, J. N. (1992) *The Islamic Movement of Iraqi Shi'as*, Boulder and London: Lynne Rienner Publishers.

Wippermann, W. (1997) *Totalitarismustheorien. Die Entwicklung der Diskussion von den Anfängen bis heute*, [Theories of Totalitarianism: The Development of the Discussion from the Beginnings until Today] Darmstadt: Wissenschaftliche Buchgesellschaft.

Wood, E. J. (2003) *Forging Democracy from Below: Insurgent Traditions in South Africa and El Salvador*, Cambridge: Cambridge University Press.

Yacoub, J. (1986) *The Assyrian Question*, Chicago: Alpha Graphic.

al-Ya'qubi, M. A (ed.) (1963) *Diwan Abi' l-Mahasin al-Karbala'i*, [The Poetry of Abu'l-Mahasin al-Karbala'i] Najaf: Matba'at al-Baqir.

Yaghoobi, A. (2008) "Anfal. The Project of Natiocide of Kurds," paper presented at the "International Conference on the Genocide against the Kurdish People," Erbil, 26–8 January 2008.

Yaphe, J. (2000) "Tribalism in Iraq, the old and the new," *Middle East Policy*, (3): 51–8.

Yildiz, K. (2007) *The Kurds in Iraq*, Ann Arbor MI: Pluto Press.

Young, T. de (1998) *Placing the Poet: Badr Shakir al-Sayyab and Postcolonial Iraq*, Albany: State University of New York Press.

Yousif, A. S. (1991) "The Struggle for Cultural Hegemony During the Iraqi Revolution," in R. A. Fernea and W. R. Louis (eds.) *The Iraqi Revolution of 1958: The Old Social Classes Revisited*, London: I. B. Tauris.

Youssef, S. (2002) *Without an Alphabet, without a Face*, trs. from Arabic by Khaled Mattawa, Saint Paul, MN: Graywolf Press.

Ypersele, L. van (2006) "Des mythes contemporains aux représentations collectives," in L. van Ypersele (ed.) *Questions d'histoire contemporaine. Conflits, mémoires et identités*, Paris: PUF.

Yusuf, Y. S. (Fahd) (1976) *Kitabat al-rafiq Fahd*, [The writings of Comrade Fahd] Baghdad: al-Tariq al-jadid.

Zahawi, J. S. (1979) *Diwan*, [Collected poetry] 2nd edn, Beirut: Dar al-'Awda.

Zayn, 'A. al- (1939) "Buwadir al-Islah fi jami'a al-Najaf, aw nahda Kashif al-Ghita'," [Reform initiatives in the mosque of Najaf, or the renaissance of Khashif al-Ghita'] *al-'Irfan*, (29), 2: 179–86.

Zeifa, H. (2004) "Les élites techniques locales durant le mandat français en Syrie (1920–45)," in N. Méouchy and P. Sluglett (eds.) *The British and French Mandates in Comparative Perspectives/Les Mandats Français et Anglais Dans une Perspective comparative*, Leiden: Brill.

Zolberg, A. (1983) "The Formation of New States as a Refugee-Generating Process," *Annals of the American Academy of Social and Political Science*, (467): 24–38.

Zubaida, S. (1991) "Community, Class and Minorities in Iraqi Politics," in R. A. Fernea and W. R. Louis (eds.) *The Iraqi Revolution of 1958. The Old Social Classes Revisited*, London and New York: Tauris.

———— (2002) "The Fragments Imagine the Nation: The Case of Iraq," *International Journal of Middle East Studies*, (34), 2: 205–15.

———— (2003) "Grandeur et décadence de la société civile irakienne," in H. Dawod and H. Bozarslan (eds.) *La société irakienne. Communautés, pouvoirs et violences*, Paris: Karthala.

———— (2006) "The Rise and Fall of Civil Society in Iraq," in H. Gülalp (ed.) *Citizenship and Ethnic Conflict: Challenging the Nation-State*, London: Routledge.

———— (2008) "Everyday Cosmopolitanism: Jews and Others in Iraq," *ISIM Review*, (22): 6–7.

Zubaydi, M. H. (1985) *Mudhakkirat 'Ali Mahmud al-Shaikh 'Ali: wazir fi hukumat al-difa' al-wataniya fi wizarat Rashid 'Ali al-Kailani al-akhira sanat 1941*, [The Memoirs of 'Ali Mahmud al-Shaikh 'Ali, Minister of Defence in Rashid 'Ali's second government, 1941], Baghdad, n.p.

INDEX OF GEOGRAPHICAL NAMES, COMMODITIES, AND THEMES

INDEX OF INDIVIDUALS
AND GROUPS

MAP OF IRAQ

Map No. 3835 Rev. 4   UNITED NATIONS
January 2004

Department of Peacekeeping Operations
Cartographic Section